Praise for *The Lincoln Miracle*

"Edward Achorn's *The Lincoln Miracle* is a rable earlier study, *Every Drop of Blood: T tion of Abraham Lincoln*. While the latter end of his presidency, the former tells lican national convention in Chicago that made his election possible and thereby changed the course of world history. Chockablock with colorful depictions of the dramatic events and deft character sketches of the leading players, Achorn's highly readable book reaches sound conclusions based on thorough research and is thus a most welcome addition to the Lincoln literature."

—Michael Burlingame, author of *Abraham Lincoln: A Life* and president of the Abraham Lincoln Association

"An exhaustively researched and detailed narrative of the 'Lincoln Miracle.'"

—Shelf Awareness

"What a good book *The Lincoln Miracle* is. It is by far the best account of that convention I have ever read, especially in featuring the collapse of William H. Seward's 'inevitable' nomination, and showing what a feat that was. *The Lincoln Miracle* projects an excitement that is rare in scholarly narrative."

—Douglas L. Wilson, two-time Lincoln Prize winner, author of *Lincoln's Sword* and *Honor's Voice*

"A wonderful story! Anyone interested in the intricacies and ironies and the deal-making and horse-trading of American politics will love this book. Although Senator William Seward of New York was the overwhelming favorite to become the Republican Party's presidential nominee at the Chicago convention in May 1860, Lincoln eventually prevailed. Edward Achorn rightly calls this the Lincoln Miracle, because, as he shows in rich and lucid prose, it was not just Lincoln's shrewd and crafty operatives but also Lincoln himself, masterful politician that he was, who brought about that miracle. Although we all know the results of the Republican Party's presidential nominating convention in 1860, Edward Achorn nevertheless has the uncanny knack of keeping us in suspense throughout all the days of the convention. With his prose rich and breathless in detail, Achorn truly makes Lincoln's nomination seem to be a miracle." **—Gordon S. Wood, Pulitzer Prize–winning author of *Empire of Liberty***

"Historian Achorn details the raucous, exciting convention and the behind-the-scenes dealings that exemplified 19th-century conventions . . . This detailed account of the convention takes the boisterous proceedings day-by-day, giving readers an in-depth look at the convention that nominated Lincoln. This finely grained and well-written account will appeal to readers interested in Lincoln or American presidential and political history." ***—Library Journal***

"Our greatest president, Abraham Lincoln, would remain unknown to Americans if not for the Republican convention of 1860, and a roller-coaster week that changed the course of history. *The Lincoln Miracle* tells the inside story with precision and panache."

—Ted Widmer, author of *Lincoln on the Verge: Thirteen Days to Washington*

"For fans of political wheeling and dealing, who find brokered conventions, Electoral College forecasts, and the down-ticket impacts of state voting trends engrossing, this is a grand book documenting a milestone in the formation of the Grand Old Party. Achorn's brisk, 400-page account is replete with all the bribery, patronage, rumors, back-stabbing, whiskey, cigars, and political calculus that went into the most consequential Presidential nomination in our history."

—National Book Review

The Lincoln Miracle

Also by Edward Achorn

Every Drop of Blood:
The Momentous Second Inauguration of Abraham Lincoln

The Summer of Beer and Whiskey:
How Brewers, Barkeeps, Rowdies, Immigrants, and a Wild Pennant Fight Made Baseball America's Game

Fifty-Nine in '84:
Old Hoss Radbourn, Barehanded Baseball, and the Greatest Season a Pitcher Ever Had

The Lincoln Miracle

Inside the Republican Convention That Changed History

Edward Achorn

Grove Press
New York

To Valerie, again

Published simultaneously in Canada
Printed in the United States of America

This book was set in 11 pt. Janson by Alpha Design & Composition of Pittsfield, NH.

First Grove Atlantic hardcover edition: February 2023
First Grove Atlantic paperback edition: February 2024

Library of Congress Cataloging-in-Publication data is available for this title.

ISBN 978-0-8021-6268-7
eISBN 978-0-8021-6063-8

Grove Press
an imprint of Grove Atlantic
154 West 14th Street
New York, NY 10011

Distributed by Publishers Group West

groveatlantic.com

24 25 26 27 10 9 8 7 6 5 4 3 2 1

Contents

The man that thinks that Lincoln quietly sat down and gathered his robes about him, waiting for the people to call on him, has a very erroneous knowledge of Lincoln. He was always calculating, and planning ahead. His ambition was a little engine that knew no rest.

—William H. Herndon

It is my belief if all the other causes had existed as they did exist, and Judge Davis had not lived, Mr. Lincoln would never have been nominated, and, consequently, never would have been elected President of the United States.

—Leonard Swett

Without Chicago we should have had no Wigwam; without the Wigwam we should have had no Abraham Lincoln; without a Lincoln we might have to day had no Government.

—Frederick Douglass

Had Abraham Lincoln died in the spring of 1860, on the eve of his first presidential nomination, he would be a forgotten man.

—Mark E. Neely Jr.

Friday, October 29, 1858

Prologue: Such a Sucker as Me

The young reporter stood on a platform alone, waiting for the train that would take him down the iron rails southeast to Springfield, twenty miles away. There was no depot building here, only a flag flapping in the evening breeze to signal to the engineer that a passenger was waiting.

It was a muggy Friday night, warm for late October in Illinois. The clouds coming in were black with moisture, even after six miserable days of gloomy skies and intermittent rain that was threatening to rot the state's potato crop.

Twenty-three-year-old Henry Villard had spent the afternoon and early evening in nearby Petersburg, attending a raucous Republican rally—one of the final events in that year's electrifying battle between the most dynamic Democrat in America, United States Senator Stephen Douglas, forty-five, and the shrewd lawyer who sought to wrest his seat from him. The "Little Giant," a five-foot-four-inch ball of energy and ambition, had been heavily favored to win another six years in the Senate, but his far less accomplished Republican challenger, a bony six-foot-four-inch former one-term congressman named Abraham Lincoln, was giving him a great deal of trouble—and making something of a national name for himself. The big Eastern newspapers had taken note of Lincoln's skill at puncturing the famous senator's arguments while advancing a forceful moral case against the spread of slavery.

Indeed, the Republican's friends now believed that he was on the cusp of pulling off a stunning victory. "Lincoln has made a magnificent canvass," circuit court judge David Davis enthused in a letter to his brother that week. Davis was probably closer to Lincoln than any other man was, and well knew his worth. The judge had spent more than a decade at Lincoln's side, crossing the prairies every spring and fall from one county courthouse to the next, stopping at taverns, eating meals with him, and often sharing a bedroom.

Davis did worry about one late development: Democratic operatives were sending Irish immigrant railroad laborers into tightly contested legislative districts to cast votes of dubious legality. "There would be no doubt of Douglas's defeat," Davis complained, if the senator were not "colonizing Irish votes." There was nothing new in the Democratic Party's creative use of the Irish vote. Eighteen years earlier, Davis had complained to a Whig friend, "If the *Irish* did not vote more than *3 times* we could easily carry the State."

The matter would be effectively settled in four days, with the election on Tuesday, November 2. Senators then were not chosen directly by voters (as they are today), but by their state's legislature. Still, everybody would know after Tuesday how the Illinois legislature would be configured, and thus whether Douglas or Lincoln would get the Senate seat when its members convened on January 5, 1859.

Like Douglas's Irish friends, the young man waiting on the platform was an immigrant and a loyal Democrat. Born in Speyer, Bavaria, Villard had stepped onto the docks of New York City six years earlier, an eighteen-year-old boy, alone and penniless, unable to speak a word of English. But bright and driven, he had hustled to learn the language. He was determined to rise above the rabble in this remarkable young country where even newcomers could turn brains and effort into riches. While millions of black slaves in the South were denied access to this dream, even some escaped slaves had risen in America to fame and success. One brilliant former slave in particular—a man named Frederick Douglass—had become a powerful orator, an influential newspaper editor, and a recognized leader in the struggle for freedom.

Villard had come out West in the late 1850s as an agent of New York's *Staats-Zeitung*, a German-language newspaper sympathetic to the pro-immigrant Democratic Party, serving as a part-time reporter while collecting the paper's bills and hawking subscriptions to its weekly edition. A fervent admirer of the Little Giant—who, in his view, epitomized the bold, can-do spirit of young America—Villard persuaded his editor to let him drop his other duties and cover the celebrated Douglas-Lincoln campaign full-time. He also provided articles for the pro-Douglas *Philadelphia Press*.

Around nine o'clock that evening, Villard heard the jangling of a horse's harness and saw a buggy approach through the gloom. A tall, stoop-shouldered figure wearing a battered stovepipe hat and lugging a faded black carpetbag clambered out awkwardly, and the buggy departed. It was the forty-nine-year-old candidate Villard had observed addressing the crowd that afternoon, using the force of his shrill, piercing voice to reach as many people as possible.

Villard had met Abraham Lincoln several times during the campaign. Like other reporters, he found the candidate disarmingly generous and engaging. But Villard could not stomach one of Lincoln's traits: his fondness for crude, sometimes dirty, tales. "I must say frankly that, although I found him most approachable, good-natured, and full of wit and humor, I could not take a real personal liking to the man, owing to an inborn weakness for which he was even then notorious and so remained during his great public career," Villard recalled. "He was inordinately fond of jokes, anecdotes, and stories. He loved to hear them, and still more to tell them himself out of the inexhaustible supply provided by his good memory and his fertile fancy. There would have been no harm in this but for the fact that, the coarser the joke, the lower the anecdote, and the more risky the story, the more he enjoyed them, especially when they were of his own invention."

The prairie politician and the prim young journalist struck up a conversation on the dark platform as they waited for the overdue train. Lincoln was interested in German Americans, who were flooding into Illinois and now constituted an important voting bloc. After half an hour, the sky began to rumble. As a storm rolled in, lightning flashed, then the heavens opened. Seeking cover, they dashed to an empty freight car on a siding and climbed inside.

They hunkered down on the floor and talked in the dark while rain drummed on the roof. The air was getting cooler.

The candidate stretching out in the shadows struck Villard as an "indescribably gawky" figure with a wrinkled, uncomely face. He had long arms with huge hands; a skinny neck too small for his collar; sallow leathery skin; a narrow, clean-shaven face with high, sharp cheekbones; a large mole on his right cheek; a big nose and oversized ears; a lazy left eye that at times drifted independently of his right eye; prominent and heavy eyebrows; and dark, almost black hair that seemed to "lay floating where his fingers or the winds left it, piled up at random," as his law partner William Herndon put it. In repose, he seemed profoundly sad, but when he broke into a little story, his face lit up with delight.

After the long campaign, Lincoln was in a reflective mood. He had delivered some sixty speeches and debated Douglas seven times—high-pressure affairs in which he had to keep his wits for hours against one of America's most combative and demagogic politicians. In October alone, Lincoln had debated his adversary three times while crisscrossing central Illinois—the fierce battleground region, since the Republicans were stronger in the north and the Democrats in the south. All told, Lincoln had traveled more than 1,300 miles that month, in sun and rain, mud and dust, explaining Republican values to thousands of voters. Douglas and his aides crossed the state in luxurious private railroad cars, their trains sometimes equipped with a flat car bearing a cannon to thrillingly boom out his presence when he had arrived in town. Lincoln was no big-time politician who could collect hefty donations from corporations or staff his campaign with men he had placed in patronage jobs. With a wife and three children to support, he had sacrificed much of his law income for months to the dream of winning a Senate seat. Unlike Douglas, he mostly traveled alone, on any number of contrivances—crowded wooden railroad cars, jolting wagons, carriages, horseback.

He was finally heading back to his hometown of Springfield, where he would be the star attraction at one last rally the next day. But Lincoln knew the area around him on that Friday night almost as intimately. He had carefully mapped out Petersburg twenty-two years earlier, while pursuing a short-lived career as a surveyor. At that time, he made his home in New Salem, a village of twenty to twenty-five families, just three miles to the south. Shortly after Lincoln left, it became a ghost town, most of its residents having moved up to Petersburg.

Though not a rich man, Lincoln had risen far from a grubby childhood, his birth and boyhood in dirty, drafty log cabins in the wilderness of Kentucky and Indiana. With little formal schooling, he transformed himself, by dint of his sharp mind and his friendly way with people, into a first-rate lawyer and a leading figure in Illinois politics. All the same, he still felt painfully embarrassed about his impoverished upbringing and poor education. To compensate, he made self-deprecating jokes and expressed surprise that people took his ambitions seriously.

Inside the dark freight car, Lincoln reminisced about clerking in a country store in nearby New Salem. In those days, he told Villard, his highest aspiration was to serve in the state legislature. "Since then, of course," Lincoln said with a laugh, "I have grown some, but my friends got me into this business" of running for the U.S. Senate. He had almost captured a seat in 1855 and had come to regard it as his dream job.

"I did not consider myself qualified for the United States Senate, and it took me a long time to persuade myself that I was. Now, to be sure," he continued with a laugh, "I am convinced that I am good enough for it; but, in spite of it all, I am saying to myself every day: 'It's too big a thing for you; you will never get it.'"

His wife had a different view of his abilities and destiny, though.

"Mary insists . . . that I am going to be Senator and President of the United States, too!" Lincoln told Villard. He roared with laughter, wrapping his arms around his knees and shaking with mirth at Mrs. Lincoln's ambition. "Just think of such a sucker as me as President!" "Sucker" was slang for an Illinois resident (the *Daily Missouri Republican* of St. Louis had called Lincoln the "tall Sucker" repeatedly during the campaign), though the word carried the hint of an unsophisticated man from the country.

Lincoln began asking the reporter probing questions, hoping to make a friend and add to his own storehouse of knowledge. How long had Villard been in America? Lincoln voiced surprise at the journalist's fluency in English after so short a time. Would many people in Germany be regarded as "infidels," as critics suggested? Villard said they did not call themselves such, but many were not churchgoers.

As the conversation flowed, Villard confessed to the older man that he did not believe in the existence of God, the divinity of Christ, or the prospect of immortality. Lincoln, as was his wont, drew out his companion without discussing his own beliefs. "He did not commit himself, but I received the impression that he was of my own way of thinking," Villard recalled.

At half past ten, the train finally appeared, noisily slowing to a screeching stop. Lincoln and Villard hurried to the platform and stepped aboard a car.

The locomotive wheezed into motion, and the pulse of its chuffing quickened. The train disappeared into the darkness, carrying a rising young reporter and a strange politician who was moving toward a heartbreaking defeat in the Senate fight but a future of greatness that not even his ambitious wife could have imagined.

Saturday, May 12, 1860

Chapter 1: Unconscious Strength

The long depot at the corner of Canal and Van Buren Streets was crawling with people on May 12, 1860. Beneath its high cupola, attendants wheeled out carts loaded with luggage. Women wearing colorful bonnets and full-length, sprawling dresses emerged into the spring sun. Men hailed horse-drawn cabs. Each incoming train of the St. Louis, Alton & Chicago Railroad unloaded masses of visitors who had come for the biggest political event in Chicago's history, the national convention of the burgeoning Republican Party, set to begin in four days. Thousands had arrived already. Many hotels were booked to capacity, and private homes were filling up.

The station stood just west of the Chicago River, which performed the service of a desultory sewer, wafting feces, industrial chemicals, garbage, ash, and the offal of slaughtered animals slowly out to Lake Michigan. The "sluggish river . . . winds its way, like an ugly black serpent, through the city," wrote one reporter who was covering the convention. Spanned by a series of iron swing bridges, it was "greasy to the touch," another observer explained, and resembled "in color and consistency a rich pea soup." It stank so fiercely that many women who ventured to shop downtown had to hold handkerchiefs to their noses. But it was also a valuable avenue of trade, bristling with vessels of all sizes, from sailing ships with towering masts moored at freight docks to chugging tugboats belching black coal smoke, mimicking the factory chimneys that filled the Chicago sky with an acrid haze. People seemed to accept the smoke and smells. They did not come here for the beauty of nature. They came to make their fortune.

That afternoon, a conspicuously weighty man—five feet eleven inches tall and three hundred pounds—stepped off a passenger car, strode through the crowd along the platform, and emerged from the depot. That morning, he had left his gracious farmhouse in Bloomington, Illinois, named Clover Lawn, with its flowers and two hundred acres of fields coming to life, and had climbed aboard a train for the five-and-a-half-hour trip to Chicago. It was a rattling ride in a wooden car with squealing metal wheels behind a noisy, smoky steam locomotive—making tedious stops at Peoria Junction, Pontiac, Odell, Gardner, Wilmington, and Joliet. Still, the 140-mile journey from Bloomington to Chicago was far faster and more comfortable than it had been just a decade earlier, when it had to be made on horseback or in a jarring carriage over rutted dirt roads through prairie fields.

The big man, forty-five-year-old David Davis, had come to Chicago on a remarkable mission. He planned to attempt the impossible, or at least exceedingly improbable, over the next several days: to make his friend, a strikingly eccentric and relatively obscure lawyer named Abraham Lincoln, the Republican nominee for president of the United States. Though he was the favorite-son candidate of Illinois and had gained some national recognition by wounding Stephen Douglas in a celebrated series of debates, few imagined Lincoln could win. Repeatedly defeated, he had not even held public office for more than a decade. But Davis was an ambitious, resourceful, no-nonsense Western man who had a way of surmounting obstacles thrown in his path.

However unsuccessful he had been in recent elections, Lincoln lived and breathed politics, and he yearned to attend the convention to witness the wheeling and dealing, and perhaps help steer the party toward victory. Unfortunately, it was considered terrible form for any candidate for the nomination to show up. Perplexed about what to do, he confessed to his friend and fellow lawyer Leonard Swett that he felt "too much of a candidate to go, and not quite enough to stay home." Lincoln regarded himself as "the humblest of all whose names were before the convention." In the end, he remained in Springfield, leaving his slim chances in the hands of Davis and other friends, who would, he hoped, follow the instructions he had given them and keep him informed by letters and telegrams.

That morning's edition of *Harper's Weekly*—a popular sixteen-page news and literature magazine published in New York City and distributed throughout the North—featured a two-page center spread of portraits of the potential Republican nominees. It was dominated, in the middle, by a large oval engraving of the delegates' overwhelming favorite: William Henry Seward, a bright, witty, and engaging U.S. senator and former governor of New York, the nation's most powerful and populous state. The centerpiece seemed fitting, because many expected that this would be Seward's convention—the nomination a tribute to his years of heroic opposition to slavery, his extensive political experience, and his talent for turning phrases that roused his supporters and enraged his opponents. Lincoln was consigned to a small picture at the bottom of the *Harper's* gallery, with the also-rans—firebrand Cassius Clay of Kentucky; colorless John Bell of Tennessee, who was no longer even a Republican candidate; and the party's first presidential nominee four years earlier, the arrogant John Frémont of California, who could find little support for another run.

In the text that followed the center spread, Seward appeared first, with the longest write-up. Lincoln was last, with the shortest description—the darkest of the dark horses, from the perspective of the *Harper's* editors. Even those who were adamantly opposed to Seward tended to overlook the Illinois lawyer. Ohio's delegates, for example, favored their nationally prominent U.S. senators, Salmon P. Chase and Benjamin F. Wade. "Our delegates have left for Chicago," Cincinnati city solicitor Rutherford B. Hayes wrote to his uncle on Friday. "After Chase, they will prefer Wade, Frémont, or some such candidate—anyone named before Seward." Only Illinois seemed to be backing Lincoln.

Davis made his way from the depot toward Chicago's premier hotel, the bustling Tremont House, at the southeast corner of Dearborn and Lake Streets, a little more than a mile away. The hotel was, remarkably, the third one built at the busy intersection by merchant Ira Couch. His first two had burned down, always a grave risk in nineteenth-century cities, with their highly flammable wooden structures and minimal firefighting forces. Rather than quit, Couch built a new hotel in 1850 that was vastly bigger and better than its predecessors—a massive six-story brick structure designed by noted architect John Van Osdel. With Chicago-style audacity, the owner adorned the rooms with fireplace mantles made of Egyptian marble, chairs of rosewood and mahogany, linen sheets on every bed, silk-lined damask curtains, and a clever system of speaking tubes and electric bells to facilitate communication with the staff. He put in steam heating, equipped the building with gaslight, installed drinking fountains in the hallways, and brought water to every floor. Ten shops at ground level, a music hall, and a railroad ticket office catered to the wants and needs of tourists and traveling businessmen. A leather-lunged porter stood in the lobby to help guide travelers to their destinations, as travel writer Lillian Foster noted, "calling out, at the top of his deep bass voice, at intervals of every ten minutes during the twenty-four hours, 'All for the Michigan Central,' 'all for the Milwaukee boat,' 'all for the Rock Island road,' until he calls over the name of almost every place in the Union." A white observation tower on the roof capped it all. Rooms went for a pricey $2.50 a day—at a time when an unskilled laborer's weekly pay was about $5.00—with parlors and additional rooms costing extra.

Some people, thinking the owner a fool or a madman to invest in something so lavish in what was still a rude Western town with filthy streets and poor sanitation, dubbed it "Couch's Folly." But, as Chicago's population almost quadrupled over the decade, exploding from less than 30,000 to more than 112,000, the hotel proved highly profitable. During the 1850s, Couch leased his building to a manager, George W. Gage, who brought in an experienced hotelier from Cincinnati, John B. Drake, to help him run the place. Since one proprietor was a Republican and the other a Democrat, the Tremont House was positioned to please "the most ultra of both sides," the *New York Daily Herald* noted—a luxury in a nation being ripped apart by vicious partisanship.

In the half-settled West, even a first-class hotel attracted a more varied and colorful clientele than would be found in the staid East. "Such a motley set!" Miss Foster exclaimed. "You meet there the nobleman and his suite; the backwoodsman in his coarse clothes and fur cap (all the same, June or January); the illustrious lady and party, over dressed; the German woman with her toys and wares for sale; and all seem to have the same object in view, a hurry to get in, and anxious to get away." In June 1859, eight-year-old Willie Lincoln wrote a letter to a friend about his visit to the plush hotel with his father, Abraham Lincoln, who often stayed at the Tremont House when he was in Chicago. "This town is a very beautiful place. Me and father have a nice little room to ourselves," Willie explained. "We have two little pitchers on a washstand. The smallest one for me the largest one for father. We have two little towels on top of both pitchers. The smallest one for me, the largest one for father. Me and father had gone to two theaters the other night."

The Tremont was already packed full that Saturday in advance of the Republican National Convention, which would commence Wednesday in a newly built auditorium five blocks away. In its preconvention guide to Chicago's hotels, the *New York Daily Herald* touted the Tremont as the best house in town, as well as a local hive of politics, "the headquarters where political intelligence of all kinds is dealt out to the inquiring multitude at all times of political excitement." The hotel was equipped with a telegraph office, that modern marvel of communications, "which will no doubt be rendered invaluable" during the convention, the *Herald* observed. On May 5, the *Herald* listed the number of delegates and their friends heading for the Tremont: New York, 50; Ohio, 88; Connecticut, 12; Massachusetts, 26; Iowa, 34; Indiana, 24; Kentucky, 6; Missouri, 30; and a few from faraway California. Oddly, there were none from Illinois, the state Davis was serving as a delegate-at-large.

After Davis reached the front desk on May 12, he discovered, to his horror, the reason: the Lincoln campaign was so disorganized that nobody had thought of booking rooms for its headquarters. Without a nerve center in the most important hotel, the campaign would surely go nowhere. Davis immediately sought out a friend, Assistant Manager Drake, who had a reputation for fawningly attending to his guests' needs. Sure enough, the accommodating Drake was able to help Davis secure space in the crowded hotel. Davis simply had to pay a premium for "the evacuation of certain rooms by private families," Swett recounted. As soon as the families had cleared out, Davis posted a sign on the door of his suite, number 74—"Illinois Headquarters"—and was in business. For the next several days, he would sit behind a large table in his rooms, directing Lincoln's friends and supporters to the places they were most needed. "Here without anybody electing him to the position, he at once became the leader of all the Illinois men," Swett marveled. "Davis was the active man, and had the business management in charge," William Herndon, Lincoln's law partner and a member of the team in Chicago, recalled. "If any negotiations were made, he made them."

When friends or neighbors needed help, David Davis was wont to roll up his sleeves and get to work. "If I were asked to state what was the leading trait of Judge Davis' character, I should say latent, unconscious strength," Swett observed. "He simply walked up to and did anything, almost impossible to be done, as a matter of course. In this way he acquired control over the most uncontrollable men, and accomplished with the greatest ease what seemed to others impossible of accomplishment." And when Davis wanted something, even the steel-willed Abraham Lincoln had trouble resisting his pressure. Davis had "that way," Lincoln complained, "of making a man do a thing whether he wants to or not."

Davis had a genial face, blue eyes, a ruddy complexion, a pleasant smile, and curly whiskers under a square jaw—no mustache. He enjoyed humor and was imbued with a sense of fun—useful traits in frontier society. He enjoyed attention maybe even more. He invested heavily in property, believing in a shining future for Illinois when the state was still an inhospitable wilderness infested with roaming prairie wolves, and his faith, though tested at times, eventually paid off, making him rich. He unabashedly adored his wife Sarah, to whom he wrote tender and romantic letters after decades of marriage and the deaths of five of their seven children in infancy. (She, in turn, fretted over him and lovingly called him "Davie.") "He had a big head and a big body, a big brain and a big heart," one woman once said of him. Swett thought Davis had fewer flaws than any man he ever met, including Lincoln. "He is the only man of whom I can say, if I had the making of him for time and eternity, I should alter nothing."

Lincoln, who never completely shook his country mannerisms, was born in poverty in Kentucky, his father an uneducated laborer. Davis was cultured and educated, born in luxury in 1815 at a slave plantation, The Rounds, at Sassafras Neck on Maryland's Eastern Shore. Nursed at the breast of a slave, he became a slaveholder himself at the age of five, when his grandfather died, willing "two Negro Boys Isaac and Charles to him and his heirs and assigns forever." (They did not remain in his possession long. The following year, his guardian sold off the boys for $125 each.) Davis's early life in the border state molded him into a conservative who hewed a middle course. He detested slavery and sympathized with those trapped in it; throughout his life, he supported a black man from Sassafras Neck named Perry Veazey, perhaps one of his childhood friends. At the same time, he reviled abolitionist leaders, writing in 1845 that they were "as corrupt and unprincipled . . . hypocrites as ever disgraced the human family." Most supporters of abolition were "honest in their motives," he conceded, but the leaders of the movement were not. They recklessly concealed the real-world difficulties of eradicating that deeply entrenched institution. They did not seem to care if their agitation ended up drowning the nation in blood.

Davis was only eight months old when his twenty-seven-year-old father, a doctor, died. After his mother's remarriage, the boy's fortune was placed in the hands of a stepfather who frittered away his inheritance of thousands of dollars, evidently using some of it to pay off his own debts. Davis tried decades later to claw back the money, but only obtained a portion from his stepfather's sureties. Though his inheritance was expected to fund his education at Yale, his stepfather sent him to a new institution that was far cheaper: Kenyon College, in Gambier, Ohio. The main college building was a large log cabin, and the student living quarters were miserably cold, but Kenyon produced, among other early alumni, future U.S. president Rutherford B. Hayes, formidable secretary of war Edwin Stanton, and two future Supreme Court justices (one of them Davis himself). After graduation, Davis finally did move on to Yale, attending its New Haven Law School, from which he graduated in 1835.

At twenty, Davis resolved to go out West to seek his fortune. Before setting off with his worldly wealth of fifty dollars (some of it borrowed) and a trunk filled with law books, Davis had one piece of important business to conduct. While working in Lenox, Massachusetts, he had fallen in love with twenty-year-old Sarah Walker, the bright and pretty daughter of the judge of probate for Berkshire County. On May 1, 1835, Davis wrote to Sarah's stern New England father for his approval of their engagement. Though poor, Davis declared his intention to earn enough money in three to four years "to support a wife as becomes a lady." Out West, he admitted, he would have to start from scratch. "I feel that I love your daughter—sincerely love her—& that the ultimate possession of her hand would be the strongest inducement that I could have to engage arduously in the business of life. I also feel that the chief object of my life could be devoted to the promotion of her happiness." He made a pledge: "Should I be so fortunate as to obtain your consent to the engagement, it shall be my object to try & evince by my conduct through life that your confidence has not been misplaced." Judge Walker refused to give his blessing, arguing that an engagement stretching out for so many years would be unfair to his daughter. If, however, in three or four years, they felt the same way about each other—and if the judge still regarded Davis favorably—they would have his consent. Davis, never one to take no for an answer, persisted until he succeeded. In three years, he married Sarah.

In his late twenties, Davis began to put on weight, eventually ballooning from two hundred to three hundred pounds. Perhaps his voracious appetite was linked to the trauma of his childhood as an unwanted and exploited boy. Davis built up his law practice, invested in land, campaigned for Whig candidates, and won a seat in the Illinois House. During that 1844 run, he found himself marveling at an unpolished Springfield lawyer and former state legislator who was campaigning hard for Whig presidential nominee Henry Clay. "Lincoln is the best Stump Speaker in the State—worked on a farm at 8 dollars a month until he was 22," he told Judge Walker. "He shows the want of early education but he has great powers as a speaker." Davis could never warm to Mary Lincoln, though. "Mrs. Lincoln is not agreeable," he told Sarah after attending one party in Springfield. When Lincoln was elected to Congress in 1846, Davis noted that Mary planned to follow him to the nation's capital and "wishes to loom largely." But her social aspirations were bound to be stymied by her rustic husband, Davis suggested. "You cant make a gentleman in his outward appearance out of Lincoln to save your life."

In 1848, at thirty-three, Davis ran for and won the position that changed his life, judge of the newly created Eighth Judicial Circuit in Illinois. Davis was not in it for the money. "The Salary I do not fight for," he told his father-in-law. "The position suits me—I like it." The court traveled across the prairies from county seat to county seat, bringing the law—and the welcome entertainment of trials—to the state's far-flung citizens. Swett, who represented clients in Davis's court many times, recalled a typical day. "Arriving at the county seat in the morning about eight o'clock, the litigants would come in, generally on horseback, [and] bring their witnesses in the same manner," he wrote. "By nine o'clock the great old Judge would occupy the bench of the log court house" and the lawyers "would be defending some criminal, brought into court from the log jail, or trying a civil case in which we had never seen the parties or witnesses, and probably never heard of the case until that morning." Many evenings were given over to fun, with Davis overseeing festivities at the local tavern. "The principal farmers called. Lincoln told his queerest stories. [State's attorney] Dave Campbell drew from a superb violin, which he never left behind, tones of sweetness." On Wednesday afternoons, the traveling show set off for the next county seat, where court was to begin all over again on Monday morning.

Judge Davis, by all accounts, sincerely tried to help people obtain justice. "He had not great erudition, and no brilliancy; he did not know, or care for, the philosophy of the law, but he was the incarnation of common-sense and sterling judgment," noted Henry Clay Whitney, a prominent lawyer on the circuit. He "shunned and abhorred all technicalities: and got right down to the essential merits of any law-suit or proposition." Davis "knew just enough law to be a great judge, and not enough to spoil him," Swett observed. "He took to justice by instinct, as the hound takes the scent." In one case, when a lawyer used a technicality to try to deprive a man of his property, Davis literally turned his back on him and suggested he talk to another judge. "Before this court you cannot steal a man's farm that way," he declared. After the sharp economic downturn of 1857, he found his court overwhelmed with claims against men who had failed to pay their bills. Davis simply announced, "This court is loaded with cases arising out of the panic. I know these men, they will pay as soon as they can. Court is adjourned to the next term."

He hated to pronounce a death sentence for murder. For understandable reasons, Davis was notably keen to protect minors from being robbed by their guardians. He was tolerant of young lawyers with limited experience, and of older lawyers who stepped out of line. "If any of the lawyers got wild, the Judge often made him stop it and go to bed to sleep it off," Swett noted. Reporting on the court's activities in 1858, the *Urbana Union* observed that "Judge Davis was as usual the personification of courtly dignity and impartiality." At times, though, his emotions got the better of him. After he found a young man guilty of brutally striking and robbing an old man who had generously given him a ride, Davis was so distracted by his own outrage that he ordered the defendant "be confined in the *Legislature of the State of Illinois for the period of seven years.*" The prosecuting attorney, Lincoln's friend Ward Hill Lamon, had to whisper in the judge's ear to substitute "penitentiary" for "legislature."

Until a web of railroads spread through the state, travel was difficult, especially for a three-hundred-pound man. Davis spent six months out on the circuit—three in the spring, another three in the fall—in all kinds of weather, including snow, sleet, rain, and biting wind, on horseback or lugged in a cart, through mud or over narrow rutted paths across plains of waving prairie grass that grew as tall as a man, and crossing unbridged streams that were often swollen. Out there, nature was still largely untouched. Swett recalled how "the quail whistled to his mate as we passed along, how the grouse with his peculiar whirr arose from his hiding places in the grasses, how the wolf fled and the red deer was startled from the grassy dell."

At roadhouses, the travelers endured repulsive food and slept on mattresses infested with vermin. "This thing of travelling in Illinois, and being eaten up by bed bugs and Mosquitoes (fleas you know dont trouble me much) is not what it is cracked up to be," Davis wrote home to Sarah. The tavern at Mount Pulaski, the seat of Logan County, was "perhaps the hardest place you ever saw," with "everything dirty & the eating Horrible," Davis observed in an 1851 letter. The lady of the house "looked as we would suppose the witch of Endor looked. She had a grown daughter who waited on the table—table greasy—table cloth greasy—floor greasy and everything else ditto. . . . I wonder if she ever washed herself. I guess the dirt must be half an inch thick all over her." Davis and the lawyers often crowded into a room to sleep, and many times they shared beds.

But Davis made the best of it. An "old pioneer" told a story of Davis's rare devotion to duty. Late one night, the judge, accompanied by lawyer Abraham Lincoln, arrived at the banks of the Sangamon River outside Decatur. Unable to see very far in the dark, Lincoln suggested turning back rather than risk a crossing. But they were due in court the next morning, and Davis, "without saying a word, plunged into the stream with his horse and swam across." Unable to find a landing, he returned to his starting point. But rather than give up, Davis went downstream to make another try. This time, he succeeded. "Then with the assistance of some farmers he built a fire on the bank of the river to show Mr. Lincoln where to land, if he chose to swim over." Lincoln, on his horse, "swam toward the light and was safely landed, and on the following morning both parties were enabled to be in attendance in court."

For the twelve years that Judge Davis served in the Eighth Circuit, he spent far more time with Lincoln than with any other lawyer. That included countless hours of plodding across the plains, fifteen miles a day or more at a stretch, with Lincoln riding on his horse "Old Buck," superseded in time by "Old Bob" and "Old Tom." Many attorneys went home when possible and caught up with the traveling court later. Not Lincoln. He loved the life of handling cases, meeting old and new friends from one end of the circuit to the other, escaping his demons of depression and difficulties at home, and telling funny stories that delighted everyone. "In my opinion, Lincoln was happy—as happy as *he* could be, when on this Circuit—and happy no other place," Davis said. He could get lost in his thoughts out there, away from the distractions of home. At rude hotels out on the circuit, Lincoln's law partner William Herndon recalled, Lincoln placed a candle on a chair near the head of the bed, "and would read and study for hours," often until 2:00 a.m. To sharpen his reasoning skills, Lincoln worked his way through the mathematical propositions contained in the first six books of Euclid. "How he could maintain his mental equilibrium or concentrate his thoughts on an abstract mathematical proposition, while Davis, Logan, Swett, Edwards and I so industriously and volubly filled the air with our interminable snoring was a problem none of us could ever solve," Herndon said.

They made an odd pair. While Davis fretted about filth and bad food, Lincoln seemed oblivious to them. Davis reached decisions quickly, with executive efficiency, and acted boldly; Lincoln mulled over problems slowly and deliberately, until he had reached a position that he considered logically unassailable. Davis was vain and loved praise; Lincoln steeled himself against both praise and criticism. Davis harbored resentments; Lincoln was quick to forgive and forget. Davis loved making money; Lincoln thought little about investing. Davis made a point of dressing well; Lincoln simply did not care. (One lawyer in Davis's court described Lincoln as wearing "a bobtail sack coat" and "jean pants that came within sixteen inches of his feet.")

Lincoln loved to campaign; Davis hated the pressure of speaking in public and selling himself to the masses. "I dread your going about Electioneering in the Sun," his wife Sarah wrote him during his 1848 run. "You must try not to get excited my dear—It makes you feverish—and does you no good." If Sarah had been ambitious, Davis might have pushed himself to seek greater political fame. "But instead of adding fuel to the flames, she throws cold water upon it, & I love her too well to thwart her views," he wrote. Mary Lincoln, by contrast, drove her husband onward, and her ambitions—and, consequently, Abraham's—extended all the way to the White House. As a girl, she had told a friend, "I am going to be the president's wife some day." Another friend, Margaret Wickliffe, recalled that when Mary dated Lincoln, she spoke of his homeliness and awkwardness, but declared, "I mean to make him President of the United States all the same. You will see that, as I have always told you, I will yet be the President's wife." Mary's sister Elizabeth Edwards called her "the most ambitious woman I ever saw," and said she "spurred up Mr. Lincoln—pushed him along and upward—made him struggle and seize his opportunities." Mary's cousin and Lincoln's first law partner, John Todd Stuart, said she "had the fire—will and ambition."

Davis tended to wear his heart on his sleeve; Lincoln was strangely and profoundly guarded about his thoughts and feelings—"the most reticent—Secretive man I Ever Saw—or Expect to See," Davis wrote. Davis had his struggles, but he found happiness at his hearth with Sarah. Lincoln was deeply depressed and often closed off emotionally. His jokes were no sign of a personal connection with others, Davis thought. They were "done to whistle off sadness." While he cared about the suffering of his fellow human beings, "Lincoln had no spontaneity—nor Emotional Nature—no Strong Emotional feelings for any person—Mankind or thing. He never thanked me for anything I did." Like others, Davis felt hurt when Lincoln put pragmatic calculations ahead of loyalty to his friends. He was miffed when Lincoln remained neutral in Davis's campaign for the judgeship, apparently balancing his friendship with a need to placate Mary, whose Yale-educated relative also sought the post. "Lincoln hadn't the manhood to come out for me in preference to Ben Edwards whom he despised. Wouldn't do it because Ben was in the family," Davis told Herndon. "I had done Lincoln many, many favors—Electioneered for him—spent money for him—worked for him—toiled for him—still he wouldn't move. Lincoln I say again and again was a peculiar man."

Yet they also shared strong similarities. They loved justice, the real thing. They were keenly intelligent and practical men. They were longtime Whigs who loved to talk and play politics. (In those days, no canons of official conduct barred sitting judges from engaging in partisan campaigns.) They both had a way with words. They loved to laugh. Davis admired Lincoln's brains and integrity so much that he asked him to fill in as judge on days he could not attend court. Yet no one seemed concerned that Davis would favor Lincoln and his clients in his rulings, since the judge himself took justice seriously. (Indeed, Lincoln won only forty of his eighty-seven cases tried before Judge Davis without a jury.) Whatever resentment may have lingered from his 1848 campaign, Davis formed a deep interest in Lincoln's political ambitions, as many of his associates did, finding his uncommon decency, self-deprecating humor, penetrating intellect, backbone, and powerful moral arguments irresistible.

In May 1850, a reporter covering the visiting court for the *Illinois Citizen*, a small newspaper in Danville, uncannily captured Lincoln's qualities. "Rough, uncouth and unattractive," he wrote, Lincoln was "stern . . . and unfamiliar . . . slow and guarded." At the same time, he was "profound in the depths of his musings. . . . He lives but to ponder, reflect and cogitate." In examining witnesses, "he displays a masterly ingenuity . . . that baffles concealment and defies deceit." In contrast with many lawyers, Lincoln did not infuse his closing arguments with sentimental appeals. He used reason, expressed in simple language. "Seizing upon the minutest points, he weaves them into an argument with an ingenuity really astonishing. . . . Bold, forcible and energetic, he forces conviction upon the mind, and, by his clearness and conciseness, stamps it there, not to be erased."

Bloomington newspaper publisher Jesse W. Fell—a mutual friend of Davis and Lincoln who sold Davis both his law practice and his farm—was among the first to urge Lincoln to seek the presidency. In late 1859, five months before the convention, Fell pressed Lincoln to provide him a biography that he could distribute to an Eastern newspaper. Lincoln replied with a brief and rather amusing 602-word sketch. "There is not much of it," he told Fell, "for the reason, I suppose, that there is not much of me."

Lincoln was born on February 12, 1809, in Hardin County, Kentucky. His parents, Thomas Lincoln and Nancy Hanks, were from Virginia. Native Americans killed his grandfather Abraham Lincoln, "not in battle, but by stealth," when he was working to clear a farm in a forest in Kentucky. "My father, at the death of his father, was but six years of age; and he grew up, litterally without education," Lincoln wrote, his misspelling ironically pointing to his own deficiencies. His parents moved the family to the wilderness of Indiana when he was seven. "It was a wild region, with many bears and other wild animals still in the woods."

He devoted a sizeable chunk of this brief autobiography to explaining a sore point, his lack of formal education. "There were some schools, so called; but no qualification was ever required of a teacher, beyond '*readin, writin, and cipherin*,' to the Rule of Three. If a straggler supposed to understand latin, happened to so-journ in the neighborhood, he was looked upon as a wizzard." That was why he entered adulthood with little schooling. "Still somehow, I could read, write, and cipher to the Rule of Three; but that was all. I have not been to school since. The little advance I now have upon this store of education, I have picked up from time to time under the pressure of necessity."

Lincoln was "raised to farm work" and continued until he was twenty-two, as he had told Davis in 1844. After that he worked as a clerk in New Salem, and served in the Black Hawk War, joining volunteers to turn away a Sauk leader named Black Hawk who brought his followers from Iowa to Illinois, evidently to reclaim ancestral land. Lincoln joked that he ran a greater risk of losing blood from mosquitos than in battle, though he did come across some slaughtered and scalped settlers. But the experience was thrilling because it gave Lincoln his first taste of his peers' approval. "I was elected a Captain of Volunteers—a success which gave me more pleasure than any I have had since," he wrote. His stint in the military, however brief, also helped him understand the ways of a lowly soldier, knowledge that would serve him well when he oversaw the largest armies America had ever seen.

He ran for state legislature and lost—"the only time I have ever been beaten by the people." After that, he was elected four times to the Illinois House. He served one two-year term in Congress, from March 1847 to March 1849, then devoted most of his attention to the law. "I was losing interest in politics, when the repeal of the Missouri Compromise aroused me again. What I have done since then is pretty well known." Lincoln concluded his autobiographical sketch: "If any personal description of me is thought desirable, it may be said, I am, in height, six feet, four inches, nearly; lean in flesh, weighing, on an average, one hundred and eighty pounds; dark complexion, with coarse black hair, and grey eyes—no other marks or brands recollected."

This pithy account of his life had the comic tone of a frontier tale, and he may well have told his story in the same manner while on the judicial circuit. Lincoln left out most of the darkness, fear, and persistent failure that surely played into his acute emotional guardedness and depression. While he cited his mother's death, which had occurred when he was nine, he did not explain how suddenly the catastrophe had struck, through "the milk sickness," nor how his father had left him and his young sister alone for months while he returned to Kentucky to seek a new wife. Uncared for, the children were soon scared, filthy, and ravenously hungry, surviving in part on dried berries their mother had set aside. Visiting his old neighborhood in adulthood, Lincoln wrote a poem about the place that was anything but nostalgic. Two lines, particularly, hinted of his childhood terror: "The panther's scream, filled the night with fear / And bears preyed on the swine." His father scorned Lincoln's attempts to educate himself and hired him out to other farmers, collecting his wages. That fueled Lincoln's hatred of slavery, which permitted an owner to reap the rewards of the labor of another human being. "I used to be a slave," he asserted. The relationship between father and son was so strained that Lincoln later declined to introduce him to Mary and his children and rejected Thomas Lincoln's plea to visit him on his deathbed in 1851. "Say to him that if we could meet now, it is doubtful whether it would not be more painful than pleasant," Lincoln icily wrote to a stepbrother. He refused to attend the funeral or pay for a gravestone.

While Lincoln accurately noted that he was only once "beaten by the people," much of his life was, in truth, scarred by defeat. His New Salem store "winked out," as Lincoln put it, plunging him deep into debt. A career as a surveyor failed, and his tools were sold off to cover debt. He failed to obtain the speakership in the Illinois House. He served only one term in Congress, where his criticism of the popular and triumphant Mexican War damaged his reputation and contributed to the Whigs' loss of his seat in the 1848 election. His attempt to obtain a federal patronage plum in 1849 from the incoming administration of Zachary Taylor in return for his years of devotion to the Whig Party failed miserably. He suffered recurring bouts of crippling depression. "I am now the most miserable man living. If what I feel were equally distributed to the whole human family, there would not be one cheerful face on earth," he confessed to a friend in 1841. People were struck by his persistent look of sadness. "His melancholy dripped from him as he walked," William Herndon said.

In 1854, his Whig friends nominated Lincoln to return to the state legislature. When Mary read of the nomination in a newspaper, she was livid, since he had already served in the legislature and had risen to Congress, however briefly. “She insisted in her imperious way that he must go to the United States Senate, and that it was a degradation to run him for the Legislature,” lawyer Henry Clay Whitney recalled. Lincoln was almost in tears as he declined the office, “the saddest man I Ever Saw—the gloomiest,” his friend William Jayne recalled. One year later, Lincoln duly sought a U.S. Senate seat, entering the fight with more votes in the legislature than any other candidate—44 compared with 41 for his Democratic rival James Shields and 5 for former Democrat Lyman Trumbull. After multiple ballots failed to secure the 50 votes he needed, Lincoln made a fateful decision. Fearing that a last-minute substitute candidate for the Democrats would prevail, he threw his support to Trumbull, thus electing him senator. “I never saw him so dejected,” his friend Joseph Gillespie recalled. “He said the fates seemed to be against him and he thought he would never strive for office again.” David Davis, who had spent a good deal of time prearranging Lincoln’s victory, kicked himself for failing to be on hand in Springfield that day. Had he been at the State House he might have used his considerable powers of persuasion—his knack for “making a man do a thing whether he wants to or not”—to swing enough votes to Lincoln. Davis would not be making the same mistake in 1860.

The turning point of Lincoln’s political life was, as he noted, the repeal of the Missouri Compromise. Passed by Congress in 1820, the compromise had limited the spread of slavery by prohibiting it in America’s northern territories. In 1854, to Lincoln’s horror, Congress replaced it with “popular sovereignty,” championed by Illinois political powerhouse and Democratic U.S. senator Stephen Douglas. Popular sovereignty gave the residents of a territory the power to vote for or against slavery within their borders. Lincoln believed intensely that the Founders had opposed slavery as an obvious contradiction of the values enshrined in the Declaration of Independence and had set it on the road to extinction, in part by banning it in the Northwest Territory that had not yet been broken into states. He was thus appalled at the implication of Douglas's scheme: that the enslavement of human beings in a territory was something that could now be voted up or down, as if the result had no moral consequence and the Declaration had no meaning. Lincoln urged his fellow citizens to recognize that slavery and freedom were incompatible. He warned that slavery must be contained to the places it existed or the economic powers behind it would insist that it be made legal everywhere. If left unchecked, Lincoln thought, Douglas's moral relativism would permit slavery to metastasize and spread to every state, North and South, undermining the freedom of all Americans.

In 1855, a conservative Whig lawyer named T. Lyle Dickey argued with Lincoln in their shared tavern room over whether slavery and freedom could permanently coexist in America. Dickey asserted that they could, as they had since the Constitution was ratified in 1788; Lincoln, sitting on the edge of the bed in his nightshirt, countered that slavery must perish in time, or the founding principles of freedom would be so weakened that they could not be sustained. They drifted off to sleep, but hours later Dickey awoke to find Lincoln sitting up in bed. "Dickey," Lincoln said, "I tell you this nation cannot exist half slave and half free." "Oh, Lincoln," Dickey replied. "Go back to sleep."

After his 1855 defeat, Lincoln had thought his political career was over, and many agreed. "Lincoln is undoubtedly the most unfortunate politician that has ever attempted to rise in Illinois," one newspaper in Urbana, Illinois, opined in 1857. "In everything he undertakes, politically, he seems doomed to failure. He has been prostrated often enough in his political schemes to have crushed the life out of any ordinary man." Lincoln could not help but compare his dismal record with the triumphant ascent of the state's most popular politician. "Twenty-two years ago . . . Douglas and I first became acquainted," he wrote in a private reflection. "We were both young then; he a trifle younger than I. Even then, we were both ambitious; I, perhaps, quite as much so as he. With *me*, the race of ambition has been a failure—a flat failure; with *him* it has been one of splendid success. His name fills the nation; and is not unknown, even, in foreign lands."

Yet Lincoln felt compelled to try yet again in 1858, seeking this time to unseat that very senator. In accepting the Senate nomination of the Republicans—the new party he had helped found in the state to oppose Stephen Douglas and his ideas—Lincoln expanded on the thoughts that had kept him up nights on the circuit. "A house divided against itself cannot stand," he declared, quoting a biblical passage well known to his listeners. "I believe this government cannot endure, permanently half *slave* and half *free*. I do not expect the Union to be *dissolved*—I do not expect the house to *fall*—but I *do* expect it will cease to be divided. It will become *all* one thing, or *all* the other." When Douglas announced his candidacy for reelection on the balcony of the Tremont House to a huge crowd gathered below, Lincoln answered his arguments the next day from the same spot, and the battle was on.

Douglas was heavily favored against his snake-bitten opponent, but he had not counted on Lincoln's skills of reasoning honed by studying Euclid and years of making closing arguments to Illinois juries. The two hammered away at each other in formal three-hour debates held outdoors before thousands of people in seven of the state's nine congressional districts, clashing in Ottawa, Freeport, Jonesboro, Charleston, Galesburg, Quincy, and Alton. The first speaker went on for an hour, the second replied for an hour and a half, and the first spoke again for thirty minutes. Douglas was sharp and snide, labeling Lincoln a radical who would destroy social cohesion and drag down white Americans. But Lincoln's intelligence, humor, eloquence, and unflinching moral character shone. At points, he left Douglas furious and sputtering. Shorthand reporters captured the pair's cutting arguments, and newspaper readers throughout the North found the little-known Lincoln an artful and impressive opponent of slavery. In the end, the candidates for the legislature backing Lincoln won more total votes than those supporting Douglas. But, because of the way the districts were drawn, the Douglas men captured more seats, guaranteeing his reelection in January 1859 when the newly elected legislators would gather to vote for senator. Lincoln had failed again.

Devastated, he told himself that, this time, his political career was irredeemably finished. Still, he was proud that he had made the fight. "It gave me a hearing on the great and durable question of the age, which I could have had in no other way; and though I now sink out of view, and shall be forgotten, I believe I have made some marks which will tell for the cause of civil liberty long after I am gone," he wrote to a doctor friend, A. G. Henry. But something happened to Lincoln on his way back home on election night, after all the rain late in the campaign. "The path had been worn hog-backed & was slippering," he recounted. "My foot slipped out from under me, knocking the other out of the way, but I recovered myself and lit square: and I said to myself, '*It's a slip and not a fall.*'"

Now, on May 12, 1860, Lincoln not only was still standing, but believed he had an outside chance at the Republican nomination for president. Everybody, of course, knew the odds were against him. "Lincoln has only the Illinois vote," the Associated Press reported that night. Already there was talk of the booby prize. "Illinois in case it fails to secure the nomination for President, wishes the Vice-Presidential nomination."

Even in the Illinois delegation, William Seward was a popular man, and the liberal northern part of the state favored him strongly. Among Seward's admirers was the boisterous former four-term congressman and current mayor of Chicago, "Long John" Wentworth, who at six feet six inches stood even taller than Lincoln. The big man had little patience for his opponents. He once reportedly told a group of unruly citizens who had gathered to hear him, "You damned fools. . . . You can either vote for me for mayor or you can go to hell." Chicagoans did vote for him, giving him a second term as mayor in March 1860. But Lincoln had left Wentworth off the list of at-large delegates he had carefully assembled to serve him in Chicago. Wentworth did not like being snubbed, and both he and the Republican newspaper he edited, the *Chicago Democrat*, seemed more supportive of the New Yorker Seward than of the Illinois candidate.

So did another of the city's Republican papers, the *Chicago Journal*. It bedecked its building—just across Dearborn Street from the Tremont House—with a huge sign. For the next several days, whenever David Davis looked out of his hotel room window he would receive a graphic reminder, in big block letters, of just who was favored to capture the nomination in Chicago:

SEWARD.

Chapter 2: The Irrepressible Conflict

Shortly before eight o'clock on that Saturday evening, May 12, 1860, the great engine of the Michigan Southern train, its big funnel-shaped stack expelling black smoke and orange sparks, pounded up the track on a long pier sunk into Lake Michigan that ran parallel to the shore. Through their windows on the left, passengers gazed at the gleaming gas lights and kerosene lamps of Michigan Avenue. The crowded train slowed as it approached and then entered the massive Grand Central Depot near the mouth of the Chicago River, squealing to a stop. With an exhausted huff of steam from the engine, the long journey from the East was over.

A cadre of strangely attired young men had been waiting for the train to arrive. They carried torches in the form of four-foot-long poles topped with tin cups filled with oil. And they wore a uniform: glazed military caps, each bound around with a red, white, and blue ribbon, and large black enameled waterproof cloaks designed to protect them from rain and any stray drops of hot oil. One member of the company carried aloft a standard bearing the arresting image of a large open eyeball—the emblem of the Wide Awakes, the new Republican paramilitary youth organization.

The Wide Awakes idea, which had sprung up just two months earlier in Hartford, Connecticut, had already become a Northern fad, leaping to Chicago and other locales, a symbol of the rapidly intensifying political passions in America. The members—many bearded, some too young to shave—wished to demonstrate the power of a young America that was ready for a change, ditching what they saw as Democratic corruption for a new and rising party that opposed the spread of slavery. They dressed up; marched in parades, shouldering their torches like muskets; and practiced complex military maneuvers, which they were only too pleased to show off to anyone who would watch.

The *Chicago Press and Tribune* found their precision striking. "The beauty and importance of a torch light procession are very much heightened by order, discipline, and regularity in marching," it noted that month. Like the baseball clubs and volunteer firefighting companies that were prominent in urban America, the movement brought young men together to expend energy, form friendships, and enjoy fraternal dinners, while giving them the sense they were doing something meaningful. "Join the Wide Awakes!" a bombastic young Republican named Trumps told the *Yonkers* (New York) *Examiner* that year. "Join the Wide Awakes, and you are a made man, a faithful citizen, and a perfect trump!" Democratic critics believed the Wide Awakes fleshed out their ranks with "all of the rowdies, bullies, and vagabonds, that can be collected together, by the promise of free suppers, and plenty of liquor to drink." Each Chicago member, however, took a pledge "that he will refrain from using profane language, or noisy demonstrations, and that he will implicitly obey the orders of his officers, and comport himself in a decent and respectful manner."

The Wide Awakes were here to greet the most distinguished leaders attending the convention, including New York governor and Seward supporter Edwin D. Morgan, a stern-visaged, impeccably dressed forty-nine-year-old with pork chop sideburns who was the powerful chairman of the Republican National Committee. With the Light Guard Band blasting patriotic songs, the Wide Awakes accompanied Morgan and his associates the three blocks to their quarters at the Tremont House. Other nationally known figures were aboard the train. America's greatest and most influential newspaper editor, Horace Greeley, the man behind the *New-York Tribune*, emerged onto the platform, as did Joshua

Giddings, a weather-beaten sixty-four-year-old Ohio congressman who had been bravely fighting against slavery, incurring the wrath of Democrats, since long before there was a Republican Party.

But perhaps the most notable passenger was a sixty-two-year-old New Yorker who was brimming with energy, graciousness, and good humor. He was a big man, at six feet one, though inclined to slouch, with broad shoulders, a ruddy and clean-shaven face, deep-set, inquisitive hazel eyes, and a prominent nose. As a veteran of America's political conventions—national and state—Thurlow Weed was in his element. A keen student of human nature, he had a passion for the intricate mechanics of politics. Genial and tactful, he thrived on securing deals, pulling levers, and motivating people to make things happen. From his position as the editor of the *Albany Journal*, in the state's capital, Weed had become a key power broker in New York and, by extension, Washington, DC. His pervasive influence behind the scenes won him the nicknames of "the Wizard of the Lobby" and "the Dictator." But his most important mission was promoting the admirable friend whose fortunes he had advanced devotedly for decades. Weed was in Chicago to secure the Republican nomination for that man, William Henry Seward—and make him the next president of the United States.

Weed needed no parade escort from the depot to his hotel. He was staying right next door at the elegant Richmond House, on the corner of South Water Street and Michigan Avenue. Though not as big or flashy as the Tremont, the Richmond maintained an exquisite standard of luxury, boasting of its luxurious modern conveniences: gas lights, steam heat, and "Hot, Cold and Shower Baths." "I have yet to see more comfort, neatness, elegance and beauty in any house of public entertainment than I have found at the Richmond House," a Kentucky visitor wrote in an 1856 dispatch to the *Louisville Daily Courier*. It "is fitted up in the most superb style, while an unusual degree of neatness and cleanliness pervades the whole establishment. . . . Beautiful cut glass, delicate china, rich plate and snow-white linen decorate the table, and the whole machinery of the house moves noiselessly and is unseen by the traveler."

Fond of working out of opulent hotels, Weed lived at the sumptuous Astor House when in New York City, where his famous suite, number 11, was known as the place "where caucuses were held, campaigns arranged, [and] senators, congressmen, cabinet ministers, governors, and Presidents made and unmade." On May 5, a week before Weed's arrival in Chicago, the *New York Daily Herald* reported that Republican politicians had been "exceedingly busy" for days at the Astor. "Thurlow Weed's room was overrun yesterday with anxious politicians. It being his last day in the city, everyone seemed anxious to see the chief; a large number stood waiting in the hall for their turn to consult with him." That afternoon was given over to final strategizing about the convention.

The chief liked to impress associates with his surroundings, giving off an aura of power and position, and he intended to lure Republican delegates to his side at the Richmond House with cigars, fine whiskey, and expensive champagne. The New Yorkers took over the ornate parlors downstairs as their "headquarters" for meetings and entertaining. Many in Weed's entourage would stay at the Richmond, too, including some of the crude types that New York politics attracted—ward bosses who drank whiskey, spat tobacco, wore big rings, laughed boisterously, slapped backs, wielded fists, and performed whatever services were required to secure victory on Election Day.

Maryland lawyer Montgomery Blair, writing to his wife on Friday, already found the Seward men as "clamorous as crows" in the city. Weed intended to make good use of them, and of the thousand Seward supporters he was importing to Chicago, sending a powerful message of his man's popularity and dominance in the party. Having left little to chance, Weed looked forward to the coming week, confident that his years of planning and hard work would bear the fruit of victory.

Like Abraham Lincoln, Edward Thurlow Weed grew up in a world far from the halls of power and elegantly appointed hotel suites. Weed was born on November 15, 1797, when John Adams was president and

George Washington was still alive, in a log cabin along a dusty turnpike between the villages of Cairo and Acra, in Greene County, New York. The family was poor, his father repeatedly in debtor's prison. Like Lincoln, Weed had next to no formal education, cobbling together only several months of schooling in childhood. And, like young Abe, the boy made up for the deficiency by reading ravenously, though books were hard to come by in rural New York. Weed long remembered his attempt to secure one prized volume. He "heard that a neighbor, some three miles off, had borrowed from a still more distant neighbor a book of great interest. . . . I started off, barefooted, in the snow, to obtain the treasure." Along the way, the boy had to stop at spots of bare ground to warm his feet, but the stinging pain proved to be worth it. "The book was at home, and the good people consented, upon my promise that it should be neither torn nor soiled, to lend it to me. In returning with the prize, I was too happy to think of the snow or my naked feet."

He grew up quickly. At eight, Thurlow went to work as a bellows blower in a local blacksmith's shop for six cents a day. Not long after, he served as a cabin boy on vessels plying the Hudson River between New York City and Albany. He ran errands for a tavern and worked at a print shop. After his father moved the family to Cincinnatus, New York, he toiled as a farm laborer and in the woods, wrapping his shoeless feet in rags, chopping wood, drawing sap, and making maple sugar—while reading books during his downtime. He labored at an iron foundry in nearby Onondaga. "That was night and day work," Weed recalled. "We ate salt pork and rye and Indian bread, three times a day, and slept on straw in bunks. I liked the excitement of a furnace life."

But he loved newspapers. With his father's help, he was apprenticed to a nearby printer. Fiercely patriotic, Thurlow joined the militia to fight in the War of 1812 when he was only fifteen, and alternated periods of service with work in his trade before being mustered out at seventeen. In 1814, while toiling in the beautiful village of Cooperstown, the restless teenager boarded with Mrs. Clarissa Ostrander and soon fell in love with her sixteen-year-old daughter, Catherine. The family, not without reason, frowned on Catherine's engagement to a journeyman printer, saying she was too young and Weed too poorly established for marriage. But like David Davis, Weed proved a stubborn man. "We communed together on the subject, and mutually agreed to hold no intercourse either by word or letter for two or three years, when, if her mind was unchanged, she was to write to me," Weed recalled. "I immediately left Cooperstown, and neither saw nor heard from her for more than three years, when a letter came informing me that time had made no change in her affections, to which I replied in similar terms."

They married on April 26, 1818, at the Presbyterian Church in Cooperstown. He was twenty; she, nineteen. Catherine proved a loving and industrious partner and mother of their four children. Newspaper work, unfortunately, could be unrewarding. At one point, the family was so poor that it survived for eight days on nothing but bread, butter, and water. "During the winter, my wife rose long before daylight, kindled her own fire, and prepared breakfast, of which we partook by candle-light, and the dawning day found me at work at the office," Weed recalled. He toiled on into the night, capping his workday by writing editorials. After he became powerful and famous, Weed often remarked that he had "commenced life with a fortune of a wife and two children, and a *cash* capital of fifty cents."

Through his newspaper work, Weed was drawn into politics, first joining a populist uprising against freemasonry, which voters perceived to be a movement of secretive and self-serving elites, and then embracing the new Whig Party. Weed got a taste of electoral politics by serving in the New York State Assembly in 1825 and 1830—his only stints in public office. He preferred working behind the scenes and exerting influence through his tart and sarcastic editorials, a journalistic innovation that attracted readers and embarrassed politicians.

However brief Weed's time in the assembly was, it was momentous. Immersed in state politics, he founded the *Albany Journal* in 1829 and made it successful and influential. In the assembly, he also met and formed a deepening friendship with a talented and sensitive young lawyer named William Henry Seward, whose slender, compact body, five feet seven inches tall, seemed alive with nervous energy. "I saw in him in a remarkable degree rapidly developing elements of character, which could not fail to render him eminently useful in public life," Weed recalled. "I discerned also unmistakable evidences of stern integrity, earnest patriotism, and unswerving fidelity. I saw also in him a rare capacity for intellectual labor, with an industry that never tired and required no relaxation; to all which was added a purity and delicacy of habit and character almost feminine."

Like Lincoln and Davis, the two New Yorkers favored the classic Whig programs of economic development through a national bank and taxpayer-backed internal improvements—the construction of canals, turnpikes, railroads, and harbors, and the enhancement of navigation on rivers—believing that the United States should be a land of opportunity for those willing to work. They supported public education and extending the vote to all white males, however poor. It seemed to Weed that, under proper management, a man of Seward's ability could make big things happen for New York, and America. "Weed is very much with me, and I enjoy his warmth of feeling," Seward wrote home to his wife. "A politician, skillful in design and persevering in execution; whose exciting principle is personal friendship or opposition, and not self-interest—that is just Thurlow Weed."

Seward had a more privileged upbringing than Weed did. He was born on May 16, 1801, in the rural village of Florida, New York, where his father, Samuel, was a leading man in the community as a physician, merchant, farmer—and slaveholder. Many New Yorkers no longer supported the institution of slavery, which the state was phasing out, but Samuel seemed a humane master. He was the only man in town who sent his slaves to school, and Seward recalled that his parents "never uttered an expression that could tend to make me think that the negro was inferior to the white person." The family had the means to provide young Seward with an education, and the redheaded boy proved a bright and eager student who devoured books. One of his family's former slaves, known in the family as Aunt Chloe, recalled proudly that "William, unlike most little boys of the village, instead of running away from school to go home, would frequently run away from home to go to school."

At fifteen, he left home to attend Union College in Schenectady, long remembering his trip up the Hudson River on a newfangled steam ship, capped by the appearance of Albany, the state capital, "so vast, so splendid, so imposing." After college, he took up the law in Auburn, New York, and joined the practice of Elijah Miller, a retired judge. Seward quickly fell in love with the judge's slim, dark-haired daughter, Frances, a bright and educated young woman who was an inch taller than Seward. They married in October 1824 and lived in Miller's large and handsome house, attended by servants. While journeying to Niagara Falls that fall, the newlyweds had trouble near Rochester, where their carriage wheel was damaged. Among those who came out to help was Thurlow Weed, then working for the *Rochester Telegraph*, who thus met Seward for the first time.

Seward was elected to the state Senate in 1830. His subsequent rise in politics, aided at each step by Weed, seemed almost charmed. In 1834—twenty-six years before he showed up in Chicago—Weed displayed an instinct for the backroom wheeling and dealing of party conventions by maneuvering the thirty-three-year-old senator into the Whig nomination for governor. Seward lost the November election and returned to the law, but Weed tried again in 1838, advancing Seward's cause for months and securing him the gubernatorial nomination on the fourth ballot at the Whig convention. In his letter of congratulations, Weed warned Seward that they were "again embarked on a sea of difficulties, and must go earnestly to work." Pro-Democratic newspapers later charged that Weed's work included importing voters from Philadelphia to help swing the election. This time, turnout was immense, and Seward won by ten thousand votes. When he finally got the news after days of counting, the governor-elect exclaimed to a friend, "God bless Thurlow Weed! I owe this result to him." Seward wrote affectionately to Weed. "The sweetness of his temper inclines me to love my tyrant," he teased him.

At thirty-seven, Seward took the oath of office and delivered a soaring, idealistic, and optimistic message to the legislature. Can anyone doubt, he asked, "that our race is ordained to reach on this continent a higher standard of social perfection than it has ever yet attained, and that hence will proceed the spirit which shall renovate the world?" Since self-government was essential to "the accomplishment of these sublime purposes," he called for a boldly liberal agenda of improvements to schools and colleges, the introduction of libraries to schools, and "the education of the colored race, as well as the white." He touted the spread of charitable institutions, called for court reform to lessen delays of justice, advocated cuts in the bureaucracy, sought election reform to thwart the notorious stuffing of ballot boxes, and pushed the Whig agenda of public investments in infrastructure. In the months ahead, he showed unusual sympathy toward immigrants and Catholics, who were detested by many Whigs and, later, Republicans.

People found him so friendly, young, and unpretentious that they could scarcely believe he was the governor. According to one story, Seward on one trip shared the seat atop a stagecoach with the driver instead of riding in comfort inside. He had trouble persuading the man that he was, in fact, New York's chief executive. When they stopped at an inn to clear up the matter, the innkeeper agreed with the driver that Seward was not the governor. "Who is, then?" Seward demanded. "Why," the innkeeper exclaimed, "Thurlow Weed!"

At the Whigs' first national convention, in 1840, Weed shrewdly maneuvered the New York delegation's crucial support behind William Henry Harrison for president rather than beloved Whig leader Henry Clay, believing the hero of the battle against the Indians at Tippecanoe could garner more votes in November. (With John Tyler as the vice-presidential nominee, the ticket ran on the catchy slogan of "Tippecanoe and Tyler too!") Weed, as usual, was right about the politics. Harrison triumphed, outperforming Seward, his coattails dragging the governor to reelection by only five thousand votes. The narrowness of Seward's victory made it clear that he had flirted with political suicide by spending lavishly on public projects and, especially, by openly embracing Catholics. He had formed a friendship with New York bishop John Hughes and advocated the use of public funds to aid Roman Catholic schools, since the curriculum of the Protestant-run Public Schools Society had a distinctly anti-Catholic undertone. His friends had pleaded with him to reconsider, but he refused. "This right hand drops off," he vowed, "before I do one act with the Whig or any other party in opposition to any portion of my fellow citizens, on the ground of the difference of their nativity or of their religion."

In 1842, Seward wisely decided against seeking reelection. His party went down to defeat in an avalanche. Regarding his political career as finished, he looked forward to returning to the law and retiring the enormous personal debts he had run up as governor, including $11,000 to Weed personally. In a letter to Weed, Seward warmly acknowledged his friend's essential role in everything he had achieved. "Without your aid," Seward wrote, "how hopeless would have been my prospect of reaching the elevation from which I am descending; how could I have sustained myself there; how could I have avoided the assaults to which I have been exposed; how could I have secured the joyous reflections of this hour?" They were joyous because he could now enjoy his superb cigars, his fine liquor, and his big Auburn home. He kept in close touch with Weed, whom he called his "late Dictator" and "my first last and best of friends."

Seward's brilliant legal mind and political experience quickly reaped financial rewards, but he also took up cases he believed served the cause of justice and humanity, even at the price of his popularity. In 1846, he defended an African American man named William Freeman who, Seward believed, was insane and unable to discern right from wrong. Some four miles outside of Auburn, Freeman had entered a home and stabbed to death a white man, his aged mother, his pregnant wife, and their two-year-old daughter. The community was incensed, and Freeman had been beaten in jail to the point that he lost some of his hearing and perhaps suffered brain damage.

Seward was determined to defend him on the grounds of insanity, though his own father-in-law pleaded with him to "abandon the nigger." Seward's wife, Frances, said her husband would not listen. "He will not close his eyes and know that a great wrong is perpetrated." His friend John Austin, the Universalist minister in Auburn, wrote in his journal of Seward's closing argument on the Fourth of July. While fireworks were erupting outside, inside the gloomy courtroom "a lone voice was pleading with all the energies of one of the mightiest minds of the age in behalf of a poor friendless demented African." The jury found Freeman guilty. Seward was so distraught over the prisoner's inability to comprehend what was going on that he "buried his face in his hands, and burst into tears—and finally seized his hat and rushed from the courtroom." But Seward won a reversal on appeal, and Freeman was deemed insane. Seward wrote to Weed after the ordeal that he was "exhausted in mind and body, covered with public reproach, and stunned with duns and protests."

By then, he was growing tired of the law and yearned to return to a position of political power. At the 1848 Whig national convention, Weed offered a deal: New York would back General Zachary Taylor, a hero of the Mexican War, for president in return for a promise to make Seward his secretary of state. Weed duly delivered the delegation, but the plan went awry when the convention chose New York's Millard Fillmore for vice president—making it impossible for Taylor to have two New Yorkers in such prominent positions. Though blocked from the cabinet, Seward took to the hustings to sell Taylor. In late September, he spoke at the Tremont Temple in Boston, to be followed on stage by a gangling Illinois congressman he had never met before, Abraham Lincoln. (On his way home, Lincoln stopped off in Albany to see the famous Weed, who took him to meet Fillmore.)

When General Taylor won handsomely, carrying the Whigs to triumph in New York, Weed had his opportunity to maneuver Seward into a U.S. Senate seat. Critics complained that Seward, who had spoken out with increasing bluntness against the horrors of slavery, was attempting to turn the Whigs into an abolitionist party. But Weed got the job done, and the legislature elected Seward senator—to the consternation, already, of Southerners. His policies marked him "as a fanatic of the deepest dye, bold, daring, reckless and malignant," the *Weekly* (Jackson) *Mississippian* warned. The paper regarded Seward's election "as ominous of evil to the South—as a blow at the constitution and the Union, likely to be as fatal as any previously struck." When Seward traveled to Charleston, South Carolina, soon thereafter, he got the cold shoulder from everyone, he told his wife, "excepting the people who stand behind the chairs at dinner"—African American slaves.

By then, slavery was threatening to rip the country apart. In the late eighteenth century, after the American Revolution greatly expanded freedom for white men and inspired the first full-scale abolitionist movement in human history, it had seemed to be an outmoded, inefficient, and immoral system that would gradually fade away. Then a Yankee inventor named Eli Whitney devised a machine that removed seeds from the cotton flower, dramatically increasing productivity and, hence, profits. His engine, or "gin" for short, transformed cotton cloth from a luxury item into one of the world's staples of clothing, boosting manufacturing on both sides of the Atlantic and greatly expanding the wealth and power of England and the United States. The cotton gin also made slavery immensely profitable and slaves immensely valuable. By the 1850s, some 1.8 million of the 3.2 million slaves in North America were feverishly producing cotton, mostly in the Deep South. By 1860, with a rising population of nearly 4 million slaves, the South was generating some 2.3 billion pounds a year, and cotton constituted a stunning 57 percent of the nation's exports. "Cotton is King," South Carolina senator James Hammond declared.

Slavery had been part of human culture going back to the dawn of civilization, long accepted as a fact of life. But in 1833, Britain banned it in most parts of the Empire, and in the United States it ran headlong into the founding principles articulated in the Declaration of Independence—that all men are created equal and endowed with rights no one could justly take away. As the cotton gin made slavery more profitable, many scoffed that the Declaration was never meant to apply to African Americans, who came to be relentlessly depicted, in everything from novels to newspaper articles to wildly successful blackface minstrel shows, as inferior to white people, if not a separate subspecies of human being.

Some contended that slaves in the South were better off than white workers, including women and children, who toiled miserably in dangerous Northern factories. Northern business owners routinely discarded employees when they became sick, injured, or too old to work, while Southern slaveowners—many of them sincere and empathetic Christians—provided housing, food, clothing, and medical care, and maintained elderly slaves until their death. But many in America took a different view. They grew increasingly troubled by the obvious horrors of slavery, endemic to any system that gives some human beings absolute power over others—the cruel wielding of the lash, unrestrained by the law, to the point of disfigurement or death; the rampant exploitation of young women as sexual slaves; the heartless separation of families, of husband from wife, and of child from mother and father, as manacled human beings were caged in filthy pens and auctioned off in public; and the misery of a human existence denied any hope of freedom and self-advancement. Southerners held that it was not that simple. They looked at attempts to limit slavery, combined with steep tariffs on imported goods, as motivated by the rapacious North's determination to weaken the South until it became a vassal region, ripe for economic exploitation. They were infuriated by Northerners' smug claims of moral superiority, when Northern greed exposed so many struggling people to abuse and neglect.

Perhaps more than any other politician, Seward set Southerners on edge. During the great Senate debate over the Compromise of 1850, designed to keep the country from splitting apart, Seward spoke movingly against a Fugitive Slave Act that would compel Northerners to return fellow human beings who had escaped to freedom. "We cannot, in our judgment, be either true Christians or real free men, if we impose on another a chain that we defy all human power to fasten on ourselves," he said. Seward defended the Constitution and said Americans have a duty to uphold it as stewards of freedom. "But there is a law higher than the Constitution," he argued—the people's allegiance to God and their own moral conscience. His three-hour speech in the Senate electrified slavery's opponents, and Seward was thrilled to see 100,000 copies of it printed and distributed to supporters by mail or at party gatherings. But Weed worried about its impact on moderate voters. The "higher law" doctrine could not help but inflame fears of disunion, since Southerners depended on the Constitution to secure their rights against a growing Northern majority. Seward was wounded by Weed's pragmatic objections, telling a friend they had "given me much pain." In Seward's own eyes, he had struck a great blow for liberty. "I *know* that I have spoken words that will tell when I am dead, and even while I am living, for the blessing and benefit of mankind, and for myself that is consolation enough."

But he would pay a price. In a show of open contempt, Southerners walked out on his second speech against the Compromise of 1850. When the House supported the plan, a disappointed Seward expressed the hope that it might help preserve the nation. "Yes, in spite of you," one representative hissed at him. New York lawyer George Templeton Strong, though a fellow Whig and friend of Seward, expressed relief in his diary that Congress had "blighted the hopes of Billy Seward and his gang of incendiaries, who wanted to set the country on fire that they might fill themselves with place and profit in the confusion."

Seward did not run for president in 1852, but he burnished his fame by aiding in the publication of three thick volumes of his writings —a staggering contrast to Lincoln's 602 scant words in recounting his own story. The *New York Times* hailed the publication as a tribute to a great American of extraordinary moral courage. "Standing upon the rock of his own personal convictions, he has withstood private persuasion, public pressure and the clamor of expediency," the *Times* observed. Seward quipped that the books were "good volumes to die on. The heresies are all in." In 1854, Seward joined the outcry against Stephen Douglas's "popular sovereignty" and the destruction of the Missouri Compromise. The barrage of praise he received after a celebrated Senate address that year included a letter from William Herndon of Springfield, Illinois, who noted that his law partner, "your friend" Abraham Lincoln, "thinks your speech most excellent."

In 1855, Seward faced the daunting prospect of seeking reelection. New York politicians who dared support him had to worry about offending their more moderate constituents. Weed had to fight hard for him. He "whipped or coaxed" the legislators in Albany "like sorry hounds," one opponent reported, until he prevailed. Seward, receiving the glad news by telegram in Washington, wrote to Weed "to express not so much my deep and deepening gratitude to you, as my amazement at the magnitude of the complexity of the dangers through which you have conducted our shattered bark, and the wonderful sagacity and skill with which you have saved us all from so imminent a wreck." Seward was indeed flirting with disaster. He and his wife, Frances, had accepted fugitive slaves in their house in Auburn as a stop on the Underground Railroad, a federal crime, and in 1859 he sold a small house nearby for next to nothing to a leading conductor on that railroad, an escaped slave named Harriet Tubman. He supported the newspaper of another escaped slave, Frederick Douglass. There was no doubt where Seward stood on the great moral question of his age.

By the mid-1850s, the politics of slavery had eaten away at Seward's Whig Party. Southern and border-state Whigs who defended the institution found themselves forced to desert to the Democrats, while many Northern Whigs sought a new political coalition. In 1854, a disparate collection of anti-Democratic Northerners who opposed the expansion of slavery coalesced into a burgeoning new party. At a state meeting that year in Ripon, Wisconsin, members adopted the name of Republican, partly in tribute to Thomas Jefferson's Democratic-Republican Party. The name caught on. Weed and Seward left the Whigs for the Republicans, helping to make the newly fledged party a national political force, the leading opponent of the Democrats by 1856.

Weed's control of New York's large Whig delegation had enabled him to play an important role in the presidential nominations of William

Henry Harrison in 1840, of Zachary Taylor in 1848, and of Winfield Scott in 1852. He wielded similar power over New York's delegation at the Republicans' first presidential nominating convention, in Philadelphia, in 1856, and might have easily secured the nomination for Seward. But Weed forced his friend to withdraw his name and, instead, enabled Californian John Frémont to win the nod. The editor had concluded that a Seward campaign would be futile at this early stage of the party's development. "We do not want him nominated for *fun*," Weed declared, explaining to one of Seward's friends that he "did not think anybody [from the new party] would be elected, and that it was better that Frémont should be sacrificed than Seward." Weed reassured a disappointed Seward that he had not been "unfaithful to a purpose which, for twenty years, engrossed my thoughts and controlled my actions"—making him president. But Seward's triumph would have to wait until 1860, when the party would be stronger. Just as Weed expected, Frémont fell short in November 1856, losing to Democrat James Buchanan, while Seward remained the darling of the Republican faithful. And the Seward-Weed partnership endured.

In 1858, while campaigning for fellow Republican Edwin D. Morgan for governor of New York, Seward grabbed headlines yet again. He delivered a speech that electrified his followers and inflamed his enemies, perhaps even more than his "higher law" address. Seward argued that America was being forced to choose between slavery and freedom; only one system could endure. "It is an irrepressible conflict between opposing and enduring forces, and it means that the United States must and will, sooner or later, become either entirely a slaveholding nation, or entirely a free-labor nation." Herndon again wrote enthusiastically to Seward, noting the striking similarities between his speech and his law partner's "House Divided" address. But Lincoln's speech had been all but ignored outside of Illinois. Seward's, by contrast, set off a firestorm, and "irrepressible conflict" became a national catchphrase, permanently fused to his name. While the speech rallied New York Republicans to elect Morgan, Southern politicians considered it a virtual declaration of war against their way of life—and perhaps a promise of a bloody civil conflict to come. Many brandished the words "traitor" and "agitator" to describe Seward, and most Southern senators ceased speaking to him.

The political heat grew so intense that Weed concluded it might be best to get him out of the country for a while. Seward set off on a nine-month-long trip to Europe, leaving New York in March 1859 aboard an oceangoing steamship, with a band playing "Hail to the Chief" and "guns firing, bells ringing, handkerchiefs waving, flags flying, and people cheering," his son Frederick recounted. European leaders greeted him warmly. The future British prime minister Lord Palmerston met with him, as did other leading politicians. Queen Victoria received him twice. In Paris, he met with Emperor Napoleon III. In Rome, he enjoyed a lengthy interview with Pope Pius IX, who hinted at the possibility of his "higher advancement." He visited Jerusalem and Egypt. A wealthy Syrian effendi named Ayoub Bey Trabulsky presented him with the lavish gift of three blooded Arabian horses, sending them on to Beirut for the trip to America. While American papers reported sporadically on Seward's lengthy trip, they devoted much more space to his prospects for the 1860 nomination. His sojourn, in a sense, gave his Republican rivals a free run for months. But Weed believed Seward was so popular with the party faithful that he could afford to fritter away much of 1859 hobnobbing with European elites and burnishing his credentials as a great man.

And indeed, as the journey neared its end, worshippers in Northern churches prayed fervently for Seward's safe return. When he reached New York aboard the ice-encrusted sidewheel steamship *Arago* on the evening of December 28, after a trip from Southampton, England, marked by violent westerly gales, snowstorms, and severe cold, word spread rapidly. In the park outside the Astor House, where Seward stayed that night, the Young Men's Republican Committee, armed with two brass cannons, fired a salute of one hundred rounds in zero-degree weather. The following day, a throng descended on a noon reception at City Hall, until it was dangerously overcrowded, with a mob outside clamoring to get in.

Well-wishers engulfed Seward, who responded with studied nonchalance. "'Be much happier to see you at the White House,' said one jostled supporter, with a smile of deep significance. 'This is a much safer place than that,' replied Mr. Seward." The esteemed lawyer William Curtis Noyes quipped, "We have a specimen of this irrepressible conflict getting in here." He was far from the only one making the joke, the *New York Times* observed. "Another repeated for the hundredth time, 'There's an irrepressible conflict going on outside.' 'I hope you'll be able to reduce it,' Seward answered." A short, stout man standing on tiptoe shouted in Seward's ear, "I hope you'll fulfill your mission!" Another little man "whispered in a confidential tone," "I want you for the next President of the United States." A man selling photographs of Seward shook his hand and asked, "D'ye want to buy a portrait Sir?" One reporter estimated that Seward's hands, right and left, were shaken nearly two thousand times within an hour.

At 2:00 p.m., still besieged, Seward called for his coat, hat, and cane, forced his way through the crowd, and stepped into a carriage. When he emerged at the Astor House, people cheered loudly, and firefighters returning from a blaze saluted him with a shrill blast of their whistle. At 5:00 p.m., Seward caught the Hudson River Railroad train for home. When he finally reached his beloved hometown of Auburn, more than 15,000 people were waiting in the cold to welcome him at the station. At his doorstep, he discovered that every clergyman in town had turned up to honor him. Touched, Seward shook hands all around before blurting out, "God bless you all, my friends!"

In October 1859, while Seward was across the Atlantic Ocean, a radical abolitionist named John Brown seized the federal armory at Harper's Ferry, Virginia, part of a mad plan to arm slaves and bring on a violent insurrection—the nightmare scenario of bloody revenge that had long haunted the white people of the South. With the help of Marines led by Robert E. Lee, Brown was arrested and, soon thereafter, found guilty of treason, murder, and inciting a slave insurrection, and he was duly hanged. Though Seward was thousands of miles away from the incident, many accused the Republicans in general, and Seward in particular, of provoking insurrection with their moralistic rhetoric and financial support. Southerners began talking darkly about seceding if such a man won the presidency in 1860. Mississippi congressman Reuben Davis spoke out bluntly on the House floor on December 8. If the Republican Party managed to get a "sectional candidate" elected to fight an "irrepressible conflict," he warned, then "we of the South will tear this Constitution in pieces, and look to our guns for justice and right against aggression and wrong." The ghost of John Brown would hover over American politics right into 1860.

Determined to impress others with his bonhomie, Seward had always tried to cultivate friendly relationships in the Senate, despite political differences. In early 1860, he invited elites of all political stripes to his Washington home for lavish dinners, which an anonymous "lady correspondent" described to the *New-York Tribune*. Servants in formal attire greeted guests and escorted them to the parlor, and later into the dining room, "where you find your name attached to the napkin placed by your plate." Seward welcomed each guest around the table by name. "Turtle soup is then served; the other courses in regular order, seventeen in number—the plates being changed for each course; wine glasses, five in number, of different size, form and color, indicating the different wines to be served." By the end of the night, Seward's guests left "doubtless convinced that their host is the man best fitted for the Presidential mansion."

At the dinner table among friends, Henry Adams recalled, Seward "threw off restraint, or seemed to throw it off," and "chose to appear as a free talker, who loathed pomposity and enjoyed a joke." The eternally cynical and acerbic Adams, grandson of one president and great-grandson of another, was struck by the senator's "slouching, slender figure," with "a head like a wise macaw; a beaked nose; shaggy eyebrows; unorderly hair and clothes; hoarse voice; offhand manner; free talk, and perpetual cigar." Adams could never be sure whether Seward was being entirely sincere or wearing a mask for political effect. But he found the New Yorker lovable and charming all the same, noticing that "Mr. Seward was never petty or personal" and that, unlike most politicians, he produced "the effect of unselfishness."

Seward even sought to be friends with, of all people, pro-slavery firebrand Jefferson Davis of Mississippi. In January 1857, Seward had come to his rescue in a raging blizzard, driving a midwife to Davis's home in Washington when his wife, Varina, had begun labor. A year later, he had attended to Davis when he was laid up in a darkened room with an agonizing eye problem, patiently explaining what was going on in the Senate in his absence. Davis, consumed by his fierce desire to defend the South, unflinchingly responded to Seward's decency and generosity with a campaign to have him hanged, after word leaked out that Seward had met with an erratic supporter of John Brown. "If I succeed in showing that, then he, like John Brown, deserves, I think, the gallows for his participation in it," Davis said. He ultimately failed to prove his charges. Seward testified to an investigating committee that "until I read in Europe of John Brown's demonstration at Harper's Ferry, I had no more idea of an invasion by John Brown at that place than I had of one by you or myself." But many agreed with Davis that the New Yorker and other anti-slavery advocates in the North were stoking violence with their incendiary rhetoric about freedom.

Seward remained immensely popular with the Republican base, though, as 1860 dawned. All he had to do to be positioned for his party's crown, he believed, was to plane down some of the sharp edges of his radical reputation. On February 29, two and a half months before the convention, Seward strode onto the Senate floor to deliver a speech that he thought would "remove all the obstacles to his nomination to the Presidency at Chicago," according to his friend Henry B. Stanton, a correspondent for the *New-York Tribune*. The gallery, crowded with women, filled up with spectators eager for the political show. Down on the floor, the famous Seward prepared to speak. Now fifty-eight, he had aged noticeably. His bushy hair, once red, had turned light ("not unlike a straw stack in shape and color," reporter Murat Halstead noted a few weeks later), his voice had become hoarser, and his great nose had become even more prominent. He retained his nervous energy, though, popping around the chamber "with school-boy elasticity" to shake hands and trade quips—"a jay bird with a sparrow hawk's bill," Halstead wrote. Studying his face, a *New York Times* correspondent found the senator to have "a small, nervous mouth" and "peculiar blue eyes, with an electric gleam in them." On the Senate floor, he "frequently fumbled with a big red silk handkerchief that lay on the table before him," reporter Noah Brooks wrote, "and occasionally blew a tremendous blast on his very long nose."

When Seward began to speak that day in the Senate, he did so without the rancor that had consumed his colleagues. "Nothing can be sweeter or more philosophic than his tone," the *Times* wrote. In response to months of venom, insults, threats, and rising passions, Seward spoke of civility and patriotic brotherhood. While defending his party's criticism of slavery, he denied that Republicans were in favor of "Negro equality" or arrayed against the South. He denounced John Brown's raid "as an act of sedition and treason, and criminal in just the extent that it affected the public peace and was destructive of human happiness and human life." He described a bright and peaceful future for America, as the nation moved "through hazes, mists, and doubtful and lurid lights" and passed beyond "all the winds of controversy" of the moment. Observers found Seward's dignified appeal to unity and the rule of law in the face of constant vilification inspiring. "So calm in temper, so philosophic in statement, so comprehensive in grasp, so passionless even in its inculpations, so far-reaching in its views, it must everywhere be recognized as a speech which no other man could have made," the *New-York Tribune* enthused. The Republican National Committee, under the control of Seward's friend Morgan, ordered 250,000 copies to be printed and handed out during the campaign. Eventually nearly twice that many went to press.

Not all Republicans were happy at what some considered an embarrassing retreat from Seward's past moral clarity. William Herndon said Seward's speech made him feel "ashamed that I am a Republican. I am like the little girl who accidently shot off wind in company—she said, 'I wish I was in "hell" a little while.'" But Seward believed he had struck just the right note of moderation in advance of Chicago. "As he handed me some copies," his friend Stanton recounted, "he said, in his liveliest manner, 'Here we go down to posterity together.' He was in buoyant spirits, seeming not to doubt that his nomination was secured." By the time of the Chicago convention, Seward seemed strong in the East and had swept up entire delegations in Western states: Minnesota, Wisconsin, Kansas, and California.

His "grand wire-puller," as the press described him, was also on the job. In February, Thurlow Weed invited Samuel Bowles, editor of the influential *Springfield* (Massachusetts) *Republican* and a friend and admirer of the reclusive poet Emily Dickinson, to dinner. Bowles came away dazzled. "He is a great man—one of the most remarkable men of our time—one whom I would rather have had such an interview with than with any President of our day and generation," Bowles enthused to a friend. "He is cool, calculating, a man of expedients, who boasts that for thirty years he has not in political affairs let his heart outweigh his judgment—and yet a man with as big a heart, as quick to feel and as prompt to act, as the best of men you and I have seen." Weed, already looking beyond Chicago, told Bowles he was "quite encouraged" about Seward's chances in November—and if the Democrats misplayed their hand at their convention in Charleston, "Seward's election would be a sure thing." Bowles, for his part, assured Weed in a March 5 letter that New England's delegates, "excepting Connecticut's," would be solidly for Seward at the upcoming convention. In Massachusetts, the delegates were "so strong for Seward as to be against anybody else." Bowles also told Weed how much he admired him personally. "Not all in political life will bear close observation. But my faith in human nature and in you was warmed and cheered by that interview."

On April 26, a correspondent for a North Carolina newspaper laid out the landscape in New York: "Not a single move has been made by any political party in this city, either in local or State politics, for more than a year, which Thurlow Weed has not influenced or attempted to influence, directly or indirectly, so as to make it promote the chances of

Mr. Seward's nomination and election." As Seward later told colleagues, "Seward is Weed and Weed is Seward. What I do, Weed approves. What he says, I endorse. We are one."

Reporters caught up with Weed shortly after he arrived in Chicago on the night of May 12, 1860. "Weed seems to be in high feather, and talks confidently of nominating Seward, and of electing him, too," Simon P. Hanscom of the *New York Daily Herald* reported. "He says the opponents of Seward cannot unite on any man, and with little or no pushing of Mr. Seward he will carry the convention. He expresses not the slightest fear of losing Pennsylvania"—a crucial state with the second-biggest trove of delegates, after New York—"and the command has gone out to keep Seward full in the front."

The power broker believed that Republicans were in superb shape for November. Rancor between Northern and Southern Democrats had "hopelessly split" that party, he assured a reporter. If, as Weed now expected, Democrats ran two tickets that fall—one Northern, one Southern—Seward would have "a good chance" to capture the White House. The swirling politics of early 1860 had created "the crowning opportunity of a life-time," according to Weed's memoir, "not to make a man President because he was a personal friend, but to raise to that splendid station one who was greater" than the men he had previously lifted to the presidency—John Quincy Adams, William Henry Harrison, and Zachary Taylor—"and at a time when the very existence of the nation was trembling in the balance." William Henry Seward, Weed believed, was the man best equipped by experience, character, and intelligence to deal with the crisis engulfing America. It was his duty to get him into the White House.

Weed's fellow Republicans also brimmed with hope that Saturday night, nowhere more than several blocks away in a massive new structure still smelling of freshly cut wood, where thousands of people had gathered under gaslight to celebrate the rise of Chicago and the impending demise of the Democrats.

Chapter 3: Temple of Liberty

Hundreds of people looking for excitement that night of May 12, 1860, went over to McVicker's Theatre, on Madison Street, built three years earlier in splendid brick and stone at a cost of more than $75,000, for a performance of *The Hidden Hand*. The smash hit comedy drama, based on the best-selling 1859 novel by a woman author named E. D. E. N. Southworth, was about a tomboyish American girl who foils injustice and achieves her dreams. Actor and theater owner James Hubert McVicker, a white man, was making "a decided sensation in Darkey impersonation" in the show, the advertisements proclaimed. The play did good business, but the eyes of thousands more Chicagoans were on a different drama that evening.

At the corner of Market and Lake Streets, near the aromatic Chicago River, a crowd buzzed around the massive doors of the Wigwam. By 7:30 p.m., the scheduled starting time of the festivities, more than seven thousand people had flowed in, each paying an admission of twenty-five cents. The celebrated Great Western Band, garbed in scarlet uniforms and under the leadership of Prussian-born William Burkhart, greeted them with sprightly classical and patriotic tunes. "And still they came," the *Chicago Press and Tribune* reported. "Gentlemen and ladies, citizens and strangers, men of all parties, all pressed in." They were eager to investigate Chicago's latest marvel, the massive building that would host the Republican National Convention, set to commence the following Wednesday.

It was a sight worth seeing. Completed in the nick of time, the wooden structure, 180 feet long by 100 feet wide, was the largest indoor auditorium in America, with a capacity "fixed by good judges, based on careful estimates, at from ten to eleven thousand," according to the *Press and Tribune*. A giant platform, with enough space to seat hundreds of delegates and reporters, ran the length of one side of the building, with committee rooms built on both ends. A massive, steeply pitched gallery, hugging the other three sides of the building, peered down on that great stage. Beneath the gallery, providing standing room, were a series of wooden tiers descending to the stage, generally following the slope of the lot beneath the building, negating the need for extensive digging. The towering wooden posts supporting the roof were "ample enough to banish all suspicion of insecurity," the *Press and Tribune* assured readers, but were positioned carefully "to interpose the least possible interruption to seeing and hearing." As a result, almost everybody had a good view. The ceiling curved from above the gallery down toward the stage, its shape cleverly designed to help project the voice of the speaker. There was no other amplification. Five huge skylights and twenty-five windows adorned with red, white, and blue curtains brought in light and air. The flat wall of the big store next door served as one of the four sides of the hall, its bricks showing behind the stage.

Like many venues of the time, the building had been designed to accommodate women in a special section. A long railing running the length of the gallery split it into two parts, the prime lower half reserved for the exclusive use of ladies and the gentlemen who accompanied them. On that opening night, women and their guests were also given privileged space on the stage on either side of the speaker's platform, where delegates would be seated in four days. The women's dresses and bonnets, in fashionably muted colors of gray, blue, lilac, and pink, brightened a hall otherwise dominated by men's dark suits.

It had all come together, like the city itself, with almost miraculous speed. Only eight weeks earlier, Chicago was still weighing its options for a venue. In 1856, the Republicans had held their nominating convention at Philadelphia's Musical Fund Hall, a symphony concert venue that easily accommodated the party's needs with two thousand seats. Some Chicagoans proposed similarly using an existing building, such as the 1,200-seat Metropolitan Hall, at the corner of Randolph and LaSalle Streets, a handsome brick structure with tall arching windows that hosted Long John Wentworth's inaugural address as mayor that spring. But, on March 14, the *Press and Tribune* exhorted the Republican faithful to think much bigger. Given the party's soaring prospects and this prime opportunity to display Chicago's brassy spirit, Chicagoans should erect a colossal wooden building—"a large, cheap, well-lighted structure, which will hold from six to eight thousand people." That would be a fitting "Republican Headquarters" for "this glorious campaign of the good year 1860."

There was a receptive audience in Chicago for such boosterism. Elbridge G. Keith, then a nineteen-year-old clerk who sold hats in his brothers' shop, recalled that the people of Chicago greeted the news of the first national political convention in their city "with boyish enthusiasm. The world must know of Chicago's manifest destiny, and now was our time to convince the doubters." At a meeting three days after the *Press and Tribune*'s harangue, the city's roused Republicans endorsed the construction of a massive new edifice—even larger than the one the newspaper advocated—at an estimated cost of $5,000. It would be called the Wigwam, a popular name given to structures erected for political gatherings, after the domed tents or huts that some Native American groups built. The powerful Democratic machine in New York City known as Tammany Hall, named after the Delaware tribe's famous Chief Tamanend, had begun the practice by calling its headquarters a wigwam.

There were several possible sites, but the most intriguing offer came from the Garrett Biblical Institute of Evanston, Illinois, then educating about sixty young men for the ministry. Its president, John Dempster, was inclined to support the Republicans, as a fierce opponent of slavery. He was devoted to logic; and finding that slavery could not be defended through the rigorous application of reason, Dempster stood "against it forever, and hates it just as he hates all lies." His institute accordingly promised the party the free use of a large vacant lot it owned near the confluence of the North, South, and Main Branches of the Chicago River.

The patch of dust and weeds was a place of significant historic importance. In 1831, when Chicago was a frontier village of twelve scattered houses, trader and river ferryman Mark Beaubien expanded his smoky log tavern on that very spot to create Chicago's first hotel, a two-story clapboard house impressively painted white with bright-blue shutters. His friend, Chief Sauganash of the Potawatomi tribe, pointed out to him that, in America, hotels were named after big men, and asked him what he would call his. Beaubien took the hint. The Sauganash Hotel proved a popular gathering place for a polyglot blend of hard-drinking traders and settlers—Native Americans, French Canadians, Anglo-Americans, and "half-breeds"—with Beaubien providing the entertainment with his lively fiddle.

As the village's most important building at the time, the hotel was the place where settlers formally incorporated Chicago as a town on August 12, 1833, and where its first local election took place (twenty-eight votes cast). Native Americans also recognized its stature. In 1835, after the Potawatomi tribe was pressured into selling its land in Illinois for much less than it was worth, eight hundred of its painted warriors, naked except for loincloths, "their eyes wild and bloodshot," performed a departing war dance on the path in front of the hotel. They looked up at the white people in the windows, one terrified guest recalled, "with hell itself depicted on their faces." But they set off peacefully to a new homeland, a reservation beyond the Mississippi River. The Sauganash Hotel passed through several owners, serving at times as a post office, a drugstore, and the city's first theater. When it burned to the ground in March 1851, after only twenty years of existence, it was already one of the last reminders of Chicago's unruly pioneer past, before the Indians were driven away and frenzied capitalism took over. Since the old Sauganash lot was located within easy walking distance of the big downtown hotels, the Republicans deemed it the ideal spot for the Wigwam.

Party members quickly fanned out into the city's wards, soliciting contributions of money and lumber. Soon thereafter, the Building Committee of the Republican Wigwam, chaired by real-estate developer Peter Page, went to work. It hired one of the city's leading architects, William W. Boyington, whose majestic limestone Chicago Avenue Water Tower and Pumping Station of 1869 still stands. Boyington kept the Wigwam's exterior much simpler, designing a great, cheap wooden box, with towers perched on two corners, each flying an oversized American flag. At the roof level between the towers on the Lake and Market Street sides were ornamental arches bearing the words REPUBLICAN WIGWAM.

Construction started none too soon, at the beginning of April. A month later, though the barnlike interior had been deliberately left "rough and unplaned," the Building Committee was scrambling to complete the Wigwam in time. Three days before the building's big Saturday night debut, Page's committee instructed the women who had been appointed to the Committee for the Decoration of the Republican Wigwam, and "any others who are willing to assist them," to gather at 9:00 a.m. at the hall "with needles, scissors, &c., equipped for action." The committee also appealed for help from young men. "Bring tacks and hammers."

A *Chicago Journal* reporter scoped out the hall later that morning. "A bevy of ladies were as busy as ants, decorating, sewing and arranging wreaths and festoons," he observed. Given their work, Chicago would "soon have a structure which will not only astonish our visitors, but also add credit to our city." Coats of arms of the states were affixed to the face of the gallery. The pillars were "twined with evergreens, and connected together with red, white and blue streamers, looped in the middle with evergreens and flowers." Busts of prominent Americans, including Whig heroes Henry Clay, Daniel Webster, and Supreme Court justice John McLean, "supported by pillars of Atlas," adorned the posts in front of the stage. Artists painted over the brick at the back of the stage, dividing the wall into faux arched panels that displayed "colossal statuary paintings" symbolizing "Liberty, Plenty, Justice, &c." A golden spread eagle hung over the platform. Outside, vendors were busy setting up stands, preparing to dispense liquor to the masses from their "Wigwam saloons," having paid $100 to $300 for prime spots. The *Press and Tribune* reporter was "pained to see that King Alcohol had begun to usurp a place in the vicinity of this noble structure." But that was a quibble. Chicagoans loved the Wigwam. "To us at that time it was a wonder," recalled the young hat clerk Keith.

The *Chicago Journal* was so enamored of the Wigwam that it took offense at a crude depiction of it published in *Harper's Weekly* on Saturday, May 12, calling the engraving a "miserable abortion." The Democratic *Daily Milwaukee News* mocked, "What made you build such an abortion, then? Next time put up a more elegant structure, if you don't want it laughed at." But the people on the ground were impressed. "Altogether the Wigwam is a success in design," the *Press and Tribune* enthused. And "when for the first time the effect of gaslight was added Saturday evening, the effect was brilliant in the extreme." The scene filled one reporter with visions of a bright future of freedom and justice for an America that had been corrupted by decadence and lies. "The sight was a grand and inspiring one; the noble structure, a voluntary gift to freedom; the sea of faces beaming with delight and kindling with the patriotic ardor of the occasion; the intermingling draperies, flags, flowers and festoons; the busts of departed sages and heroes benignantly looking down upon a scene which they had dimly prophesied but never seen, the peeling music; all conspired to form a glorious omen of the future—a prophetic sign, large with golden promise of a glorious harvest of truth and right next fall."

With its gas lights flaring amid evergreens, unfinished wood, and cloth bunting, the Wigwam "must have been one of the most dangerous fire traps ever built in America," historian Bruce Catton aptly noted. But the *Press and Tribune* found the big, crude edifice a "worthy object of pride to all our citizens," and sure to "know many glorious rallies during the summer and fall to come." A reporter tested the acoustics, roaming to the farthest reaches of the gallery. Wherever he went, he "could hear distinctly the fuller tones of the speaker's voice." The convention orators had a treat ahead of them: "The rare privilege of being listened to by an audience of over ten thousand persons under one roof."

There was one big problem: construction costs had skyrocketed to nearly $6,000, and contributions had fallen short by some $2,000. Rather than "tax private liberality"—i.e., tap rich Republicans—to pay the contractors, the committee hit on the idea of charging admission to a "Grand Republican House-Warming," featuring "ceremonies, music, speaking, singing, and glorification generally." Chicagoans were sure to turn out. "Boys, let there be a rouser," the *Press and Tribune* urged. "Come up and put a shoulder to the wheel," the *Chicago Journal* added on Saturday, "for tonight the ball begins to roll and the signal guns of the approaching contest between Freedom and Slavery will be fired. Let every man be at his post." When some ten thousand people paid their two bits to get in—a $2,500 gate take—the debt was more than retired.

Like a remarkable number of men in his city, Peter Page had seized on a difficult task and delivered spectacularly. He could feel justifiable pride as he rose at 7:30 p.m. to begin the event, as its master of ceremonies.

Page's first task was to call up the Reverend Dr. Robert Wilson Patterson, pastor of the Second Presbyterian Church, for the invocation. The tall preacher had trained for the ministry at the famed Lane Theological Seminary in Cincinnati, under Lyman Beecher, a brilliant Presbyterian minister who openly embraced controversy, believing Christianity compelled its practitioners to right moral wrongs. One of Beecher's thirteen children was a young woman named Harriet, who in 1852 published the novel *Uncle Tom's Cabin*, a pulse-pounding bestseller that roused many white Americans against slavery by depicting black slaves as fellow human beings tragically entrapped by a cruel system. She married another of Patterson's professors, biblical scholar Calvin E. Stowe, and formed a social circle that included many who detested slavery, among them the courageous lawyer Salmon P. Chase, now a U.S. senator and candidate for president at the Wigwam.

As a student, Patterson was haunted by the wrong of slavery and moved by the arguments of abolitionist William Lloyd Garrison. As a leading Presbyterian minister at a national general assembly in 1857, he helped draft a statement asserting the natural right of human beings to liberty and opposing the sale of slaves for gain and the separation of husbands from wives—a statement that Southern ministers bitterly opposed as an ungenerous attempt to "agitate" the slavery issue and split the church. By the time he rose to lead the prayer at the Wigwam, the reverend understood all too well the passions that were tearing apart the nation and the consequences of the upcoming election. "Oh God, we pray that thou wilt continue to smile upon us," he said, "blessing . . . all portions of our common country, North, East, South, and West. Come not out in wrath against us, but forgive us our national sins, our ambitions and pride, our oppressions and our forgetfulness of others. We pray thee give wisdom to our rulers and to all the people in the discharge of their official duties, and grant, we entreat thee, to us that our peace and unity may still be preserved." Peace and unity in America increasingly seemed to require divine intervention.

The invocation out of the way, Page rose to praise the work done on the Wigwam, making it a point to pay "a happy tribute to the zealous and well-bestowed services of the ladies in putting the finishing and tasteful touches to the work." Then his cohort, E. S. Williams, a Chicago lawyer and president of the city's Young Men's Republican Club, came forward to read letters from prominent Republicans in response to invitations to Saturday's event.

Massachusetts senator Charles Sumner sent his regrets. A brilliant, highly educated man and a former Harvard law professor, he was most famous for a horror that had befallen him on May 22, 1856, when an enraged South Carolina congressman named Preston Brooks walked onto the Senate floor and bludgeoned him nearly to death, leaving him unconscious in a pool of his blood. In a Senate speech two days before the attack, Sumner had openly mocked the congressman's kinsman,

South Carolina senator Andrew Butler, for claiming to represent chivalry and honor while defending crimes committed in the name of slavery. In Sumner's eviscerating words, Butler had taken "a mistress . . . who, though ugly to others, is always lovely to him; though polluted in the sight of the world, is chaste in his sight;—I mean the harlot Slavery." Southerners treated Brooks as a hero for chastising Sumner, and well-wishers sent the congressman dozens of new walking canes to replace the one that he had broken over the senator's skull. But Brooks's violence shocked many Northerners, opening their eyes to what they increasingly saw as the brutality and barbarism underlying slavery, and the lengths to which Democrats would go to silence any criticism of the institution. As a result, untold thousands of voters became Republicans. Sumner long suffered from weakness, nightmares, and agonizing headaches. Though he declined the invitation to travel to Chicago and open the Wigwam, he offered his encouragement. "I rejoice in the omens which I see in all directions," the senator wrote. "One of these is the enthusiastic energy with which the Republicans of Chicago are prepared to welcome the great Convention, whose duty it will be *to organize victory*."

Frederick Hassaurek, the twenty-seven-year-old editor of Cincinnati's German-language newspaper the *Volksblatt*, or "People's Journal," pleaded sickness and "the pressure of business," though he would be coming to Chicago within days as an Ohio delegate. An eloquent bilingual speaker, Hassaurek, the son of a Viennese businessman and banker, spoke for millions who had fled oppression in Europe to start a new life in America. He had "torn himself from all the dear scenes and associations of his native country, to escape the tyranny of a brutal monarch, and enjoy the sweets of freedom and our Republican institutions." The editor represented an increasingly important voting bloc to the Republicans: freedom-loving German Americans who rejected the Democratic Party. That spring, the *Cleveland Daily Leader* described Hassaurek as a Republican "treasure," rating him "one of the most popular, stirring and effective speakers in the country. Unassuming, modest in appearance, he speaks words of fire, inflaming the hearts of his hearers with love of liberty."

Page and Williams had also invited a Republican hero from a border state, a region whose votes the party was hard-pressed to obtain. Cassius Marcellus Clay of Kentucky, who hoped to be a presidential or vice-presidential nominee in the coming days, was a man of astonishing courage. The son of one of the richest planters and slaveowners in Kentucky, he had, like the Reverend Patterson, been drawn to the anti-slavery message of William Lloyd Garrison. Clay freed his slaves, became an ardent advocate of emancipation, and founded the Republican Party in his state—all of which made him a target for violence, which he returned in full measure, sometimes disfiguring or even killing his enemies with a knife he wielded efficiently. Clay found it fitting that Illinois, one of the birthplaces of the Republican Party, was hosting "the convention of gallant patriots who are to select the generals and the flag which shall lead us on to victory." While he would not be in Chicago in person, "I am now and will be present in spirit . . . believing that I and you have but one end in mind—the union of these States and the liberties of mankind."

The struggles of Sumner, Hassaurek, and Clay spoke of the hatreds now threatening to destroy a great republic that had been designed to funnel such passions through a system of law and peaceful elections. After the replies of these leading Republicans were read, a lesser figure rose to address the crowd: Aaron Goodrich, a genial fifty-two-year-old Seward delegate from the two-year-old state of Minnesota. A former chief justice of the Supreme Court in the Minnesota territory and a founder of the Republican Party there, he was an acolyte of high bombast, even by the gaseous standards of his age. The judge thanked "the ladies for their zeal, their energy, and their taste, as manifested during the past week, in preparing these decorations, these garlands and bouquets. These flowers, too, which are around us, we thank you for. They are emblems of innocence and beauty. As they bloom upon this spot, they will mark your bloom, and that of those who shall come after you." Mothers, sisters, and daughters, he believed, would be called upon soon to provide essential aid "in this impending crisis—this conflict that is now about to be waged, and which will never cease until the great Republican party shall take charge of the nation." While women did not possess the vote, they wielded enormous influence—indeed, they determined the outcome of elections, the judge maintained, to the crowd's appreciative applause. "I say it is meet that the ladies of Chicago should be present on this occasion."

Goodrich also pleased the audience with a promise that history would soon be made in this building—that "before the close of the coming week, the standard bearer of the Republican party will be nominated and that the nomination will go out before the people of the United States, and in November, he will be triumphantly elected President of the United States." For generations to come, the Wigwam would stand as a sweet reminder "of a proud epoch in the history of your country, and in my imagination I look down the vista of time and see the school boy at his desk—three thousand years from today—"

At that moment, the Wide Awakes, fresh from their mission of escorting Republican dignitaries to the Tremont House, marched into the Wigwam, their Light Guard Band blasting a patriotic tune, to the delight and applause of the crowd. After the diversion, the judge returned to his address, speaking of the Old Testament, familiar to every educated or religious person in the audience. He recalled the miseries that the Israelites endured as slaves, and the plagues God inflicted on ancient Egypt. God was again testing His people, Goodrich postulated—this time, Americans, who confronted an anguishing plague of acrimony that threatened to break into widespread violence. "But the day of the coming out from the land of Egypt and the land of bondage is at hand," he promised, "and here the leaders that shall bring us up, will be chosen."

The Minnesota judge could hardly believe what had happened to Chicago since he had passed through the area in 1835, when he was in his twenties. A boggy wilderness that one early settler described as "a mighty lonely, wet place" had been transformed, as if by magic, into a great, pulsing city. "It is now twenty-five years since I trod the grassy prairie whereon now stands this goodly, this mighty Babylon of the West," Goodrich said. "I behold opulence, splendor, taste and all that indicates a high order of civilization where there was the barren waste. I am filled with emotion when I contemplate the changes that the quarter of a century has wrought."

He was not exaggerating. In 1835, Chicago—"*Checagou*," French settlers had called it, after a Native American word meaning "place of the wild onion"—was a small cluster of primitive cabins around Fort Dearborn on the picturesque banks of the Chicago River. By 1860, its population had exploded to more than 112,000, making it the ninth-largest city in America. And new people poured in every day—more than half of them foreign-born, desperate for work in the factories, slaughterhouses, and lumber yards. "Its bustle and life quite dazzle the eyes and brain of an old fogy used to Kentucky quiet," a correspondent for the *Louisville Daily Courier* wrote in 1856 (the same visitor who lavishly praised the Richmond House). He discovered, to his surprise, that Chicago, though still growing like a hothouse radish, had "all the habits of a great city, and an air of settled maturity, full of immense warehouses and palatial residences," with a high society like that found in New York or New Orleans. "Isn't it strange," he asked, that Chicago "should have risen within less than a quarter of a century from the center of a marsh, changing a perfect wilderness into a beautiful metropolis? What other country in the world can afford a parallel with this change?" The Kentuckian was struck that when he went to a new theater during his visit, he found workers finishing the stage and hanging the curtain right in front of the audience just before the show. Chicago did not wait around; it got things done quickly and moved on to the next challenge. The city's insatiable spirit of innovation made it the ideal location, many believed, for a convention of forward-thinking Americans who wanted to stop slavery in its tracks.

The irresistible force of change in this city sprang from two sources: its remarkable location and the energy and daring of the people who had come there. Chicago was perched between the Great Lakes and a tributary of the Mississippi River, and when the Illinois and

Michigan Canal was completed in 1848, the two great waterways of North America were joined. Timber from Michigan and Wisconsin flowed in, to be distributed throughout the country. Gigantic stinking slaughterhouses arose along the river, packing the meat that was served up on America's tables. Railroads quickly capitalized on Chicago's central location. By 1860, more lines met at Chicago than anywhere in the world. Senator Stephen Douglas used his clout to push through federal aid in 1850 for the mighty Illinois Central Railroad—a win-win for Douglas, since it dramatically boosted both the local economy and his own wealth. While Douglas was working on the legislation, financiers with interests in Washington helped him quietly purchase seventy-five acres along the line's direct right of way, and thousands more in the Chicago area, the value of which exploded as the railroad was built. Ease of transportation, in turn, stimulated manufacturing. Cyrus McCormick, inventor of a reaping machine that dramatically increased productivity on the nation's farms, was turning out four thousand reapers a year in Chicago by 1860. The revolution he wrought in farming—doubling the nation's wheat acreage—boosted the city's incredible grain-holding and transportation business. By 1858, twelve giant slate-covered "grain houses," taller than the highest church steeples, dominated Chicago's skyline. Business barons became fantastically wealthy, and began to build stunning, stone-turreted mansions.

Chicago was ill-equipped, however, for growth of this speed and ferocity. For one thing, its increasing volume of garbage gave rise to a massive infestation of rodents, who nested below the wooden planks that served as sidewalks along the muddy streets. Carl Schurz, a brilliant German freedom fighter who immigrated to the United States in 1852, experienced the darker side of Chicago during his 1854 tour of the Midwest. Arriving by train after midnight, he found no room at the Tremont House and two other hotels. Lugging his valise, he became lost and, utterly exhausted, dropped down on a curb. Schurz then beheld, to his horror, innumerable rats swarming under the gaslights. "As I was sitting still, they playfully scampered over my feet. Efforts to scare them away proved unavailing. I sought another curbstone, but the rats were there too." After that welcome, Schurz seemed less impressed with Chicago than other visitors were. "Excepting the principal public edifices, hotels, and business houses, and a few private residences, the town was built of wood. The partly unpaved and partly ill-paved streets were extremely dusty in dry, and extremely muddy in wet, weather. I noticed remarkably few attempts to give dwelling houses an attractive appearance." The residents appeared to be obsessed with making money, and little else. "Everybody seemed busy—so busy, indeed, that I was almost afraid to claim anybody's time and attention."

The Reverend Henry Ward Beecher, brother of the author of *Uncle Tom's Cabin*, was struck by the frenzy during one visit. "The river is choked with craft, and the harbor is filled with vessels. The streets are filled up with boxes and bales, the stores are like hives in spring weather, with swarms going in and out with incessant activity;—buying and selling, buying and selling, buying and selling,—that is Chicago," he wrote. "It fairly smokes and roars with business." Journalist Noah Brooks studied the residents' frantic spirit at the iron bridges spanning the Chicago River, which constantly pivoted either open or shut. They "no sooner discharge one accumulation of people and teams than they fly open wide to allow the passage of some sort of lake craft, and smoking funnels and screeching steam-whistles go past in an almost unceasing stream," Brooks wrote. "As soon as the bridge closes again, the impatient crowd rushes madly on, giving a stranger the impression that the Chicagonians are an active race, given to gymnastics and slightly crazed."

Mary A. Livermore, an abolitionist and temperance reformer who had left the civilized East when her husband accepted a position as Universalist minister in Chicago, was appalled by this hectic, filthy city. When she arrived in the 1850s, the sidewalks were merely boards placed on the prairie soil, and "green and black slime oozed up between the cracks in wet weather, splashing the face of the pedestrian and befouling his clothes." In lieu of sewers, deep ditches had been dug on both sides of streets. "In wet weather the streets were rivers of mud; in the dry season they were veritable Saharas of dust. The prairie breeze not only kept the dust in perpetual motion, but caught up the litter and *debris* strewn about the streets, and sent that whirling through the air in clouds that blinded the eyes, and choked the throat and nostrils." People bore it with good humor, because they were here to make money, and they believed better times were ahead. They even joked about their discomforts. At one point, a large omnibus got stuck in the mud on Clark Street and could not be extracted before the ground froze solid. Someone attached a signboard that remained all that winter: "Keep off the grass!"

As the population exploded, robbery and violence proliferated. Vagrants haunted the downtown. Streetwalkers, rip-off artists, and pickpockets made their rounds. Men chewing tobacco spat streams of yellow-and-brown saliva everywhere. Concert saloons, gambling halls, and houses of prostitution flourished within strolling distance of the Wigwam and the hotels. Their owners paid protection money to politicians, who in turn ordered the city's small police force to look the other way. Some particularly dubious haunts prospered along Wells Street, east of the river, an area described as an "aggregation of vileness." A diminutive Yorkshireman named Roger Plant and his Liverpool-born wife who was twice his size ran one of the most notorious houses, the bucolically named "Under the Willow" at the corner of Monroe Street. "Every window of the den displayed on a flaring blue shade, in large gilt letters, the legend 'Why Not?'" one resident recalled—as in, why not enjoy sex and liquor? "The place was a refuge for the very nethermost strata of the Underworld—the refuse of the bridewell. Only by seeking the bottom of the malodorous river could its inmates go lower—as they sometimes did."

Worst was the disease. As outhouses steadily contaminated the groundwater, clean drinking water became increasingly difficult to come by. Epidemics swept the city year after year, including typhoid fever, dysentery, and, in 1854, a terrifying visitation of cholera, which killed 6 percent of the population. It struck quickly and cruelly. Someone seemingly well at midday could be dead at night, after hours of agonizing cramps, diarrhea, and vomiting. Since wells were suicidally polluted, people purchased fresh water from carts that plied the city.

They took care to boil even that. A good underground sewer system could not be installed because Chicago stood on marshy land, only a few feet above the level of the lake.

In typical Chicago fashion, city fathers adopted an incredibly bold solution in 1856. The entire city would be lifted, its buildings raised by as much as twelve feet, with immense amounts of dirt carted in to fill the space beneath them, refashion streets, and cover sewer pipes. At their own expense, owners of big buildings had to hire engineers, who used giant jackscrews to lift the structures slowly, preventing any cracked bricks, broken windows, or other damage. In the case of hotels, guests were undisturbed while the process was going on. Citywide, the transition took well over a decade.

By the time of the Republican convention, some buildings had been lifted while others had not, creating a town of "ups and downs" for pedestrians. "When you walk along even the principal streets," one visitor observed in 1857, "you pass perhaps a block of fine stone-built stores, with splendid plate-glass windows (finer than any in New York), with good granite pavement in front: a few steps on you descend by three or four wooden steps to the old level of the street, and find a wooden pavement, in front of low, shabby-looking wooden houses." The Tremont House had yet to be raised, making it look as if it were sunk into the ground, "and only the high granite curb-stone, over which you have to clamber, reminds you of the reform yet to come."

The guidebook *The Tricks and Traps of Chicago* warned that "side-walk oglers" liked to position themselves under the steep up-and-down stairs to catch the sight of women's legs. And those steps could be dangerous, particularly at night, especially for pedestrians who had been drinking, the same guidebook warned. "To a strictly sober and temperate gentleman, absorbed, perhaps, in the consideration of some momentous commercial interest, it is not too pleasant to be suddenly confronted in the way by a flight of stairs; and to one who is not strictly sober and temperate, it is not agreeable to be tumbled headlong *down* a flight of stairs or off a perpendicular precipice." Convention delegates—a class of visitors known to imbibe—had to watch themselves.

After the cholera horror of 1854, the city began pumping in cleaner water from Lake Michigan. But small fish were drawn to the warmth of the water along the shore, where they were sucked into the pipes and poured out into the city's sinks and bathtubs. "It was no uncommon thing to find the unwelcome fry sporting in one's washbowl, or dead and stuck in the faucets," wrote William Bross, a city council member in the 1850s. Fish also found their way into the city's hot-water reservoir, "where they would get stewed up into a very nauseous fish chowder," to "the horror of all good housewives." Worse than any of this was that the newly buried sewer pipes simply discharged waste into the Chicago River, which flowed into Lake Michigan. Most of the time, the water drawn from the lake, while muddy and fishy, "was comparatively good." But when the wind blew strongly from the south, the current changed, and sewage became mixed "into an abominably filthy soup" that was "pumped up and distributed through the pipes alike to the poorest street gamin and to the nabobs of the city."

The Republican convention had come to this roaring, half-finished city through the efforts of a shrewd local lawyer and political operator. Born and educated in New York, Norman B. Judd relocated to Chicago in 1836, when it was still a village—another Easterner seeking his fortune in the rising West—and quickly took on the job of town attorney, and then alderman. He served in the state Senate for a time and became a top railroad lawyer. He was a Democrat until the party's growing insistence on protecting slavery made him a Republican. In December 1859, he traveled to New York's Astor House—where Thurlow Weed held sway—to pitch Chicago as the 1860 convention site to the executive committee of the Republican National Committee, headed by Seward's friend and ally Governor Morgan.

David Davis did not like or trust Judd, considering him "a contemptible fellow" who had maneuvered to get Lyman Trumbull, "a Democrat—dyed in the wool," elected to the U.S. Senate over the ex-Whig Abraham Lincoln in 1855. Davis believed that Judd, who oversaw Lincoln's 1858 Senate run, cost him that race as well, even though Judd was behind the ingenious plan to rope Stephen Douglas into the famous series of debates. To be sure, the lawyer ran hot and cold on Lincoln. In 1859, Judd scoffed at an Illinois newspaper editor's support of Lincoln for president, saying the journalist had to be joking. "I am astonished that any one should think of his nomination when we have first class statesmen in our party like Lyman Trumbull, Salmon P. Chase and John M. Palmer," Judd exclaimed. Lincoln, for his part, seemed incapable of holding resentments, and he recognized that Judd's talents served his own ambitions well. "It seems to me he has done more for the success of our party than any man in the State," Lincoln later noted, "and he is certainly the best organizer we have." Lincoln, indeed, worked carefully to strengthen his friendship with both Judd and Trumbull. When a rumor began to circulate that Lincoln would attempt to topple Trumbull in 1860, Lincoln hastened to reassure the senator it was a lie. "Any effort to put enmity between you and me is as idle as the wind," Lincoln wrote. "I cannot conceive it possible for me to be a rival of yours, or to take sides against you in favor of any rival."

In accordance with the universally acknowledged truth that any senator who looks in a mirror sees a president staring back, Trumbull harbored some thoughts of obtaining the 1860 nomination as a compromise candidate should the delegates deadlock. In angling for a Chicago-based convention, Judd may thus have intended to help his close ally if Lincoln fell short, as expected. Neither man, though, appeared to have much of a shot, and Judd's overriding interest may have been boosting the local economy and his own prominence (he was running for governor at the time). Lincoln, for his part, did not seem to grasp that home-field advantage might significantly boost his chances. "I find some of our friends here, attach more consequence to getting the National convention into our State than I do," he wrote to Judd on December 14, before the lawyer set off for New York.

At the Astor House, advocates pressed the claims of Buffalo, Pittsburgh, Philadelphia, Harrisburg, Washington, DC, Cleveland, Cincinnati, Indianapolis, and St. Louis, as well as Chicago. A man from Wheeling even made a strong case for that city, then located in Virginia—though the committee reasonably concluded that holding the Republican convention in a slave state might be deemed an unnecessary show of "bravado" that would inspire "acts of annoyance or menace" by Southern zealots. The committee, trying to appear even-handed, turned down states with strong favorite sons: New York (William Seward), Ohio (Salmon Chase), Pennsylvania (Simon Cameron), and Missouri (Edward Bates). The District of Columbia had no electoral votes back in 1860, and Indianapolis had too few hotel rooms. Chicago made sense as a city that could handle big crowds—in a swing state that Republicans needed to win in November. Moreover, the goal of Seward's supporters was to make sure none of his chief rivals benefited from the location of the convention. They seem to have accepted Chicago because they believed no serious threat to Seward would emanate from Illinois. The "selection of Chicago, is regarded as a triumph of the Sewardites," one journalist reported.

Judd, forty-five, though already hoarse from "hallooing," looked ecstatically happy as he took the stage at the Wigwam's grand consecration Saturday night. The promise he had made to the Republican National Committee—that Chicago would "do all that any other city could do and more too"—had been redeemed "fully and completely" by the erection of "this glorious Wigwam," he told the applauding crowd. But in the coming days, he said, the Wigwam would be more than just a political auditorium. Though "cheap in its construction" and "rapid in its execution," this place would prove to be sacred to the cause of freedom. "This is essentially, emphatically the temple of liberty," Judd asserted. The delegates who would gather here would be able "to say to the free people of the United States—'We have placed in the Presidential chair a man who will slay the aggression of slavery.'" The audience roared its approval.

Before he left the podium, Judd invited up John Johns, a most unusual delegate from Iowa. A virtual embodiment of American rugged individualism, Johns was a grizzled hunter, coroner, and itinerant Baptist preacher, eking out a living far from population centers near the abandoned military post of Fort Dodge. In January that year, he had created a stir when he showed up at his state's Republican convention, in glaring contrast to the well-dressed professional politicians, in homemade clothes of jean trousers and shirt. "He wore a 'knitted cap of blue and white yarn that ran up to a peak, whence a tassel flared and flirted jauntily' with every motion of his head," according to one report. "His thin gray hair, his long unkempt beard, and his thoroughly weather-beaten appearance were true witnesses of his sixty winters." Yet the tough old bird won a place in the delegation with his passionate patriotism.

Refusing to be cowed by Southern threats of secession should a Republican be elected in November, Johns "became vehement," daring Southerners "to rebel against the expressed will of the people—daring them 'to pluck a single star from the galaxy represented on the flag.'" Johns vowed to make it to Chicago to vote for Seward even if he had "to walk all the way." It had almost come to that, Judd informed the Wigwam crowd. The man trooped 150 miles on dirt paths to a railroad station in Iowa City, where he could catch a train—the first one he had ever seen—to the convention. "He is a live Republican, you may be sure," wrote L. D. Ingersoll for the *Burlington Daily Hawk-Eye*, in Iowa. Ingersoll scooped up Johns earlier that Saturday when the delegate arrived in Chicago. "I took great pleasure in piloting the old gentleman around, this morning, for which he returned hearty thanks, he never having been, as he said, to market but once and to mill but twice, in all his life." He "feels a little odd in this town, which is not very scattering," Ingersoll added.

On the Wigwam platform, Johns made some "brief remarks that were sound and sensible," scoring some "telling hits" before ceding the stage to more seasoned orators. D. M. Cheeseman of California brought up the 1859 killing of U.S. senator David Broderick, who, though a Democrat, was widely regarded as another victim of the barbarous violence behind slavery. David Terry, a defender of slavery who lost his reelection as California's chief justice after he stabbed a man to death, taunted the anti-slavery Broderick until the senator felt he must challenge Terry to a duel. Terry, who provided the guns, supposedly supplied Broderick a pistol with a hair trigger that went off before the senator could take aim. The judge then coolly gunned down his adversary. Before a crowd of thousands in San Francisco gathered for the funeral, Republican U.S. senator Edward D. Baker of Oregon denounced the killing as a political assassination "poorly veiled under the guise of a private quarrel," and "the consequence of intense political hatred." The invocation of Broderick's memory at the Wigwam was one more sign of the poisonous miasma that hovered over the country. A few days later, the Wigwam's Committee on Decorations approved a request by Californians to place a portrait of the martyred Broderick, though a Democrat, alongside the state's coat of arms, draped in mourning. The committee expressed the hope that "the *honor* to his *memory*, as shown by the great free city of the North West, will inspire his friends in his own State to desert a corrupt party"—the vile Democrats.

Henry S. Lane, fifty-nine, "a thin, angular man, as quick as a cat, and with a voice like a trumpet," in the words of the *New York Daily Herald*, took his turn at the podium. The Republican candidate for governor of the important swing state of Indiana, he would become one of the most influential men in Chicago in the coming days. Iowa correspondent Ingersoll sized him up. "I suppose Col. Lane is the ugliest man in Indiana," he reported. "His head is about the size of your fist, and is covered with iron gray hair—his eyes are deep sunken, and his mouth is a vast receptacle for food and tobacco. When he speaks, he often bends his body so that the portion above the hips makes a perfect right angle with his long, slim legs, and anon he throws his head back so far as to have the upper portion of his person at an angle of about 45 degrees." But he was undeniably a powerful orator.

Lane told the crowd he would keep his remarks short, "having traveled two hundred miles in the dust to-day" from the "smoke" of his own fiercely fought campaign. But he thought it important to note that the country now faced an unavoidable decision, "disguise it as we may," about the fate of slavery. A disagreement that began as a cloud no bigger than a man's hand "has rolled up until it has almost excluded every ray of hope," he said. "We did not desire this contest; we have sought to avoid it by every possible means, but it has been brought upon us contrary to our wishes." Hope for the survival of America and its ideals would begin to be restored with the election of a Republican president that November, Lane maintained. "I do not know who that Republican may be," he said, but he ran through four possibilities, each garnering loud approval: Supreme Court justice John McLean, senator Salmon Chase, Massachusetts governor Nathaniel Banks, and "that distinguished, trusty, and tried statesman of New York," William Seward. Lane did not reveal that he had come to Chicago on a determined mission to derail that distinguished statesman's nomination, for fear that Seward would ruin his own chances of being elected in conservative Indiana. Over the next six days, Lane would warn anyone in earshot that Seward must be defeated if Republicans were to prevail.

Perhaps the sentimental favorite of the night was a gray-haired sixty-four-year-old congressman from Ohio who had been bravely fighting the spread of slavery for decades, defying ostracism and open death threats. After arriving at the Grand Central Depot on the Southern Michigan train, Joshua R. Giddings had hustled straight to the Wigwam. "You embarrass me exceedingly with so much noise," he said in response to raucous applause. Noting that another scheduled speaker had begged off, complaining of exhaustion after his long journey, Giddings said, "I sympathize with him, for I expect to be old myself some time," a line that drew laughter. "But the burden and heat must fall on us young men at present," he added, which drew more.

The six-foot-two-inch Giddings revealed that the scene at the Wigwam astonished him. "This is entirely unexpected—this vast audience, this elegant hall prepared for the cause of Republicanism, the hearty sympathy which seems to pervade the whole assembly, the enthusiastic cheering, the sentiment, the feeling." When he began his lonely fight against slavery's spread, things had been much different. "I stood in Congress without a single sympathetic heart," he said. "I had no conception of living to behold the time when I should see this the prevailing sentiment throbbing in every heart." He had been censured by the House in 1842 for even speaking out against slavery, in violation of the gag order then in effect. Now, eighteen years later, against all expectations, and against rising threats of violence, Americans were returning to the ideals of their founding. "We have come here with our souls baptized with the love of truth, justice and liberty," he declared. "We know we shall have a man who maintains these doctrines"—a sixteenth president who supports "the rights of the people, those great, immutable, unchangeable truths, for which your fathers and mine contended on the hundred battle fields of the revolution. We are fighting those battles over again." In the days just ahead, Giddings told the crowd, the people gathered in Chicago would do something of immense consequence. "My friends we are come here on a great and important errand. The eyes of the country, the eyes of the whole civilized world, are upon us."

When the program ended, the crowd poured out onto the gaslit streets, chattering with excitement. Some delegates headed for the bars and brothels, while Weed, Davis, and the other managers went straight to work, opening intense lobbying for delegates' votes. On that Saturday night in May, those thronging Chicago seemed to sense, after years of painful compromises over slavery, that a profound change was in the air, and that Republicans—formed of political flotsam and jetsam only a few years earlier—were on the brink of leading the nation toward its destiny of freedom.

Sunday,
May 13, 1860

Chapter 4: Star after Star

As a city that had sprung up almost overnight, Chicago was, to a remarkable degree, a place packed with strangers. Most of its residents had been born and raised elsewhere. Tormented by homesickness, many sought out others from their former states to share meals and memories. That quirk of Chicago turned out to be a blessing to the convention-goers. In the weeks leading up to the great gathering, residents joined together to assist the visitors from their states of origin. In many cases, they were waiting right at the train station to give the delegates and guests a warm welcome and escort them to the places where they would lodge, in hotels, halls, or private homes.

Chicago's Committee of the Sons of Maine was typical. Its members stayed in close contact with Republicans in the Pine Tree State, trying to form an accurate count of who was coming. At first, 178 were expected to make the long trip to Chicago, a number so big that the chairman of the reception committee pleaded with transplanted Mainers "to open their hands and their hearts, or their houses, to welcome their brethren from Maine." Some of the visitors might be very welcome indeed. "It will increase the interest of all to learn that we have the promise of greeting some of Maine's fair daughters, to stir up the hearts of many by sweet reminiscences."

But in early May, a new burst of interest in the convention obliterated the earlier projections. John A. Poor, a Portland lawyer, entrepreneur, railroad promoter, and editor of the *Portland Daily Advocate*, was helping to organize his delegation's journey to Chicago. He warned the Sons of Maine on May 3 that as many as three hundred men and women were now coming—thanks to a disaster that had befallen Democrats at their party's national convention in Charleston, South Carolina. "The news to-night, of their disgraceful capitulation, renders the triumph of the Republicans certain, and will add to the number of those already booked for Chicago," Poor wrote. "The 'irrepressible conflict' has swept the Democratic Party from power forever, and some of those who ranked themselves as Douglas Democrats last week, are now Republicans."

Certain triumph might have been an overstatement, but Poor was right: catastrophe had struck the Democrats in Charleston. The party's Southern members had given up on seeking the middle ground to win national elections, leaving its Northern members to fend for themselves. While the Republican Party would almost certainly benefit, what would become of the nation was anyone's guess. A savage civil war was one possibility.

The Democratic Party, founded by supporters of Andrew Jackson in 1828, had assumed immense power by selling itself to voters as the only way to prevent the North and South from tearing apart. In the spring of 1860, Democrats controlled the presidency and the Senate, while the burgeoning Republicans held only a plurality of the House. Democrats also dominated the Supreme Court, which, as one editor put it, "never omitted an opportunity of showing its regard for the institution of slavery." Washington was effectively a Democratic stronghold.

Stephen Douglas had every hope of being nominated in Charleston in late April. The party's incumbent president, James Buchanan, elected in 1856, had declined to seek the office again. Having endured a fusillade of abuse throughout his presidency, he had no appetite for more, even if the delegates were willing to ignore his unpopularity. No other Democrat approached the political stature of Douglas.

The Little Giant had established himself as a bold and dogmatic fighter, and a man who could get things done, a symbol of the muscular new West. He was also an unabashed white supremacist who had little concern for black Americans, taking every opportunity to employ the contemptuous N-word—already considered vulgar—in his public addresses, though the Senate clerks often cleaned up the official record by substituting "negro." White Americans, including immigrants, widely shared his views, and his own state of Illinois had enacted some of the toughest laws in the nation restricting free black people—indeed, it tried to keep them out altogether, on the grounds that they would place a burden on the public. "We do not wish to make our state an asylum for all the old and decrepit and broken-down negroes that may emigrate or be sent to it," Douglas said in one Senate speech. "We desire every other state to take care of her own negroes, whether free or slave, and we will take care of ours." Douglas believed that treating all races equally was ridiculous, because all races were not the same, in intelligence, work ethic, or capacity for inventive genius. The "sad and melancholy results of the mixture of the races in Mexico, South America and Central America," he argued, served "as a warning to our Revolutionary fathers to preserve the purity of the white race." For years, Douglas had been courting the South assiduously, trying to win over that section without canceling his support in the North, a most precarious balancing act.

Both Northerners and Southerners believed the fate of slavery hinged on one question: whether it was allowed to expand to new territories or was quarantined where it existed. Expanding slavery would permit it to grow and thrive; quarantining it would signal it was under control and on the path to extinction. But even that was a proxy for a more fundamental question: whether slavery was simply a part of human civilization, as it had been for millennia, or a grave moral wrong. Douglas, who did not seem to care which way Americans came down on that question, thought he could set aside the whole divisive dispute before it split his party and ruined his presidential prospects. He had pushed through the Kansas-Nebraska Act in 1854, giving the voters in the territories the power either to introduce slavery into their new states or to exclude it. The onus would thus be on them—not on the Congress, the president, the North, or the South.

But "popular sovereignty," as he branded the scheme, proved to be no solution at all. Opponents of slavery regarded it as a plot to expand slavery to territories where it had long been prohibited, and ultimately to spread it through the entire North. Defenders thought any ban on slavery, by the voters or anyone else, was unconstitutional, denying slaveowners their just property rights. Where Douglas's voting scheme was first put to a test—in the Kansas Territory—both sides sought to tilt the outcome by rushing in as many settlers (and guns) as possible. Intimidation, bloodshed, arson, retaliation, and voting fraud ensued, leading to savage eruptions of violence that resembled guerilla warfare. Far from decreasing tension over slavery, Douglas had significantly ratcheted it up. He had filled the ranks of the Republican Party with disgruntled Democrats. And when he refused to endorse pro-slavery voting results in Kansas that were blatantly fraudulent—splitting with Buchanan on the issue, to the president's fury—he earned the hatred of many in the South, who henceforth regarded him as a viper and a traitor.

Still, the Democrats might have attempted to do the usual in Charleston—produce a bland platform that dodged the most divisive issues and nominate a candidate who could appeal to both sections of the country. With 303 electoral votes in contention, 152 were needed to win the November election. The solid South and the border states would provide 120 of them—and Douglas might easily pick up the remaining 32 needed in the North, postponing the threat of disunion yet again.

The problem was that a growing number of Southerners no longer regarded compromise as the safe path. Alabama newspaper editor William Lowndes Yancey, for one, had been advocating, for years, the creation of a new Southern confederacy that would end any further need for painful and dangerous concessions. If the South were to assert its independence, Yancey held, white Southerners could finally stop living in fear and anxiety. Slavery would be secure, and Southern society would not be at risk of imminent destruction. Southerners would no longer have to share a country with people who constantly disparaged them and their institutions, intolerably attacking their sense of honor and self-respect. They would no longer be subject to high tariffs on imported products that Southerners needed, inflicted by Northern politicians who catered to wealthy manufacturers. At Charleston, Yancey intended to end, at long last, the bowing and scraping to the North. He was only too willing to see the party—and, hence, the nation—come apart.

Many white Americans staunchly believed that God, or "nature's law," had made black people their intellectual inferiors. "This is *fact*, unchanging, immovable, everlasting fact, fixed by the hand of the Almighty," argued the notoriously racist New Yorker Dr. John H. Van Evrie in his introduction to *The Negro's Place in Nature*, a pseudoscientific paper by British anthropologist James Hunt. "We know the *fact*, and God holds us responsible only for our mode of dealing with it, and when we willfully shut our eyes, disregard and ignore it altogether, and impiously strive to degrade our race *down*, or to force the Negro *up*, to 'impartial freedom,' or a forbidden level, we are blindly striving to reverse the natural order, and to *reform* the work of the Almighty." In the view of many white Americans, most people of African descent needed the structure provided through slavery—housing, food, medicine, employment, religious instruction—to survive in dog-eat-dog America.

Hence, Southern leaders regarded the abolitionists' dream of freeing millions of slaves as almost unthinkable, even beyond the loss to slaveowners of $2 billion in human property. They believed many black people, left to their own devices, would quickly sink into poverty and turn to crime and violence, reducing the region to an enfeebled condition that would leave it vulnerable to ruthless exploitation by Northern economic interests. These newly freed masses might seek vengeance against their former oppressors, igniting a race war, bloody and tragic for both sides. Even if that did not happen, white people, unlikely to accept subservience, would surely employ brute force against former slaves to maintain their governments and their power. In short, these leaders believed, abolition would wreck the South for both blacks and whites. As South Carolina senator John Calhoun argued in 1850, slavery "cannot be destroyed without subjecting the two races to the greatest calamity, and the section to poverty, desolation, and wretchedness." That is why Southerners felt "bound, by every consideration of interest and safety, to defend it." Since the Southern people had no real choice in the matter, Calhoun argued, Congress could preserve the nation only "by adopting such measures as will satisfy the States belonging to the Southern section, that they can remain in the Union consistently with their honor and their safety."

Such leaders were outraged at rising criticism of what was a legally sanctioned and time-honored system that had existed in America for almost 250 years. They believed abolition groups had been formed to foment insurrection and destroy the public's peace and safety, and they were appalled that the North refused to enact laws to stifle this relentless agitation. The North's own prosperity, they pointed out, had been built on slavery, through the slave trade. For a long time, Northerners had even claimed that trade was sanctified by God. One writer recorded that in Rhode Island a "highly respected elder, whose 'ventures' in slaving had usually turned out well, always returned thanks, on the Sunday following the arrival of a slaver in the harbor of Newport, 'that an overruling Providence has been pleased to bring to this land of freedom another cargo of benighted heathen, to enjoy the blessing of a Gospel dispensation.'" Until the trade was banned in 1808, Northern slave ships helped plant the institution throughout the South. Those ships even helped to fund the great colleges of the North, including Harvard, Yale, Princeton, Columbia, and Brown. Southerners deemed it the height of hypocrisy for the North to denounce slavery now, after having squeezed immense wealth out of it.

White Southerners, infuriated by ceaseless attacks on their character and morality, were particularly angered and insulted by Northern efforts to contain slavery. For example, Robert Toombs, a United States senator and wealthy Georgia planter, insisted that Southerners had every right to bring their property into the territories, whatever the North might say. "I will never surrender. In my judgment this right, involving, as it does, political equality, is worth a dozen such Unions as we have, even if each were a thousand times more valuable than this," he told the Senate. "Deprive us of this right," and the United States becomes "your government, not mine. Then I am its enemy, and I will then, if I can, bring my children and my constituents to the altar of liberty, and . . . I will swear them to eternal hostility to your foul domination."

In 1857, the United States Supreme Court ruled, in essence, that Toombs was right: no one could justly interfere with the right of slave-owners to carry their property into free states or territories. The court had taken up the case of Dred Scott, a slave who sued for his freedom after he was brought into Illinois and the Wisconsin Territory, where slavery was prohibited. As Chief Justice Roger Taney explained in his majority opinion, black people had no standing to sue for redress in federal courts because they "had for more than a century before been regarded as beings of an inferior order; and altogether unfit to associate with the white race, either in social or political relations; and so far inferior, that they had no rights which the white man was bound to respect; and that the negro might justly and lawfully be reduced to slavery for his benefit. He was bought and sold, and treated as an ordinary article of merchandise and traffic."

Despite the fierce political battles waged, and often won, in slavery's defense, such men as Toombs did not seem to grasp—perhaps they could not face—that the relentless force of modernization was already, and inexorably, undermining the institution. Railroads and telegraph wires were utterly transforming America. Ideas and information now spread rapidly. Newspapers had become cheap to produce and distribute. Travel had become dramatically easier and less expensive. Once-isolated communities were now linked to each other. People were obtaining food and goods from distant places. The West was becoming accessible for settlement. As distances shrank, the pace of daily life accelerated, making the clock a much more important tool. The nation was experiencing an extraordinary boom in population, productivity, technology, and wealth. Immigrants poured in by the millions, making the number of slaves an ever-smaller percentage of the total population. As the nation of isolated villages disappeared, power shifted to the urban North, where Americans exalted individual liberty, rags-to-riches success, and robust democracy. Slavery, as a brutally coercive system of labor that ran counter to ideals of freedom, stood increasingly exposed and vulnerable in such a country.

In the face of this roaring change, Southern leaders stubbornly defended their languid, hierarchical society. One South Carolina planter voiced his disgust with the "noisy, brawling, roistering *progressistas*" who demanded that the graceful South be remade into an imitation of the frantic, greedy North. Edward A. Pollard, who was born and raised on a Virginia slave plantation and became an editor of the *Richmond Examiner*, postulated that the differences between the rapacious, judgmental North and the gracious, generous South went all the way back to their original settlers. "The intolerance of the Puritan, the painful thrift of the Northern colonists, their external forms of piety, their jaundiced legislation, their convenient morals, their lack of sentimentalism which makes up the half of modern civilization, and their unremitting hunt after selfish aggrandizement are traits of character which are yet visible in their descendants. On the other hand, the colonists of Virginia and the Carolinas were from the first distinguished by their polite manners, their fine sentiments, their attachment to a sort of feudal life, their landed gentry, their love of field-sports and dangerous adventure, and the prodigal and improvident aristocracy that dispensed its stores in constant rounds of hospitality and gaiety."

Many Northern visitors to the South formed an entirely different impression. They could not help observing how backward the region was. William Seward, during an 1835 trip to Virginia, found "an exhausted soil, old and decaying towns, wretchedly-neglected roads, and, in every respect, an absence of enterprise and improvement." He saw only one explanation. "Such has been the effect of slavery."

* * *

If Northern and Southern Democrats agreed on anything by 1860, it was contempt for Seward's rising Republican Party, which in their view threatened the constitutional order, the only thing that held America together. Many Democrats refused to speak of the detested group without attaching the prefix "black" to it. "Black Republicans" was a racially loaded term, implying that the party fanatically placed the interests of blacks before those of whites. The *Montgomery* (AL) *Confederation* labeled Black Republicans "the very worst enemies of our country." The *Detroit Free Press* warned that if the government in Washington "shall fall into black republican hands, and if a serious attempt be made to enforce the doctrines of the black republican party, as they have been proclaimed by SEWARD, HALE, SUMNER, WADE, GIDDINGS and other recognized leaders of that party, the disruption of the Union will speedily ensue."

During his 1858 reelection campaign, Stephen Douglas cited Abraham Lincoln's party as a key reason the tall lawyer had to be defeated. "I am opposed to organizing a sectional party, which appeals to Northern pride, and Northern passion and prejudice, against Southern institutions, thus stirring up ill feeling and hot blood between brethren of the same Republic," Douglas said in a speech at Bloomington, Illinois, in the moderate center of the state. "I am opposed to that whole system of sectional agitation, which can produce nothing but strife, but discord, but hostility, and, finally, disunion."

During their debates, Lincoln felt compelled to deny Douglas's politically poisonous charges that, as a "Black Republican" out to sow division, he sought equality and marriage between races. "I am not, nor ever have been, in favor of bringing about in any way the social and political equality of the white and black races," Lincoln said. He could hardly say anything else and have a prayer of winning. "I am not nor ever have been in favor of making voters or jurors of negroes, nor of qualifying them to hold office, nor to intermarry with white people; and I will say in addition to this that there is a physical difference between the white and black races which I believe will forever forbid the two races living together on terms of social and political equality." Because of their differences, one race would have to be deemed superior to the other, Lincoln conceded, "and I as much as any other man am in favor of having the superior position assigned to the white race." But that did not mean "the negro should be denied everything," Lincoln said, before unleashing one of his characteristic witticisms. "I do not understand that because I do not want a negro woman for a slave I must necessarily want her for a wife. My understanding is that I can just let her alone."

In the eyes of Democrats, the emblem of Black Republicanism was William Seward. He was, the *New Orleans Bee* asserted, "beyond all doubt the [Greek god-warrior] Ajax Telamon of the party; the man who gave it being and breath; who nurtured its sickly infancy and fostered it with earnest solicitude until it attained its present formidable proportions; who dared bravely and boldly in the face of an assembled multitude to avow its ultimate purposes; who originated the axiom of the existence of an irrepressible conflict between slavery and freedom; who is the head and font of Black Republicanism; who in the United States Senate is ever its cool, watchful, wary, sagacious, bland, keen and indefatigable advocate; who, in fine, by his talent, his position, his high standing, and his prologued services has ever been deemed preeminently worthy [of] the most exalted honors his party can bestow."

The *New York Daily Herald* believed that Democrats could defeat Seward and his movement by taking the middle ground in Charleston, appealing to both North and South. In the wake of John Brown's attempted insurrection, the mood in America had shifted. "A reaction has begun in the Central and Northern commercial States against the revolutionary and destructive mania which has taken hold of the black republican party," it noted, and conservatives were readying themselves for "the fight of self-preservation against Seward and his fanatical followers." The *Herald* pleaded with Democrats to "recognize the greatness of the emergency that is before them, and, putting aside their petty local fancies, adopt a platform broad as the Union, and place upon it a man who will command the confidence of the conservative feeling now everywhere aroused by the sense of danger." But such appeals fell on deaf ears. A large chunk of the delegates at Charleston had bigger concerns than beating Seward in November. For starters, many Southerners simply could not stomach the idea of Stephen Douglas as their nominee.

Murat Halstead was struck by the animosity even before he reached Charleston. The journalist was riding on a train filled with Democratic delegates when it slowed to a stop at a village called Social Circle, in rural Georgia, giving the passengers a chance to grab a bite before continuing their journey. The son of an Ohio farmer, Halstead had learned to read at four, and in boyhood plowed through such weighty tomes as *Plutarch's Lives*, the works of the Jewish historian Josephus, Rollin's *Ancient History*, and *Revolutions in Europe*. In his teen years, while attending Farmer's College, he took on odd jobs for local newspapers and discovered his life's passion. A lively stylist with a sharp eye for detail and a rare desire to report the facts without partisanship, he was, at thirty, an editor and part-owner of the *Cincinnati Commercial*, in a position to assign himself to cover the juicy story of the 1860 national political conventions. The machinations of these gatherings fascinated him, and he happily stepped off the train forty-five miles east of Atlanta to share a table with a group of delegates, including one from Indiana, another from Kentucky, and a pair from Mississippi.

The delegates passed a bottle of "private whiskey" around, and the Mississippians proposed a toast to the "health of the nominee." Asked if that included Douglas, the Mississippians said no, because the South would never go along with the divisive Northerner's nomination. When the Indiana man countered that Jefferson Davis was a prime example of the party's divisive "Southern fanatics and fire-eaters," the Mississippians bristled, insisting that all Davis had ever done was defend the constitutional rights of the South. The Indiana man protested that he could criticize Davis if they could knock Douglas, prompting one of the Mississippi delegates to shoot back that "Davis was a patriot, and

Douglas was a traitor, d—d little better than Seward—that was the difference."

Delegates overhearing this bickering shook their heads in dismay "and talked of stormy times ahead and the peril in which the party would be placed" if Southerners persisted in their refusal to compromise with the North. Halstead wrote that the Mississippians seemed to regard the Democratic Party as their personal property, like a slave, "and rather a worn out" one who was "welcome to die." Democrats who, like the Indiana man, put party first and were prepared to support the nominee, whoever he was, were dealing with Southerners who claimed they would act only from "principle." An unnamed Alabama delegate told Halstead the same. He was not interested in another artfully worded platform, open to interpretation so that both the friends and foes of slavery could accept it, nor would he endure a crafty Northern politician like Douglas. "There must be no Douglas dodges—no double constructions—no Janus-faced lying resolutions—no double-tongued and doubly damned trifling with the people." If the Democratic Party would not stand up for a strict construction of the Constitution, he asked, what good was it?

Some of the Southerners carried with them copies of the 1858 Lincoln-Douglas debate at Freeport, Illinois. In that debate, Douglas, replying to Lincoln's pointed interrogation of his popular sovereignty idea, had declared that voters in the territories could indeed still thwart slavery, despite the Dred Scott ruling, by declining to pass local legislation protecting it—common sense, really, since the people could always find ways to frustrate a court decree that they considered impractical. But to Southerners, who regarded the ruling as the bulwark of their rights, Douglas's response to Lincoln was anathema.

The arriving delegates found Charleston a beautiful city, its oak trees dripping with Spanish moss, its elegant homes catering to planters who came for the social life and ocean breezes, its lovely Battery and promenade looking out on the half-built Fort Sumter in the harbor.

With its tasteful vistas and conservatism, Charleston made a striking contrast to the brassy, burgeoning Chicago of the Republicans. Democrats had chosen their city as a gesture of generosity toward their Southern brethren. But, as the epicenter of the rigid Southern views that Halstead had already encountered, the city was anything but hospitable to the Douglas forces. They could expect most of the gallery, adorned with Southern belles, to cheer on any effusions of Southern pride and treat Northern efforts at conciliation with silent scorn or worse. The *Charleston Mercury*, the voice of Southern rights, greeted the delegates with a belligerent editorial calling on the South to defend itself. "She has now no other alternative, but to raise up the lifeless body of the Democratic party, by restoring to it living principles, and putting it into power, or to dissolve the Union." Meanwhile, President Buchanan, out for revenge against Douglas, sent his top wirepullers down to Charleston. They employed patronage and threats to try to turn the convention against the Little Giant.

On April 20, Douglas's most notorious critic, Alabama's William Lowndes Yancey, checked into the Charleston Hotel, the headquarters of the Southern delegates. Halstead took the time to study the celebrated man closely. "He is a compact, middle-sized man, straight limbed, with a square built head and face, and an eye full of expression." Strangely, his manner was "mild and bland," belying his image as a radical. "No one would be likely to point him out in a group of gentlemen as the redoubtable Yancey, who proposes, according to the common report, to precipitate the Cotton States into a revolution, dissolve the Union and build up a Southern empire."

The hard-drinking Douglas men, meanwhile, settled into the Mills House and Hibernian Hall, where boxloads of James W. Sheahan's *Life of Stephen A. Douglas* had been deposited, there for the taking. On the hall's second floor, hundreds of cots, "with white spreads and pillows," were arranged in rows and marked with states' names, all for the Douglas supporters. "They were full of enthusiasm—rampant and riotous—'hot as monkeys'—and proclaim that the universal world is for the Little Giant." But Halstead could see right away that Yancey spelled trouble for Douglas. "I very much doubt whether the Douglas men have a leader competent to cope with him in the coming fight," he wrote. "It is quite clear that while the North may be strongest in votes here, and the most noisy, the South will have the intellect and the pluck to make its points."

Things started off well enough for Douglas when the convention opened on Monday, April 23. His floor managers persuaded the delegates to ditch the "unit rule," under which some state delegations were compelled to vote unanimously for one candidate. That meant that Douglas could pick off votes from states where he did not hold the majority—perhaps boosting his total by forty. Every bit would help, since two-thirds of the convention's delegates were needed to win the nomination. But trouble was brewing behind the scenes. At a caucus of Southern states, delegates from Arkansas, Georgia, Florida, Louisiana, Mississippi, and Texas decided they would follow the lead of Yancey's Alabama on the important matter of the party platform. Yancey insisted that it contain a guarantee of protection of slavery in all the territories. Without that pledge, his people would walk. Such a platform, of course, would be entirely unacceptable to Northerners, who simply could not be elected on it. In a Senate speech months earlier, Douglas had tried to caution Southerners that a Democratic nominee could not carry even a single Northern state "on the platform that it is the duty of the Federal Government to force the people of a territory to have slavery if they do not want it."

A committee charged with working out a platform came back with clashing versions. The pro-Douglas minority report basically sought to adopt the conciliatory platform of the 1856 Democratic convention in Cincinnati, which had floated the party safely to victory, adding some language attempting to placate the South—suggesting the fate of slavery should be left to the courts, which had already ruled in favor of property in human beings. The pro-Southern majority report, by contrast, was explosive—containing an explicit statement that Congress had no power to ban slavery in the territories or prohibit slaves from entering them, "nor any power to destroy or impair the right of property in slaves by any legislation whatsoever." The battle over those two approaches would, in a matter of days, tear the party apart.

On Friday, April 27, Yancey delivered what Halstead called "the speech of the Convention," an hour-and-a-half tour de force in favor of the pro-Southern platform. "Mr. Yancey is a very mild and gentlemanly man, always wearing a genuinely good-humored smile looking as if nothing in the world could disturb the equanimity of his spirits," Halstead reported. "There was no question after he had been on the platform a few minutes that he was a man of remarkable gifts of intellect and captivating powers as a speaker." In simple and resonant language, Yancey reiterated what Calhoun, Toombs, and other Southerners had been saying for years about Northern attacks on slavery. He tried to explain how the Southern people felt. "Ours is the property invaded; ours are the institutions which are at stake; ours is the peace that is to be destroyed; ours is the honor at stake—the honor of children, the honor of families, the lives, perhaps, of all." Yancey and his colleagues were not in favor of dissolving the Union per se, he explained. But the Union *would* be dissolved unless American voters made it clear that they would protect slavery—and, hence, protect the South. The time for dodging was over. The Southerners wanted to know where they stood this fall, not later. Their patience had run out.

By that point, Northern delegates had run out of patience themselves. They had compromised to maintain an allegiance with the South, while Republicans gained power and patronage at their expense. Now, Northern Democrats were being commanded to "put their hands on their mouths and their mouths in the dust," Halstead noted. "Gentlemen of the South," exclaimed Ohio's George A. Pugh, "you mistake us—you mistake us—we will not do it." Pugh's impassioned address "had not the silvery music, the grace and polish, that distinguished the oration of Mr. Yancey, but it was keen, shrewd and telling," Halstead remarked. "The hall was still, as it was understood that Pugh was the spokesman of Douglas, and that the fate of the Democratic party was at issue." When a delegate called for the convention to settle the matter with a vote on the platform, a frenzy erupted. "In an instant the house was in an uproar—a hundred delegates upon the floor, and upon chairs, screaming like panthers, and gesticulating like monkeys." One man, Halstead noted, cried out "'like some strong swimmer in his agony,' emitting 'a bubbling groan.' . . . The poor fellow thought the party was about to bust and the thing die—so he shrieked for the salvation of the Democratic party." The vote was postponed.

After adjournment on that Friday, the Democrats reconvened Saturday, only to squabble fruitlessly. Though Sunday, April 29, was ostensibly a day of rest, delegates worked hard behind the scenes, with Douglas's operatives trying to stop the pro-Southern platform and conjure up the two-thirds support he needed for the nomination. They promised, by one estimate, ten times more jobs than Douglas could conceivably deliver if elected. One Northern delegate passed the time by wandering down a Charleston side street, where he came across a sign that said, SLAVES FOR SALE. He walked in and said he would like to buy a nice woman. The salesmen "told him they could sell him a very fine seamstress." He asked to have a look, and they brought out "a clever mulatto girl, well dressed, and, like a great many of her race, sporting considerable jewelry, ear-drops, finger-rings, etc. Her qualities as a seamstress were dwelt upon" and the price fixed at $1,500. That was the going rate, evidently, for a young woman who was obviously intended to serve as a sex slave. The man begged off and departed, better acquainted with the institution that threatened to split America apart.

The convention resumed on Monday, April 30, "with a curious mingling of despair of accomplishing anything, and hope that something will turn up." Northern visitors, many of them Douglas supporters who had come to Charleston for good times and a raucous celebration, began departing, leaving the galleries increasingly to Douglas's opponents. Even so, it appeared at first blush that the Douglas forces might be back on top. The convention approved the Douglas platform over the Southern one, reaffirming the wishy-washy 1856 Cincinnati platform—or, as the South now called it, "the Cincinnati swindle." But that proved only to be a signal flare for the party's destruction. For, at that point, several Southern delegations, one after another, got up to say farewell and leave the hall.

Alabama was first. "There was a shudder of excitement, a universal stir over the house, and then for the first time during the day, profound stillness," Halstead noted. Leroy Pope Walker, "a tall, slender, pale gentleman, able in controversy and graceful in movement," declared that Alabama would leave because "justice has not been done the South." Mississippi, Louisiana, South Carolina, Florida, and Arkansas delegations followed. The ladies crowding the gallery "favored the secessionists with their sweetest smiles, and with nods and glances of approval, a delighted fluttering of fans and parasols, and even occasional clapping of hands." Like many in the hall, a lawyer from Illinois named Richard T. Merrick could scarcely believe what was happening. He rose and pleaded with the Southerners to reconsider. A Mexican War veteran and former Maryland legislator, Merrick had left that state three years earlier to make his fortune in the great Northwest. He came to Charleston hoping "to join in fraternal concord and mutual love with my Southern brethren of the Democratic party." Instead, he now found "star after star madly shooting from the Democratic galaxy." The implications horrified him. "Does it presage that, hereafter, star after star will shoot from the galaxy of the Republic, and the American union become a fragment, and a parcel of sectional republics?"

After adjournment that day, people gathered in groups on street corners, and even in the center of the road, talking over the startling developments. Love for the Union seemed to have expired. Sympathy for the Southern seceders, naturally, ran strong in Charleston. "It is now believed that nearly the whole South will go out, and there may be an attempt to organize two 'National Democratic' parties," Halstead wrote. At 11:00 p.m., under beautiful moonlight, "which silvered the live oaks along Meeting Street, and made the plastered fronts of the old houses gleam like marble," the reporter strolled to a mass night rally of Southern delegates. "People hurried by, looking excited and solicitous.

There were still groups about the corners, and the conversations were full of animation. Presently I heard a band of music and shouts of multitude." The Mills House and Magnolia Hall, which in previous days had been filled with animated Douglas supporters, looked dark and deserted. In front of the elegant Charleston County Court House, said by many to be the model for the White House in Washington, the journalist found the street filled with thousands of joyous and excited people, chanting, "Yancey! Yancey!" When that man of the hour rose to speak, he called for the South to stand together and demand constitutional protection of slavery, come what may. It seemed that a new country was being born. "Perhaps even now," Yancey suggested with delight, "the pen of the historian was nibbed to write the story of a new revolution." Someone in the crowd cried, "Three cheers for the Independent Southern Republic!" The throng readily complied.

Nothing could be the same after that. When the convention reconvened the next day, fifty Southern delegates were gone. A few who remained made the case that even worse would follow if the convention made Douglas its nominee. One insisted the institution of slavery was "a patriarchal one, and beneficial alike to master and slave." Another argued that it was "right, socially, politically, morally and religiously." If it were to be abolished, he said, "civilization would go back two hundred years." Indeed, he called on Democrats to fight for the resumption of the importation of African slaves, a notion that drew both laughter and applause. Solomon Cohen of Savannah, Georgia, begged the convention to understand that the South was in deadly earnest—and that its wishes must be respected. "I will stay here until the last feather be placed upon the back of the camel—I will stay until crushed and broken in spirit, humiliated by feeling and knowing that I no longer have a voice in the counsels of the Democracy of the Union—feeling that the Southern States are as a mere cipher in your estimation—that all her rights are trampled under foot." He would stay, that is, until the convention nominated Douglas.

That would not happen any time soon, it readily became apparent. Chairman Caleb Cushing, a Massachusetts man who nevertheless sympathized deeply with the South, ruled that the nominee must obtain two-thirds of the delegates originally in the hall, not two-thirds of those remaining. When Douglas received only 145 ½ of the 202 required on the first ballot, it was immediately obvious that he would fall far short. Eleven more ballots, with similar results, followed that day. Douglas remained far and away the leading candidate, but he was not popular enough to carry the convention.

Many delegates were coming around to the grim realization that, even if the party could be stitched back together, no candidate would command enough support to carry the Democrats to victory in November. "I hear it stated here a hundred times a day, by the most orthodox Democrats and rampant Southerners, 'William H. Seward will be the next President of the United States,'" Halstead reported. "And I have heard this remark several times from South Carolinians: 'I'll be damned if I don't believe Senator Seward would make a good President.' The fact is, there is a large class to whom the idea of Douglas is more offensive than Seward." Northern Democrats, for their part, were enraged over the turn of events. Some of Douglas's supporters declared openly and earnestly that they would join the Black Republicans. They "use language about the South, her institutions, and particularly her politicians, that is not fit for publication," Halstead wrote. "Their exasperation and bitterness toward the South . . . can hardly be described. Many of them would not lift a finger to prevent the election of Seward to the presidency."

After grinding through fifty-seven ballots without producing a nominee, the Democratic convention adjourned on Thursday, May 3, resolving to reconvene in Baltimore on June 18. Douglas's team, though crushed, retained hopes that, by then, Democrats would replace the Southern bolters with new delegates committed to the party's survival. Lacking any clear direction, a rump convention comprised of the secessionists and their sympathizers decided to meet on June 11 in Richmond to determine what to do. Visitors and delegates rushed to their hotels, crammed their carpetbags with their clothing, paid their bills, and jumped on trains bound for home.

While some Douglas men believed the party could still be saved, Alexander Stephens, a Whig-turned-Democrat and former congressman from Georgia, saw only tragedy ahead. The Charleston convention, he told a friend, meant "that men will be cutting one another's throats in a little while. In less than twelve months we shall be in a war, and that the bloodiest in history." Stephens believed that Douglas, while imperfect, was "one of the foremost defenders of constitutional rights in the country." But he had no confidence that the party would come to its senses in Baltimore. "The party is split forever," Stephens said. "The only hope was at Charleston. If the party could have agreed there we might carry the election. As it is, the cause is hopelessly lost."

Halstead also saw bleak times ahead for the Democrats. After the disaster in Charleston, he wrote, "the Chicago Convention has all the cards in its hands to win the next Presidency and the spoils of the Federal Government."

On the afternoon of Sunday, May 13—ten days after the Democrats fled from their disastrous convention in Charleston—a crowd gathered to pray in Chicago's Republican Wigwam. The service began with a hymn, as the worshippers raised their voices in song. Then the Reverend Zephaniah Moore Humphrey, pastor of the First Presbyterian Church, stood up to deliver the opening prayer. The erudite Humphrey, regarded as an unusually courageous and principled man, was related by blood to none other than John Brown, the radical abolitionist. His father, Amherst College president Herman Humphrey, was a first cousin of Brown. Indeed, the condemned leader of the raid on Harper's Ferry had written to Herman in November 1859, while awaiting his execution in Virginia. Brown noted that he would be the first in the family line to die in such a manner, but added, "I neither feel mortified, degraded, nor in the least ashamed of my imprisonment, my chains, or near prospect of death by hanging. I feel assured 'that not one hair shall fall from my head without the will of my Heavenly Father.'" In commenting on Zephaniah's bravery—he had, in addition to defying slavery, chased away a thug who broke into his house—his friends noted: "Something of the sturdy John Brown blood was flowing in those veins."

After Humphrey concluded his prayer and the gathering sang another hymn, the Reverend Henry Cox of the Methodist Church delivered the sermon to the Wigwam gathering. It was founded on the text of Joshua 3:17, which told of the miraculous journey of the ancient Jews. They had been able to cross to safety in the Promised Land when the River Jordan miraculously turned dry. He urged his audience at the Wigwam to grasp "the necessity of a thorough dependence on the Word of God."

Chapter 5: The Man in the White Coat

Sunday was no day of rest for the political managers and delegates in Chicago. With their own crossing to the Promised Land suddenly opened by the Democrats' stunning division, they worked intensely to advance their candidates for president. None was toiling more determinedly than an eccentric forty-nine-year-old newspaper editor who had arrived Saturday night on the same train as Thurlow Weed. He nursed a bitter resentment against Weed, and he had come from New York City to kill the presidential hopes of William Henry Seward.

Horace Greeley was, without much doubt, the biggest star in American journalism and the most celebrated man in Chicago that day. Even his shabby, old-fashioned attire was famous, widely lampooned in political cartoons and newspaper editorials—particularly his white linen coat and his battered old beaver hat "redolent with antediluvian rust." Some thought Greeley dressed this way to promote his image as a working-class philosopher, though he was, by May 1860, a national celebrity running an extremely lucrative business. "His dilapidated hat, his worn out white coat, (which he took care to inform the world was purchased second-hand,) his thick and dirty boots, were designed to bear out the impression of his philosophic indifference to worldly matters," the *Brooklyn Daily Eagle* scoffed that month. But Greeley did, in truth, consider his life's mission more important than wealth. He had toiled hard for decades as an ink-stained printer and editor, and he genuinely felt a kinship with the downtrodden in America. Most notably, as founder and editor of the mighty *New-York Tribune*, he had spent years fighting the spread of slavery, which made him almost as hated in much of America as William H. Seward was.

Greeley was pale and wan, with small, close-set eyes behind wire-rimmed glasses, tousled graying hair on his expansive balding head, and fleecy whiskers under his chin. He spoke in a high-pitched, rather squeaky voice. The great showman P. T. Barnum, a friend and dining companion, once described him as "a gangling, wispy-haired, pasty-cheeked man, high-domed and myopic, with the face of somebody's favorite grandmother." But in print, Greeley's virile defenses of freedom moved a nation. He "is personally as placid and harmless as a lamb; but politically as remorseless and unmerciful as a tiger," the *Richmond* (Virginia) *Dispatch* observed. He spoke the common people's language, using catchy, colloquial words to drive home his points. "I can write better slang than any editor in America," he boasted. Greeley is best known, to this day, for the phrase, "Go West, young man," which quickly entered the American lexicon and remained embedded there. While he seems not to have used those exact words in any of his writing, they did express his sentiments. Greeley looked on America as the place where dreams could come true, and he repeatedly urged the young to seek their fortunes in the freewheeling states and territories that pioneers had carved out of the wilderness.

While other editors focused on lurid crime stories and political scandals, Greeley was determined to produce a paper for the "virtuous and refined." He called himself a "public teacher," and he wanted to shape opinion rather than simply reflect it. To that end, he constantly advocated progress, seeking better schools, less corrupt government, greater freedom for black people and women, less alcohol abuse, more infrastructure, and less poverty. He deplored the treatment of Native Americans. He advocated for utopian communities. He promoted the work of New England writers Ralph Waldo Emerson and Henry David Thoreau and published, among other foreign correspondents, German philosopher-in-exile Karl Marx and feminist author Margaret Fuller, who became a particular friend. "Mr. Greeley, I like, nay more, love," Fuller wrote to her brother Eugene. "He is, in his habits, a slattern and plebian; in his heart, a noble man." Even his friends admitted that, at times, he pushed fringe, if not crackpot, ideas. "Had God granted him a little plain practical sense, Horace Greeley would have been a great man," New York diarist George Templeton Strong wrote after his death. Many regarded Greeley as a mercurial figure swept along by his enthusiasms rather than anchored in cold, hard reason. There was something about the man—an earnestness, exuberance, and optimism, bordering on wide-eyed naivete—that made people poke fun at him.

Greeley did connect with readers, though. By 1860, his daily *Tribune*, produced every Monday through Saturday, was the city's second most popular daily, behind the *New York Daily Herald*. But his weekly edition, published Wednesday morning and mailed throughout the country, was spectacularly popular, with a circulation of well over 200,000—the highest in the world. Since each copy tended to be handed around, actual readership might have been one million sets of eyes per week. In many poor and rural homes, particularly in the Western states, it was said, the only printed material to be found was the Bible and the *New-York Weekly Tribune*. Ralph Waldo Emerson, writing to Scottish essayist Thomas Carlyle in 1854, quipped that Greeley, by means of his weekly edition, had become "the right spiritual father" of Midwesterners and "does all their thinking and theory for them, for two dollars a year." During his own lecture tour of the region, Emerson had appeared hard on the heels of Greeley. He was struck that people from the heartland flocked to the editor's talks, some "coming thirty to forty miles to hear him speak." That same year, English-born schoolmaster James Parton produced a colorful, full-length biography of the editor. "I undertook the task simply and solely because I liked the man, because I gloried in his career, because I thought the story of his life ought to be told," Parton explained.

Such a man did not only publish news; he made it. Even during Greeley's journey from New York to Chicago for the Republican convention, he drew press attention. The *Cleveland Leader* noted that Greeley was among a "good load of delegates and others" who had arrived in Cleveland Saturday morning from the East—a load that included New York governor Edwin D. Morgan, congressman Joshua R. Giddings, and "other notables." They boarded a steam-powered propeller boat, the *Galena*, to travel across Lake Erie to Detroit, and from there, took the Michigan Southern Railroad into Chicago Saturday night. Henry Clay Whitney, an Illinois lawyer and friend of Abraham Lincoln, spotted Greeley walking unpretentiously from the depot to the Tremont House, "lugging a huge leather satchel, which he would change from one hand to the other every little while." There, Greeley settled in with fellow members of his delegation—representing not his home state of New York but Oregon, of all places.

Oregon, which had become a state only a year earlier, controlled six seats at the convention. With no cross-continental railroad yet in operation, an overland trip to Chicago through territories that would become Idaho, Wyoming, and Nebraska, and on into Iowa and Illinois, was expensive and time-consuming, taking four or five weeks. Even communications with Oregon were difficult. No transcontinental telegraph yet reached the state, and news had to come by pony express or by a roundabout route across the Isthmus of Panama. When the Republican National Committee in early 1860 moved up the convention from June to May, Oregon officials suddenly had to scramble to fill their allotted seats. They awarded one to twenty-three-year-old Frank Johnson of Oregon City, for example, because they had little money for expenses, and the young man was already planning to travel east to resume his studies at Colgate Theological Seminary, in Hamilton, New York. He could stop off in Chicago along the way. Two other seats went to Oregon men, including Joel Burlingame, the father of Republican congressman Anson Burlingame of Massachusetts. One remained unfilled. The last two were given, oddly, to Horace Greeley and another anti-slavery man, Massachusetts congressman Eli Thayer.

Greeley had never set foot in Oregon. He had even opposed its admission as a state, fearing its Democratic politicians would strengthen the pro-slavery forces in Congress. Furthermore, Oregon had already instructed its Republican delegates to back Seward for president. Yet Oregon's Leander Holmes, who could not attend because of the change of date, informed the state party in March that "he has empowered Horace Greeley to act in his stead and cast his vote for Edward Bates." Greeley later insisted that an invitation arrived unsolicited from Holmes, and "I did not feel at liberty to refuse the duty thus imposed on me."

Greeley had been writing glowingly in the *Tribune* about Bates, who seemed like the last candidate who would enjoy support in far-off Oregon. According to one account, it all went back to Oregon pioneer Jesse Applegate, who had been aided early in life by Bates and greatly admired him; Applegate had urged Holmes to send his proxy to Greeley. Oregon gave Greeley an opportunity to get in on the action, not just report on it. Backed by his fame and influence in the party, he was suddenly able to wield power in Chicago—right on the Wigwam stage and in the committee rooms.

The Oregon invitation was a godsend, because Greeley would never have been permitted to join the New York delegation, as an intractable Bates man. He had broken from the powerful political boss who controlled it, Thurlow Weed—the very man who had recognized Greeley's talent when he was a nobody and helped him become perhaps the most formidable force in the publishing world.

Born on February 3, 1811, on a small farm in the rolling, rocky hills of Amherst, New Hampshire, Greeley grew up, like many Americans, in a world of hard labor punctuated by the recurring misery of hard times. His father, Zaccheus, though reduced to a life of physical toil and financial troubles, shone above his neighbors—even local clergymen—in his knowledge of the Bible, which he could quote profusely and accurately. Horace's mother, Mary, was an indefatigable worker, a trait she handed down to her son. "She worked," one resident recalled, "in doors and out of doors, could out-rake any man in the town, and could *load* the hay-wagons as fast and as well as her husband. She hoed in the garden;

she labored in the field; and, while doing more than the work of an ordinary man and an ordinary woman combined, would laugh and sing all day long, and tell stories all the evening." At two, Greeley began to look at the family Bible with great fascination. At four, he could read, even before he could pronounce some of the longer words. Like Weed and Lincoln, he became a passionate autodidact, and scoured his rural region for books he could borrow. He was said to have read through the Bible when he was six; consumed the *Arabian Nights* at eight; read *Robinson Crusoe* at nine, Shakespeare at eleven, and piles of histories, romances, and other tales at twelve, thirteen, and fourteen. He seemed so lost in his thoughts that some took him for "a natural fool," until they discovered that the boy was phenomenally intelligent.

Poverty, disruption, and separation hounded his childhood. When Horace was ten, the Greeley home was seized, and the family fled to Vermont, lest his father be imprisoned for failing to pay his debts. There, neighbors recalled, Zaccheus performed any odd job he could find, and the family survived on a bleak diet of bean porridge. Though friends of the family proposed to fund an education for the startlingly gifted child, his parents were too proud to accept such charity. At eleven, Greeley ran away from home, hoping to become an apprentice printer. He made it to Whitehall, about nine miles away, where he inquired about working at the newspaper but was turned away because he was too young. He glumly returned home. At fifteen, he spotted an advertisement seeking an apprentice printer at the *Northern Spectator* in East Poultney, Vermont. This time, his father gave the boy permission to walk the eleven miles to see about it. He got the job. Horace was in a strange place, far from loved ones, doing difficult work, when he got word that his struggling father was moving the family yet again, this time to Erie County, in far western New York. "The parting was a sore trial to me," Horace recalled, "and I was almost persuaded to go off with them, my place being then hard and disagreeable, but I said goodbye and went back to my cold, strange home with a dry face but a sore heart."

He learned the painstaking trade of setting type, inking typeface, and operating the press. In his off hours, he raced through all the books in the small public library. He joined the local debating society, where his prodigious memory for names, places, dates, statistics, and quotes helped him shape his opinions and make a compelling case for them. His strange nature was evident. "I doubt if, in the whole term of his apprenticeship, he ever spent an hour in the common recreations of young men," Amos Bliss, editor of the *Spectator*, recalled. Horace passed Bliss's office on his way to daily meals but seemed so absorbed in his thoughts that he did not recognize the editor's presence. The boy constantly kept "his head bent forward and his eyes fixed upon the ground." Already stubbornly independent, Horace refused to waste time on dance lessons or gambling, but he excelled at cards and chess. In a nation of heavy drinkers—the whiskey jug helped hard work go easier—he embraced temperance, rejecting not only alcohol but such stimulants as coffee and tea. By the time he was sixteen, he was in many ways the Greeley of middle age. The residents of East Poultney, like hundreds of thousands of Americans later, greatly respected his opinions and his knowledge. "He came, at length, to be regarded as a sort of Town Encyclopedia, and if any one wanted to know anything, he went, as a matter of course, to Horace Greeley," biographer Parton wrote.

Though the boy's annual salary was a paltry forty dollars, he scrimped and sent as much of the pittance as he could to his debt-fleeing father, who moved the family once again, to northern Pennsylvania near the New York line, where he cleared woods and built a log cabin. At twenty, at the end of his long apprenticeship, Horace rejoined his family, making a four-hundred-mile, twelve-day journey, some of it by slow canal boat and steamboat, but much of it on foot, on an injured leg. After undergoing a quack treatment with electric current that left a red scar on his leg, Greeley set off for New York City, where he took on a variety of printing jobs, eventually coming to edit a weekly newspaper focused on literature and ideas, the *New-Yorker* (no relation to the modern magazine).

In New York, he readily adopted liberal ideas—some of them considered bizarre novelties. Raised in a Congregational home, he turned to the Universalists and became immersed in their society in the big city. He embraced the teachings of Sylvester Graham—inventor of the graham cracker—who frowned on sexual stimulation, especially masturbation, and advocated exercise, cold baths, open windows, sleeping on hard mattresses, drinking only cold water, and eating a strict vegetarian diet, including bread made of coarsely ground wheat or rye. In the 1830s, boardinghouses operating on Grahamite principles sprang up, and Greeley chose to live in one on Barclay Street in New York. Residents were required to rise at 5:00 a.m. for exercise and to be in bed by 10:00 p.m. They shared two vegetarian meals a day.

There he met a fellow occupant, a twenty-two-year-old schoolteacher named Mary Youngs Cheney, who became his wife. Though their marriage survived until her death in 1872, it was a difficult one. "Molly," as Greeley called her, suffered from poor health, mental and physical. She seemed to loathe marital relations and told Horace at one point that she contemplated leaving their marriage "because her fire would not burn." Greeley called their home "Castle Doleful." Five of their seven children died young. Some may have perished from neglect. In 1846, Molly left one sickly infant daughter for long stretches of time in her basket, while she "often said she wished her dead on account of the labor and anxiety she caused," Greeley wrote to Margaret Fuller. Molly kept the couple's beloved son Arthur, nicknamed "Pickie," in diapers until he was nearly four and whipped him repeatedly when he challenged her, fueling his anger and anguish. "When beaten, as he was when we rode out last Saturday," Greeley wrote, "he looks her in the eye with an aspect of indignation and grief, yelling, 'O you ugly creature!' He does not get whipped so often as he did, for his Mother has adopted the plan of shutting him in the upper chamber, which speedily brings him to subjection." After the boy died of cholera at the age of six, the devastated mother sought to reconnect with him through a spirit medium. She pressured Greeley to hire eleven-year-old Kate Fox, who with her sister had made sensational headlines by supposedly reaching the dead through mysterious rapping on a table at their home. Though Kate claimed to bring Molly in contact with Pickie's spirit, she detested the bossy woman and the home's Grahamite diet of bran bread, sometimes-rancid porridge, and puddings. Through it all, Greeley left his domestic life mostly to Molly and focused on work he deemed to be of national importance.

Among his other passions, Greeley jumped into Whig politics. In 1837, as a great depression weighed down on the nation, the *New-Yorker* was struggling, the editor unable to pay his bills. Unbidden, Thurlow Weed came to the rescue. He was casting about for an editor for a weekly newspaper that would advocate for Whig candidates, including Seward. Impressed by the *New-Yorker*, Weed paid a visit to its office. Up a flight of rickety stairs, Weed found a skinny twenty-six-year-old man "with light hair and blond complexion, with coat off and sleeves rolled up," standing at the case of moveable type, his composing stick in hand. Greeley took the job to supplement his *New-Yorker* income, and Weed raised the money to fund the Albany-based *Jeffersonian*. It first rolled off the press in February 1838 and contributed later that year to a sensational Whig victory in the presidential and legislative races. As Greeley began shuttling back and forth between New York and Albany, staying in Weed's house, his long and close relationship with Weed and Seward blossomed, a partnership that he later called "the firm." He described Seward as "the finest fellow I ever knew."

In 1841, Greeley folded the *New-Yorker* into the newspaper that would make him famous, the *New-York Tribune*. He started in an attic, with a staff of ten men. Whig friends fronted the money. Weed probably helped, since he had been pushing for a cheap daily paper that would reach out to working-class Whigs in New York. But Greeley, characteristically, wandered off the Whig plantation. During the dark winter of 1837–38, he was haunted by terrible scenes of "filth, squalor, rags, dissipation, want, and misery" in his Sixth Ward, and in the 1840s he began touting a form of socialism to address the needs of the poor. Recognizing the creed ran counter to Whig values of hard work, freedom, and independence, Weed expressed his concern to Greeley. The young editor lashed back. "I am ever ready to defer to your superior experience and judgment,—only convince me that I am wrong on any point, but do not assume to dictate or lecture me," Greeley responded testily. "I would hope, also, that we may still be friends . . . but if I can only enjoy your friendship on terms of humiliation, let us be strangers henceforth." They remained friends. Weed believed the prickly editor was still useful to the Whig cause, though he increasingly looked on him as a loose cannon.

In 1846, Greeley spoke out passionately against Democratic president James Polk and the Mexican War, which he regarded as a project of the Southern "slaveocracy," designed to bring new slave territory into the Union to bulk up its political power. "The laws of Heaven are suspended and those of Hell established in their stead," he wrote as the war dragged on. "It means that the Commandments are to be read and obeyed by our people thus—Thou *shalt* kill Mexicans; Thou *shalt* steal from them, hate them, burn their houses, ravage their fields, and fire red-hot cannon balls into towns swarming with their wives and children."

In July 1847, Greeley and Weed visited the fledgling city of Chicago for the first time, leading the New York delegation to the Chicago River and Harbor Convention, organized to protest President Polk's veto of a bill supporting infrastructure improvements. More than ten thousand conventioneers showed up. Edward Bates of Missouri was named chairman. The just-elected Whig congressman from Illinois, Abraham Lincoln, addressed the crowd at one point, as did Weed, who later lavished praise on Bates, expressing the hope that he would serve the public for years to come. "The nation cannot afford to be deprived of so much integrity, talent, and patriotism," Weed wrote. But Greeley arguably stole the show. "Every word that [Greeley] uttered was full of truth and wisdom," Weed proclaimed.

Weed's shrewd promotion of Mexican War hero Zachary Taylor as the Whig nominee for president in 1848 put Greeley in something of a bind, since he had been a bitter critic of the war and believed Henry Clay was far better qualified. By then, Greeley hungered for public office himself, with the opportunity to exert power directly. He mentioned the governorship as one option—and, failing that, the lieutenant governorship. He even mulled seeking a U.S. Senate seat. Weed, trying to keep the Whigs as strong as possible and concerned that Greeley was too quirky and truculent, hit on the expedient of testing him in one office without doing the party too much harm. After Greeley agreed to make a speech supporting General Taylor for president, Weed helped him win a campaign to fill out the few remaining months of the term of a New York Democratic congressman who had been ousted for election fraud. The *Tribune* editor went to Washington and joined such figures in the Thirtieth Congress as Alexander Stephens and Robert Toombs of Georgia, Joshua Giddings of Ohio, Andrew Johnson of Tennessee, and Abraham Lincoln of Illinois.

In the scant time available to him, Greeley made a distinct impression, for better or worse. Incapable of going along to get along, he seized on issues that could not help but infuriate his House colleagues. Notably, he attacked them for boosting their income by claiming excessive travel expenses. The *Tribune* reported, for example, that Abraham Lincoln had charged the government for a 1,600-mile trip from Illinois, when he might have reached the capital by a route half that length—thus cheating the taxpayers out of $676.80. "The usually travelled route for a great many members of the last Congress was an exceedingly crooked one, even for politicians," Greeley opined. He boasted to Margaret Fuller that, within a few weeks of assuming office, he had made himself "the most thoroughly detested man who ever sat in Congress, enveloped by a crowd who long and pray for a chance to extirpate me." Greeley irritated his colleagues constantly by interrupting the flow of business on the floor, wasting everyone's time. He pushed quixotic legislation, trying to ban the Navy's grog ration to sailors and change the name of the United States of America to Columbia, since Columbus beat Amerigo Vespucci to the hemisphere and thus was the one who merited recognition.

Senator Seward, looking in on the House, informed Weed that he was not impressed with their friend's performance. "He won't let them adjourn until three o'clock, and martyrizes himself five or six times a day by voting against the whole House. I am sorry, but who can reason with him?" Greeley, enjoying his taste of political power, hoped to move into a diplomatic post or the cabinet when his term was over, but Weed could not, or would not, make it happen.

Greeley's frustration finally boiled over in the 1850s, precipitated by one of his former staffers. Henry J. Raymond bolted from the *Tribune* to found, in September 1851, a rival newspaper that would compete for the same pool of Whig readers but hew to the party line more faithfully. It was called the *New York Times*. Acting in secrecy, Raymond hired away reporters from other papers, including the *Tribune*, instructing them to say nothing until the last minute. After the *Times* was up and running, Greeley found that even his friend Seward had betrayed him. Breaking a longstanding agreement to give him advance copies of his speeches, Seward handed them to Raymond's paper instead. Greeley snapped at Seward that "the *Times* is your special organ and its filibustering editorials and general negation of principle [are] especially agreeable to you. . . . I do not dispute your right to *make* it your organ. . . . I only ask for such treatment as you would cheerfully accord to your bitterest enemy."

In 1854, Greeley confronted Weed in his Astor House suite and bluntly asked whether, at long last, "the time and circumstances were favorable to his nomination as Governor." Weed pleaded that he could no longer control the gubernatorial nomination of the fractured Whigs. When Greeley asked about the post of lieutenant governor, then, Weed was just as discouraging. He noted that Greeley was a notorious advocate of temperance. The party could not win over working-class voters if it had a strong anti-liquor candidate for governor, in Myron Clark, and another for lieutenant governor. Weed, who seemed perpetually blind to Greeley's festering feelings, believed that these pragmatic arguments had assuaged the editor. He "left in good spirits," Weed recalled.

Then Greeley discovered which candidate Weed and Seward *were* supporting for lieutenant governor: his archenemy Henry J. Raymond. After Raymond's election, the *Tribune* editor sat down and wrote Seward a long letter. "It seems to me a fitting time to announce to you the dissolution of the firm of Seward, Weed and Greeley, by the withdrawal of the junior partner," Greeley declared. He recounted their sixteen-year relationship and all he had done to advance the causes dear to them. But now he would go his own way. "I am sure Weed did not mean to humiliate me, but he did it," particularly in the choice of lieutenant governor. "No other name could have been put on the ticket so bitterly humbling to me as that which was selected. The nomination was given to Raymond; the fight left to me."

Weed apparently had no idea that Greeley had angrily dissolved the "partnership." Seward quietly put Greeley's 1854 letter away, evidently sparing his friend Weed its peevish words. But the dissolution of the firm proved to be permanent, with fateful consequences for Seward, Weed, and the United States.

Diehard Whigs tried to prop up their dying party for as long as possible. But by the mid-1850s, the party's professionals recognized that to survive in a changing America they would have to form a new coalition of anti-Democrats. Greeley enthusiastically supported the idea and recommended "some simple name like 'Republican'" for it. But, as in his Whig days, he continued to place his own values above loyalty to the nascent party. Notably, in 1858, he sang the praises of Democrat Stephen Douglas after the senator broke with President Buchanan over Kansas. Greeley then supported the senator's reelection over Abraham Lincoln, believing (quite presciently, in truth) that Douglas's continued presence on the national stage would keep the Democratic Party bitterly divided, greatly increasing the chances for a Republican presidential victory in 1860. Seward and Weed seemed to agree, since their early promises of support for Lincoln vanished like the morning mist. Greeley even worked with Midwesterners to try to persuade Douglas to join the Republicans, while lecturing Lincoln's incredulous law partner William Herndon that the party's members ought to stop being such sticklers over the spread of slavery to the territories. "The Republican standard is too high. We want something practical," Greeley told him.

Lincoln, who believed Douglas's indifference to slavery was both deeply immoral and extremely dangerous, argued that Republicans would lose their whole reason for being if they embraced such a man. "What does *The New York Tribune* mean by its constant eulogizing, and admiring, and magnifying [of] Douglas?" Lincoln asked with a rare note of bitterness. If it was Greeley's intention to sacrifice the Republicans in Illinois, "we would like to know it soon; it will save us a great deal of labor to surrender at once." Herndon could hardly believe that the bold champion of freedom in New York whom he had admired for years was unmoved by the mighty battle between right and wrong taking place in Illinois. "Who would know by Greeley's paper that a great race for weal or woe was being fought all over the vast world-wide prairies of Illinois? Who would. It is strange indeed," Herndon wrote to Boston transcendentalist minister Theodore Parker. Lincoln, reticent to form resentments, told himself that Greeley was no doubt doing what he thought was best. But Lincoln could not help being miffed. "Greeley is not doing me right," he complained to Herndon. "His conduct, I believe, savors a little of injustice." Lincoln's supporters agreed, urging him to take on the Eastern establishment and Douglas at the same time. "Our business is war, war, war on them!" congressman John Wentworth, later the Chicago mayor, wrote to Lincoln. For his part, Lincoln engaged in the battle with all his might, very nearly toppling the powerful Douglas.

Greeley, meanwhile, persisted in underrating Lincoln's importance to the Republican Party and to the nation.

In 1859, Greeley decided to "go West" himself, making a journey overland from New York City to California, recording his impressions along the way. Two other journalists came along to cover the famous editor's antics, one of them Henry Villard. Greeley waved farewell to the comforts of civilization when he left Chicago on May 12, writing, "Chocolate and morning journals last seen on the hotel breakfast-table." At successive stages of the trip, he said goodbye to room-bells and bathtubs, beefsteaks and washbowls, potatoes and eggs, bootblacks, and even benches for meals (he found himself sitting on boxes and sacks). He visited troubled Kansas, speaking to its brave opponents of slavery. He took a jolting stagecoach from St. Joseph, Missouri, to Denver, Colorado.

Along the way, a herd of stampeding buffalo overturned the carriage, leaving Greeley so severely cut and bruised that he had to be carried off the coach when it reached its destination at the Denver House. That so-called hotel was really a large log cabin without interior walls, where hard-bitten miners gathered to drink and gamble while guests tried to sleep on board bedsteads separated from the action only by low partitions. Customers brandished guns, and bursts of shooting periodically erupted out front. On his third night there, Greeley felt compelled to address the rowdy clientele. "Friends, I have been in pain and without sleep for almost a week, and I am well-nigh worn out. Now I am a guest at this hotel, I pay a high price for my board and lodging, and I am entitled to rest during the night. But how can I get it with all this noise going on in this place?" Greeley spoke for nearly an hour, Villard wrote, "and was listened to with rapt interest and the utmost respect. He succeeded, too, in his object. The gambling stopped, and the bar was closed at eleven o'clock as long as he stayed." Some miners did, however, play a trick on the credulous Easterner during the daytime, "salting" a mine with gold flakes to dupe Greeley into believing that they had struck it rich so that he would promote their operation.

In Salt Lake City, he had a long interview with Mormon leader Brigham Young. His subsequent trip from Nevada to California became the stuff of legend. Mark Twain recounted the tale, which was incessantly retold out West, in his 1872 book *Roughing It*.

> Horace Greeley went over this road once. When he was leaving Carson City he told the driver, Hank Monk, that he had an engagement to lecture at Placerville and was very anxious to go through quick. Hank Monk cracked his whip and started off at an awful pace. The coach bounced up and down in such a terrific way that it jolted the buttons all off Horace's coat, and finally shot his head clean through the roof of the stage, and then he yelled at Hank Monk and begged him to go easier—said he

> wasn't in as much of a hurry as he was a while ago. But Hank Monk said, "Keep your seat, Horace, and I'll get you there on time!"—and you bet he did, what was left of him.

Back in New York, what was left of Greeley continued to confound expectations. Warning that Republicans faced an electoral disaster in 1860 unless they toned down their anti-slavery message, he made a case in early February for nominating the most conservative candidate possible—Edward Bates of the slave state of Missouri. Though respected for his brains and integrity, Bates seemed an odd, even bizarre, choice for a crusading editor who had long championed the bold and urbane Seward. Many Americans had never even heard of the man. Squat and stuffy, Bates seemed older than his sixty-six years. He was an old-fashioned, stern-visaged, white-bearded St. Louis jurist who had fought in the War of 1812. Born to wealth in Virginia, the well-educated Bates had nobly turned against slavery and freed the slaves that his father had handed down to him, drastically shrinking his inheritance. But slavery was not his political focus. He thought government should promote Western growth.

Bates had never really warmed to the Republicans, since he considered himself a classic Whig—polite, sophisticated, and dedicated to economic advancement—and disliked agitation over the slavery issue. Indeed, Bates had flatly refused to join the Republicans in 1856, choosing to remain with the fading and almost comatose Whig Party. He even presided over the party's national convention, where the Whigs nominated the supremely bland former president, Millard Fillmore of New York. Fillmore had already been chosen by the American Party, widely derided as the "Know-Nothings," as its candidate. He appealed to conservatives who detested politicians' endless bickering over slavery and the way America was being transformed by rampant immigration. (After the election, Mary Lincoln, who disliked her foreign-born maids, joked to her sister, "If some of you Kentuckians, had to deal with the 'Wild Irish,' as we housekeepers are sometimes called upon to do, the South would certainly elect Mr. Fillmore next time.") In the end,

Fillmore won only the eight electoral votes of Maryland. After the Whigs' defeat, Bates remained in a kind of conservative Limbo, still wary of joining the Republicans. "Madame Bates," a *New York Daily Herald* correspondent sneered, "is the personification of weakness." Even Greeley conceded that he was "old-fogish." Joseph Medill of the *Chicago Press and Tribune* would brand Bates a "fossil of the Silurian era."

But heading into the 1860 Republican convention, Bates was thrilled by signs that he had a serious shot at winning the presidential nomination of the party he had long spurned. The time seemed ripe for the Republicans to choose a conservative who might carry the border states and dampen the South's ardor for secession. In addition to Greeley's support, Bates had the impressive backing of the Blairs, the most prominent political family in America. They were headed by the crafty sixty-nine-year-old Francis Preston Blair, who owned a mansion across Pennsylvania Avenue from the White House and had long been a confidant of presidents, starting with "Old Hickory," Andrew Jackson. As one reporter noted, "there had not been a turn or a twist in national politics for thirty years that he had not been more or less concerned in." Observing Blair at the 1856 Republican convention, Murat Halstead found him to be "a little old gentleman, thin, slender, and feeble in appearance, yet moving about with considerable activity." He thought old Blair's face was "spoiled by a badly fitting set of false front teeth, which his upper lip is unable to hide. Then he is given a top-heavy appearance by the fact that his head is too big for his body, and his hat too big for his head." All the same, the Republican delegates found him impressive. "He is treated with distinguished consideration, and the mention of his name is invariably followed by uproarious applause. . . . The old fellow's big, bald head glistens with intelligence." Democrats, by contrast, thought it almost inconceivable that a Jackson man had betrayed their party for one that advanced the rights of blacks.

"Old Frank Blair" was already working the delegates in Chicago Friday night when a reporter for the racist, Democratic *Cincinnati Enquirer* spotted him. Blair was "the ugliest man in America," the correspondent asserted. "And he looked a deuced sight uglier in my eyes, from the fact of having been the confidential associate of Old Hickory, and now the confidential associate of Black Republicans. If he is ugly, he is smart, as is generally the case. I am devilish ugly myself, but not as ugly as Frank Blair; and I am smarter than he, for I have never deserted the straight-haired for the wooly-heads." Blair's impressive sons, both delegates to the 1860 convention, were also on the Bates team: stout, redheaded, resolute Missouri congressman Frank Blair, thirty-nine, whose courageous fight against slavery in a border state had won him a national reputation; and trim, dapper Maryland lawyer Montgomery Blair, forty-seven, who had served as U.S. solicitor general and worked on the case supporting Dred Scott's claim to freedom. With Greeley on their side, this was a formidable operation prepared to topple Seward in Chicago.

The old man acknowledged that "the ultra Republicans" in the Northern states still loved Seward. But the "middle men & middle states undoubtedly look to Bates as the safest man to prevent secession or to suppress it." That made Bates more electable, in Blair's view, and thus more likely to be "the choice in Chicago—In my opinion he is preferable to Seward in every respect." Months before the convention, even some of Bates's opponents had concluded that he was ready to claim the Republican crown. Judge George Hoadley of Cincinnati warned candidate Salmon P. Chase that "the same clique" that nominated John Frémont in 1856—namely, the Blairs—was "in on the plot" to nominate Bates in 1860. On February 6, he bluntly informed Chase: "Neither you nor Mr. Seward stand a chance. You will not be offended by my frankness. . . . Edward Bates is . . . certain to be nominated."

Others thought it preposterous that the Virginia-born conservative could prevail in a Republican convention. "Who can believe that Seward and his followers would ever permit the republican organization to be taken out of his hands by such a silurian nondescript as Bates?" the *New York Daily Herald* asked. Even if Bates were nominated, the Seward forces would never accept him, and the Republican Party would "be demolished and disorganized by admixture of Southern mire with

Northern metal, like the image seen by Nebuchadnezzar, whose feet were part of iron and part of clay, and which, for want of any principle of cohesion, fell in pieces and were scattered as chaff before the wind."

But the Bates boom was only one sign of the party's growing concerns about Seward's electability. When conservative New Jersey chose its delegates to the Chicago convention at a meeting on March 9, a call for three cheers for Seward produced "hisses . . . as prominent as the hurrahs." Even at New York's heavily pro-Seward Republican state convention in Syracuse on April 18, delegates conceded that they might have to choose a compromise candidate in Chicago. "Devotion to the success of the Republican party and its principles was clearly stronger than personal attachments," the *New York Times* reported. "Desire for success was paramount."

While Seward still seemed stronger, at least on paper, than any other Republican, Bates could almost taste victory as the convention approached. Samuel Bowles's influential *Springfield* (Massachusetts) *Republican* and John D. Defrees's *Indianapolis Daily Atlas* joined Greeley in endorsing him, as did numerous other Indiana papers. Orville Hickman Browning, a friend of Abraham Lincoln, privately assured Bates that the Illinois delegation, after casting its requisite favorite-son vote for Lincoln, would swing to him. A Pennsylvania man told Bates that almost half of the state's big delegation supported him. "And that, considering the favorable signs in other States, he thinks will make my nomination sure," Bates wrote in his diary.

Intense pressure on Republicans to choose a "safe" candidate came from outside as well. A new moderate party had been formed, appealing to Americans who disliked the mounting hatred between Democrats and Republicans and were terrified by the prospect of disunion. It wrapped up its convention just two days before Greeley, Weed, and Davis arrived in Chicago.

The Constitutional Union Convention, held in Baltimore on May 9 and 10, represented a last-ditch effort by conservatives—mostly well-to-do former Whigs—to hold America together and avert the bloodbath that Alexander Stephens envisioned. The Constitutional Union delegates gathered in an old church, with galleries on three sides, all festooned in red, white, and blue. Behind the president's chair hung a full-length portrait of George Washington beneath an outstretched American eagle. Venerable men who yearned for a return to a less contentious past—essentially by ignoring slavery—filled the aisles. They still hoped that the "irrepressible conflict" might be repressed. "There were crowds of good-looking gentlemen, talking of the prospect of redeeming the country," reported Murat Halstead, who had stopped off in Baltimore before heading to Chicago. "The delegates seem to be in high spirits. . . . The general foolishness of the two great parties has given the third unusual animation." Such young and idealistic Republicans as Oregon's Frank Johnson, on the other hand, branded the assemblage "'ye Old Fogie' Convention."

The delegates easily nominated Senator John Bell of Tennessee, a former Whig congressman and secretary of war, for president. Another former Whig won the nod for vice president: Edward Everett of Massachusetts, a man with an astounding resume—senator, congressman, governor, secretary of state, minister to Britain, president of Harvard University. One orator called it the "kangaroo ticket, with all the strength in its hind legs," in the form of the overqualified Everett. The platform was short and sweet: "the Constitution as it is, and the Union under it, now and forever," as Kentucky politician Leslie Combs described it. Platitudes prevailed. During the convention's two days, the participants scrupulously avoided any discussion of slavery. "Patriotism" and "Union" were the watchwords.

The grandson of Patrick Henry, whose ringing declaration of "Give me liberty, or give me death" helped inspire America's founding, delivered the convention's most notable speech. A longtime Whig from Tennessee, Gustavus A. Henry pleaded with Americans to preserve their precious inheritance. "With what face could we meet the wondering nations," he asked, "if by strife and hate and blinded councils, and the blasted sway of demagogues accursed, we throw away the richest heritage that God ever gave to man, blot out our fair escutcheon to all coming time, deliver down our names to be accursed, teach despots that freedom is but a dream, quench its fair light wherever it might dawn, and bid the lovers of mankind despair?" On a lighter note, Combs drew laughs with his sarcastic jabs at the two major parties: the "harmonious" Democrats, "who have lately agreed together so beautifully at Charleston," and "the 'irrepressible conflict' philanthropists about to assemble at Chicago."

Conservative papers hailed the party's actions. The *Augusta* (GA) *Chronicle and Sentinel* opined that Bell and Everett "are not demagogues, seeking power at the expense of the public good and the public peace, but plain, old-fashioned patriots, like the fathers of the Republic." While they "have almost too much honesty, fidelity, and capacity, we fear, for this corrupt and degenerate age," the paper prayed that "they might allay the fratricidal strife which bad men and mere politicians had wickedly or foolishly aroused" and that, if elected, they might enforce the laws and treat the states equally, thus preserving "our beloved Union."

For all the excitement in Baltimore, it seemed doubtful John Bell would carry a single Northern state—or a Deep Southern one, if the Democratic Party snapped in two, as now seemed likely. Perhaps the Constitutional Union Party might serve as a spoiler, collecting enough border states to deny any candidate an electoral college majority and thus throw the election into the House of Representatives. But the party, however weak, posed an obvious menace to the Republicans. Bell and Everett threatened to siphon away the votes of conservative Whigs, making it harder for Republicans to beat the Democrats. "This whole movement of the Conservative-Constitutional-Union-Know-Nothing-Old-Whig fossils is a miserable farce," the pro-Seward *Chicago Journal* complained. The Whigs in 1856 had accomplished nothing except to help elect Democrat James Buchanan, and they "are trying the same despicable game all over again." But that gave weight to arguments that the Chicago convention must nominate someone who could appeal to moderates—someone other than Seward.

* * *

In the furious row over the fate of slavery that spring, the prominent voices were those of white Americans. No African Americans participated in any of the major party conventions, not even the Republican one. "I could not be a member of the Republican party if I were so disposed; I am disenfranchised; I have no vote; I am put out of the pale of political society," Robert Purvis of Philadelphia, who had a black grandmother, told the American Anti-Slavery Society, which met in New York on May 8 and 9. "How could I, an Abolitionist, join a party that styles itself emphatically the 'white man's party'? . . . The Republicans may be, and doubtless are, opposed to the extension of slavery, but they are sworn to support, and they *will* support, slavery where it exists."

Even the election of Seward, "the noblest Roman of them all," would not end slavery, Purvis argued. With a weaker man, along the lines of Franklin Pierce or James Buchanan, the evils of slavery would be more readily exposed, and "we will have an irrepressible conflict that all men can see and understand"—a revolution bringing about emancipation. Many in the anti-slavery movement shared his disdain of Republicans, rating them half-hearted at best. "Every one knows—or ought to know—that the leaders of the Republican party do not believe in equal rights, and have never made an effort in any State in which they had the power, to remove from the colored man the political and legal disabilities which oppress him," the *Anti-Slavery Bugle* of Lisbon, Ohio, pointed out.

Purvis was especially disgusted with Horace Greeley. He quoted from an editorial the famous slavery opponent had published in his *New-York Tribune* on February 29. "We love liberty, equality, justice, humanity," Greeley wrote, ". . . but we do not like negroes, and heartily wish no individual of that race had ever been brought to America. We hope the day will come when the whole negro race in this country, being fully at liberty, will gradually, peacefully, freely draw off and form a community by themselves, somewhere toward the Equator, or join their brethren in lineage in Africa or the West Indies."

Still, Purvis believed it was inevitable that slavery would perish, whoever was elected. "The Anti-Slavery cause is onward; its doctrines are destined to triumph in this country; and no party can succeed that refuses to acknowledge it," Purvis said. "Slavery will be abolished in this land, and with it, that twin relic of barbarism, prejudice against color."

Three days after the American Anti-Slavery Society meeting ended, and two days after the Baltimore convention adjourned, the Bates team was on the ground in Chicago, operating from the Tremont House—Greeley, Francis Blair, his bold son Frank, Indiana editor John D. Defrees, and the campaign's young manager Charles Gibson, an ardent admirer who had studied law under Bates. Frank Blair was as confident about Bates's chances as his father was. "I tell you we shall yet get the old man nominated at Chicago and carry the Country for him at the election in November," he wrote. If not, Republicans could go hang themselves. "After Bates, I don't care a d—n." The senior Blair told reporters on this Sunday that he counted over sixty votes for Bates on the first ballot, second only to Seward, who he predicted would come in with eighty-five. That would position Bates beautifully to push on to victory, by making him the obvious alternative to Seward.

Weed and Seward had been cautioned for weeks about Greeley's intentions, but they did not want to believe their old friend would betray them, beyond occasionally touting Edward Bates on his editorial pages. Julius J. Wood, a former New Yorker and friend of Greeley, Seward, and Weed, smelled a rat. He paid Seward a visit in Washington, warning him that Greeley was out to ruin his campaign. Seward dismissed his concerns, but Weed thought it wise to sound Greeley out. One Sunday morning in Manhattan, according to the *Tribune*'s city editor, Franklin J. Otterson, Weed and Seward appeared at Greeley's preferred house of worship, the Universalist Church on Broadway, and pushed their way into Greeley's pew. But "this was a church service, and besides,

Greeley was not just then in a mood to talk with Weed and Seward," so nothing was discussed. Otterson asked what the text of the sermon had been. "The text?" Greeley responded, his eyes lighting up. "Let me see. It was in Isaiah:—'My thoughts are not your thoughts, neither are your ways my ways.'" At that, Greeley "burst out with a cackling peal of laughter that was heard throughout the outer office."

But on one Sunday—perhaps the same one—Greeley did come to see Weed at the Astor House. Wood, who was also there, recalled that he ran into Greeley in the hallway, where Greeley predicted that the Republicans "shan't nominate Seward. We'll take some conservative man," quite likely Bates. Wood immediately went to Seward's room to report these remarks. The senator assured him that Weed and Greeley had just met, and they remained on the friendliest terms. "Greeley has just been here with Weed. Weed brought him up here. You were wrong in what you said to me at Washington about Greeley; he is all right," Seward said. "No, I was not wrong. Greeley is cheating you. He will go to Chicago and work against you," Wood insisted. "My dear Wood," Seward replied, "your zeal sometimes gets a little better of your judgment."

Weed also tried to calm Wood's fears that night at the Astor House, telling him that no one would be able to block Seward's march to the nomination. "But the Blairs, . . . Mr. Greeley, and others are certainly hard at work," Wood insisted. "Yes," Weed said, "but something more than their opposition will be required to accomplish the defeat of a man upon whom the people have set their hearts." Weed simply could not accept that his old friend would, in the end, defy the party's passionate base. He believed Greeley was, at heart, kind and generous, and would come around to Seward, who had fought for freedom valiantly at his side. When pro-Seward sentiment swept state conventions in early 1860; "when State after State, with unanimity and emphasis, declared for Governor Seward; and when a politician of Mr. Greeley's experience and knowledge was scarcely at liberty to doubt the result, we did not expect to encounter his obstinate opposition," Weed wrote in his *Albany Journal*. But even Greeley's admiring biographer, Parton, reflected later that "Horace Greeley is a human being" who was crushed by Weed's failure to support his political aspirations. He had a motive for destroying Seward. "He may not have been conscious of the fact; but men are often unconscious of the motives which really control their conduct." What's more, Parton added, "the election of Mr. Seward to the Presidency would place Mr. Thurlow Weed in a position of commanding influence, and give a rival newspaper advantages of inestimable value."

Greeley had been underrated as a child, as a struggling young man, and even now, as a famous editor. Dismissed as naive, flakey, and unreliable, he had been denied public power and position in New York. But the *Tribune* editor would soon demonstrate that he was, in truth, a most dangerous adversary—a brilliant and stubborn advocate who was supremely confident that he knew better than others. Greeley had been hard at work from the moment he arrived in Chicago Saturday night. On Sunday, his "sharp voice" could be "heard high over the din of conversation at the Tremont House" in his effort to get "the old fossil" Bates "into the ring," the *New York Daily Herald* reported. The *Chicago Journal*, noting that Greeley had undermined the party's values two years earlier when Lincoln was battling against Stephen Douglas, thought the man in the white coat was up to no good. "It would seem that he is seeking to accomplish a like purpose again, by discharging poisoned arrows at Mr. Seward and his friends." Mayor Long John Wentworth, sensing the strength of the Bates forces, cautioned in his *Chicago Democrat* that the party must not water down its principles for the sake of winning an election. "Much as success is desired by us," he wrote, "we would prefer to fight four years longer to making any compromise of these eternal principles of justice and liberty that called the republican party into existence."

But the argument of electability did seem to resonate with delegates. Addressing the Missouri delegation at its Tremont House headquarters that Sunday morning, Greeley "remarked . . . with evident gratification, that he was much surprised at the feeling for Mr. Bates, and felt very much encouraged at the prospects," a correspondent for the *Missouri Democrat*, in St. Louis, reported. The writer concurred with

Greeley. "I have heard a great deal of discussion, and the only debatable subject has seemed to be Bates or Seward. For every Seward man with his strong personal preference and his ultra Republican views, I have found a moderate, yet firm Bates man, tenacious of his candidate's soundness and most strenuous in his views of availability." John J. Mudd, a thriving Chicago merchant who had relocated from St. Louis, was working hard for Bates too, making "plain and logical" arguments "about the necessity of running such a man as Mr. Bates in Southern Illinois, in Indiana, Ohio and Pennsylvania," the crucial swing states filled with conservative voters. The reporter assured his readers that "Mr. Bates has nothing to fear from McLean, Chase, Cameron, or Lincoln. The contest seems to be narrowed down to Bates and Seward for first choice." The Missouri men, in short, thought "that our candidate has an excellent chance. All are in fine spirits."

Still, the power of Seward was undeniable. "Undoubtedly the outside influence of this city is against us," the St. Louis reporter conceded. "The New York representatives, who are in great numbers, and men of high talent, are most enthusiastic, and are uncompromising for a radical man." Over at the Richmond House, the *New York Daily Herald* reported, Weed appeared to be fully in command, issuing "orders to his faithful lieutenants" to charm or cajole the incoming delegates. He was confident that Seward would be nominated and that the Pennsylvania delegation would ultimately swing around and support the New Yorker.

But Weed would quickly discover, to his dismay, that Greeley was doing more than singing the praises of Bates; he was poisoning delegates' minds against Seward, and his reputation for courage and integrity made him highly persuasive. At the same time, a threat was emerging from another quarter. Judge David Davis of Illinois, like many others in Chicago, recognized that Seward could be stopped only if delegates were willing to rally around one opposition candidate. Weed thought such a unified effort was unlikely; the delegates seemed committed only to their favorite sons, and when those lesser lights faded, they would support their party's leader. But Davis had spent his first hours in Chicago sounding out politicians from the swing states. The fear that Seward would hurt Republicans in November was far stronger than he had imagined, and Davis believed that these delegates would be desperate enough to unite behind a lesser candidate if their favorite failed—ideally one less controversial than Seward but still acceptable to the party's earnest anti-slavery base.

Chapter 6: The Taste *Is* in My Mouth

From their home base at the Tremont House, Jesse K. Dubois was working closely with Judge Davis that Sunday to advance Abraham Lincoln's chances. The forty-nine-year-old politician had a long history with Lincoln. In the 1830s, when they both served in the Illinois House of Representatives, Lincoln enlisted the support of the blue-eyed, auburn-haired Dubois in efforts to relocate the Illinois capital from Vandalia to the sleepy village of Springfield. Dubois and others who voted for the move told their constituents that the capital needed to be closer to the state's center. "But in reality we gave the vote to Lincoln because we liked him, because we wanted to oblige our friend, and because we recognized him as our leader," Dubois recalled. With his humor, strength of character, and intelligence, Lincoln attracted allegiance from the start of his career.

Like many faithful Whigs, Dubois joined the Republicans reluctantly. A conservative who did not want to be tainted by radicalism, he grudgingly attended their May 1856 state convention in Bloomington, arriving in time to capture the nomination for state auditor, an elected office. But once there, he was riveted by Lincoln's keynote speech against the Kansas-Nebraska Act. As the convention broke up, Dubois approached his friend Henry Clay Whitney, seized him "by the arm with a painful grip," and exclaimed, "Whitney, that is the greatest speech ever made in Illinois and it puts Lincoln on the track for the Presidency." With Mary Lincoln and Bloomington *Daily Pantagraph* publisher Jesse Fell, he was one of the first to perceive that this tall, ungainly, largely self-educated lawyer might be presidential material.

As excited as Dubois became that day, Lincoln was quite familiar with his friend's political caution. Two years later, when Lincoln was preparing for his Senate run, Dubois visited his office and found him scribbling with a pen. "Lincoln, what are you writing?" he asked. "I am writing something which you may or may never see," Lincoln replied evasively. Dubois pressed him to share it. "No, sir, I have said I will not," Lincoln insisted. It turned out to be his "House Divided" speech, which his allies would regard as dangerously provocative in declaring that freedom and slavery could not ultimately survive alongside each other—that one or the other would inevitably prevail. Such an idea was heresy in the South, and anathema to Illinoisans who sympathized with that region. Lincoln later explained to Dubois, "I would not read it to you because I knew you would make me change it—modify & mollify." Come what may, America's core commitment to freedom was at stake, and Lincoln felt compelled to explain why Stephen Douglas must be stopped. "I . . . was willing to perish with it, if necessary," Lincoln said. Horace Greeley and others in the East had been touting Douglas as a de facto Republican, but the speech would set Lincoln far apart from the Democrat. After it, no one could doubt who was the true Republican. "Mr. Lincoln did this because he wanted to cut the winds out of *Seward & others*," Dubois wrote.

Having been elected state auditor in 1856, Dubois had moved to Springfield, just across Eighth Street and a few houses down from Lincoln's home. The two men and their families bonded. They visited each other frequently, and their children played together. Mary Lincoln, in one letter to Dubois, extended her best wishes to "your wife, whom I have always loved so much." Jesse's son, Fred, recalled that "Mrs. Lincoln was a constant visitor in our home and a most intimate friend of my mother." The families enjoyed horseraces together. "Mr. Lincoln and my father and some other friends would get into the family carriage, accompanied always by some of us boys, and drive out to the grounds," Fred recalled. "Mr. Lincoln was a good judge of horses and he and his companions would often place a small wager on the results of the race." Some memories were less pleasant. Jesse Dubois recalled walking with Lincoln to his house for breakfast one morning. Mary Lincoln had some "aristocratic company" from Kentucky and had asked her husband to head downtown and buy some meat. She greeted Lincoln and Dubois at the door. "Upon opening the paper of meat she became enraged at the Kind L had bought," Dubois wrote. "She abused L. outrageously and finally was so mad she struck him in the face," drawing blood. Rubbing the blood off, Lincoln told Dubois they should leave, and they walked away, without breakfast.

During the long years of their friendship, Lincoln revealed to Dubois an indelible memory from his early twenties, when he helped his family move from Indiana to Illinois during the "rough and cold" month of March 1830, driving a wagon pulled by oxen. The wagon came to a swamp spanned by a corduroy wooden bridge, which was covered by a layer of ice, leaving only posts exposed to guide the way. Lincoln could not make the frightened oxen proceed "without apparent cruelty," though he coaxed and threatened the beasts. Reluctantly, he had to use the lash, "cutting open the hide," which finally drove the oxen to move forward, their hooves breaking through the thin ice. Halfway over, Lincoln discovered the family dog had gotten out of the wagon and was stranded in the swamp, emitting "a kind of despairing howl." Though fearful of the danger, Lincoln took off his shoes, rolled up his pants, climbed out of the wagon, and "jumped into the Cold water, the sheets of ice hitting his shins." He reached the dog, who was "frightened nearly to death," and carried him back to the wagon. The pet huddled by the feet of Lincoln's stepmother, Sarah, "scared half out of his wits." When the family finally reached the other side after the harrowing crossing, the dog did not want to come out of the wagon. Lincoln had to "haul him out by force." Once on dry land, the canine "cut up such antics as no dog Ever did before: he ran round and round Abe & laid down at his feet—got up and ran round and round again and again: he seemed—was grateful to Abe, his benefactor." Lincoln capped the story with an admission of his fear. "Well, Jesse, I guess that I felt about as glad as the dog."

Now, Jesse Dubois was in Chicago, trying to carry his neighbor across a treacherous landscape of a different sort. On that night of Sunday, May 13, Dubois scrawled out a hopeful note, addressed simply to "Hon. A Lincoln, Springfield, Ill.," the envelope bearing a brown three-cent George Washington stamp, duly postmarked "Chicago." Dubois informed Lincoln: "Judge Davis is furious, never saw him work so hard and so quick in all my life."

Shortly after Lincoln delivered the 1856 speech that so moved Dubois, Lincoln was out on the circuit, staying with his fellow lawyers at the American House in Urbana. After court, Lincoln and Davis typically retired to the room they shared, while Whitney fetched the *Chicago Press*, brought in by train, and returned to read it to them. The hotel had one serious defect. Its host, John Dunaway, would madly beat an earsplitting gong at the front door every mealtime, greatly irritating Lincoln, Davis, and Whitney, whose room, with its open window, was directly overhead. On one hot, dry day, when the court cases had been dull, Whitney returned to the hotel and discovered that the offending gong had mysteriously disappeared, and that Dunaway was searching desperately for it. When Whitney reached his room, he instantly recognized the culprit. "Lincoln sat awkwardly in a chair tilted up after his fashion, looking amused, silly and guilty, as if he had done something ridiculous, funny and reprehensible." Davis was amused, too, but said, "Now, Lincoln, that is a shame. Poor Dunaway is the most distressed being. You must put that back." Lincoln had secreted the hated gong between the top of the dining room table and its false bottom, where it would never have been found. But, overcome with guilt, he snuck downstairs with Whitney and returned it to its place, "after which he bounded up the stairs, two steps at a time, I following."

That week, Whitney read to Davis and Lincoln from the Chicago newspaper that the Republicans had chosen John Frémont for president. The following day's paper contained the fascinating information that, although the delegates unanimously nominated former senator William L. Dayton for vice president, an impressive 110 votes had been cast in an earlier test ballot for somebody named Lincoln. Davis and Whitney were thrilled. Lincoln shrugged off the report. "I reckon that ain't me; there's another great man in Massachusetts named Lincoln, and I reckon it's him," he said. But in fact, Abraham Lincoln had been pushed by an Illinois delegate named William B. Archer, who had served in the legislature with him. The next edition of the paper included some of the floor debate. Someone had asked, "Will Lincoln fight?" and was assured that he would. "Lincoln betrayed no other feeling except that of amusement, at the sole qualification demanded," Whitney recalled.

In the immediate aftermath of his crushing Senate loss to Stephen Douglas two years later, Lincoln believed his political career was over. Jesse Fell thought differently. Lincoln's compelling moral case for freedom—in plain and often folksy language that connected with people—had impressed everyone who read about it. One month after the election, Fell grabbed Lincoln outside the courthouse in Bloomington and pulled him over to his brother's law office across the street for a private chat. He informed Lincoln that everywhere he had gone that year—in New England, New York, New Jersey, Pennsylvania, Ohio, Michigan, and Indiana—someone had asked him who this Lincoln was, this man tying Douglas in knots. "I have a decided impression," Fell told Lincoln, "that if your popular history and efforts on the slavery question can be sufficiently brought before the people, you can be made a formidable, if not successful, candidate for the Presidency." Lincoln was skeptical. "Oh, Fell, what's the use of talking of me for the presidency, whilst we have such men as Seward, Chase and others, who are so much better known to the people, and whose names are so intimately associated with the principles of the Republican party? Everybody knows them; nobody, scarcely, outside of Illinois, knows me."

Yet Lincoln, though beaten down, never quite lost all hope that he could gain a public position that would help him advance the cause of freedom. One night in January 1859, after the legislature formally reelected Douglas as senator, Lincoln joined a strategy session of prominent Illinois Republicans in the first-floor library at the State House. Memories are hazy, but the group apparently included such close friends as Leonard Swett, Jesse Dubois, and Norman Judd. As Whitney recalled, Dubois suggested "putting Lincoln up for a place on the ticket, either for President or Vice-President—one or the other." When Lincoln tried to object, his colleagues interrupted him, and Lincoln held his tongue. Perhaps he concluded that a favorite-son presidential candidacy in 1860, however hopeless, might help him retain his popularity with state Republicans until he could compete again for a Senate seat in a few years. Shortly after the meeting, a reporter asked Lincoln for his reaction to the formal election of Douglas. Lincoln replied "that he felt like the Kentucky boy, who, after having his finger squeezed pretty badly, felt 'too big to cry, and too badly hurt to laugh.'"

Law partner William Herndon contended that Lincoln never stopped plotting his potential advancement. "His ambition was a little engine that knew no rest," he wrote. But Lincoln's ambition ran on the tracks of sagacity and caution. At least initially, he seemed to believe what he said—that he was ill-equipped for the presidency and would not make a serious candidate. But he quite brilliantly concocted a plan that would maximize whatever chances he had. Any such bid, Lincoln realized, even as a placeholder for a later Senate run, would have to be kept under wraps for as long as possible. He lacked the following, fame, and financial support of the leading Republicans, and any announcement of his intentions would appear arrogant and foolish, sure to irritate others in the party. Throughout 1859 and well into 1860, he thus tamped down any talk of his candidacy. "He had his burning and his consuming ambition, but he kept his secrets and opened not," Herndon observed.

Lincoln even shot down an early show of support in Illinois. On April 13, 1859, Thomas J. Pickett, who had touted Lincoln for president in his *Rock Island Register*, proposed a dramatic event. He would gather Republican editors from around the state to jointly announce they would back him for president. Lincoln hastily snuffed out the idea. "I must, in candor, say I do not think myself fit for the Presidency," he wrote Pickett. "I certainly am flattered, and gratified, that some partial friends think of me in that connection; but I really think it best for our cause that no concerted effort, such as you suggest, should be made." He made a similar statement to Ohio lawyer and former congressman Samuel Galloway. "I must say I do not think myself fit for the Presidency."

Instead of touting himself directly, Lincoln prepared the ground for Republican success in November 1860. He worked hard to persuade fellow Republicans around the country to hammer on just one issue—stopping the expansion of slavery—while soft-pedaling or ignoring others that offended voters or divided the party. Keep it simple and don't pick fights, he advised. Thus, Lincoln frowned on a January 10, 1859, speech by Maine congressman Israel Washburn, who blasted Oregon for blocking free black people from entering the new state. Seward, the party's moral leader, had also criticized the new state on that score. Lincoln surely agreed with both men, but he realized that many voters still supported such Black Codes—Illinois itself had one—and it would not be helpful to antagonize them. Lincoln urged Republicans to "consider whether it would not be better and wiser, so long as we all agree that this matter of slavery is a moral, political and social wrong, and ought to be treated as a wrong, not to let anything minor or subsidiary to that main principle and purpose make us fail to cooperate."

Lincoln similarly sounded an alarm over the efforts of Ohio Republicans to undermine the Fugitive Slave Act, which many voters saw as an integral part of the 1850 compromise to save the Union. To be sure, Lincoln despised the law, which gave authorities additional powers to re-enslave people who had escaped to freedom. "I hate to see the poor creatures hunted down, and caught, and carried back to their stripes, and unrewarded toils," he wrote privately in 1855. Yet Lincoln believed the Republicans would only hurt themselves by attempting to get a plank into the 1860 party platform calling for the law's repeal.

Indeed, that effort was "already damaging" them in Illinois, he informed Ohio governor Salmon P. Chase in a June 9 letter. Such a plank would "explode" the convention, Lincoln warned. "Once introduced, its supporters and . . . opponents will quarrel irreconcilably." Lincoln stressed he was not arguing the merits, only the politics. "I assure you that the cause of Republicanism is hopeless in Illinois, if it be in any way made responsible for that plank. I hope you can, and will, contribute something to relieve us of it."

Lincoln made a similar plea in a July 6 letter to Indiana congressman Schuyler Colfax. He urged him to help "hedge against divisions in the Republican ranks generally, and particularly for the contest of 1860. The point of danger is the temptation in different localities to '*platform*' for something which will be popular just there, but which, nevertheless, will be a firebrand elsewhere, and especially in a National convention." He cited some examples: a "movement against foreigners" in Massachusetts; an effort in New Hampshire to treat obedience to the Fugitive Slave Law as a crime; Ohio's proposed plank to overturn that law; and the flirtation of Kansas Republicans with Douglas's "squatter sovereignty" as a solution to the vicious struggle over slavery there. "In these things there is explosive matter enough to blow up half a dozen national conventions, if it gets into them," Lincoln warned. Seward had won the hearts of Republicans with his bold pronouncements and policies, but Lincoln believed the party had to be more cautious and pragmatic to win over swing voters. Republicans should narrow their focus to getting elected, without sacrificing the core principle—no extension of slavery. "In a word, in every locality we should look beyond our noses; and at least say *nothing* on points where it is probable we shall disagree."

If Lincoln was not publicly running for president in 1859 and on into 1860, Stephen Douglas most emphatically was. Still hoping to win over Southern Democrats without losing Northerners, he continued to defend his "popular sovereignty" idea, most notably in an extraordinary, densely argued 18,000-word article in the September issue of *Harper's Magazine*. Painstakingly laying out the historic and intellectual basis of the idea, Douglas insisted that the "fathers of the Revolution" had recognized the right of the people to local self-government, including decisions about slavery. The senator blasted Seward's "irrepressible conflict" and Lincoln's "house divided" stances, arguing these two politicians had made clear that they would permit "no peace on the slavery question—no truce in the sectional strife—no fraternity between the North and South, so long as this Union remains as our fathers made it."

The piece appalled Lincoln. He strode into the office of Springfield lawyer Milton Hay and, "without a salutation, said: 'This will never do. He puts the moral element out of this question. It won't stay out.'" Lincoln, who owed whatever national prominence he enjoyed almost entirely to his battles with Douglas, was only too happy to reply through a series of speeches that fall in Ohio and Indiana. He pounded home basic themes. Slavery, Lincoln contended, was ultimately incompatible with America's founding principles—notably the Declaration of Independence, which held that "all men are created equal" and that governments could not justly deny human beings their God-given rights. Although forced to accept the hard reality of slavery, the Founders adopted "a policy restricting the spread of slavery" by barring it from the Northwest Territory, so that "the whole country looked forward to the ultimate extinction of the institution."

The Founders, Lincoln argued, were on the side of freedom, not slavery, even if slavery had to be accepted for a time. He quoted his eloquent hero Henry Clay, arguing that if Douglas and his allies hoped to reverse the movement toward universal freedom unleashed by America's founding, "they must go back to the era of our independence, and muzzle the cannon which thundered its annual joyous return on the Fourth of July; they must blow out the moral lights around us; they must penetrate the human soul and eradicate the love of liberty." That was something he did not believe they could do. In his speeches, Lincoln mocked Douglas's indifference to slavery in simple and memorable language: "He is so put up by nature that a lash upon his back would hurt him, but a lash upon anybody else's back does not hurt him." As Lincoln's popularity as a speaker grew, invitations flowed in, all making him better known. He went to Wisconsin and violence-torn Kansas.

He even started to catch the attention of leading presidential campaigns. On October 20, 1859, Lincoln's friend Norman Judd, the Illinois member of the Republican National Committee, received an oddly peremptory telegram from Thurlow Weed: "Send Abram Lincoln to Albany immediately." Judd, perplexed, forwarded it directly to Lincoln. "What it means I don't know nor do I know what to advise," Judd wrote. "I take it that Thurlow Weed is not so green to think he can get you into a combination with his pet Seward and it must be something else and probably of importance—I am in a fog about it." Lincoln ignored the fog and the summons.

Four days after Weed's telegram, a supporter of Pennsylvania presidential hopeful Simon Cameron asked Lincoln to form a partnership with the senator, political boss, and wealthy banker and transportation mogul. The letter was evidently part of a coordinated strategy by Cameron's men to nail down Illinois's support before the 1860 convention. In early October, the *Lancaster Examiner and Herald*, located in the county where Cameron was born, had published an editorial touting its native son for president and Lincoln for vice president, which was sent to newspapers throughout Illinois and even printed up as a flyer for distribution there. Lincoln artfully dodged. "As to the ticket you name, I shall be heartily for it, *after* it shall have been fairly nominated by a Republican national convention; and I can not be committed to it *before*," he said. Lincoln stressed that he was working for the success of the Republican cause by serving "in the ranks," and would continue to do so unless the party—"as I think not probable"—nominated him for president or vice president.

Believing his debates with Douglas two years earlier would give him a toehold in history, even if nothing else did, Lincoln had been working since late 1858 to get the transcripts published as a book. To that end, he carefully collected copies of the most accurate press accounts and used scissors and paste to assemble them into a scrapbook, which he sent to prospective publishers. The initial response was chilly. But on December 7, 1859, Lincoln got welcome news from George M. Parsons, chairman of the Republican State Central Committee of Ohio, that the party would sponsor the printing of the debates by a Columbus publisher, Follet, Foster and Company, in early 1860, essentially for use as an anti-Douglas document during the upcoming presidential campaign. Not wishing to distract from the drama and power of the debates, Lincoln asked that they appear without an introduction or any other editorial adornments. Though fond of Lincoln, the *Chicago Press and Tribune* viewed the book mostly through the lens of its harm to Douglas. "It contains, perhaps, the most forceful statement of Mr. Douglas's political opinions, and a complete and triumphant exposition of their danger and unsoundness," the paper opined in February 1860. "It sets forth with great clearness the fundamental doctrines of the Republican party, and has the proof, in Mr. Douglas' impotent assaults upon them, of their necessity and beneficence." Yet even as a weapon against Douglas, the volume could not help but boost Lincoln's reputation.

There were other signs his star was ascending. In late October, Lincoln received an invitation to speak at Henry Ward Beecher's Plymouth Church, in Brooklyn. He eagerly accepted, welcoming this opportunity to make his mark in the New York metropolitan area, though he asked that the date be moved to February 1860. He needed time to prepare. Lincoln spent one hundred dollars on a new suit and set to work at the State House library, digging into the Founders' views on slavery, intending to devote his speech to his usual topic—refuting Douglas. He wanted to make it exactly right, powerful enough to impress the severe critics in the East. "No former effort in the line of speech-making had cost Lincoln so much time and thought as this one," Herndon wrote.

After Lincoln checked into the Astor House, in New York, he discovered that the Young Men's Republican Union had taken over sponsorship and had moved the speech to the hall of the Cooper Institute (also known as the Cooper Union) in Manhattan. The Union's board members happened to include Horace Greeley and New-York *Evening Post* editor William Cullen Bryant, both of whom were working ardently to derail William Seward's candidacy. Lincoln was, in fact, the third in a series of speakers they had brought in to offer alternatives to the popular New York senator. On January 25, congressman Frank Blair Jr.—touting Edward Bates of Missouri for president—argued that Republicans needed a candidate from the border states to restrain hotheaded Southern leaders bent on disunion. On February 15, Cassius M. Clay of Kentucky, a candidate for president himself, made a characteristically belligerent speech, arguing that the Southern secessionists must be dealt with harshly. He had been fighting such men for twenty years, he argued. "They can't drive me out, gentlemen. . . . Put me at the head of the United States and I will whip them."

Once ensconced in Manhattan, Lincoln strolled the streets, bought a new stovepipe hat, and posed for a full-length portrait by Mathew Brady, who skillfully de-emphasized his skinny neck, big ears, drooping left eyelid, and disheveled hair, providing the dignified image later used to acquaint America with Lincoln's rugged, beardless face. Mason Brayman, a fellow Illinois lawyer, met Lincoln at his hotel and took him to dinner. Lincoln seemed oblivious to the frowns of Eastern snobs, making little effort to disguise his country roots. He had trouble deciphering the menu at a posh restaurant even after the waiter translated the French, but when the waiter mentioned beans, "Lincoln's face brightened and he made a quick gesture. 'Hold on there, bring me beans. I know beans.'" When a group of admirers, including a leading Republican and respected New York lawyer, Yale-educated William M. Evarts, stopped by the table to say hello, Brayman wrote, Lincoln "turned half round and talked 'hoss' to them—introduced me as a Democrat, but one so good tempered that he and I could 'eat out of the *same rack, without a pole between us.*'"

Not nearly as cultivated and well educated as Blair and Clay, Lincoln rose on the night of February 27 in his shiny new suit, which he had unfortunately wrinkled by cramming it into his trunk, to address 1,500 spectators at the Cooper Institute. Greeley and Bryant watched from the stage as Lincoln commenced in his high-pitched voice, with his rural Midwestern accent. One eyewitness was at first mortified. "I was greatly disappointed. He was tall, tall,—oh, how tall! and so angular and awkward that I had, for an instant, a feeling of pity for so ungainly a man." When Lincoln began to speak, though, "his face lighted up as with an inward fire; the whole man was transfigured. I forgot his clothes, his personal appearance, and his individual peculiarities. Presently, forgetting myself, I was on my feet like the rest, yelling like a wild Indian, cheering this wonderful man." Lincoln won over the crowd without histrionics. As he did when addressing a jury on the circuit in Illinois, he spoke simply, directly, and methodically, laying brick of evidence atop brick and appealing to his listeners' reason and morality.

He examined the men who created the Constitution, to see how they viewed the expansion of slavery. By Lincoln's tally, twenty-three of thirty-six signers later supported, through their votes, at least some limitations on slavery in the territories—a powerful argument against Douglas's contention that the Founders had wanted the people of local jurisdictions to decide the matter. That being the case, Lincoln argued, Republicans were simply embracing the approach of the Founders. Though the Democrats, especially in the South, smeared them as radicals out to destroy America, it was fairer to call them conservatives. If people wished to stop the divisive debate over slavery, Lincoln had a solution: "Go back to that old policy. . . . If you would have the peace of old times, readopt the precepts and policy of the old times."

In the wake of abolitionist John Brown's attempt to incite a bloody slave uprising four months earlier, outraged Democrats accused Republicans of fomenting insurrection and creating vicious sectional hatreds. It was a powerful political argument, because many Americans did believe that incessant criticism of slavery was tearing the country in half. Lincoln explained that Republicans held no animus toward the South and wished the Union to live on, strong and united—that it was Southern radicals who were claiming that the election of a "sectional" president would compel them to break the country in two. "That is cool. A highwayman holds a pistol to my ear, and mutters through his teeth, 'Stand and deliver, or I shall kill you, and then you will be a murderer!'" Lincoln understood that Southerners wanted slavery to be regarded as a positive good, but that did not mean Republicans should feel compelled to placate them. "Thinking it right, as they do, they are not to blame for desiring its full recognition, as being right; but, thinking it wrong, as we do, can we yield to them? Can we cast our votes with their view, and against our own? In view of our moral, social, and political responsibilities, can we do this?"

Republicans were willing to maintain slavery where it was—in the slave states. They only sought that the country return to the idea of slavery that the Founders held: that it was wrong and should not be permitted to spread—that, as Lincoln put it, it should "be put in the course of ultimate extinction." Lincoln insisted that this point of view was moderate, humane, and conservative—not radical, and not an imminent threat to the South's way of life. "Neither let us be slandered from our duty by false accusations against us, nor frightened from it by menaces of destruction to the Government nor of dungeons to ourselves. LET US HAVE FAITH THAT RIGHT MAKES MIGHT, AND IN THAT FAITH, LET US, TO THE END, DARE TO DO OUR DUTY AS WE UNDERSTAND IT," he said, capitalizing the conclusion of his address.

The speech was a triumph. Rather than shrink from the battle, Lincoln had expressed, clearly and forcefully, the morality, compassion, and patriotism underlying the Republican cause. Lincoln's emphasis on siding with the Founders—rather than denouncing the Constitution, as some ardent opponents of slavery did—helped cloak him with conservatism. The address electrified the party faithful, as did his short tour of New England, with stops in Rhode Island, New Hampshire, and Connecticut. The honorarium from the Cooper Institute speech, which paid for the trip, permitted Lincoln to visit his eldest son, Robert, at his preparatory school, Phillips Exeter Academy, in New Hampshire, where the boy was receiving further education after failing to get into Harvard. (Robert later joked that he did his part to boost his father's national aspirations by flunking fifteen of his sixteen entrance examinations, thus prompting him to come East.) At each stop, Lincoln reiterated that Republicans were the true conservatives in the slavery debate, not the revolutionaries, as the Democratic press falsely asserted. He even defended Seward repeatedly for his most notorious phrase. When the "idea that slavery is right, and the idea that it is wrong" collide, Lincoln explained, they "do actually produce that irrepressible conflict which Mr. Seward has been so roundly abused for mentioning." People were drawn to this unpolished man from the West with his moral vision, delivered with unexpected power. To be sure, Lincoln did not return to the West as a top-tier candidate. Greeley, for example, continued to back Bates, and Illinois seemed to be the only state that regarded Lincoln as presidential material. But he had aroused the interest of the Eastern press.

In Springfield, William Herndon detected a change in his law partner's mood. "Seward was the great man of the day, but Lincoln had demonstrated to the satisfaction of his friends that he was tall enough and strong enough to measure swords with the Auburn statesman," Herndon recalled. Lincoln, he noted, had no money and no organization to speak of. "Seward had all these things, and, behind them all, a brilliant record in the United States Senate with which to dazzle his followers. But with all the prestige and the experience the [senator] was no more adroit and no more untiring in his pursuit of his ambition than the man who had just delivered the Cooper Institute speech."

Before Lincoln went East, a twenty-five-year-old reporter for the *Chicago Press and Tribune* named Horace White gave the undeclared candidate a heads-up. "Friend Lincoln," he wrote. "You must get yourself in training for the presidency. Do not be surprised if the *Press & Tribune* break ground for you in a few days." White had traveled thousands of miles alongside Lincoln during the 1858 Senate campaign, and he had come to deeply admire this odd man who veered between sad introspection and infectious laughter. "There was more difference between Lincoln dull & Lincoln animated, in facial expressions, than I ever saw in *any other human being*," he later wrote. As White had hinted, the paper began a barrage of enthusiastically pro-Lincoln editorials on February 16 that continued right through the convention. It stressed the essential point of Lincoln's electability—his popularity in Illinois and Indiana, and his fine chances in Pennsylvania and New Jersey, all of them crucial swing states that the Republicans had lost in 1856. Managing editor Joseph Medill went to Washington in early 1860, specifically to probe the party's presidential politics and Lincoln's chances. Seward, who had long enjoyed the newspaper's support as the nation's most eminent Republican, confronted him at a reception for the British ambassador. The senator "'blew me up' tremendously for having disappointed him—'gone back on him'—and preferring that 'prairie statesman,' as he called Lincoln," Medill recalled. "He dismissed me from his presence, saying that hereafter he and I would no longer be friends."

Lincoln, by contrast, made every effort to get and keep all the friends he could. To have any real shot at the nomination, he would have to make sure that the Illinois delegation sent to Chicago was unified behind him. If Lincoln could not even muster the support of his own state, his advocates would have little luck persuading anyone that he could be a serious candidate. Unfortunately, Lincoln confronted nasty divisions among Illinois Republicans that threatened to tear that effort apart. Long John Wentworth, the former congressman and Chicago mayor, had been feuding viciously with Chicago lawyer and party leader Judd. Wentworth was the editor of the *Chicago Democrat*—a Republican paper despite its name—and Judd was associated with the rising *Press and Tribune*, both papers competing for the same pool of readers, like the *Tribune* and *Times* in New York, a situation rife with tension. Judd publicly branded Wentworth "a most corrupt liar and knave," while Wentworth tore Judd to shreds on the pages of the *Democrat*. Lincoln needed both men on his side—not to mention their allies. David Davis, for example, sided with Wentworth and believed Judd was a conniving backstabber. Complicating the tense situation, Judd was competing for the Republican nomination for governor against two of Lincoln's other friends: Leonard Swett, who was particularly close to Lincoln and Davis, and Richard Yates.

Wentworth seemed lukewarm toward Lincoln at times. In 1859, he was using his pages to praise such old Whigs as John Bell of Tennessee and Edward Bates of Missouri—or, as Judd put it in a letter to Lincoln, "whoring after Strange Gods, men who have never had any affinities or connection with the Republican party." Things went from bad to worse when Judd sued Wentworth for libel, seeking $100,000 in damages. With the skill of a technician defusing a timebomb, Lincoln deftly issued a statement endorsing Judd's loyalty and integrity, while persuading him to withdraw his suit against Wentworth. Judge Davis, meanwhile, urged Lincoln to make Wentworth one of the state's at-large delegates at the convention. And, with the convention only three weeks away, Davis urged Lincoln to appoint Wentworth as his own Thurlow Weed, manager of his presidential bid. "Do like Seward does, get someone to *run* you," Davis said, adding, "you could not have a more Effective or efficient friend—He will not desert you until I do." To be sure, the mayor was supporting Seward in his *Chicago Democrat*, Davis admitted, but he was doing that only because "the Germans in Chicago love Gov Seward." Lincoln ignored the advice—wisely, because Wentworth was an ambitious, independent, and even obnoxious man, ill-suited for the job that Davis eventually felt compelled to take on himself in Chicago.

While Lincoln scrupulously remained neutral, Wentworth fiercely fought his enemy's gubernatorial bid, trying to prevent Judd delegates from winning seats at the May state convention in Decatur. That endangered Lincoln's meticulous efforts to send a unified delegation to Chicago. "I am not in a position where it would hurt much for me to not be nominated on the national ticket; but I am where it would hurt some for me to not get the Illinois delegates," Lincoln confessed to Judd on February 10. "Your discomfitted assailants are most bitter against me; and they will, for revenge upon me, lay to the Bates egg in the South, and to the Seward egg in the North, and go far towards squeezing me out in the middle with nothing." Lincoln, who had deftly defended Judd's character against Wentworth's attacks, asked plaintively, "can you not help me a little in this matter, in your end of the vineyard?" That may well have triggered the shift in the *Press and Tribune*'s treatment of

Lincoln that quickly incurred Seward's wrath. After months of remaining neutral, the newspaper began to tout his presidential prospects. "You saw what the *Tribune* said about you. Was it satisfactory?" Judd asked Lincoln.

While Lincoln employed his extraordinary political skills to keep the Illinois Republicans from careening apart, he successfully performed the high-wire balancing act of remaining confidential friends with both Judd and Wentworth. Judd's help with the *Press and Tribune* proved invaluable, while Wentworth offered Lincoln some very sound advice in a February 7 letter. "Look out for *prominence*," Wentworth warned him. "When it is ascertained that no one of the prominent candidates can be nominated, then *ought* to be your time."

On the night of February 8, Lincoln met with Orville H. Browning, a gifted Illinois lawyer and friend. Browning was an old-time Whig who backed Edward Bates on the practical grounds that he could carry enough conservative votes to win in November. Lincoln understood the argument. "He thinks I may be right in supposing Mr. Bates to be the strongest and the best man we can run," Browning wrote in his diary. Lincoln even observed—quite realistically—that Bates might do better in Lincoln's own Sangamon County than he himself would. "He says it is not improbable that by the time the National convention meets in Chicago he may be of the opinion that the very best thing that can be done will be to nominate Mr. Bates." But Lincoln, with his conditional phrases, kept his options open. He thought moderate Supreme Court justice John McLean of Ohio might have been a strong candidate, but at seventy-five he was too old to be taken seriously. "If he were ten years younger he would be our best candidate," Lincoln wrote to senator Lyman Trumbull in March. Even David Davis, while remaining a staunch Lincoln ally, expressed little confidence in his friend's nomination. "It seems to me from this standpoint now, as if it would either be Mr. Bates or Govr. Seward," Davis wrote on February 20 to a lawyer from Beardstown, Henry E. Dummer.

Certainly, Lincoln was not being treated like a major candidate less than two months before the convention. Henry Clay Whitney, who stayed with him at the Tremont House in Chicago toward the end of March while Lincoln handled an important land case in U.S. district court, was struck by how few people came to visit the supposed contender. "Lincoln himself entertained a merely possible hope of success," Whitney noted. He had time one night to go out to dinner with friends. He had time on another night to travel forty miles north to deliver a speech in Waukegan, though he had to stop soon after he began speaking because of repeated alarm bells in the town, initially thought to be the result of Democratic hijinks. "Well, gentlemen, let us all go, as there really seems to be a fire, and help put it out," Lincoln said. He had time on a third night to go see Rumsey & Newcomb's Brass Band and Hooley & Campbell's Minstrels at Metropolitan Hall, a building that had been considered a possible site for the Republican convention. The highlight of the blackface show was a new song by Dan Emmett, a runaway hit in the South called "Dixie's Land," with its catchy chorus: "*Den I wish I was in Dixie, Hoo-ray! Hoo-ray! / In Dixie land, I'll took my stand to lib and die in Dixie.*" "Lincoln was perfectly 'taken' with it: and clapped his great hands, demanding an *encore*, louder than anyone," Whitney recalled. During the evening, Whitney turned to Lincoln and observed that he might be nominated in that building. Lincoln replied, "It is enough honor for me to be talked about, for it."

During Lincoln's stay in Chicago, only "two men of any note whatever" visited him at the Tremont. One was a lawyer. Another was hard-drinking Mayor Wentworth, "who had partaken largely, just before, of the cup which cheers," Whitney recalled. Lincoln also had time, during breaks from court, to pose for Chicago sculptor Leonard W. Volk, who had cast a popular bust of Stephen Douglas (the cousin of Volk's wife) and was hoping to have similar luck with sculptures of his Senate opponent. To negate the need for several more sittings, Lincoln endured having Volk make a life mask of his face, a painful process when the cast was removed, ripping out any facial hair that had not been scrupulously covered. Five weeks later, on May 4, a *Chicago Press and Tribune* reporter dropped by Volk's studio to look at his completed works—a life-sized bust of Lincoln, and a miniature version designed to be placed in a cabinet. "Everyone who has seen them, at once pronounces them to be 'Old Abe' himself," the reporter enthused.

In April, as time was rapidly running out before the convention, a Connecticut admirer asked Lincoln for the names of some people who were pushing him for the presidency. He replied with a list of men who seemed likely to help, starting with David Davis. Lincoln continued to stress, however, that the party must come first. While claiming "no greater exemption from selfishness than is common, I still feel that my whole aspiration should be, and therefore must be, to be placed anywhere, or nowhere, as may appear most likely to advance our cause."

"Nowhere" seemed Lincoln's probable assignment in the weeks before the national convention. Norman Judd, a shrewd political tactician, believed that Seward could be stopped only if the battleground states united against him. "Cannot a quiet combination between the delegates from New Jersey, Indiana and Illinois be brought about—including Pennsylvania. United action by these delegates will probably control the convention," Judd wrote his friend Lyman Trumbull on April 2. Trumbull was maneuvering behind the scenes in Washington to create such a combination, but not always to Lincoln's advantage. That month, Trumbull reached out to Justice McLean with a flattering message, informing him that he was "the only person who can be nominated in Chicago in opposition to Seward." Because Trumbull expected that Lincoln's support would evaporate after the first ballot, he advised McLean that "I think we could also give you Illinois."

Several days later, in an eight-page letter, Trumbull frankly informed Lincoln that the outlook was bleak. The senator had been speaking with experienced politicians in Washington. "When urging your claims," he told Lincoln, "I am almost always met with the remark, 'if you are going to nominate a man of that stamp, why not take Seward.' There seems to be a disposition in the public mind to associate you together, from the fact, I suppose, that you have both given expression to a similar sentiment in regard to the ultimate extinction of slavery."

Politicians paired Lincoln's "house divided" with Seward's "irrepressible conflict," both problematic. And since Lincoln was seen as a lesser man, Seward "would most likely succeed" if the nomination came down to a fight between the two.

But could Seward be nominated? Those opposed to him insisted he could not, since too many voters regarded him as a radical. Politicians from Connecticut, Rhode Island, New Jersey, Indiana, and Pennsylvania believed Seward would drag down the ticket in their states, Trumbull wrote, "& I must confess the letters I am daily receiving from Central & South Ill. lead me to doubt if he could carry our State." But who could stop Seward? "If it can be done at all," the best bet was McLean, Trumbull argued, even if he was old and tired, with "infirmities" that might give some delegates pause. Bates, the darling of the conservatives, could not be nominated, Trumbull believed, because immigrant voters were against him. If Seward for some reason dropped out, Lincoln might be in a strong position, "for if Seward's friends were to see that he could not succeed, I think they would be quite as likely to rally upon you as any one." Still, the "McLean movement is daily gaining strength, & even now looks formidable; but I want to know your views."

In his response, Lincoln informed Trumbull, in his halting manner, that he was indeed running for president, and seriously. "The taste *is* in my mouth a little," Lincoln wrote. With the proviso that this made him a biased observer, he shared his analysis. Among McLean, Bates, and Seward, McLean would help Republicans in Illinois the most, drawing swing voters who would secure the legislative seats crucial to Trumbull's Senate reelection. Bates would be second strongest; Seward, the weakest. Lincoln then broached a touchy issue: He warned Trumbull to send no more letters to people stating that he supported any other candidate than Lincoln. Any impression that he was opposing Lincoln would damage Trumbull's reelection chances. "There are men on constant watch for such things out of which to prejudice my peculiar friends against you," Lincoln wrote. It is not clear whether Lincoln was making a veiled threat to bring down Trumbull if he opposed him for president, or whether he was in truth concerned about Trumbull's reelection. "I have hesitated some to write this paragraph, lest you should suspect I do it for my own benefit, and not for yours; but on reflection I conclude you will not suspect me," Lincoln wrote.

Lincoln knew that Trumbull was right—he could not topple Seward directly. He continued to pursue his cautious strategy. While the Seward and Bates forces openly scrapped for votes, beating each other up in the process, Lincoln would undercut no one, intimidate no one, and quietly position himself as an acceptable second option for as many delegates as possible. "My name is new in the field; and I suppose I am not the *first* choice of a very great many. Our policy, then, is to give no offence to others—leave them in a mood to come to us, if they shall be compelled to give up their first love," Lincoln wrote to his Ohio friend Samuel Galloway. This approach would treat everyone justly, while "leaving us in a mood to support heartily whoever shall be nominated." It was particularly important to refrain from disparaging Seward, who was regarded as the shining light of the party even among many of those who doubted he could be elected. Those instructions were clearly conveyed to Lincoln's supporters. At Chicago, they would not "present Mr. Lincoln as a rival to Mr. Seward, but rather as an admirer and friend," wrote James G. Blaine, a rising Maine politician who was at the convention.

To make his claim as a strong second choice convincing, though, Lincoln would need the support of at least one more state on the first ballot. The best hope was neighboring Indiana, which had no favorite son, was wary of Seward, and was friendly to Lincoln, who had spent most of his childhood there. On May 1, Lincoln wrote to Cyrus M. Allen, a delegate and lawyer from Vincennes, advising him that David Davis or Jesse Dubois, "one or both," would be in Chicago on Saturday, May 12, and would meet up with him. On May 2, Lincoln shared his estimate of his strength with Ohio lawyer and delegate Richard M. Corwine. Illinois, and no other delegation, Lincoln speculated, would be with him unanimously on the first ballot, though his sources ("men who ought to know") had informed him "that the whole of Indiana might not be difficult to get." Ohio was divided, "and yet I have not heard that anyone makes any positive objection to me. It is just so everywhere as far as I can perceive."

His men on the ground in Chicago would have to make a compelling case that he would do well in the swing states in November. His reputation for pragmatism, integrity, moral courage, and shrewd intelligence—as readily displayed in the Douglas debates—would help, as would his remarkable personal story.

But before he could achieve anything, Lincoln first had to secure the unanimous support of his own Illinois delegation. The state convention, meeting in Decatur, would decide that.

As Lincoln had recounted to his friend Dubois, the Lincolns' traumatic trip in March 1830 across the ice-crusted landscape into Illinois brought them to Decatur's primitive town square. There to meet them was John Hanks, a cousin of Lincoln's mother, Nancy. He led the family to his small farm ten miles west of the square, on the banks of the Sangamon River. In the months that followed, Lincoln had to work hard to survive. He joined Hanks in splitting thousands of rails—mostly bur oak and walnut—for the Lincoln and Hanks farms and those of their neighbors.

In the three decades since, Lincoln had returned to Decatur many times, doing less physically exhausting but far more stimulating work while making his rounds with Judge Davis on the Eighth Judicial Circuit. He was back in town on Wednesday, May 9, for the 1860 state convention, a week before the Republican National Convention. It was to be held in a rude, temporary, tarp-covered structure that was named a wigwam, like the massive auditorium the ladies were then decorating in Chicago. Overseeing the Decatur preparations was a boisterous local Republican and Mexican War veteran named Richard J. Oglesby, who had the instincts of a showman. Before the convention, he hit on a brilliant idea. Oglesby contacted John Hanks, and the two rode out to the old Lincoln homestead, keeping their mission to themselves.

As the state convention proceeded, Long John Wentworth could claim a partial victory. The mayor's enemy Norman Judd lost his race for governor when Richard Yates captured the nomination on the fourth ballot. But Lincoln's months of painstakingly maintaining neutrality and soothing wounded feelings paid off in the convention's vote to make him the state party's nominee for president and, more important, to require the delegates to vote as a unit in Chicago initially—all for Lincoln, none for Bates, Seward, or McLean. His superb skill at handling difficult people and assuaging egos had won him the unanimous delegation he needed if he was to compete. A crowd of about nine hundred people who had stuffed themselves into the small wigwam, with thousands standing outdoors, were wild with enthusiasm for the man they had known for years. Lincoln, who was hovering near an opening in the back, could not squeeze through to the stage, so the crowd lifted the gangly lawyer and passed him forward over their heads, an undignified spectacle endorsed with thunderous applause.

Then Oglesby announced that "an old Democrat of Macon county" had come bearing a gift. As the audience wondered, in marched Hanks and a Decatur carpenter named Isaac Jennings, each carrying a fence rail upright. Connecting the rails at the top was a horizontal board bearing a homemade banner:

ABE LINCOLN
THE RAIL CANDIDATE
FOR PRESIDENT IN 1860

The crowd exploded with chants of "Lincoln! Lincoln!" When he reached the stage, Hanks asked, "How are you, Abe?" Lincoln replied, "How are you, John?" Never one to romanticize his past, Lincoln seemed embarrassed by the sudden appearance of the weather-beaten rails he had supposedly split. He conceded they might have been his, but joked, "I could make better ones than these now." All the same, a potent symbol had been born, capturing Lincoln's rugged past and remarkable rise in the world—the kind of rags-to-riches story that Americans ate up. From then on, he was known as "the Railsplitter."

After the show, Lincoln sprawled on the grass under a tree outside the wigwam with Davis, Judd, Swett, and other key supporters. The apportionment of delegates to the national convention was loosely based on the size of a state's congressional delegation doubled. Illinois had been granted twenty-two. Most of the delegates were chosen in local party gatherings around the state, but Lincoln had direct power over the selection of four at-large seats. With the aid of his allies, he carefully selected Davis, Judd, German American Gustave Koerner, and Orville H. Browning. Though Browning supported Bates, Lincoln was sure a man of his talent and intelligence could be useful.

Four days later, on Sunday night, Dubois was at the Tremont House, writing Lincoln his breathless letter about the weekend's hard work. "We are here in great confusion," he wrote, "but things this evening look as favorable as we had any right to expect." Dubois and Davis had discovered that Indiana "is very willing to go for you, although a portion are for Bates." Eight of the Ohio delegates "are urging you on with great vigor." Pennsylvania delegates were dead set on favorite son Cameron, "but that Starch must be taken out of them." Dubois had also spoken several times to George Ashmun, a Yale-educated former Massachusetts congressman and state House speaker who, surprisingly, "talks very kindly" and "is not for Seward." Dubois even found Iowa delegates who were willing to go with Lincoln on the first ballot. Mayor Wentworth, meanwhile, "is for you to day in good faith," though no one could "tell what he may do tomorrow."

Another of Lincoln's friends on the ground, a lawyer and aspiring Kansas politician named Mark W. Delahay, also thought things looked promising. Lincoln had stayed with Delahay and his wife, a distant Lincoln relative, when speaking in Kansas in 1859. In March 1860, Lincoln lamented privately to the thirty-two-year-old that he "can not enter the ring on the money basis"—something Seward unquestionably could—but he promised to give Delahay one hundred dollars to cover expenses if he went to Chicago as a delegate. When Kansas Republicans chose Seward supporters as delegates instead, Lincoln promised to pay for the trip anyway. Delahay may not have been the best man to send to Chicago. He tended to drink excessively, blow through money, and fly off the handle. But Lincoln welcomed the Kansan's help, while reining him in with careful instructions. He urged Delahay to focus on the Iowa and Minnesota delegations, and cautioned him to "keep cool under all circumstances." As for the Seward men from Kansas, "Don't stir them up to anger."

The grateful Kansan wrote Lincoln on Sunday night that he had dutifully brought delegates from Iowa, Minnesota, and Kansas to Judge Davis's rooms at the Tremont House. He also conveyed the big news that Horace Greeley was right there in the hotel, "telling a Crowd now around him" that Bates could carry New York. (Delahay quickly perceived that Greeley's quest was about more than Bates: "I think he is Calculated rather to injure Seward.") Delahay further informed Lincoln that Cameron's men were still trying to get him on the ticket as vice president—an offer the Lincoln men flatly rejected. Such "a move would appear like a '*Slate*' and Seward is too potent here to attempt such a meeting," Delahay wrote, adding, "his friends would probably *Slate* us, if it were done." Delahay was pleased that several Massachusetts and New Jersey delegates informed him that they "are for a success" rather than for riding the Seward bandwagon to defeat. All in all, "matters have been looking up," Delahay wrote, adding, "I have been up late & Early and am perfectly *cool* & hopeful."

In a third letter, written after midnight, the spelling-challenged Illinois state treasurer, William Butler, informed Lincoln that the team desperately needed help: "we want all our deligates on hand it was a grate oversight in their not Coming early." Still, "your chances are brightening," he wrote, saying delegates from Indiana, Iowa, Maine, and New Hampshire had expressed strong support, with those from Pennsylvania and some from Ohio "inclineing for you" on later ballots. He added, "We have procured a Parler at the Tremont House making the best fight we can, we are in good spirits will keep you advised."

A Massachusetts delegate named Edward L. Pierce, a former law partner and Senate aide to Salmon P. Chase, was picking up the same intelligence about unrest in the battleground states. In his own letter from Chicago that Sunday, Pierce broke the bad news to Chase that, in his opinion, he could not win the nomination. But neither could Seward. "The pressure against him from Pennsylvania, Indiana and Illinois is as strong as it can possibly be," Pierce wrote. "One hundred Thurlow Weeds cannot nominate Seward if he does not happen to suit the fancy of the hour." There were no guarantees, of course, that these early shoots of hope would survive the intense heat of the days ahead. Dubois assured Lincoln, "we will do our best and if we fail we must submit."

Over at the Richmond House, the picture looked much different. Submission to failure—particularly at the hands of a mere prairie statesman—was the last thing Weed contemplated on Sunday night, as he awaited the arrival of massive trains the next day stuffed with ecstatic Seward supporters.

Monday, May 14, 1860

Chapter 7: River of Iron

Some of the visitors to Chicago woke up Monday morning in the city jail, courtesy of Mayor John Wentworth. "Long John made his usual whorehouse Sunday night visit," Chicago grocer Edward Hempstead reported to his relative, Republican congressman Elihu B. Washburne of Illinois. This time, the mayor's weekly dragnet of the brothels ensnared some convention delegates, to the outrage of Chicagoans. "Many of our citizens are indignant," Hempstead quipped, "as we do not include the Calaboose in our festivities."

One of the houses of ill repute that Wentworth's police raided, the Democratic *Chicago Times* reported, was "the new and costly establishment of Kate Howard," a well-known Chicago madam. She had made national news in 1857 for her response to discovering a thirteen- or fourteen-year-old Canadian girl named Ida May on her 118 Wells Street doorstep. The girl had come to Chicago to meet up with her father, but he was nowhere to be seen. A stranger who took a keen interest in her told her that the Tremont House was no place for a young lady and sent her to Howard's brothel with a letter, obviously hoping to reap some of the proceeds of a valuable young teen on the sex market. The madam would have none of it. "He has sent you to a house of prostitution," she informed the girl, "and I am the keeper of it; but I have not forgotten that I was once an innocent child like yourself, or that I once had a mother, as perhaps you have, and I will protect you and defend you, outcast as I am." Howard put Ida up at the home of a respectable German family in the neighborhood, paying her room and board until she was safely "restored to the arms of her father."

Now, three years later, the men rounded up in the madam's house included three Republican delegates from Ohio, the *Times* reported, "but we have been unable to ascertain the names of any of them. Their names do not appear on the lockup record—at least not their *real* names—and the officers of the institution are of course profoundly ignorant in regard to the matter." In the eyes of the mayor's political enemies, the whole purpose of his whorehouse visits was to extort money from the victims in return for the police's silence. Chicago's *Western Railroad Gazette* found it all deliciously amusing. "Our Brobdingnagian Mayor" had been looking forward to the arrival of the conventioneers "with feelings of delight akin to that with which a lean spider looks forward to the brisk fly time of summer," the paper maintained. "His favorite method of replenishing the city finances (reduced to a deplorably low ebb) is by arresting and fineing boys of mature growth who go to naughty places, and are nabbed by his policemen (accomplished experts in the business) and after that, rebuked by this embodiment of all the virtues and released on the payment of a swinging fine." When the delegates that weekend were "caught in haunts other than the orthodox 'Wigwam,'" money proved efficacious, as usual. "Several dollars if not more were got in the way to help grease the creaking wheels of our city government."

The arrests did not appear in Monday morning's *Chicago Press and Tribune*, but the paper did report excitedly that two "monster trains"—packed with extraordinary numbers of conventioneers—were expected that night at the Grand Central Depot. The city was planning a noisy and colorful welcome, something that would get Convention Week off with literal fireworks.

Since Friday, people from as far away as Maine had been gathering in the Buffalo area for the Monday morning departure of the great trains. Late Saturday night, the Massachusetts delegation and its attendants arrived in Buffalo, 250 in all, including the thirty-piece Patrick Gilmore's Boston Band, just back from serenading the Democratic convention in Charleston. (Three years later, Gilmore would write the poignant war song "When Johnny Comes Marching Home.") Many of the travelers enjoyed spending the weekend with likeminded Americans, particularly those who loved and admired William H. Seward. They looked forward to the great man's nomination for president, presaging a glorious new era for the nation, with courageous leadership and greater devotion to freedom and human rights. At Bloomer's Hotel, on West Eagle Street in downtown Buffalo, a huge Seward banner "of the richest silk" was on display, featuring a life-sized portrait of the senator by noted artist Thomas Hicks and bearing words from his February 29 speech in the Senate, the one Seward was sure would propel him to the nomination: UNION AND LIBERTY, COME WHAT MAY, IN VICTORY AS IN DEFEAT, IN POWER AS OUT OF POWER, NOW AND FOREVER. The delegates were bringing it to Chicago.

Isaac Platt, the fifty-six-year-old editor and publisher of the *Poughkeepsie Eagle* in New York, had vowed never to attend another national convention. Bitter experience had taught him "that such bodies were not attractive in any sense, that while they contained many honest and pure men, it was impossible to keep them free from an almost incalculable amount of dishonesty and corruption, so that the tendencies of their deliberations were generally more likely to lead to wrong than right results." But Platt considered Seward's nomination so crucial to America's well-being "that I could not feel content to remain at home when anything could be done to render his success more certain." Elected an alternate delegate, and hoping to help his friend and fellow editor Thurlow Weed in Chicago, he set off from home Saturday morning, catching a train on the Hudson River Railway. He arrived that night at Niagara Falls, America's top tourist spot, where he waited out the Sabbath doing little "beyond viewing the mighty cataract, which appeared more interesting and wonderful than ever."

Twelve years earlier, Abraham Lincoln had visited the Falls on his way back to Illinois after sharing a stage in Boston with Seward and meeting his friend Weed in Albany. The magnificent scene moved him to take up his pen. "By what mysterious power is it that millions and millions are drawn from all parts of the world to gaze upon Niagara Falls?" Lincoln mused in a private reflection. He was staggered by the amount of water that fell—hundreds of thousands of tons per minute—and pondered a corresponding marvel, that the sun had to lift just as much weight elsewhere, through constant, silent, undetected evaporation, followed by rainfall, to produce such a torrent. But what struck Lincoln most forcefully was that the falls had been ceaselessly pounding since before the dawn of human civilization. "When Columbus first sought this continent—when Christ suffered on the cross—when Moses led Israel through the Red Sea—nay, even when Adam first came from the hand of his Maker; then, as now, Niagara was roaring here. The eyes of the species of extinct giants whose bones fill the mounds of America have gazed on Niagara, as ours do now. Contemporary with the first race of men, and older than the first man, Niagara is strong and fresh to-day as ten thousand years ago. The Mammoth and Mastodon—now so long dead that fragments of their monstrous bones alone testify that they ever lived, have gazed on Niagara. In that long—long, time never still for a single moment. Never dried, never froze, never slept, never rested."

A frail New York girl named Mary King, her lungs gravely weakened from a bad cold, was among the throng at the Falls on Sunday. A doctor had suggested that her family convey her to the open West, where she would find cleaner and drier air. Luckily, her great-uncle was a big man—former New York governor John Alsop King, a leading member of the state's ecstatically pro-Seward delegation to the Republican National Convention. With a private railroad car at his disposal, he offered to take Mary and her father as far as Chicago. From there, they would go off on their own to St. Paul, Minnesota, to stay for a while with her aunt. After Mary climbed onto the train leaving New York City Saturday night, her imposing great-uncle—"tall, dark, superbly built, holding his head high"—introduced her to their fellow passengers, "men selected for their patriotism and political integrity." As she recalled years later, she met wealthy merchant and longtime Weed ally Simeon Draper, "with his eagle's beak and merry blue eyes"; shipping magnate and former congressman Moses H. Grinnell, "with his white whiskers and generally well-groomed English look"; and banker, lawyer, and community leader Richard M. Blatchford, "a sturdy patriot and a man of deep religious feeling," who had, among other things, served as one of the commissioners overseeing the creation of Central Park. Henry J. Raymond, editor of the *New York Times*, was in the car, as were Nathaniel B. Blunt, "a politician in whom there was no guile," and his daughter. The "best" people—brilliant, educated, sophisticated, accomplished, wealthy, philanthropic—were going to Chicago to nominate Seward. When the train reached Niagara Falls early Sunday morning, Mary childishly imagined that the governor had stopped there "for the pleasure and convenience of the invalid girl," though hundreds of men and women filled the other cars.

After Sunday church services concluded, her great-uncle held court at the sprawling International Hotel, with its spectacular view of the thundering falls, receiving friends all afternoon and evening. An English visitor found the hotel to be "on a scale to match Niagara. The drawing-room is a gorgeous immensity of plate-glass, gilding and upholstery. You walk over a prairie of carpeting." Tourists were struck most, though, by what went on in the massive dining room, which conveyed an impression of "infinite space, infinite eating, infinite clatter." The hotel's highly trained black waiters, whose race conveyed an image of impeccable service in nineteenth-century America, made every meal a show. "A vast regiment of negro waiters parade, march, counter-march, and go through a series of distracting evolutions, to the music of a full band playing in an alcove. There is a march for them to enter; a three-four movement for soup; a *piscicato* passage for fish; the covers come off to a crash of trombones, cymbals, and gongs; and so the whole dinner goes off to appropriate music, with an accompaniment of champagne corks like the firing of skirmishers." On that Sunday, though, neither the Falls nor the hotel show occupied center stage. As one reporter noted, "Niagara scenery possessed but a limited interest in comparison with the all absorbing topic of who would be our candidate in the present National contest." Most thought Seward.

The next morning, at 4:30 a.m., the travelers were awakened for the journey west. "A hurried breakfast at 5 o'clock in the morning did not naturally put one in good condition for a long day's ride," Isaac Platt noted, but "we soon forgot the inconvenience of the hour in the exciting scene." Two great trains, filled with delegates and party activists, left Buffalo at the same time: 6:00 a.m.—one taking a southwestern direction from Buffalo on the Lake Shore and Michigan Southern Railway, which hugged the southern shore of Lake Erie; and the other on the Great Western Railway, which picked up passengers at Niagara Falls, passed over the great Suspension Bridge, and moved on through Ontario before connecting with the Michigan Central Railroad in Detroit.

The superintendents of the lines decided to make it a "trial of speed"—a race to Chicago, pushing the limits of 1860 technology. "It will be run through with care and yet at high speed, the utmost precautions having been taken to guard against accident," the *Chicago Press and Tribune* promised. Railroad accidents were something to be wary of. Five years earlier, the grand opening of the Gasconade Bridge in Missouri had ended in disaster when the span broke under the weight of its inaugural train crossing, killing thirty-one people, including leading citizens of St. Louis. The following year, two trains collided, killing as many as sixty-seven people and injuring more than one hundred. In 1859, an embankment collapsed near South Bend, Indiana, plunging cars and passengers into a torrent of water, killing at least forty-two people and injuring fifty more. Modern travel could be deadly, but Americans were willing to risk it to get where they wanted to go rapidly.

Soon after leaving Buffalo, the gleaming Lake Shore train, which had been freshly painted and "presented a beautiful appearance," pulled into the depot at Dunkirk, New York, to pick up delegates deposited by the Erie Railroad. It was quickly evident that many citizens regarded this trek to Chicago as more than a simple journey, or even a thrilling race. Worried about rising hatreds, violence, and corruption, and infused with patriotic fervor, people thronged the station to pay tribute to the men who were about to choose a leader who would meet the dire threat confronting America. "The gaily decorated engines, the waving flags, patriotically inscribed, the huzzaings of the multitude, and the booming of the welcoming cannon, formed a scene which will long live in the memory of those who were so fortunate as to witness it," wrote one reporter. When the train reached Cleveland, two thousand people greeted it with cheers, while artillery perched on a hill fired a salute. At another station in Ohio, a passenger noted, "there were gathered the largest group of ladies that we had yet met. It seemed as if the whole feminine division of the country round about had gathered to give a God speed to the train."

The race to Chicago was not without mishaps. After pushing an average of forty-seven miles per hour early in the journey—lightning speed for the time—the Lake Shore engine burst a steam pipe, making the train thirteen minutes late chugging into Erie, Pennsylvania. Still, for a time, the velocity was breathtaking. The passengers "gazed with amazement" at the scenery flashing by "as the huge train dashed along, and occasionally, when a 'mile a minute' was accomplished, the 'boldest held his breath,' and the timid ones quaked in their boots."

Behind a new engine, the *Huron*, the journey "went merry as a marriage bell" for a while. "The road was in excellent order, the rails were as firm as the rock of Gibraltar, while the entire absence of dust was a noticeable feature to those who had provided themselves with linen coats and calico caps with which to keep clean their more sombre suits." The engineer invited Joseph Howard of the *New York Times* to ride with him up front. "The whistle nearly blew my ears off; the rushing air wore out my eyes; the jogging of the engine as it leaped from rail to rail all but broke the end of my backbone off; my hat, which was blown away in less than a minute after we started, was caught by the fireman in a miraculous manner; and every nerve in my body, jumped, squirmed and wired, as relentlessly the iron steed kept up to 'time,'" Howard reported.

The train covered twenty-nine miles in thirty minutes. Few humans in history had traveled faster. "While we were going at this terrific speed—while the mileposts succeeded each other so swiftly that they seemed like fence-stakes, and while the various growths of wheat, oats, potatoes and corn, looked as if they were planted in a heap, the engine would jump, leap, skip and roll, like a frightened horse, and in a 'dreadful unsartin' manner." After he caught his breath, Howard studied the "quiet, uncommunicative" engineer. "He was as calm as a May morning. He pulled a rod, and an unearthly scream was heard. He pushed another one, and the speed, already like the arrow's dart, became that of the lightning's flash. All was under his control, and I could but admire the coolness, the firmness of purpose and quickness of execution which he unconsciously exhibited." It was clear that a new age of technological prowess was upon America.

News swept through the passenger cars that the train, pushed to its limits, would arrive in Chicago at 8:15 p.m., more than an hour before anyone thought possible. "But man proposes and God disposes." Between Toledo and Chicago, both pumps aboard one engine broke. On another, a steampipe erupted. "If I had not broken engines on my best running ground, I should have made the time from Toledo to Chicago in six hours," Michigan Southern superintendent John D. Campbell lamented. Still, new engines were brought in, and the race resumed.

In the end, the Lake Shore Line narrowly beat the competition. The engine, bearing a placard that read THE IRREPRESSIBLE CONFLICT GOES ON, pulled into the depot at 9:15 p.m. Monday. The journey covered 538 miles, including stops, in fifteen hours and fifteen minutes—miraculously fast in comparison with the weeks-long journey endured by pioneers heading west just a generation earlier.

The competing Great Western Railway train—for which a staggering 1,500 tickets had been sold by Friday—had some challenges, too. It confronted steeper grades and was the weightier of the trains, its passenger and baggage cars "all heavily loaded." It started its journey over one of the marvels of the modern age, the Niagara Falls Suspension Bridge, completed in 1855 under the leadership of German-born John A. Roebling, who later designed and built the Brooklyn Bridge. Editor Platt rated it a "wonder of the world, almost equal to the Falls." Given the engineering mishaps of the time, the 825-foot-long span was not for the faint of heart. "Those who have never crossed it in the cars cannot begin to realize the fearfulness and grandeur of the sight of a train filled with passengers stretching nearly across the river, at the height of two hundred and fifty feet above the angry waters, the whole suspended on four cables, in which a break under the great weight would send all to instant destruction," Platt wrote. "The most fearful view is when the car you are in reaches the middle of the river, as the cables there descend below the track, and on looking out you find yourself as it were suspended in mid air, without visible support." Though the bridge seemed stable enough, "there is a sensation of relief on reaching the river's bank and passing off upon the solid earth."

The mood on board was celebratory. At the bridge, the great silken banner that had been on display in Buffalo was unfurled, and New York men "decorated everyone who would wear them with badges lettered 'Seward,'" wrote Simon P. Hanscom of the *New York Daily Herald.* The reporter was amused that the wealthy New York elites had to share the vicissitudes of 1860s train travel with the common Seward supporters, and "all ate the same luxuriant sandwich, swallowed the same cinders, enjoyed the same festive doughnut, nibbled the same African cracker, gnawed the juicy railroad station beef, hung in epicurean delight over the delicious pie, and exerted their imaginative faculties upon the rural coffee and the provincial whiskey." Hanscom called it "a touching and a dusty scene. All your famous equalizers—dirt and politics, hunger and thirst—did the work of fraternization as the extremes touched." During the engine's required stops along the way to take on water,

Gilmore's Boston Band climbed down and played an assortment of tunes, including "God Save the Queen" in tribute to the Canadians and their head of state, Victoria.

Despite the stops, the train arrived fifteen minutes early in Windsor, Ontario, where the passengers were to transfer to a ferry that would take them across the Detroit River. Thousands of people had made their way that morning to the Windsor docks to await the appearance of the "Black Republicans," hoping "to see what a Massachusetts abolitionist and a New York city republican look like," scoffed the *Detroit Free Press*, a ferociously Democratic newspaper. The reporter covering the scene frowned not only on the "blk. rep." contingent but also on such shocking manifestations of modernity as loose pants on a female. "A woman in a Bloomer dress absorbed the attention of the crowd," he reported, "until the cars arrived in a cloud of dust." As the Light Guard Band struck up "Hail Columbia," officials formally greeted the passengers. "The delegates were too tired and dirty and hungry to stand any such nonsense, and hurried on board of the boat without ceremony."

Eager to mock the Republicans, the writer remarked that the rough reality of Seward's supporters jarred with the party's pretentions of moral superiority. "We had naturally expected, judging from the fiercely virtuous airs which the party arrogates to itself, to have met a solemn procession of long-haired, sanctimonious individuals, with white chokers on their necks and hymn-books on their arms." Instead, the reporter beheld the "unmistakable Bowery swing of that redoubtable hero," Tom Hyer, America's most celebrated professional boxer, who was lending his considerable prestige to his fellow New Yorker Seward. "Close at his heels followed the Seward element, looking very dusty and cross, and seemingly anxious to get at the long-necked bottles which peeped from their pockets here and there." Two other famed pugilists, Scottish-born Patrick Brannigan—known as "Scotty of Brooklyn"—and Boston's Ed Price, also made their appearance. In those days, boxers fought with bare knuckles, and members of polite society—and, in many cases, local police—regarded them as no better than thugs. "As they sailed under the Seward banner, it was conjectured that they were the muscle portion of the irrepressible conflict," ready to intimidate the forces of "Bates and the rest of the opposition at the critical moment." The *Buffalo Daily Courier* punned that the boxing champion was there to advance Seward's "Hyer law doctrine."

Delegates and friends crowded onto a Michigan Central train for the second leg of the journey to Chicago. The *Cleveland Daily Leader* promised a good ride. "The Michigan Central, in all its appointments, is one of the best railways on the continent. The track is solid and smooth, the grades very trifling, and the curves next to nothing." With three sets of wheels on the undercarriage instead of the usual two, great speed was possible "with much less than the usual jar." The line's handsome passenger cars were equipped with "canvass dusters down to the track," intended to protect travelers "from that almost intolerable nuisance which fills, eyes, ears, and lungs on most railroads" on days when there were no rainclouds to "act as track sprinklers" and suppress the dust. The route passed through the best cultivated and most settled portions of Michigan. One passenger wrote of the beauty of the countryside that Monday in May, observing "long lines of furrows stretching off on either side of the track, the intervening spaces filled with the just springing wheat and grass of bright green."

Newspapers in upstate New York sent the delegates off with a poem titled "The Chicago Convention":

They come, they come, a gallant host,
The chosen guard of freedom's van;
From city, plain and sea girt coast,
To choose and crown the coming man.

A nation beats her morning drum,
And bids her sons to her behest,
From North, from South, from East they come
To clasp the hand of golden West.

The Empire State, proud, leads the van,
And throws her Seward's banner forth,
The champion of the rights of man,
The lion of awakened North—

. . . From all the free States of our land,
Amid the shouts of Union rise
Too long has waved the dastard hand,
Of traitors, 'neath more southern skies.

In addition to name-checking Seward, the unsigned poem touted Massachusetts governor Nathaniel Banks, Missouri's Frank Blair, Senator John Hale of New Hampshire, Pennsylvania's Simon Cameron, and Kentucky's Cassius Clay—but not the obscure Abraham Lincoln. It noted that the tyrannical czar of Russia had already moved to end serfdom, while the United States, the land of the free, continued to expand slavery. But the Chicago convention would change that, the poet predicted. The Republicans would yet wave the "banner of a nation FREE" over "Slavery's hateful shrine."

Then onward to the golden West,
Ye chosen guard of freedom's van;
We'll blaze upon our banner's crest,
A triumph for the coming man.

Maine's delegates wrote their own lyrics about the historic railroad trip to the tune of "The Star-Spangled Banner," concluding:

So harness the steam horse, and fill up the car,
We sweep to Chicago, we annihilate space,
By this River of Iron; the distance so far,
Is spanned in two days of "this wonderful race,"
The sea and the West, are united as one,
So fill up the fire-box, and loosen the brakes,
We move toward the West, with the speed of the Sun,
From the Gem of the Sea to the Queen of the Lakes.

The fate of humanity, in no small measure, seemed to be riding on those rails. "The eyes of the nation are turned toward this convention; the hopes of America rest in the keeping of the true hearted men who compose the Chicago Convention. No other assemblage possessed as much power, or wielded as great an influence for good, in this country, since that one whose deliberations culminated on the 4th of July, 1776," wrote one Washington correspondent on May 11. While the Founders had created America's extraordinary republic, he argued, it remained for the current generation to perfect their work. "Shall we, upon whose shoulders has fallen the mantle of liberty, hand down to succeeding generations the holy doctrines for which Washington and his compeers passed through the Revolution? or shall we, scullion-like, desert the post of duty at the first approach of the advancing foes to Virtue, Liberty and Independence? The duty of the Chicago Convention is plain; nominate a candidate who will carry out the wishes of the founders of the Government."

John A. Andrew, a Massachusetts delegate running for governor, found that "along the whole line of that immense travel, wherever we stopped to reinvigorate the iron horse, there we were met by a crowd of the citizens of Michigan or Indiana, surrounding the trains, with waving hats, with streaming banners, with vociferous voices and animated countenances, calling aloud, in cheering tones, their words of welcome" to the delegates. Some men even "threw themselves across our track, determined that the train should not proceed until they had seen one, and another, and another of the men who had come to represent the patriotism and the wisdom" of Republicans from the East. Mary King recalled that, at every stop, the train was "met always by crowds of excited men who insisted on a speech" from her great-uncle, "and ever his voice rang out clear and firm for the Union and for our candidate, the only man who, under God, could save the nation—New York's noble son, the wise, true statesman, William H. Seward. Loud applause followed his stirring words." At station after station, the *Chicago Press and Tribune* reported, crowds waved, fired cannon, and played music, "and from farm houses the ladies waved their handkerchiefs, and farmers in the fields swung their hats as the train passed by."

Along the journey, speed took its toll. "Our train was obliged to stop twice to cool heated axles, and this delayed our arrival in time," a passenger noted. At one point, the axles grew so hot that the bottom of a car caught fire and had to be disengaged from the train and left behind. In the desire to win the race to Chicago, the railroad pulled off an extraordinary stunt—no doubt highly dangerous in an age before air brakes. At Michigan City, "it was necessary to change engines, and in order not to lose time" the train was run along the track at fifteen miles per hour, while its engine was decoupled and run onto a siding. Meanwhile, a "gaily trimmed" engine was moving on the track ahead, and the train caught up and was coupled to it. Thus, the engines were switched *without stopping the train*—AN UNEXAMPLED RAILROAD FEAT, as one headline put it. The daring and ingenuity of modern America seemed to know no bounds. Such a world of progress and invention would surely have little place for slavery, a relic of humanity's barbaric past. On board, the passengers convened a hasty meeting, chaired by Governor King, and passed a resolution expressing thanks to the railroad for the speed and safety of the trip and the comfort extended the passengers. New York delegate Thomas Murphy, an Irish American merchant, took up a collection to award seventy-five dollars to the daring engineer—probably more than a month's pay.

Trains roared in from the West, too. In Atchison, Kansas, on Friday evening, a correspondent for the *Weekly Atchison Champion* set off with that state's delegates. Their train roared through Missouri and Illinois before reaching Chicago around noon Sunday. Though an accident up the line in Illinois delayed their arrival by several hours, the reporter found the trip pleasant enough, particularly on the new route from Atchison to St. Joseph, Missouri, with "less of that annoying and everlasting jolting and jostling of passengers on it than on any road over which we have passed." The immense flat stretches of green and fertile farmland they passed through were lovely, he wrote, but he assured readers back in Kansas that there was no place like home. "I saw but little like our beautiful rolling prairies . . . swelling and falling as gracefully as the waves of Lake Erie; and, indeed, whether it be considered infatuation or not, I do not believe there is a country on the face of the Earth that will compare with Kansas."

Once in Chicago, he found plenty of support for his delegation's choice, William Seward. Writing Monday from the Briggs House, he predicted Seward would win the nomination on the first or second ballot. The New Yorker could have been nominated four years earlier in Philadelphia, "but his election was not then thought sure, and so he withdrew. Now, however it is different. . . . You can set it down as certain that Gov. Seward is a candidate for the nomination this time, and will not be withdrawn, and as equally certain that if nominated he will be elected."

Leonard Swett rolled into Chicago from Bloomington that Monday without fireworks or fanfare. The tall, willowy lawyer made his way through the crowds to the Tremont House, where he located the Illinois headquarters. There, he discovered his fellow Bloomingtonian, Judge David Davis, fervently issuing instructions to a small but dedicated cadre of men who had spent years with Lincoln and had come to love him. On Swett's arrival, Davis made a startling statement: "If you will put yourself at my disposal day and night, I believe Lincoln can be nominated." Until that moment, Swett had not regarded his friend's bid as serious. But Davis had carefully assessed the political situation on the ground, and he believed he could overcome the obstacles to Lincoln's nomination, if everyone worked hard enough. "I assented to his proposition, and immediately the service was begun." For the next four days, Swett would not sleep more than two hours at a stretch.

If a miracle was in the making, it would not be Swett's first. It was a wonder that he was even alive on that Monday in Chicago. Born near Turner, Maine, in 1825, Swett had been raised and educated in that state, attending Colby College and then reading law in Portland. His life changed forever after he enlisted in the Mexican-American War, was shipped off to Mexico, and came down with a terrible fever, perhaps a symptom of mosquito-borne malaria. In his weakened, sweating, and shivering state, he overheard a doctor say he would be dead in forty-eight hours. With other desperately sick soldiers, Swett was sent back to New Orleans on a hospital ship. During the journey, one-third of the wretched passengers died, their corpses tossed overboard, but Swett somehow clung to life. On July 8, 1848, he was mustered out at the Jefferson Barracks in St. Louis.

Swett resolved to get back to Maine, on foot if by no other way. But with his six-foot-two-inch body shriveled to a skeletal 123 pounds, Swett made it only halfway across Illinois before he lost the strength to go on. A schoolmaster named George Washington Minier recalled sitting outside the little hotel in downtown Bloomington one day, when he "saw a tall, gaunt, emaciated young man come up the street just able to walk." Minier reached out to him. "He told me he was a discharged soldier, he lived in a distant state, that his people did not know his whereabouts and that he had come to Bloomington to die, and when he breathed his last he wished me to write his parents of his fate. I encouraged him and told him that God still had work for him to do." Minier provided food and shelter, getting the veteran back on his feet. Within two months, Swett had risen like a modern-day Lazarus. He was helping Minier at his school and reading law again. His weight climbed to 155 pounds. By the middle of January 1849, Swett was practicing law, and he decided later that year to seek cases on the Eighth Judicial Circuit.

During the fall session, the twenty-three-year-old lawyer set out for Danville, Illinois. Arriving after dark, he sought out the circuit's judge at the wooden, two-story McCormick House. Informed he could find David Davis and ex-congressman Abraham Lincoln in a room upstairs, Swett climbed up "the unbanistered stairway," nervous about interrupting so great a man as a judge. "In response to my timid knock two voices responded almost simultaneously, 'Come in.' Imagine my surprise when the door opened to find two men undressed or rather dressed for bed, engaged in a lively battle with pillows, tossing them at each other's heads." One, a heavyset man, "leaned against the foot of the bed and puffed like a lizard." The other combatant "was a man of tremendous stature" who "was encased in a long, indescribable garment, yellow as saffron, which reached to his heels, and from beneath which protruded two of the largest feet I had, up to that time, been in the habit of seeing." This "apparition, with the modest announcement, 'My name is Lincoln,' strode across the room to shake my trembling hand." Swett was stunned. He "was certainly the ungodliest figure I have ever seen."

Swett became a fixture on the Eighth Judicial Circuit, putting in more time in its courts than anyone but Davis and Lincoln. Henry Clay Whitney called the three "the great triumvirate" of the circuit. Ten years younger than Davis and sixteen years younger than Lincoln, Swett quickly established himself as a brilliant trial lawyer. He estimated that, by May 1860, he had worked ten thousand cases with or against Lincoln. "I know him as intimately as I have ever known any man in my life," Swett wrote to his lifelong friend and former school roommate Josiah H. Drummond, a state senator and former House speaker back in Maine. In small tavern rooms, the heavy Davis often occupied one bed, and the tall and slender Swett and Lincoln tended to share the other.

Personable and well respected, Swett ran for governor of Illinois in 1860, at thirty-four, only to lose the nomination at Decatur a week before the Chicago convention. Like Davis, he felt the sting of Lincoln's cold refusal to support him at a crucial hour. Lincoln carefully avoided making an endorsement in the gubernatorial race, saying he was "very anxious to take no part between the many friends, all good and true," who were seeking the position. He could not afford to split the state party's support for his presidential bid. But like Davis, Swett admired Lincoln so much that he rose above his wounded feelings and worked his heart out for him. He proved to be a most valuable ally in Chicago.

During his first forty-eight hours in Chicago—before many of the delegates arrived—Davis had discovered an unexpectedly severe case of the jitters among the professional politicians from the swing states. In the wake of John Brown's frightening attempt to ignite a slave uprising, voters seemed increasingly concerned about anti-slavery rhetoric. Swing-state politicians now thought they would suffer in November if their presidential nominee could be stereotyped as a radical—as Seward surely would be. With enough time and effort, Davis believed he could persuade nervous delegates that Lincoln, despite his defeats and his lack of experience, was the best alternative.

Lincoln could not match the New Yorker's powerful organization and well-financed army of supporters. He relied on the efforts of a cadre of loyal colleagues, the fruit of his gift for making friends: his law partner William Herndon, his former law partner Stephen T. Logan, and his sometime partner Ward Hill Lamon; other lawyers from the Eighth Judicial Circuit, such as Swett, Henry Clay Whitney, John M. Palmer, and Burton C. Cook; Illinois newspapermen Jesse Fell, Joseph Medill, and Charles Ray; a handful of state officials, including auditor Jesse Dubois, treasurer William Butler, secretary of state Ozias M. Hatch, and former lieutenant governor Gustave Koerner; and allies Lincoln had collected here and there, including Taylor Hawkins, the mayor of Keokuk, Iowa, and the rather hapless Mark Delahay of Kansas. Though few in number, they were "tireless, sleepless, unwavering and ever vigilant friends," Swett noted—and most were savvy and pragmatic operators, their talents sharpened in testy local elections and prairie courtrooms.

Sitting behind a large desk at his suite in the Tremont, gathering constantly updated intelligence, Davis directed the Lincoln forces where they were most needed. The judge quickly organized "committees of visitation," making good use of the varied backgrounds of his Westerners, most of whom had come from somewhere else. He assigned Illinois lawyer and politician Samuel C. Parks, who was born in Middlebury, Vermont, to lead a group to meet with the Vermont men; "and he had me, from the State of Maine, organize a delegation and visit my old friends from the Pine Tree State, and every man was to come back and report to him," Swett wrote. "And so he labored with all, issued his orders to all, and knew the situation of every delegation." He also inspired his men to work as a team for Lincoln. The state party had instructed the delegation to vote as a unit for Lincoln, but the unity was something of an illusion. Of the twenty-two delegates, "there were eight who would have gladly gone to Seward," Swett noted. "They intended in good faith to go for Lincoln, but talked despondingly and really wanted and expected finally to vote" for Seward. The judge had to keep those Seward men battling for Lincoln for as long as Illinois was in the hunt.

Davis instructed his team to drive home one practical point: if the delegates had to move on from their favorite, Lincoln would be the best alternative as the most "available"—that is, electable—candidate. He was thus the one most likely to help candidates further down the ticket, as well as bring in the bumper crop of federal patronage positions that would follow a Republican victory in November. Though he was an outspoken opponent of slavery, Lincoln had offended fewer voters and made fewer political enemies than other vocal critics of the institution, mainly because he was more cautious and less well known. He had upset neither pro-immigrant nor anti-immigrant groups. Struggling Americans who worked hard to get ahead would connect with Lincoln's extraordinary personal story as a man who had risen from nothing. In fact, people had already begun to talk about that. In February, newspapers widely circulated a brief account of an old man in Macon County, Illinois, who recalled that Lincoln in his youth "would split rails by daylight, and then study surveying by candle light. He was as honest as the sun." The integrity of "Honest Old Abe" would appeal to voters who believed Washington elites had become lawless and corrupt. He was untethered to anything like the New York political machine.

These were powerful arguments to the party's professional politicians, who were practical men. What they cared about most was winning elections, obtaining power, and dispensing jobs. Which candidate might make the best president in a national crisis was a consideration, but decidedly a secondary one. The *Chicago Press and Tribune* appealed to their naked self-interest in an editorial Monday touting Lincoln to the arriving delegates: "Constables are worth more than Presidents in the long run, as a means of holding political power. The Legislature is of vastly more consequence to particular States than their delegations in Congress. We look to Mr. Lincoln to tow constables and General Assembly [members] into power. . . . The gods help those who help themselves."

The leaders of the Indiana delegation were among the loudest in insisting the party must back a man who stood a better chance than Seward. But they wanted something in return for their support. "Nearly the entire delegation from Indiana came there with the specific design of securing control of the fat Interior Department in case of Republican success," Henry Clay Whitney wrote. "They had agreed on a secretary of that department—Caleb Smith; a Commissioner of Indian Affairs, William P. Dole, formerly of Indiana; and on candidates for some of the minor offices. They then opened their political huckster shop and spread out their votes for inspection." Davis needed Indiana if Lincoln was to emerge from the first ballot as more than a favorite-son candidate. Lincoln had strong connections with Indiana Republicans, and he had served in Congress with Smith. Davis had something to work with if he decided to trade public offices for support—and, more pressingly, if he could persuade the delegation that the Illinois lawyer was a serious alternative to Seward. Indiana initially seemed to be split between Edward Bates and John McLean, the leading moderates. But the Lincoln team spent Saturday, Sunday, and Monday lobbying its delegates intensely, Swett recounted.

Almost as encouraging, the crucial state of Pennsylvania, though wed to Simon Cameron on the first ballot, appeared to be up for grabs. That was a surprise to Thurlow Weed, who had cultivated the Pennsylvanians for years in anticipation of Seward's nomination. Weed teamed up with Cameron in 1856, trying to boost Republican candidates, though one ally judged the Pennsylvania state organization "a set of Pollitical Hoars." For a time, it seemed that grateful Pennsylvanians would be solidly in Seward's camp. In March 1859, Seward traveled to Harrisburg to see Cameron. "He took me to his house, told me all was right. He was for me, and Pennsylvania would be," Seward wrote to

Weed. In April 1860, Cameron asked Weed to stop by for a chat, either in Washington or Philadelphia, perhaps hoping to secure his promise of a position in a Seward administration. But the meeting never came off. "You know why we left Pennsylvania alone," Weed wrote to Seward cryptically after the convention. Perhaps he did not want Seward drawn into Pennsylvania's bitter intraparty fight between the Cameron forces and the supporters of Andrew G. Curtin, who was running for governor and considered Cameron a disgrace. Weed had discovered during his first hours in Chicago that, after all his efforts, Pennsylvania was not a sure thing for Seward after all.

The Lincoln men's number-one mission was to prevent the nomination of Seward on the first ballot. Their secondary goal was to obtain one hundred votes for Lincoln on that ballot, enough to signify that Lincoln was Seward's key competitor. Under their plan, Lincoln would then inch up in subsequent ballots, creating the appearance that the delegates were spontaneously swinging behind him. Pennsylvania might well deliver the coup de grâce, demonstrating to the delegates that Lincoln could outmuscle his opponents for the biggest swing state. "Everybody who knows politicians knows that what they worship is the god of success," Swett observed.

As of Monday, the prospect of implementing this plan seemed surprisingly good. Four members of the team sent Lincoln letters that day, all revealing they were nearly giddy with excitement. "Things are working; keep a good nerve—be not surprised at any result—but I tell you that your chances are not the worst," Nathan M. Knapp, a lawyer, longtime friend, and delegate from Winchester, Illinois, wrote exuberantly. After talking things over with swing-state delegates, Knapp believed that Lincoln, rather than Bates or McLean, might emerge as the compromise candidate. The Lincoln men could sell the Illinoisan as less conservative than Bates—and thus more appealing to the party's base. And he was far younger, more alert, and more energetic than the elderly McLean. "We are laboring to make you the second choice of all the Delegations we can where we cannot make you first choice. We are dealing tenderly with delegates, taking them in detail, and making no fuss." Knapp urged Lincoln to stay calm. "Be not too Expectant but rely upon our discretion. Again I say brace your nerves for any result."

In a letter headed "*Profoundly Private*," Charles H. Ray, the editor-in-chief of the *Chicago Press and Tribune*, informed Lincoln that his friends were "at work for you hard, and with great success." The team already believed that Lincoln's support would extend beyond Illinois on the first ballot, "and after that it will be strongly developed." But deals would have to be made by "a few trusty friends" of Lincoln. "A pledge or two may be necessary when the pinch comes," Ray wrote. Like Knapp, the editor cautioned Lincoln to resist overconfidence, something that Ray himself seemed to be having a hard time doing. "Don't be too sanguine. Matters now look well and as things stand to-day I had rather have your chances than those of any other man. But don't get excited."

Illinois treasurer William Butler informed Lincoln that New York and Pennsylvania were helpfully at each other's throats. "Sir I wrote you yesterday evening, the Pennsylvania & Newyork delegates are quarling. the Pennsylvania delegation will not gow for Mr Seward under no Circumstances. they tell us to Stand fast Never gow to Mr Seward they are much excited." The New York forces said the reverse. "The Newyork men tell us to stand firm dont gow to Mr. Camron." Both states, desperate to win the backing of Illinois, proposed "to run you for Vice President," but "we have persistently refused to Suffer your name used for Vice President on any Ticket."

Butler, sixty-two, was unusually close to Lincoln. He first saw Lincoln decades earlier, paddling down the Sangamon River in a canoe. "He was as ruff a specimen of humanity as could be found. His legs were bare for six inches between the bottom of pants and top of socks." But Butler quickly warmed to the unusually bright and affable young man. He encouraged Lincoln to take up the law. When Butler moved to Springfield, he invited the young man to board with his family, which Lincoln eventually did in 1841 and 1842, before marrying Mary. "You know he was always careless about his clothes," Butler recalled.

"In all the time he stayed at my house, he never bought a hat or a pair of socks, or a coat. Whenever he needed them, my wife went out and bought them for him, and put them in a drawer where he could find them." Butler paid off $400 of Lincoln's debts and stubbornly refused to accept repayment, even years later. "He came to me with the money a few years ago. I told him not to mention the subject again if he did not wish to offend me. Has been grateful," Butler said in 1860. The two old friends had broken apart for nearly a decade over local political patronage, and Butler had bitterly denounced Lincoln. But Lincoln, as usual, worked hard to restore the bond, refusing to take offense or hold grudges, and Butler had become one of his tireless workers in Chicago.

Mark Delahay, Lincoln's boisterous friend from Kansas, told the candidate, "The Stock is gradually rising." He confirmed that the leading campaigns were urging Illinois to accept the vice presidency, "but we are not biting at the Bate." The team was carefully following Lincoln's instructions: "We are not pressing too hard your Claims, we are making friends every where." Like Butler, he reported that New York and Pennsylvania were bitterly at odds, with New York whispering that a former Democrat like Simon Cameron could never win the Republican nomination; "this all to my mind looks as well as we could wish." Some of the Pennsylvania delegates had revealed to Delahay that they were "quite as well satisfied with [Lincoln] as with Cameron." But the Lincoln men needed reinforcements, Delahay stressed. He told Lincoln to "send up all your . . . friends who can prudently aid in the outside Pressure." Delahay even urged Lincoln to come to Chicago himself, to run the operation and make his case in the flesh. That seemed to be the last thing Judge Davis and Jesse Dubois wanted. It was considered impertinent and rude for a serious candidate to be on hand. More important, the two may have feared that Lincoln would interfere with their negotiations—perhaps by objecting to their promises of public offices in return for delegate votes. Whatever the reason, the prospect of Lincoln's presence so horrified them that they fired off a brusque telegram that Monday:

To A Lincoln
Dont come unless we send for you
Dubois & Davis

The thousands of visitors already in town had much more than politics to entertain them that evening. Brothels were busy, saloons were full, and theaters were open for business. The owners of McVicker's Theatre, a short walk from the downtown hotels, hoped to reap a financial windfall from the convention. "Strangers are respectfully informed that the FAVORITE PLAYS of the Season will be presented during the present week," they announced in that morning's *Press and Tribune*. That night at eight o'clock, McVicker's presented "the greatest comedy of the day," the wildly popular *Our American Cousin*. It was the play Abraham Lincoln would be enjoying five years later when actor John Wilkes Booth snuck up behind him in his box, aimed a gun at his head, and pulled the trigger.

Massachusetts congressman Charles Francis Adams—the son of President John Quincy Adams, grandson of President John Adams, and father of the brilliant young Henry Adams—recorded in his diary Sunday that his dear friend William Seward had left the city of Washington and returned to his home in Auburn, New York, "expecting that his nomination will be followed by a resignation of his place in the Senate." Seward was preparing for what seemed inevitable. "In all probability I shall never return to the Senate again," he told his colleagues earlier that month. As *New-York Tribune* correspondent J. S. Pike noted, he "a thousand times declared his aims and his expectations of being the Republican candidate, and had settled into the fixed habit of regarding his nomination as an absolute certainty."

Seward always felt happy and secure in Auburn, surrounded by thousands of citizens who revered him. "His popularity is universal. He is beloved by all classes of people, irrespective of partisan predilections. No work of public utility is undertaken unless he has a lending and a helping hand in it," a correspondent for the *New York Daily Herald* observed that year. "On all sides, among all classes of politicians, I find that sentiments of respect and esteem prevail in favor of Gov. Seward, and no one refers to him without expressing unhesitatingly their entire confidence in his uprightness and unselfish public spirit." He had expanded his father-in-law's 1816 brick house, adding a dining room, kitchen, and private office to its ten rooms. He kept a well-stocked library. All was "fitted up with exquisite taste." Painted a cream color, with sculpted lions atop its main gate, the mansion looked from the main road like "an Oriental villa in subdued form." The four-acre grounds abounded with vines teeming with Isabella grapes for wine and trees that would be laden with plump fruit in the fall. Seward made a point each year of distributing any unused apples among the poor. Pretty paths wound through full-grown shade and ornamental trees—elm, rock maple, locust, horse chestnut, ailanthus, and hazelnut—and led to a cozy summer house amid clambering vines and shrubs. On Monday evening, Unitarian minister John Austin visited Seward and strolled the placid grounds with him. "He appears entirely cool and calm, and not in the slightest degree excited," Austin noted in his journal.

That same evening, after leaving Kalamazoo, the Michigan Central train carrying hundreds of Seward supporters "emerged on to the shore of Lake Michigan, in time to see the after tints of a glorious sunset." It approached Chicago on a fine, clear night, a little after 9:30 p.m. For twelve solid minutes the lengthy train, hauled by an engine named the *Rambler*, slowly rumbled down the long pier just offshore. In honor of the arriving delegates, Chicagoans had lit their homes along the entire length of Michigan Avenue, "and a most magically beautiful effect was the result, the lights flashing back from and multiplied countlessly in the waters of the Lake shore basin," the *Chicago Press and Tribune* reported. As the headlight of the *Rambler* passed Twelfth Street, a rocket from Park Row signaled to thousands waiting along the lakeshore and in the Grand Depot that the train was coming. Bonfires roared along the lake, cannon fired by the Chicago Light Artillery shook the air, and fireworks flew into the sky, shot up from the foot of Jackson Street.

The paramilitary Wide Awakes, their ranks swelled by new volunteers, took their places near the depot with flaming torches. Six short, sharp screams of the steam whistle announced the train's arrival.

The station had been cleared of other cars to make room for throngs of cheering people, many of them ladies. "No one who saw the scene . . . will ever forget it," the *Press and Tribune* reported. "The artillery pealing, the flight of the rockets, the gleaming windows from the entire residence front of our city, the vast depot edifice filled with the eager crowd, the excursion train safe from its flying trip across the peninsular State, about to land its passengers, many of them for the first time, on the Western shore of Lake Michigan, all constituted a *tout ensemble* wonderful and rare." The crowd's cheers, Platt noted, "fairly shook the earth." The *Herald*'s Hanscom captured the chaos: "The cannons began to boom, the rockets to soar, the small boys to hurrah, the police to get into everybody's way, and the dense crowd which filled the great railway station and all the streets adjacent, to push and elbow and generally annoy each other . . . all to look at a couple of hundred of hungry, fatigued, and ill-humored politicians, covered with dust."

However friendly, the crowd was a mixed blessing. "To get from the cars into the open streets required much patience and perseverance," Platt reported. Little Mary King, who arrived exhausted, had never seen anything like the frenzied grown-ups mobbing the New Yorkers. "Terrified, I stared at the crowd pushing and pressing on us; but my uncle called upon our strong man," a "prize-fighter and gentleman"—probably Tom Hyer—to guide her to the Richmond House. "Clinging to his strong arm, the tired, delicate girl was speedily and safely landed at the hotel, and soon forgot the dangers she had passed in a sound, dreamless sleep."

There was little sleep in store for Thurlow Weed, who greeted New York's leading delegates and escorted them to the hotel. He had strategy to discuss. In the two days Weed had been in Chicago, he had discovered the full extent of Horace Greeley's betrayal and heard rising talk that Seward was in trouble. But his confidence was not shaken. Chicago mayor John Wentworth assured the New Yorkers

Monday that Illinois Republicans, despite their affection for Lincoln, would dutifully swing to Seward on later ballots. A Vermonter, writing from the Tremont House to the *Burlington Times* that day, also rated Seward's chances highly. "Long John Wentworth is ubiquitous among the delegates, and stoutly upholds the cause of William the Irrepressible," he reported. "Mr. Seward . . . looms up decidedly above the other candidates," enjoying great strength with "masses of the North West and of New England," on top of his rock-solid New York base. A correspondent for the *Daily Gazette* in Janesville, Wisconsin, reported that "the bulk of the party" was for Seward. "The energetic, active men of the party are united in his favor," while those who opposed Seward were motivated by fear rather than enthusiasm. They either worried about his strength in this or that state, or wished "to propitiate some dead faction, or fossilized party"—meaning the Whigs and Bates.

After a day spent crossing the country, finding ecstatic crowds at every depot waving flags and cheering them on, Seward's supporters could not help but feel elated. "The advent of the Seward delegations from the East into Chicago was the spectacular event of the pre-convention days," Kansas delegate Addison G. Procter recalled. Seward's backers "went to Chicago with the joy, pride and self confidence of a bridegroom marching to his wedding feast," the *New York Daily Herald* observed. The New Yorker was not over the hump, but he seemed to be within about sixty votes of capturing the nomination on the first ballot, Procter wrote, and he could rely on "many of the most noted political manipulators of his party under the leadership of Thurlow Weed, the most adroit politician of his day," to collect the remainder.

And now, thanks to the day's arrivals on the river of iron, Weed had hundreds more supporters around him, including men of great intelligence, respectability, and accomplishment. "The New York delegation was for Seward to a man. And for him absolutely, unreservedly—first, last, and all the time, without any second choice," journalist Isaac H. Bromley wrote. "To them Mr. Seward seemed the central figure of the whole movement, its prophet, priest, and oracle." They believed the cause of liberty would lose its fervor if cowardly Republicans surrendered the moral high ground and refused to nominate the party's courageous leader. "Without him it would be the play without Hamlet. They were vociferous, aggressive, boisterous, and they had brought with them from New York outsiders and workers and brass bands who filled the streets with processions and the nights with music to such an extent that the Seward enthusiasm seemed ubiquitous and all-absorbing."

Just a week earlier, as critics who were backing rival candidates blasted away at the frontrunner, Weed had reassured Seward that the delegates, once they arrived in Chicago and sensed his appeal, would embrace his strong leadership in this hour of national peril. "I too rely on the tone of the times and temper of the Delegates, to overrule Aspirations, Jealousies and Animosities," Weed wrote. In the end, he believed, the delegates would swallow their fears, do the right thing for America, and nominate the great man who, through long years of courage and devotion, had led their Republican Party to the brink of a stunning victory for freedom.

Chapter 8: Deutsches Haus

While the trains were thundering on to Chicago that Monday, Abraham Lincoln sat down in Springfield to jot a quick letter to Carl Schurz, the chairman of the Wisconsin delegation at the Chicago convention: "Allow me to introduce my friend, Jesse K. Dubois, our Illinois State Auditor. Yours truly A. LINCOLN." Though Schurz was an earnest supporter of Seward, Lincoln wanted his neighbor Dubois to speak with the man who was arguably the nation's most admired German American.

Germans had been pouring into the country for decades, to the point that they had become an important factor in elections, in some places holding the balance of power. By 1860, more than 1.3 million residents hailed from the German states, 31 percent of the nation's foreign-born population, second only to the Irish, who stood at 39 percent. But Irish immigration had peaked in 1851, and German immigrants were now flooding into America at a faster clip than any other nationality. They flocked to the region then known as the Northwest, forming particularly big and powerful communities in St. Louis, Cincinnati, Milwaukee, and Chicago. Lincoln recognized their importance to the nation, as voters, laborers, creative entrepreneurs, and leaders in politics, medicine, academia, and journalism. And he certainly knew they would play a role at the Chicago convention. All seven Northwestern states included foreign-born delegates, most of them German.

Schurz was a prime example of the priceless human capital that had flowed to America in the mid-nineteenth century, as educated, freedom-loving Germans fled from intense harassment and subjugation by their authoritarian governments. While studying at the University of Bonn, Schurz had joined the rebel military forces that were battling the powerful Kingdom of Prussia in 1848–49, seeking to depose King Frederick William IV. When the rebels were forced to surrender the fortress of Rastatt in July 1849, the twenty-year-old narrowly escaped capture and possible execution by the Prussian army by crawling to freedom through a sewer and fleeing to Switzerland. Schurz made international news with another audacious exploit in 1850. Returning to Germany in disguise and dispensing hefty bribes, he helped his beloved professor, the poet and freedom fighter Gottfried Kinkel, make a daring escape from Spandau Prison in Berlin, using a rope to rappel down the side of the building.

Schurz fled to America in 1852 at the age of twenty-three, starting a new life from scratch. Using a German-English dictionary, he painstakingly taught himself English—first by reading the *Philadelphia Ledger*, then by delving into great English literature, up to and including the works of Shakespeare. In little time, he became a superb English writer and orator, and a champion of the expansion of freedom in America. "I look upon this gentleman as one of the most intellectual, philosophical and eloquent orators of the country," wrote a correspondent in Chicago for Iowa's *Burlington Weekly Hawk-Eye*. "In person, he is of medium size, with scarcely anything but the fire of his eye blazing through his steel-bound spectacles to indicate an extraordinary man."

During Lincoln's 1858 run against Stephen Douglas, Schurz came out to Illinois on the Republican Party's behalf, delivering speeches in English and German to the state's German American voters. (In one address, he introduced the phrase "irrepressible conflict"—a month before Seward used it.) In October, Schurz took a train to Quincy, where a debate between Lincoln and Douglas was to take place. At one stop along the way, a tall, beardless man in a rusty black dress coat and a battered stovepipe hat, carrying a gray woolen shawl and an old umbrella in his left hand, climbed aboard. The men on the train "addressed him in a most familiar style: 'Hello, Abe! How are you?' and so on. And he responded in a similar manner: 'Good-evening, Ben! How are you, Joe? Glad to see you, Dick!' and there was much laughter at some of the things he said, which, in the confusion of voices, I could not understand." A state committeeman hauled Schurz over to meet Lincoln. Though the German stood more than six feet tall, he had to lift his head to look into "that swarthy face with its strong features, its deep furrows, and its benignant, melancholy eyes." Schurz had met many rough Western men during his journeys, "but none whose looks seemed quite so uncouth, not to say grotesque, as Lincoln's."

But Schurz quickly discovered the man's extraordinary tact and modesty. He treated Schurz like an old friend, sitting down with him in the crowded passenger car. "In a somewhat high-pitched but pleasant voice he began to talk to me," sharing some insights on his battle with Douglas. Lincoln, who believed he could learn a great deal by listening to other people, asked Schurz about his activities in Illinois and about his thoughts on the campaign. During the back-and-forth, Lincoln told "all sorts of quaint stories, each of which had a witty point applicable to the subject in hand," Schurz recalled. "He seemed to enjoy his own jests in a childlike way, for his usually sad-looking eyes would kindle with a merry twinkle, and he himself led in the laughter; and his laugh was so genuine, hearty, and contagious that nobody could fail to join in it."

A year later, Schurz visited with a more prominent and somber Republican, Ohio governor Salmon P. Chase, who then fancied himself a leading contender for the party's presidential nomination. At Chase's sprawling, turreted Columbus mansion, Schurz met the candidate's effervescent daughter Kate, who hoped to serve as the princess of Washington society at the side of her thrice-widowed father the president. "She was then about eighteen years old, tall and slender, and exceedingly well formed," Schurz recalled. He greatly admired her father for his bold and brave stance against slavery and for his eloquent speeches. When they talked in his library, Chase did not attempt to conceal his ardent desire to be nominated and elected president in 1860. At the risk of offending his host, Schurz frankly shared his belief with Chase that if the delegates were going to nominate "an advanced anti-slavery man, they will nominate Seward." Chase firmly disagreed, insisting that "he could not see why anti-slavery men would place him second in the order of leadership instead of first." But Schurz could detect a "note of sadness in his tone," and knew that his opinion had wounded Chase. The man suffered from a bad case of "presidential fever," Schurz realized; Chase believed "that he owed it to the country and that the country owed it to him that he should be President."

Like many liberal German Americans, Schurz considered Seward the man of the hour, not Chase or some dark horse like Lincoln. In that belief, he fully represented his Wisconsin delegation to Chicago. Every member regarded Seward as the leader in the hard struggle against slavery. "From him we received the battle-cry in the turmoil of the contest, for he was one of those spirits who will go ahead of public opinion instead of tamely following its footprints," Schurz noted. "He would compress into a single sentence, a single word, the whole issue of a controversy; and those words became the inscriptions on our banners, the pass-words of our combatants. His comprehensive intellect seemed to possess the peculiar power of penetrating into the interior connection and of grasping the general tendency of events and ideas, things and abstractions; he charmed our minds with panoramic views of our political and social condition and the problems to be solved; his telescopic eye seemed to pierce even the veil which covers future developments; and while all his acts and words were marked by a thoroughgoing and uncompromising consistency, they were, at the same time, adorned with the peculiar graces of superior mental culture."

Young liberals—Schurz was thirty-one at the time of the convention—believed that the best approach for Republicans was to "take the boldest course" and make "the most resolute appeal to the love of liberty, and to the generous impulses of the popular heart." They feared, above all, "a lowering of the standard of Republicanism" through a "half-hearted platform" and the nomination of a "compromise" man who, while ostensibly an enemy of the Democrats, would lack the will or the nerve to take on the powerful men advancing slavery. "Such a candidate was presented in the person of Mr. Edward Bates of Missouri," Schurz noted, "an old Whig who was supposed to be against slavery in a mild, unaggressive way." Prominent Republicans were selling him as the man who could "convince the timorous throughout the country that the Republican party in power would carefully avoid any disturbance." The question was who would prevail: the bold, young, and idealistic wing of the party, or the more cautious professionals focused on the spoils of victory and hoping to assuage Southern firebrands?

That Monday, the Bates forces made their big push. A committee of prominent and successful men—*New-York Tribune* editor Horace Greeley; congressman Frank Blair; *Indianapolis Atlas* publisher John D. Defrees; Bavarian-born insurance company president John C. Vogel; world-renowned civil engineer and bridge builder James B. Eads; and Dr. Adam Hammer, whose Bavarian Brewery in St. Louis was later absorbed into the Anheuser-Busch operation—issued a circular to the delegates in Chicago, which was carried in newspapers nationwide.

These powerful men pointed out that Bates had been born in one slave state and had long lived in another, and was a man of such principle that he had emancipated his own slaves. His nomination would refute critics' charges that Republicans were a "sectional" party representing only free Northern states. Moreover, his election in November would "render fire-eating and threats of dis-union . . . probably futile," greatly lessening the risk of a terrifying civil war. Given that Bates was an old Whig himself who hated slavery agitation, his nomination would cut the ground out from under John Bell and the Constitutional Union Party, inducing "those hitherto known as Americans, Old Line Whigs, Union men, &c., to cooperate heartily with us in rescuing this country from the hands into which she has been permitted to fall." Pennsylvania and New Jersey would be safe with Bates, along with Indiana, Illinois, and Oregon, placing the party's victory "beyond controversy." The very name of Bates would serve as an "olive branch to the various parties which earnestly desire the overthrow of the filibustering, slavery-extending, sham Democracy, as a proffer of fraternization and kindly regard." While the Bates manifesto did not mention the name of William H. Seward, it argued by inference that border states would regard Seward's nomination as a selfish and divisive gesture by the Republicans. Select Bates "in a generous and magnanimous spirit," the statement advised, "and you will have vindicated our cause from the unjust but damaging imputations of sectionalism."

The argument appealed powerfully to many of the delegates who were alarmed about Seward's prospects in the swing states—and worried about how the Southern fire-eaters might react after November. But a carefully designed plot to explode Bates's candidacy was already underway. German Americans planned, over the next two days, to make it all but impossible for cautious Republicans to consider the Missouri judge as their nominee, however much Greeley and the Blairs touted him and tore down Seward.

The Republicans in 1860 were a motley collection of interests, drawn together by their opposition to Democrats. As Lincoln noted in his "House Divided" speech, "*strange*, *discordant*, and even, *hostile* elements" had been "gathered from the four winds" to make the party. There were anti-slavery men. There were prohibitionists devoted to curbing the misery caused by alcohol. And there were American-born Protestants concerned that unbridled immigration was warping the country's values, culture, and workforce. Many of these nativists loved freedom and opposed slavery.

Not surprisingly, immigrants overwhelmingly preferred the Democratic Party, which welcomed them warmly, accepted their religions, made no effort to suppress their customs—including their freedom to drink—and rushed them into elections as quickly as possible. Immigrants, by and large, were willing to go along with the party of slavery. Struggling to survive as they put down roots in America, they could spare little sympathy for Southern slaves, who seemed to be the chief concern of the Republicans. And they had no desire to compete for jobs against freed slaves. That included most Germans, who yearned for peace and stability, and to be left alone. As one German pamphleteer wrote during the 1856 campaign, "Our own children are closer to our heart than the children of the Negroes."

Immigrants particularly hated and feared the American Party, nicknamed the "Know-Nothings" due to its origin as a secret society. (When outsiders asked about the society, its early adherents were advised to reply, "I know nothing.") More of a populist movement than a professional political organization, it fed on the discontent of working Americans who had paid the price for the massive influx of poor immigrant laborers in the mid-nineteenth century, which increased competition for jobs and put downward pressure on wages. Those drawn to the American Party scorned political elites, proudly waved the American flag, fought for labor rights, supported robust freedom of speech, denounced the rise of slums and crime, and frowned on the big-city corruption that was fueling election fraud. Many believed that Catholicism was incompatible with self-government, individual liberty, and freedom of conscience, since Catholics were supposed to be loyal to an authoritarian system dominated by a pope in Rome. In their view, Catholicism promoted ignorance, superstition, and devotion to a hidebound hierarchy rather than the American values of reason, science, and societal advancement. Consequently, they insisted on a sharp separation between church and state, and ardently fought against taxpayer support for Catholic schools. Many of them particularly loathed impoverished and uneducated Irish immigrants, regarding most of those who ended up in America as little better than lazy, thieving drunkards. As Irish immigrants flooded into Boston, nativist ideas caught fire even in Massachusetts, arguably the most progressive state in the Union.

In the eyes of the popular nativist group the Order of United Americans, relentless immigration was destroying the nation from within. It had to be stopped by patriots who were prepared to strike back without warning. The OUA's monthly magazine captured that spirit in an illustration it regularly published, depicting a strong arm descending from a cloud to strangle a venomous serpent baring its fangs.

But worries about the impact of untrammeled immigration extended far beyond nativist groups. New York diarist George Templeton Strong, a public-spirited Whig, voiced horror at the way Democrats exploited ill-educated newcomers to control elections. "It was enough to turn a man's stomach—to make a man abjure republicanism forever—to see the way they were naturalizing this morning at the [City] Hall . . . the very scum and dregs of human nature," he wrote in 1838. Former New York mayor Philip Hone made similar complaints about the hordes of "low Irishmen" infecting the system. "These Irishmen, strangers among us, without a feeling of patriotism or affection in common with American citizens, *decide the elections in the city of New York*," Hone wrote. "They make presidents and governors, and they send men to represent us in the councils of the nation, and, what is worse than all, their importance in these matters is derived from the use which is made of them by political demagogues, who despise the tools they work with."

Many adherents of the American Party reluctantly turned to the Republican Party in the late 1850s, viewing the rising party as their best hope for halting the destruction of the republic by Democrats and their immigrant hordes. William H. Seward and Thurlow Weed had built up the Republican Party to the point that it had become the only serious alternative to the Democrats, while deftly undermining the Know-Nothings. "Mr. Seward had been the determined foe of that party," wrote James G. Blaine of Maine. "In battling for the rights of the negro, he deemed it unwise and inconsistent to increase the disabilities of the foreign-born citizen. His influence, more than that of any other man, had broken down the proscriptive creed of the American Party, and turned its members into the Republican ranks. But many of them came reluctantly, and in a complaining mood against Mr. Seward." Seward had set hardcore nativists' teeth on edge by openly supporting public funding of Catholic schools and by treating New York archbishop John J. Hughes with great respect.

By 1860, Seward was persona non grata with many Know-Nothing voters—one reason that delegates from swing states were worried about the New Yorker as their standard-bearer. By contrast, Abraham Lincoln, not wishing to divide the forces opposing the Democrats, said little about the Know-Nothings in public, a silence that led some to suspect him of being a secret member. Privately, though, Lincoln expressed fierce contempt for the movement. "I am not a Know-Nothing—that is certain," Lincoln wrote to his friend Joshua Speed in 1855.

> How could I be? How can any one who abhors the oppression of negroes, be in favor of degrading classes of white people? Our progress in degeneracy appears to me to be pretty rapid. As a nation, we began by declaring that 'all men are created equal.' We now practically read it 'all men are created equal, except negroes.' When the Know-Nothings get control, it will read 'all men are created equals, except negroes and foreigners and Catholics.' When it comes to that I should prefer emigrating to some country where they make no pretense of loving liberty—to Russia, for instance, where despotism can be taken pure, and without the base alloy of hypocrisy.

When members of the American Party tried to recruit Lincoln in 1854, he flatly rejected them and explained why. Men whose ancestors had pushed aside Native Americans were now trying to block newcomers who "were not fortunate enough to come over as early as we or our forefathers," Lincoln said. "Gentlemen of the committee, your party is wrong on principle." Characteristically, he told them a story. One morning, an Irish immigrant named Patrick was out hoeing Lincoln's garden. They began talking about the Know-Nothings. "I asked Pat why he was not born in this country. 'Faith, Mr. Lincoln,' he replied, 'I wanted to be, but my mother wouldn't let me.'"

Yet the rumors that Lincoln was a Know-Nothing persisted. During his 1858 Senate campaign, Lincoln heard that the story was "still being told, and insisted upon, that I have been a Know-Nothing." In a letter to a farmer who lived in Meredosia, Illinois, Lincoln stressed "that I am not, nor ever have been, connected with the party called the

Know-Nothing party, or party calling themselves the American party. *Certainly* no man of truth, and I *believe*, no man [of] good character for truth can be found to say on his own knowledge that I ever was connected with that party."

Germans came in for their full share of the general prejudice against foreigners. "Germans were persecuted by American mobs with as great a brutality, and as diabolic a cruelty, as that with which Europeans have ever been persecuted in China, Chinese in California, or Jews in Rumania," recounted Anton C. Hesing, who came to America from Lower Saxony in 1839 and rose to become a newspaper publisher. He recalled "how packs of native Americans, drunk with the desire to kill, burned down churches of the 'damned Germans'" and "how peaceful Germans were hunted down and butchered in the streets of Louisville." Nativists were disgusted that American cities, for blocks and blocks, had been filled with foreigners speaking nothing but German, selling German goods, holding German celebrations, attending German churches, running German schools, and reading German newspapers. They could see that German ideas were transforming America in myriad ways.

Germans, for example, introduced Christmas customs that included exchanging gifts and decorating an evergreen tree. They treated Sunday as a day for festive family activities, fit for drinking, picnics, and games, while American Protestants tried to keep it God-focused by locking it down with blue laws. And they drank lager beer rather than the hard liquor Americans commonly consumed. "Ten years ago it was impossible to find a glass of lager beer in New York," the *New York Daily Herald* noted in June 1859. Thanks to German immigrants, it had "become an institution of the city. . . . It is everywhere—on every block almost of the leading thoroughfares; in the American public houses as well as in the German saloons, and even in the first class hotels. It has become a fashionable drink in private houses. The quantity of lager beer now consumed in New York is truly amazing." For their part, educated Germans initially found America to be a cultural wasteland, largely devoid of good beer, classical music, and fine art, and they set about addressing those deficiencies.

Critics of the Germans believed the changes being wrought went far beyond beer, art, and Sunday activities. New York nativist Thomas Richard Whitney contended that former German freedom fighters were the vanguard of atheism, socialism, and communism, "Red Republicans" bent on destroying law and order in America—"malcontents of the Old World, who hate monarchy, not because it is monarchy, but because it is restraint. They are such men as stood by the side of Robespierre." The *Sentinel*, a Democratic paper published in Maquoketa, Iowa, unleashed a similar diatribe in 1859, branding German Republicans as "busy-bodies, and mischief-makers in every community where they reside. They were driven out of Germany in '48 for their clannishness and meddlesomeness. They ignore the Bible, and all revealed religion . . . and act on the motto, 'live while we live.' They aim at anarchy in politics, morals, and religion, and are a curse to any country or community."

The rise of a powerful prohibition movement during the 1850s—advanced by Protestant ministers and reformers who sought to limit the horrors of alcohol addiction—struck many immigrants, particularly beer-loving Germans, as a threat to their way of life. Maine drew national attention in 1851 with the first outright ban on alcohol. By 1855, twelve states had followed. Such newspapers as the *Journal of the American Temperance Movement* led the charge, often overstating the success of the reform. It argued, for example, that after the passage of the Connecticut law in 1854, "almost every grog shop and tavern bar in the State has been closed with the happiest results; that drunkenness is much at an end" and "that the people at large rejoice in the deliverance."

In Chicago, the prohibitionist movement exploded into violence in 1855. Nativist mayor Levi Boone, anticipating that the state of Illinois would support prohibition in its own upcoming referendum, ratcheted up tensions by closing German beer taverns on Sunday, while hiking license fees so high that many immigrants could no longer afford them. When Germans chose to defy the mayor and serve beer on

Sunday anyway, his newly uniformed and enlarged police force—whose foreign-born officers had been replaced by men born in America—apprehended some two hundred people. Protesters, infuriated by the arrests, massed around the Cook County Court House on the day of their trials and, inevitably, clashed with police. The crowd grew, as more armed Germans swarmed downtown from their neighborhoods north of the Chicago River—the *Nordseite*, as even native Chicagoans had taken to calling it—until the mayor ordered the bridges swung open, no longer able to be crossed. Overzealous police then shot at Germans who were trapped on the opened Clark Street Bridge and unable to escape. In the end, the public relations debacle was so complete that the city abandoned its crusade and reorganized the police department. Boone did not dare run for reelection. And the referendum to make Illinois a "dry" state failed by 54 to 46 percent. "The Germans turned out to a man, and, it was charged, also to a woman, voting against the law," wrote German-born Illinois lieutenant governor Gustave P. Koerner. Women, of course, could not legally vote.

Despite the Republicans' nativist and prohibitionist tinge, many German Americans, particularly highly educated men who had fled oppression after the failed revolutions of 1848 and 1849, embraced the party. While German Catholics, for the most part, allied with the Democratic Party, many German Protestants detested slavery and wanted to join the fight for freedom in America. They despised Democratic president James Buchanan for failing to defend naturalized American citizens who had returned to visit their native Prussia only to be seized by authorities and forced into the military. And they abhorred the political corruption in the Democratic Party.

Their apostasy was not well received by German Democrats. During one speech in Watertown, Wisconsin, Carl Schurz found himself pelted with rotten eggs and denounced as "*ein verdammter Republikaner*"—a damn Republican. But by spring 1860, Chicago's German wards were rolling up large majorities for Republicans for the first time, helping to elect Long John Wentworth as mayor. The Democratic *Chicago Times*, disgusted with this turn of events, described the local German Americans as "imported barbarians," and the "offscourings . . . of outcasts from the serfs of Europe"—a "noisy, ragged, dirty, and miserable looking drove of imported 'voting cattle,'" the "rag-tag and bob-tail of creation." After the election, the *Times* complained, Germans were out on the streets "hooting like so many savages" in celebration.

While voting Republican, these Germans remained hypersensitive to any flirtation by party members with Know-Nothingism. They were deeply concerned, for example, that a growing number of Republicans were touting Edward Bates for president, after he had criticized the party just four years earlier and presided over the Whig convention that chose Millard Fillmore as its nominee, the candidate of the nativist American Party. (Fillmore also warmly accepted the nomination of the notorious Order of United Americans, saying he felt "peculiarly flattered" by the gesture.) Even more troubling to German Republicans was the 1859 passage of a constitutional amendment in Republican Massachusetts requiring naturalized citizens to wait another two years before they could vote—effectively rendering them second-class citizens. Republican governor Nathaniel P. Banks, sensing a shift toward Americanism, supported the amendment, riding the anti-immigrant wave to reelection. All the way to Chicago, conservatives touted him as a possible nominee in 1860, one who would appeal to Know-Nothing voters in the border states. New York and Connecticut Republicans began mulling such an amendment in their states.

The amendment was one of those volatile diversions Lincoln had hoped Republicans would avoid. He did not want to be drawn into a bitterly divisive immigration debate. At the same time, he did quietly support German Americans. In 1856, Lincoln worked behind the scenes to help George Schneider, editor of the influential German-language *Illinois Staats-Zeitung*, insert an anti-nativist plank in the state Republican platform. Lincoln deftly honed the wording to keep it from splitting the party. Schneider then got it placed, word for word, in the national Republican platform. That year, Lincoln also came to the rescue of a leading German American orator, Friedrich Hecker, who had fought for freedom in Germany alongside Carl Schurz. While Hecker was out speaking on behalf of the Republican Party, his Illinois house caught fire and burned down—possibly the work of an arsonist—and Lincoln raised money to help him rebuild. Sensitive to Hecker's pride, Lincoln wrote to him: "I have started a proposition for this, among our friends, with a prospect of some degree of success. It is but fair and just; and I hope you will not decline to accept what we may be able to do."

In May 1859, another former German revolutionary, Theodore Canisius, editor of the *Illinois Staats-Anzeiger*, Springfield's German newspaper, queried Lincoln about the Massachusetts Amendment. Lincoln replied in a carefully worded letter that he knew would be picked up by other newspapers. He began by cautiously defending the Bay State's right to do as it pleased. "Massachusetts is a sovereign and independent state; and it is no privilege of mine to scold her for what she does. Still, if from what she *has done*, an inference is sought to be drawn as to what I *would do*, I may, without impropriety, speak out," Lincoln wrote. Then he made clear that he sided with the immigrants.

> I say then, that, as I understand the Massachusetts provision, I am against its adoption in Illinois, or in any other place, where I have a right to oppose it. Understanding the spirit of our institutions to aim at the *elevation* of men, I am opposed to whatever tends to *degrade* them. I have some little notoriety for commiserating the oppressed condition of the negro; and I should be strangely inconsistent if I could favor any project for curtailing the existing rights of *white men*, even though born in different lands, and speaking different languages from myself.

In his quest to help German Americans, Lincoln went so far as to secretly purchase the *Staats-Anzeiger* rather than let it fail, leaving Canisius in place as editor with instructions to advance the cause of the Republican Party. (He had hoped to enlist the financial support of Norman Judd and the Republican State Committee, but apparently ended up using $500 from his firm's income. "Herndon, I gave the

Germans $250 of yours the other day," he breezily informed his law partner.) A year later, Lincoln shrewdly awarded one of his four precious at-large delegate slots at the national convention to Lieutenant Governor Koerner, a former German revolutionary and a fellow lawyer. Lincoln grasped that it would be important to get the word out in Chicago that he was a friend of German Americans.

As Bates gathered strength in early 1860, thanks largely to Horace Greeley's powerful promotion, German American Republicans worried that the party was about to sell its soul. At Indiana's state convention on February 22, Theodor Hielscher, editor of the Indianapolis *Freie Presse*, pushed a resolution—transparently aimed at Bates—"instructing the delegates to Chicago to vote for no candidate for the nomination who was not a good Republican in 1856." The convention rejected the measure, but Hielscher had succeeded in putting German American concerns on record. In Bates's own Missouri, a similar protest erupted. Carl Daenzer, editor of the St. Louis *Westliche Post*, complained that the state party had fallen under the control of "the finest models of Missouri fire-eaters,—rabid pro-slavery men,—old Know-Nothings, Whig-Whigs, and office-hunting ex-republicans." At the state convention, some respected German Americans backed Bates, but several stood up and walked out in protest.

A German American gathering in Davenport, Iowa, on March 6 stridently denounced Bates, noting that the 1856 Whig nominee, ex-president Fillmore, had embraced the American Party's anti-immigrant platform, which among other things declared, "Americans must rule America, and to this end native-born citizens should be selected for all State, Federal, and Municipal offices of Government in preference to all others," and proposed that immigrants be required to live in America for a whopping twenty-one years before being considered for citizenship. And while Bates now indicated he would be willing to change his stripes and become a full-fledged Republican, he would take office at the age of sixty-seven and could not be trusted to "truly, faithfully and vigorously execute Republican principles in the impending crisis." Therefore, the Iowa German Americans declared, "we . . . under no circumstances will vote for the Hon. Edward Bates." Theodor Olshausen, editor of *Der Demokrat*, a German-language paper in Davenport, voiced the hope that the resolutions would gain widespread distribution in newspapers and might even persuade "Mr. Horace Greeley . . . to revise his calculations somewhat."

Greeley did not revise his calculations, and German Americans persisted with their implied threat that they would walk if Bates became the nominee. "No matter what course the majority of the republican party may pursue, we for our part shall always and immutably remain true to the *principles* of *liberty* and *humanity* which we heretofore have considered identical with those of the republican party," Olshausen vowed. A correspondent named GERMANICUS made the threat explicit in a letter to the *Cleveland Plain Dealer*: "If Bates, Banks, or any other man of their stripe should be preferred by the Chicago convention, you may be assured that not one hundredth part of the German Republican vote will be cast in his favor. . . . To be beaten under the leadership of Chase, Seward or any other true Republican is less injurious than with a party-man of today."

In a February meeting, the members of the German Republican Club of Peoria, Illinois, drew national attention by backing Seward and adopting a resolution stating that "no man who has not heretofore been identified with the Republican Party can get their support for the presidency, even if such a man should be nominated at Chicago." Illinois congressman Owen Lovejoy, an abolitionist friend of Lincoln, praised the Germans' firm stand against compromise. "We have dallied and played a hide-and-seek policy with the slaveholding despotism long enough. It is time now to square it around and hit it in the eyes," Lovejoy wrote. "Let us have a standard bearer who can inspire confidence and awaken enthusiasm, and we will kindle a fire that will burn the sham Democracy to the lowest hell." *New-York Tribune* reporter Fitz Henry Warren said much the same thing, privately disagreeing with his boss about the fusty Bates. "For God's sake let us look to life and not to resurrection for our success in '60," he wrote to the *Tribune*'s Washington correspondent James S. Pike. He questioned the wisdom of going into the bowels of a slave state for a candidate.

During the winter and spring, German Americans also mounted a sustained attack on the Massachusetts Amendment. On the eve of the anniversary of the battles at Lexington and Concord, Schurz went into the belly of the beast, speaking on April 18 at Boston's Faneuil Hall. He asked Massachusetts to live up to its hard-won reputation as a champion of liberty and equal rights. The United States, Schurz argued, was meant to be "the Republic of equal rights," not a land where different classes of citizens had different degrees of legal privilege. Under Lincoln's careful leadership, Illinois Republicans at their state convention in Decatur in 1860 placed a plank in their platform opposing any change in naturalization laws, including such discrimination against naturalized citizens as in the Massachusetts Amendment.

On March 7, the German Republican Club of New York, fearful that the Bates movement was growing, decided the time had come to rock the Republican establishment. It issued a national call to German Republicans to gather in Chicago on Monday, May 14—on the week and in the city of the national convention—to make their concerns plain to the delegates. Such a meeting was bound to create intense political pressure on the convention. Some, even in the German American community, believed it was a bad idea, too divisive and sure to foster long-term resentments. What would become of the Germans' clout if the convention went with Bates? Should Germans present themselves as a special interest, or should they present themselves as common citizens? Would German Republicans really prefer to see Stephen Douglas elected? Lincoln's friends Carl Schurz and Gustave Koerner were among those who remained silent about the plan.

But German Americans around the country began to prepare for a trip to Chicago, their representatives selected by their local clubs. As the German Republican Club of Newark noted, the need for the meeting was "generally recognized by the Germans," who believed that the preservation of their rights could be best advanced "by a vigorous, decided, and common action before the nomination." The pro-Democrat *Detroit Free Press* savored the unrest in the German camp, noting that Republicans would be doomed without the German vote. "If it is taken from them in any single states except possibly Massachusetts and Vermont, they immediately go into a minority. It is not necessary that they should be given to their opponents, but let that vote be silent during a single election and there is not a single state in the Union, with these two exceptions, in which the party would not be beaten." Many Republican strategists shared that view.

During convention week, the German Americans met at the Deutsches Haus—also known as the German Hall and the German Theatre—on the corner of North Wells and Indiana Streets. The three-story brick building, constructed in 1856, was a short walking distance north of the downtown, across the Wells Street Bridge and on past the enormous Gibbs, Griffin & Company warehouse and the Chicago & Galena Union Railroad station. With a large American flag flapping atop the building, it functioned as a German community center, hosting clubs, lodges, bands, lectures, and dances—including a concert and ball on February 17, 1860, advertised as the "greatest affair of the season," with "Police in attendance to exclude entirely all improper characters." Now it was hosting the cream of German American society—an extraordinary group of professors, politicians, physicians, ministers, writers, lecturers, and editors, selected by their fellow Germans for their ability, character, and influence.

Many papers thought the German gathering was a plot to advance the political fortunes of the leading candidate at the Wigwam—a "Seward move," as the *Springfield* (Massachusetts) *Republican* put it. The *New-York Tribune* accordingly pooh-poohed the conference, reporting in a dispatch Sunday night, perhaps sent by Horace Greeley, before the meeting even took place: "The German convention is repudiated and denounced by the Germans generally and will amount to nothing." Attendance was sparse at the Deutsches Haus on the first day, Monday.

In a dispatch that night, the *Tribune* reported: "The German convention today did nothing—only eight delegates were present. They could not even pass a resolution demanding that the National Convention should denounce the famous Massachusetts Two Years Amendment." Greeley's paper added wishfully: "The German friends of Judge Bates are increasing."

Other reporters also downplayed the importance of Monday's gathering. "There was no convention and the idea of holding one during the sitting of the national convention met with no favor," the Associated Press reported. The German Americans running the meeting evidently told the press they were not holding an official convention and that all this was informal, to avoid creating an impression that they were being divisive or threatening. But the gathering would, in truth, prove enormously consequential, particularly after new arrivals on Tuesday and Wednesday swelled the crowd to hundreds.

On Monday, the early attendees quickly resolved that the national party's platform must include a plank "recognizing perfect equality and protection to all citizens at home and abroad, and declaring against any extension of the present term of naturalization, and against any discrimination between native and adopted citizens as to their qualifications as voters." Intriguingly, they took a straw poll, signaling their support for four candidates: New York senator William H. Seward, Ohio senators Salmon P. Chase and Benjamin Wade, and the local favorite, Illinois lawyer Abraham Lincoln. Glaringly missing was the name of Edward Bates, though the Bates supporters had issued their much-touted "address" that day. "Greeley is hard at work for poor old Bates, his pet," noted a correspondent for the *Daily Democrat and News* of Davenport, Iowa, "and has put forth a circular with one of his usual Tom-fool arguments why Bates should be nominated and trying to do away with the objections of the Teutonic element to that old fossil." German objections, it was soon clear, would not be so easily done away with.

On Tuesday, the gathering at the Deutsches Haus resumed in earnest. With more than two hundred now in attendance, the conference named William Kopp, editor of the influential *New York Demokrat*, as its chairman. And it began passing a series of resolutions expressing "the sentiment of the majority of German Republican voters of the Union." The resolves urged Republicans at their national convention to pass a platform that included some elements of key importance to German Americans: a strong and "progressive" plank against slavery; support for a Homestead Act that would help immigrants and other Americans obtain homes out West; and a specific condemnation of the Massachusetts Amendment.

On Wednesday, the conference's final day, the German Americans shifted to the vitally important presidential race. Though Lincoln's friend Gustave Koerner did not specifically mention the Deutsches Haus gathering in his memoirs, he arrived in Chicago that day and evidently attended. He did recall that at "German localities" in Chicago the presidential nomination was passionately debated. "The feeling for Seward was decidedly the strongest," Koerner wrote. "I was almost the only one who advocated the claims of Lincoln, not only as the best and purest, but also as the most available candidate." By then, the Bates forces, belatedly recognizing that this gathering Greeley had been downplaying could prove disastrous to their candidate, realized they must show up and make a case for Bates.

The Bates team did include some prominent Germans. Adam Hammer and John C. Vogel had signed Monday's Bates manifesto, while Missouri's delegation included such leading German Americans as writer and politician Friedrich Muench; editor and doctor Karl Ludwig Bernays; and lawyer, editor, and politician Arnold Krekel. At the Deutsches Haus, the men "tried to defend their position as supporters to Bates," according to an Associated Press dispatch. But they met "with no encouragement whatever." The eloquent Carl Schurz was "among the most earnest opponents of Mr. Bates," along with Dr. Adolph Douai of Boston, a bold writer, orator, and education reformer who had been driven out of Texas for advocating abolition in the German-language newspaper he edited in San Antonio. In Boston, he had founded the city's first kindergarten. In the end, the German Americans passed a resolution pledging their support for any candidate for president or vice president who backed a strong platform "and has never opposed the republican platform of 1856, nor has ever been associated with the spirit of the Massachusetts Amendment." The meaning was clear: neither Bates nor Massachusetts governor Banks would be tolerated.

Greeley continued to push Bates as the best candidate, ignoring the Germans' opposition. But others recognized that the widely respected and influential men meeting in the Deutsches Haus, representing untold thousands of voters, had to be taken seriously. Needing every possible vote in November, Republican leaders could ill afford to let the German Americans sit out the election or bolt to a third party. The upshot of the three-day Deutsches Haus gathering was this: politicians fearful of losing the swing states would have to find someone other than Bates or Banks to promote as their alternative to the controversial Seward or Chase.

Tuesday,
May 15, 1860

Chapter 9: Moving Heaven and Earth

Murat Halstead was anxious to get to Chicago to start reporting on the convention for the *Cincinnati Commercial Gazette*. But his trip from Baltimore, where he had been covering the Constitutional Union Party's nomination of John Bell, was anything but easy. On Friday, heavy rains triggered a landslide on the Pennsylvania Central Railroad between Harrisburg and Pittsburgh, killing no one, luckily, but creating long delays and stranding carloads of travelers.

Like Halstead, many of them were Chicago-bound. At 1:00 a.m. on Saturday, delegates from Lancaster, accompanied by a correspondent for the local *Daily Evening Express*, made their way to the depot under a drenching rain, with plans to reach Pittsburgh by 2:00 p.m. But after seven hours of travel, they had to hunker down later that morning at the depot in Harrisburg, their route blocked by the landslide. The United States Cornet Band from Philadelphia stepped onto the portico to entertain the crowds while everyone waited. At last, the immense train pushed out from Harrisburg, fourteen cars long and filled with delegates from Pennsylvania, New York, Massachusetts, Rhode Island, and other states. As it approached the site of the landslide near Mifflin, the train cautiously slowed and squealed to a halt. A second massive train was waiting on the other side of the slide, and a "small army of laborers and assistants very speedily transferred the baggage" from one train to the other, while the passengers walked gingerly to the waiting cars.

Such work-arounds could themselves be dangerous. "While one train was standing on the track," according to one press report, "its passengers having been transferred, the second slide took place, carrying with it an immense mass of earth, rock, and trees, which caught the three rear cars of the train, carrying them, with the track into the Juniata [River]." In a stroke of luck, the train was empty at the time. "No one, who has never seen the like, can imagine the terribleness of one of these fearful land-slides," wrote another convention-bound traveler. "Think of the whole side of a vast mountain, covering many acres of ground, being precipitated upon the valley beneath, burying everything, with which its huge mass comes in contact, away from human sight. Such was the case here." Fortunately for later travelers, the damage to the line itself was quickly repaired. "As soon as the dirt and rocks were removed—which caused some thirty hours hard labor, with a large force of hands—the trains passed over as before."

With schedules disrupted, the Pennsylvania delegates had to wait in Pittsburgh all day Sunday for a train to take them to Chicago. To the professed horror of Democratic newspaper editors, they decided to spend the time marching in the streets behind their flashy Philadelphia band, which belted out "profane music"—a shockingly irreligious act on a Sunday. Republicans liked to "boast of their morality and decency," the *Holmes County Farmer* in Millersburg, Ohio, huffed, but "no person ever heard of Delegates to a Democratic convention parading the streets of a city on the Sabbath day preceded by a brass band."

Halstead, too, had to wait for a Pittsburgh, Fort Wayne and Chicago Railway train that was six hours late. Stoking the Cincinnati journalist's annoyance were the obnoxious Seward men equipped with "private bottles," who filled the crowded cars when the train got up and running. Most of the "Irrepressibles," as they had taken to calling themselves, were "unsound," and "rather disposed to boast of the fact"—drunk and proud of it. By Halstead's estimate, the quantity of hard liquor consumed on the journey to Chicago was greater than on any train bound for the Democratic convention in Charleston. Some of the Republicans were appalled that members of their "painfully virtuous party" were conducting themselves in that manner, Halstead noted, and travelers from Ohio's religious Western Reserve were "thrown into prayers and perspiration by some New Yorkers who were singing songs not found in hymn books."

Amid the carousing, Halstead contemplated the passing landscape. The men of the North, he noticed, had developed land far more extensively and beautifully than slaveholders and poor farmers in the South. "I have not had any disposition to speak in disparaging terms of the Southern country, but it is the plain truth that the country visible along the road from Baltimore to Harrisburg alone, is worth more by far than all that can be seen from Charleston to the Potomac," he wrote. "In the South few attempts have been made to cultivate any lands other than those most favorably situated, and most rich. But in Pennsylvania, free labor has made not only the valleys bloom, but the hill-tops are radiant with clover and wheat. And there are many other things that rush upon the sight in the North as contrasted with the South, that testify to the paramount glory of free labor."

A train of twelve passenger cars packed with Pennsylvania delegates finally arrived in Chicago sometime after 2:00 a.m. Tuesday, several hours behind the big ones that had raced in from Buffalo. Even at that wee hour, the Wide Awakes were waiting. As soon as the travelers stepped out of the cars, they joined in an immense torchlight procession, marching to their lodgings near the intersection of Randolph and Wells Streets: the Briggs House, a first-class, $2.50-a-night hotel, and the Metropolitan Hotel across the street, a less fancy $2.00-a-night affair. "After arriving at the Hotel, we were not long finding, and turning into our beds, when old Morpheus came to our relief and banished from our thoughts all care for politics," the correspondent for the *Daily Evening Express* reported.

The reporter did not sleep for long. Stepping out on a bright, sunny morning onto streets that were "literally alive with a rushing multitude," he headed straight for the famous Wigwam. "That the

Chicagoans are a wide-awake, go-ahead people, a stranger has only to visit this structure to be convinced," he wrote, marveling at its immensity, its decorations, and the speed of its construction. Inside, he found workmen and some of "the ladies of Chicago, who seem to manifest the liveliest interest in the arrangements," applying the final touches, beautifully adorning the hall with pictures, wreaths, and flowers before the convention's opening the next day. As for the political situation, the "friends of Senator Seward are here in great numbers, and will make a most determined fight for his nomination. Thurlow Weed, who is Seward's engineer, conducts the fight with much ability. His carriers are circulating through the crowds and talk Seward with great vehemence."

One of the most effective advocates now on the scene was lawyer William M. Evarts, the suave chairman of the New York delegation, who went from hotel to hotel expounding on Seward's rare strengths. Evarts was "a splendid man, when you consider him intellectually," Iowa journalist L. D. Ingersoll observed. "He is an excellent speaker, having a good voice and graceful manner, with not a bit of the immortal spread eagle in his manner." Fellow journalist Isaac H. Bromley shared Ingersoll's admiration. Evarts's "smooth-shaven, classical features and strong profile" distinguished him "from the vulgar crowd." The "dignity of his carriage and repose of his manner" stood "in marked contrast with the fussy and uneasy Greeley, who was shambling around in an aimless disjointed way." There was already talk that the eminent and articulate lawyer would succeed Seward in the Senate. "Even those who most decidedly differed from him followed him from one delegation to another allured by the charm of his words," wrote James G. Blaine. "He pleaded for the Republic, for the party that could save it, for the grand statesman who had founded the party, and knew where and how to lead it. He spoke as one friend for another, and the great career of Mr. Seward was never so illumined as by the brilliant painting of Mr. Evarts." Even a Lincoln supporter found himself charmed. "No one who then heard Mr. Evarts can ever forget the exquisite tenderness with which he pronounced the name of William Henry Seward," he noted.

By the time Halstead reached Chicago on Tuesday, it was mobbed. "The city swarms like a bee-hive," reported the *Chicago Press and Tribune*. "Hotels are full. Multitudes of our private residences have their quota of guests, and on every side . . . the work of President-making" was in progress. Three trains on the Pittsburgh, Fort Wayne and Chicago Railway that day brought in thirty-five carloads of passengers, including two marching bands. The Illinois Central and other lines also arrived filled with passengers, tens of thousands all told. The Associated Press estimated Tuesday that there were already forty thousand visitors in the city. "The weather is warm and the political thermometer very high," the *New York Daily Herald* reported. "The city is full of strangers, and the Convention creates the greatest excitement. It is a perfect political saturnalia." Halstead set out for the Tremont House, where he hoped to make sense of the maelstrom of political talk.

Harvard-educated lawyer Nathaniel Collins McLean rolled into Chicago at around ten o'clock that morning. He had come to aid the longshot presidential campaign of his father, John McLean. The seventy-five-year-old associate Supreme Court justice, best known for writing a scathing dissent to the court's notorious Dred Scott decision, appealed to moderates like Illinois senator Lyman Trumbull, who argued that McLean was the candidate best poised to derail Seward—at least until Abraham Lincoln advised Trumbull to stop making that case. But the justice lacked any real organization, while two other Ohio candidates, Salmon P. Chase and Benjamin Wade, seemed to have a stronger presence. McLean was essentially a name, and little more—an alternative to Seward if the convention could settle on no one else.

The big argument against him was his age. Born before the ratification of the Constitution and the presidency of George Washington, McLean had served as postmaster general decades earlier in the cabinet of President Andrew Jackson, until Jackson put him on the court in 1829. Some professed to have seen McLean falling asleep during oral arguments, fueling doubts that he could energize the young party. "He would kindle as much enthusiasm in the ranks as a eunuch or a mummy," the *New York Daily Herald*'s Washington correspondent asserted. "It strikes me that the great fault with him is his youth," an unnamed politician quipped to the *Springfield Republican*, in Massachusetts. "It won't do to run a boy; an airy, flighty, skipping youngster like Johnny McLean. Why he is only 94, some people say only 84. . . . For my part I would prefer a man who had reached the mature age of 130 or even 140." The judge did have the support of one influential Ohio congressman in Chicago, the aged Tom Corwin, a former senator, governor, and U.S. Treasury secretary who bore the nickname "the Wagon Boy" for his heroic work supplying the army of General William Henry Harrison during the War of 1812.

At first, Nathaniel McLean could not find a room in packed Chicago. He wrote to his wife from "a brother lawyer's office upon whom I have been sponging. He has invited me to stay with him but I prefer to be at the hotel"—presumably the Tremont, where the Ohio delegates were residing. McLean spent all Tuesday picking up political intelligence and touting his father, at one point working his way through the hotel, which he found unbelievably crowded. "It is almost impossible to move about in the halls without tearing off the buttons from your coat. It is now four o'clock and I have been on my feet nearly all day and feel very tired, but I must keep going in order to learn all the news." Among other things, he learned that Thurlow Weed was hard at work, and probably buying support. "The friends of Mr. Seward are moving heaven and earth for his nomination and it is said that much money is being expended for his interest. This may all be slander but I fear not." The New Yorkers' hard sell had created some resentment among the supporters of the other candidates, making Seward's long-term prospects in Chicago doubtful, McLean believed. "If Seward is not nominated in the beginning his chance say the wise ones is gone."

As for his father, "I scarcely know what to say in regard to the Judge. He has many warm friends who are working for him very earnestly. It seems to be the policy not to push him forward from the beginning of the fight, but to hold him in reserve on a compromise when the other factions shall have found out that their favorite cannot be nominated." Chase, the strongest Ohio candidate going in, "is out of the question" for the nomination, McLean reported, "and only has influence enough left to do harm." Whatever happened, he thought things would move quickly. "I should not be astonished at the nomination of Seward" almost immediately, the justice's son wrote. "The result will soon come and I can only hope for the best."

A correspondent for the Democratic *Erie Observer* in Pennsylvania found the political picture incoherent that afternoon. "Babel was never so near being enacted again as in this convocation," he wrote. Advocates from various states all seemed adamant that their favored candidate must win, or the party and country would go to hell. "And so it is, in bar-rooms, at street corners, and wherever the subject is discussed. Greeley is here leading the forces in opposition to Seward. Weed is here leading the Seward forces, and trying his best to check-mate the bran-bread philosopher. . . . On the whole it is about the closest fight we have witnessed for many a day." By contrast, Isaac Platt, the editor and publisher of the *Poughkeepsie Eagle*, thought his man Seward would easily prevail. The "claims of Senator Seward were so much superior to those of other candidates" that there seemed "little difficulty in securing his nomination," Platt noted. In addition, "we felt satisfied that the expediency doctrine"—the idea of choosing a second-rate man because he was more electable—had proven so disastrous for the Whigs in the 1840s and 1850s that the Republicans would not make the same mistake in 1860 by rejecting Seward.

In the chaotic hours before the convention, Carl Schurz and the Wisconsin delegation paid a visit to Thurlow Weed in his opulent parlor at the Richmond House, seeking instructions about advancing the candidate's chances. The idealistic Schurz had looked forward to meeting the high-minded leaders of the New York operation—Governor Edwin D. Morgan, *New York Times* editor Henry J. Raymond, the silver-tongued Evarts, and the essayist and transcendentalist George William

Curtis. Instead, Schurz found Weed surrounded by a group of men, "some of whom did not strike me as desirable companions"—grubby New York politicians, "apparently of the lower sort," who had come to Chicago to employ the blunt tactics that worked back home. These men, Schurz recalled with disgust, "talked very freely about the great services they had rendered or were going to render." They "treated members of other delegations with no end of champagne and cigars, to win them for Seward, if not as their first, then at least as their second choice, to be voted for on the second or third ballot." They hinted to influential delegates that patronage or campaign funds would follow Seward's nomination and election. "They had spent money freely and let everyone understand that there was a great lot more to spend." And the New Yorkers were already making a show of themselves in Chicago by marching with brass bands and Seward banners, demonstrating that their candidate enjoyed passionate support.

But the New Yorkers struck many as obnoxious. They "assume an air of dictation which is at once unwarranted & offensive, & which I think will create a reaction," James Blaine wrote to his mentor and fellow Mainer, Senator William Pitt Fessenden. At the same time, Democratic editors lambasted Seward's operation. Weed had brought with him "a whole squad of roughs and fighting men, under the lead of Tom Hyer, to be used for the promotion of Seward's interests," the *Detroit Free Press* contended. "These men wear badges with his name upon them, and will, no doubt, do efficient service at the fitting opportunity." The editor added scathingly that the aura of violence was appropriate: "John Brown represented him at Harper's Ferry, and it is fit that Tom Hyer should represent him at Chicago."

At the center of it all, Thurlow Weed was using his well-honed political skills and almost magical powers of persuasion to try to overcome resistance to Seward. He "moved as the great captain," Schurz recounted, "with ceaseless activity and noiseless step, receiving their reports and giving new instructions in his peculiar whisper, now and then taking one into the corner of the room for a secret talk, or disappearing with another through a side door for transactions still more secret." Weed, he explained, was "a man of mysterious powers; as a political wizard able to devise and accomplish combinations beyond the conception of ordinary mortals; as the past-master of political intrigue and stratagem; as the profoundest judge of men's abilities, virtues, and failings; as the surest calculator of political chances and results; and as the guide, superintendent, and protecting genius of William H. Seward's political career." Blaine recalled that "Mr. Weed, though unable to make a public speech, was the most persuasive of men in private conversation. He was quiet, gentle, and deferential in manner. He grasped a subject with a giant's strength, presented its strong points, and marshaled its details with extraordinary power." Another man in Chicago that week found that Weed's "motions are as rapid as a rope-dancer's; his eye heretofore dull lights up with an expression both powerful and charming; he speaks quick and short and always in a low tone, smiling you into acquiescence, and looking you into conviction with his sincerity; he calls with his finger, and changes proceedings with a word. Marvelous is his power over man—indescribable it is felt, not seen; you act upon his convictions, not your own, and know not when or how the substitution was made."

There were differing opinions of his character. "His opponents denounced him as a selfish and utterly unscrupulous trickster," Schurz wrote, "while his friends emphasized the fact that he secured offices for ever so many friends, but never any for himself, except a public printer's place which was profitable in revenue, but very modest in rank. In this respect, therefore, his ambition passed as disinterested." Though Weed devoted himself intensely to Seward's advancement and enjoyed a "singular intimacy" with him, "it cannot be said that Thurlow Weed turned Seward's rise in influence and power to his own material advantage." Still, Weed left Schurz with the impression that he would apply ethically dubious means to achieve his political ends, including trading public offices for support. "I may not have been quite just to him in this opinion, but it was strengthened by the spectacle I saw before me at the moment I speak of—the tall man with his cold, impassive face and with the mysterious whisper of his high voice, giving directions to a lot of henchmen, the looks and the talk and the demeanor of many of whom made me feel exceedingly uncomfortable." While Schurz remained a staunch supporter of candidate Seward, he began to fear that a President Seward "might find himself burdened with a mass of obligations incurred in his behalf," which he could not shake off without breaking his word or damaging the public. "I disliked to think of Mr. Seward sitting in the presidential chair with just this Mentor behind him."

Seward's men stressed one point to party insiders: New York had money to spread around, mother's milk to politicians. Those who supported Seward could count on financial aid. All that cash would get out the vote, which in theory would more than offset any damage done by Seward's radical reputation. But some were troubled about how Weed had acquired all that money. Republicans, after all, were promising Americans that they would end the sickening corruption that pervaded the government. But over its winter session, the Republican-run New York legislature had passed a plan dividing New York City into grids for public transportation, and men representing rail lines had evidently bribed politicians to get their share of an extremely lucrative monopoly. Many regarded the whole scheme as Weed's brainchild, and they suspected that kickbacks to the Republican Party had filled the war chest that would fund the politicians who backed Seward.

In a May 6 editorial, the *Detroit Free Press* contended that the "corruption and bribery in the late black republican Legislature of New York, in which Thurlow Weed, Speaker Littlejohn, and other of the chief workers for Seward are deeply implicated," would soon be exposed. The *New York Post*, which opposed Seward, reported that vast sums of money had been spent to secure the passage of major legislation during the winter session—especially on the city railroad bills, which cost assorted interests $250,000 in "money or stocks." A Weed agent was reportedly collecting bribes. New Hampshire newspaper publisher George G. Fogg thought all this reflected poorly on Seward. "He won't steal, himself, but he don't care how much his friends steal," Fogg said. Connecticut senator James Dixon, who favored Edward Bates, complained in a letter a few weeks before the convention that Seward was "surrounded by a corrupt set of rascals," and that a Seward "administration would be the most corrupt the country has ever witnessed."

A Washington correspondent for the Democratic *New York Daily Herald* sniffed out these concerns. But he argued that Seward was so popular with Republicans that they would shrug off any faults. "The convention would not reject him even if he should spit in the faces of the delegates." In the same vein, the writer cynically dismissed the idea that Weed would cause Seward any harm.

> It is objected that his election would inaugurate Thurlow Weed and the Albany lobby at Washington. Many open their eyes in holy horror and look aghast at the doings of the late republican Legislature of the State of New York and ask if that is Sewardism. But these very men, the hour that Weed goes to Washington, rush to his room, and hang upon his words as if they didn't know what to order for dinner without consulting him. The fact is, Weed is a man of talent—almost of genius—and the republican party is not overstocked with brains, and if all that is alleged against him were known to be true, he would still be ruler and king in his party. Whatever other effect the misdeeds of the New York republican Legislature may have, Mr. Weed has no reason to apprehend any injury to himself from them.

In his memoirs, Schurz compared Weed with Mephistopheles, the demon in German folklore who used his fantastical powers to seduce Faust—represented by Seward—with transitory power and glory. Those who knew Weed better understood that he was intensely loyal, warm, and sentimental, that he was willing to put others above himself, and that he profoundly desired to help America survive and prosper.

Weed had forged ahead in the teeth of terrible personal losses. In the spring of 1851, his bright, generous, and energetic thirty-year-old son, James, who was often at his side, died from what doctors deemed an attack of inflammatory rheumatism. "He was so robust and was so seldom ill that we never thought of *his* being the first summoned. But thirty years of exemption should have found us better prepared for chastisement," the heartbroken father wrote, seeking solace in his Calvinist faith. In 1858, he spent months at the bedside of his wife, Catharine, who was dying slowly with excruciating spasms. On April 26, their fortieth wedding anniversary, she took off her ring and said, "I shall not live through the day." But she struggled on in misery until July 3.

When possible, Weed loved to be in his chair at his hearthside each night from ten to eleven thirty, reading for pleasure. His favorite author was Charles Dickens, the great novelist of love, kindness, and redemption, whose *Dombey and Son*, *The Pickwick Papers*, *David Copperfield*, *Bleak House*, "and the rest, he knew almost by heart, having read and re-read them with unabated enjoyment an innumerable number of times." His spontaneous gestures of kindness were legion, some little known.

In one rather Dickensian incident, Weed was sitting in an Albany barber's chair on a cold winter evening in 1846 when he heard the latest city gossip: a physically deformed, ill-natured writing teacher "of intemperate habits" named Chapman had died of delirium tremens, a fact that neighbors were unaware of until alerted by the frantic cries of his four-year-old daughter. A constable dealt with the body and planned to take the girl to an almshouse in the morning. Fifteen minutes after this discovery, Weed was at the tea table in his home, recounting the tale to his wife and children. His wife asked where the little girl was—and was surprised that Weed had not bothered to find out. His son James rose from the table asking if he should not find out what had happened to the girl, and his eldest daughter met Weed at the front door to pursue the investigation. "Now all this was what I hoped, but fearing that others might not share in the spontaneous sympathy which I felt for the offspring of a hateful dwarf, an offspring which, for ought we knew, might inherit his deformities, I imparted the information to my family with apparent indifference," Weed recalled.

Relieved that his family would support his mission of mercy, the political boss set off to locate the child. He found her sitting alone on a stool in the house of a milliner named Mrs. Woolley, where she was staying until the morning. "Mary," said the milliner, "this gentleman wants to see you." A "delicate mite of a girl came over where I was seated and extended her hand to me with a look of confidence and reliance which will never be forgotten," Weed recalled. To his question "Will you go home with me?" she replied promptly, "Yes sir." Mrs. Woolley exclaimed "that she was glad enough to cry, to think that the child would have such a home." At the Weed house, his family was "waiting impatiently, and gave the newcomer as hearty a welcome as if she had been a lost and recovered member of the household, and with that slight frail creature, as she crossed our threshold, came a joy which grew brighter and higher year after year, as her beauties and graces of mind were unfolding, until, like others too good for this world, she was removed to another."

Weed researched the girl's past, recovering a small trunk with a locket containing a miniature portrait of her English-born mother, who had perished in illness. He learned that the mother's first husband had died of cholera, "that she was in person and manners attractive and ladylike, and that she had evidently been accustomed to good society." She was said to have married the dwarfish Chapman to support her children; he had lied that he had money, including a Mississippi plantation. Despite the loss of her parents, Mary "was always cheerful, and sometimes joyous," Weed recounted. A favorite with the neighborhood children, she "derived pleasure from dolls, toys, pictures, and flowers, at intervals; but her constant study was to be diligently useful, to learn household duties, and to help her mother and sister." Before Mary was seven, Weed recalled with pride, she made him a shirt that was exhibited at the American Institute in New York, winning a silver medal as "the best specimen in plain sewing."

Late in 1854, the girl developed a severe lung infection that plagued her for months. "Two days before her death, up to which time she had been very hopeful, she expressed a desire to sit in the rocking-chair, and, turning her feet out of bed, discovered that they were swollen," Weed recalled. "Lifting her eyes to mine with an expression which I too well remember, she quietly said, 'Has it come to this?' Young as she was, she instantly recognized the fatal significance of her discovery." She died on October 28, 1855, at the age of twelve. The supposedly selfish and utterly unscrupulous trickster never forgot the anguish of seeing this beloved child die. Over the span of seven years in the 1850s, Weed had lost his grown son, his young adopted daughter, and his wife of forty years. He threw himself into his work, focusing his aspirations on Seward.

Soon after they arrived in Chicago, the Kansas delegates were invited to a meeting with Weed at the Richmond House. "We had a touch of trepidation as we contemplated being ushered into the presence of this noted political mogul, but we braced up our courage and went," recalled Addison G. Procter, a twenty-one-year-old delegate from the town of Emporia. After they entered his parlor and sat around a large table, Weed quickly "dispelled all terror." He stood by the table and addressed the delegates individually, "calling each of us by name, which appealed to us as something remarkable, seeing that our introduction was so informal." Weed's uncanny ability to connect a face with a name was one of the secrets of his remarkable political success. "He was an attractive man and very interesting."

After complimenting the Kansans on their courageous struggle for freedom, Weed made his pitch for Seward. The Republicans had lost in 1856 with "that boy Frémont" because he "had not one single quality to commend him for the Presidency." The Republicans must not make that mistake again. "We are facing a crisis; there are troublous times ahead of us. We all recognize that. What this country will demand as its chief executive for the next four years is a man of the highest order of executive ability, a man of real statesmanlike qualities, well known to the Country, and of large experience in national affairs." Seward was precisely that man. He had demonstrated superb executive abilities as governor. He had established himself as a statesman and a political philosopher. He had strong experience in foreign relations. "We expect to nominate him on the first ballot," Weed said, "and to go before the Country full of courage and confidence." He thanked the delegates for the call and gave each a friendly handshake at their parting. Weed's confidence was being conveyed back to Auburn, New York. Seward's neighbor John Austin recorded in his diary Tuesday that the candidate "received a telegraphic dispatch from Chicago assuring him everything looks promising."

The Kansans had hardly made it back to their rooms at the Briggs House, Procter recalled, when Horace Greeley entered, "dressed in his light drab suit with soft felt hat which he threw carelessly on our table. A clear red and white complexion, blue eyes and flaxen hair, he looked, as he stood there, for all the world like a well-to-do dairy farmer fresh from his clover field." Greeley thanked them for their work in strife-torn Kansas, then got to the point. "I suppose they are telling you that Seward is the be all and end all of our existence as a party, our great statesman, our profound philosopher, our pillar of cloud by day, our pillar of fire by night," Greeley said, "but I want to tell you boys that in spite of all this you couldn't elect Seward if you could nominate him." Americans would regard Republicans as a purely sectional party if Seward topped the ticket. In that case, the New Yorker would have to sweep the North to win. But he could not carry New Jersey, Pennsylvania, Indiana, or Iowa, Greeley insisted, "and I will bring to you representative men from each of these states who will confirm what I say."

Greeley did precisely that. Samuel J. Kirkwood, governor of Iowa; Henry S. Lane, running for governor of Indiana; and Andrew G. Curtin, running for governor of Pennsylvania, all came and spoke against Seward. The "bright looking, enthusiastic, young" Curtin, forty-five, made a particularly strong impression on Procter. He told the Kansans that James Buchanan had carried Pennsylvania by fifty thousand votes—a deficit the Republicans would have to make up to prevail. "I could not win with Mr. Seward as our candidate," he insisted. Procter was struck by the effort Greeley was putting into stopping Seward. "I doubt if Horace Greeley slept three consecutive hours during the entire session of that convention," he recalled.

Greeley was going around saying that Seward could not even win New York in November and claiming that twenty of the state's delegates were against him. "He misled many fair minded men," Weed later informed Seward. "He was not scrupulous." A handful of prominent New Yorkers had come to Chicago solely to work against Seward, among them lawyer David Dudley Field, who joined the forces backing Judge Bates. "The traitors from New-York were few in number, but most violent and unscrupulous," Weed wrote. His fellow New York editor Isaac Platt found Greeley's campaign contemptible. "In his zeal here," wrote Platt, Greeley "gave a clear exposition of his treachery to the principles he had advocated for ten years past. While he talked of Bates he surely knew that his nomination would completely demoralize and ruin the party and its principles, that success, were it possible in such a candidate, would be worse than defeat, because the victory would be a fruitless one. But he cared nothing for all that."

Despite Greeley's fierce lobbying, Weed believed he could put Seward over the top by winning over roughly one-third of the 150 delegates who came to Chicago free from state instructions and empowered to vote for any candidate. Alternatively, he might flip delegations committed to a candidate by making deals. He tried various means of doing so—including buying support with campaign cash and shopping the vice presidency around. Montgomery Blair recalled that the Seward forces proposed putting his elder brother, Frank Blair, on the ticket, but the Blairs refused to abandon Bates. Should Seward fall short on the first ballot, Weed hoped to gather sufficient delegates on the second—men like the eight Illinois delegates who supported Seward but were compelled to vote for Lincoln initially. But none of this was going to be easy.

Weed tried to recruit the Indiana delegation through Henry S. Lane, though the gubernatorial hopeful had been out speaking against Seward to the Kansas delegation and others. Lane's wife, who was in Chicago, recalled years later that Weed took her husband out one evening "and pleaded with him to lead the Indiana delegation over to Seward, saying they would send enough money from New York to ensure his election for Governor, and carry the State later for the New York candidate." Lane "indignantly refused," according to his wife. He evidently feared that, money or no money, Seward's name at the top of the ticket would spell defeat. "Elections in the city of New York may be carried with money, but it has but little influence upon the minds of people who inhabit this side of the mountains," a correspondent for the *Wabash Express* in Terre Haute, Indiana, wrote in his Tuesday report. New Yorker Platt found the Indiana delegation's posture infuriating, writing that "few pens could do justice" to its stubbornness. "Had the occasion been a national agricultural fair the first impression of any outsider would have been that the state had resolved to bear off the premium in the exhibition of *asses*, especially on account of the superiority of their *braying*. It was clear that they had been sent to perform one duty only, and that was to howl against Mr. Seward, that he could not carry the state."

Recognizing that Indiana refused to budge toward Seward, the Lincoln men had been lobbying the state's delegates since Saturday to make Lincoln their first choice, rather than Bates or McLean—evidently with some success. At its caucus Tuesday morning, the delegation conducted a straw poll. Seward got one vote, and Chase one. McLean got "four or five," the *Wabash Express* reported. The remaining delegates were "about equally divided between Bates and Lincoln," though the writer predicted that Lincoln ultimately would be the choice "of a majority, if not all our delegation." If Seward was not the nominee, he thought, Lincoln would be.

Worst of all, Weed faced vexing and unexpected problems with the crucial Pennsylvania delegation. Pennsylvania was one of the places where the radicalism of the Republicans carried such a bad odor that the state party did not even dare carry the name; its delegation came to Chicago as the representatives of the People's Party, a fusion of anti-Democratic elements, rather than as Republicans. (Similarly, the New Jersey delegation represented the Opposition Party.) But Simon Cameron had repeatedly promised Seward his support, and his brother and son were on hand to enact his wishes, along with Alexander Cummings, editor of the Philadelphia *Evening Bulletin*. Unfortunately, none of the three, when pressed in Chicago, would say anything about supporting Seward on later ballots. "They did, however, assure me that [Cameron] would be kept in the field until I could see them again," Weed later told Seward. As for now, most of the Pennsylvania delegates were against Seward; "every friend" of Cameron, "inside and out, were violent and denunciatory—all saying you could not carry the state." The Seward forces considered all this "cold ingratitude," since Weed had sent Alexander K. McClure, chairman of the Republican State Central Committee, "material aid" to help carry the elections in Philadelphia that spring.

Even in New England, long considered a Seward stronghold, there was trouble. Senator James F. Simmons of Rhode Island—later expelled from the Senate for corruption—"was here very hostile" to Seward, Weed reported. In early April in Rhode Island, a radical candidate for governor associated with Seward had been throttled by William Sprague IV, a wealthy industrialist backed by Democrats, Know-Nothings, and conservative Republicans. Combined with a shockingly narrow victory for Republicans in Connecticut, that sent chills through the ranks of Republican politicians, to the delight of such Democratic newspapers as the *Rock Island Argus* in Illinois: "All honor to glorious *little* Rhode Island! She has broken the back bone of New England sectional disunion abolition know-nothingism, and drove a wedge which will split that party 'from turret to foundation stone.'" The Democratic *Providence Post* read the result as a direct repudiation of "higher lawism"—the values of William Seward. "It was most emphatically a contest between Union and Disunion—between Loyalty and Treason—between Conservatism and Radicalism," the *Post* declared.

Thirty-one-year-old Charles C. Nourse, an Iowa delegate from Des Moines, was one of many who worried about the damage Seward would do the party in November. "To me, Governor Seward was a dangerous radical. He had been intimately associated for over a decade with the extreme opponents of slavery," Nourse recalled. "He had used expressions in his speeches that seemed to us then to indicate he was in favor of abolition or emancipation." He was certainly poison in the southern counties of Iowa that Nourse knew well. There, Seward's support of Catholics and hostility toward the American Party had offended many Know-Nothing voters.

Finding so much unrest, Boston lawyer and gubernatorial candidate John A. Andrew set out to discover who might be more electable than Seward. Heading a committee of delegates from Massachusetts and other New England states, Andrew met that Tuesday with the representatives of four key "doubtful" states—Pennsylvania, New Jersey, Indiana, and Illinois. As New Jersey lawyer Thomas H. Dudley recalled, Andrew informed them that Massachusetts and other New England states favored Seward, but they cared most about victory in November. If New England's delegates could be persuaded that another candidate had a better chance to win, they would gladly support him. But the anti-Seward forces could not yet say who that might be. "You delegates all say that William H. Seward cannot carry the doubtful States," Andrew said. "When we ask you who can, you from New Jersey give us the name of William L. Dayton, a most excellent and worthy man in every way, and entirely satisfactory to us; but when we go to Pennsylvania, they name Simon Cameron; and Indiana and Illinois, Abraham Lincoln. Now it is impossible to have all these three candidates." Unless the four states could agree on an alternative, "we from New England will vote for our choice, William H. Seward of New York." The delegates found his statement powerful, but they were still unwilling to ditch their favorite candidate. "To break from them and vote for some one else was not a very easy or pleasant thing to do," Dudley noted.

With the convention's opening only a day away, Weed realized that far more delegates were skittish about Seward than he had expected. "The Seward men are not a little frightened at the earnest opposition to him from all quarters except New York," the *New York Daily Herald* reported in a dispatch that Tuesday. On Monday, Seward's nomination had seemed inevitable, the newspaper wrote, "but many of his former supporters are beginning to think that it would be equivalent to party suicide."

THE WINNING MAN—ABRAHAM LINCOLN, the *Chicago Press and Tribune* headlined its editorial that morning. Aimed at the delegates now thronging the city, the editorial conceded that Seward was "the first choice of perhaps a majority of the rank and file of the party," and that Cameron, Chase, Bates, Wade, McLean, and Maine senator Fessenden had much to recommend them. But the fifty-one-year-old Lincoln, "without the ripe experience of Seward, the age and maturity of Bates and McLean, or the fire of Fessenden and Wade, has that rare and happy combination of qualities" that made him their superior—for he was the best compromise candidate. "Seward men, Bates men, Cameron men and Chase men can all accept him as their second choice."

Lincoln had never announced he was seeking the presidency and had never pledged anything in return for support, the editorial argued. Hence, he could enter the campaign with "no clogs, no embarrassment." While he was a strong opponent of slavery, "nature has given him the wise conservativism" of mind; he instinctively hated to sow ill will and tended to avoid strident language. His support for moderate tariffs—a crucial point with Pennsylvania, which was dependent on manufacturing—was acceptable to all voters outside the South. Born in Kentucky, a border slave state with conservative leanings, he "had never departed" from the founding principles taught him from birth. Though he carried no stain of Know-Nothingism, he was acceptable to most followers of the American Party, because he celebrated the Founders and the Declaration of Independence. And given his incredible rise from poverty, "there is enough of romance and poetry in his life to fill all the land with shouting and song. Honest Old Abe!" In sum, the paper argued, "Mr. Lincoln *can be elected*." Conveniently left off the list, of course, were Lincoln's recurring defeats and his infinitesimal executive experience—limited to running a two-man law office.

While anyone could see the newspaper was blatantly partial to Lincoln, its arguments—repeated incessantly by the Lincoln men—wormed their way into delegates' ears. To be sure, the Illinois men could not deny that the Seward forces were impressive. "The New York men were more cultured and scholarly than we," recalled one Illinoisan. "They were better and more appropriately dressed for such an occasion. They wore their neat business suits, to which they were accustomed; while we, especially those of us who were from the country, were dressed in our 'Sunday clothes,' to which we were not accustomed." But the Lincoln men believed they could countermand that effect. "Being upon our own ground, in our own State, in a city that was new, and living among those who, like ourselves, were all from somewhere, we had a certain advantage over the New York men, for we knew better how to reach men from all parts of the country."

On that day before the convention began, Lincoln was in the thick of the fight, thought William Butler, the orthographically challenged treasurer of Illinois. There had been "no material change in Sentiment of public opinion amongst deligates Since yesterday," he reported to Lincoln in a hastily scrawled letter from the Tremont House. "The Strife between dilegates from New York & Pennsylvania Still rage high." Butler noted that Thaddeus Stephens, an acerbic congressman from Pennsylvania who had been born with a club foot, was spreading the word that the state "was lost" with Seward as the nominee, but that the party "Can Carry it by 20,000" with Judge McLean or Lincoln heading the ticket. Stephens was pledged to Cameron "but frankly Says it will not do." Cameron could not carry the convention, and his delegates would have to look for an alternative after an early ballot or two.

In one of the more striking developments that Tuesday, New York's squat, fat, and fidgety senator Preston King visited Butler that morning and "braught with him" a Mr. Street of Oneida County in Upstate New York. "After interducing him Mr King left." Street "entered into what he termed a confidential Conversation," offering a deal. If Lincoln would consent to having his name placed on the ticket with Seward, $100,000—a vast sum in 1860—could be placed "in the proper hands" to carry Illinois and Indiana. "I promptly told him under no Circumstances Could your name be used in a Second place on the Ticket," Butler informed Lincoln. Though Butler quickly rejected the Seward team's offer, the big dollar amounts being thrown around rattled him. "I am a little afraid of this eliment," he confessed; "to [what] extent it may be used I Cant say."

Disappointingly, two Chicago editors—Mayor Long John Wentworth, of the *Chicago Democrat*, and Charles L. Wilson, of the *Chicago*

Journal—were now "both against you," Butler noted. A piece in Wentworth's *Chicago Democrat* touting Seward's chances particularly upset the Lincoln men. "Wentworth has come out in his paper for Seward this morning, Weed having made a bargain with him. This will hurt Lincoln as he declares Seward can carry our state," Chicago German leader Herman Kreismann wrote that day to congressman Elihu B. Washburne. "I for one think [Wentworth] is a 'dog, and unworthy to be called a member of our party,'" fumed Lincoln's Kansas friend, Mark Delahay. Lincoln supporter John M. Palmer spotted Wentworth going "around the hotels talking for Seward and endeavoring to discredit Lincoln," until the Lincoln team "detailed a man to follow him around and denounce him." On that Tuesday, Butler confessed that he did not know what to make of it all. "I feel much incouraged though you Must be prepared for defeat," he told Lincoln. "I will Keep you advised as well as I Can Others I persume knows more than I & will wright." He wrapped up hurriedly. "I must Stop evrything all is Confusion & noise."

For his part, Delahay still believed that Seward would fall short of the delegates needed—and that Lincoln was as strong as any alternative. A straw poll conducted on a train from Columbus, Delahay reported, found 73 votes for Seward to 65 for Lincoln, with only 15 for Chase, 10 for Bates, and 4 for McLean. But the Kansan feared that the Seward team had been energized by the arrival of the great trains packed with his supporters. "I Cant say any thing more like encouragement now than in my last; the large recruits by the trains last Evening have proven rather a Stimulant to the Seward men not that they have, as we can perceive, made him any stronger, but they come in such Great numbers that they have a head quarters at Every Hotel," he wrote Lincoln. They could reach into all the delegations.

Delahay was also worried about pro-Seward Southern delegations, which struck many observers as shady. In a dispatch sent that night, Horace Greeley's *New-York Tribune* flatly warned that the Texas delegation was "bogus," comprised of men who lived far from the Lone Star State. The New Orleans *Picayune* later reported that the Texas delegation was "got up" in Grand Haven, Michigan, a state where

Seward was immensely strong, and that "not one" of its members "has ever been within one thousand miles of Texas." Delahay seethed that "if any body is nominated by this species of fraud, I think it will give sufficient offence to Defeat the party—many Republicans swear they will not support any man nominated under such circumstances."

Meanwhile, rumors spread that the Blairs were now trying to get Bates on the ticket as vice president, which if true might well have finished off Lincoln. "How it will end," Delahay told Lincoln, "I cant predict—I am quite worn out and am unable to write a letter. I have lost so much rest." Delahay stressed that he did "not dispair by any means. But believing that good sense may ultimately prevail, I am hopeful and shall continue on," conducting himself as Lincoln had urged: "I have given no offinse, But have made many friends."

Operating on a much smaller scale than Seward's forces, the Lincoln men received an important infusion of help Tuesday, not from the arrival of a thousand supporters aboard monster trains but from the appearance of one unheralded traveler. Orville Hickman Browning, fifty-four, had left his thriving town of Quincy, located on the Mississippi River, at 5:30 p.m. Monday, then transferred to a sleeping car at Galesburg, finally rolling into Chicago Tuesday. The lawyer might have seemed an improbable Lincoln advocate. Like Greeley and the Blairs, he personally favored Edward Bates. In Browning's view, the slave-state judge offered the party significant political advantages. He would "strengthen our organization in the South, and remove any apprehension in the South of any hostile purpose on the part of Republicans to the institutions of the South—to restore fraternal regard among the different sections of the Union—to bring to our support the old whigs in the free states, who have not yet fraternized with us, and to give some check to the ultra tendencies of the Republican party." But Browning's admiration of Bates did not seem to faze David Davis. Like the other Illinois delegates, the Quincy lawyer was bound by the state party's instructions to back Lincoln through at least the first ballot. Until then, Davis believed, Browning's eloquence might do the cause some real good.

Indeed, the moment Browning checked in with Illinois headquarters, Davis grabbed him and Tom Marshall—an Illinois lawyer friend—and hustled over to the Briggs House to visit the pro-Seward Maine delegates. At the members' request, Browning shared his insights about Lincoln. He had met Lincoln in 1836, as a fellow Whig legislator, and had often crossed paths with him on the legal circuit. They were both from Kentucky. Among other things, Browning stressed Lincoln's personal story, his extraordinary rise from poverty. The trio then called on the New Hampshire delegation, and at night visited the rooms of the Massachusetts men, where again Browning spoke.

The Virginia delegation was also on the itinerary. Meeting for the first time Tuesday, the Virginians decided to take a straw vote, which revealed that Seward had "more friends than all the others," reported a correspondent for that state's *Wheeling Daily Intelligencer*. Soon after, the Lincoln men asked to meet with the delegation. Five or six men—Browning probably among them—"urged most warmly the claims and qualifications of the 'gallant Abe,' the man 'whose first act had been to maul rails and whose last had been to maul Douglas.' Our delegation listened to them long and patiently and weighed every argument they put forth." There was something compelling about Lincoln's story and the way these men told it. "At the close of the conference, there was a decided good feeling for Lincoln," the correspondent wrote. "I think that the friends of Seward and Bates, if they find the nomination of either impossible or impolitic, will go strong for Lincoln. I should not be a bit surprised to see Lincoln the nominee of the Convention."

The day's work confirmed Lincoln's sagacity in selecting Browning as one of his four at-large delegates, trusting that he would do more for Lincoln as part of the delegation than he would have outside the fold. "Prospects very good," Jesse K. Dubois reported to Lincoln in a telegram, adding, "We are doing everything Illinois men acting nobly Browning doing his duty." Indeed, Davis and Dubois felt increasingly optimistic as they canvassed the delegates. While state leaders were busy weighing their options, most of the rank and file seemed to like Lincoln. The two fired off another telegram, informing their friend that they were "moving heaven & Earth" for him. They added hopefully, "nothing will beat us but old fogy politicians the heart of the delegates are with us."

Murat Halstead, making the rounds on his first day in Chicago, reported that the great "curiosity of the town"—aside from the Wigwam itself—could be found at the Dearborn Street headquarters of Schurz's Wisconsin delegation. Visitors flocked there to view a seven-foot-long, forty-pound bowie knife, manufactured by the New England Cutlery Company, of Wallingford, Connecticut. It was a gift to the Wisconsin delegates from the slave state of Missouri, in tribute to congressman John Potter, a man who had proved himself willing to fight for his beliefs—literally—in Washington.

Through most of the 1850s, Southerners had formed the impression that Northerners were effete cowards who would back down if challenged. But a new breed of populist Republicans had been winning elections—men determined to give their opponents a taste of their own medicine. Republicans were now fiercely resisting Democrats who had long resorted to intimidation and censorship to get their way. The Maine-born Potter was one. When a fistfight erupted on the House floor on February 6, 1858, the Wisconsin congressman got smack in the middle of it. Grabbing the back of the head of Mississippi congressman William Barksdale to punch him in the face, he was astonished to find the firebrand's hair come off in his hand, revealing that the pugnacious Mississippian wore a toupee. In early 1860, when Southerners made noises about silencing his Illinois colleague Owen Lovejoy, Potter fiercely—if not offensively—defended the abolitionist's right to address the House. Hotheaded Democrat Roger Pryor of Virginia rose and challenged Potter to a duel, which Potter quickly accepted. When the Wisconsin man named "bowie-knives" as his weapon of choice, however, the Virginian promptly backed down, rejecting such a "vulgar, barbarous, and inhuman" form of dueling as beneath his dignity. The nickname of John "Bowie-Knife" Potter was born.

The giant knife in Chicago bore the inscription PRESENTED TO JOHN F. POTTER BY THE REPUBLICANS OF MISSOURI. On the opposite side was a motto: "Will always keep a 'Pryor' engagement." Republicans relished this symbol of their growing defiance of the Democrats. "A very pretty compliment from southern men to northern pluck," wrote a correspondent for the *Buffalo Daily Courier*, who saw it lying on top of a piano. "It is a rather significant instrument, and means a good deal more than it says," wrote a correspondent for the *Daily Gazette* of Janesville, Wisconsin. One thing it meant was that people were increasingly seeing violence as the way to resolve political disagreements.

Halstead was struck by the crowds in Chicago, vastly bigger than those in Charleston and Baltimore had been. "The Tremont House is so crammed that it is with much difficulty people get about in it from one room to another," he wrote. The most noteworthy figures there, he reported, were the Bates men Francis P. Blair and Horace Greeley. "The way Greeley is stared at as he shuffles about, looking as innocent as ever, is itself a sight. Whenever he appears, there is a crowd gaping at him, and if he stops to talk a minute with someone who wishes to consult him as the oracle, the crowd become as dense as possible, and there is the most eager desire to hear the words of wisdom that are supposed to fall on such occasions." Fed up with Greeley's incessant pontification, one wag took a silk Seward badge and discreetly pinned it to the back of the editor's white coat. Numerous newspapers made fun of the editor for racing around Chicago for hours with the "irrepressible badge" on his back.

As the evening came on, heavy drinking commenced. Soon after arriving in Chicago, a *Cincinnati Enquirer* reporter overheard a man in a shop speculating that the visitors must be Democrats, given the size of crowds packing the saloons. But "the truth is," he wrote, "the Republican delegates and outsiders are demonstrating, by unceasing practice, that though they may dislike slavery, they have no dislike of 'Old Bourbon' that is made under its auspices."

Hordes of thirsty politicians also swarmed into the hotel rooms that served as states' headquarters. Iowa's was a notable example.

William Penn Clarke, chairman of the delegation, harbored political ambitions, having nearly won a U.S. Senate seat in 1858, and he had taken care to secure an impressive room at the Tremont House, on the theory that his hospitality would win him support. Unfortunately, Iowa delegate Nourse observed, some of the state's delegates "liked wines and Kentucky Bourbon more than was good for them," and these "gay lords had plenty of encouragement to indulge their fondness for spirits."

Clarke himself, who did not imbibe much, found that his guests "ordered such liquors as they desired and had the costs charged to the 'Iowa Headquarters.'" With the delegates deciding the fate of the nation, they did not trouble themselves "to think of such prosy matters" as paying for their beverages. "In the furious excitement just preceding and following the nomination they totally forgot that they had ordered or were ordering all sorts of high priced liquors." When the convention was over, the Tremont House presented Clarke with a staggering bill. "It took his breath," Nourse noted, "but he had to pay it and he realized as never before the benefits of fame among politicians."

That night, some fifteen thousand people headed for the Wigwam for a "magnificent rally," the *Press and Tribune* reported, "exceeding in numbers and enthusiasm any previous meeting" in the great building. About five thousand people had to be turned away. With their convention now just hours away, Republicans spoke about the serious challenges ahead. Without naming Seward, Indiana's Godlove S. Orth stressed that the convention must choose a nominee who could triumph in November. "Occasionally I hear some irrepressible Republican say they must go for this or that man. They say defeat is better than victory without their particular man. I don't believe in the doctrine. . . . I go in to win," Orth declared. New York militia general James W. Nye, by contrast, praised Seward immoderately, to the point of likening him to Jesus Christ, declaring that he "will be for this nation 'the resurrection and the life' of freedom." But whoever was nominated, Nye said, the forces of freedom faced a terrible struggle ahead. "Every inch will be disputed. Every inch of ground has to be soaked in the life blood of patriotism. . . . I speak to you therefore, fellow-citizens, with a heart burdened with anxiety." General Nye called on old men to share their wisdom, and young men to "buckle on your armor and march to the battle field of glory. I invite you not with implements of war. I bid you arm yourselves with the freeman's privilege and the tyrant's foe, the ballot." The retreating Democratic Party, he promised, "will fall before you for fear of your power, and run from the sense of their own wrongs."

At the Richmond House, merchant Simeon Draper and shipping magnate Moses H. Grinnell threw a lavish dinner party for the New York delegates. The banner of the life-sized Seward that had hung at Bloomer's Hotel in Buffalo was now on display at the Richmond, and his acolytes were in high spirits. An Associated Press dispatch that night reported that Seward seemed to be in decent shape. "The chances appear to be," the dispatch said, "that the superior tack of Seward's friends and the distracted state of the opposition will carry him through successfully." Despite warnings that Seward would damage Republicans in some states, his men were staunchly refusing to give up, rejecting a shameful abdication of principle for the "sake of spoils," the *New York Times* reported. Even so, they were "compelled to acknowledge to themselves that the speck" of opposition "has become a cloud, and may yet be a storm, pregnant with disaster to themselves and ruin to the party." A similar metaphor occurred to a *Cincinnati Enquirer* correspondent, writing at 9:00 p.m. He thought that Seward was "decidedly in the foreground," but he believed there was "a very black cloud in the distance." The reporter was distinctly unimpressed, though, with the Lincoln men's sales pitch. "His principal argument is that he split rails a good while ago, and his followers bring that forward as a convincing argument that he is 'the man of the people.'"

Well into the night, delegates and their friends paraded down Chicago's streets. Lincoln supporters marched behind Gilmore's Boston Band, while the "Irrepressibles" followed Chicago's Light Guard Band, a superb group that featured many German immigrant musicians. Thousands watched them, the *New York Times* noted, "attracted by the music, and the frequent orations delivered at every corner." Lincoln enjoyed something of a home-field advantage, as Chicago men hung his banners across the streets. The horse-drawn city buses were festooned with "Lincoln flags and Lincoln tokens."

Amidst the music and raucous noise, some visitors tried to grab some sleep before the convention opened. Nathaniel McLean finally obtained a hotel room by bunking with two other men. "The last thing I remember was sundry yells given by some excited person in the hall below, but what about I cannot tell. Whiskey was probably the cause." At the Tremont, Halstead's noisy roommates "were in magnificent condition" that night. "They were 'glorious'—'o'er all the ills of life victorious,' and, to use the expression which is here in everybody's mouth every minute, they were irrepressible until a late hour." Early Wednesday morning, Halstead was awakened by an angry debate among them, "and rubbing my eyes, discovered that they were sitting up in bed playing cards to see who should pay for gin cocktails all around, the cocktails being an indispensable preliminary to breakfast."

With the hour of the convention fast approaching, "the agitation of the city is exceedingly great," Halstead reported. Drunk, sober, or hungover, thousands turned their eyes to the Wigwam.

Wednesday, May 16, 1860

Chapter 10: Things Is Working

Wednesday opened warm and clear, and the hotel dining rooms were humming with people having breakfast. Hotelkeepers estimated there were more people in Chicago now than during the National Fair in 1859, when some thirty thousand guests flooded the city. At the Tremont House alone, there were fifteen hundred people "stowed away," as Murat Halstead put it. Outside, people were scurrying. "Our street cars run in every direction loaded with passengers, while there is hardly a carriage, hack or wheeled vehicle of any kind that has not been brought into active and constant requisition," Chicago's *Western Railroad Gazette* noted. When a reporter for the *Wheeling Daily Intelligencer* of Virginia left his hotel, he found himself plunged into "thousands and tens of thousands of people on the street." Every five minutes, he heard the shrieking whistle of an arriving or departing train and could "see a great many people with valises and carpet sacks in their hands, hurrying here and there." Van Amburgh's Circus was running sideshows along the streets, while Sands' Ale wagons, Joy & Frisbie ice wagons, and assorted bakery wagons, all accompanied by bands, competed for space with taxi buggies, family carriages, and horse-drawn rail cars. A cashier at one saloon told a reporter for the *North Iowa Times* that he expected to rake in $3,000 for the week through billiards, cigars, and drinks—and that there were plenty of first-class establishments doing just as much business.

Reporters who had visited Chicago just a few years earlier were stunned by the transformation. "It seems almost fabulous, when we reflect, that all this has been done even in our recollection. That these extended streets, those marble faced private residences, those immense business houses, the chequered net work of rail roads, this hum of busy life that is every where present, have been created—sprung into reality —within the last twenty-five or thirty years," wrote a correspondent for the *Wabash Express* of Terre Haute, Indiana. "It is wonderful, gloriously wonderful, and illustrates not only the energy, the will and the determination of the Anglo-American race, but the advantages of free institutions." The city's evolution was "a marvel," the *Cleveland Daily Leader* declared. "The surprise of strangers at the growth and grandeur of Chicago was universal."

Some visitors had qualms. A *Boston Evening Transcript* reporter observed that the booming metropolis was "not half finished, and everything about it bears the marks of unhealthy development." Hovels squatted alongside the splendid new warehouses and homes, and "the streets are in wretched condition." But the best of Chicago was impressive. A man touring the city with members of the Pennsylvania delegation marveled at the posh residential street of Michigan Avenue, paved and one hundred feet wide, with two beautiful rows of shade trees and "scores of palatial dwellings occupied by the wealthy citizens." The houses looked out on the blue of Lake Michigan. "A more desirable location for a home would be hard to find." At the upscale shopping district of Lake Street, the touring group discovered workers ratcheting up an entire block of buildings on the street's south side. "Imagine a block of five-storied brick houses—two hundred feet in length—being raised some five feet with several thousand Jack screws, by the aid of a steam engine stationed at the edge of the pavement, the people in the stores selling goods as though nothing strange were occurring—such a sight we beheld."

Chicago "has had its ups and downs, in street grades and other things as well," Simon P. Hanscom of the *New York Daily Herald* reported, "but its broad avenues, magnificent buildings, splendid shops, and fine private residences, show that there is a solid foundation for this miraculous prosperity." The writer found this bursting city a perfect expression of the American character. "Here may be seen, as in a stereoscope, all our strong points and all our weak points—all our headlong haste to be rich—all our contempt for old forms and ceremonies—all our ridiculous parvenu affectation—all our real energy, enterprise and perseverance, opposed to which no difficulties are insurmountable—all our extravagance at the bung and our economy at the spigot—in fact, all the idiosyncrasies of Young America may be summed up in the single word Chicago." The residents appeared to be as excited as the visitors. In Chicago, Hanscom noted, "the mania for politics is universal," and the population "seems a mercurial, restless one, always looking for a new excitement and plunging into it headlong. . . . Even the women and children talk politics along with their candy and crochet."

In the halls of the Tremont House, Halstead observed, well-dressed men were packed so tightly that they were "crushing each other's ribs, tramping each other's toes, and titillating each other with the gossip of the day." Though virulently anti-Republican, the *Chicago Times* described them as "perhaps as fine a looking body of men as was ever assembled in the Union. No one who would see them would ever suppose they entertained their extravagant and dangerous political sentiments that they pretend to believe in." Arriving in Chicago that morning after a night of little sleep, thanks to the boisterous Republicans aboard his train, a correspondent for the *Quad-City Times* of Davenport, Iowa, found the place "positively black with Republicans from all sections of the North; the hotels are running over with them to such an extent that it is next to impossible to find a sleeping place; the private houses are full, the saloons and restaurants are full, and if one may judge from the haul of Ohio delegates made by Long John's police force the other night, the houses of a questionable character are likewise plentifully supplied with them." As if the crowds were not big enough already, excursion trains loaded with visitors kept arriving all morning, afternoon, and night. Earlier in the week, guests had appealed to hotelkeepers for single rooms. Now, newcomers were reduced to begging, "Oh, give me a *cot*!"

Halstead encountered men gathered in little groups, chatting and whispering conspiratorially, "as if the fate of the country depended on their immediate delivery of the mighty political secrets with which their imaginations are big. There are a thousand rumors afloat, and things of incalculable moment are communicated to you confidentially, at intervals of five minutes." Halstead found the gossip ludicrous. Many were saying that morning, for example, that Ohio dark horse Benjamin Wade was on the rise, along with Abraham Lincoln. "The Bates movement, the McLean movement, the Cameron movement, the Banks movement, are all nowhere. They have gone down like lead in the mighty waters," Halstead wrote. "'Old Abe' and 'Old Ben' are in the field against Seward. Abe and Ben are representatives of the conservatism, the respectability, the availability, and all that sort of thing." He dismissed the talk that Lincoln might be the nominee as typical "twaddle." A correspondent for the rival *Cincinnati Enquirer* was astounded by the little-known politicians being touted in Chicago. "This is the city where they raise large brick houses six and seven feet from their foundations without breaking a pane of glass or cracking the plaster of a single room," he wrote. "That is a great feat, but nothing to the feats attempted to be practiced here in raising small men into high position."

In his report published in the *Cincinnati Commercial* that morning —so juicy that all fifty copies delivered to the Tremont House were quickly snapped up—Halstead exposed a devious plot in the Ohio delegation. It seemed that Wade was using the convention to wrest political power from his Senate colleague Salmon P. Chase. Many of the delegates, Halstead reported, planned to use the "unit rule"—under which the state would unite on a single candidate for each ballot—to vote for Chase on the initial ballot, making a mere show of support, only to switch to Wade thereafter. The article had a "telling effect," James Elliott wrote to his friend Chase. Now alerted to the conspiracy and fearful that Wade would derail their man's political future, Chase supporters blocked the unit rule and threatened to defect to Seward if the Wade forces persisted—something that might well set off a pro-Seward stampede in the convention. Wade's supporters were so horrified by that prospect that they quickly backed off, and instead tried to persuade the influential Halstead to support their man. "Great efforts were made to get an expression from him that he favored Wade over Seward, but they were unsuccessful," Elliott wrote. Kentucky's Cassius M. Clay, who favored Chase if his own candidacy faltered, fumed that "Bluff Ben" Wade was a "trickster . . . who envied Chase's high character and fame" and "set up for himself to divide the Ohio delegation, and thus throw Chase out of the contest."

In sum, the Ohio delegation was hopelessly split, and thus unable to wield much influence in Chicago. Chase had none of Lincoln's gift for mending fences and unifying Republicans in his backyard. "If you had been backed up by Ohio as Seward was by New York or Lincoln by Illinois, your nomination could easily have been procured," Elliott told Chase. Instead, another friend wrote, the state's "position was humiliating to Ohioans—there she stood a Giant—fettered—clothed in the garments of a Dwarf—without influence over each other, or respect from abroad." As another correspondent put it to Chase, the delegation "hatched wooden eggs."

In his *Chicago Democrat*, mayor Long John Wentworth noted that veteran politicians had been pouring in from Washington all week, many of them fearful of a Seward nomination and a number supporting Senator Wade. But Wentworth noted something else interesting: "Mr. Lincoln was either the first or second choice of every man." Rather than further inflame divisions in the party, Wentworth recommended that Seward choose Lincoln as his running mate, or Lincoln choose Seward, and be done with it. "We are satisfied that Gov. Seward's friends will go for Lincoln before they will for Wade. And we are also satisfied that the Wade men will go for Lincoln before they will for Seward," he wrote. The sticking point, of course, was that neither Seward nor Lincoln was willing to relinquish the top slot.

The *Cincinnati Daily Press* urged readers to be wary of these speculative rumors, produced, the paper said, only because journalists on the ground needed to report *something*. "The friend of some candidate, say Seward, treats them to a 'nipper' and every thing seems to them rose-colored, and straightaway they report to their metropolitan journal that Seward stock is high; that his friends have plenty of money and free whisky. Anon, a sore headache follows, and they pronounce Seward on the wane, and that his nomination will be a great affliction to the party," the editor quipped. "A mild tonic with a quiet Wade man brings a report that 'Wade is looming up,' and is prominent in the back ground, as a candidate to fall back on for a compromise. Then a supper and fixings, with a lot of Bates managers from St. Louis, causes the report to be sent specially over the wires that Bates stock is rising, and there is a disposition to select a conservative national candidate, and to nominate to win."

In such preconvention conjecture, few were touting the prospects of the party's narcissistic 1856 nominee, John C. Frémont. His California friends, reading the mood in Chicago, effectively pulled the plug on Wednesday. They distributed an April 12 letter written by Frémont in which he declared, with a note of wounded pride, that he would have no interest in the party's 1860 nomination if he were required to fight for it. In the beginning of the 1856 contest, "if I had neither political prestige, nor party organization, I had, at least, no organized bodies opposed to my nomination. Now the case is wholly different," he wrote with some bitterness. Of course, this left open his acceptance of the nomination if the convention could agree on no other candidate. But it seemed unlikely the convention would ignore all the contenders, and few politicians on the scene seemed terribly ruffled by the idea that Frémont was out of the running. With a serious chance of winning the White House in November, Republicans would not squander the nomination on a sacrificial lamb again.

The convention was set to start at noon—on the fifty-ninth birthday of the party's hero, William H. Seward. The *Racine Democrat*, in Wisconsin, theorized that the Republican National Committee, dominated by Seward supporters, had chosen this day purposely when it decided to move the convention up from its scheduled June opening. "The change of time was cooked up in New York by his political friends . . . to retrieve his falling popularity with his party," the *Democrat* held. Others read the date simply as an omen that Seward was destined to capture the party's crown. Just as strikingly, the Democratic convention in Charleston had opened on April 23, the birthday of its favorite, Stephen Douglas, a fact that political writers had made much of earlier in the year. That had turned out to be no charm for Douglas. "Since the [Democratic] Convention has proven a dismal fizzle, we have heard but little concerning Douglas' birth-day," the *White Cloud Kansas Chief* observed. "We would call this little circumstance to the attention of members of other parties, who are indulging in a similar species of nonsense." Meanwhile, several newspapers noted wryly that the Democrats were set to reconvene in Baltimore on June 18—the anniversary of Napoleon's debacle at Waterloo.

The *Press and Tribune* continued its hard push for Lincoln. Determined to pound home the basic points to delegates, the paper Wednesday morning simply reran its Tuesday editorial, THE WINNING MAN—ABRAHAM LINCOLN. The paper also announced that it had hired "a competent corps of short-hand writers" to record all the action at the convention for publication the next day and would have extra copies on sale at its 51 Clark Street office. Reporters covering the convention, meanwhile, faced a scramble for credentials to get inside the Wigwam, big as it was. It had limited seats on the platform for journalists, with more than nine hundred applications for them; in the building all told there were eight hundred spots held for reporters, most of them in the gallery, but more than fifteen hundred requests. The *North Iowa Times* correspondent described a reporter's daily routine as leaving his hotel and "being squeezed almost to death on the street, and quite to death if you happen to get into the sanctum."

By 11:00 a.m., anxious crowds of "Irrepressible Conflicters," as reporters styled the Republicans, thronged the Wigwam's twenty-foot-wide doors. "Vast as the Wigwam is, not one-fifth of those who would be glad to get inside can be accommodated," Halstead noted. Women who had toiled on the decorations stood at the entrances, awaiting their reward: the enjoyment of the convention from a seat in the ladies' gallery. Men were pushier. "The door keepers were of Roman firmness and the door-posts stout," barring the mob from packing the Wigwam before others could enter, the *Press and Tribune* reported. At half past eleven, the guards admitted ticket holders, delegates, and members of the press through assigned doors, "and the tide began to flow in, in a steady stream." Then ladies and their guests were permitted entry. Finally, the doors were flung open to the general public, and with "one grand rush," the crowd "filled, packed and condensed every part of the hall its billows of rushing, excited, humanity had access to"—including the area under the galleries where, as another reporter put it, men stood and stared "like superabundant calves." The delegates from Pennsylvania, all wearing white hats, staged a grand entrance, marching en masse behind a band from the Briggs House to the Wigwam, "making a very impressive show," the *Pittsburgh Daily Post* reported. The crowd cheered their entrance.

Large placards identified the locations of the state delegations. They occupied both sides of the massive stage—half of the delegates to the left of the podium and half to the right. The advantage of that setup was that "the delegates could be seen from all parts of the auditorium and none of the proceedings lost by the audience," wrote Isaac H. Bromley, covering the convention for the *Norwich* (Connecticut) *Morning Journal*. The disadvantage was that the division made it hard for delegates to confer, since they were seated in two separate blocks. But the show took precedence, Bromley noted. "Something of convenience was sacrificed to dramatic effect."

The states seemed to be haphazardly placed—in neither alphabetical nor geographical order. In truth, they had been carefully positioned by Lincoln's friend Norman B. Judd. He had persuaded the Republican National Committee to bring the convention to Chicago, and he had landed the task of creating the seating chart. Years later, Judd's son Edward recalled that, shortly before the opening of the convention, "father returned home late at night, and, assuming that my mother was asleep, before he made ready for bed, quietly lighted a lamp on the table in the far corner of the room, and busied himself with paper and pencil." After half an hour, his wife approached him and heard him exclaim, "By cracky, Abe's nominated." The Chicago lawyer had shrewdly positioned the entire New York delegation in a place of honor in the forefront of the platform, to the right of the podium. Judd surrounded that state with Seward's strongest supporters. He put the wavering delegations on the other side, near Illinois and Indiana. That would make it easy for the Lincoln men to communicate with them later during the balloting, and all but impossible for the Seward men to get over there. In the center, between the two wings of delegates, were the scores of journalists allowed on the platform. In short, Judd's seating arrangement hemmed in the New Yorkers and left the Lincoln men "ideally placed for missionary work." Joseph Medill of the *Press and Tribune* later claimed he helped Judd with the plan. "It was the meanest political trick I ever had a hand in in my life," he told a journalist, with "an irresistible look of mock contrition."

Finally, the hour of the convention approached. For those who had struggled for years to hem in slavery, the moment was packed with emotion. A *Chicago Journal* editor reflected that the telegraph wires would soon hum with the news of the man nominated to lead the Union through the dark times ahead. "The scene is such as a man beholds but once in a lifetime. Along a thousand lines of a continent's open palm, Wisdom and Patriotism have come pilgrims, and the men on two seaboards are waiting for a voice from Chicago. That voice will utter a name, and its syllables will flash along the lightning's spidery web from border to border; unnumbered tongues will speak it; unnumbered pens record it; hearts will cherish it; hands will uphold it. It will be a name to rally a host, to win a battle, to honor a principle, to bless a land." The delegates who had gathered in the Wigwam were doing more than dividing political spoils, he asserted; "they are adding a chapter to the story of a struggle that has slavery on one side and liberty on the other."

Some compared the convention's work to the Founders' creation of a new nation. To the delegates "has fallen the duty of restoring that government, where it has grown weak and suffered from the ill-use of vandal hands," the *Buffalo Morning Express* declared that day. "Like all nations that run a swift race to greatness, and become heated in the noon blaze of prosperity, our country has grown forgetful in late years of the vigilance that alone preserves the perfect order of government.... Unfit and undeserving men have gained the trusts designed for the greatest and best, and they have abused them. Cunning, and dishonesty, and selfishness, have usurped the functions of wisdom and patriotism in the guidance and direction of authority." The founding principles "have been discarded by our modern rulers," replaced with "shallow dogmas" designed to deceive the public. The government had become "dark and secret and deceitful." Americans were "blind too long" to "these insidious and alarming changes," but an awakening was underway. Growing numbers of citizens now recognized the dire threat to their nation. "Millions strong, they wait to-day with breathless anxiety and hope, the action of that body of men assembled in Chicago, to whom has been delegated the choice of the 'man for the emergency:'—the man about whom they can rally in fervent faith, and march with irresistible determination to the rescue of the Union and its government."

Carl Schurz, who had grown up under oppression, found the packed building "a grand and inspiring sight. It was a free people met to consult upon their policy and to choose their chief. To me it was like the fulfillment of all the dreams of my youth." Some "10,000 people were gathered to-day as participators or spectators," the *New-York Tribune* reported, "and the animation passing, as by electric shocks, through them, made them one in sympathy and action." Those fortunate enough to get inside gave the venue rave reviews. Though it was essentially a "barn-like structure, made of rough timber," it was "decorated so completely with flags, banners, bunting, etc., that when filled it seemed a gorgeous pavilion aflutter with pennants and streamers," the Connecticut journalist Bromley recalled. "Everybody, citizens and strangers, delegates or outsiders . . . all fell in love with the Great Wigwam," the *Press and Tribune* asserted. It gave the "spectators a sight few of them will ever forget, a sight and hearing of the most remarkable political Convention in spirit, enthusiasm, and inevitable destiny of result that ever assembled in the history of our politics."

Shortly after noon, Edwin D. Morgan, governor of New York, chairman of the Republican National Committee, and supporter of Seward, brought down his gavel with a sharp rap, opening the convention before the largest audience that had ever been assembled indoors in America. In reading the formal call to convene, he addressed not only the Republican Party but also the People's Party of Pennsylvania and the Opposition Party of New Jersey—an unavoidable reminder that the Republicans' radical brand was still problematic in swing states. The Reverend Zephaniah Moore Humphrey, pastor of the First Presbyterian Church, offered the opening prayer, three days after he had performed the Sunday service at the Wigwam. The delegates then elected David Wilmot as the convention's temporary president by unanimous acclaim, and Morgan turned the proceedings over to him.

A Pennsylvania congressman, initially a Democrat, Wilmot was a longtime hero to those who believed that slavery, as a great moral wrong, ought to be contained. "No man in the Convention was better known than he," Bromley noted. In August 1846, he introduced his famous Wilmot Proviso as an attachment to an appropriations bill, barring slavery from all the territories obtained through the Mexican-American War. "It stuck like wax," Abraham Lincoln recalled, and it passed the House. Though it failed in the Senate, it ignited fierce debate over the expansion of slavery and the meaning of America. When Lincoln served in the next Congress, he recalled, the "'Wilmot Proviso' or the principle of it, was constantly coming up in some shape or other, and I think I may venture to say I voted for it at least forty times; during the short term I was there. The Senate, however, held it in check, and it never became law." The honorary presidency of the convention was a way for Republicans to thank Wilmot for that historic service. Illinois delegate Orville H. Browning was not impressed. "He is a dull, chuckel headed, booby looking man, and makes a very poor presiding officer," Browning wrote in his diary. A Vermont correspondent concurred, at least about Wilmot's looks. "His appearance does not give promise of his intellectual strength," the reporter wrote. "He has red hair, a red round face, and looks rather heavy and stupid."

In taking the podium, Wilmot, forty-six, expressed his deep gratitude for the "undeserved honor" bestowed on him. "I shall carry the recollection of it, and your manifestation of partiality with me until the day of my death," he said. Wilmot spoke briefly about the challenges Republicans faced in fighting the powerful forces behind slavery that had infested the federal government. He sounded the conservative theme that Lincoln had advanced at the Cooper Institute three months earlier. "It is our purpose to restore the Constitution to its original meaning; to give to it its true interpretation; to read that instrument as our fathers read it," Wilmot said. "That instrument was not ordained and established for the purpose of extending slavery within this country; it was not ordained and established for giving guarantees and securities to that institution. Our fathers regarded slavery as a blot upon this country. They went down into their graves with the belief, that but a few more years and that blot would be extinguished from our land."

Wilmot lamented that the slave power had become so dominant that it was able to censor speech throughout the South and punish those who advocated for liberty. "Whose rights are safe where slavery has the power to trample them under foot? Who to-day is not more free to utter his opinions within the empire of Russia, or under the shadow of the despotism of Austria than he is within the limits of the slave states of this republic?" If slavery were now permitted to spread to all territories and to the North itself, he warned, the freedoms Americans had long enjoyed would be increasingly under attack. Wilmot argued that "the safety of our liberty" depended on Republicans winning the election and restoring the Constitution as recognized for sixty years, before a "new dogma was started," falsely asserting that the nation "was established to guarantee to slavery perpetual existence and unlimited empire."

Setting to work on formal business, Wilmot called out the names of America's states as part of organizing the convention. Most garnered loud applause. Each delegation responded to the call by naming one member to serve on the convention's executive committee. When he got to the names of Southern states that had sent no delegations because Republicans were reviled within their borders—Tennessee, Arkansas, Mississippi, Louisiana, Alabama, Georgia, South Carolina, North Carolina, and Florida—the crowd hissed, laughed, or both.

The great anti-slavery congressman from Ohio, Joshua Giddings, won applause by declaring that he hoped the convention would conclude its business by 3:00 p.m. the next day—thus avoiding, he did not have to say, the agonizingly protracted disputes that destroyed the Democrats' convention in Charleston, leaving behind toxic hatreds. The convention then created a Committee on Permanent Organization, to choose its permanent president; a Committee on Credentials, to determine whether Seward's Southern delegates were legitimate; and a Committee on Business, to handle other details.

Horace Greeley, the *New-York Tribune* editor who was improbably if not preposterously representing Oregon, immediately got into the middle of the action, making motions. At one point, Ohio delegation chairman David K. Cartter—who confusingly spelled his last name with two *t*'s—moved "to amend the proposition of a gentleman from Oregon or New York, Mr. Greeley, I am not sure which," drawing laughter from the Wigwam crowd. "I accept the amendment of the gentleman from Maryland or Rhode Island, I am not particular which," Greeley replied, winning more laughter and applause. In his battered white coat, "Horace Greeley was the most conspicuous, as he was certainly the most picturesque, figure on the platform," Bromley recalled. Everybody in the audience seemed to know him. "There's old Greeley!" people in the crowd exclaimed.

Wilmot's limitations as a presiding officer became clearer after one delegate made a grand announcement: the Chicago Board of Trade had invited the delegates to an excursion on the lake at 5:00 p.m., on the assumption that the convention's business for the day would be over by then. After the invitation was greeted with gushing statements of gratitude and approved by unanimous acclaim, a lengthy and chaotic discussion ensued about whether the pleasure jaunt made sense. The convention needed to take a break that afternoon so that the committees could meet and deliberate. The plan for the moment was to reconvene at 5:00 p.m., exactly when the pleasure cruise was to start. Someone suggested holding a night session, permitting delegates to first enjoy the excursion. Someone else noted the Wigwam had scheduled a display of precision military maneuvers that evening. Furthermore, delegates needed time to have dinner and attend to their other plans. New York senator Preston King expressed appreciation for the Board of Trade's invitation but argued it should not drive the convention's schedule. "Our object here is business, not pleasure," King pointed out. In the end, the delegates decided to skip the cruise and reconvene at 5:00 p.m., as planned, giving the members of the committees three and a half hours to meet, and giving carpenters time to come in and put some finishing touches on the Wigwam. After the building emptied, an immense crowd waited outside during the entire intermission, hoping to get back in when the doors reopened.

Taking advantage of the recess, Nathaniel McLean sat down to write a letter to his wife. "Today all is confusion and no one can tell the result," he informed her. His father, associate justice John McLean, seemed to be going nowhere. "The Ohio delegation I am sorry to say are playing the fool by splitting up and dividing their strength upon men who cannot possibly get the nomination. Chase and Wade of Ohio are the first choice of different factions, and neither Chase or Wade could by any possibility get the nomination," he wrote. "Yet knowing this," they were unwilling to "throw their votes for the Judge," even though they could "nominate him beyond all question" if they did so. McLean was dismayed that delegates from his own state had chosen to "*misrepresent* the sentiment of the people" and put their allegiances and ambitions above Ohio's interests. Seward still enjoyed more support than anyone,

McLean reported, though such savvy observers as Pennsylvania congressman Thaddeus Stevens insisted that the New Yorker could not be nominated. "All however is doubt and confusion and a very little matter may change the whole phase of affairs. Wise counsel it is best hoped will prevail among the delegates, but for the present we can only hope for the best."

McLean hoped to get a seat in the Wigwam when the convention resumed after 5:00 p.m., "but I do not know that I can succeed as only delegates are admitted on the first floor, and gentlemen *with ladies* in the gallery. As I have no lady to go with me I must try to get a ticket from a delegate and go in as if I had a right to a seat." Those who had been frozen out of the first session or forced to stand through it had learned their lesson quickly: if they wanted a seat, they would need to gain admittance to the ladies' gallery; and to do that, they would need a woman on their arm. Accordingly, female escorts were suddenly in high demand. Some men, Halstead reported, found schoolgirls on the street and paid them a quarter each to help them get safely inside. "Other girls, those of undoubted character (no doubt on the subject whatever)" were much sought after. One such woman, who was offered half a dollar to help a man in, declined, saying she had already done so twice at each of the three main entrances and was afraid she would be arrested if she tried again.

Halstead was amused to find men resorting to the use of women who—by the casual prejudices of the time—were of low status. "An Irish woman passing with a bundle of clothes under her arm was levied upon by an 'irrepressible,' and seeing him safely into the seats reserved for ladies and accompanying gentlemen, retired with her fee and bundle." When another "irrepressible" tried to get in with "an Indian woman who was selling moccasins" in the street, however, the policeman at the door drew the line, insisting that "a squaw was not a lady." That prompted a bitter argument. "The young Republican protested indignantly against the policeman's decision, claiming equal rights for all womankind." Those who had no women to help them prepared to storm the entrances. When the doors were finally open to unaccompanied men, "the rush for places was tremendous." The standing room under the galleries, with a capacity of about 4,500, filled up in five minutes. Voracious pickpockets worked the crowd, looking to lift watches and wallets from men whose attention was riveted on the stage.

At 5:15 p.m., the convention resumed. The first order of business was yet another debate about the lake excursion. Morrow B. Lowry, a wealthy merchant from Erie, Pennsylvania, and an acquaintance of John Brown (he had visited the condemned terrorist in his jail cell in November 1859), explained that the Board of Trade, having received the convention's initial approval, had immediately readied the fleet of boats required to hold all the delegates, set to leave the dock at Rush Street Bridge, near the Richmond House. "They say that if we are pressed with business we can hold the Convention on the decks of their vessels if we desire it, and we can, so they say, have cabins for rooms to caucus in," Lowry noted, proposing an adjournment at 6:00 p.m. "I suppose that we are here on important business," Rowland Hazard Jr., a mill owner and abolitionist from Rhode Island, observed laconically, and the delegates agreed, voting down Lowry's idea.

The convention quickly approved its executive committee's choice of a permanent president, former Massachusetts congressman George Ashmun, fifty-five, a bright, capable, and respectable ex-Whig with a balding head, prim whiskers under his chin, and deep rings under his eyes. The same Vermont reporter who knocked Wilmot's appearance described Ashmun as "gentle, manly, affable, and yet admirably skilled in parliamentary tactics, and never embarrassed by the confusion which is inevitable in a convention of five hundred men, met together for the first time to transact such important business." Two Seward men—Preston King and Carl Schurz—solemnly escorted him to his chair, "the one short and round as a barrel and fat as butter, the other tall and slender," Halstead observed. "The suggestion of Don Quixote and Sancho Panza was too striking for the assembled multitude to resist," Schurz recalled, "and a titter ran over the convention" that threatened to break into "a general guffaw."

In his brief remarks, Ashmun argued that the long railroad journey many delegates had undertaken to Chicago "could only have been made upon some solemn call; and the stern look which I see on every face" confirmed "the deep sense of the solemn obligation" that the delegates felt. They had come "for the purpose of rescuing the government from the deep degradation into which it has fallen" under the presidency of James Buchanan. "I think we have a right here today, in the name of the American people, to impeach the administration of our general government of the highest crimes that can be committed against a constitutional government, against a free people, and against humanity."

Halstead poked fun at one of Ashmun's observations—his fatuous claim that he had heard nothing but expressions of "brotherly kindness" among the delegates in Chicago. Ashmun either had not gotten out much or was hard of hearing, the journalist remarked. "He certainly could not stay long among the Seward men at the Richmond House without hearing unkind and profane expressions used respecting brother delegates of conservative notions. He would very frequently hear Brother Greeley, for example, who is hated immensely by them, called a 'd—d old ass.' Indeed, that is a very mild specimen of the forms of expression used." But all in all, Ashmun made an excellent presiding officer, Halstead concluded: "His clear, full-toned voice was one refreshing to hear amid the clamors of a Convention. He is cool, clear headed and executive, and will dispatch business," moving things along briskly. Norman Judd completed the induction ceremony by presenting Ashmun with a beautifully carved gavel on behalf of the mechanics of Chicago. It was hewn from the oak of the *Lawrence*, the flagship of Commodore Oliver H. Perry, who famously proclaimed during the War of 1812, "Don't give up the ship!" As Judd told the Wigwam crowd, that "should be a motto for every Republican of this convention." And after the November election, he added, the nominee chosen here would be able to send a dispatch to Washington "in the language of the gallant Perry, 'We have met the enemy, and they are ours.'"

On a more serious note, the convention approved a Resolutions Committee, tasked with drafting the all-important Republican platform, a document of great significance in nineteenth-century politics. When the names of its members were read out, three received tremendous applause: Frank Blair, Carl Schurz, and Horace Greeley. The *New-York Tribune* editor lapped up the acclaim, Halstead noted with amusement. "Greeley had the greatest ovation, and though there is an impression to the contrary, those who know him well know that nobody is more fond of the breath of popular favor than the philosophic Horace."

At that point, the convention moved to adjourn for the day. Somebody suggested reconvening at nine the next morning. "Make it ten!" many voices called out. "Nine o'clock is too early," protested Francis Palmer Tracy, of San Francisco, a forty-five-year-old minister, orator, and ardent enemy of slavery who had helped found the Republican Party in California. "I have come a long way, many thousand miles, to attend this convention and am tired and I can't get up so early." Committees were also meeting in the morning and would have little time to thrash out differences before nine. With a ten o'clock restart approved, the convention's work for Wednesday was done. But an intense struggle continued in the hotel rooms, halls, and lobbies of Chicago, as men grappled with the question of who would "bless a land" as the party's nominee for president.

In Auburn, New York, Unitarian minister John Austin went to his neighbor William H. Seward's house after tea that birthday afternoon and enjoyed "a long and pleasant" discussion with the senator. Seward modestly declined to proclaim his imminent victory. "He does not express a positive opinion as to his nomination by the Republican Convention which met in Chicago to-day, but I drew the inference from his conversation that he conceives the probabilities to be strongly in his favor," Austin wrote in his journal. "He received a telegraphic dispatch saying that although there was a strong opposition to his nomination, on the part of timid and disaffected members of the Convention, yet his friends were sanguine he would win the nomination." Indeed, in a telegram sent to Seward that day, James Watson Webb, editor of the *Morning Courier and New-York Enquirer*, assured him there was "no cause for doubting" his victory.

To some on the scene, Seward seemed to be gaining ground. Horace Greeley looked "very much discouraged" when he visited the Kansas delegation sometime Wednesday, delegate Addison G. Procter recalled. "He seemed tired and depressed," gripped with the fear that Seward would win on the first ballot the following day. Greeley continued to pitch Bates as a man who would "make a good candidate and an able President if elected." Asked about the contender people seemed to be talking about more and more, the Illinois lawyer Abraham Lincoln, Greeley spoke slowly as if weighing his words carefully. "Lincoln is a very adroit politician. He has a host of friends out here in Illinois who seem to see something in him that the rest of us haven't seen yet. He has a very interesting history that would make good campaign literature, but the trouble with Lincoln is this, he has no experience in National affairs, and facing a crisis as we all believe, I doubt if such a nomination would be acceptable. It is too risky an undertaking. I think Bates would be safer."

GOV. SEWARD'S NOMINATION MORE PROBABLE, the *New-York Tribune* headlined Greeley's own dispatch from Chicago at 10:40 p.m. Seward's men had reportedly received assurances from the New Jersey and Virginia delegations. "I can only say that the advocates of Gov. Seward's nomination, who were much depressed last night, are now quite confident of his success," Greeley telegraphed. "I should say that the chances of his nomination are now about even." The editor's tireless lobbying for Bates did not seem to be working. "Mr. Lincoln appears to have the next best look," Greeley conceded.

A great split had opened in the party's ranks, Halstead now perceived. "The Republicans have all divided into two classes, the 'Irrepressibles' and the 'Conservatives.'" Though Lincoln's men were evidently making progress, the so-called conservatives were still fragmented among several candidates, and it was unclear any of them had enough votes to stop Seward. "The greatest excitement prevails in every place. Nothing is talked of but 'who is going to get the nomination?'" wrote the editor of the *Racine* (Wisconsin) *Daily Journal*, who had turned his newspaper over to "the devil and all hands" and come to Chicago. ("If a paper is not smart enough to run itself a few days, it is not much of a paper," he told readers.) "The friends of Seward are largely in majority, but the greatest, and in some instances the most bitter opposition is manifested toward him. The suckers [i.e., Illinoisans] go in for 'Old Abe,' with a very determined face. It would not surprise us if Wade, Lincoln or Bates should come up as a compromise candidate and receive the nomination, but when the question will so soon be decided speculations are useless."

One of Old Abe's top suckers, lawyer Leonard Swett, met that day with David Davis and the team to discuss strategy. They realized that, ironically, they had done perhaps too good a job since Saturday advancing Lincoln as the electable alternative to Seward. For a year, Lincoln had held back, not wishing to expose himself to ridicule or attack until the last possible moment. As Swett later told Lincoln, his supporters now feared that his "strength was augmenting with sufficient & perhaps too great speed." As party insiders started to take Lincoln seriously, they began to weigh the effect his nomination would have on their access to power and patronage. Lincoln's men had to take steps to make sure that "your increasing prominence did not create jealousies & counter combinations."

The huge Pennsylvania delegation had to be handled with particular care. Davis sent Swett that day to conduct some delicate diplomacy through a Pennsylvania friend, John W. Shaffer, who "had the confidence" of that state's delegation. Swett quickly realized something was seriously amiss. "The first thing I discovered was a reluctance to talk with me freely," Swett recounted to Lincoln, "but finally he admitted that the Cameron men would not go for you as a second choice but would go to Wade." As usual, patronage was at the bottom of the matter. The eight Seward supporters in the Illinois delegation, though pledged to vote for Lincoln on the first ballot, had been spreading the word that a victorious Lincoln would deny jobs to supporters of Seward and Cameron. The Seward men of the Northwest, in particular, "would be annihilated," thanks to the resentments of the powerful people behind Lincoln—namely, the editors of the *Press and Tribune* and their close associates, Norman Judd and Illinois lawyer Ebenezer Peck.

Swett had stumbled onto a nest of fears and jealousies that might destroy Lincoln's whole campaign. After hastily consulting Davis, Swett gathered all the friends he had in the Seward and Cameron camps and employed his talents as a trial lawyer highly effective at swaying juries. "My assurance to them was this—That I knew you to be a fair minded man & if elected you would treat all fairly," he later informed Lincoln. Indeed, they would be rewarded as if they had been "original friends" if they performed "service to you by way of preventing combinations against you & perhaps aiding in one or the other Element to come to you." After Swett heard out their complaints, he made a solemn pledge: "I agreed to hold myself personally responsible to them for general fairness, and agreed forever to forfeit their confidence if it was not done." It seemed to work. The men who had harbored fears about Lincoln promised to go to the Pennsylvania and New York delegations "& try to get you as their Second Choice."

By then, it was dawning on some Pennsylvania delegates that Cameron was a "dead cock in the pit." That only ratcheted up the anger and discord in the state's political ranks. At the Briggs House that morning, a correspondent for the state's *Erie Observer* witnessed a bitter argument between a Cameron supporter and an opponent that almost came to blows. "As it was, 'liar,' 'puppy,' 'slink,' 'coward,' 'scoundrel'" were among the epithets they "hurled at one another's head thick and fast," he reported. "We were looking on as complacent as a summer's morning, and thinking to ourselves how beautiful it was to see brethren dwell together in harmony." A big question loomed: Once "this great Pennsylvania humbug" was out of the picture, "where will the Pennsylvania delegation go?" A correspondent for the *Daily Evening Express* of Lancaster got some answers at a delegation caucus that day. The members leaned toward supporting Cameron on the first ballot, supporting McLean on the second, and dividing their vote on the third among Lincoln, Bates, and Seward. The writer regarded that as a significant victory for Lincoln. "This change from Cameron to McLean and from McLean to Lincoln, will have a great influence in favor of the latter," he wrote, "and from the enthusiasm which is gradually raising up in his favor I would not be surprised to see him eventually nominated."

Mark Delahay, in his daily letter to Lincoln, reported excitedly that Lincoln seemed to be emerging as the leading alternative to the frontrunner. "Unless Seward has strength sufficient early in the Ballotting to give him the nomination, You I think will be nominated." Even so, Delahay fretted that Seward might be gaining support, thanks to the help pouring in from New York. "Greely [*sic*] told me awhile ago that it was impossible to nominate Seward; I hope this is the Case, but I am not free from fears I confess. . . . N York continues to send in reinforcements, Bankers, Rounders, Gamblers and Blowers are thick from that City." The Seward men were making deals, even though, for more than a year, they had peddled patronage "in the market & sold out many times—until it is mortgaged a foot thick." Whatever happened, Delahay pledged to fight on. Like Judd, he quoted Commodore Perry. "I am not discouraged & shall never give up the Ship while a rope remains to be handled, But I am fatigued greatly with loss of rest &c."

Illinois treasurer William Butler, "wrighting in the Room where all is fuss and Confusion," was brimming with overconfidence. He told Lincoln that Indiana—the crucial second state he needed—now intended to stand behind him, along with much of Iowa and New Hampshire. After joining Davis and Jesse K. Dubois in a meeting with the Massachusetts delegates Wednesday, Butler thought that state would "gow for you" as well. Ohio intended to support Salmon P. Chase initially and Benjamin Wade on the second ballot, but if Lincoln hung in, the Buckeye State might shift to him after that. Seward's men, however, still expected to win. "Sewards friends feel a little sore this evening, but Seem to be in good Spirits," Butler wrote. "Mr Seward will not be nominated all hands seem to Conceede this except Newyork." But he added a note of caution to his friend: "I think your Chance good yet be prepared for defeat."

Trying to cover every angle, the Lincoln forces met that night to discuss the manipulation of the Wigwam audience. They were concerned that Weed, who did not seem to miss a trick, had imported a throng of boisterous New Yorkers to scream their support for Seward during the upcoming balloting for the presidential nomination. Weed well understood the propensity of human beings to follow the herd. One-sided bellowing might well capture the emotions of wavering delegates, setting off a stampede for the New Yorker. The Lincoln forces decided there and then that "the West should be heard" as well, Chicago lawyer Isaac Arnold recalled. They knew of a Chicago man "whose voice could drown the roar of Lake Michigan in its wildest fury; nay, it was said that his shout could be heard on a calm day, across the lake." Word went out to him. Burton C. Cook, a lawyer and delegate from the Illinois River town of Ottawa, knew another man who lived on the river, "a Dr. Ames, who had never found his equal in his ability to shout and huzzah." Unfortunately, he was a Democrat. But with no time to spare, Cook telegraphed him to come to Chicago by the first available train.

Those screamers would have to be backed by scores of Illinois men. Fortunately, there were plenty in Chicago, if a way could be found to squeeze them into the Wigwam. H. M. Russell, a rough-and-ready thirty-three-year-old from Urbana, a grocery store owner and former stagecoach driver, took charge of organizing them. Russell was twenty-one when he first met Lincoln. He was then working at his uncle's Champaign House, which catered to Judge Davis and the traveling lawyers of the Eighth Judicial Circuit. Russell recalled "looking after the wants of the judge and of the attorneys, attending the fires in their rooms, carrying water and cigars as needed," and waiting on the dining room table. "I at once took a liking to Mr. Lincoln, because of his gentleness and friendliness—so different from most of the other attorneys. Mr. Lincoln was always pleasant in asking for things and in thanking for them when they were brought to him." His kindness to a young man of no apparent importance in 1848—as to many others during his life—would have consequences in Chicago in 1860.

Scrounging for votes anywhere he could find them, David Davis seemed to be offering a variety of jobs in a Lincoln administration. George Blakey, handling Cassius Clay's efforts in Chicago, said the Lincoln men told him Clay could be secretary of war or of the navy if he could swing Kentucky over to Lincoln. Weed was working Blakey at the same time, hinting at a spot on the ticket for Clay—a prize he had now dangled multiple times before candidates from various states, including Illinois. That night, Iowa politician and Lincoln supporter Hawkins Taylor took the pulse of his state's delegates. He rushed off a letter to Lincoln informing him that few of the Iowans supported him for president, but every one of them would back him for vice president. Whatever Lincoln thought of the vice presidency, it held no appeal to his ambitious wife. When a Dr. Ritchie visited the Lincolns in Springfield that week, the topic of Taylor's letter, which had just arrived, came up. Mary Lincoln turned to her husband, "spoke up in a hard, bitter manner and said, 'If you can not have the first place, you shall not have the second.'" Lincoln's men, fortunately, were working hard for first place, fending off constant schemes by Seward's men to sideline Lincoln by putting him second on the ticket. "They literally overwhelmed us with kindness," recalled John M. Palmer, an Illinois lawyer and one of the founders of the state's Republican Party.

A "grave and venerable judge" from New Jersey, for example, kept "insisting that Lincoln shall be nominated for Vice-President—and Seward for President." Palmer and Davis decided to go over to the Richmond House to meet with the eighty-three-year-old jurist, retired state Supreme Court chief justice Joseph Coerten Hornblower. The judge "praised Seward, but he was especially effusive in expressing his admiration for Lincoln. He thought that Seward was clearly entitled to the first place, and that Lincoln's eminent merits entitled him to second place," Palmer recalled. A former Democrat, Palmer had an idea for stopping Hornblower's talk. He warned the judge that "there are 40,000 Democrats in Illinois" who would oppose a ticket made up of Seward and Lincoln. "We are willing to vote for Mr. Lincoln with a Democrat on the ticket," he said, "but we will not consent to vote for two old Whigs." Hornblower angrily asked, "Judge Davis, is it possible that party spirit so prevails in Illinois that Judge Palmer properly represents public opinion?" Davis, himself an old Whig, played along. "Oh," he replied, "oh, my God, Judge, you can't account for the conduct of these old Locofocos," the Whig nickname for Democrats. They would "certainly" do as Palmer suggested, Davis informed Hornblower. "There are 40,000 of them, and, as Palmer says, not a d—d one of them will vote for two Whigs." Palmer and Davis left the judge "in a towering rage" about this Palmer fellow and the petty partisanship of the state's former Democrats. When they got back to the Tremont House, Palmer complained, "Davis, you are an infernal rascal to sit there and hear Hornblower berate me as he did. You really seemed to encourage him." Davis said nothing, "but chuckled as if he had greatly enjoyed the joke."

All in all, the Lincoln men were doing reasonably well that Wednesday. Dubois sent Lincoln, his Eighth Street neighbor, a hasty telegram: "Prospects fair friends at work night & day tell my wife I am well." Norman Judd, having seated the delegates to Lincoln's advantage and provided the beautifully carved gavel for the convention, fired off another telegram to Lincoln: "Dont be frightend Keep cool things is working."

As it turned out, the Board of Trade did carry out its excursion that evening. Though few delegates were available, about five hundred people in town for the festivities boarded four beautiful schooners—the *Imperial*, the *San Jacinto*, the *Maple Leaf*, and the *Grey Eagle*—all of them lashed together and tugged out into Lake Michigan from the Rush Street Bridge by the steam-driven boat *McQueen*. The guests included "prominent citizens from almost every State in the Union," entertained on board by the ubiquitous Gilmore's Boston Band. Julian S. Rumsey, chairman of the board's executive committee and owner of a prominent

Chicago shipping company, called the crowd's attention to the immense grain storehouses that now lined the banks of the Chicago River, and spoke about the explosive growth of the city over the previous twenty years. Edward F. Noyes, a young Republican lawyer from Ohio destined to be that state's governor, thanked the Board of Trade for the treat and praised Chicagoans for their wonderful Wigwam and warm hospitality. Turning to Democratic politics, he quipped that if there was any doubt about what Senator Seward meant by the "irrepressible conflict," there was none after the collapse of the Charleston convention. Far from uniting the Democrats, Stephen Douglas's squatter sovereignty had created an almost miraculous opening for Republicans. As "the children of Israel walked through the Red Sea, its waters on each side being as walls," Noyes said, "so would the Republican party walk through the political sea, with Squatter Sovereignty as a wall on the one hand and slavery on the other." At half past eight the boats returned to the harbor and hundreds disembarked onto terra firma, "highly delighted with the trip."

In the parlor of the Tremont House, members of the Resolutions Committee got to work on the platform. The group quickly concluded that too many men, all trying to have their say, were involved. To produce a platform "with any degree of promptness," a smaller group was needed, Gustave Koerner of Illinois recalled. Accordingly, the committee selected seven of its members, including Greeley, Schurz, and Koerner, to come back with a platform. After toiling all evening, the seven agreed to reconvene in the morning.

While some tired delegates yearned for rest, many others chose to celebrate long into the night. They "seize all the chances after adjournment for looking about, seeing, and enjoying" the city, the *Western Railroad Gazette* noted. "President making, strikes an outsider, as a pretty jolly affair all around." Gilmore's Boston Band marched off the boats and over to the Metropolitan Hall, where it played a program of music "full of richness and beauty" to a packed house. The Hooley & Campbell Minstrel Troupe entertained another sellout crowd at Kingsbury Hall. The Wigwam filled up all over again for the flashy drill of the

U.S. Zouave Cadets, under the command of a twenty-three-year-old Chicago law clerk and self-styled major named Elmer Ephraim Ellsworth. Mimicking real soldiers—the Zouave troops of the French army, prominent in North Africa—the eighty young cadets wore flashy red fez-style hats, short open-fronted blue jackets, and baggy red trousers. In their remarkably acrobatic performance, they executed maneuvers with a rapidity and precision that mesmerized the crowd. "They fall prostrate in open ranks, fire, load while lying on their backs, leap forward, fall, fire, and reload, with the rapidity and precision of usually drilled soldiers standing erect," the *Cleveland Daily Leader* enthused. "Their trot charge of bayonets under the Zouave yell is irresistibly terrific." Bloodshed might be coming, but war in May 1860 still was a thrilling show that killed no one.

The white-hatted Pennsylvania men got up a torchlight parade that night, marching through the streets behind Philadelphia's United States Cornet Band and Pittsburgh's Duquesne Grays' Band. Ominously for Seward, they carried a large transparency declaring, PENNSYLVANIA ASKS FOR A UNION AND CONSERVATIVE CANDIDATE AND PLEDGES 20,000 MAJORITY, while shouting for "Cameron and Lincoln"—a ticket they still hoped would propel political boss Simon Cameron to the nomination. From a balcony in front of the Metropolitan House, Pennsylvania politicians roared speeches to the large crowd attracted by the music and lights. New York editor Isaac Platt watched with growing dismay. "Every one of their orators began by telling how much he reverenced Senator Seward, how much he was prepared to do for him, and then branched off declaring that it would be impossible for him to carry Pennsylvania. This one string was harped on the whole evening. Additional declarations that the state *could* be carried for *Bates*, or *McLean*, or *Cameron*, or *Wade*, but never for Seward, were made over and over again to the crowd," Platt lamented.

Elsewhere, alcohol consumption took precedence over politics. In a dispatch that night, the acerbic correspondent for the Davenport *Democrat and News* noted that the "braves" and "squaws" of the Wigwam were demonstrating a decided taste for "fire-water." "Drinks and fights are quite frequent," he reported, with heavyweight boxing champion Tom Hyer serving as "a sort of private policeman" to aid the Seward men. Some delegates were so drunk that they "let out the most important and private secrets of the caucus rooms," and had to be watched by their friends. "We are quite certain that the Reverend and holy Henry Ward Beecher would be very much shocked could he but see the enormous wickedness and dissipation going on at the assembling of his disciples."

At the Tremont House, the wickedness and dissipation went on almost all night. "At two o'clock this morning part of the Missouri delegation were singing songs in their parlor," Halstead reported. "There were still a crowd of fellows caucusing—and the glasses were still clinking in the barrooms—and far down the street a brass band was making the night musical." Men enjoyed the hotel's billiard tables for much of the evening. But just before midnight, the hotel staff halted all play and dragged mattresses on top of the tables. Looking in, a *Press and Tribune* reporter counted one hundred thirty men making use of the billiard tables for relief "from the fatigues of the day." Many felt themselves fortunate to find such a bed in a city overrun with strangers.

Nathaniel McLean, who had been working nonstop ("the only really quiet time I have is when writing in my friends office and in bed"), did not even attempt to go to his hotel room until just before midnight. Once there, amid the sounds of revelry, he collapsed into sleep. The next day might well be historic. The delegates could end the agony of suspense by taking up nominations—which, given the Democrats' catastrophe at Charleston, might be tantamount to choosing the first Republican president.

Thursday,
May 17, 1860

Chapter 11:
For Want of Tally Sheets

And still they came. Masses of people, "expecting the nomination to be made today and desiring to be present," poured into Chicago overnight, Murat Halstead reported Thursday. The crowd was "mighty and overwhelming; it can only be numbered by tens of thousands." In the hotels, the crush was even worse than on Wednesday. "Two thousand persons took breakfast at the Tremont House," Halstead marveled. The burgeoning crowds, a correspondent for the *Wisconsin State Journal* of Madison contended, were a measure of the "transcendent interest" Americans had taken in the proceedings in Chicago. "This vast multitude . . . speaks in significant language of the profound and persuasive sense" that the American people were about to rebel against the forces of slavery and immorality. "It is but the first manifestation of the popular whirlwind which is rising to sweep from the high places it has dishonored and betrayed a corrupt and profligate administration."

That morning's *Chicago Press and Tribune* listed some local attractions that might supplement the convention. Visitors who wished to take home a memento of the Wigwam could find "one of the best views to carry away" at the 113 Lake Street gallery of Alexander Hesler, who was selling prints of the "beautiful photograph" of its exterior he had captured on Wednesday. Hesler was famous for lugging his bulky equipment and sensitive chemicals into the great outdoors, to record spectacular nature scenes. (America's most beloved poet, Henry Wadsworth Longfellow, was said to have held Hesler's daguerreotype of Minnehaha Falls in his left hand while writing his famous 1855 poem "The Song of Hiawatha.") But Hesler was also a superb studio portrait photographer. In 1857, he captured an unforgettable image of the irredeemably roughhewn Abraham Lincoln, notable for the subject's mop of outrageously tousled hair, as if Lincoln had just stepped out of a shower.

In the realm of sculpture, Leonard Volk's studio in the Portland Block, at the corner of Dearborn and Washington Streets, was open from 9:00 a.m. to 5:00 p.m. There, prospective buyers could view "his statues of Senator Douglas, busts of Abraham Lincoln, and other works." For those interested in sports, the Prairie Club of Chicago was hosting the celebrated Union Club of Cincinnati in a "grand Cricket match," with a band in attendance, at 10:00 a.m. at the open grounds of the former West Madison Street. Cricket was contending with the rising game of base ball—then two words—for dominance as the most popular field sport in America.

But the convention's selection of a presidential nominee was the consuming passion of the assembled masses. In what might be its last opportunity to sway delegates, the *Press and Tribune* offered its requisite pro-Lincoln editorial on the front page, THE MAN WHO CAN WIN, again making a pragmatic argument that the lawyer was the most electable man in the field. It displayed a chart showing that neither Democrats nor Republicans held the majority in the key states of Iowa, Illinois, Indiana, Ohio, and Pennsylvania, necessitating the nomination of a candidate who could win over supporters of the old Whig Party and the American Party. The liberal Seward was not that man. Lincoln, with his "known conservativism," would be "acceptable by reason of his birth-place, political antecedents and constitutional moderation, to that belt of country without the acquiescence of which no man can win."

Before they could get to the presidential nomination, the delegates would have to deal with two big challenges: establishing the rules for the vote and approving a party platform outlining the Republicans' values and aspirations. That morning, committees were hard at work on those challenges in closed hotel parlors. At the same time, an enormous crowd of less studious conventioneers was forming outside the Richmond House to make a striking show of one candidate's popularity. More than three thousand men from New York and Michigan, the tassels of their Seward badges fluttering in the spring breeze, lined up in the sun behind a splendidly uniformed marching band for a parade to the Wigwam. At their head they carried the gaudy banner with Seward's life-sized likeness. One of their orators stood "upon a doorstep, with hat and cane in his hands, . . . haranguing them as a captain might address his soldiers marching to battle," Halstead reported. As the lead band blasted out a popular tune—"O Isn't He a Darling?"—the delegates stepped off, four abreast, "in a cloud of dust." Trooping down the middle of the dirt streets of Chicago, a block from the stinking river, the "Seward procession was [as] heedless of the dust as regular soldiers, and strode on with gay elasticity and jaunty bearing." As they passed the Tremont House—the headquarters of Lincoln, Bates, and other "opponents of 'Old Irrepressible'"—they gave "three throat-tearing cheers for Seward." Thurlow Weed was doing everything in his power to whip up enthusiasm for the New York senator. "It will be a clear case, if he is not nominated, that the failure cannot be charged to his friends," Halstead wrote. "Few men have had friends who would cleave unto them as the Sewardites to their great man here."

The impressive display of strength, a seeming harbinger of Seward's nomination later that day, galled many delegates. Distraught Pennsylvanians, repeating the theme of their speeches the previous night, warned anyone who would listen that they would be "immediately ruined" if Seward were nominated. Most of the New Jersey men shared that opinion. The Indiana men "look heartbroken at the suggestion that Seward has the inside track, and throw up their hands in despair. They say [gubernatorial candidate] Henry S. Lane will be beaten, the legislature pass utterly into the hands of the Democracy, and the two Republican Senators hoped for, be heard no more," Halstead reported. Both Pennsylvania and Indiana, the political strategists knew well, would hold elections in October. Republican cohesion and strength in those battles would serve as a harbinger of national victory in November and buck up Republicans throughout the North. Defeat in those two states, by contrast, would signal an oncoming disaster. Illinois men warned that Seward's "nomination would kill off Lyman Trumbull and give the legislature into the hands of Democrats to make the next Congressional appointment." Given the amount of power and patronage at stake, professional politicians in these states could ill afford to nominate Seward, even if they thought he would make the best president of any of the candidates.

Though these fears ran like a fault line beneath the convention, Seward's loyalists, from Weed on down, ignored them. "Amid all these cries of distress," Halstead noted, "the Sewardites are true as steel to their champion, and they will cling to 'Old Irrepressible,' as they call him, until the last gun is fired and the big bell rings." Nathaniel McLean, son of candidate John McLean, wrote that the Seward men that morning "have no doubt of the nomination of Seward." One dark-horse candidate seemed to be gaining strength, but McLean found it hard to believe that the delegates would turn to him. "Lincoln of Illinois seems to be very prominent just now, and although an honest man with talent enough for many places, yet totally unfit in administration capacity for President," McLean wrote. "Lincoln is I believe entirely honest and a very clever fellow, but we want something in addition to this in a President."

Still seeking a feasible alternative to Seward, the Indiana and Pennsylvania delegations gathered that morning two blocks away from the Tremont House, at Chicago's seven-year-old Court House, to hear a last-ditch appeal by Edward Bates's supporters. The great white building, bounded by LaSalle, Washington, Clark, and Randolph Streets, contained several municipal departments, including a jail in the basement, the mayor's office on the first floor, and a large courtroom and a city council chamber on the second floor. Chicago citizens and visitors, out for a good political show, packed the courtroom to watch. Frank Blair did not disappoint. He made an impassioned plea for Bates as the man most likely to win in November and unify the country. Spooked by the hostility toward Bates expressed at the Deutsches Haus, Blair brought along prominent German-born Americans to attest to the man's brilliance and character, including Frederick "Far West" Muench, a beloved early pioneer and writer, and Arnold Krekel, a respected lawyer and editor who would later win appointment as a U.S. district judge. When David Davis got wind of the session, he immediately dispatched Koerner and Orville Browning to try to counter Blair's presentation.

Koerner caught the end of Blair's address and sat through the speeches of the Germans. The delegates had seemed receptive. Then, no doubt to Blair's discomfort, he cried out for permission to speak in front of the Illinois crowd. "The moment I named Lincoln the cheers almost shook the court house," he recalled. While Blair and his ally Charles Gibson looked on helplessly, Koerner voiced disgust that his fellow Germans could think of supporting Bates, who had endorsed a Know-Nothing ticket in St. Louis municipal elections and presided over the 1856 Whig convention that chose Know-Nothing nominee Millard Fillmore as its candidate. Koerner insisted "in all candor" that, "outside of St. Louis and a few German settlements represented by Krekel and Muench," no German Americans would vote for Bates. "I for one would not, and I would advise my countrymen to the same effect." Browning—ironically, a Bates supporter—then spoke about Lincoln's admirable conservatism as a former Whig. While a strong advocate of America's founding principles, "Lincoln had always opposed Native Americanism. This would secure him the foreign Republican vote all over the country." Browning concluded with "a most beautiful and eloquent eulogy on Lincoln," acquainting the delegates with the special qualities of the man his Illinois friends and neighbors had come to know. The emergency intervention of Koerner and Browning stunned the Bates men and transformed the meeting.

After the speeches, the delegates went into a secret session, Koerner recalled, and there the Indiana men agreed to support Lincoln. Many Pennsylvanians, meanwhile, previously supporters of Bates on later ballots, wanted to make Lincoln their second choice, behind

Cameron. But as subsequent events demonstrated, the Lincoln men would have to do much more to win over either of those states. "Both sides are trying to buy off Pennsylvania from Cameron, but the bargain is not yet consummated," the *New York Daily Herald* reported that day. "Greeley says that whoever buys off Pennsylvania must pay well for it."

The great Seward parade reached the Wigwam, the delegates poured into their seats, and other New Yorkers got into the building as best they could. In the well of the Wigwam, in front of the platform, the tireless Gilmore's Boston Band serenaded the audience. When the big building could hold no more, the doors were closed, and tens of thousands of men in business suits and women in colorful, flowing dresses found themselves stranded outside. Rather than leave, most clustered around the Wigwam in the pleasant May weather, waiting for news to trickle out. Someone passed a message inside to George Ashmun, the president of the Republican National Convention: "Sir—Can you not arrange to send out some effective speaker to entertain twenty thousand Republicans and their wives outside the building?"

Shortly after ten o'clock, with a thwack of his gavel hewn from Commodore Perry's flagship, Ashmun called the convention to order. For all the talk of Republican unity and brotherhood, the divide between the Seward men and the more conservative delegates became instantly apparent. The Committee on the Order of Business, in a majority report, recommended that the nominee should be decided, in effect, by a two-thirds vote of the delegates, which would drag out the contest and make it difficult for Seward to win. The Seward men, represented by the committee's minority, leapt up and shouted, "No! No!" Former Ohio congressman David K. Cartter suggested that, before resolving that difference, the convention first hear from the Committee on Credentials.

That committee, it turned out, had accepted all the delegations—including the "bogus" one from Texas. Former congressman Timothy Davis of Gloucester, Massachusetts, rose and objected to the ruling,

The leading Republican candidates for president as presented in *Harper's Weekly*, May 12, 1860. William Seward was the clear favorite; Abraham Lincoln (lower left) was almost an afterthought.

Judge David Davis.

Joshua R. Giddings.

DELEGATE'S CARD.

Admit David Davis

TO THE

REPUBLICAN NATIONAL CONVENTION.

E. D. Morgan

Ch'm'n Rep. Nat. Com.

David Davis's delegate card for the Republican National Convention.

Francis P. Blair.

The Deutsches Haus.

The Tremont House.

The Wigwam, May 18, 1860.

Inside the Wigwam, May 19, 1860.

William H. Seward.

Thurlow Weed.

Simon Cameron.

Salmon P. Chase.

Edward Bates.

Henry S. Lane.

Stephen A. Douglas.

Mary A. Livermore.

Horace Greeley.

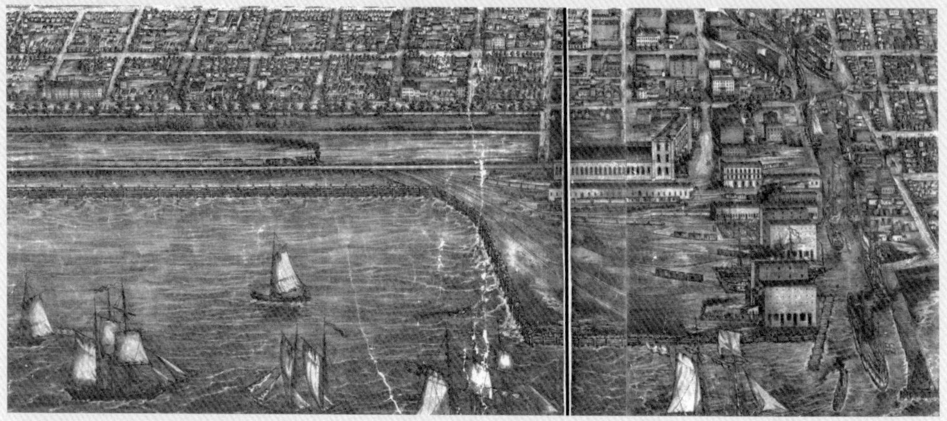

Train on causeway approaching Chicago's Grand Central Depot in 1857 bird's-eye view map.

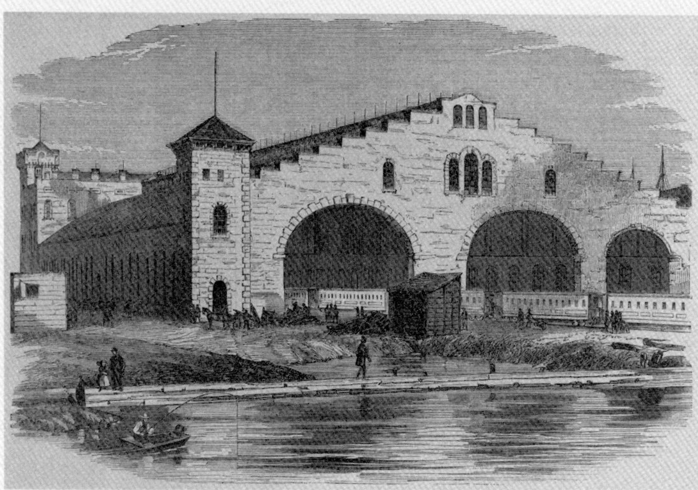

Grand Central Depot, Chicago.

Currier & Ives illustration of a fast train, c. 1864.

PROCESSION OF THE WIDE-AWAKE CLUB OF HARTFORD, CONN., ON THURSDAY, JULY 26.—FROM A SKETCH BY OUR SPECIAL ARTIST.

A procession of the Wide Awakes in Hartford, July 26, 1860.

Carl Schurz.

Tom Hyer.

John Wentworth.

Currier & Ives cartoon satirizing Horace Greeley's role in bringing about the defeat of William Seward at the Chicago convention. From left to right, James Watson Webb, Horace Greeley, Henry Raymond, and in the water, William Seward, holding the famous letter by Greeley dissolving the "political firm" of Seward, Thurlow Weed, and Greeley.

Abraham Lincoln, Springfield, Illinois, May 20, 1860, two days after his nomination, by William Marsh.

The Lincolns' front parlor, Springfield, Illinois.

Mary Todd Lincoln.

Campaign rally at the Lincolns' house, August 8, 1860.

The Lincolns' house at Eighth & Jackson Streets in Springfield, Illinois, in 1860. Lincoln stands in front with his son Willie, while son Tad rides the fence.

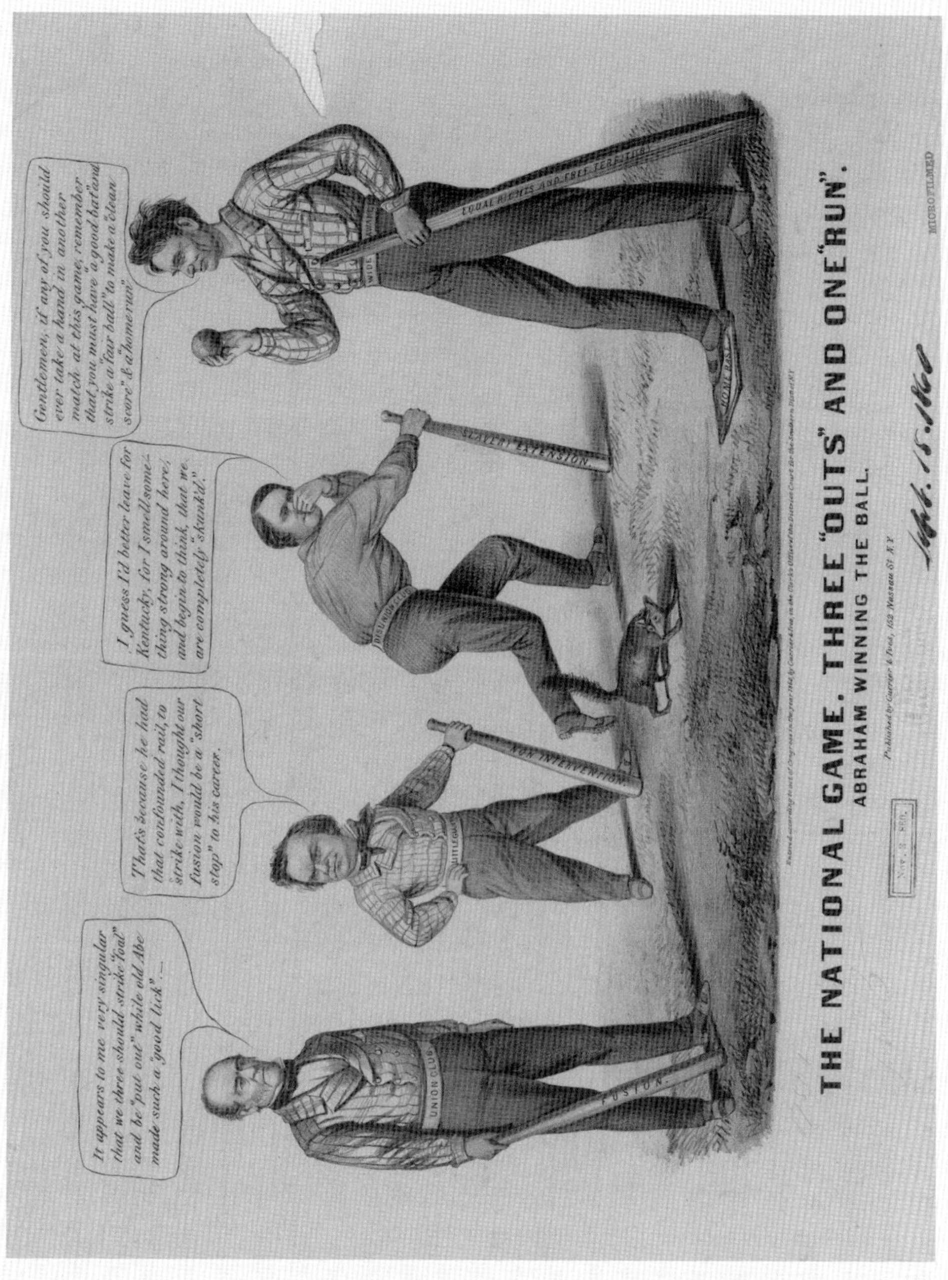

Currier & Ives pro-Lincoln cartoon inspired by the rising game of base ball (two words then). As the Railsplitter, Lincoln carries a rail instead of a bat. From left to right are his opponents in the 1860 presidential race, John Bell, Stephen Douglas, and John Breckinridge. The cartoon is full of amusing baseball jargon.

1860 campaign lithograph of the Republican ticket, Abraham Lincoln and vice presidential nominee Hannibal Hamlin of Maine.

moving that the question of Texas be sent back to the committee. The celebrated David Wilmot then kicked over a hornet's nest by questioning the legitimacy of *all* the Southern states represented in Chicago—not only Texas, but also Maryland, Virginia, and Kentucky, as well as the District of Columbia and the territories of Kansas and Nebraska. "I can see nothing better calculated to demoralize a party, and to break it up, than just such a proceeding," Wilmot declared. "Why, sir, this nomination is to be the nomination of the Republican Party in the Union, not the nomination of respectable gentlemen who may belong to the Republican Party in Virginia, Maryland, or Kentucky." For good measure, Wilmot took a shot at the two-thirds rule, winning a "tremendous cheer" with a call for "plain old Republican rule, that the majority—the real majority—shall control" the nomination.

The defenders of the Southern delegations returned heavy fire. John H. Ewing, of Washington, Pennsylvania, said he was shocked that a Republican convention could "ever adopt such an outrage as to disenfranchise our friends that come from the Southern States. Why, sir, I was mortified at such a sentiment coming from my distinguished friend from Pennsylvania. . . . We all come here as Republicans, and those who came here from the states named deserve ten times more credit than those who came here from the free states." That was not merely hot air. When Virginia Republicans held their state convention in Wheeling two weeks earlier, the city's *Union* newspaper called on armed citizens to shut it down by force. "*Where is the old Virginia pride, the hot impetuous nature and fiery spirit, once so prompt to resent any insult cast upon her glorious old name?*" the paper asked, with emphasis. "It must be dead indeed when we stand coolly and unconcerned, while those arch traitors are plotting in our very midst, the vilest treason; counselling opposition to her tried, trusty and time honored institutions."

Charles Lee Armour, of Frederick, Maryland, rising to address the Wigwam, explained that a man who admitted to being a Republican in a Southern state risked serious injury or worse. The Republican state convention in Baltimore just three weeks earlier, for example, had been infiltrated by "Roughs" and "hard boys," in the words of the

New York Times, who overturned benches, hurled missiles, called on the crowd to "Kill the scoundrel" speaking, and traded punches with police officers who tried to eject them. Armour was there. "I faced the mob in Baltimore"—an attack planned by the "menial hirelings" of the Democratic Buchanan administration, he told his Chicago audience. When Armour got home, he added, "I . . . found that I had been burned in effigy and suspended by the neck because I dared to avow myself a friend of freedom." He pointed out that Wilmot, by contrast, lived in a free state, breathing free air. Yet he and the men there did not even dare to call themselves Republicans. "I claim to be as true a Republican as the distinguished member of the 'People's' party from Pennsylvania," Armour said, his sarcasm drawing laughter and applause. Halstead was impressed. "I have seldom heard so plump a speech," he wrote. When Armour "left the floor the author of the Wilmot Proviso had gone to grass and come to grief."

George Blakey of Kentucky then piled on, expressing astonishment that Wilmot would seek to oust the delegates from his state, when he and other Kentuckians had voted for Wilmot for vice president at the 1856 convention. "Can I be forgiven for that sin?" he asked sarcastically, drawing more laughter and applause. Tempers flared, as one man after another defended his state's honor. Wilmot protested that he simply wanted to be sure that the party's key decisions were made by actual Republicans who really represented their states. "I am told that the gentlemen who are here from Texas, or a majority of them, are not residents of the state at all, and they have no Republican organization in the state," Wilmot said.

Halstead found the debate "really entertaining and full of fire. There has not been in any previous Republican Convention sharpshooting so keen, and sarcasm so bitter and incisive." But others thought the party should move on. "I am in favor of less talk and more work," Aaron Goodrich of Minnesota declared, to cries of "Good, good!" and "No more speeches now!" The delegates, by then wondering about the Texas delegation and hungry for lunch, voted to recommit the report to the Committee on Credentials and adjourned until that afternoon.

* * *

During the break, William Butler scrawled a quick letter to Abraham Lincoln. The convention's upcoming votes on the doubtful delegations and the percentage needed to nominate would reveal Seward's strength, he advised Lincoln. "The Newyork men will fight hard on these two points a defeat on either whips them." Indeed, the Seward men spent their lunch break pushing hard to get their way. Butler also told Lincoln that he had clearly become Seward's chief rival. "The hole contest as now Spoken of is between you and Seward. though your Vote may start off Small," Butler wrote. Still, on that afternoon, with the balloting for the nomination expected to begin a few hours later, it remained anyone's guess who would triumph. "We have done all that Can be done If whiped, we expect to meet defeat Knowing we have done all in our power."

Back in Springfield, Edward L. Baker, editor of the *Illinois State Journal* (no relation to Edward D. Baker, the California senator), picked up on a new threat. Lincoln, who had written countless unsigned editorials for the paper over the years, was Baker's friend and ally. When the editor found a troubling piece in the *Missouri Democrat*, a St. Louis paper partial to Bates, he quickly alerted the candidate. The paper had published a message from a Seward supporter. Trying to explode the effective marketing of Lincoln as a conservative, the writer quoted from Lincoln's speeches to show he was in truth as radical as Seward—an idea which, if it took hold in Chicago, might destroy the whole argument of Lincoln's "availability."

With the window of opportunity to change minds rapidly closing, Lincoln marked a copy of the article to lay out the facts. "I agree with Seward in his 'Irrepressible Conflict,' but I do not endorse his 'Higher Law' doctrine," Lincoln scrawled in the margin in pencil. He could hardly dispute the idea of an irrepressible conflict, since he had made virtually that point in his "House Divided" speech. But as a fierce defender of the rule of law, Lincoln found it reckless of Seward to speak of a higher law than the Constitution. Lincoln gave the paper back to

Baker, who rushed off to catch the next train to Chicago. There, he would hand it over to David Davis for his use in lobbying delegates, if it were not already too late.

Lincoln included a stern addendum in the margin, underlined for emphasis: "*Make no contracts that will bind me.*" No political novice, he surely knew his men would be discussing deals in Chicago. Perhaps he wanted people to think that he did not approve. Perhaps he wanted to limit the damage. Given the anti-corruption mood sweeping the nation and his nickname of "Honest Abe," Lincoln would not have wished to be saddled with a reputation for selling government positions to win office—and he certainly wanted to control as much patronage as he could, understanding that he would have to dispense it to the right people to maximize his support in Washington, if it ever came to that. Then he opened a remarkable letter from Chicago headed "'*Confidential*' *Confidential*" that insisted vastly *more* such deals must be made in Chicago, rather than none.

Lincoln's mercurial Kansas friend, Mark Delahay, was the author. He sounded panicked. Frustrated with his colleagues' inability to wrest the nomination from Seward, Delahay tattled to Lincoln that David Davis and his cohorts had turned out to be hopelessly weak, bound by a sense of propriety while waging the brutal war of presidential politics. Unfortunately, the other side was not as punctilious. Seward men "are desperate gamblers and I am well acquainted with their appliances to accomplish an end—your men are I regret to say too honest to advance your Prospects as surely as I would like to see." While Davis was "a good Judge doubtless," and Jesse Dubois and Butler were "honest & faithful," they were "unacquainted with New York Polaticians— I live among them & have suffered at their hands." If the Lincoln forces would only empower men from the Ohio, Pennsylvania, Massachusetts, and Iowa delegations to distribute "what ever Patronage they respectively are or would be entitled to from the administration," Lincoln would easily win. "The story would be told to morrow & you would beyond doubt be nominated— But this will not be done as your men (for this purpose) are straw men; I know that you have no relish for such a

Game; But it is an old maxium that you must fight the devil with fire." Lincoln surely viewed the letter with a degree of horror, though he probably thought Davis was shrewd enough to resist putting the power of patronage in others' hands, to be dispensed like candy, destroying Lincoln's reputation for probity and his power to control the party. Like Butler, Delahay reported that the battle had come down to Seward versus Lincoln, but he too was bracing for defeat. "We are still hopeful but it is only because we have the man of acknowledge[d] merit—it is not on account of superior skill and management; if we are beat this will be the last time I shall ever be heard of in Polatics."

With time rapidly running out in Chicago, Illinois delegates spent the Wigwam lunch break at an emergency meeting in the Briggs House with fellow delegates from Pennsylvania, New Jersey, and Indiana. All were trying to figure out some way to stop Seward before it was too late. But even at this late hour, the anti-Seward men found it impossible to agree on a candidate. Other states' delegates did not concur with the Illinois men that Lincoln had become the only feasible alternative. "Much discussion was going on, and it was very evident that nothing could be agreed upon in this sub-convention," New Jersey delegate-at-large Thomas H. Dudley recalled. Lincoln's friend Norman Judd, acting on a suggestion from Dudley, proposed that a select committee of twelve—made up of three men from each of the four states—be appointed to figure something out. The members would be men who had played prominent roles over days of politicking in Chicago, including David Davis of Illinois, Caleb B. Smith of Indiana, and David Wilmot of Pennsylvania. The subcommittee planned to meet at Wilmot's room at 6:00 p.m.—if, that is, the convention had not nominated Seward by then.

At 3:15 p.m., Ashmun gaveled the convention back into action. He first acknowledged the massive crowd that had been standing outside since morning. Vast as the Wigwam was, he observed, "twice as many honest and wise heads are there as here." In response to that morning's request for a speaker, Ashmun announced that Governor Alexander Randall of Wisconsin, a noted stemwinder, would take on the task. The good-natured Wigwam crowd applauded warmly, then began chanting "Corwin! Corwin!" in reference to a more celebrated orator, the "Old Wagon Boy," congressman and former governor Tom Corwin of Ohio. California's Francis Palmer Tracy stood up and declared, "I think Mr. Corwin had better go out with Gov. Randall," drawing laughter.

The Committee on Credentials, after its meeting at the Richmond House, reported that it had decided to recognize all the states—a big victory for Seward. The conservatives on the panel, holding a one-vote majority, could have thwarted Seward's men, but they sensed that the mood on the convention floor favored accepting the Southern delegations, and they did not want to split the party. At first it was not clear whether the most controversial delegation of all was included in the recommendation. Cries of "Texas! Texas!" rose from the floor. Jacob Benton of New Hampshire, chairman of the committee, stood up to explain that, in the scant time available during the break, the panel had taken testimony. Witnesses persuaded the committee that the "delegates from Texas—resident delegates who are here in attendance" were legitimate. They were chosen on April 12 in a "mass convention" in Austin, requested by three hundred registered voters. The call for the convention had been published in two German-language newspapers and advertised around the state, Benton asserted.

The whole idea of such a convention seemed far-fetched to many observers, given Texans' violent hostility toward Republicans and abolitionists. That very week, Northern newspapers reprinted a horrifying report by the *New-York Tribune* about a white peddler who made his way to Buchanan, Texas, sixty miles southwest of Dallas. The unnamed young man, thought to be a Yankee, had with him a wagonload of maps and books, mainly Bibles and other religious works. He also had a few copies of Hinton Rowan Helper's 1857 book *The Impending Crisis of the South*, an analysis of the economic damage done by slavery that might well have stirred even more outrage in the South than *Uncle Tom's Cabin*. An enraged mob, the story alleged, seized the peddler, flogged him, stripped him, and covered him in tar. Then, after a black slave (under torture) accused him of forging a pass to help him escape, the men passed a rope around the peddler's neck, threw the other end over a limb, raised him until his toes barely reached a pile of sticks and twigs they had heaped on his wagon, and applied a torch, burning him alive until his shrieks of agony were heard no more. On the day the Republicans in Chicago ratified the Texas delegation, Abram M. Gentry, president of the Texas and Louisiana Railroad, informed a New York crowd that there could not possibly be any such entity as a Republican Party of Texas. Only two parties existed in the state—the Democratic and the American—for the simple reason that Texans harbored a murderous hatred of Republicans. "No man could have assembled anywhere in Texas to elect delegates to the Chicago convention and lived until morning," Gentry asserted.

But the Texas delegation was in, and the Seward men were thrilled about it. Shouts of "Good! Good!" greeted the report, along with loud applause. The convention approved it unanimously. Another important Seward victory followed, when the delegates voted to substitute the minority report of the Rules Committee for the majority report. The nominee would therefore be elected with a simple majority—far easier for Seward to reach than two-thirds of the vote. With 466 delegates now officially approved, that meant Seward would need only 234 votes to win. If the convention's actions that afternoon were tests of Seward's strength, as Butler had argued, the New Yorker had proved his power.

The delegates turned to the party's proposed platform, pounded out just that day. The select group of seven members of the Committee on Resolutions had reconvened early that morning at the Tremont House to finish its work. One of its aggressively opinionated members, Horace Greeley, insisted on a plank that vigorously supported protective tariffs, craved by manufacturers in Pennsylvania—and opposed by rural states, whose residents did not want to have to pay artificially high prices for goods. The others on the committee recognized that they risked dividing the party with too strong a tariff measure.

Abraham Lincoln had addressed the explosive issue with his usual circumspection the previous Saturday. He wrote a cautious letter that might be shared with delegates, though only if the issue came up in Chicago, addressing it to a trusted acquaintance from Pennsylvania who was attending the convention: Dr. Edward Wallace, brother of the Lincolns' family doctor in Springfield. "I now think the Tariff question ought not to be agitated in the Chicago convention," Lincoln instructed Wallace. But any delegates who cared about Lincoln's tariff position should be confident that he would neither use his executive powers to force a tariff law on the nation nor veto a "reasonable one" passed by Congress.

Lincoln's man on the platform committee, Illinois's Gustave Koerner, reflected that wary approach. "We did not consider the tariff question at this particular time as of primary importance," Koerner recalled, "and we humored" Greeley with a vaguely worded plank supporting protection that "did not essentially differ from former Democratic declarations on the same subject." Greeley accepted the language. He was less happy with another plank, one that strongly repudiated Stephen Douglas's popular sovereignty idea. Greeley's reaction was perhaps understandable, given that he had all but supported Douglas's Senate reelection in 1858. "Here, of course, we did not yield, but condemned the doctrine most emphatically," Koerner wrote. Greeley, clearly upset, "left the committee, and did not further participate in our discussions of the platform."

Without advancing radical proposals that might turn off swing voters, the platform of seventeen planks was chock-full of measures that delighted delegates. It opposed the expansion of slavery to the territories; called for a homestead law helping Western settlers obtain government land cheaply; denounced Democratic perfidy in threatening disunion and fostering government waste and corruption; assured voters that Republicans opposed a military invasion of the South to end slavery, making it explicit that the party rejected the bloody approach of John Brown; and backed internal improvements and federal aid for a railroad to the Pacific coast. With Carl Schurz and Koerner serving on the committee, it also included the German American plank insisting on the rights of naturalized citizens and implicitly knocking

Massachusetts. The *New York Daily Herald* sneeringly dubbed it the "Teutonic naturalization resolution, Schurz's lager beer invention." But the paper had to admit that the platform overall aimed at moderation, reflecting Republicans' fears of a "rising tide of conservative feeling among the masses of the people. . . . Here we have a platform in which any demagogue north of Mason and Dixon's line may find a text to suit his audience, expressed in language pliable and elastic enough for any purpose."

The *Daily Pantagraph*, in David Davis's hometown of Bloomington, Illinois, by contrast, found the platform oak-solid. "Its sentiments are plain, outspoken, and appeal directly to the hearts, the judgment, and the patriotism of the people. Step on it, ye doubting, wavering, hesitating souls; every plank is sound, and will carry you and our common country safely and triumphantly through the fog and shoals now besetting the Ship of State." When the platform was read out at the convention, its support for tariffs, however vague, thrilled delegates from the manufacturing states. "Pennsylvania went into spasms of joy over the 'Tariff Plank,' her whole delegation rising and swinging hats and canes," Halstead reported. The Wigwam seemed so happy with the platform that David Cartter of Ohio moved that the convention accept it whole without discussion.

Amid confusion, his fellow Ohioan, Joshua R. Giddings, rose to object. The tall, stocky, white-haired former congressman, who had been cheered loudly Saturday night at the Wigwam, was revered by many in this audience for his stalwart decades-long battle against slavery, defying ostracism and death threats. He did not go along to get along. During a debate on the House floor fourteen years earlier, his words had inflamed a Louisiana congressman, who cocked a pistol and declared, "I'll shoot him! By G—d, I'll shoot him!" When a Georgia congressman armed with a pistol and a heavy sword cane approached, Giddings shouted defiantly: "Come on! The people of Ohio don't send cowards here!"

Now this unflinching man was about to precipitate a debate over the meaning of the Republican Party.

* * *

Giddings's fellow Buckeye David Cartter tried to shut him up and hustle through approval of the platform, but the "convention was not willing to treat the old Ohio abolitionist with rudeness," recalled Illinois lawyer Isaac N. Arnold. Though it "was obviously afraid of his radicalism," the convention voted 301 to 155 to permit discussion.

Giddings pointed to the second of the seventeen planks. It pledged the party to support the principles of the Declaration of Independence, but Giddings wanted to add more explicit language: "That we solemnly re-assert the self-evident truths that all men are endowed by their creator with certain inalienable rights, among which are those of life, liberty and the pursuit of happiness"—a passage that drew cheers from the Wigwam crowd—and "that governments are instituted among those men to secure the enjoyment of those rights."

The safest thing for the Republican Party to do, pragmatists knew, was give lip service to the Declaration and move on. The Declaration was a dangerous document, because it asserted that all men were equally endowed with rights—a notion that simply did not square with the continued existence of race-based slavery. "Many members of the convention were still very afraid of abolitionism," Arnold noted. "The party was far from homogenous, and there was danger of a rupture." Practical politicians could see plainly that even voters who considered slavery evil would be repulsed by any attempt to emphasize that all men, black and white, should be treated equally. Yet Republicans could not run away from the Declaration. They had built their party around the founding ideal that every human being was endowed with sacred and inviolable rights.

"All men are created equal" was a phrase that the Founders, and particularly the Declaration's brilliant author, slaveholder Thomas Jefferson, could not have failed to recognize as an implicit rebuke of chattel slavery. The idea of universal rights at the heart of the Declaration was certain to fatally weaken the institution. As Republicans saw it, the founding generation had hoped that slavery, though embedded in the Southern states at that moment, would gradually die off, while freedom took root and flourished. That prospect had been dashed by Eli Whitney's invention of the cotton gin, which dramatically transformed the economics of slavery. But the Declaration had lived on as a measure of how far the country had come and how far it had fallen short of its ideals.

As the great black leader Frederick Douglass stated in an Independence Day speech in Rochester, New York, in 1852, "The signers of the Declaration of Independence were brave men. They were great men, too, great enough to give frame to a great age. It does not often happen to a nation to raise, at one time, such a number of truly great men." But they and their nation had failed to extend the blessings of liberty to black Americans.

> I am not included within the pale of this glorious anniversary! Your high independence only reveals the immeasurable distance between us. The blessings in which you, this day, rejoice, are not enjoyed in common. The rich inheritance of justice, liberty, prosperity and independence, bequeathed by your fathers, is shared by you, not by me. The sunlight that brought light and healing to you, has brought stripes and death to me. This Fourth of July is yours, not mine. You may rejoice, I must mourn.

The continued discussion of the Declaration through the eighty-four years since 1776 picked at a national wound that would not heal. Many white Northerners feared the prospect of ill-educated freed slaves streaming into their states, competing for jobs, intermarrying with white people, and contributing to crime. Equal rights for all remained a utopian, even a radical, notion.

No Republican had clung to the Declaration more tenaciously than Abraham Lincoln. In 1854, Lincoln spoke of his hatred of the principles of popular sovereignty, which held that people could vote to spread slavery: "I hate it because of the monstrous injustice of slavery itself. I hate it because it deprives our republican example of its just influence in the world—enables the enemies of free institutions, with plausibility, to taunt us as hypocrites—causes the real friends of freedom to doubt our sincerity, and especially because it forces so many really good men amongst ourselves into an open war with the very fundamental principles of civil liberty—criticizing the Declaration of Independence, and insisting that there is no right principle of action but *self-interest*."

During their debates in 1858, Stephen Douglas repeatedly mocked Lincoln for contending that the sacred rights of humanity applied to black people. "Now, I say to you, my fellow-citizens, that in my opinion the signers of the Declaration had no reference to the negro whatever when they declared all men to be created equal," Douglas asserted. "They desired to express by that phrase, white men, men of European birth and European descent, and had no reference either to the negro, the savage Indians, the Fejee, the Malay, or any other inferior and degraded race, when they spoke of the equality of men." During the campaign, Lincoln voiced dismay that this view was spreading—the notion that the founders did not mean "all men" when they said "all men." "If you have been inclined to believe" that, Lincoln said, "let me entreat you to come back. Return to the fountain whose waters spring close by the blood of the Revolution. Think nothing of me—take no thought for the political fate of any man whomsoever—but come back to the truths that are in the Declaration of Independence." The ideals it encapsulated mattered more than the election of any one man, Lincoln insisted. "I charge you to drop every paltry and insignificant thought for any man's success. It is nothing; I am nothing; Judge Douglas is nothing. *But do not destroy that immortal emblem of Humanity—the Declaration of American Independence.*" More recently, in an 1859 letter to the organizer of a Boston dinner in honor of Thomas Jefferson's birthday, Lincoln marveled that Jefferson had introduced "into a merely revolutionary document, an abstract truth, applicable to all men and all times, and so to embalm it there, that to-day, and in all coming days, it shall be a rebuke and a stumbling-block to the very harbingers of re-appearing tyranny and oppression."

In savaging Lincoln during the 1858 campaign, Douglas compared "his negro-equality doctrines" and "the enormity of his principles" with those of the most extreme Republicans. "Did old Giddings, when he came down among you four years ago, preach more radical abolitionism than that?" Douglas asked an Illinois crowd. "No, never!" angry Democrats shouted in response. Now, here in Chicago, old Giddings stood up on the Wigwam stage to explain why he wanted the 1860 platform to quote the Declaration. "I offer this because our party was formed upon it. It grew upon it. It has existed upon it—and when you leave out this truth you leave out the party," he said. The crowd cheered lustily. "Everybody knew him as one of the champions of the anti-slavery cause," Carl Schurz noted. "He had pleaded for that cause with undaunted courage and fidelity when even in many parts of the North no one could do so without danger. It was the religion of his life." Massachusetts congressman Eli Thayer—oddly representing Oregon, like his friend Greeley—rose to object, saying, "It is not the business, I think, of this Convention . . . to embrace in its platform all the truths that the world in all its past history has recognized." That, too, won applause, and the convention voted down Giddings's amendment, preferring the safer route of saying little.

With that, "Mr. Giddings, a look of distress upon his face, his white head towering above the crowd, slowly made his way toward the door of the hall," Schurz recalled. Delegates begged Giddings not to go. "But he considered everything lost, even honor," Halstead wrote. The New York delegation assured him the matter would be taken up again, but Giddings "left the Convention—actually seceded in sorrow and anger." Though some in the hall thought Giddings was behaving like a child, the walkout of a venerable anti-slavery hero threatened to embarrass the Republicans.

Wilmot moved that the planks be taken up separately. The delegates were restless, eager to move along to voting for their presidential nominee, and voices rang out: "No!" "Take them in a lot!" But debate began.

Wilmot objected to the German American plank, which criticized "state legislation" that denied new citizens their full rights, an obvious jab at Massachusetts. He noted that the fourth plank pledged to maintain "the rights of the States, and especially the right of each State to order and control its own domestic institutions according to its own judgment exclusively." When the chairman of the committee, a Yale-educated Pennsylvania judge named William Jessup, pointed out that Republican criticism of a state's policy was not the same thing as advocating that the federal government overturn it, Wilmot withdrew his objection.

Though no one was now formally protesting the plank, Carl Schurz grabbed the opportunity to make an impassioned speech in favor of it. He played his strongest card: the voting power of immigrants. "The German Republicans of the Northern States have given you 300,000 votes," he said, to the crowd's applause, "and I wish that they should find it consistent with their honor and their safety to give you 300,000 more." But Germans would find honor and safety in the party only if Republicans took a stand against prejudice. As he knew well from the discussions of the Resolutions Committee, many party strategists feared the plank would cost Republicans the votes of former Know-Nothings in the swing states. "You go to calculate, will prejudice give us more votes or will right give us more votes," Schurz said. "Let me tell you one thing, that the votes you get by truckling to prejudice will never be safe; while those votes which you get by recognizing constitutional rights may every time be counted upon." A man covering the convention for the *Daily Evening Express* of Lancaster, Pennsylvania, was deeply impressed. He described Schurz as "slimly built, with a bright, blue German eye, that burns into you and wins your heart at once." He was a "fascinating" speaker, using beautiful English with little hint of a German accent, "and sentences roll from his lips as smooth and as rounded as those of Macaulay," the famous British historian and Whig politician, "but possess more fire."

The eloquent German-born newspaper editor Frederick Hassaurek of Cincinnati then spoke. He was in favor of the plank "not because I am an adopted citizen, but because I claim to be a true American." Long before he came to America, he told the delegates, he had studied Washington and Jefferson as mighty champions of liberty and enemies of tyranny. "I loved this country before my eyes ever beheld its hospitable shores," he said. "Gentlemen, as one who has suffered the stings and oppressions of despotism, I claim to be doubly capable of apprehending the blessings of liberty." The crowd cheered loudly. "Gentlemen, I have seen the nations of Europe smarting under the arbitrary rule of despots, and I know what an inestimable treasure, what an incalculable boon freedom is." He insisted that America had "a nobler purpose than to be the mere means of fortifying, protecting and propagating the institution of human servitude"—the Democrats' relentless agenda. Thus, the nation should not betray its principles by creating a dual system of justice. During his brief plea, the crowd interrupted Hassaurek fourteen times with cheers.

Gustave Koerner sat amid the Illinois delegation, directly behind the Massachusetts men, as the debate unfolded. John A. Andrew, running for governor of Massachusetts, paid little attention until his state's name was mentioned. He turned and exclaimed to George S. Boutwell, a former governor, "That will never do! That is aimed at our State." With that, Andrew stood up and cried for recognition: "Mr. President!" Given that Andrew was a "fiery, energetic, and most eloquent" speaker, Koerner recalled, "it is hard to tell what might have happened to the resolution, had he been recognized by the chair." Boutwell had served on the Resolutions Committee and had warned that that plank could damage Republicans, but he had come to recognize that the measure was "all important to keep the German Republicans in line." The ex-governor quickly grabbed Andrew's shoulders "and sought to push him down," as Koerner, "sitting right behind him, took hold of his coat tails and held him down." While Andrew "was looking around with the greatest astonishment," the discussion moved on to another topic.

Then "a young man of strikingly beautiful features," in Carl Schurz's words, took the floor. At thirty-six, George William Curtis was one of the stars of the convention: brilliant and articulate; an ornament of New York society; a prolific essayist, popular lecturer, journalist, editor, and author of six books so far. A slender man with lustrous hair and long sideburns, he was a friend of the famous transcendentalists in and around Concord, Massachusetts, and had helped Henry David Thoreau build his little one-room cabin just uphill from a cove of Walden Pond. "No man was ever more honored in the character of his raisers than I," Thoreau wrote in his 1854 book *Walden*. "They are destined, I trust, to assist at the raising of loftier structures one day."

The lofty structure that Curtis was now raising was the 1860 platform of the Republican Party. He proposed an amendment to the second plank, adding these words: "That all men are created equal; that they are endowed by their Creator with certain inalienable rights; that among these are life, liberty and the pursuit of happiness; that to secure those rights, governments are instituted amongst men, deriving their just powers from the consent of the governed." Great applause broke out, while men jumped up, seeking recognition. Eli Thayer protested that the convention had already voted down an amendment to the plank, a fair point.

Curtis then observed a man across the aisle from his own seat, "a sturdy sandy-haired man, who sat carelessly swinging one leg and foot over the arm of the seat, and squirting tobacco juice on the floor, apparently indifferent to every thing that took place." As Ashmun prepared to rule on Thayer's objection, the man, "by a sudden spring raised himself erect upon his feet, standing on the seat, and with a voice that commanded the chair so that he instinctively turned and could not help recognizing the speaker, exclaimed, 'Mr. President!'" It was Frank Blair, the Bates man from Missouri. He came to the rescue of the Seward man Curtis, arguing that the New Yorker was referring to the second clause of the plank, rather than the first that Giddings had addressed. The discussion was permitted to go on, eating up valuable time.

Rising, Curtis pleaded with the delegates to exhibit courage. He asked them if, while meeting "upon the free prairies of the West, in the summer of 1860," they would "dare to wince and quail" rather than repeat the words that "great men enunciated" in Philadelphia in 1776—men who, everyone knew, might well have been hanged for treason. The crowd thundered its applause. "This was a strong appeal and took the convention by storm. It was a great personal triumph for Curtis," Halstead reported. Samuel P. Oyler, an English-born lawyer and prosecutor "from one of the negro-hating districts of Indiana," as a Kansas reporter put it, still objected. "I presume that all Republicans here are in favor of the Declaration of Independence. Does it necessarily follow that we must publish it in our platform?" Members of the crowd yelled, "Yes!" "Well, then it is there now," Oyler protested. "Put it in twice!" someone yelled.

There was no restraining the emotions stirred by Curtis's appeal to patriotic valor. "His classical features, literary fame, pleasing style as a speaker, and the force of his case, called attention to him, and gave him the ear of the Convention, and gave him the triumph," Halstead wrote. "There was such earnestness in his manner, such pathos of entreaty in his tone, that the audience stretched out and listened to him as it had listened to no one before," added Connecticut journalist Isaac H. Bromley. Schurz, no mean orator himself, never forgot Curtis's appeal: "As he stood there in that convention, towering over the vast multitude, his beautiful face radiant with resolute fervor, his singularly melodious voice thrilling with impassioned anxiety of purpose, one might have seen in him an ideal, poetic embodiment of the best of that moral impulse and lofty enthusiasm which aroused the people in the North to the decisive struggle against slavery."

The amendment passed, and Joshua Giddings, his faith in the Republican Party restored, walked back onto the platform. Isaac Arnold described the moment: "It was touching to see old Mr. Giddings, as he went up to Curtis, and throwing his arms around his neck, exclaimed: 'God bless you, my boy. You have saved the republican party. God bless you.'" Giddings rejoined his Ohio delegation. The pragmatic Edward Bates, back in St. Louis, was less impressed, complaining that the platform "lugs in the lofty generalities of the Declaration of Independence for no practical purpose I can see, but needlessly exposing the party to the specious charge of favoring Negro equality—and this only to gratify a handful of extreme abolitionists, led on by Mr. Giddings." The *Cincinnati Enquirer* was appalled. The incorporation of the Declaration's language into the platform signified that, in the eyes of Republicans, "a negro is as good as a white man, if not a little better, and that a slaveholder has no right to the involuntary service of his slaves. How they will make the South howl should they succeed in securing the control of the General Government!"

At around 6:00 p.m., the delegates approved the entire platform unanimously. Halstead, though a veteran of many conventions, found the crowd's response astounding. "All the thousands of men in that enormous Wigwam commenced swinging their hats, and cheering with intense enthusiasm; and the other thousands of ladies waved their handkerchiefs and clapped their hands," he reported. "The roar that went up from that mass of ten thousand human beings under one roof was indescribable." No one had ever seen or heard anything like it at a political convention. "A herd of buffalos or lions could not have made a more tremendous roaring." The *Chicago Journal* reported that thousands "sprang to their feet, and cheers upon cheers, deafening, tumultuous, and rapturous, went up from every throat. Men waved their hats, ladies their handkerchiefs, reporters their written pages and all screamed with very joy. This wild excitement was kept up for some ten or fifteen minutes. It was a scene that will never be forgotten by those present, a spectacle that was worth a man's lifetime to witness. It made one feel good all over."

One task remained: to nominate a candidate. Seward's great moment neared. Minnesota's Aaron Goodrich stood up to call for adjournment for the day. Voices cried out, "No, no!" and "Ballot, ballot!" "I withdraw the motion and move that we now proceed to ballot for a candidate to the Presidency," Goodrich sheepishly declared. Another delegate followed with a formal motion to adjourn, which the convention defeated.

Cincinnati lawyer Richard M. Corwine moved that the balloting begin. There seemed to be great confusion on the floor, with cries of "Ballot! Ballot!" breaking out. Lincoln's former law partner Stephen T. Logan had a letter from Lincoln in his pocket, authorizing Logan to withdraw his name from contention when the time was right. That time might have come very soon.

Had the balloting proceeded at that moment, "Seward would have been nominated beyond the question of a doubt," Pennsylvanian Andrew G. Curtin insisted. Thurlow Weed's tactics had worked like a charm all day, and Seward's strength had been proven over and over. When Wilmot questioned the dubious delegations, Halstead noted, Seward's men "made a beautiful fight," in part by "putting forward men to strike the necessary blows who were not suspected of Seward-ism." When Seward's opponents tried to pass the two-thirds measure, his men had made "a splendid fight" against that rule, making the idea so "odious" that two-thirds of delegates rejected it. As the cherry on top, Seward's men had come to the rescue of old Giddings, though the Ohio delegate had been working behind the scenes against the New York senator. With his eloquence, Curtis had demonstrated the magnanimity of the Seward forces, their dedication to the cause of freedom, and their willingness to treat even men outside of the fold with justice and support. The wild emotion greeting the approval of the platform suggested the crowd was just as ready to be swept away with the nomination of Seward as president.

But his men had made, perhaps, one fatal mistake. Instead of hustling things along, they had indulged in lengthy arguments about the Declaration of Independence and the German amendment plank. All that had pushed the voting for president past 6:00 p.m., when delegates were getting hungry and ready for a break. One of Seward's opponents, Ohio's David Cartter, seized control of the floor and shouted, "I call for a division of ayes and nays, to see if gentlemen want to go without their supper." Derisive laughter and cries of "Call the roll!" greeted the request.

At that moment, fate intervened. The chair announced that the presidential tally sheets "are prepared, but are not yet at hand, but will be in a few minutes." A quick vote might have nominated Seward, perhaps leading to his election as president in November against a divided Democratic Party, putting him in charge at the nation's darkest hour. But the prospect of a further delay took the spirit out of the famished delegates, and a desultory vote on adjournment began. The chair declared the motion carried, and the delegates poured out of the Wigwam, to reconvene at 10:00 a.m. Friday. For a want of tally sheets, Seward was not going to be selected that evening. On such slender threads hangs the destiny of nations.

Two hundred miles to the southwest, Lincoln was in downtown Springfield, dealing with whatever pressure he felt. One of the people who saw him there that afternoon was James Gourley, a shoemaker who had long lived in the small house backing up to Lincoln's. They knew each other so well that Lincoln at times came to Gourley's door in slippers and an old pair of pants, with only one suspender up, asking to borrow milk. Inside, Lincoln risked banging his head on the low ceiling. "Jim," he told his neighbor, "you have to lift your loft a little higher." Lincoln joked to Gourley's wife that "little people had Some advantages: it did not take quite So much wood & wool to make their house & Clothes."

On that Thursday, Gourley, who ran a shop downtown, saw Lincoln out playing ball. Two blocks north of the state capitol stood a vacant lot that had been leveled and smoothed to serve as a handball court. Nearby were the offices of the *Illinois State Journal*. In that space, residents played a game called "fives" against the store's windowless brick side, using a rubber ball wrapped in twine and covered in leather. One player hurled the ball against the wall, while the other used the flat of his hand to drive it back. "It was a very strenuous game," Jesse Dubois's son, Fred, recalled. The lawyers and other men working downtown tended to play it "just before the evening meal, and there was always a large crowd on the sidewalk and in the street outside the vacant lot to watch."

Another Springfield boy, John Langdon Kaine, remembered watching Lincoln compete several times—including on one proud day, when the lanky lawyer asked the boy, by name, to take his coat. Kaine admired the unexpected dexterity of the stooping lawyer he often saw trudging around Springfield, arms behind his back. Lincoln had a peculiar gait, without any spring in his step, planting his feet flat on the ground instead of rolling from heel to toe. "His legs seemed to drag from his knees down," one observer said, "like those of a laborer going home after a hard day's work." At the handball court, though, he seemed to come alive. "His agility was surprising in view of his usual deliberate, almost indolent manner," Kaine recalled, "and his long legs and long arms gave him a remarkable range of play." An aspiring lawyer named Charles S. Zane recalled that Lincoln "loved this game," the only physical sport Zane ever saw him indulge in. "This game makes my shoulders feel well," Lincoln explained. It also helped steady his nerves, no doubt, as the hours and minutes ticked away before the balloting for the Republican presidential nomination.

In Auburn, New York, William H. Seward seemed to feel less of a need to blow off steam. As he had all week, he spent some time at home that afternoon in pleasant conversation with his neighbor, the Reverend John Austin. That evening, after dinner, Seward sent again for Austin. "This intimacy with Gov. Seward is part of a long and deeply cemented friendship which has existed between us for nearly fourteen years," the reverend boasted in his journal. Seward wanted to share some wonderful news he had just received—a telegram from New York congressman Eldridge Spaulding in Chicago: "Your friends are firm and confident that you will be nominated after a few ballots." New York governor Edward D. Morgan offered a similar assurance in another telegram: "We have no doubt of a favorable result tomorrow." Seward, Austin wrote, produced "a dispatch he had just received from Chicago, assuring him that his nomination was beyond a contingency." Seward was in good spirits. "He appeared quite hopeful and happy."

David Davis, utterly exhausted, had a few short hours to try to change the course of history. Somehow, before the convention gathered the next morning, he would need to concentrate and strengthen the opposition to Seward. But Davis thought he could do it. He sent Lincoln a terse telegram. "Am very hopeful dont be Excited nearly dead with fatigue telegraph or write here very little." Davis did not want Lincoln interfering with what he had to do.

Overnight Thursday, May 17, to Friday, May 18, 1860

Chapter 12: Lincoln Ain't Here

As the delegates poured out of the Wigwam through the streets of Chicago that Thursday evening, they "seemed to electrify the city," Murat Halstead reported. "The agitation of the masses that pack the hotels and throng the streets, and are certainly forty thousand strong, was such as made the little excitement at Charleston seem insignificant." Some thought the crowd was even bigger than Halstead estimated it to be. Special rates offered by both Western and Eastern railroads—including a fifteen-dollar roundtrip ticket between Buffalo and Chicago, dirt cheap for the time—brought in enormous numbers. And it was obvious that many who had made it into the Wigwam were Seward enthusiasts. "The cheering of the thousands of spectators indicated that a very large share of the outside pressure was for Seward," Halstead reported. "There is something almost irresistible here in the pressure of his fame." As the Wigwam rapidly emptied that Thursday evening, two prominent Seward supporters forged a bond. Carl Schurz made his way to George William Curtis, whom he had never met, to thank him for his moving comments about the Declaration of Independence. "We became friends then and there," Schurz recalled, and they remained so for life.

In the hotels, saloons, restaurants, and, surely, brothels, the Seward enthusiasts made their presence felt that night. "The New Yorkers here are of a class unknown to Western Republican politicians," Halstead informed his readers in Cincinnati. "They can drink as much whiskey, swear as loud and long, sing as bad songs, and 'get up and howl' as ferociously as any crowd of Democrats you ever heard, or heard of. They are opposed, as they say, to being 'too d—d virtuous.'" A Seward man who recognized another on the street was likely to slap him on the back and roar, "How *are* you?" while the other responded, "How are you, hoss?" in a fashion reminiscent of a wild night in bourbon country—or as Halstead put it, in a "style that would do honor to Old Kaintuck on a bust." Even those not getting drunk were "doing that which ill-tutored youths call 'raising h—l generally.'" And they simply loved Seward. "They hoot at the idea that Seward could not sweep all the Northern States, and swear that he would have a party in less than a year that would clean out the disunionists from shore to shore." Certain of victory, they "did not fear the results of caucusing that night, though they knew every hour would be employed against them."

Not everyone on the Seward side was drinking. Thurlow Weed's men spent the night doggedly lobbying the delegations, scooping up last-minute supporters, and reiterating the case they had made all week. They emphasized Seward's practical advantages of "known ability, of great experience, of large acquaintance," as well as his "ability to . . . finance a hard campaign," which would "help to overcome any factional opposition in the doubtful states," Kansas delegate Addison G. Procter recalled. They sent out their bands to entertain delegations and hosted a lavish "champagne supper" at the Richmond House, during which their guests reportedly drank down three hundred bottles of bubbly. "This may be an exaggeration, but I am not inclined to think the quantity overstated, for it flowed freely as water," Halstead observed. At 10:30 p.m., Weed, joined by two highly distinguished New York lawyers, William M. Evarts and William C. Noyes, received a pledge from the New Hampshire delegation to swing to Seward on the second ballot. Ohio remained split, but five delegates supporting Salmon P. Chase promised Weed that they would line up for Seward after Chase "was dropped." Joshua Giddings, champion of the Declaration of Independence, and Tom Corwin, the celebrated orator, assured Weed that "they were for [Seward] as against Lincoln."

With all this unfolding, the Seward men were universally "in fine feather," Halstead reported. "They entertain no particle of doubt of his nomination in the morning." At that point, they were far from the only ones. Few people in Chicago believed it was possible to stop the senator now. "His friends had played their game to admiration and had been victorious on every preliminary skirmish" that day. "When the platform had been adopted, inclusive of the Declaration of Independence, they felt themselves already exalted on the pinnacle of victory." Although they had been thwarted when the convention adjourned before the voting on the presidential nomination commenced, they were "displeased but not disheartened." George G. Washburn, editor of the *Elyria Independent Democrat* of Ohio, summed up the mood that night. "The Seward men are in good spirit, and nearly every body expects his nomination to-morrow, on the second or third ballot."

Horace Greeley, by contrast, was "absolutely 'terrified,'" and regarded Seward's impending nomination "in defiance of his influence [as] a cruel blow," Halstead wrote. With the vociferous Irrepressibles dominating the convention, "the conservative expediency men—Greeley, the Blairs, the Republican candidates for Governor in Pennsylvania, Indiana, and Illinois—are hard pressed, sorely perplexed, and despondent."

As Seward's team waxed confident, the Lincoln men were "working like tigers to secure the scattering votes," wrote editor Washburn. While Davis and his associates could not afford to throw champagne dinners or send out marching bands, they maximized their meager resources. Their key challenge was winning delegates, but they also sought some way to break Thurlow Weed's control of the crowd's emotions. Earlier that day, the mobs of his roaring men in the Wigwam, including loud roughs headed by boxing champion Tom Hyer, had threatened to set off a stampede of support for Seward's nomination. The delay in balloting had given the Lincoln men a welcome chance to regroup. Fortunately for Lincoln, the two Illinois fellows with "stentorian voices" who had been sent for Wednesday arrived at the Tremont House Thursday evening. Lincoln delegate Burton C. Cook devised a plan for Friday's session of the convention. The two lead shouters, backed by crowds of Lincoln supporters, would set up on opposite sides of the Wigwam. When Cook, up on the platform with the delegates, "took out his handkerchief, they were to cheer, and not to cease until he returned it to his pocket." The stereophonic cheers for Lincoln would envelope the delegates and crowd, creating the illusion of universal support. There were now plenty of people in Chicago who could be mobilized for the effort. Leonard Swett noted that, while Seward men had poured in from the East early that week, "we were aided" later in the week "by the arrival of at least 10,000 people from Indiana and Central Illinois." Of course, the Wigwam had been packed Wednesday and Thursday with Seward enthusiasts bearing visitors' tickets courtesy of the party's pro-Seward leaders. Getting hundreds of Lincoln screamers into the crowded building was another thorny problem that would have to be solved that night.

As if the team's tasks were not challenging enough, *Illinois State Journal* editor Edward L. Baker appeared at the Tremont House with his annotated copy of the *Missouri Democrat*. The men struggling to secure the nomination were none too happy to receive Lincoln's imperious and impractical dictate: "*Make no contracts that will bind me.*" They loved Lincoln for his intelligence, his courage, and his moral integrity. But if they adhered to such a demand, they would be effectively disarmed in the crucial final hours of negotiations in Chicago. Henry Clay Whitney recalled that Lincoln's order infuriated the exhausted team. "Everybody was mad, of course. Here were men working night and day to place him on the highest mountain peak of fame, and he pulling back all he knew how," Whitney wrote, wondering, "What was to be done?" Jesse Dubois barked, "Damn Lincoln!" The more polished Leonard Swett said, "I am very sure if Lincoln was aware of the necessities—" Lincoln's former law partner Stephen T. Logan began arguing with his current one, William H. Herndon. Finally, David Davis "cut the

Gordian knot." The big judge who had led Lincoln across a swollen river on the prairie would not give up now. He simply brushed aside Lincoln's order. "Lincoln ain't here, and don't know what we have to meet, so we will go ahead as if we hadn't heard from him, and he must ratify it." If Davis had no authorization from Lincoln to sell offices, he would lie to delegates that he did.

Davis knew that deals had to be made, above all, with two vital states. Indiana, which had no favorite-son candidate but was dead set against Seward, had pursued two goals in Chicago since Saturday: finding an electable alternative to the New Yorker and securing ample patronage in the next administration. Some in its delegation wanted the promise of a cabinet seat—secretary of the interior—for former congressman Caleb B. Smith. Delegate-at-large Judge William T. Otto later told a friend that Smith secured the post on spurious grounds, exploiting the desperation of the Lincoln team at a moment when it "was pledging everything in sight to insure Mr. Lincoln's nomination." The bargain was unnecessary, Otto claimed, because "none of us cared for Smith." Once "we got to Chicago and looked over the ground all were for Lincoln." As William Butler had informed Lincoln, Indiana delegates had been leaning toward him since at least Tuesday. But Smith was the chairman of the delegation, and the pledge of a cabinet position for Indiana surely helped solidify its support.

The other big prize, Pennsylvania, remained elusive. Senator Simon Cameron controlled most of its delegation, using his power to launch his candidacy for president, but many inside and outside Pennsylvania considered the political boss essentially dishonest. Years earlier, Cameron had served as a commissioner to settle claims of the Winnebago Indians, and the charge that he had cheated them earned him the unwelcome monikers of "Old Winnebago" and "the Great Winnebago Chief." Pennsylvania lawyer and Republican activist Thomas M. Marshall regarded the politician as disgustingly corrupt, asserting that he could "go through a dark alley at midnight, and the first man I caught would make a better President than Simon Cameron." The sardonic congressman Thaddeus Stevens later discussed his fellow

Pennsylvanian's moral probity with Lincoln. "I don't think he would steal a red-hot stove," Stevens observed. Lincoln himself reportedly commented that Cameron's "very name stinks in the nostrils of the people for his corruption." The Pennsylvanian's whole presidential campaign, Illinois lawyer Ward Hill Lamon contended, was "a mere sham, got up to enable Cameron to make a bargain with some real candidate, and secure for himself the lion's share of the spoils in the event of a victory at the polls." No one could dispute that Old Winnebago was a smart political operator proficient at obtaining power. It would hardly be out of character for him to use the delegation as his tool to secure a patronage-laden cabinet post.

In truth, Cameron did have enthusiastic supporters who believed that the shrewd, successful banker and businessman might burst through the borders of Pennsylvania and attract wider support for the presidency. They "had been fed upon meat," Halstead quipped—filled with confidence and strength, certain that Pennsylvania was vital to the party's victory in November, and that other delegates would thus have to bow to their wishes in Chicago. Their sales pitch for "Sim" Cameron, as they familiarly called him, was simple: "He was the only man, they a thousand times said, who would certainly carry Pennsylvania." But his men had been unable to persuade other swing states to accept Cameron.

Weed had gone into the convention believing that Cameron was soundly in his camp and that the Pennsylvania delegates would ultimately swing behind Seward. "Seward had a good tariff record"—the all-important issue to Pennsylvania—"and his friends would spend money enough in the State to carry it against any Democratic candidate who was a possibility," Halstead noted. "The flood of Seward money promised for Pennsylvania was not without efficacy." Pennsylvanians spread the word that Seward "would *spend oceans of money*."

But, while the delegation overwhelmingly backed Cameron, it proved unwilling to invest in Seward. For one thing, these men did not represent Republicans alone but, rather, the People's Party, an amalgamation that included Seward-averse nativists. Cameron, as a former

Democrat and Know-Nothing, reflected its tendencies. But even those without nativist leanings believed a ticket with Seward at the top, tinged with radicalism, would prove electoral poison in Pennsylvania. Gubernatorial candidate Andrew G. Curtin, like his counterpart Henry S. Lane in Indiana, was certain the New Yorker would inescapably drag him down to defeat, and he spread that warning throughout the convention. Some in the delegation were plotting to get behind the moderate candidates Edward Bates or John McLean as soon as Cameron was out of the picture. On the night before the balloting, Pennsylvania was still weighing its options.

After all, the delegates in Chicago "were not free from selfish ambitions nor unfamiliar with the arts by which these ambitions are promoted," Connecticut journalist Isaac H. Bromley observed. "They were altogether human; and whoever believes, on account of what followed their work, that they were saints or even unselfish philanthropists, that they pursued no devious ways, resorted to no intrigues, and drove no sharp bargains, makes a mistake."

Shortly after the convention broke for the day, a fateful meeting began in the rooms of Pennsylvanian David Wilmot at the Briggs House. It was the session that had been arranged during the lunch break, a gathering of twelve leading men, three each from Illinois, Indiana, New Jersey, and Pennsylvania. Their goal was to rally around a candidate who might stop the New Yorker cold. For the next five hours they wrangled. Unless they could agree on an alternative—Cameron, Dayton, Lincoln, *someone*—it seemed clear to the political observers in Chicago that Seward would win.

Later that night, with his deadline for the morning edition of the *New-York Tribune* fast approaching, Horace Greeley poked his head in. The man in the white coat departed despondently and went to a telegraph office to report his disappointing news. The *Tribune* printed his telegram in Friday morning's paper:

GOV. SEWARD WILL BE NOMINATED

CHICAGO, *Thursday, May 17*—11:40 p.m.—My conclusion, from all that I can gather tonight, is, that the opposition to Gov. Seward cannot concentrate on any other candidate, and that he will be nominated. H.G.

The *New York Daily Herald* concurred. "The opposition to Seward is not fixed on any man," it reported in a midnight dispatch. "If some effective combination is not made to-night, Seward may be nominated to-morrow. As matters stand, such a result is not improbable." Halstead telegraphed much the same to his *Cincinnati Commercial*. As he noted the next day, "every one of the forty thousand men in attendance upon the Chicago convention will testify that at midnight of Thursday-Friday night, the universal impression was that Seward's success was certain." Seward's men could sense it. "The New Yorkers were exultant. Their bands were playing, and the champagne flowing at their headquarters as after a victory." The *New York Times*, whose editor Henry Raymond was there fighting for Seward, exuded confidence. "It is impossible to predict the result with any certainty, but Mr. Seward's prospects are just now decidedly good. His opponents will find it impossible to unite on any candidate, and the general impression is that his nomination is simply a matter of necessity," the *Times* reported. "The only man on whom there is any hope of uniting is Mr. Lincoln, and very little progress is made in the effort. The prospect is that when the several States find that they cannot carry their own candidate, they will all fall back upon Mr. Seward."

In a 10:00 p.m. dispatch, a correspondent for Lincoln's hometown newspaper, the *Illinois State Journal*, reported that "the skillful and practical New Yorkers are active and confident of success. Their organization is well drilled, powerful, and united, and its influence is felt in every direction." The "tremendous outside pressure at work in Seward's favor," the correspondent noted, "would dampen the ardor of men less earnest and bold than the friends of Lincoln." Fortunately, he added, Lincoln's fate was in the hands of men who "lack neither judgment nor pluck, and he will not be abandoned while there is a ray of hope." Win or lose, they deserved "the cordial thanks of every friend of the noble Lincoln for the adroitness displayed in guarding his interest."

But after the journalists sped off to file their reports, just beating their deadlines, the committee of twelve inched forward. A New Jersey man suggested that the panel's members give their opinion, through a straw vote, on which of their favorite-son candidates would fare best with the full convention. Here Davis's deal with Indiana proved invaluable. With Caleb Smith and the other two representatives from Indiana presumably joining Illinois, Lincoln outpolled Cameron and Dayton. A New Jersey delegate then asked the three men from Pennsylvania if that state would agree to give up on Cameron and support Lincoln on later ballots if New Jersey did the same with Dayton. "The committee from Pennsylvania stated that they had no power to bind their co-delegates, but that they were prepared to recommend it, providing the committee from New Jersey would do the same," Thomas H. Dudley of New Jersey recalled. "Abraham Lincoln, so far as this committee of twelve from the four doubtful states was concerned, was agreed upon as the candidate for the Presidency."

At 1:00 a.m., the New Jersey supporters of William L. Dayton met at the Richmond House. Dayton, fifty-three years old, was a fine man, a former U.S. senator and current state attorney general. The son of a mechanic and farmer, he projected energy and strength, with a strong nose and a full head of hair, including a sweeping bang on his forehead. At the Republican convention in Philadelphia four years earlier, he had won the party's nomination for vice president, drawing far more votes than the obscure Lincoln. But Dayton's backers, recognizing the weakness of their position on the eve of balloting in Chicago, could only do so much for him. They were here representing the Opposition Party—meaning opposition to the Democrats. As in Pennsylvania, Republicans in New Jersey were forced to form a coalition with the

Know-Nothings and old Whigs to have a fighting chance at the polls. They knew their electoral prospects were dim unless they derailed Seward. Informed of the decision reached by their three representatives on the committee of twelve, most of the New Jersey men "ratified it and agreed that after the complimentary voting was over they would vote for Lincoln." New Jersey, of course, insisted that its abandonment of Dayton would be conditional on Pennsylvania's abandonment of Cameron. The Pennsylvania delegation would not meet until 9:00 a.m., leaving everything up in the air until then.

In the time remaining, the various candidates tried to mop up support from individual delegates and smaller states. "There were hundreds of Pennsylvanians, Indianians and Illinoisans who never closed their eyes that night," Halstead wrote. Around 1:00 a.m., the journalist saw Indiana gubernatorial nominee Lane prowling the halls of the Tremont House. He was "pale and haggard, with cane under his arm, walking . . . from one caucus room to another." Lane had "asserted hundreds of times" that Seward at the top of the ticket "would be death to him," and he was promising to quit his campaign, rather than invest more money and hard work in a hopeless pursuit, if the New Yorker won the nomination. His warnings had begun to sink in. For days, Lane "had been toiling with desperation to bring the Indiana delegation to go as a unit for Lincoln." With his delegation prepared to do that, he was now working alongside the Lincoln men "to bring the Vermonters and Virginians to the point of deserting Seward." They were trying to persuade as many delegates as possible to join with the battleground states and vote for "success rather than Seward," however much those delegates admired the man.

All night, the gaslit, dusty streets of Chicago were alive with processions and brass bands, while the headquarters of the delegations boomed with laughter, clinking glasses, and oratory. At the Richmond House, waiters cleared away hundreds of drained champagne bottles. A Wisconsin correspondent noted that the mood was bright, despite the fight over the nomination. Everybody seemed happy about the platform, which would provide "a grand opening" to the campaign, he wrote. "A blaze has been kindled that will burn brighter and brighter, and in November next will sweep over every free State, and make considerable progress in several of the border slave States. No one can doubt that [is] what we are seeing here." Ohio editor Washburn wrote that he would be thrilled with either of the leading candidates. "They are both glorious fellows, and the certainty that the one nominated will be the next President, makes the contest one of surpassing interest. To-morrow will determine it, and after that all will be Seward men or Lincoln men." The hard work of swaying any malleable delegates went on. "There was not much sleep for anybody that night," Bromley wrote.

At the Briggs House, the committee of twelve, having settled on Lincoln as its weapon to stop Seward, decided to sound each other out about the vice president. The members fixed on a man from one of the border slave states, congressman Henry Winter Davis of Maryland. The conservative former slaveowner from the East would certainly provide a balance to Lincoln, an anti-slavery Northerner from the West. There was one problem: Davis, a former Whig, was a Know-Nothing and not a Republican. But he had earned the admiration of Republicans for siding with the party on the contentious question of electing a House speaker that year, while incurring a vote of censure by the Democratic legislature of Maryland. The committee appointed Lincoln's manager, David Davis—who happened to be the congressman's first cousin, having grown up in the same house with him—to telegraph him and ask whether he would accept if nominated. The members then adjourned, agreeing to keep their proceedings secret, apart from necessary discussions with the four state delegations involved. For that reason, Thurlow Weed and his team had no idea what was about to hit them.

Sometime that night, the Lincoln men invited the leading Pennsylvania men to the Tremont House, including John P. Sanderson, a lawyer, author, former editor of the Philadelphia *Daily News*, and former chairman of the state's Know-Nothing Party; Joseph Casey, a lawyer and former Whig congressman; and Andrew H. Reeder, who had famously lost his job as governor of the Kansas Territory when he refused to rubber-stamp a fraudulent election ostensibly approving slavery. There they met with Davis, Logan, Swett, and their Illinois friend William P. Dole, a former Hoosier who hoped to land a job in the new administration. Joseph Medill of the *Press and Tribune* recalled that he was waiting at the Tremont House for word of the result when he saw Davis come down a flight of steps. "Damned if we haven't got them," the judge said. Pennsylvania would swing to Lincoln after Cameron. Medill asked how he did it. "By paying their price," Davis replied. Medill recalled something Lincoln had told him before the convention: "I want that big Pennsylvania foot brought down on the scale."

Years later, Cameron insisted that he had stood by Seward, as promised. He claimed, as if wounded deeply, that Davis and Swett "bought all my men—Casey and Sanderson and the rest of them. I was for Seward. I knew I couldn't be nominated but I wanted a complimentary vote from my own State. But Davis and the rest of them stole all my men. Seward accused me of having cheated him." In truth, Cameron was only too happy to have Davis "steal" his men. After the convention, Casey informed Cameron that the deal had been struck with Davis only "after everything was arranged carefully and unconditionally in reference to yourself." The Lincoln fellows, he noted, were willing to make a deal. Seward's men, by contrast, "refused to talk of anything but his unconditional nomination." Casey and his team apparently demanded no less than the patronage-rich post of treasury secretary for Cameron—a prospect that initially appalled Medill, given the man's sordid reputation. But Medill's *Press and Tribune* colleague Charles H. Ray told him, "Oh, what is the difference? We are after a bigger thing than that; we want the presidency, and the treasury is not a great stake to pay for it."

The "commerce between Illinois, Indiana and Pennsylvania" had led to a deal that proved beneficial to all parties, journalist Bromley later wrote. Lincoln had become those states' compromise choice for president, and former Indiana congressman Caleb Smith and senator Simon Cameron had been promised positions in a Lincoln cabinet. Charles Gibson, a lawyer and tireless advocate for Bates, wrote to the Missouri judge with disgust that his team, at one point, had secured nineteen votes from Indiana and fifteen from Pennsylvania, but that "Judge Davis, Lamon, and Swett, traded off a cabinet position to Caleb Smith for our Indiana votes and another place in the cabinet to Simon Cameron for our Pennsylvania vote." As Ward Hill Lamon asserted, the Pennsylvania delegates had been split between Bates and McLean as their choice after Cameron. "But Cameron was in a fine position to trade, and his friends were anxious for business."

"All Hail Pennsylvanians!" read a headline in the next morning's Chicago *Press and Tribune*. "All Pennsylvanians in this city are requested to meet at the Metropolitan Hotel this (Friday) morning at nine o'clock. Sons of the Keystone State fail not to attend. By order of E. Poulson, Ch'n Com. of Arrangements." That was the hour when that state's delegates were to gather just across the street, at the Briggs House, to hear the recommendation of the committee of twelve.

One of the most momentous days in American history dawned on Friday, May 18, as a dim orange-yellow band of light formed on the horizon of Lake Michigan, presaging a rising sun that painted the church steeples and monstrous grain elevators of Chicago. The rats that swarmed over the city at night, foraging on bits of rubbish, retreated beneath the wooden sidewalks and to their burrows underground. Swarms of humans had been out all night, too, their brass bands and loud celebrations filling the streets and hotel rooms, and many groggy delegates faced the new day without having gone to bed. At the Tremont House, David Davis received a telegraphed reply from his cousin: the Maryland congressman was unprepared to declare himself an outright Republican and thus would not accept a nomination. The convention would have to come up with its vice-presidential candidate without advice from the committee of twelve.

"I feel more confident of Mr. Seward's success this morning than ever before," wrote a correspondent for the *Wisconsin State Journal*. "His friends are full of hope, and laboring with a zeal worthy of the cause and the man. They must succeed, and in their success the country will rejoice." The *Chicago Democrat*, edited by mayor Long John Wentworth, predicted that the convention would wait until Saturday to nominate Seward, since Fridays were regarded as "Hangman's Day." "The friends of other candidates have mistaken their proper course towards Seward, and he is now stronger than he was when the convention assembled," the *Democrat* wrote. "It is astonishing what a hold Gov. Seward has upon the masses of the people. The coopers, the carpenters, the blacksmiths, the tailors, the printers, the shoemakers, the masons, the artisans, the free laborers generally are for Seward, *over and above all other men*. When once nominated, the enthusiasm in his favor will be perfectly crushing in its effect upon the politicians who are now opposing his nomination." There were still some in the Illinois delegation endeavoring to create an impression that Lincoln would not accept the vice presidency, the *Democrat* admitted. "These men know better. They know Lincoln will serve."

In Washington that morning, Senator Hannibal Hamlin, a former Democrat who had helped found the Republican Party in Maine, sat down to write a letter to his wife, Ellen, back in Bangor. Though most of the Maine delegation backed Seward, the pragmatic Hamlin had instructed it to weigh the alternatives in Chicago, since he was concerned about Seward's ability to carry the swing states. "To-day I presume Seward will be nominated at Chicago. If so we must make the best of it, though I am sure a much wiser nomination could be made," he wrote Ellen.

Confronting such widespread feelings, the Chicago *Press and Tribune* that morning published a final front-page appeal, A LAST ENTREATY. As Halstead noted, "It was evidently written in a despairing state of mind, and it simply begged that Seward should not be nominated." The editorial warned that Republicans should not count on the divided Democratic Party to ensure their victory in November; they must back a candidate who had a fighting chance of carrying the "doubtful" states. The paper cited one measure of how precarious the condition of Republicans was in Indiana and Illinois: "We refer to the Black laws"—statutes "more infamously despotic and unjust" than any in the notorious realms of Naples or Cairo. Through these blatantly unjust laws, which sharply curtailed the movement of black people and helped slave catchers put them back in chains, "slavery is virtually established within the jurisdiction of the two states." Yet "the Republican party in neither State had ever been able to repeal" them. Idealistic delegates who were prepared to nominate their bold champion, the *Press and Tribune* argued, should pause to consider the brutal realities Republicans confronted.

The editorial mentioned neither Lincoln nor Seward by name, but the message was clear. "We ask, we entreat, we implore" the convention to nominate a candidate who was "radical up to the extreme limit of the platform" but not susceptible to the sort of attacks Democrats would hurl "against one prominent gentleman now in the field and in high favor." With the nomination of a less controversial candidate, "a triumph may not be a thing of infinite labor, and prolonged and painful doubt, but a certainty from the moment that the choice of the Convention is declared." The editorial begged the delegates to pay careful heed to the concerns expressed by politicians from the battleground states, "else an inglorious and fatal defeat stares us in the face" in November. "For the sake of all that the party would accomplish, we entreat the Convention to act with the prudence, wisdom and foresight which the crisis demands," the paper wrote, adding somewhat forlornly, "We believe that all will yet be well."

One column over, the newspaper published a post submitted by the Seward men:

> **Attention! Friends of Seward.**
>
> The warm friends of Mr. Seward are requested to meet this morning, at 9 o'clock promptly, at the Richmond House, for the purpose of escorting the New York and Michigan delegations to the National Convention to the Wigwam.
>
> Turn Out! and let the escort show by its magnitude and enthusiasm, the admiration entertained in Chicago for the greatest living American Statesman and Patriot.
>
> By the order of the Committee.

In Auburn, New York, thousands of area residents prepared for a grand celebration the moment the telegraph flashed the report from Chicago announcing that this great statesman and patriot, their famous son, had been chosen as the Republican nominee for president of the United States. "A cannon was taken from the Armory and planted in the Park, the cannoneers were stationed at their posts, and fire lighted, the ammunition ready, and all waiting for the signal to make the city and county echo to the joyful news," the *Auburn Democrat* reported. "Sundry baskets of champagne were carted to one of our hotels, preparatory to a general salute of small arms in the celebration." Cayuga County "poured itself into Auburn. The streets were full," wrote New York journalist and abolitionist Henry B. Stanton. At Seward's own house on South Street, the "grounds overflowed with his admirers. The trees waved themselves on the lawn as if betokening coming victory." At the gate out front, between two posts topped by sculpted lions, another loaded cannon was placed, to be fired in celebration. Flags were readied to be raised.

On that bright morning, no one gathered around the two-story frame house at the corner of Eighth and Jackson Streets in Springfield, Illinois. Long accustomed to defeat, Abraham Lincoln left home and trudged downtown in his business suit and frayed stovepipe hat, head bent in thought. That morning's *Illinois State Journal*, which he usually read out loud at the office, contained the dispatch from Chicago with its elegiac tone, reporting the great confidence of the Seward forces and arguing that Lincoln's men deserved credit for the hard fight they had made. Meanwhile, life in that capital city of ten thousand people went on as usual, especially around Springfield's public square, dominated in the center by the State House.

In the *Journal*, local businesses—Lincoln knew them all well—advertised their ample wares. M. M. Van Deusen's drugstore, on the square's west side, boasted that it carried the finest soda water in America—Empire and Congress brand—the "best corrector of the stomach and bowels. A bottle taken in the morning will cool the coppers of a man sooner than anything else. It will keep you cool when the weather is hot, lively when everything is dull, and will drive away the blues." Grocer Rudolph Hugy, on Adams Street across from the Baptist church, had fresh lake fish for sale, "nicely dressed and preserved in ice, delivered daily." Conrad Loch invited readers to visit his shoe store on Fifth Street, where they could "open their eyes on about as big a show of superior footwear as was ever beheld by mortal." Isaac B. Curran's jewelry store, on the square's south side, not far from Lincoln's office, announced that it had secured the services of a Miss Summer, "expert hair braider, who can turn out as fine work as ever was seen," weaving jewelry and other adornments into women's hair. George W. Chatterton's shop, located near Van Deusen's drugstore, advertised an array of "clocks, watches, jewelry, musical instruments and sheet music," and announced that it now had "Wheeler & Weston's celebrated sewing machine" in stock.

Lincoln resorted to some of his favorite diversions that morning, friends recalled. Having caught a night train back from Chicago, editor Edward Baker played more "fives" with Lincoln near the offices of the *Illinois State Journal*, then repaired to an "Excellent & neat Beer Saloon" to play a game of billiards. The city was buzzing with political speculation, and the tables were full. Baker had a beer. Lincoln helped pass the time by pulling out jokes from the vast store of country humor he kept in his memory, delighting in making his male friends and neighbors roar with laughter. He often prefaced a joke with the statement "That reminds me of a story." Lincoln usually laughed louder than his listeners did, his mouth wide open.

Lawyer Christopher C. Brown, who worked in the office of Lincoln's first law partner, John T. Stuart, recounted that the presidential hopeful "was very nervous" that morning and "told vulgar Stories &c vehemently." Some could be very vulgar, indeed. Brown recalled that Lincoln, in 1859, had traveled eighty or ninety miles to attend his wedding, where the women were attired in their best hoopskirts. On the morning of the ceremony, Lincoln asked him, "Brown, why is a woman like a barrel?" Brown could not say. "Well," Lincoln said, "you have to raise the hoops before you put the head in." Brown knew well that "when intensely excited Lincoln told stories"—and on that Friday, Lincoln "was nervous, fidgety." Something that morning reminded Lincoln of the story of Revolutionary War hero Ethan Allen's visit to England after America had won its independence through years of bloody conflict with the armies of King George III. As Lincoln recounted, Allen's English hosts poked fun at Americans, particularly George Washington, and even hung a picture of the revered general in the outhouse. When they asked if Allen had seen it there, he answered no, but added that it was a very appropriate place for an Englishman to keep that picture. When they asked why, he explained that there "is Nothing that Will Make an Englishman Shit So quick as the Sight of Genl Washington." The delegates marching, meeting, and balloting in Chicago did not know everything, perhaps, about this roughhewn man who had a taste for the presidency.

At 9:00 a.m., just an hour before the reconvening of the convention, the Pennsylvania delegates met in the Briggs House. After some arm-twisting, they agreed to go along with the committee of twelve. But it was a surprisingly close thing. "The bargain was fulfilled, but not without difficulty," Lamon recounted. "Cameron's strength was more apparent than real," and some delegates still favored Bates and McLean for the later ballots. But with the help of the red-haired, red-faced David Wilmot, who liked Lincoln, the Cameron men managed to sway the members to commit to the Illinois lawyer, though only by a narrow majority of six votes in the fifty-four-member delegation.

An immense crowd had formed outside the Wigwam by nine o'clock, with thousands desperate to get inside for the final act of a great national drama. At that hour, the Wisconsin delegates, accompanied by supporters who called themselves the "Badger Boys," met at their headquarters at the Rice Block. Behind the Racine Bugle Band, they marched to the Richmond House to join the massive, four-blocks-long parade that was forming. The Seward men there "abounded in confidence," Halstead reported. To be sure, the "air was full of rumors" that the battleground states had caucused overnight, but "the opposition of the doubtful States to Seward was an old story; and after the distress of Pennsylvania, Indiana & Co., on the subject of Seward's availability had been so freely and ineffectually expressed from the start, it was not imagined their protests would suddenly become effective."

A thousand men, wearing their silk Seward badges, lined up behind the magnificent Dodworth Band of New York, which was "brilliantly uniformed," with "epaulets shining on their shoulders, and white and scarlet feathers waving from their caps." Boxing champion Tom Hyer led the procession. Thurlow Weed sent them off, a Vermont correspondent wrote, with the promise "that the deed was done, and they had only to go over to the Convention and ratify it." Under the guidance of their well-known leaders, they marched down the streets of Chicago "in a style that would have done credit to many volunteer military companies."

Halstead thought that the Irrepressibles might have protracted their march too much, because when they arrived, a shock awaited them. They could not get into the Wigwam, despite angrily waving their official tickets guaranteeing them admission. "Torrents of men had rushed in at the three broad doors until not another one could squeeze in," and the Wigwam was jammed with more than twelve thousand people. Every seat and every inch of standing room and aisle space was full. This was a real blow, undermining Weed's painstaking and costly effort to fill the building with men who would scream at the mere mention of the name of William H. Seward.

Halstead called it a "misfortune," but evidently luck had nothing to do with it. The Lincoln men had been working through the night on the extraordinary project—a scheme involving "a political 'turn of the wrist,' known only to wicked Chicago," in the words of Lincoln's friend Henry Clay Whitney. While the Seward men were out marching, the Lincoln supporters robbed them of their Wigwam seats. "I got our hooters in while the New Yorkers were parading," boasted H. M. Russell of Urbana, the young tavern worker Lincoln had treated kindly. He had "helped organize the coup," managing to sneak about three hundred Lincoln men into the Wigwam, while keeping out the equivalent number of Seward supporters. Stories differ about how the Lincoln men did it, but according to one account, the stratagem involved the printing of counterfeit tickets, "which, all through the night, were signed with the names of officers of the convention by a group of young men mustered for the purpose." They successfully kept hundreds of noisy Seward supporters out of the building, limiting them to "curbstone enthusiasm," as Lamon put it. "It was plain to see that all the local influence that could be packed into the building had been gathered to make demonstrations and help the game against Mr. Seward," fumed *Poughkeepsie Eagle* editor Isaac Platt. After roaring their hearts out on Wednesday and Thursday, the Seward men "had to be content with their two days' largess, already enjoyed, in which there was no political utility," Whitney mused. The Lincoln men intended to put their strengthened cheering section to good use.

The *Press and Tribune* estimated that there were now eighty thousand visitors in the city. Perhaps twenty-five thousand or more of them were in and around the Wigwam. "Stores were closed, and seemingly, the whole city was there," Lincoln's friend Leonard Swett wrote. Around the building, stretching out for blocks, a mass of humanity stopped up the streets. "Gaily attired ladies, with expansive crinoline, and unhooped damsels from the rural districts of the Sucker State, were contending with equal spirit for available places in the galleries," wrote a correspondent for the *Daily Evening Express* of Lancaster, Pennsylvania. "Men from all sections of the great Republic—from Maine to Florida, and from the rock bound shores of the Atlantic to the golden sands of the Pacific—were wedged together in a compact mass, and struggling, with the best humor, for an inside view of the Convention." Reporters stood on a narrow staircase, waiting for the press entrance to open, while hundreds of fellow journalists, desperate to get inside, gathered on the ground below them. "When the door was opened, those near the steps were taken up bodily by those behind, and literally forced through the narrow entrance, the door-keepers vainly striving to keep them back," wrote a correspondent for the *Elyria* (Ohio)

Independent Democrat. "Being in this crowd, your correspondent found him safely inside without any knowledge of how he got up the steps, or through the door." A line of men was stationed on the roof. One looked down on the speaker's stand, Swett wrote, "catching from an open skylight the proceedings within and reporting to his next man, and so on to the man in front of the building, who, with stentorian lungs, announced to the thousands in the street." Somebody hauled a cannon up on the roof to be fired when the convention made its nomination, heedless of the danger a wayward spark might pose to the thousands packed tightly below in the wooden building.

Inside the Wigwam, a brief kerfuffle erupted when a marshal noticed, to his horror, that a woman was up onstage with the reporters. Mary A. Livermore, a thirty-nine-year-old writer covering the event for her husband's Chicago-based Universalist newspaper, the *New Covenant*, bore a ticket admitting her to the densely packed press section and had dressed in black to try to blend in with the men. The guard would have none of it. "In stentorian tones that rang throughout the building, while his extended arm and forefinger pointed me out, and made me the target for thousands of eyes, he ordered me to withdraw my profane womanhood from the sacred enclosure provided for men, and 'go up higher,' among the women," in the ladies' gallery. As she rose to go, her husband, the Reverend David Livermore, tried, without luck, to intercede. But the reporters around her ordered her to "Sit still!" and advised the marshal to "Dry up!" After a heated argument involving the reporters, the marshal, police, and her husband, Mrs. Livermore was left in peace. "The unconventional West was new to me," she recalled, "and I was a good deal disturbed by this episode, which no one but myself seemed to remember ten minutes later."

One reporter up on the platform, twenty-seven-year-old Isaac Bromley, struggled to contain his emotions as the hour of decision approached. "Looked at from the stage, the shimmer of its gay decorations and the flutter of its constant movement dazzled the vision, while the confused and inarticulate buzz of voices and hum of conversation bewildered the sense," he wrote. "It was not easy to untangle oneself from it sufficiently to get the scene in perspective." Nearby on stage, under the Kansas sign, twenty-one-year-old delegate Addison Procter awaited "the battle of the ballot," knowing the delegates had at last come "face to face with the demand for a duty we could not shirk, or we would not if we could." With the nation careening toward a catastrophic upheaval—with Southern politicians all but promising disunion if a Republican were elected president—Procter and his fellow delegates had to choose a candidate. "We felt the full weight of the responsibility," understanding that their decision "might involve the very existence of the Republic. . . . The coming events were casting their dread shadows before us." The young man found it an ordeal. "All I can say is—we simply put our trust in God," he recalled.

A Vermont reporter studied the faces of the New York delegates, who were within "hand-shaking" distance of him. "Their countenances were beaming with the assurance of anticipated success," he wrote. Greeley arrived, also expecting Seward to prevail. "I could not see how a concentration of the anti-Seward force was to be effected," he wrote. Seward's friends—"not by way of bravado, but in perfect good faith"—asked their opponents about their preference for vice president, "regarding their own success for the first place as a matter of course." They knew they had to bring together all sides of the party to have the best hope of winning the White House in November.

David Davis was with the Illinois delegation. By then he was all but flattened with fatigue, but he was prepared to rally any wavering delegates, even one-on-one, to Lincoln's side. The Lincoln forces—men from the prairie who lacked Thurlow Weed's money, organization, and experience—had done an extraordinary night's work. "Lincoln will be nominated. I think he is the second choice of everybody," one ecstatic Lincoln booster, John F. Farnsworth, telegraphed that morning to fellow Illinois congressman Elihu B. Washburne. But few others thought so. Indiana lawyer, newspaperman, and politician John Defrees and others sent dispatches to their friends in Washington indicating that Seward was about to be nominated. At the Capitol, "the Republican side of the House looked gloomy and desponding, with but few exceptions,"

Indiana congressman Schuyler Colfax, a supporter of Edward Bates, noted. "Two or three even of the New York members said frankly that their Districts would be lost in that event. On the Democratic side, they were joyous & hopeful; for every one of them had insisted that we would nominate the New York Senator, &, did not conceal their desire that we should."

Thurlow Weed arrived at the Wigwam, too, reassuring his supporters that Seward was in a strong position. Weed believed that his years of effort were about to earn his dear friend the nomination, the culmination that Seward so richly deserved and the torn country so desperately needed. "Mr. Weed's hand directed all the movements of the canvass, and his advice was followed with unquestioning confidence," the *Autobiography of Thurlow Weed* recounted. "For weeks his whole heart and brain were absorbed in the thought of putting Mr. Seward at the head of the Chicago ticket. So well were arrangements made for that result that defeat seemed out of the question. Mr. Seward looked to his nomination almost as one does upon an accomplished fact, and so did Mr. Weed."

In Auburn, Seward received a last telegram from Chicago before the balloting began. It was from his distinguished friends William Evarts, Senator Preston King, and Richard Blatchford: "All right. Everything indicates your nomination today sure."

Friday, May 18, 1860

Chapter 13: Yonder Goes Lincoln

The Reverend H. K. Green, pastor of the Tabernacle Baptist Church of Chicago, opened Friday's session with a prayer. His growing church ran a school for impoverished children in the city's slums and supported ministers who were speaking out for freedom in "Bleeding Kansas." Now, without mentioning the word "slavery," he beseeched God that America might survive the oncoming crisis of hatred and division, while preserving the freedoms that the Founders and their successors had secured at a great cost. "O, we entreat Thee, that at some future but not distant day, the evils which now invest the body politic shall not only have been arrested in their progress, but wholly eradicated from the system," he prayed. "And may the pen of the historian trace an intimate connection between that glorious consummation and the transactions of this Convention." During the quiet of the solemn prayer, cheers from outside the Wigwam could be heard through the open windows. The vast throng outdoors was listening to speakers in three or four meetings going on at the same time.

Convention president George Ashmun followed the reverend to the platform to make an appeal, "not merely to the gentlemen of the Convention, but to every individual of this vast audience." He had heard the shouts of the Seward men on Wednesday and Thursday, and he may have seen evidence that Lincoln supporters were prepared to match them. Ashmun asked that those in attendance "remember the utmost importance of keeping and preserving order during the entire session—as much silence as possible," and that they, "to the utmost of their ability, refrain from any demonstrations of applause that may disturb the proceedings of this convention." There was little chance the excited audience would comply.

At that point, a speaker reminded the convention that a motion advanced Thursday by Aaron Goodrich of Minnesota was on the table—to proceed to ballot for a candidate for president of the United States. "Question, question!" men cried out.

Montgomery Blair of Maryland interrupted, evidently making one last bid to strengthen his family's candidate, Edward Bates. Blair asked that five additional delegates from Maryland be permitted to participate. While Maryland had originally planned on sixteen delegates, only eleven had come to Chicago and been approved by the convention. But on Thursday night, Blair had magically scrounged up five more men. Maryland delegate Charles Lee Armour, a Seward supporter who had powerfully defended his state's delegation on Thursday, got up to speak, warning the convention that mischief was afoot. The Bates men had convened that meeting without alerting the pro-Seward members, he said, and filled up the delegation "with outsiders"—men who were unknown to Armour and who surely did not live in Maryland. "God Almighty only knows where they live," Armour declared, to laughter and applause. President Ashmun rejected the new delegates, ruling that Maryland must make do with the delegates previously approved—delivering yet another victory to the Seward forces.

The moment of truth finally seemed to arrive. William M. Evarts, forty-two, the elegant chairman of the New York delegation, called for attention. "I rise—" he said, only to be interrupted. "The Pennsylvania delegation is not provided with seats," cried out a voice. "Get them in quick!" someone else yelled. The Pennsylvania men had been delayed by their discussion and vote that morning and by their subsequent parade from the Briggs House and Metropolitan Hotel. Entering the Wigwam, they found that interlopers had taken their seats onstage. A note was slipped to Ashmun explaining the situation. Delegates were passing "their tickets over the railings and through the windows to their friends who are not entitled to them," permitting nondelegates to get onto the stage and fill seats. As if speaking to children, Ashmun instructed the delegations "to insist that no person except their delegates shall occupy their seats. If they will do this with rigor every delegate in the room will be accommodated." With some difficulty, the Pennsylvania delegates ejected the intruders and took their seats.

One of the intruders was Joseph Medill of the *Press and Tribune*. Instead of going to the press section, he plopped himself down among the Ohio delegation, where he had no business being. Seven years earlier, Medill had cofounded the *Cleveland Leader*, so he knew many of the delegates well. David Davis, fearful that the Ohio delegation might swing from Chase to Seward, had enlisted Medill to use his connections to try to steer votes to Lincoln, perhaps by making yet one more deal. "I took my seat among my old friends of the Ohio delegation, as I personally knew nearly all of them, and did what missionary work I could," Medill recounted. An outraged Joshua R. Giddings "soon espied me, and, without ceremony, ordered me out," unleashing a "little speech for my benefit and the edification of the Ohio delegates within hearing." Others, though—almost certainly those who hoped to derail Chase and Seward—"came to my rescue and told me to stay, and I did, and we had a nice little argument. I remained with the Ohio men." When all the delegates were in place, 465 were in the hall. That meant the nomination could be captured with 233 votes, the simple majority.

At last, the serious work began. "In the order of business before the Convention," Evarts declared, "Sir, I take the liberty to name as a candidate to be nominated by this Convention for the office of President of the United States, William H. Seward." A lifetime of work by Thurlow Weed had led to this moment. The audience erupted "with a deafening shout," Leonard Swett wrote, "which, I confess, appalled us a little." The efforts to tamp down the Seward enthusiasm did not seem to be working. The New Yorker's supporters roared loud and long. Then Norman Judd, the Chicago lawyer who had brought the convention to that city, stood up. "I desire on behalf of the delegation from Illinois, to put in nomination, as a candidate for President of the United States, Abraham Lincoln, of Illinois." Here the Lincoln men fought back. "The response was prodigious," Halstead wrote, "rising and raging far beyond the Seward shriek."

The nominations of favorite sons flowed in quickly. Thomas H. Dudley of New Jersey nominated William L. Dayton. Andrew H. Reeder of Pennsylvania nominated Simon Cameron. David H. Cartter of Ohio nominated Salmon P. Chase. Frank Blair of Missouri nominated Edward Bates. Thomas Corwin of Ohio nominated John McLean. But it became instantly clear which two candidates were dominant. "The only names that produced 'tremendous applause' were those of Seward and Lincoln," Halstead reported. "Everybody felt that the fight was between them, and yelled accordingly." Given the intense shouting contest that followed, journalist Isaac H. Bromley mused, "one might have supposed that the choice between them was to be governed by the volume of sound."

When Caleb B. Smith of Indiana rose to second Lincoln's nomination after the other favorite sons were nominated, "the response was absolutely terrific," Halstead observed. The Western men were determined to prove themselves. "The idea of us Hoosiers and Suckers being outscreamed, would have been as bad to them as the loss of their man," Swett wrote. "Five thousand people at once leaped to their seats, women not wanting in the number, and the wild yell made soft vesper breathings of all that had preceded. No language can describe it. A thousand steam whistles, ten acres of hotel gongs, a tribe of Comanches, headed by a choice vanguard from pandemonium, might have been mingled with the scene unnoticed." The pro-Seward party leaders had obviously committed a colossal blunder five months earlier when they approved Chicago as the convention site—on the basis that Illinois had no serious presidential aspirant.

But the Seward supporters were not content to be beaten in the shouting match, even on Lincoln's home field. When Austin Blair of Michigan seconded Seward's nomination, Halstead wrote, the "effect was startling. Hundreds of persons stopped their ears in pain. The shouting was absolutely frantic, shrill and wild. No Comanches, no panthers ever struck a higher note, or gave screams with more infernal intensity." As Halstead looked out at the great amphitheater from the stage, "nothing was to be seen below but thousands of hats—a black, mighty swarm of hats—flying with the velocity of hornets over a mass of human heads, most of the mouths of which were open. Above, all around the galleries, hats and handkerchiefs were flying in the tempest together. The wonder of the thing was that the Seward outside pressure should, so far from New York, be so powerful."

Yet the screaming contest was not over. When former Whig congressman Columbus Delano of Ohio joined in seconding Lincoln's nomination, "the uproar was beyond description," Halstead reported. "Imagine all the hogs ever slaughtered in Cincinnati giving their death squeals together, a score of big steam whistles going (steam at 160 lbs. per inch), and you conceive something of the same nature." Halstead had thought the Seward screaming could not be surpassed, but the Lincoln men had done it, "and feeling their victory as there was a lull in the storm, took deep breaths all around, and gave a concentrated shriek that was positively awful, [and] accompanied it with stamping that made every plank and pillar in the building tremble." Indiana gubernatorial candidate Henry S. Lane leapt on top of a table, "and swinging hat and cane, performed like an acrobat." He seemed to scream something—"his mouth was desperately wide open"—but no one could hear what. Halstead looked over to the solid Seward delegations: New York, Michigan, and Wisconsin, which Judd had bunched together in his floor plan. "Many of their faces whitened as the Lincoln *yawp* swelled into a wild hozanna of victory." The screaming surely informed Seward's opponents that Lincoln was their best hope.

While the nominations were going on, Joseph R. Hawley, editor of the pro-Republican *Hartford Evening Press*, turned to his Connecticut journalism colleague Bromley, seated at his elbow at the press table. "Why don't you hurrah?" asked Hawley, who had been screaming along with the crowd. "I don't know why I did not, but I remember I felt queer and only said, 'I can't hurrah; I should cry if anyone touched me.'" The frenzy inside the Wigwam obviously bore some connection to the passions raging beyond these walls, North and South, threatening to crack apart the country. The heat in the Wigwam grew intense, particularly for women garbed in multiple layers and long dresses. Four ladies among the spectators fainted, the *Press and Tribune* reported, "and were carried from the building senseless." One man "took a fit" and "had to be removed through one of the windows."

It was time to vote. The states were called, one by one, from east to west. Maine awarded ten votes to Seward but, surprisingly, six to Lincoln. Swett's lobbying of his native state had evidently had some effect. New Hampshire gave seven of its ten votes to Lincoln. Vermont gave all of its ten votes to Senator Jacob Collamer, a complimentary gift to a native son whom no one took seriously, but a blow to Seward, Halstead thought, since it showed that the Green Mountain State was "hostile or indifferent" to him. Massachusetts gave twenty-one of its twenty-five votes to Seward—Weed had hoped for a clean sweep—but Rhode Island and Connecticut, whose elections earlier in the year indicated voters had qualms about Seward, gave him none. Seward, who was expected to be strong in New England, emerged with only thirty-two votes against the other candidates' forty-nine.

Then it was New York's turn. Evarts rose to declare, "with a swelling tone of pride in his voice—'The State of *New York* casts her *seventy votes for William H. Seward!*'" The load of votes "was a plumper, and there was slight applause, and that rustle and vibration in the audience indicating a sensation," Halstead wrote. But the happiness of the New Yorkers was short-lived. Pennsylvania, which permitted fractional votes, surprised no one by casting forty-seven and a half of its fifty-four votes for Cameron. But Virginia, expected to be solid for Seward, reported fourteen votes for Lincoln and only eight for Seward. "The New Yorkers looked significantly at each other as this was announced." Then followed a bigger surprise: Indiana gave all twenty-six of its votes to Lincoln. The state had been expected to spread them out among the conservative candidates, notably Bates and McLean. "The solid vote was a startler, and the keen little eyes of Henry S. Lane glittered as it was given." Lane knew that he had a chance to stop Seward and save his own campaign.

When the Maryland delegation came to vote, another war broke out, as the Bates forces again attempted to pull a fast one. Delegation chairman Francis S. Corkran announced all its eleven votes for Bates. Seward man William E. Coale leapt to his feet. "I object to that. I am a freeman in Maryland, although surrounded by slavery. If I were going to look for a place to be immolated on the altar of slavery I should not come to Chicago." Delegates shouted "Order!" Armour jumped in. "I will present the point of protestation a little clearer than my aged friend has," he said. "Call the roll!" men shouted. President Ashmun asserted that the vote of a state was not a matter for debate. But Armour insisted, informing those in the Wigwam that the state convention in Baltimore had soundly rejected attempts to mandate that the delegation vote as a unit. The delegates believed "then and now that we were free to cast our votes for the man of our choice, and we claim that right on the floor of the Convention." Armour won applause and cries of "Good!" Frank Blair of Missouri, rising to protect the Bates vote, protested that the rules required that each vote be reported by the state's chairman. "I desire to know whether this Convention is to be governed by its rules or not?" he asked in his best tone of wounded propriety. But the convention took the matter up and voted that Maryland could split the vote. Eight votes went to Bates, and three to Seward.

It was another Seward victory, but a petty one. Thurlow Weed had not foreseen the onslaught of opposition to Seward—and, worse, that this opposition had been organized and was rallying around one candidate. Abraham Lincoln, the inelegant, self-educated prairie lawyer who had endured defeat after defeat, was suddenly a serious challenger to the sophisticated, erudite, experienced Seward. And, while the New Yorker was far in the lead for now, the balloting revealed that Seward would be in grave danger if Lincoln could collect the votes now going to Cameron and Bates.

The secretary, having tallied the votes, read out the results of the first ballot:

William H. Seward, New York	173 ½
Abraham Lincoln, Illinois	102
Edward Bates, Missouri	48
Simon Cameron, Pennsylvania	50 ½
John McLean, Ohio	12
Salmon P. Chase, Ohio	49
Benjamin F. Wade, Ohio	3
William L. Dayton, New Jersey	14
John M. Reed, Pennsylvania	1
Jacob Collamer, Vermont	10
Charles Sumner, Massachusetts	1
John C. Frémont, California	1

Davis and the Lincoln men, though not nearly as experienced in delegate counting as Weed, had hit their target almost exactly. "Our programme was to give Lincoln 100 votes on the first ballot," Swett wrote, with more to follow later.

No one having received a majority, the secretary announced that the convention would proceed to a second ballot. The vote tally raced across the nation on its telegraph wires.

In Auburn, New York, the Reverend John Austin dropped in on his neighbor at about eleven that morning. They talked for about an hour. "He was sanguine—nay, almost certain of his nomination," Austin wrote. After dinner, knowing that the balloting must be going on in Chicago, the reverend clung to the telegraph office nearby. "About 3 o'clock the account of the first ballot was received. I took it and went immediately to Gov. Seward's," Austin recounted. "I found him in his arbor garden." Nothing evidently seemed amiss to Seward. "He received the statement without the movement of a muscle of his countenance. It was considered as favorable as could be expected for the first ballot."

The crowds in Auburn agreed. "Loud shouts rent the air, and the zealous adherents of the 'Irrepressible' champion were with difficulty restrained from letting 'the kettle to the trumpet speak; the trumpet to the cannoneer without, the cannon to the heavens, and the heavens to the earth,' in proclamation of the joyful tidings," the *Auburn Democrat* reported, quoting from Shakespeare's *Hamlet*.

In Springfield, Illinois, Lincoln, who restlessly played ball and told jokes that morning, headed for the humble law office of Lincoln & Herndon. It was located up three flights of steps in the Tinsley Building, which was dominated by Seth Tinsley's multistory dry goods store, at a prominent corner on the south side of the public square. The office was not much to look at. "The furniture," recalled Gibson Harris, who had studied law there, was "somewhat dilapidated, consisting of one small desk and a table, a sofa or lounge with a raised head at one end, and a half dozen wooden chairs. The floor was never scrubbed. If cleaned at all it was done by the clerk or law student who occasionally ventured to sweep up the accumulated dirt. Over the desk a few shelves had been enclosed; this was the office bookcase holding a set of *Blackstone*, *Kent's Commentaries*, *Chitty's Pleadings*, and a few other books." At one point, the dust in a corner grew so thick that seeds that had leaked out from seed packets given to Lincoln had started to sprout. The windows were as filthy as the floor.

Charles S. Zane, who was studying law with Lincoln's friend James C. Conkling, was in Lincoln & Herndon's office that Friday morning, talking with another law student, when the candidate came in. "Well boys, what do you know?" Lincoln asked, and he plunked himself down in a chair. Zane informed him that Springfield lawyer and editor John E. Rosette had returned from Chicago on the morning train and "thinks your chances for the nomination are good." Lincoln asked Zane if he knew Rosette's reasons for thinking so. During the conversation, Edward L. Baker, the editor of the *Illinois State Journal*, rushed in to read to Lincoln "a telegram which said the names of the Candidates for nomination had been announced to the Convention" and that Lincoln's name "was received with greater applause, than that of any other candidate."

Concluding he would get no work done that day, Lincoln left soon after, with the law clerks in tow, cutting through the square and across the wide and dusty Sixth Street, to enter the city's telegraph office on the north side of the park, near the offices of the *Illinois State Journal.* He wanted to be on hand when the results arrived in Springfield. "After waiting there some time the telegraph of the first ballot Came over the wires," Zane recalled. "From the manner in which Mr. Lincoln received this dispatch it was my impression that it was as favorable as he expected."

The vote tally suggested to Lincoln that Seward would fail. "His opinion was or had been that if Mr. Seward did not get the nomination on the first ballot or come near to it he would not be likely to get it at all," Zane recalled. And, just as his supporters in Chicago had predicted, it was Lincoln—and not the more famous Chase, or the respected conservatives Bates or McLean, or Pennsylvania's Simon Cameron, or Ohio dark horse Ben Wade—who had emerged as Seward's strongest rival.

If there was any time during the balloting to lobby the wavering delegates, Lincoln's men alone could do it. Judd had clumped the strong Seward delegations together on the opposite side, beyond the press section. David Davis and his team, by contrast, had immediate access to those who might still be swayed. Between ballots, the convention clamored to resume the voting without delay. "Every man was fiercely enlisted in the struggle," Halstead wrote. "The partisans of the various candidates were strung up to such a pitch of excitement as to render them incapable of patience." Cries of "call the roll" were "fairly hissed through their teeth."

East to west, it began again. Maine repeated its vote. But New Hampshire added two votes for Lincoln, increasing the margin to nine to one. Weed, who thought he had extracted a promise from the delegation to swing to Seward on the second ballot, had been misled. Then Vermont, expected to turn to Seward after voting for favorite son Collamer on the first ballot, swung entirely to Lincoln, ten to none. "This was a blighting blow upon the Seward interest," Halstead reported. "The New Yorkers started as if an Orsini bomb had exploded." A Vermont reporter employed the same image, writing that "had a bomb-shell been thrown into the N.Y. camp it could not have produced greater consternation. They foresaw the inevitable doom that awaited them." Judge Davis's careful cultivation of the Vermont delegation had borne fruit. The state delivered on its promise to swing to Lincoln on the second ballot. Lincoln had beaten Seward thirty-six to thirty-three in New England, of all places, with thirteen votes scattered among other candidates. New Jersey, which had promised to go with Lincoln on a later ballot, still clung to Dayton.

Then came the hardest blow. The secretary called for the vote of Pennsylvania. Few knew what the state would do. Seward men thought it would splinter among many candidates, with most perhaps supporting the New Yorker after Cameron was out of the picture. Despite their promises, the Cameron men had not consulted with Weed before the vote. Davis hoped his overnight deal, and the morning vote, would hold. As it turned out, one man clung to Cameron, but the delegation threw nearly all its strength behind Lincoln, with forty-four delegates shifting to him. The big foot of Pennsylvania had come down on the scale, to the abject horror of Weed. "The fate of the day was now determined," Halstead wrote. New York must now have expected "'checkmate' in the next move," but "sullenly proceeded with the game, assuming unconsciousness of her inevitable doom." On the second ballot, Seward had gained eleven votes, but Lincoln had increased by a whopping seventy-nine. Even Swett admitted that was "a little more than we had calculated."

Men could hardly believe what they were seeing. The courageous, highly qualified, beloved leader of the Republican Party was going down. The secretary read out the results of the second ballot:

William H. Seward, New York	184 ½
Abraham Lincoln, Illinois	181
Edward Bates, Missouri	35
Simon Cameron, Pennsylvania	2
John McLean, Ohio	8
Salmon P. Chase, Ohio	42 ½
William L. Dayton, New Jersey	10
Cassius M. Clay, Kentucky	2

"It now dawned upon the multitude that the presumption entertained the night before, that the Seward men would have everything their own way, was a mistake," Halstead wrote. The Sewardites had either been bluffing or they had been badly fooled, like almost everyone else. Even inexperienced observers could see that most of the delegates who had supported other candidates would swing behind the lawyer from Illinois. It was possible that some of the Chase men might move to Seward, but the Bates, McLean, and Dayton supporters certainly would not.

At that moment, Medill grabbed David Cartter, chairman of the Ohio delegation. As Halstead described him, Cartter, a former congressman, was "a large man with rather striking features, a shock of bristling black hair, large and shining eyes, and is terribly marked with the smallpox. He has also an impediment in his speech, which amounts to a stutter." It was "altogether appropriate," the reporter rather unkindly added, that such a damaged man served as chairman of the divided, ineffective Ohio delegation. One Cleveland man later described Cartter to Lincoln as "neither honest brave or wise. He is doubtless a man of some ability on the stump, and that is all. . . . His manners are course and repulsive, and [he] has not the benefit of a mind well regulated and pure, he can strut and swell like a toad in a rage, but he can never play the gentleman, or persuade himself to be a true friend." Medill informed Cartter that if Ohio now threw its support behind Lincoln, Chase could "have anything he wants." Cartter asked, "H-how d-d'ye know?" Medill answered, "Ask Judge Davis. He holds the authority from Lincoln."

Unaware of the deals that Davis had struck overnight, *New York Times* editor Henry J. Raymond believed that the crowd's screaming for Lincoln had swayed mindless delegates. Illinois men had successfully packed the hall, and the Vermont delegates—in defiance of their own constituents, who favored Seward—were "the first to catch the contagious impulse," Raymond asserted. Right "down to the time of taking the first ballot there had been no agreement among the opponents of Seward as to the candidate upon whom they should unite. The first distinct impression in Lincoln's favor was made by the tremendous applause which arose from the ten thousand persons congregated in the Wigwam, upon the presentation of his name as a candidate,—and by the echo it received from the still larger gathering in the street outside." He could not help but conclude that the brilliant and experienced Seward was being swept away by the passions of a mob.

Seward man Isaac Platt, covering the convention for the *Poughkeepsie Eagle*, dismissed the shouting as artificial. "It did not look to me like enthusiasm," he wrote sourly. Rather, it was "a continuous yell by the same men as long as their breath held out, and a strife to see who could make the most noise. I am free to say I would not give a farthing for all such enthusiasm that can be raised in the country." But the *New York Daily Herald* found it all devilishly clever. The Lincoln men, "by the artful contrivance of a big wigwam, which would admit a large number of spectators, managed to get into the convention a strong expression of local feeling in favor of a man comparatively unknown out of Chicago and the State of Illinois." Through this tactic, "the enthusiasm of the delegations in favor of their true party leader was overborne and crushed out."

No one having received a majority, the secretary announced that the convention would proceed to a third ballot.

* * *

Maine, New Hampshire, and Vermont held their ground, but Massachusetts shifted four votes to Lincoln. Lincoln picked up two votes in Rhode Island. He was now, presumably, in the lead. All but one delegate from New Jersey finally dropped Dayton, shifting eight votes to Lincoln and five to Seward—less support than was promised for Lincoln, but helpful nonetheless. When Ohio was called, Cartter announced twenty-nine votes for Lincoln, to only fifteen for Chase and two for McLean, a terrible blow to Seward. People began whispering, "Lincoln's the coming man—will be nominated on this ballot." Amid the delegations, Bromley noticed, "there was a great deal of hurrying back and forth, swift consultations, pulling and hauling, and hubbub generally." At the same time, the audience's shouting and demonstrations had quieted down. "The excitement was too intense, the nervous strain too severe, to resolve itself in noise."

Midway into the tally, Halstead stopped paying any heed to the other candidates' votes and concentrated on Lincoln's alone, to determine whether he would hit the winning total of 233. "I saw under my pencil as the Lincoln column was completed, the figures 231 ½—one vote and a half to give him the nomination. In a moment the fact was whispered, about a hundred pencils had told the same story. The news went over the house wonderfully, and there was a pause." New York, Michigan, Wisconsin, California, and Minnesota, as well as the Kansas Territory and the District of Columbia, had remained 100 percent loyal to Seward, but it was not enough. During the balloting, Bates man Charles Gibson sought out Weed and asked if New York might shift its votes to Bates, to keep the battle going, at least for a while. Weed answered that he believed Lincoln's nomination was certain, but if the third ballot produced no winner, he would attempt that act of desperation. Gibson rushed across the stage to tell his fellow Bates supporter, Horace Greeley.

But it was too late. Halstead knew what would happen first. A politician seeking his little place in history would grab the spotlight.

"In about ten ticks of a watch," Ohio's Cartter stood up and attracted President Ashmun's attention. Halstead reported his stuttering remarks: "I rise (eh), Mr. Chairman (eh), to announce the change of four votes of Ohio from Mr. Chase to Mr. Lincoln." The deed was done.

A silence fell over the hall. "The nerves of the thousands, which through the hours of suspense had been subjected to terrible tension, relaxed, and as deep breaths of relief were taken, there was a noise in the Wigwam like the rush of a great wind in the van of a storm—and in another breath the storm was there. There were thousands cheering with the energy of insanity," Halstead wrote. "Nearly every member of the Illinois delegation was so overcome with unexpected joy that they sat silently shedding tears," the *New York Daily Herald* reported. But not for long. The shrieks exceeded even what went before. On the platform near Bromley, "Henry S. Lane was executing a war-dance with some other dignified delegate as a partner; the Indiana men generally were smashing hats and hugging each other; the Illinois men did everything except stand on their heads; hands were flying wildly in the air, everybody's mouth was open, and bedlam seemed loose." Lane's crazed excitement also caught the eye of L. D. Ingersoll, the correspondent for the *Burlington Weekly Hawk-Eye*, of Iowa. "Standing next to the railing of the platform, his tall, limber form bowed backward and forward, as shout after shout escaped his lips." The nomination of Lincoln, the writer noted, "has secured his election as Governor of Indiana beyond a doubt." At the same time, the "ladies in the gallery rose to their feet and cheered with might and main."

The Republicans were staking their fortunes on an ungainly man of the people—who had split rails in his youth, who had risen by his own effort, who told jokes to ward off his devastating depression, and who had suffered crushing disappointments in his middle age but stubbornly persisted in his quest to preserve and expand the freedom that America promised. John A. Andrew, a Seward man, found his Massachusetts delegation surrounded by "a peal of human voices, a grand chorus of exultation, the like of which has not been heard on earth since the morning stars first sang together, and the sons of God shouted for joy." The Illinois delegates "leaped to the top of the benches on which they sat, and as by one motion of one man, hats were swung and thrown aloft in air, coats themselves streaming like banners in the breeze." Andrew saw old men with "quivering lips and streaming eyes, and hearts so full of joy they could not check their emotion." Edwin O. Gale, a prosperous twenty-eight-year-old Chicago druggist who managed to get into the Wigwam that day, remembered looking upward. "In that direction shouts and handkerchiefs, hats and umbrellas went so high that their owners never saw or heard of them again. Men were beside themselves. Old, grizzly-bearded fellows acted like boys, and appeared reckless of consequences to themselves or their belongings" for the sake of making "a wild demonstration." All over the Wigwam, a Pennsylvania eyewitness noted, "men yelled like incarnate furies; women waved their handkerchiefs, fans and parasols, all exhibiting the most exuberant feelings of joy." Reporter Mary A. Livermore found herself engulfed by raging men. "The billows of this delirious joy surged around me, as I sat amid the swaying, rocking forms of men who had sprung to their feet and grasped each other by the hand, or had fallen into one another's arms, and were laughing, crying, and talking incoherently."

The man on the roof "demanded by gestures at the skylight" to know what had happened. One of the secretaries, clutching a tally sheet, shouted up, "Fire the Salute! Abe Lincoln is nominated!" As the cheering in the Wigwam subsided, the audience could hear the crowd outside erupt. The sound of the exterior celebration whipped up the Wigwam crowd all over again, and the "shouting was repeated with such tremendous fury that some discharges of the cannon were absolutely not heard by those on the stage. Puffs of smoke, drifting by the open doors, and the smell of gunpowder, told what was going on." Chicago was in a frenzy. Before the reverberations of the first cannon had faded away, Isaac N. Arnold noted, "a hundred thousand voters of Illinois and the neighboring states were shouting, screaming, and rejoicing at the results." For the next seventeen minutes, the cannon boomed every thirty seconds, reviving the cheers each time. The *Press and Tribune* called it a "Babel of joy and excitement." An *Indianapolis*

Journal writer struggled for a way to describe the madness. "The whole house was a boiling, tossing sea of heads, except in the little eddy of New York. No words can describe the scene. No noise I ever heard would compare with it."

Someone carried in a large oval photograph of Lincoln in a gilt frame that had hung in one of the side meeting rooms, and held it up on a pole "before the surging and screaming masses." The delegates grabbed the signs identifying the state names, ripped them out of their sockets, and swung them above their heads in celebration of Lincoln's nomination. "The New Yorkers sat like marble statues all the while, and when urged by their outside friends, as a matter of policy, to join in the general tumult, they respectfully declined," the *New York Daily Herald* reported. "Some of the Sewardites were so overcome by the defeat of their favorite that they cried like heart broken children." The Seward men, who had gone to Chicago with such joy, would have to return to New York "like Rachel, weeping and refusing to be comforted," the *Herald* noted. "They were not even accorded the poor privilege of naming the candidate" when Seward fell short; "but Lincoln was thrown in their faces without so much as saying by your leave." When delegates from other states rushed to grab the New York standard and swing it with the rest, the sullen New Yorkers defended it angrily, refusing to let it be removed.

Reporter Livermore was not at all sure the convention's rejection of Seward and embrace of a compromise candidate was a good thing. "It seemed to me these demonstrations were made rather because the anti-slavery principle had triumphed, than because Mr. Lincoln himself was a special favorite. The great majority knew him only as a country lawyer, and not very distinguished at that." Wondering if Lincoln was a "humbug" who was pretending to be "anti-slavery just now for the sake of getting votes," she asked a Massachusetts reporter beside her, "Is it *certain* that Mr. Lincoln is an uncompromising anti-slavery man?" He assured her Lincoln was.

Lincoln's old friend David Davis stood on stage, drained physically and emotionally. He "threw his great arms around a friend and cried like a child," Swett recalled. The judge was so overcome with emotion, his friend Jesse Fell recounted, that, for hours to come, he broke into tears when "grasping hands of congratulating friends." Horace Greeley, the disappointed office seeker, beamed happily at the defeat of his former friend. Thurlow Weed, a reporter noticed, pressed "his fingers *hard* upon his eyelids to keep back the tears."

William Evarts turned to George William Curtis, who had so eloquently defended Joshua Giddings the day before, and joked ruefully, "Well, Curtis, we have at least saved the Declaration of Independence."

For some reason, the thoughts of German American leader Carl Schurz raced to a great man he had met in Ohio in late 1859, "who, I imagined, sat in a quiet office room at Columbus with a telegraph near by clicking the news from Chicago. Not only had the prediction made to him a few months before become true, but it had become more terribly true than I myself had anticipated." Salmon P. Chase had never scraped together more than forty-nine votes—had never even enjoyed the unanimous support of his own state. "No doubt he had hoped, and hoped, and hoped against hope—no American afflicted with the presidential fever ever ceases to hope—and now came this disastrous, crushing, humiliating defeat. I saw that magnificent man before me, writhing with the agony of his disappointment, and I sympathized with him most profoundly." But, for now, "the whole City of Chicago shook with triumphant cheers for Lincoln," and Schurz had to prepare to shift Wisconsin's votes from his beloved Seward to the winner.

In the chaos, nothing but shouting and cheering could be heard, a correspondent for the *Buffalo Daily Courier* reported. "Western fellows" were different from Easterners, he explained, "taking a sample of the men who have been staying at the house I am at, six feet and over, with constitutions like the oxen they raise on their prairies, and lungs of prodigious capacities, they can halo longer and louder than almost any other men you will meet." While the cannon was still booming, half a dozen men were standing on their seats screaming for recognition so that they could switch their states' votes to Lincoln. Before the secretary could announce the results of the third ballot—formally declaring Lincoln the nominee—delegations demanded to be heard.

Party unity would be essential going forward. But would the devastated New Yorkers fully support Lincoln? "New York! New York!" members of the audience cried out. The chairman of the delegation, Evarts, finally claimed the floor. "Physically," observed Iowa correspondent Ingersoll, Evarts "does not amount to much, being rather small of stature, and of no very prepossessing appearance. Nevertheless, you can see that he is a man of decision, nerve, and backbone." A silence fell on the Wigwam "so profound that you might have heard a pin drop anywhere in the vast building," one reporter wrote.

"Mounting a table," *New York Times* correspondent Joseph Howard recounted, "with grief manifest in his countenance, his hands clenched nervously, and every nerve quivering with excitement," Evarts began to speak. He noted the delegation had come to Chicago with unanimous support for a noble son "who had served the state from boyhood up, who had labored for and loved it." Out of love for the great republic and for liberty, the delegation had voted unanimously for Seward. "For, gentlemen, it was from Gov. Seward that most of us learned to love Republican principles and the Republican Party." Evarts concluded with an emotional appeal for unity. Seward's "fidelity to the country, the constitution and the laws; his fidelity to the party and the principle that the majority govern; his interest in the advancement of our party to its victory, that our country may rise to its true glory, induces me to assume to speak his sentiments, as I do, indeed, the opinions of our whole delegation when I move you, as I do now, that the nomination of Abraham Lincoln, of Illinois, as the Republican candidate for the suffrages of the whole country for the office of Chief Magistrate of the American Union, be made unanimous." Those who heard Evarts's appeal, Howard noted, "could not fail to be impressed with the idea that a man who could have such a friend must be a noble man indeed." The correspondent for the *North Iowa Times* found it a "brief and beautiful eulogy," though it "resembled a funeral sermon rather than a cheerful acquiescence" in Lincoln's nomination.

John A. Andrew of Massachusetts spoke of his state's love of liberty —of Bunker Hill, of Lexington and Concord, of the brilliant political philosophers who spoke at Faneuil Hall, and of the Massachusetts Constitution, which had banned slavery even before the nation was born. "The affection of our hearts and the judgment of our intellects bound our political fortunes to William Henry Seward . . . the brightest and most shining light of this political generation." In "the thickest and hottest of every battle" for freedom, Andrew noted, "there waved the white plume of the gallant leader of New York." But Massachusetts was ready to fight now for Abraham Lincoln. "We know that this cause of ours is bound to triumph, and that the American people will, one day, be convinced, if not in 1860, that the path of duty and patriotism leads in the direction of the Republican cause."

Ingersoll looked over at Horace Greeley. "All this time, there sat, just to my right, the white-haired, small-eyed, breeches-rolled-up Philosopher of the *Tribune*, calm as a placid lake on which no zephyr blows, and, beyond all peradventure cool as a cucumber. With his head on his cane, he was ruminating, doubtless, on the transitoriness of all things in general, and the downfall of Bates in particular," wrote Ingersoll.

Schurz, speaking for Wisconsin, insisted that, "even if the name of William H. Seward should remain in history an instance of the highest merit uncrowned with the highest honor," his "ambition will be satisfied with the success of the cause which was the dream of his youth, and to which he has devoted all the days of his manhood." With a platform as noble as the one the Republicans had passed, and with a candidate "who so fairly represents it, as Mr. Lincoln does, we defy all the passion and prejudice that may be enforced against us by our opponents. We defy the whole slave power and the whole vassalage of hell."

Austin Blair of Michigan made what Halstead called "the speech of the hour." At "your behest here today," he told the delegates, Michigan "lays down her first, best-loved candidate to take up yours, with some bleeding of the heart, with some quivering in the veins; but she does not fear that the fame of Seward will suffer, for she knows that his fame is a portion of the history of the American Union; it will be written and read and beloved long after the temporary excitement of this day has passed away, and when Presidents are themselves forgotten in the oblivion which comes over all temporal things. We stand by him still. . . . We marshal now behind him in the grand column which shall go out to battle for Lincoln." There was more regret than celebration in these speeches.

Still in a daze over Lincoln's win—at first unable to speak, "almost disabled" by emotion—Orville Browning got up to put in a word for Illinois. "We are so much elated at present that we are scarcely in a condition to collect our own thoughts, or to express them intelligently to those who may listen to us," he began. But he wanted to stress the state's admiration for Seward. The men of Illinois fought against him "solely because we believed here that we could go into battle on the prairies of Illinois with more hope and more prospect of success under our own noble son." No lover of liberty could do other than to venerate Seward's name, Browning said. "On this occasion, I desire to say, only, that the hearts of the Illinois delegation are to-day filled with emotions of gratification for which they have no utterance. We are not more overcome by the triumph of our noble Lincoln, loving him as we do, knowing the purity of his past life, the integrity of his character, and devotion to the principles of our party, and the gallantry with which we will be conducted through this contest, than we are by the magnanimity of our friends of the great and glorious State of New York in moving to make this nomination unanimous." Lincoln had shown strong judgment in sending Browning, though initially a Bates man, to Chicago.

With that, the motion was carried. "No human body could attend to business after such a scene," the *New York Times* reported, so at about 1:30 p.m., the convention moved to adjourn and to reconvene at 5:00 p.m. Before going, the delegates approved Evarts's suggestion that a committee of the chairmen of the delegations meet at 3:00 p.m. at the Richmond House, obviously to settle on a vice-presidential nominee. Evarts also asked his fellow New Yorkers to convene immediately after adjournment at their Richmond House headquarters, surely to figure out whether they wanted a say in the matter.

Women exited the building with their fashionable clothing crushed and ruined by the mob. The "crinoline which entered in the a.m., in all its glory was undiscernible on its exit," a reporter noted. Thirty thousand people surrounding the Wigwam were cheering maniacally. "There were bands of music playing, and processions marching, and joyous cries heard on every hand, from the army of trumpeters for Lincoln of Illinois, and the thousands who are always enthusiastic on the winning side," Halstead wrote. But he noticed that those who had screamed inside the Wigwam and had stood at a pitch of excitement for hours "were hardly able to walk to their hotels. There were men who had not tasted liquor who staggered about like drunkards, unable to manage themselves." The Seward men "were mortified beyond expression, and walked thoughtfully and silently away from the slaughterhouse, more ashamed than embittered." They accepted Lincoln's nomination, "but did not pretend to be pleased with it," and they were not hopeful Lincoln would be elected. "It was their funeral and they would not make merry."

In Cleveland, as in many cities, residents anxiously awaited the news. "The anxiety was by no means confined to politicians, for we heard a diminutive apple girl gravely ask a customer if Seward was nominated," reported the *Cleveland Morning Leader*, Medill's old paper. The sidewalk in front of the *Leader* office's bulletin board was "crowded with men waiting for the first flash of the electric current which should tell the story." Then a special dispatch arrived. A messenger rushed into the office to have it set in type, shouting to all in earshot, "*Lincoln on the third ballot!*" People snapped up copies of a hastily printed extra that newsboys loudly hawked in the streets. The newspaper removed a photograph of Lincoln from the office and hung it on the front door, attracting the interest of the crowds in the street, who had no idea what the man looked like. "It must be confessed that our standard bearer is not remarkable for beauty, as the world goes, but has an air of sturdy independence and manliness, which attracts by its very singularity."

* * *

In Auburn, the Reverend Austin was conversing with Seward about the first ballot when Theodore Dimon, the senator's personal doctor and friend, rushed into the garden with news of the second and third ballots. "As he drew near us, he threw up his hands and exclaimed aloud—*Oh, God, it is all gone, gone, gone! Abraham Lincoln has received the nomination!!*" Austin was staggered. "His voice thrilled my heart with an agonizing sensation which it is totally impossible to describe. Had a thunder bolt from a clear sky struck Gov. Seward dead at my feet, I should not have been more startled or shocked!" The minister looked at Seward. "A deadly paleness overspread his countenance for an instant, succeeded instantly by a flush, and then all was calm as a summer morning." Seward resumed talking about the balloting, "and was the most composed man of the three or four who were present."

Austin could barely believe it. "I never was more disappointed and pained in my life by an event so sudden and unlooked for. Had we not been made so confident of success by the dispatches which had been received for several days. But to be elevated to such a degree, and then suddenly plunged down by an overthrow totally unlooked for, made the revulsion more cutting and painful." It was appalling. "The Republican Party have made a sad and fatal mistake. Through an over-ardent desire for success and in an unworthy distrust of the strength and permanency of their principles they have thrust aside a great and good man who was the Founder and Father of their Party, and whose only offense has been unwavering fidelity to its principles, and adopted a candidate who, although a good and true man, was comparatively obscure and unknown. I fear they will see the day when they will deeply regret this ungrateful and cruel abandonment."

The *Auburn Democrat*, savoring the embarrassment of the great local Republican, reported that Dr. Dimon arrived at Seward's front gate "so pale, trembling and speechless with agony, that even the lions that guard the Governor's mansion were moved to tears." The doctor's "woe-begone face told that the 'Defender of the Rights of Man' was sacrificed on the altar of expediency—sacrificed for Abraham Lincoln, a bar-room politician, who, compared with Gov. Seward, is as 'satyr to a Hyperion'"—another *Hamlet* reference. "The house of joy was turned into a house of mourning." The doctor instructed the artillerymen, who were waiting for a signal, to go home. There would be no cannon blasts in Auburn for Lincoln's nomination. "The Doctor approached them—his face as long as one of the rails that 'Honest Abe Lincoln' used to split—and ordered the cannon back to the armory. He 'would not fire for a democratic victory,' and was so little a soldier that he could not see the utility of firing at a funeral." Henry B. Stanton painted a similar scene. "The flags were furled, the cannon was rolled away, and Cayuga county went home with a clouded brow." The pro-Seward *Auburn Daily Advertiser* reported that Lincoln had won the nomination and added, "We have no time nor heart for comment."

Seward's fifteen-year-old daughter, Fanny, wrote in her diary that her father came into the house and "told Mother and I—in three words, 'Abraham Lincoln nominated.'" She was struck that he took the defeat "with philosophical & unselfish coolness." While his friends "feel much distress—he alone has a smile." The Reverend Austin, who found that Friday "one of the most painful and trying days of my life," left soon after, while other friends of Seward flocked to his house to offer their heartfelt sympathies.

Austin could not stay away. He called twice more at the Seward house, in the afternoon and evening, and joined other gentlemen in gathering around the senator, as at a wake. "I also went into Mrs. Seward's room and had a conversation with her on the subject. I found her calm and self-possessed, and not disposed to murmur in the least, at the sudden turn affairs had taken." Frances Adeline Seward, fifty-four, had been married to Seward for thirty-five years and disliked the ways of Washington. Whatever she felt about the news, she knew that her husband's lifelong political dream had been crushed. "This is a most affectionate woman," Austin wrote. "While we were sitting in the Governor's room, after the sad intelligence had arrived—(some six or seven gentlemen being present) she came in, spoke a few words to each of us, threw her arms around the Governor's neck, kissed him and retired! Faithful, true and loving wife!"

Abraham Lincoln waited in the telegraph office in Springfield for the report of the second ballot. When it came in around noon, it showed that Pennsylvania had swung to him, and that Lincoln had all but closed the gap with Seward. "This I thought from his manner he considered as virtually deciding the nomination," recalled Charles Zane. Confronted with this stunning turn of events, Lincoln did not wait for the final vote. He left the building and went over to the second-story headquarters of the *Illinois State Journal* next door, where he could burn off nervous energy talking with the folks gathered there.

The others remaining at the telegraph office closely studied the operator when a further report came clicking in. The man working the machine threw down his pencil, "evidently excited," Zane recalled. Then, taking it up, he wrote down the dispatch straight from the Wigwam and, according to the *Chicago Journal*, handed it to a messenger boy, who hurried over to the *Illinois State Journal* offices, where Lincoln was chatting with people. The boy gave it to Lincoln. "TO LINCOLN YOU ARE NOMINATED," it read. "He took the paper in hand, and looked at it long and silently, not heeding the noisy exultation of all around," the *Chicago Journal* reported. "When the second ballot came I knew this must Come," he said quietly. After studying it at length, he put the note in his vest pocket.

Zane was struck by the nominee's composure. "He received all with apparent coolness from the expressions playing on his Countenance however a close observer Could detect Strong emotions within." Telegram after telegram quickly followed. "Abe Lincoln: We did it, glory to God," wrote delegate Nathan M. Knapp, a fellow Illinois lawyer, from Chicago. "Abraham Lincoln: You're nominated & elected," wrote Springfield resident J. J. Richards, who quickly followed with:

"Hon. A. Lincoln: You were nominated on 3rd ballot." More news from the Wigwam came over the wire: "Hon. A. Lincoln: Vote just announced. . . . On motion of Mr. Evarts of New York, the nomination was made unanimous amid intense enthusiasm."

Lincoln did not stay at the newspaper office for long. He quietly remarked, "There's a little woman down at our house would like to hear this. I'll go down and tell her." Mary, after all, had long believed his brilliant mind and talent might make him president, even when Lincoln himself had treated such ambitions as a joke. The quote appeared in newspapers across the country, an early harbinger of Lincoln's charmingly down-to-earth nature.

Word quickly leaked out onto the street and shouts for Lincoln began. Someone told Lincoln, "I suppose we will soon have a book containing your life now," to which Lincoln replied that there was not much in his life to write about. (He had expressed much the same to Jesse Fell half a year earlier, when submitting a 602-word autobiography: "There's not much of it for the reason, I suppose, that there is not much of me.") At the foot of the stairs leading down from the newspaper office, Zane recalled, a group of "Irish & American Citizens" congratulated the nominee. "Boys," he joked, "you had better come and shake hands with me now that you have an oppertunity—for you do not Know what influence the nomination may have on me. I am human, you Know."

Lincoln's neighbor James Gourley recalled that Lincoln was "agitated—turned pale—trembled" as he walked home from the *Journal* office. For years, Lincoln had just been Lincoln to the people of Springfield—the homely, smart, good-natured lawyer who was away half the year working the judicial circuit; the father of rambunctious—some said rude and spoiled—boys, and the husband of a bright and loyal but sometimes cantankerous wife; the country entertainer who told knee-slapping jokes around potbellied stoves in downtown stores and offices; and the politician who had gotten himself some national notoriety by almost toppling the Little Giant, Stephen Douglas. Suddenly, a major party with a strong chance of winning in November had chosen this very Lincoln as its candidate for president of the United States.

As the tall man in the stovepipe hat strode on with his lumbering gait, his fellow citizens turned and looked at him "with a feeling of great satisfaction . . . mingled with Considerable of pride," Zane recalled. People pointed at him and said, "Yonder goes Lincoln." He had "grown in their interest that morning."

Chapter 14: The Dirty-Shirt Ticket

For the first time, a man from Illinois had been nominated for president, and Chicagoans began to celebrate. Joy & Frisbie, which supplied the city with ice from massive ice houses in suburban Crystal Lake, quickly rounded up all forty of its horse-drawn delivery wagons and sent them out behind a marching band, "much to the amusement of spectators for its novelty and much to their own advantage as an advertisement," the *Chicago Press and Tribune* noted. Out on Lake Michigan and the Chicago River, men festooned their vessels with American flags. "The steamtugs are whistling out their gratifications, drums are beating, children in the streets cry out for Lincoln, and the Douglas men look glum," the *New York Daily Herald* reported.

During the convention's lunch break, Murat Halstead observed an Illinois man roaring at a dinner table at the Tremont House, making a profanity-laced speech about Lincoln's victory to his immediate neighbors, none of whom he knew. "Talk of your money and bring on your bullies with you!—the immortal principles of the everlasting people are with Abe Lincoln, of the people, by—." The prairie lawyer had done it without Thurlow Weed's well-oiled political machine or Tom Hyer's fists. "Abe Lincoln has no money and no bullies, but he has the people by—." A waiter approached and asked what the man would like to eat. "Go to the devil—what do I want to eat for? Abe Lincoln is nominated,

G—d—d it; and I'm going to live on air—the air of Liberty by —." In a moment, though, the man requested the bill of fare, and ordered "a great deal of everything." As Halstead wrote, "He swore he felt as if he could 'devour and digest an Illinois prairie.' And this was one of thousands."

Telegrams bombarded the nominee. Jesse Fell, Lincoln's longtime Bloomington friend, reported from Chicago: "City wild with Excitement—from my inmost heart I congratulate you." Lincoln's friends and fellow lawyers Ward Hill Lamon and William W. Orme wrote: "God bless you we are happy & may you ever be. Your success is sure in November as it has been today." Lincoln's friend and fellow lawyer William M. Dickson, whose wife was a first cousin of Mary Todd Lincoln, telegraphed from Cincinnati: "My humble congratulations great Enthusiasm our guns thundering all over."

With dollar signs in their eyes, publishers and writers immediately clamored for Lincoln's blessings. An official of Follett, Foster and Company, of Columbus, Ohio, publisher of the Lincoln-Douglas debates, telegraphed Lincoln to notify him that "we have announced your biography." The company asked that Lincoln "please designate your pleasure if any as to who the writer shall be." Horace White, the twenty-five-year-old *Press and Tribune* reporter and friend of Lincoln, was already lobbying for the job, telegraphing the nominee that "I shall probably be appointed your Biographer in behalf of Follett Foster & Co." The "matter is under consultation among your friends," he informed Lincoln, promising to "go immediately to Springfield" if chosen. (As it turned out, a twenty-three-year-old named William Dean Howells—later one of the masters of nineteenth-century American literature—won the nod to write the official biography.) D. B. Cooke and Company, a Chicago concern that published railway guides, lawbooks, city directories, and political books, telegraphed Lincoln that it had been "Engaged to Edit a volume of your life & speeches," begging him to "give no one else the preference." It urged: "Answer at once." Instantly, Lincoln had become a red-hot commodity.

Several people thought that a moment of high drama could cap the convention and set the party aflame. Since Springfield was only about two hundred miles away, they proposed rushing Lincoln up to accept his nomination in person and rouse the Republicans before they departed for home. "There is great of enquiry made is Mr Lincoln coming up," J. J. A. Wilson telegraphed Lincoln. "What can I say you are Expected." J. J. Richards informed Lincoln by telegram: "The Republicans of the United States assembled at the wigwam want you here tonight will you come." Charles H. Ray, the editor-in-chief of the *Press and Tribune*, also telegraphed, suggesting Lincoln might arrive Saturday: "I congratulate you. Shall you be up tomorrow morning answer." A correspondent for the Bloomington *Daily Pantagraph* reported as fact that Friday: "A special train has been sent after Mr. Lincoln; it will arrive with him this evening."

All this horrified David Davis, already exhausted after a nerve-racking week. He evidently feared that Lincoln's sudden appearance in Chicago would set off a catastrophic explosion. Despite the sad speeches by Seward supporters moving that Lincoln's nomination be made unanimous, the party was far from unified. The New Yorkers were furious and needed time to cool down. Lincoln's closest friends and allies raced to the telegraph office and fired off a barrage of frantic messages. "Dont come here for God's sake," Davis telegraphed, adding, "You will be telegraphed by others to come It is the united [advice] of your friends not to come this is important." Leonard Swett telegraphed: "Dont let any one persuade you to come here." Similar telegrams poured in from Norman Judd, Jesse Dubois, William Butler, Chicago grain merchant Solomon Sturgis, and Gustave Koerner. Charles Ray amended his earlier telegram, joining with fellow journalists John Locke Scripps and Joseph Medill to inform Lincoln that they had consulted with Pennsylvanians, who felt he should not come "till after New York has gone home." Davis shot off a second telegram: "Write no letters & make no promises till You see me—write me at Bloomington when to see you—I must see you soon." He surely needed to see him to explain how Illinois obtained the votes that put Lincoln over the top. Whether or not the pile of panicked telegrams influenced him, the cautious Lincoln stayed put.

In Chicago, people were still scratching their heads over what the convention had just done. "The nomination of Abram Lincoln, although not entirely unexpected, took even his friends by surprise," observed a *Philadelphia Press* correspondent, who did not yet know the candidate's first name. "He was as little known to the delegates of the Republican party assembled in the Convention as he is known to the country at large, and this was shown by the fact that no one attempted to discuss his character or the effect of the nomination upon the country at large." The only thing that seemed to matter to the delegates was whether he was more electable than Seward.

New York Times correspondent Joseph Howard, racing to complete his report before the final post of the day, found it difficult to write. He too was exhausted, struggling to form his words while pandemonium engulfed the Tremont House. Everybody was drinking. "The rooms of the Massachusetts Delegation are directly opposite mine, and Gilmore's band is now in there playing 'When Swallows Homeward Fly.' The rooms of the Pennsylvania Delegation are 'round the corner,' and the Pittsburgh band strikes up 'Hail Columbia,' after which the 'Light-guard band' of Chicago, which is stationed in the Hall below, gives us the benefit of the 'Star Spangled Banner;' so you see we have pretty lively times," he wrote. Mark Delahay, the self-centered Kansan whose stay in Chicago had been funded by Lincoln, also wrote a letter at the Tremont, his last to Lincoln from the convention. "I am excited & exhausted," he told his friend. This "is the happiest day of my checkquerd life."

The party's leaders had little time for dinner and celebrations. They needed to choose a vice president before the convention resumed at 5:00 p.m., and they did not have time to consult the party's nominee—one of the consequences of having no candidates on hand at the convention. The most important task at this point was to soothe the New York men, who were enraged about the day's events and did not care who knew it. A *Buffalo Courier* correspondent visited their headquarters at the Richmond House that afternoon and concluded that "such another sorry set of fellows are not in this city." The New Yorkers blamed one man above all for the disaster: *New-York Tribune* editor Horace Greeley, who had the audacity to be there at the headquarters, mingling with the crowd and carrying on as if he had done nothing wrong. "They accuse Greeley of stabbing Seward, and say he shall be paid for it," the *Courier* correspondent wrote. "The curses heaped upon the head of the old man are loud and deep, such as men who have been disappointed in long cherished hopes, may be expected to indulge in." Some delegates even cursed Greeley to his face, "and he did not seem to exactly relish the position he has placed himself in."

Pro-Seward editor Isaac Platt was furious. The Republicans' shameful abandonment of Seward, he contended, had been "brought about by the machinations of his enemies," including "mercenaries sent under pay to do the dirty work of demagogues in the distance, who, jealous of him they assailed, were ashamed to appear themselves." With them "were knaves, fools and cowards," who were "ready to second any treachery as pretexts offered." Greeley, he believed, had betrayed his principles by backing Edward Bates. The *Tribune* editor surely knew that such a candidate would divide Republicans and depress the party's base, dimming its prospects for victory in November. The party's betrayal of Seward would have been all for nothing, Platt contended. For all his rhetoric about saving the nation, Greeley intended only "to stab Mr. Seward at every point and prevent his nomination. His course called forth expressions of indignation from every quarter, as it was well known that jealousy of Thurlow Weed, whom he is anxious and ambitious to supplant, was his moving motive."

Tall, handsome, silver-haired James Watson Webb, editor of the *Morning Courier and New-York Enquirer*, who admired Seward so much that he named one of his sons William Seward Webb, also pointed the finger straight at Greeley. Believing that four-fifths of America's Republicans, including a large majority of delegates, had favored Seward, Webb had been sending the senator encouraging telegrams from Chicago.

He did not realize until it was too late that delegates' minds had been poisoned "by apprehensions created *by his friend* Greeley." The blameless Seward had been "sacrificed to the most infamous and systematic falsehoods, having their foundation in personal malice and the desire of revenge," Webb reflected bitterly in his newspaper.

The correspondent for the Democratic *North Iowa Times* visited the New York headquarters with some fellow journalists and discovered "a scene of madness" that no Lincoln man could have imagined. They "listened to groans for Lincoln, cheers for Seward and *for Douglas*, and denunciations of 'the baseness of the Pennsylvania delegates' till we became sorry for the Empire boys." Older Seward men looked sad, and younger ones were furious. The men there thought that the thirty-five electoral votes of New York had been traded for the "merest *chance*" of eleven from Illinois. "No cheers could be got" for Lincoln, while "Horace Greeley was threatened with a universal effigy burning throughout New York."

Democratic papers saw it much the same way as the Seward delegates. A highly amused editor at the *Richmond Dispatch* in Virginia suggested that Seward should have taken greater care to avoid the fangs of the viper Greeley. "This illustrious personage of the white hat is considered by some in his party to be so guileless, inoffensive and ignorant of the world, that he can be trampled upon with impunity. But Greeley has shown that he can bite the heel that treads on him, and that there is venom enough in his composition, when scientifically condensed and energetically ejected, to annihilate the king of beasts." Lincoln's triumph, he wrote, was merely a byproduct of "the intrigues of Horace Greeley and old Blair . . . who, though they could not obtain the nomination for Madame Bates, their first love, yet prevented the success of the apostle of higher law." Seward, it seemed, had somehow given offense to Greeley, "and he has never been forgiven though it was he who first raised the editor of the *Tribune* to importance." In Chicago, Greeley had taken his well-timed revenge. Seward "fell, covered with innumerable wounds, most of them in his back. In his dying agony he turned a reproachful look on Greeley, and, in the words of stabbed Caesar to Brutus, exclaimed, '*Et tu quoque, Brute!*'"

New York Times editor Henry Raymond found the betrayal no laughing matter. Like Platt, he believed this execrable convention had turned out to be about one thing: destroying Seward. And "in that endeavor, Mr. Greeley labored harder and did tenfold more than the whole family of Blairs, together with all the Gubernatorial candidates." In his postmortem published the following week, Raymond argued that Greeley had influence on the Republican delegates only because he had advanced the cause of freedom for decades. Greeley had defended Seward's courageous stand against the Know-Nothings. He had urged his reelection to the Senate in the face of bitter opposition. He had been known to be his friend and loyal supporter. "These things gave him a hold upon the Republican sentiment of the country, and a weight of authority in everything relating to Gov. Seward," far beyond the influence of the Blairs. Greeley abused that trust to bring Seward down. "Mr. Greeley was in Chicago several days before the meeting of the Convention," Raymond noted bitterly, "and he devoted every hour of the interval to the most steady and relentless prosecution of the main business which took him thither—the defeat of Gov. Seward. He labored personally with delegates as they arrived—commending himself always to their confidence by professions of regard and the most zealous friendship for Gov. Seward, but presenting defeat *even in New-York*, as the inevitable result of his nomination."

His words carried weight, Raymond argued, because everyone believed Greeley was still friendly with Seward. They were unaware of his private letter angrily dissolving the firm of Seward, Weed and Greeley after his friends had blocked his rise in politics. Had that story been known in Chicago, "it would have disarmed the deadly effect of his pretended friendship" with Seward, "upon whom he was thus deliberately wreaking the long hoarded revenge of a disappointed office-seeker." Delegates would have realized that his actions were "stimulated by a hatred he had secretly cherished for years." But Seward had kept the letter secret, and even Weed and Raymond knew nothing about it.

Thus, Greeley was "protected by the forbearance of those whom he assailed," while he remained "strong in the confidence of those upon whom he sought to operate."

Even some of Seward's opponents agreed that Greeley had made all the difference. "Greeley slaughtered Seward and saved the party," Indiana editor John D. Defrees wrote to congressman Schuyler Colfax during the convention's afternoon break. "He deserves the praises of all men, and gets them now. Wherever he goes he is greeted with cheers"—except, of course, at the headquarters of pro-Seward states. Greeley, for his part, continued to insist Bates would have been the wisest choice. As for Seward, Greeley wrote, "I was never insensible to his many good and some great qualities, both of head and heart. But I did not and do not believe it advisable that he should be the Republican candidate for President." Privately, Greeley complained that others should not have left it to him to fight Seward, "considering where I live and the power of the sore-heads to damage me." Unfortunately, other Seward opponents had been scared off by "fear of Weed's resentment"—Schuyler Colfax among them. "I don't think you wanted to come face to face with Weed in a case wherein his heart was so set on a triumph," Greeley complained to the calculating congressman. "I ought not to have been obliged to expose myself to the deadliest resentment of all the Seward crowd, as I did. But what I must do, I will, regardless of consequences."

Greeley would survive the boiling contempt of his fellow New Yorkers, the *Buffalo Courier* writer predicted. The people of the West still loved him. Even at the Richmond House headquarters, he remained "a popular man among the sturdy farmers of this region, and he was followed about the room, by people of this class and others, curious to hear him talk on the questions absorbing the thought of every one here." But the Irrepressibles would leave Chicago spitting with anger about Greeley's betrayal. In their minds, he had shoved Seward off the cliff, and they would never forgive him for it. Led by Weed, they would eventually have their revenge.

* * *

All this bitterness and rage was a bad thing for the party. Victory in November would be impossible without New York's heap of electoral votes—nearly a quarter of the 152 needed. And Republicans seeking office in other states, including crucial Pennsylvania, would find themselves hard-pressed without New York's money. Something had to be done to mollify the Empire State.

Prior to the 3:00 p.m. gathering of delegation chairmen, Greeley, of all people, went to New York governor Edwin D. Morgan to ask if he would accept the nomination for vice president. It did not go well. "Governor Morgan not only declined to accept it himself, but he declined to suggest any one of Seward's friends for the place," Pennsylvanian A. K. McClure wrote. "Not only Governor Morgan, but Mr. Evarts and Mr. Weed, all refused to be consulted on the subject of the Vice-Presidency, and they did it in a temper that indicated contempt for the action of the convention." They did not want to put their stamp of approval on the Republicans' spineless treatment of Seward. Some delegates proposed New York senator Preston King—the short, rotund Seward ally who had been part of the effort to bribe the Illinois delegation three days earlier. But King, too, scorned the idea, refusing to be considered. The "first act" of the Seward men after Lincoln's nomination "was to declare that New-York would not accept the Vice-Presidency under any circumstances," Raymond wrote, "and their next was to designate Hamlin, of Maine, as their choice, so far as they had any."

Senator Hannibal Hamlin, a friend of Senator King, was a former newspaper editor who had served as a Democratic congressman in the 1840s, before the uproar over the Kansas-Nebraska Act led him to speak out with increasing vehemence about slavery and the ugly politics sustaining it. By 1856, he had cofounded the Republican Party in Maine, and his leadership helped it win control of the legislature. For a short time, he even served as governor. The *New York Daily Herald* described him as a sloppy dresser but rated him "a pleasant, good looking, middle aged, middle sized man, with a complexion and hair and eyes as dark as those of Daniel Webster. He has a musical voice, is a good speaker, and in both houses of Congress has had a large experience in public affairs."

The senator was, in some ways, an inspired choice. He could provide some needed balance for the ticket—an Easterner to offset a Westerner, a former Democrat to offset a former Whig, an elected Washington insider to offset an unelected outsider from Illinois. Maine was a Seward state, suitable to be rewarded by the New Yorkers. On top of that, his "standing as a parliamentarian . . . peculiarly fitted him to preside over the Senate," one of the only constitutional tasks of vice presidents, his grandson Charles Eugene Hamlin noted. McClure believed the delegation chairmen found the Maine man attractive "simply because he was a representative Republican fresh from the Democratic party." That was no small point. The former Whigs and Democrats who comprised the party had fought like cats and dogs for decades before becoming Republicans, and ill will and jealousies persisted. Both wings had to be appeased.

On the minus side, Maine, with its meager stash of eight electoral votes, was a minor state that already was in the Republican column. If the delegates had been capable of thinking rationally, they might have considered a former Democrat from crucial Pennsylvania—say, political boss Simon Cameron, given his ability to deliver that state's electoral jackpot of twenty-seven votes, or congressman John Hickman. But Pennsylvania had plunged the fatal knife into Seward's back, and the New York men were in no mood to reward it. At their 3:00 p.m. meeting, the delegation chairmen agreed that Hamlin would serve as well as anyone under the circumstances.

While most Seward supporters were busy sulking and cursing Greeley, one New Yorker decided he wanted to meet the men from Illinois who had somehow outgeneraled the brilliant tactician Thurlow Weed. The avuncular James W. Nye, forty-four, a delegate, political player, and militia general who had entertained listeners at railroad stops Monday and at the Wigwam Tuesday night, made his way over to the Tremont House. There, Isaac N. Arnold recounted, "the Illinois delegation was in session, anxiously considering how the friends of Seward and Weed could be satisfied, so that they would give the ticket their cordial and hearty support." The clean-shaven, pudgy Nye knocked at the door and told the man answering that he had a message for Illinois. Norman B. Judd warmly welcomed him. "What can Illinois do for New York?" Judd asked. "Name it, and if in our power, consider it done." Nye weighed the offer. "Well," he said, "if you sucker boys will please send an Illinois school-master to Albany to teach Thurlow Weed his political alphabet, we will be greatly obliged." The generous joke broke at least some of the ice.

At the Capitol in Washington, senator Stephen Douglas received a stunning telegram from New York congressman John B. Haskin at about 2:30 p.m., alerting him that the Republican Party had nominated, of all people, his gangly Illinois adversary. Around that time, several House members, including Indiana Republican Colfax, wandered over to the Senate, itching for news. They carefully examined the dispatch, doubting its authenticity, since "several forged ones" about Lincoln's nomination had been circulated before even the second ballot was taken at Chicago, Colfax recalled. The *New York Daily Herald* reported much the same. "By most people it was supposed to be a hoax, played off by some wag upon the Little Giant, the report seemed *prima facie* so very absurd, improbable and incredible."

But confirmation of the absurd and improbable report came at about 4:00 p.m. By the time Colfax got back to the House chamber, members had interrupted business and were exchanging "hearty congratulations." They seemed delighted, since they regarded the obscure Lincoln as far more electable than the controversial Seward. "I do not think there were a dozen out of our 112 [House Republicans] who did not join in the rejoicing, & all was hilarity, confidence, & enthusiasm on our side," Colfax wrote to Lincoln that night, perhaps trying to butter him up after initially opposing his nomination. The Democrats, by contrast, "looked depressed & disappointed." Some Democratic members from Illinois told Colfax confidentially that "they were not confident of saving their State," even if Douglas managed to become their nominee.

Even some New Yorkers "seemed delighted," Illinois senator Lyman Trumbull informed Lincoln by letter that evening. Ohio senator Benjamin Wade opined that "the election was settled—that our success was certain." The Democrats, by the same token, "were taken aback—They were all looking to Gov. Seward's nomination." Trumbull heard that his Illinois Senate colleague, Douglas, "told a friend that it was no use to disguise the fact, that it was the strongest nomination which could have been made, that no man could get as many votes by thousands in the North West as you—I think it finishes his prospects." The man who, for decades, had outshone Lincoln in the battle for political success was suddenly in danger of being outflanked for the ultimate prize.

Senator Douglas strode into the House chamber that afternoon "& surprised every one by the hearty & eulogistic manner in which he spoke of you," Colfax informed Lincoln. "He told me, in the presence of a score of Dems. & Reps, that though he often met his fellow-Senators in debate none of them had ever proved so hard a match as you—that no stronger nomination than yours could have been made"—and "that your selection would kindle a glow of enthusiasm that no one else could have effected &c &c &c." In the Senate campaign two years earlier, Lincoln had bruised Douglas so badly in Illinois that the Democrats lost the popular vote to Republicans, and the senator had clung to his seat only because the legislative districts were shaped to favor Democrats. During their debate at Freeport, Illinois, Lincoln had maneuvered Douglas into stating a position that pried him apart from Southern Democrats, effectively ruining his chances for the nomination in Charleston. Douglas, more than anyone, knew how dangerous an adversary the folksy, joke-telling Springfield lawyer was.

Celebrations were erupting all over Chicago. At the first lull in the booming of cannon outside the Wigwam after Lincoln's nomination, a "stentorian voice" called out, inviting Pennsylvania residents to convene at the state's headquarters. A short time later, eight hundred to a thousand "sons of the Keystone" stood outside the Briggs House and the Metropolitan Hotel. A correspondent for Pennsylvania's *Daily Evening Express* of Lancaster noted that these men well understood the central role they had just played—that, without their efforts, Seward would have been "nominated without a doubt." The Philadelphia Cornet Band went to the front, and the parade stepped off. A "wild enthusiasm" had seized the men. "The 'boys' were perfectly frantic, and went in, 'regardless of expense.'" Looking for something to shoulder that would symbolize the Railsplitter, they rushed into a broom store on Randolph Street and bought out its stock "in about two minutes." They bolted into a hardware store and stripped it of all its rakes in as little time, and "vandal hands" made off with a pile of rails lying by the road. "All along the route they carried the tidings of Lincoln's nomination, and everywhere they met with the heartiest responses." The correspondent for the *North Iowa Times* was somewhat less impressed. "At the head was a hatless gent carrying a stick of basswood to indicate that Mr. Lincoln was handy with an axe. Farther along was another silly looking josey with a piece of scantling on his shoulder, supposed to represent the *first rail* that 'Old Abe' split." Symbolism had quickly replaced substance, and the deplorably unsophisticated crowd had triumphed. The writer overheard a Seward man from Wisconsin muttering, "the *brains* of the party feel insulted."

At 5:00 p.m., the delegates returned to the Wigwam for the concluding session of the convention. The Pennsylvania contingent, freshened by their parade in the spring air, carried a large banner onto the platform, winning loud applause: PENNSYLVANIA GOOD FOR 20,000 MAJORITY, FOR THE PEOPLE'S CANDIDATE, ABE. LINCOLN. The nomination of a vice president quickly began. Abel Carter Wilder, a Kansas merchant who had bravely fought for freedom in that territory and had been chosen the Leavenworth delegate over Lincoln's friend Mark Delahay, nominated Pennsylvania congressman John Hickman. David Cartter, the stuttering former congressman from Ohio who had put Lincoln over the top, enjoyed the privilege of nominating the choice of the smoke-filled room, Hannibal Hamlin, who received tepid applause.

Former Massachusetts governor George S. Boutwell nominated the state's current governor, Nathaniel P. Banks, whose presidential aspirations had crashed in Chicago. Morrow B. Lowry of Erie, Pennsylvania, who had visited with the jailed John Brown just before his execution, nominated Andrew H. Reeder of his state, the brave former governor of Kansas.

The loudest cheering, by far, greeted Indianan Caleb B. Smith's nomination of the pugnacious, knife-wielding Kentuckian Cassius M. Clay. "If the multitude could have had their way, Mr. Clay would have been put on the ticket by acclamation," Halstead contended. As a Southerner from a slave state, Clay might have helped make the case that the Republicans were not a purely Northern concern. But party leaders passed the word that "Mr. Hamlin was a good friend of Mr. Seward," Halstead wrote. "He was geographically distant from Lincoln, and was once a Democrat. It was deemed judicious to pretend to patronize the Democratic element, and thus consolidate those who were calling the Convention an 'old Whig concern.'" On the first ballot, Hamlin garnered 194 votes to 101 ½ for Clay. That signaled an impending landslide. On the second ballot, Hamlin outscored Clay 367 votes to 86, with 13 for Hickman, and it was done. The crowd greeted the nomination with only polite applause. "The faithful yelled themselves out for Lincoln, and had no voice for Hamlin," the *New York Daily Herald* reported. Mayor Long John Wentworth was pleased enough to fire off a telegram to Lincoln: "Senator Hamlin is Vice Prest no man could be better for you." Though Wentworth had spent much of the week lobbying for Seward, telling reporters that "nobody ever seriously thought of Lincoln for president," he seemed unconcerned that any of that would damage his relationship with Lincoln.

Kentucky delegate George D. Blakey, a wealthy farmer representing Clay's state, dutifully moved that the nomination be made unanimous. Then the clean-shaven Indiana congressman Caleb Smith—"Cale" Smith, as everyone called him—rose to address the Wigwam. Standing five feet eight inches tall, with thin brown hair on a nearly bald head, he spoke with "a shrill, musical and clear" voice, correspondent L. D.

Ingersoll noted, "like higher notes of a bugle. When he becomes fully aroused, he can be heard distinctly in every part of the great Wigwam." He was aroused now, and he lent his considerable oratorical firepower to eulogizing Clay's remarkable courage. "It is a very easy matter for us who live upon soil unstained by slavery; who breathe the free air of States where the manacles of the slave are never seen, and their wailings are never heard, to advocate the principles of the Republican party; but gentlemen, to advocate those principles upon the soil of slavery itself, in the very face and shadows of their altars and false gods, requires a degree of moral heroism of which but few of us can boast." With such men fighting against slavery, the flag of freedom would someday "wave in triumph" over America, Smith promised. "Let me assure you, gentlemen, that when that banner which is now trailing in the dust shall be borne aloft in triumph, and its glorious folds shall be expanded to the winds of heaven, you will see inscribed upon its brightest folds in characters of living light the name of Cassius M. Clay."

The convention quickly made the nomination unanimous. William McCrillis, a lawyer and state representative from Bangor, rose to thank the delegates for placing a son of Maine on the ticket. He noted that thousands of Mainers had migrated to Illinois—that the bones of many of them were buried in Western soil—while those who had stayed put would hail Lincoln's nomination "with one spontaneous, loud, long and continued shout of enthusiasm and applause." Even so, the choice of Hamlin "was a matter of surprise to nearly everybody, and perhaps no one so much as himself," the *Lancaster Daily Evening Express* correspondent noted. "He was not even talked of in that connection previous to his name being submitted." *New York Times* correspondent Joseph Howard lost a bet he had made during the break that the ticket would be Lincoln-Hickman, or Lincoln-Banks.

Tying up loose ends, the convention voted to send a group of delegates representing each state—headed by convention president George Ashmun—to meet with Abraham Lincoln in Springfield the following day. Joshua Giddings, making a last appeal for American freedom, persuaded the convention to pass a resolution expressing sympathy with those in the slave states who had been "exiled from their homes on account of their opinions"—and holding Democrats responsible "for these gross violations" of free-speech rights.

Valedictory addresses spilled out. "We have now completed the great work for which we are assembled here. We have presented to this country a ticket which will command the love and admiration of Republicans everywhere, and the respect and esteem of the entire country," Caleb Smith said. "I feel that we stand upon a rock and the gates of hell cannot prevail against it." Smith also touched on Lincoln's life story, sure to be a focus of the coming campaign. Some "thirty years ago on the southern frontier of Indiana you might have seen a humble, ragged boy, barefooted, driving his oxen through the mountains, and who, by his own exertions, has elevated himself to the pinnacle which has now presented him as the candidate of this Convention. He is a living illustration of the enterprise which characterizes the West, and every western heart will throb with joy when the name of Lincoln shall be presented to them as the candidate of the Republican party." Ingersoll admired the little speech but noted that Smith spoke with something of a lisp. "When he becomes fully aroused, the lisp passes away, but it is amusing enough to hear him say 'Mithter Prethident' or 'Fellow Thitithens.'"

Fellow Hoosier Henry S. Lane, who had celebrated Seward's demise earlier that day by dancing on a table and swinging his cane, joined Smith in hailing the convention's work. "No event in the history of the United States" since the signing of the Declaration of Independence "is more sublime and impressive than the event which has this day been inaugurated in this vast presence of the freemen of the United States of America." The "torch of civilization" had been handed to Republicans, and "I ask you to bear it aloft and upward in the light of free institutions, until this whole world shall glow with the light of our illumination." He also scourged the Democrats, urging the delegates to "sternly rebuke the disunion spirit which now disgraces the politics of the United States, and to burn, hissing hot, into the brazen front of the Southern Democracy the brand of disunion, as God marked Cain, the first murderer."

During these final speeches, members of the audience made "loud cries" for Horace Greeley to speak. "Applause and hisses" greeted them, the *New York Daily Herald* reported, revealing the ugly fissure in the party and the anger of Seward men. While Greeley remained seated, the bombastic Adam Goodrich of Minnesota rose to call on "citizens and strangers, ladies and gentlemen," to make a "triumphal procession" that night. He moved that they gather at the head of Washington Street on Michigan Avenue and make a winding march down major downtown streets—Lake, Dearborn, Randolph, Franklin, and back to Lake—to the Wigwam for a "grand ratification" meeting, celebrating the day's nominations. Proceeding to another topic, he sought a resolution of appreciation for "the hospitality, taste, zeal and munificence displayed by the ladies and gentlemen of the city of Chicago, in aid of the great Republican cause." When he tried to make a third motion, cries of "No speech" interrupted Goodrich. "I am charged with other matters. Be yet patient," he implored. "No, no!" and "Dry up!" cried the audience. The crowd wanted to adjourn and begin celebrating. Goodrich felt wounded. "I am not in the habit of being halloed down, even by opponents, and certainly not friends, and the friends of the cause that I claim to be an humble advocate of." "If you are a friend, let us go home," a man retorted, drawing laughter. When Goodrich continued, the audience became "impatient and vociferous in their calls" to move along. Eventually, he sat down.

Wrapping things up, President Ashmun thanked the delegates for their kindness to him and revealed that he knew the nominee. "It was my good fortune to have served with Mr. Lincoln in the Congress of the United States, and I rejoice in the opportunity to say there was never elected to the House of Representatives a purer, truer, nor more intelligent and loyal Representative than Abraham Lincoln." With the help of "God who giveth the victory, we will triumph," he said. Finally, the president moved to adjourn. The delegates heartily approved. The gavel came down, and raucous celebrations became the new order of business on that spring evening in Chicago.

* * *

"Torrents of liquor were poured down the throats of the multitude," Halstead reported. The effect became quickly apparent. "Everybody seems to have, for the time, laid aside their gravity and become again boys. The city is wild with excitement," a correspondent for the *Illinois State Journal* in Springfield wrote. "At the Illinois headquarters in the Tremont was assembled a set of the craziest men I ever saw. Their demonstrations were such as to defy competition from the inmates of any Lunatic Asylum." The Lincoln men made speeches, hugged each other, sang songs, and delivered "cheers which almost raised the roof."

At the closing of the convention, one hundred guns thundered from the roof of the Tremont House, "their echoes caught up and answered from other parts of the city almost as soon as their flashes were seen across the night sky." Many buildings, including the giant warehouse of A. Huntington, Wadsworth and Parks on Lake Street, were illuminated with multicolored lights in the windows. A massive bonfire of leaping yellow, orange, and red flames, thirty feet in circumference, raged in front of the Tremont House, reddening the night sky for miles around. Another blazed before the Metropolitan Hotel. The *Chicago Press and Tribune*, which had fought hard for Lincoln, went all out. "From turret to foundation," the building was lit by "the brilliant glare of a thousand lights which blazed from windows and doors with a most attractive and beautiful effect." Rails stood on both sides of the counting room door—said to be two of the three thousand that had been split by "honest Old Abe" thirty years earlier at Decatur, by the Sangamon River. "On the inside were two more, brilliantly hung with tapers whose numberless individual lights glistened like so many stars in contrast with the dark walnut color of the wood." The employees strung an immense transparency on the front of the building over the main door: FOR PRESIDENT, "HONEST OLD ABE."—FOR VICE PRESIDENT, HANNIBAL HAMLIN.

Though rain had started falling, crowds collected in front of hotels. Shouldering their rails, rakes, and brooms, men set off marching. A score of bands were out, sending their cheering music through the downtown. Lights everywhere shimmered in the puddled streets. A unity parade stopped on Clark Street in front of the *Press and Tribune*, where the marchers "rent the air with soul inspiring cheers," returned with joy by the paper's one hundred employees. Hundreds gathered in front of the Briggs House, where Andrew Curtin, the Pennsylvania gubernatorial candidate who had fought all week to bring Seward down, pledged the Republicans would carry the state by twenty-five thousand votes. According to one report, the Pennsylvanians in Chicago got so worked up that they telegraphed Decatur "for *the whole fence* that Old Abe had put up in 1830." Chicagoans shot off rockets, which hissed into the darkness and "clove through the air like fiery telegrams to the sky." Thousands of men and boys in their Wide Awake uniforms marched in precision with flaming torches, the light dancing on their shiny black cloaks.

But the Seward men still stewed in anger. George Dawson, covering the convention for Weed's *Albany Evening Journal*, seethed over the perfidy of the New Yorker's enemies. "Misrepresentation has achieved its work," he wrote. "The timid and credulous have succumbed to threats and perverseness. To please a few thousand men of equivocal principle and faltering faith, millions of loyal hearts have been saddened. The recognized standard bearer of the Republican party has been sacrificed on the altar of fancied availability." Dawson denounced the "bitter hate" of Seward's foes. "The result is less a defeat of Wm. H. Seward than a triumph of his personal enemies."

The correspondent for the *Missouri Republican*, a Democratic paper in St. Louis, saw only gloom for the Republicans. "The New Yorkers are mad as March hares, and swear they would as soon go for Jeffn. Davis, Judge Douglas, or any other candidate, as for this third rate, rail splitting Lincoln," he wrote. "A great deal of trading was going on last night, Lincoln's friends furnishing every delegate an office who would vote for him." One New Yorker who had blown $1,900 in Chicago trying to get Seward nominated launched into a speech in front of the Tremont House, predicting that Douglas would carry the Empire State overwhelmingly. An "indignation meeting" took place at the Richmond House, where men freely bet that Lincoln would lose by twenty thousand votes in New York. "Delegates are almost afraid to go back there, fearing the wrath of the people." Boxer Tom Hyer complained that his friends wanted "to quit the miserable, truckling republican party" and get behind "some man of prominence for president" who could win. "It commenced to rain as soon as Lincoln was nominated—this, and the day being Friday, hangman's day, are bad signs."

German-born Gustave Koerner of Illinois discovered a subdued crowd at the Deutsches Haus, where German American visitors from around the country were mulling the day's events. "I found them generally very despondent," Koerner recalled. "Seward, or even some other radical Republican, such as Wade or Chase, had been their choice. They believed that Lincoln's nomination would not meet with half the enthusiasm that Seward's would have met with, in which they were very much mistaken." On the other hand, the convention had brought the ax down on their nemesis Edward Bates. One group of German Americans formed "a large procession" in Chicago that night to promote the Republican cause.

Addison G. Procter, the young Seward delegate from Kansas, sought out the Michigan delegation at the Adams House to arrange to join them on a free train ride from Chicago to Detroit, after which he would head back East to Massachusetts, where he grew up. At the luxurious hotel, he found Governor Austin Blair exhorting Michigan's depressed delegates "to forget their disappointments (for Michigan had been for Seward from start to finish) and unite for an enthusiastic beginning to the campaign." The cars of the special Michigan Central train departing early the next morning would be decorated with slogans and a portrait of the candidate, "setting the ball to rolling for Lincoln," as some delegates put it. Still, Procter knew many people would be asking why in God's name the convention chose Lincoln over the party's most esteemed man. "Though the Seward element, especially those from New York, made a splendid showing of graceful yielding to the will of the majority, we all felt that a campaign of education was before us," Procter recalled. The *North Iowa Times* reporter detected a similar mood. Republicans that night "generally remarked that Lincoln would run better than Seward," he noted, "but they as generally admitted that the 'mother' was taken out of their vinegar."

Pennsylvania's Curtin ventured bravely into the black heart of depression, paying a call on New York's Governor Morgan, chairman of the Republican National Committee, that night at the Richmond House. "He treated me civilly, but with marked coolness," Curtin recalled. Curtin then visited Weed, who could barely contain his contempt. "You have defeated the man who of all others was most revered by the people and wanted for President," Weed told him, hinting that Curtin and Henry S. Lane could now effectively go to hell. Curtin's ally A. K. McClure had a similar experience with the New York boss that night. "I found him sullen, and offensive in both manner and expression. He refused even to talk about the contest, and intimated very broadly that Pennsylvania, having defeated Seward, could now elect Curtin and Lincoln."

The Lincoln men were deeply worried. That night, a rumor that Seward would support Lincoln "spread like wildfire, and the Illinois delegates took heart from it, for they had been expecting the worst, the New Yorkers having shown unmistakably that they were bitterly dissatisfied with the defeat of their favorite," the *Philadelphia Press* reported. But no one could be sure the gossip was true. At some point, a New Yorker named Humphreys forced his way through the raucous crowds at the Tremont House to the Illinois headquarters. A former Bloomington man, he sought out a current resident, Leonard Swett. Humphreys informed Swett that Weed was "feeling badly" and suggested that some of the Illinois men "ought to call on him." That seemed like a good idea to Swett, who asked Humphreys if he would introduce him to Weed. Humphreys begged off, saying he did not know the political boss well. But Swett and his fellow Bloomingtonian David Davis decided to go over to the Richmond House anyway, alone and uninvited.

They found the famous man, whom they had never met, in his room with his unmarried, devoted forty-one-year-old daughter Harriet. The Illinois men appeared to irritate him less than the Pennsylvanians did. Weed did not seem angry. Nor did he complain about anyone. He spoke with sadness, confessing that the day's events had been the most crushing political disappointment of his life. "I hoped to make my friend, Mr. Seward, President, and I thought I could serve my country in doing so," Weed said. Swett had not expected this. "He was a larger man intellectually than I anticipated, and of finer fibre. There was in him an element of gentleness and a large humanity which won me, and I was pleased no less than surprised."

Davis and Swett tried to sound Weed out on the coming campaign. "I informed them very frankly," Weed recalled, "that I was so greatly disappointed at the result of the action of the convention as to be unable to think or talk on the subject; that I was going to pass a few days upon the prairies of Iowa, and that by the time I reached Albany I should be prepared to do my duty for the Republican cause and for its nominees." Weed owned land in Iowa, and he had made plans to inspect it with Harriet and a small group of friends, taking advantage of a railroad-sponsored junket to the Hawkeye State for two hundred delegates and several journalists. The New York political boss was plainly in no hurry to return home, where people would want to ask questions about his disaster in Chicago. Davis and Swett urged him to stop by Springfield and meet with Lincoln before he headed back East. Weed seemed reticent, but they cajoled him into promising to let them know when he could be in Springfield. They would meet him there and formally introduce him to their friend.

Thousands of people out marching on the wet streets of Chicago reached the Wigwam before 8:00 p.m. for the ratification rally. The big building again filled up to capacity, leaving three thousand people outdoors. Women were more excited than anyone. By the estimate of the *Press and Tribune*, they occupied 90 percent of the gallery, and most of the rest of the hall. Frank Lumbard—a crooner with a warm tenor voice who had toured with the blackface minstrel shows of Dan Emmett, composer of the hit song "Dixie's Land"—sang "The Star-Spangled Banner." New York's General Nye reduced Joshua Giddings to both laughter and tears with his emotive speech. Chicago mayor

Wentworth capped an eventful week by presenting a ceremonial flag on stage to representatives of the Sixth Ward, home of the Wigwam.

Dispatches from New York, Philadelphia, and other cities were read to the crowd, winning loud cheers. They reported that "ratification meetings were assembling, guns firing, processions upon parade, etc., throughout the whole country." Republicans across the nation, though stunned by the news, seemed enthusiastic about Lincoln, to the relief of party leaders. Even in New York, men fired cannons and cheered. To be sure, many were saddened that the man who had sacrificed so much for the party had been denied his reward. As one New Yorker attending a city ratification rally put it, "Seward had shaken the bush, but Lincoln had caught the bird."

Providing the Democratic Party spin, the Albany correspondent for the *New York Daily Herald* claimed that there was "no enthusiasm" for Lincoln that night in Thurlow Weed's city. The news of Seward's defeat "came down upon the republicans here with the most crushing weight. Their countenances displayed unutterable disappointment. More than any other persons, they walked the streets in the semblance of pallbearers." And New Yorkers thought Lincoln no substitute for their great man. The moment his nomination was announced, the correspondent claimed, Albany's Republican activists lamented that "the campaign was already ended," fearing that the Democratic nominee, whoever he might be, would be able to "'walk over the course' with scarcely a competitor." The scene was similar in Rome, New York, according to its *Daily Sentinel*. The Republicans there looked "as though they have lost all the friends they ever had."

But there were no regrets evident at the Wigwam. At a "late hour," the *Press and Tribune* reported, thousands of people flowed out of the building and went home, "satisfied that victory had perched upon the banner under which they are fighting." The great wooden hall that had hosted a remarkable convention—one that would arguably change the course of world history—shut its doors for the night and went dark.

The city stayed open. "Chicago is in a blaze of glory tonight," the *New-York Tribune* reported at 11:30 p.m. "Bonfires, processions, torchlights, fireworks, illuminations, and salutes, have filled the air with noise and the eye with beauty. 'Honest Abe' is the cry in every mouth, and the 'irrepressible conflict' against Slavery and corruptions opens with great promise and immense enthusiasm. It is impossible to exaggerate the good feeling and joy that prevail here."

That evening, word arrived in the nation's capital that Hamlin had been chosen for vice president—a nomination almost as surprising as Lincoln's. According to the *New York Daily Herald*'s Washington correspondent, insiders quickly dubbed the pairing "'the dirty-shirt ticket,' for while 'Old Abe' is said to be [a] rough piece of timber for the White House . . . Hamlin is about the most slovenly man in appearance that we have had as a candidate for vice president" in decades. Without commenting on the imperfections of his wardrobe, the Washington correspondent of the *Chicago Press and Tribune* described Hamlin as a humble man, "pleasant and genial in his demeanor, with an utter absence of *hauteur*, which often attaches to rank—in a word, he is a *perfect Democrat*." Moreover, his wife, Ellen—the sister of his first wife, Sarah, who died in 1855—"is one of the most beautiful and accomplished ladies that have for many years appeared in Washington society."

Hamlin was in his rooms at the Washington House, at Third Street and Pennsylvania Avenue, around 9:00 p.m., enjoying a quiet game of cards with a Senate colleague when the sound of boisterous men was heard downstairs, followed by loud pounding at his door. Hamlin opened it to see a slew of Republican politicians gathered in the hallway. "Good evening, Mr. Vice President," they said. "What do you mean?" Hamlin asked. "You have been nominated for Vice-President," they told him. "But I don't want the place," Hamlin protested. The men persuaded him he must take it, lest it appear he opposed a ticket headed by Lincoln.

"Well, dear," Hamlin wrote to Ellen, "I presume you were as much astonished as myself at my nomination for Vice President." In Bangor, where Ellen was that night, bonfires, music, and a one-hundred-gun salute announced the ticket. Hamlin's sister Vesta Holmes wrote to him from Calais, Maine, about her reaction to the news: "I could not believe it, it took me so by surprise. But when I heard bells ringing, guns firing, and men shouting, I took it for a fact." The news made her think of their childhood friend Pat Carey. A fortuneteller told Pat that, in his old age, he would ride in a handsome carriage, "on the doors of which was to be the motto, 'Who'd have thought it'? Now it seems to me if you should ever arrive at the honor of being Vice-President the same motto might not be inappropriate."

The Hamlin family's shock was widely shared. "We at Washington had no other thought but that Mr. Seward would head the ticket, and that Mr. Lincoln, or some other Western man, would be selected for the second place," wrote Republican senator Henry L. Dawes of Massachusetts. "Our hearts were broken with disappointment." During the hours between news of Lincoln's and Hamlin's nominations, the "time was spent in nursing our anger." In Hamlin's honor, his hotel was quickly "illuminated" with light in each window, and the city's Republican Association sent out word to its members to form a march to the Washington House behind the Marine Band. Upon arrival, the band struck up "Hail to the Chief," and the nominee emerged onto a balcony to say a couple of words. "The night was gloomy, and the crowd was more so," Dawes wrote. But Hamlin's humble words "lifted the cloud and let in the light."

"You have assembled to congratulate each other upon the doings of our recent Convention at Chicago, the result of which has come over the telegraph wires," Hamlin said. The great honor of his nomination had come unbidden, he acknowledged, but he felt a solemn responsibility to accept the burden. Hamlin praised Lincoln, hoping to assuage doubts about the Illinois lawyer. Lincoln was "a man of comprehensive and vigorous intellect, and fully equal to the position designated," he assured the crowd. Then he turned to the growing national crisis. Republicans, he pledged, would "preserve the integrity of the Union, with the full and just rights of all the states." That would ensure that "our government will remain a blessing to us all, and our country a refuge in which the man of every creed and every clime may enjoy the securities and privileges of institutions of freedom, regulated by law." By the time Hamlin concluded, Dawes recalled, "we were ready to lay aside our idol and pledge our loyalty to a new leader." Hamlin was so proud of the speech that he sent Ellen copies of several newspapers that carried accounts of it.

The crowd then marched to the residence of Lincoln's fellow Illinoisan, Senator Trumbull, to serenade him. When he went to the stoop to speak, the political hatreds that threatened the Union suddenly flared up. Washington was a Southern town, with slave markets and limited tolerance for Republican ideas, and a noisy mob of Democrats formed on the other side of the narrow street, clamoring for Stephen Douglas, asking about John Brown, and jeering at Trumbull. "For nearly five minutes the hissing and groaning was so great that Mr. Trumbull could not proceed," the Washington correspondent for the *Press and Tribune* reported. "Do you ask where were the police? I answer, the Mayor is a Douglas man."

Illinois congressman Elihu B. Washburne followed, at which point the rowdies stretched a rope across the street to harass and trip up the Republicans. While Washburne was speaking, Democrats pelted the crowd with stones and brickbats, precipitating a panic, as the members of the Marine Band, among others, took to their heels. Washburne called on the remaining Republicans "to stand firm and, if necessary, to die in their tracks, rather than submit to the outrage of these hirelings of a corrupt Administration." He was able to finish his speech, and no one was seriously injured, but the whole affair exposed the savage emotions tearing at the Union, threatening even a traditional gathering celebrating a nomination. The spirit of mutual tolerance essential to a republic seemed to be gone. The Republicans resolved to prepare for violence the next time. "The outrage has caused great indignation among the Republicans, and they feel disposed hereafter, when they hold their meetings, to go armed to defend themselves," the *Press and Tribune* man noted. Republicans were increasingly determined to fight Democrats—with fists, knives, and guns—rather than surrender to intimidation. "Free speech cannot be successfully put down even in this slave-market," the writer promised. God only knew how the Democrats, North and South, would react if a Republican administration took over in Washington.

Springfield was "in a blaze of excitement" over the stunning elevation of its son. Shortly after word came around noon, residents made plans for a one-hundred-gun salute, and the booming of cannon began. "It was kept up during most of the afternoon," the *Illinois State Journal* reported. Bells rang out from the city's churches for hours. Flags flew from the State House, the Republican headquarters, the *Journal* offices, and private homes. The bright faces of Springfield's residents showed their "sincere pleasure at the nomination of our distinguished townsman for the highest office within the gift of the people." Even Democrats had nice things to say, the pro-Lincoln paper claimed. Some "were candid enough to admit that 'Old Abe's' nomination was a bad thing for [Democrats], and they were honest enough to say that they would rather vote for Mr. Lincoln than for some members of their own party." A hastily arranged mass meeting was held that night at the State House, with speeches and songs. After it adjourned at nine o'clock, a crowd formed behind the Young America Silver Band to march to Lincoln's home at Eighth and Jackson.

In front of the two-story house, handsomely painted light brown with dark-green shutters, two of Lincoln's sons, seven-year-old Tad and nine-year-old Willie, excitedly took positions on fence posts to watch the festivities. (Lincoln's other son, sixteen-year-old Robert, was at Phillips Exeter Academy in New Hampshire when the news arrived. "I will write home for a check before he spends all his money in the campaign," the teenager quipped to a classmate.) As a crowd of thousands formed, people "made loud calls for Mr. Lincoln, and they were soon gratified by seeing the tall form of the next President in front of them." If he was nervous or excited about his sudden elevation, he did not show it. Years of struggle and disappointment seemed to have worn down his emotions. When the cheering subsided, Lincoln spoke. "He did not suppose the honor of such a visit was intended particularly for himself, as a private citizen, but rather to the representative of a great party." Those looking for partisan shots at the Democrats had to be disappointed. Lincoln announced he would make no statements "on the political questions of the day," referring the crowd "to his previous public letters and speeches." Lincoln would uphold that policy of caution throughout the campaign, as the threat of civil war lowered over the country.

Wrapping up his remarks, Lincoln said he "would invite the whole crowd into his house if it was large enough to hold them." A voice cried out: "We will give you a larger house on the fourth of next March," the day of the inauguration. Lincoln continued: since everyone would not fit, "he would merely invite as many as could find room." The crowd responded with "deafening cheers" and "in less than a minute Mr. Lincoln's house was invaded by as many as could 'squeeze in!' The invaders were warmly received and many of them had the pleasure of shaking the right hand of their hospitable host." What Mary Lincoln made of so many people tromping through her home was not recorded.

The pretty town of Auburn, New York, by contrast, had gone deathly quiet, and William Henry Seward sat down to write. He might have been forgiven for setting aside all his responsibilities that day, but he chose to serve others, despite his searing disappointment. In a characteristic show of decency, Seward penned a brief unsigned editorial for Saturday's edition of the *Auburn Daily Advertiser* when it became clear no one else had the heart to do it: "We place the names of Lincoln and Hamlin at the head of our columns, with pride and satisfaction. No truer exposition of the Republican creed could be given, than the platform adopted by the Convention contains. No truer or firmer defenders of the Republican faith could have been found in the Union, than the distinguished and esteemed citizens on whom the honors of the nominations have fallen." Seward also took the time to write a letter to a dear friend who he knew would be suffering, seeking to ease his pain:

> My dear Weed,—
>
> You have my unbounded gratitude for this last as for a whole life of efforts in my behalf.
>
> I wish that I were sure that your sense of disappointment is as light as my own. It ought to be equally so, if we have been equally thoughtful and zealous for friends, party, and country. I know not what has been left undone, that could have been done, or done that ought to be regretted.
>
> You see I am not expecting you to stop here on your way home, although Mrs. Seward and I have hoped that Harriet might stay with us a day or two.
>
> Ever faithfully yours,
> William H. Seward.

The business of the convention over, thousands of people rushed for the trains leaving Chicago that night. *Cincinnati Commercial* editor Murat Halstead left on a late run of the Pittsburgh, Fort Wayne and Chicago Railway. Every seat of its eleven cars was filled, and passengers stood in the aisles and corners. Many aboard, Halstead noticed, were no longer physically capable of celebrating. "I never before saw a company of persons so prostrated by continued excitement," he wrote. "The Lincoln men were not able to respond to the cheers which went up along the road for 'Old Abe.' They had not only done their duty in that respect but exhausted their capacity." Long after midnight, at every village that had a station, the passengers found "tar barrels burning, drums beating, boys carrying rails; and guns, great and small, banging away." Weary conventioneers who yearned for rest were out of luck. They were "plagued by the thundering jar of cannon, the clamor of drums, the glare of bonfires, and the whooping of boys, who were delighted with the idea of a candidate for the Presidency who thirty years ago split rails on the Sangamon River—classic stream now and forevermore—and whose neighbors named him 'honest.'"

But, since Lincoln had no high office, no national profile, and no formal education, the question now was whether the party's elites would risk their time, money, and influence on such a man.

Saturday, May 19, 1860

Chapter 15: Six Feet Four

Before catching the special train bound for Iowa, a correspondent for the *Yonkers Examiner* scribbled out his report that morning. Though he was among the multitude of New Yorkers who had come to Chicago for William H. Seward's nomination, he had already set his jaw and accepted the great man's shocking defeat. "This morning, we of New York, have dried our eyes. Noble as was our hero, the Cause is grander still," he wrote.

Across the North that morning, readers opened their Republican newspapers to see two new names anchored at the top of the opinion column, heading the list of endorsements: "For President, Abraham Lincoln, of Illinois; For Vice President, Hannibal Hamlin, of Maine." In the few hours between learning of Lincoln's nomination and going to press, editors—Republicans and Democrats, Union Whigs and secessionists —scrambled to provide readers with perspective about this man and his victory. For most Americans, Lincoln remained an unknown. Many editors did not even get his name right yet, calling him "Abram."

Some ardent pro-Seward editors swallowed their pride and swung dutifully to Lincoln. James Watson Webb, who had threatened in his *Morning Courier and New-York Enquirer* to bolt from the party if Seward was not nominated, promised Saturday morning to "*bow to the decision*" of the convention—"and bow with cheerfulness." Weed's own *Albany*

Evening Journal said New Yorkers would find Lincoln to be a strong second-best to Seward. The *Chicago Journal*, which had adorned its building with a giant SEWARD sign, was ready to support Lincoln heartily. "We have summered and wintered with the gallant old leader, and have long since learned to love him as a true and good man." Such Seward devotees as Isaac Platt were reassured by the way David Davis and his team went about selling Lincoln—not by tearing down Seward, but by proposing Lincoln as an alternative should the leading candidate falter. Others worried, though, that the rejection of Seward would depress the party's base and make it difficult for Republicans to capture New York in November.

Some editors attributed Seward's defeat to the odor of corruption in his ranks. Delegates had feared his election would "transplant Thurlow Weed and his lobby from Albany to Washington, and entail disgrace upon the party from the day it entered into power," the *Buffalo Commercial Advertiser* argued. As one Republican told the newspaper on Friday: "We owe Mr. Seward everything; he founded the party, and built it up to greatness; our debt to him is incalculable; *but we won't pay it in hard cash to Thurlow Weed*." Connecticut's *Hartford Courant* saw the rising tide of populism in Lincoln's victory. The delegates reflected the Northern public's burgeoning disdain for the corrupt political class that had led the country to the brink of a terrifying crisis. "The People want one of *themselves* for President; they are sick of heartless diplomats and politicians by trade, who have grown grey in the corrupting atmosphere of Washington." Even Seward "has been too long separated from the People, too much pampered with the honors and emoluments of office, to lie very close to the popular heart." Lincoln, on the other hand, "will be hugged to the people's hearts like a second Andrew Jackson."

If Republican editors thought this self-made lawyer would do, many Democratic papers, inaugurating nearly five years of abuse, quickly deemed Lincoln little short of a disaster for his party and the country. Some played into intense fears that if Lincoln became president white Americans would be at each other's throats and enslaved African Americans might eventually be freed. "Lincoln is a traitor," the unabashedly racist *Daily Democrat and News* in Davenport, Iowa, declared that Saturday. "He was born in the South, in the noble old State of Kentucky, whose institutions he now conspires to overthrow, whose hearthstones he wishes to desolate, whose wives and mothers he threatens to surrender to the brutality and lust of the beastly African." It was Lincoln, the editor insisted, "and not Seward, who first advanced the brutal and bloody doctrine of the 'irrepressible conflict.' . . . He it was who declared that States should not exist, part free and part slave, and showed that he needed but the opportunity to cry havoc and let slip the dogs of war upon the land that gave him birth. . . . Such a man is Lincoln, and he has found men base enough to reward him for his treason."

Conservative papers worried that the Republicans had blown an opportunity to reduce tensions by putting someone from a slave state on the ticket. One pro-Bates man wrote to the St. Louis *Evening News* that the nomination of Northerners for both president and vice president "does not look right, and never can be made to look right to the masses of this country, who really love the Union."

Lincoln's hardscrabble background also fueled Democrats' criticism. "Lincoln—ignorant of his mother tongue, unable to write a line of English grammatically, without the least distinction as a legislator or statesman . . . is preferred by the Black Republican Convention to the orator, the scholar, the statesman of New York!" the *Daily Democrat and News* exclaimed. Lincoln's upbringing, the *Richmond Examiner* in Virginia asserted, would make him even more dangerous than Seward. "The latter has talents and ambition which might have operated to restrain his prejudices; but the former, an illiterate partizan, is without talents, without education, possessed only of his inveterate hatred of slavery and his openly avowed predilections for negro equality to recommend him to his party." Given such a prospect, Lincoln's election "will most certainly disrupt the Federal Union," the paper warned. The *Lancaster Intelligencer* in Pennsylvania dismissed Lincoln as a "roughhewn village politician . . . always ready for the rough joke and the foul and filthy double entendre . . . possessing neither education nor refinement." The *Western Railroad Gazette*, in Chicago, laughed that Lincoln had shown boys that they no longer needed an education to rise in America. "When your mother wants you to learn ugly, hard words, don't you do it, but go right off into the woods and *split rails*."

Editors wrote with no clear sense of the catastrophe that would soon envelop America. Under the Republicans, the editor of the *New Orleans Daily Crescent* warned, "the institution of slavery is to be attacked in every conceivable mode—for nothing else will satisfy the fanaticism at the North which overshadows every just and conservative sentiment." Should the Union Party or Democrats fail to stop Lincoln in the upcoming election, he added darkly, "some other mode can doubtless be agreed upon." Two years later, his New Orleans, the largest metropolis in the South, would be a conquered city under U.S. military control.

In the North, Robert G. Harper, editor of the *Adams Sentinel*, hailed the nominations of Lincoln and Hamlin, calling them "men of marked ability, and eminently worthy of the high honor conferred on them," and predicting that their "triumphant election will administer a just rebuke to the present reckless national administration, and restore Government to what the Fathers of the Republic designed it to be." The paper was published in Adams County, in the sleepy crossroads town of Gettysburg, Pennsylvania, where gas pipes were being laid that week through its principal streets, to soon serve Pennsylvania College down the road and the Lutheran Theological Seminary up the hill. In three years and two months, Gettysburg would be pockmarked with bullet holes and battered by artillery shells, its surrounding rocky hills and rolling green fields covered with the dead and broken bodies of thousands of young men, after the bloodiest battle in American history.

At the Tremont House, New York politician Andrew B. Dickinson spotted Greeley as he was preparing to leave Chicago for home and angrily confronted him. The "air was fairly blue with vituperation," an eyewitness recounted, Dickinson "charging him with the basest ingratitude" toward Seward and Weed. "I never saw a man get such an awful dressing.

Greeley couldn't get a word in edgewise." The *New York Daily Herald* joked that, after Greeley had made such a spectacle of himself at the convention, money was being raised to "buy Greeley a new suit of clothes to replace his present seedy raiment—a white coat, a pair of boots, (both fellows,) and a pair of pantaloons which will be long enough to cover them." The paper refused to contribute because it did not want to reward Greeley for "the defeat of Mr. Seward, who is a far better man in every way than Abe Lincoln." But it would attempt to raise "five cents toward a new white summer hat for Greeley, who is reported to have had on a shocking bad rusty old tile the last time he was seen in Chicago."

That same morning in Chicago, Joshua R. Giddings, the staunch defender of the Declaration of Independence, wrote a note of congratulations to Lincoln. It was also an implicit warning to beware of political corruption. Lincoln had been nominated, Giddings wrote, "upon two grounds 1 That you are an honest man. 2nd That you are not in the hands of Corrupt or dishonest men." He urged Lincoln to "permit no designing men to Lay you under apparent obligations, but keep yourself and the office pure and separate from the corrupting influences which have beset our public men." Lincoln, seemingly unaware of the "obligations" Davis had incurred, replied that he was grateful his nomination came to him "without conditions." He added: "May the Almighty grant that the cause of truth, justice, and humanity, shall in no wise suffer at my hands."

The great exodus from Chicago was well underway that morning. At nine o'clock, to the booming of cannon and the shouts of "Old Abers," the enormous Iowa special pulled out of the Chicago & Rock Island Railroad depot, gradually picking up speed as it headed west, its sixteen cars filled with scores of delegates and journalists, including *New York Times* correspondent Joseph Howard, as well as Thurlow Weed and his daughter. "As seems to be the custom in this Western country, a liberal supply of whisky, brandy and cigars was provided," Howard wrote, "and—as, also, seems a Western custom, . . . the said beverages and smokables were speedily and persistently taken care of." Passing beyond the outskirts of Chicago, the train entered onto a great prairie that stretched as far as the eye could see. "Oh, it was beautiful. Limitless, apparently, in extent, unbroken in line by a solitary tree, and covered to the depth of two feet by that most beautiful of herbage which so richly carpets the fertile soil of God's great green earth," Howard enthused. He never tired of the passing landscape. "The crops of corn and other grains, grass and so on, were very forward, while the orchards were full of trees all heavily laden with the fruit promising blossom."

But the mood aboard the train was not all that happy. Many delegates still stewed over what they regarded as the convention's reckless nomination of a second-rate man. Lincoln's supporters, including one "sucker friend" wearing "ragged trowsers," endeavored to persuade "desponding Sewardites" that Lincoln would be a better candidate and make a fine president. They only ignited debates that "became personal, bitter and taunting." Many residents along the way seemed just as divided. While interested crowds greeted the train, Howard wrote, there was not "any great display of enthusiasm." At a stop at Joliet, John C. Underwood, a Virginia lawyer, farmer, abolitionist, and delegate, tried to rally the crowd. He got some cheers, "but it was cold and almost dead." An African American man climbed aboard the train to beg. He "approached the passengers and stated his little case, enlarged upon his trials, and wound up with an appeal to every Republican to help a friend and brother along." His tale of woe struck Howard as suspicious, but one prominent New Yorker led the way in showing compassion: "Weed gave him a dollar, and the rest followed in sums varying from ten cents to a half a dollar."

That evening, at around six thirty, the train finally reached the Mississippi River. "The sun, in its going down, had cast its last far rays upon it, and like a silver mirror, burnished and bright, in all its beauty it reflected the overhanging foliage," Howard wrote. The train slowed and rumbled over a long bridge from Rock Island, Illinois, to Davenport, Iowa, with its distinctive series of wooden arches resting on stone piers, as the passengers gave "three cheers for the Father of Waters." Three years earlier, the railroad had hired none other than Abraham Lincoln to defend its right to span the Mississippi with that very bridge, after the steamboat *Effie Afton* crashed into an abutment. Lincoln had prevailed.

Entering the city, the train pulled to a stop in front of a beautiful brick hotel, the Burtis House, where the Davenport Light Infantry and a throng of local citizens waited. A reporter for the city's *Daily Democrat and News*, which had labeled Lincoln a traitor in that day's edition, reported on the booming of cannon and the music of bands, but found the crowd's response muted. After remarks by Governor Samuel J. Kirkwood and a few other orators, everyone entered the Burtis House, crowding its saloons.

By eight thirty, people had begun gathering in front of the Republican Club on Second Street for a grand political rally, and by nine, "a perfect sea of human beings were stretched along the line of that thoroughfare." But, again, the crowd reaction was mixed. "There was a fair attendance of citizens, of all parties," and good music by a local band, "but no real enthusiasm for the ticket," claimed the Democratic *Rock Island Argus*. When Judge Eleazer K. Foster, a delegate from Connecticut, got up to speak, the crowd repeatedly pelted him with cries of "Louder!" He sought forgiveness, pleading that he had yelled so much in Chicago "that I find my voice has become too hoarse for much more service at the present time." Virginia delegate Underwood tried to laugh off the not-very-funny threats of Southern secession should Lincoln be elected. "I have been talking with some of the disunionists lately, and I come to-night to tell you that I think they have made up their minds that they won't dissolve the Union just yet," he joked. "They say they are a little afraid that if they should dissolve the Union that the laboring men of the North and the Yankees would not let it stay dissolved." Other speakers, acknowledging the profound disappointment of Seward men, felt they had to defend their choice of Lincoln. "I believed that I was discharging an honest duty, not only to my State, but to the nation at large," Iowa delegate Charles C. Nourse explained.

Thurlow Weed was not enjoying himself. For all the hoopla, "the nomination was coldly received here," he later informed Seward. "The assembled crowd were almost silent until New-York was mentioned."

* * *

The flamboyantly decorated Michigan Central campaign train set off that morning to the East, bound for Detroit. Michigan governor Austin Blair had telegraphed stations along the line, urging local Republicans to "meet the train with all the enthusiasm they could muster," recalled Kansas delegate Addison G. Procter. During stops, speakers worked to whip up the waiting crowds. While some gave "three cheers" for Governor Blair, Procter was shocked by how little enthusiasm people showed for the Republican nominee. From Niles to Detroit, "not one crowd offered a single cheer for Lincoln," he recalled. "It was a nipping frost all the way and set us all to thinking, what next? The further we went East, the more pronounced this showing of disappointment became." Later, when Procter tried to set up a Lincoln Club in Kansas to promote the candidate, he found that a prominent local Republican refused to get involved. "You fellows knew at Chicago what this country is facing," the man told Procter. "You knew we are up against the most critical time in the life of this Nation. You knew that it will take the very best ability we can produce to pull us through. You knew that above everything else these times demanded a statesman and you have gone and given us a *rail splitter*. No, I will not preside or attend." Despite the ringing applause for Lincoln's nomination in Republican papers, Procter believed a great deal of work would be required to win over the rank and file. The Republicans needed to get Seward out on the trail, to lend his luster to the campaign.

The party's leaders were eager to get to Springfield to size up the man they had chosen. Some officials had heard tales of Lincoln's miserable education and crude manners, and, despite the assurances of the Illinois men, they worried they might discover that they had made a terrible mistake. A special Illinois Central train of three cars behind the railroad's fastest locomotive waited that Saturday morning at Chicago's Grand Central depot. The railroad treated its guests to a breakfast that "abundantly provided against the contingencies of a famine," a correspondent from Lancaster, Pennsylvania, reported with enthusiasm. At 10:00 a.m., after the convention president George Ashmun, the delegation leaders, a band, and several journalists had climbed safely aboard, the train glided out of the depot "and was soon whistling over the magnificent prairies of the west."

The passengers were festive, and the landscape was alive with wild game—prairie chickens, jacksnipe, ducks, and partridges that flew from their covers every few yards. "At every railroad station we passed in daylight we were received with demonstrations of joy," recalled one celebrity passenger, Carl Schurz. During a stop at Urbana, the Philadelphia Cornet Band disembarked to play, drawing hundreds of people from the stores, gardens, and workshops within earshot of the station. When the townspeople discovered where the train was bound, they supplemented the music with "long, loud and enthusiastic shouts for Honest Old Abe." Soon, the crowd "was irrepressible," demanding speeches, the *Press and Tribune* man observed. An array of Republican stars stepped forward: Governor Edwin Morgan of New York; the stuttering David Cartter of Ohio; Judge William D. Kelley of Pennsylvania, noted for his "tall form and sonorous eloquence"; and the silver-tongued Schurz. The next stop was Decatur, where Lincoln's family had come after its cold, hard journey from Indiana. A large crowd stood on the platform as the train approached, greeting the delegation with round after round of joyous applause. The past was on everyone's mind. "In the vicinity of that place his father lived, and there Abe chopped cordwood and split rails for many of the old settlers yet alive."

Lincoln's old friend and ally Gustave Koerner was already in Springfield, having beaten the notification committee by catching an earlier, regularly scheduled train. Knowing that the meeting—a sort of coming-out party for Lincoln—would send an important signal to the nation, Koerner wanted to help Abraham and Mary Lincoln with any necessary preparations. He brought with him a noted political fixer, the long-bearded Chicago lawyer and state representative Ebenezer Peck, who had helped Lincoln develop his strategy for his Douglas debates two years earlier. Welcomed into Lincoln's home, Koerner and Peck glanced into a room on the right, the small family room that the Lincolns deemed a library because it included a case containing several books. They immediately detected a problem. A long table had been set out, "on which stood many glasses, a decanter or two of brandy, and under the tables a champagne basket." A servant informed them, "This is for the Chicago folks."

Mary Lincoln greeted the visitors, asking what they thought of the spread. They did not mince words. "We told her at once that this would hardly do," Koerner recalled. As the party's nominee, Lincoln had to be wary of any signals he sent through the press. He needed the votes of the prickly Protestant prohibitionists who made up a significant percentage of the Republicans back East. Serving liquor was a bad idea. Mary, raised in a fine Kentucky home and steeped in the values of Southern hospitality, "remonstrated in her very lively manner, but we insisted on dispensing with this hospitality, which we appreciated ourselves, but which might be construed." Koerner peremptorily ordered the servant to remove the liquor, while "Mrs. Lincoln still argued with us." Lincoln—who did not drink, had never served liquor in his home before, and was feeling his way around the protocols of national politics—thought it best to intervene. "Perhaps, Mary, these gentlemen are right. After all this is over, we may see about it, and some may stay and have a good time." The alcohol was removed from sight.

The liquor crisis averted, Peck and Koerner took a few minutes to sit down with Lincoln in the parlor across the hall to share their impressions of the convention, "which of course interested him very much." Peck, "a very witty and lively talker," got Lincoln laughing with "some very humorous remarks." Laughter was always the best medicine when Lincoln was under pressure.

That evening, "almost the whole population" of Springfield gathered at the depot to welcome the notification committee. When the train approached after seven o'clock, the city's proud residents greeted it with blasting cannon, strains of martial music, and loud hurrahs. As the great men disembarked, the crowd gave three cheers each for New

York's Governor Morgan, Missouri's Frank Blair, and former Massachusetts governor George S. Boutwell, and "three cheers and a tiger"—meaning a raucous roar—for all the delegates from Pennsylvania, who had effectively nominated Lincoln. With some difficulty, the committee formed a procession through the mob, making the twelve-minute walk to the Chenery House, at Fourth and Washington Streets. "Rails formed a prominent feature of the procession," noted the Lancaster correspondent. "I rather suspect there was not a single unemployed rail in the entire town." Along the way, the men, women, and children of Springfield cheered gleefully. Several buildings were "brilliantly illuminated." The *Press and Tribune* found the welcome of Lincoln's friends and neighbors moving—"a tribute in which there was no sign of envy or jealousy."

By the time the delegates rolled into Springfield, Ebenezer Peck had left Lincoln's home and was at the Chenery House to oversee matters there. The hotel, which did not have to worry about appeasing prohibitionist voters, laid out a nice spread of food and liquor for the famished and thirsty travelers, who were now in a hurry. Having arrived late, they had to eat and drink, make another twelve-minute walk to Lincoln's house to formally notify him of his nomination, and return downtown, where some were slated to appear at the State House for that night's grand ratification meeting. Given the time crunch, the officious organizers decided to exclude ladies from the ceremony at Lincoln's house. Even "the presence of Mrs. Lincoln was not expected or, in fact, desired," Lincoln biographer Jesse W. Weik wrote later, basing his account on the memories of eyewitnesses. Peck had the thankless task of persuading Mary to make herself scarce. All too familiar with her "mercurial disposition," he attempted to enlist Springfield residents to do the dirty work. "But it happened that the Springfield people were also familiar with Mrs. Lincoln's peculiar temperament," and they refused to intervene. "Go tell the lady, yourself," they retorted.

After enjoying their refreshments, the committee of delegates, accompanied by forty to fifty outsiders, set off for Lincoln's house. As they approached the front gate sometime after eight, they found two young boys standing by the posts, forming a welcoming committee. "Good morning, gentlemen," the boys said, though it was night. "Are you Mr. Lincoln's son?" William K. Evarts, chairman of the New York delegation, asked the older boy, nine-year-old Willie. "Yes, Sir," he said. "Then let's shake hands," Evarts replied. "I'm a Lincoln, too," seven-year-old Tad piped up, "whereupon several delegates, amid much laughter, saluted the young Lincoln," a correspondent for the *Chicago Journal* reported.

They were welcomed indoors. To the left of the front hall was the formal parlor—with the family's best mahogany furniture and priciest wallpaper, its cream-colored background adorned with gray tendrils, leaves, and flowers, highlighted with gold leaf—a space strictly off-limits to the Lincolns' rambunctious boys. As the members of the committee "filed in gravely," Weik noted, "the first person they saw was Mrs. Lincoln dressed in her finest, bedecked with flowers, and graciously awaiting them in the parlor!" Either Peck had not mustered the courage to say anything or Mary had stood up for herself. In anticipation of the gathering, the Lincolns had rolled back the folding doors that divided their two parlors—the rear one had been a bedroom before they added a second floor—to create one large room. Lincoln stood on the threshold of the back parlor, leaning on an armchair. To Schurz he seemed "tall and ungainly in his black suit of apparently new but ill-fitting clothes, his long tawney neck emerging gauntly from his turned-down collar, his melancholy eyes sunken deep in his haggard face." Lincoln bowed stiffly as the delegates filled the front parlor. "Most of the members of the committee had never seen him before, and gazed at him with surprised curiosity," Schurz noted. "He certainly did not present the appearance of a statesman as people usually picture it in their imagination."

An awkward silence followed. Then Lincoln realized he was in charge, and he motioned for George Ashmun to begin. With the "subdued earnestness of manner appropriate" to a moment imbued with historic importance, Ashmun spoke. "I have, sir, the honor in behalf of the gentlemen who are present, a committee appointed by the Republican convention recently assembled at Chicago, to discharge a most pleasant duty," he began. "We have come . . . to notify you that you have been selected by the convention of Republicans at Chicago, as their candidate for President of the United States." Ashmun, on behalf of the committee, also presented Lincoln with the party's platform. "Sir, at your convenience we shall be glad to receive from you such a response as it may be your pleasure to give us."

Standing with his hands clasped in front of him, "Mr. Lincoln listened with a countenance grave and earnest, almost to sternness, regarding Mr. Ashmun with the profoundest attention," the *Journal* reported. The *Press and Tribune* man thought Lincoln seemed unmoved, beyond an "unnatural paleness" in his face "and a compressed lip." But Koerner saw more in his old friend's somber face. "Mr. Lincoln looked much moved, and rather sad, evidently feeling the heavy responsibility thrown upon him." Then Lincoln stepped forward, and "with a voice as clear as a bell, in natural tones and with slow and distinct utterances," made a carefully worded reply to Ashmun. "Mr. Chairman and gentlemen of the committee, I tender you, and through you the Republican National Convention, and all the people represented in it, my profoundest thanks for the high honor done me. Deeply, and even painfully sensible of the great responsibility which is inseparable from that honor—a responsibility which I could almost wish had fallen upon some one of the far more eminent men and experienced statesmen whose distinguished names were before the Convention, I shall, by your leave, consider more fully the resolutions of the Convention, denominated the platform, and without unseasonable delay, respond to you, Mr. Chairman, in writing—not doubting now, that the platform will be found satisfactory, and the nomination accepted." Since Lincoln knew about his nomination and had studied the platform well before the committee arrived, all of this had the aura of kabuki theater. "And now," he concluded, "I will no longer defer the pleasure of taking you, and each of you, by the hand."

The brief and artful reply—"appropriate, earnest, and well-shaped," Schurz thought—seemed a great relief to everyone. "Men who had taken up the notion from Mr. Lincoln's *soubriquet*, that he was a rough diamond, who would not shine in the White House, that he was a stump orator only, popular with the masses but unused to occasions which require tact and polite address, were astonished by his manifestations of ease and grace," the *Press and Tribune* correspondent wrote. They had come to Springfield fearing "that the man who had mauled rails, driven oxen, and tugged at the flat-boat oar, could not have that polish which the etiquette of the *salons* requires." Those fears, he claimed, "fell dead forever." As one New Englander told the *Chicago Journal*'s correspondent, "I was afraid I should meet a gigantic rail-splitter with the manners of a flat-boatsman, and the ugliest face in creation; and he's a complete gentleman."

Another reporter in the room, Charles Carleton Coffin, studied Lincoln as he concluded his reply and began shaking hands. "The lines upon his face, the large ears, sunken cheeks, enormous nose, shaggy hair, the deep-set eyes, sparkling with humor, and which seemed to be looking far away, were distinguishing facial marks." There was something about this man "which commanded instant admiration," Coffin noted. "A stranger meeting him on a country road, ignorant of his history, would have said, 'He is no ordinary man.'" Schurz was not so sure. With some delegates, "an undertone of resignation and of suppressed doubt was perceptible," he recalled. Those meeting Lincoln for the first time and "unused to Western men and Western ways . . . could not quite conceal their misgivings as to how this single-minded man, this child of nature," would deal with the complex crisis bearing down on America. Yet Lincoln's good humor undeniably charmed them. "His rough and ready manners, his hearty grasp of the hand, make all who come in contact with him feel perfectly at home. His memory is remarkable—he called gentlemen by name whom he had not seen for years," wrote the Lancaster correspondent, adding that Lincoln had "a fist *a la* Hyer."

The notables waiting to shake that big fist included Massachusetts gubernatorial candidate John A. Andrew; gray-headed Rhode Island senator James F. Simmons; Missourian Frank Blair, who had tried his best to nominate Bates; "brave old" George Blakey of Kentucky, who had tried to get the vice-presidential slot for Cassius Clay; Joel Burlingame of Oregon; and "burly, loud voiced" David Cartter of Ohio. Lincoln's greeting of Pennsylvania's Judge Kelley was perhaps the most memorable moment. "A smile, like the sun shining through the rift of a passing cloud sweeping over the landscape, illuminated his face, lighting up every homely feature, as he grasped the hand of Mr. Kelley," journalist Coffin recalled.

"You are a tall man, Judge. What's your height?" Lincoln asked.

"Six feet three; what is yours, Mr. Lincoln?"

"Six feet four."

"Then Pennsylvania bows to Illinois. My dear man, for years my heart has been aching for a President that I could *look up to*, and I've found him at last in the land where we thought there were none but *little* giants."

Lincoln often broke the ice by talking about such uncontroversial and reassuringly human matters as height or home. It worked again. "There was a bubbling up of quaint humor, fragrant with Western idiom, making the hour exceedingly enjoyable," Coffin wrote. Like others that night, Andrew was struck by Lincoln's extraordinary visage. "My eyes were never feasted with the vision of a human face, in which more transparent honesty, and more benignant kindness were combined with more of the intellect and firmness which belong to masculine humanity," he said a few days later. When Andrew got his turn to shake Lincoln's hand, he quipped that Massachusetts could claim him as one of its sons, since the Lincoln name was an old one in Plymouth County. "We'll consider it so this evening," Lincoln replied. After introducing several leading men to the nominee, Ashmun urged the rest to present themselves. "Come up gentlemen," Lincoln's friend Norman Judd called out, "it's nobody but old Abe Lincoln."

It was all a smashing success, the *Chicago Journal* said. "Mr. Lincoln bore himself during the evening with dignity and grace. His kindly and sincere manner, frank and honest expression, unaffected, pleasant conversation, soon made every one feel at ease, and rendered the hour and a half which they spent with him one of great pleasure to the delegates." After greeting each man, Lincoln directed him across the hall to meet with Mrs. Lincoln in the library, adding he could find a drink in there. "You must be thirsty after your long ride."

The five-foot-two-inch Mrs. Lincoln, whose care and taste had turned this house into an attractive and fashionable home, received her guests "with the grace and intelligence which have made her a distinguished ornament of the excellent society of the capital," the *Press and Tribune* reported. The visitors seemed anxious to meet the woman "to whom the hospitalities and social influences of the White House will be entrusted." The *Journal* man assured readers that "this amiable and accomplished lady" could adorn any drawing-room and would "do the honors at the White House with appropriate grace." He described her as "a very handsome woman, with a vivacious and graceful manner," and as "an interesting and often sparkling talker. Standing by her almost gigantic husband, she appears petite, but is really about the average height of ladies." The Lancaster man noted that Lincoln's home "is plainly but neatly furnished, and contains an interesting family, especially the hostess, who is a fine specimen of the accomplished western lady." Coffin was struck that there was a plain table in the room with a pitcher of cold water on it and glasses, but no wines or liquors. An Associated Press dispatch conveyed that fact to newspaper readers across the country, strengthening Lincoln's reputation for temperance and frugality.

As the smiling visitors said their farewells and walked down Lincoln's front steps, Judge Kelley turned to his fellow delegate Schurz and remarked, "Well, we might have done a more brilliant thing, but we could hardly have done a better thing."

The big wigs marched off to the State House for the great ratification meeting, behind the music of the Young America Silver Band and the German Saxe Horn Band. The *Press and Tribune* correspondent was dazzled: "Every Republican house around the square was illuminated, the State House was a blaze of light, the air was filled with exploding rockets and the ears of all were stunned by the booming of cannon and the resonant cheers of the happy multitudes glad to do honor to their neighbor who had received as a free gift one of the highest honors that can be bestowed on any man. The people were fairly wild with delight." Climbing the stairs, the delegates entered the chamber of the House of Representatives, which was overflowing with Springfield residents—the very room where Lincoln had delivered his "House Divided" speech two years earlier.

Frederick Hassaurek, the German-born Cincinnati editor who had made a stirring defense of equal justice and the Declaration of Independence two days earlier at the Wigwam, "electrified his audience for upwards of an hour" with a speech that "repeatedly brought down the house with volleys of deafening cheers." He saw Lincoln's nomination "as the harbinger of a certain victory over the slavery Democracy in November next." David Cartter followed with "a most glorious tribute to our Standard bearer, 'glorious old Abe,'" promising that Lincoln's nomination could be tantamount to victory if Republicans did their job. He was "rapturously applauded." Congressman Amos Tuck of New Hampshire lauded "Mr. Lincoln's sterling and distinguished qualities as a man and a statesman," winning cheers "again and again." Ex-governor Boutwell of Massachusetts pledged that Lincoln "would meet [with] the cordial and hearty approbation of the Republicans of the Old Bay State," and would win the state in November by a margin that would "put to shame" all the previous Republican triumphs. Judge Kelley made "*the* speech of the evening," filled with promises that Lincoln would unite all of the opposition "to the pie-bald Democracy" in the crucial state of Pennsylvania. Carl Schurz wrapped up the night. While he "paid a glowing tribute to Mr. Seward," he contended that Lincoln's nomination would secure the triumph of the Republican cause.

Since presidential candidates did not then, as a practice, campaign for themselves—as Lincoln would not—it was important that the party's best speakers get involved. The meeting made it clear that these talented politicians, at least, would "enter into the canvas with zeal and determination, which are the sure messengers and harbingers of success," Springfield's *Illinois State Journal* asserted. After the speeches, fireworks, cannon blasts, and bonfires raged on into the night. "As long as the rockets and powder were to be had and as long as there was one throat capable of a cheer, the demonstrations were kept up."

At midnight, the train that had brought the delegates rolled out of Springfield, disappearing into the darkness. From Chicago, the party leaders would set off for home. Satisfied that Lincoln would not unduly embarrass them, they would toil for the next six months to get him elected. In doing so, they would ignite a savage war that would eradicate the curse of slavery at an unimaginable cost.

Aftermath

Chapter 16: The People Decide

As rain poured down on Davenport, Iowa, on Sunday, May 20, Thurlow Weed finally got around to scrawling a letter to his friend, William H. Seward. Weed wrote as if he wanted to crawl away somewhere and cower in shame. "I have slight inclination to think, or speak, or write, and less to go where I shall be seen or questioned." But he felt he owed Seward an explanation for the disaster in Chicago.

Weed laid out the conspiracy of the "malignant" Horace Greeley and others from New York; the stubborn opposition of the Pennsylvania delegates; the unstoppable avalanche of delegates toward Lincoln, who had been regarded initially as nothing more than vice-presidential material. The bright future that Weed had envisioned was now shrouded. He had looked forward to "a pleasant close of political duty" in November and a foreign trip after Seward's election to the White House. Instead, he was contemplating a quick escape. "Now I go to Europe in July, or remain, as you wish," he wrote glumly. Reining in his emotions, Weed offered some pragmatic political advice to Seward. "Whatever your ultimate purpose may be, I cannot doubt that a prompt and cheerful acquiescence in the Nomination, and an early return to Washington, is not only wise, but a duty."

Seward was working on the first task, though his heart did not seem to be in it. As a human being, with the bloated ego of a politician, he was finding it hard to rise above what had happened. After writing his generous unsigned editorial Friday, the senator pointedly declined to headline the official New York celebration of the Lincoln nomination, making the rather flimsy excuse that he needed to be at home for the reconstruction of his burned-out barn. In a formal statement turning down the organizers, Seward struck a pose of stoicism, insisting that his friends had put his name in nomination in Chicago, not he. "The disappointment, therefore, is their disappointment, not mine." But the glaring absence of any mention of Lincoln's name belied his posture of indifference. Coldly, Seward predicted that his supporters would not "hinder or delay, or in any way embarrass the progress of" the Republican cause—in other words, they would do the bare minimum of swallowing their pride and declining to hamper efforts to elect Lincoln. The *New York Times* approvingly ran Seward's missive on its front page.

Seward's friends remained distraught that the party had nominated a man they regarded as the New Yorker's shabby inferior. "The rail candidate forsooth!" an Ohioan wrote to Frances Seward. "I confess to a disposition to *rail* at him, & much more at the convention for its self-stultification." Another friend from out West wrote, "When I got the news, I felt as if I didn't want to have any thing more to do with white men's politics, and about ready to go out and live among the Potawatomies." Seward was no doubt gratified to find that his fellow Auburn residents felt much the same. "When I went out to market this morning, I had the rare experience of a man walking about town, after he is dead, and hearing what people would say of him," Seward told a friend. "I confess I was unprepared for so much real grief, as I heard expressed at every corner." People kept coming by Auburn not to "console" Seward, "but to be consoled."

Times editor Henry Raymond, visiting Seward at Auburn on May 22 on his way back from Chicago, found Seward ready to quit the thankless world of politics. He would not resign immediately, after all, but would faithfully serve out his Senate term, which continued until March 4, 1861. Then he planned to enjoy a well-earned retirement. During Raymond's visit, Seward divulged a long-kept secret: Greeley had written Seward an angry letter in 1854 dissolving his alliance with Seward and Weed, arguing that they had failed to support his political ambitions. From the perspective of Raymond, and no doubt Seward, Greeley thus had a hidden motive for his relentless opposition in Chicago. Outraged, Raymond sat down in Auburn and wrote out his piece accusing the *Tribune* editor of base and vindictive conduct. Its appearance in the *Times* two days later led Greeley to demand publication of his 1854 letter in full, believing it would show he had behaved honorably. After Seward produced it, its reprinting in newspapers nationwide effectively hung out the party's dirty laundry for inspection, exposing a split in the Republican ranks that Democratic editors found deliciously entertaining. In the *Albany Evening Journal*, Weed later stated that he had not known of the letter and wished it had never surfaced. "It jars harshly upon cherished memories," he wrote. "It destroys ideals of disinterestedness and generosity which relieve political life from so much that is selfish, sordid, and rapacious." That may have been Weed's polite way of calling Greeley all those things.

Greeley only irritated the Seward faithful further when, at the New York meeting ratifying Lincoln's nomination, he urged the Republicans to move on, declaring, "The past is dead: let the dead bury the dead, and let its mourners, if they will, go about the streets; while we devote ourselves to the living present." But Greeley would not so easily put the political assassination behind him, Democratic editors predicted. His hands were "smeared with the innocent blood of the Republican chief," and "the ghost of Seward will continue to haunt him," the *Daily Milwaukee News* promised. "Like Lady Macbeth in her sleep, he rubs his hands and cries, 'Out, out, damned spot!' But the blood stain remains, and all great Neptune's oceans cannot wash it away."

On May 24, as the *New York Times* opened fire on Greeley, Thurlow Weed arrived in Springfield, Illinois, to visit with Abraham Lincoln. The two tall men, possessing perhaps the two shrewdest political minds in the country, compared notes in Lincoln's parlor, with David Davis and Leonard Swett sitting in. "Both men were remarkable in stature and appearance," Swett noted. "Both had rough, strongly marked features, and both had risen by their own exertions from humble relations to control of a nation whose destinies they were then shaping." Lincoln opened by declaring he would like Seward to be in his cabinet. They immediately began discussing the campaign. The Deep South would be against the Republicans, but the other states were worth discussing. Which ones were safe? Which ones had to be fought for? In which ones should the Republicans expend money and effort, and how much? Who should be enlisted to help? They ended up talking for five hours.

Though they had met briefly earlier in 1848, Weed found this session a revelation. "I found Mr. Lincoln sagacious and practical," he recalled. "He displayed throughout the conversation so much good sense, such intuitive understanding of human nature, and such familiarity with the virtues and infirmities of politicians, that I became impressed very favorably with his fitness for the duties which he was not unlikely to be called upon to discharge." As Swett later recalled, "Mr. Lincoln and Mr. Weed, to use our rough phrase, naturally 'took to each other' from the very day they met," and "their relations grew gradually more agreeable and friendly" from that point on. Lincoln seemed surprised that, for once, a fellow politician asked for nothing in return for his efforts. As he told Senator Lyman Trumbull, Weed "saw me; but he showed no signs whatever of the intriguer. He asked for nothing; and said N.Y. is safe, without condition." Lincoln observed that Weed and, later, a fellow New Yorker had asked for "*fairness*, and fairness only. This, so far as in my power, they, and all others, shall have."

On the same day that Weed met with Lincoln, Seward wrote to his friend, thanking him for his "kind and generous" Davenport letter. "I know who my friends were, and how generously, faithfully, and devotedly they acted," he assured Weed. He was of two minds on Weed's trip to Europe. As a friend, Seward would like to see him flee politics and enjoy himself, but he warned that Republicans were in danger. Referring to the detested Greeley, Seward posited that the "egotism and ambition on the part of the chief leader of the late movement, now unavoidably the leader of the Republican party, will, in six months, bring everything to a dead stand"—defeat in November—"and you may then be able to save all." Seward did not yet believe that Lincoln was in fact running the Republican Party—or, perhaps, that he was even capable of it.

On May 30, Seward wrote his wife, Frances, a self-absorbed letter about his journey back to Washington as a beaten man. The trip included a stop in Albany, where Weed was waiting at the depot to meet him for the first time since the convention. "Weed was subdued, gentle, sad," Seward recounted. While Lincoln was surrounded with admirers and intriguers, Seward had become yesterday's news. Between Albany and New York City, Seward was at one point alone in the darkest corner of the car, when a policeman with an Irish brogue approached him. Seward recorded the scene, including the officer's flipping of his initials:

> "Have I the honor to speak to the Honorable H. W. Seward?"
>
> I answered: "My name is Seward."
>
> "Well sir," said he, as he gave a warm pressure of the hand, "I cannot leave the cars tonight without invoking the blessing of God upon you," and immediately retired. He was gone, and everybody else. I was alone."

In Washington, his fellow New York senator, Preston King, who had declined the vice-presidential nomination in Chicago, met him at the depot and conveyed him home. "It seemed sad and mournful," Seward wrote. The faces of his friends "all seemed like pictures of the dead." Congressmen Elbridge Gerry Spaulding and Israel Washburn Jr. came by during dinner, "and we talked of Chicago, and their trials and disappointments, until midnight." At the Senate on May 29, Republicans came up to greet him, "but in a manner which showed a consciousness of embarrassment, which made the courtesy a conventional one." All that day, "good men" came to see him. "Their eyes fill with tears, and they become speechless, as they speak of what they call 'ingratitude.' They console themselves with the vain hope of a day of 'vindication;' and my letters all talk of the same thing. But they awaken no response in my heart."

Seward visited with Charles Francis Adams, the son of one president and grandson of another, and his wife, Abigail, "and found them generous, kind, and faithful as ever." Adams had written to him after the Chicago disaster, urging him to forge on in politics. "Your services are more necessary to the cause than they ever were," Adams wrote, and "your own reputation will gain more of permanency from the becoming manner in which you meet this disappointment than it would from all the brilliancy of the highest success." But Seward was adamant: he was done with the political game.

Lincoln embraced his era's traditional view that it was undignified for a presidential candidate to campaign for himself. Others would have to introduce him to the voters. When the editor of the fiercely pro-slavery *Charleston Mercury*, in South Carolina, got a gander of Lincoln's portrait published in the May 26 edition of *Harper's Weekly*, he was quick to express his revulsion. "A horrid looking wretch he is!—sooty and scoundrelly in aspect; a cross between the nutmeg dealer, the horse-swapper, and the night man, a creature 'fit evidently for petty treason, small stratagems and all sorts of spoils.' He is a lank-sided Yankee of the uncomeliest visage, and of the dirtiest complexion. Faugh! after him what decent white man would be President?" At the other extreme of the political spectrum, abolitionists voiced disgust with Lincoln and his party. "Who is this huckster in politics? Who is this country court advocate? Who is this who does not know if he has got any opinions?" asked Wendell Phillips, speaking at the New England Anti-Slavery Convention on May 30. "What is his recommendation? It is that nobody knows good or bad of him." Seward had done "as much as any man in politics has done" to marshal opposition to slavery. But the party sidelined him "because of those efforts—nothing else."

Lincoln's fortunes were linked to the Democrats' convention, which reconvened in Baltimore in June. If the party could somehow heal the split of May, it might have a solid chance to win in November. Alas for the Democrats, squabbling commenced almost as soon as the delegates and spectators crowded into the Front Street Theatre. After Southern delegates had stormed out in May, some new delegations, slightly less hostile to Douglas, had been elected in some states. But Caleb Cushing of Massachusetts, the former U.S. attorney general presiding over the convention, refused to accept them in place of the previous delegations, who were also in attendance. For three days, a credentials committee tried to resolve the dispute, while tensions rose between supporters of Stephen Douglas and hardline Southerners. On June 21, when everyone crowded into the theater again to hear what had been decided, a section of the floor alarmingly gave way. No one was seriously hurt, and carpenters hastened to repair the damage, but the mishap was an omen of the disaster to come.

The majority report favored seating most of the new delegates, while the minority insisted on the states' original delegations. At the request of the New York delegation, the convention adjourned to mull things over until the next day, Friday, June 22. By then, the only thing that seemed likely to save the party was the capitulation of its Northern members to the South, through Douglas's withdrawal. The senator's powerful supporter, Dean Richmond, a railroad magnate and longtime New York Democratic Party chairman, happened to have a letter in his pocket from Douglas offering to bow out. "If my enemies are determined to divide and destroy the Democratic party, and perhaps the country, rather than see me elected, and if the unity of the party can be preserved and its ascendency perpetuated by dropping my name and uniting upon some other reliable non-intervention and Union-loving Democrat, I beseech you, in consultation with our friends, to pursue that course which will save the party and the country without regard to my individual interest," Douglas had written. But that was the rub: a "non-intervention" Democrat was one who supported Douglas's idea of letting local voters decide whether slavery should exist in a territory, while most Southern delegates supported federal intervention to protect the institution. And a "Union-loving" Democrat, by Douglas's definition, was increasingly difficult to come by in the South. Finding no such potential nominee in the works, Richmond kept the letter safely in his pocket.

By the time the convention approved the pro-Douglas majority report on June 23, most of the Southern delegates, repeating their actions in Charleston, had walked out. Caleb Cushing also resigned his post as presiding officer, unhappy that the original delegates had not been seated. Only a few Southerners remained to decry what was happening to the party. "In the name of common sense, have we not enough of higher law, revolutionary, abolitionist scoundrels in the North to fight without fighting our friends?" S. M. Moffat of Virginia exclaimed, to little effect.

Douglas, receiving more than two-thirds of the remaining delegates' votes, quickly won the nomination for president. But the anti-Douglas delegates had gone over to the Maryland Institute, where they declared themselves the real Democrats. After Cushing strolled in, they made him their presiding officer, to great applause, happy to add his imprimatur of legitimacy to their gathering. The delegates chose Vice President John C. Breckinridge, of Kentucky, as their nominee on the first ballot, followed by a vote to make it unanimous. When the Democrats left Baltimore that night, there were two Democratic Parties and two Democratic nominees.

Such Southern moderates as Virginian Robert E. Lee, then a lieutenant colonel in the 2nd United States Cavalry, still hoped the Democrats might settle on one candidate. "If . . . Douglas would now withdraw & join himself & party to aid in the election of Breckinridge, he might retrieve himself before the country & Lincoln be defeated," Lee wrote to his friend Major Earl Van Dorn on July 3. But Lee knew that was unlikely. "Politicians I fear are too selfish to become martyrs."

With the vote divided between four major candidates, two outcomes seemed possible: either no one would amass enough electoral votes to win, throwing the presidential election into the House; or Lincoln would be elected, possibly precipitating secession of the Southern states. "No one, this side of the mountains, pretends that any ticket can be elected by the People, unless it be ours," Lincoln wrote a friend.

Whether he could cross the threshold of 152 electoral votes was the question.

Lincoln spent the months until November in a kind of suspended animation, waiting for the voters' verdict and obstinately refusing to comment on the crisis engulfing the country. He dealt with a barrage of patronage-focused letters and visitors, while working with Weed and party leaders to craft a campaign strategy and form a cabinet. In a lighter moment, Lincoln received a new stovepipe hat fashioned by a Brooklyn hatter from a supporter back East. As Lincoln put it on his head and walked to the mirror, he turned to Mary with a twinkle in his eye. "Well, wife, there is one thing likely to come out of this scrape, any how," he said. "We are going to have some *new clothes*!" Still, it was clear well into the campaign that darkness was descending over the nation. Lincoln made an extraordinary confession that October, confiding to a visitor that he would have preferred a full term in the Senate, "where there was more chance to make [a] reputation and less danger of losing it—than four years in the presidency."

The nation seemed swept on riptides of emotion. In the North, thousands of men carried rails or marched in nighttime parades as Wide Awakes. Lawyer George Templeton Strong described a thousand Wide Awakes striding in precision down Broadway in October amid the eruption of roman candles and rockets, as ninety thousand New Yorkers cheered. The "procession moved along under a galaxy of fire balls—white, red, and green. I have never seen so beautiful a spectacle on any political turnout." To the tune of "The Old Gray Mare," tens of thousands sang out the lyrics of a campaign song, "Ain't You Glad You Joined the Republicans?" In the South, editors portrayed Republicans as greedy monsters bent on America's destruction. Many Southerners believed Lincoln was an uncultured demagogue who would free the slaves, unleashing anarchy on the region. Leaders prepared the way for disunion. Northern Democrats warned that blacks were determined to achieve political and social equality. Noting Frederick Douglass had come out in favor of Lincoln, the shamelessly racist *Holmes County Farmer* in Millersburg, Ohio, opined: "That's all right. Niggers vote in

New York, as they do in many places in Ohio, and elsewhere. Certainly the niggers should make as much noise as the nigger worshippers. The Black Republicans who consider themselves as no better than niggers should aid in giving Fred's paper a large circulation."

The nation's big states of Pennsylvania and New York would decide the election. Facing intraparty warfare in Pennsylvania—as the bitter squabbling between the forces of senator Simon Cameron and gubernatorial hopeful Andrew Curtin persisted—Lincoln sent Davis and Swett to investigate. Davis spent all of August 4 in Harrisburg with Cameron, finding him "a genial, pleasant, and kind hearted man," as he informed Lincoln. The senator's mood may have been improved by some notes Davis had brought from Lincoln explaining his views on tariffs. Cameron found them "abundantly satisfactory," and promised Davis that there was "not a shadow of a doubt" that both Lincoln and Curtin would carry Pennsylvania. Weed met with Cameron a week later. "He was well pleased with the visit of Judge Davis, and will go to work earnestly," Weed assured Lincoln. "He is by far the strongest man and best worker in the State."

Meanwhile, in Pennsylvania, New York, and New Jersey, Lincoln's opponents—seeing no way to save the nation except by throwing the election into the House—formed a "fusion" ticket, trying to persuade all supporters of Douglas, Breckinridge, and John Bell to gang up against the Republican. According to one report, the fabulously wealthy New Yorker William B. Astor, hoping to stave off a ruinous civil war, alone contributed one million dollars to the effort. When fusion reared its head in Indiana, Lincoln sent Davis to that key swing state. The judge subsequently wrote to Weed that the Hoosier State was "in great danger." Financial assistance "should be sent at once. *Men work better with money in hand.*" German speakers would also help. "I believe in God's Providence in this Election," Davis told Weed, "but at the same time we should keep our powder dry." Party leaders made sure Indiana Republicans received additional money to conduct campaign operations and an enthralling German American orator in the form of Carl Schurz.

As the weather and the campaign heated up, Seward rethought his plan to retire from politics. He could no longer stand aside. Seward conceded to Weed in July that "some part, perhaps a considerable one, of the responsibility of electing [Lincoln] rests upon us." In August, he began traveling, speaking out at whistle stops and events along the way. During the next few months, Seward made speeches in Maine, New Hampshire, Vermont, Massachusetts, New York, Pennsylvania, Ohio, Michigan, Indiana, Illinois, Wisconsin, Missouri, Minnesota, Iowa, and Kansas. At town after town, Seward was greeted by troops of Wide Awakes and enormous crowds, accompanied by bands and firing cannon. One member of his entourage, young Charles Francis Adams Jr., found Seward's energy and intelligence amazing, noting, "I never could understand where, when or how he then prepared the really remarkable speeches he delivered in rapid succession." Minnesota's Adam Goodrich told Seward during one stop, "You are doing more for Lincoln's election than any hundred men in the United States."

The New Yorker delivered his longer speeches mostly in solidly Republican areas where he knew he would be greeted with wild acclaim, leading some in the party to wonder just what he was up to. "The truth is, we want no aid where he is going, & I cannot see the necessity for, or the policy of this intended demonstration," James E. Harvey, a longtime Philadelphia newspaperman, wrote uneasily to Lincoln on July 27. Meanwhile, Seward persisted in treating Lincoln with decided coolness. In an interview with the *New York Daily Herald* in August, Seward "had very little to say about Lincoln, further than that he should receive his support." He "did not even smile" when told that, during a campaign rally in Springfield, Illinois, frenzied Lincoln supporters had raided his winter woodpile for logs that they believed he had split. Seward only "quietly expressed his confidence in the integrity, single mindedness and capability" of Lincoln.

A trip to Springfield later underscored Seward's evident antipathy to Lincoln. In July, the nominee's supporters urged Seward to visit, an idea Lincoln warmly endorsed in a postscript, writing, "I shall be personally much gratified to meet him here." Seward icily declined the invitation, and only condescended to stop briefly in Lincoln's hometown on October 2 when his trip to Chicago made it impolitic to skip Springfield altogether. Yet Seward would not deign to visit Lincoln at his office or home. Instead, Lincoln was compelled to wait humbly for Seward's train with hundreds of people on the depot platform, and then had to climb on board to seek out the New Yorker. As Lincoln "elbowed his way up to Seward's seat his countenance was lighted up with an expression of pleasure and good humor," Simon P. Hanscom of the *New York Daily Herald* reported. Seward, by contrast, showed none of his usual bonhomie. After Lincoln approached, Seward delivered a calculated snub. Seward rose from his seat, "shook hands with him, introduced him to the ladies and gentlemen in his company and, then, without entering into a conversation of even formal courtesy with him resumed his seat."

Charles Francis Adams Jr. found Lincoln an amusing specimen of country bumpkin, noting in his diary that "'old Abe' was a revelation. There he was, tall, shambling, plain and good-natured. He seemed shy to a degree, and very awkward in manner, as if he felt out of place, and had a realizing sense that properly the position should be reversed. Seward too appeared constrained." During the hasty meeting, Seward heard the crowds clamoring for him to speak. "As if glad to abbreviate . . . the interview," he went out onto the platform and made some brief remarks, predicting the Republicans would carry New York by sixty thousand votes.

Then he left immediately for Chicago, where all-out Sewardmania erupted later that day, with police forcing back the crowds to get the New Yorker through. In perfect fall weather, Seward spoke for an hour and a half to tens of thousands of people from a stand set up outside the Wigwam. While Chase gave a few speeches and Edward Bates none, Seward traveled thousands of miles and made dozens of speeches before the election, working himself to the edge of exhaustion. But "he very rarely, and then only in the curtest manner, spoke of the republican candidate for the Presidency," Hanscom observed. "He recognized that the flattering demonstrations that attended his tour were made in honor of himself personally, and had little or nothing to do with the republican cause or candidate." None of his travel mates tried to stifle talk that Seward would have made a better president. "Seward would have been more or less than human if he did not, to a very considerable extent, share in the feeling. His heart was not in the cause of Lincoln and Hamlin."

David Davis, attending the Eighth District Circuit Court and sweating out the campaign news, was worried and lonely. In September, he accompanied his wife, Sarah, and daughter Sallie as far as Detroit—from there those two were going on to visit family back East—and returned to Bloomington alone. "Oh, how lonesome this house is without loved ones," he wrote Sarah. "I felt a chill through me when I entered the house last night. The loved ones make home—without them what really constitutes home is gone." A raucous Democratic rally in town had left him frazzled. "If this election is unsuccessful I will bid a good bye to politics—shall consider that the idea the people are capable of self government is a heresy."

To his immense relief, the Republicans won the state elections in Indiana and Pennsylvania in October. It was a particularly close call in Indiana, as Henry S. Lane—who had warned that Republicans would lose with Seward heading the ticket—was elected governor by less than ten thousand votes. Davis wrote Sarah that he felt so excited that "it is right hard to hold Court." The results pointed to Lincoln's triumph in November and the defeat of a man Davis heartily detested, Stephen Douglas. "I consider Douglass [*sic*] the most arrogant demagogue that ever disgraced humanity, & if he could run through this race & not get a single . . . Electoral vote then I should consider the spirit of justice satisfied," Davis wrote.

Douglas himself saw the writing on the wall, telling a colleague, "Mr. Lincoln is the next president." Breaking with tradition against candidates campaigning, he set off on a courageous speaking tour through Southern states, no longer because he believed he could win, but to denounce secession and urge his fellow Democrats to sustain the Union after the election. On the steps of city hall in Norfolk, Virginia, he insisted that no man should vote for him unless he wanted to see "the Union maintained and preserved intact by the faithful execution of every act, every line and every letter of the written Constitution which our fathers bequeathed to us." Asked if secession would be justified if Lincoln were elected, Douglas replied with an emphatic no. "The election of a man to the presidency by the American people, in conformity with the Constitution of the United States, would not justify any attempt at dissolving this glorious confederacy." At Raleigh, North Carolina, Douglas was even more emphatic. "Yes, my friends, I would hang every man higher than Haman who would attempt by force to resist the execution of any provision of the Constitution which our fathers made and bequeathed to us." He hoped to reach Southerners still loyal to the United States, letting them know not all Democrats backed secession.

With Pennsylvania and Indiana evidently safe, Davis wrote Sarah on October 12 that it was becoming ever clearer that Lincoln would win the White House. "His wife is very ambitious and is in high feather now I have no doubt." Yet the circuit judge did not wish to trade places with his old friend. "I would not give my dear wife for the Presidency of this Union," he told Sarah. "All the honors of the world pale beside my undying love for you." In a letter later that month, he recalled their courting days in Lenox, Massachusetts. "What delightful rambles, charming rides, & pleasant talks we had. . . . Oh, the witchery of your eyes & smile & oh, how you magnetized your devoted lover *then* & your equally devoted lover *now*," he wrote. "The Earth to us was spanned by a rainbow." At Springfield on October 13, Davis visited Lincoln with the great Ohio orator and politician Tom Corwin. "Mr. Lincoln looked as if he had a heavy responsibility weighing on him. The cares & responsibility of office will weigh on him," Davis observed. On into November, the judge worried about the future that Lincoln confronted. "A fearful responsibility will devolve on Mr. Lincoln if he is elected in view of the feelings of the Southern people towards us," Davis wrote

Sarah. He prayed that Lincoln "may act with prudence, judgment and discretion & that he may hand the government over to his successor with his own honor untarnished, & the people united & happy."

On October 15, Grace Bedell, an eleven-year-old girl from Westfield, New York, wrote Lincoln a letter. "Have you any little girls about as large as I am if so give them my love and tell her to write to me if you cannot answer this letter." Grace's father had been to a fair, the girl wrote, and had brought home pictures of Lincoln and Hamlin. Grace asserted that Lincoln "would look a great deal better" with a beard, "for your face is so thin. All the ladies like whiskers and they would tease their husbands to vote for you and then you would be President." Though swamped with business, the amused Lincoln wrote back four days later. "I regret the necessity of saying I have no daughters. I have three sons—one seventeen, one nine, and one seven, years of age. . . . As to the whiskers, having never worn any, do you not think people would call it a silly affectation if I were to begin it now?" But Lincoln did begin growing his iconic beard.

Nearly five million American men went to the polls on November 6, a robust turnout of 81 percent of registered voters. With Southerners threatening secession should Lincoln win, the *New York Times* urged voters to reject this "direct and haughty attempt to domineer by terror over the Northern mind." The people had a right to elect the candidate of their choice, and the "North will elect Abraham Lincoln," the *Times* asserted. "So be it, good friends," replied the editor of the *Charleston Mercury*. "We have not the least objection. America is a free country. Do as you choose, and so will we." On the big day, Lincoln observed that "elections were like 'big boils'—they caused a great deal of pain before they came to a head, but after the trouble was over the body was in better health than before." He "hoped that the bitterness of the canvass would pass away 'as easily as the core of a boil.'"

That night, Lincoln awaited the election returns in downtown Springfield. As the results were brought to him, he "accepted everything with an almost immovable tranquility," a *New-York Tribune* reporter observed. At ten thirty, Thurlow Weed telegraphed that the news in New York "was satisfactory so far, only it was not conclusive." Pennsylvania went strongly for Lincoln, as did the New England states. When encouraging news from New York began to flow in, Lincoln admonished his happy companions, "Not too fast, my friends. Not too fast, it may not be over yet." When yet more results arrived, Lincoln's neighbor Jesse K. Dubois asked, "Well, Uncle Abe, are you satisfied now?" A smiling Lincoln replied, "Well, the agony is almost over, and you will soon be able to go to bed."

Finally, a message came that Lincoln had carried New York, sealing his election. He read the dispatch "with evident marks of pleasure." After well-wishers congratulated him, Lincoln remarked, "I feel a great responsibility. God help me, God help me." Though he won Illinois handily, Lincoln carried Springfield by all of sixty-nine votes, and he lost his own Sangamon County by forty-two—a prophet without honor in his own conservative county.

Lincoln would have to serve as a minority president, having won only a little more than 39 percent of the national vote—the second smallest percentage by the victor in the nation's history, ahead only of John Quincy Adams's 31 percent in 1824. Lincoln's 180 electoral votes, though, were more than enough. He won 1,855,993 votes, to 1,381,944 for Douglas; 851,844 for Breckinridge; and 590,946 for Bell. The Democrats combined won significantly more popular votes than the Republican. Even if the voters of Douglas and Breckinridge were added together, though, Lincoln would have captured enough electoral college votes to win the presidency.

Breckinridge won Delaware and swept the Deep South, obtaining seventy-two electoral votes. Douglas carried only Missouri and a portion of New Jersey, for twelve electoral votes. Bell took the border states of Virginia, Kentucky, and Tennessee, winning thirty-nine electoral votes. Lincoln's strength was confined entirely to the North. In the Deep South, his name was not even on the ballot, and even in Virginia, he won barely 1 percent of the vote.

With the matter settled, Lincoln finally went home. By the time serenaders arrived at Eighth and Jackson, Mary had already lost patience with the masses' demands on her husband, even before he assumed the presidency. She reportedly "cursed—swore and held him back, so that it was with difficulty that he went out to meet the people."

Lincoln famously filled his cabinet with his rivals for the nomination. He sought to enlist support across the breadth of the party, a sign of his confidence in his ability to keep these obstreperously egocentric politicians in check. Lincoln, overlooking Seward's snub in the railroad car in Springfield, coaxed Seward to accept the top slot of secretary of state.

Lincoln denied businessman and senator Simon Cameron the treasury job—and contemplated leaving him out of the cabinet altogether. "All through the campaign my friends have been calling me 'Honest Old Abe,' and I have been elected mainly on that cry," Lincoln told Pennsylvania politicians who came to pitch Cameron. "What will be thought now if the first thing I do is to appoint C[ameron], whose very name stinks in the nostrils of the people for his corruption?" Cameron's manager at the convention, Joseph Casey, felt the need to nudge Swett. "From the things that occurred when I was at Springfield my mind has since been in doubt as to whether Mr. Lincoln has been made *fully acquainted* with the conversations between you & Judge Davis on the one side, & myself, on the other, at the Tremont House, the night before the nomination," Casey wrote pointedly. Swett complained to Lincoln that Cameron's friends were repeatedly pressuring him and Davis to deliver appointments. "Yet on the whole, from what occurred at Chicago I think they have a right to do it," he conceded. Deciding Pennsylvania must be represented on the cabinet, and perhaps wishing to honor the deals made in his name, Lincoln reluctantly named Cameron secretary of war.

The other man the Lincoln forces had evidently made promises to at the convention, Caleb B. Smith, was duly selected for interior secretary. Lincoln appointed the brilliant Chase to Treasury, made

Bates, a former judge, his attorney general, and named a cranky New Englander, Connecticut newspaper editor Gideon Welles, as his navy secretary. Montgomery Blair, who had fought at Chicago for Bates, won the job of postmaster general. William L. Dayton of New Jersey, some of whose delegates flipped to Lincoln, did not end up in the cabinet, but won the prized post of minister to France.

The hatreds stirred by the election, Lincoln soon discovered, failed to dissipate like a healed boil. For Southern leaders, the prospect of a president who hated slavery signaled the doom of their way of life, and states immediately began moving to secede from the Union. South Carolina departed on December 20, followed quickly by Mississippi, Florida, Alabama, Georgia, Louisiana, and Texas.

In early 1861, Seward, still convinced he was a greater man than Lincoln, was in Washington, acting as a virtual spokesman for the incoming administration. Hoping to forestall the South's secession by postponing the struggle over slavery to a later day, he advised the president-elect back in Springfield that "every thought that we think ought to be conciliatory, forbearing and paternal." Horace Greeley went further, contending that the Southern states should be permitted to secede in peace. Many still hoped that the South might be placated if Republicans quickly retreated from the positions that the voters had just endorsed. But Lincoln was of sterner stuff, insisting that Republicans must "hold firm, as with a chain of steel" to the principle of containing slavery, lest their long struggle be for naught, and the losers of the election be permitted to veto the voters' will. On February 4, 1861, Southern representatives gathered in Montgomery, Alabama, to form what they called a new nation, the Confederate States of America. Seward's on-and-off friend in the Senate, Jefferson Davis of Mississippi, was named its president.

The divisions in the Republican Party so evident at the Chicago convention persisted months later, as Seward's critics called for his removal from the cabinet. Greeley's *Tribune* charged that Seward "regards himself as the center and soul of the incoming administration, and Mr. Lincoln but an ornamental appendage thereto." There was a good deal of truth to the charge. Seward believed himself the nation's leading Republican, indispensable to the new administration's success, and he was determined to save the nation by wielding as much power as possible. This mission, he worried, would be fatally undermined by the strong and contentious men Lincoln was appointing. Evidently hoping to pressure Lincoln into naming a more Seward-friendly cabinet, he submitted his resignation just days before the inauguration.

Though Lincoln badly needed the support of New York and its powerful leader, he firmly rejected Seward's attempt to control the cabinet. "I can't afford to let Seward take the first trick," he told his secretary John G. Nicolay. Without budging, Lincoln managed to talk Seward out of bolting. But he made clear that he needed and respected the New Yorker's advice, including about his inaugural address, a crucial statement about the secession crisis. Seward suggested thoughtful changes that Lincoln accepted, making the speech less combative. Notably, Seward proposed a poignant, hopeful addendum about the bonds that Americans yet shared, speaking of the "mystic chords" proceeding from "so many battle fields and so many patriot graves." Lincoln loved the idea, but he transformed Seward's touching prose into unforgettable poetry. "I am loath to close," Lincoln said, as he delivered the speech on March 4, 1861. "We are not enemies, but friends. We must not be enemies. . . . The mystic chords of memory, stretching from every battlefield and patriot grave to every living heart and hearthstone all over this broad land, will yet swell the chorus of the Union, when again touched, as surely they will be, by the better angels of our nature."

One month into the administration, with the South gearing up to seize U.S. forts in South Carolina and Florida, Seward believed Lincoln was failing. After discussing his concerns with Thurlow Weed and Henry Raymond, he wrote a remarkable letter headed "Some thoughts for the President's consideration." In it, Seward complained that the administration was "yet without a policy either foreign or domestic," and urged Lincoln to precipitate a foreign crisis to draw the feuding states together. Whatever policy was adopted, it must be pursued vigorously, he told Lincoln. "Either the President must do it himself and be all the while active in it, or devolve it on some member of his cabinet. . . . It is not my especial province. But I neither seek to evade nor assume responsibility." He seemed to be suggesting that Lincoln was not up to the job of chief executive, but that he, Seward, was willing to pitch in and save the nation by assuming greater responsibility. Refusing to take offense, Lincoln wrote out a reply, patiently explaining that the administration *did* have a policy—one that the cabinet supported—of holding onto the forts for as long as possible. He added that if something was to be done to change the administration's policies, "I must do it"—and no one else. Lincoln evidently did not send Seward this letter, but rather discussed its points with him.

For a time, Seward continued to fear Lincoln's ineptitude. Using Seward's ideas, Raymond's *New York Times* published a scorching editorial headlined, WANTED—A POLICY. But as Seward worked alongside Lincoln during the first few months of his administration, sharing long talks with him, he came to recognize the president's extraordinary political savvy, personal warmth, and steely will. He ceased trying to take over. In June 1861, Seward wrote his wife, "Executive skill and vigor are rare qualities," and declared that the "President is the best of us."

On Friday, April 12, 1861, Southern batteries opened fire on Fort Sumter in Charleston Harbor, forcing its surrender. Lincoln called for seventy-five thousand volunteers to suppress "combinations too powerful" to be stopped by law enforcement, and a remorselessly bloody and revolutionary civil war was on, one that would drag out for four years, claiming as many as 750,000 American lives, while ultimately freeing four million enslaved human beings.

All of this would have come as a shock to those packed into the Wigwam in May 1860, Connecticut journalist Isaac H. Bromley noted. "If anyone had said that within the next Presidential term slavery would be abolished, and the slaves made free citizens, he would have been listened to very much as one would who predicted that the Mississippi would presently run north." Many of the attendees would find their lives changed forever. "A year later it is not improbable that from a quarter to a half of the male citizens in the Wigwam were in military uniforms," Bromley wrote. "It was a thick curtain that hung before the Chicago Convention of 1860. Behind it were preparing the most bewildering transformations that ever dazzled the eyes of mortal man."

Epilogue: Unconscious Instruments

In February 1861, Weed got some measure of revenge on Horace Greeley for his efforts at the Chicago convention. When New York Republican legislators met in their all-important caucus to choose a new senator to replace Seward, Weed's man was William M. Evarts, the distinguished lawyer who had placed Seward's name in nomination in Chicago. His top opponent was none other than Greeley, seeking political office yet again, this time in defiance of Weed. While Evarts initially led Greeley, the *Tribune* editor steadily gained strength in the balloting. Suddenly, Greeley shot ahead of Evarts and seemed poised to win the Senate nomination on the next ballot.

"Pale as ashes," Weed sat just outside the assembly chamber listening to the tallies, so preoccupied that he lit a new cigar without realizing he already had one in his mouth. Jumping to his feet, he frantically told his lieutenant, "Tell the Evarts men to go right over to Harris—to *Harris*—to HARRIS!" His legislators dutifully swung from Evarts to state Supreme Court justice Ira Harris, a longtime friend of Seward, who vanquished Greeley by a margin of sixty to forty-nine. Though Weed was unable to elect his first choice—evidence that his power was waning—he had stopped the man who in his eyes was behind the Chicago debacle. Weed boasted to newly elected Kansas congressman

Abel C. Wilder after the battle that he had "paid the *first* installment on a large debt to Mr. Greeley."

Mr. Greeley would prove a thorn in Lincoln's side for much of the war. At first, he urged Lincoln to let the Southern states go in peace. After the attack on Fort Sumter, he shifted, calling for military force to bring the region under control. "What in the world is the matter with Uncle Horace?" Lincoln asked at one point. "Why can't he restrain himself and wait a little?" For day after day, Greeley's *Tribune* headed its editorial column FORWARD TO RICHMOND! FORWARD TO RICHMOND! FORWARD TO RICHMOND! creating enormous political pressure for an attack by green troops in July 1861. The first Battle of Bull Run, in Virginia, on July 21 proved a Union disaster, as the raw army fled the field and staggered back into Washington. In its wake, Greeley seemed to suffer a nervous breakdown, confessing to Lincoln in a hand-wringing letter that he had not slept for seven nights. If the Southerners could not be beaten, Greeley said, then Lincoln must end the war, or "every drop of blood henceforth shed in this quarrel will be wantonly, wickedly shed, and the guilt will rest heavily on the soul of every promoter of the crime." He signed off, "Yours, in the depths of bitterness." Lincoln filed the letter and kept on fighting for the Union.

In August 1862, Greeley published a famous editorial, "The Prayer of 20 Millions," hoping to pressure Lincoln to free the slaves. Lincoln had already decided to issue his Emancipation Proclamation, but without revealing that fact, he used the opportunity to make a vital point, crucial to maintaining political support for the war: "As to the policy I 'seem to be pursuing' as you say, I have not meant to leave any one in doubt," he wrote Greeley in a public response.

> I would save the Union. . . . If there be those who would not save the Union, unless they could at the same time *save* slavery, I do not agree with them. If there be those who would not save the Union unless they could at the same time *destroy* slavery, I do not agree with them. My paramount object in this struggle *is*

> to save the Union, and is *not* either to save or to destroy slavery. If I could save the Union without freeing *any* slave I would do it, and if I could save it by freeing *all* the slaves I would do it; and if I could save it by freeing some and leaving others alone I would also do that. What I do about slavery, and the colored race, I do because I believe it helps to save the Union; and what I forbear, I forbear because I do *not* believe it would help to save the Union." But Lincoln added: "I have here stated my purpose according to my view of *official* duty; and I intend no modification of my oft-expressed *personal* wish that all men every where could be free.

One of the effects of Lincoln's Emancipation Proclamation was a flood of former slaves into the Union ranks as soldiers—something almost unimaginable when the war began. Eventually, 180,000 African Americans served, turning the tide of the war. Black leader Frederick Douglass urged their enlistment. "There is no time for delay," he wrote in March 1863. "The iron gate of our prison stands half-open. One gallant rush from the North will fling it wide open, while four millions of our brothers and sisters shall march out into Liberty!"

The Wigwam served for years as a hall for large gatherings, but it never hosted another national political convention. When the Prince of Wales, the future King Edward VII, visited Chicago in September 1860, mayor Long John Wentworth, in the words of the *New York Times*, "took him everywhere, and showed him up as a manager would an elephant." In a quick tour of the city, Wentworth made sure to show the prince the Court House, the grain elevators, the waterworks, and, of course, the great Wigwam. In 1867, Frederick Douglass visited the city and spoke about the momentous events of seven years earlier. "Without Chicago," Douglass said, "we should have had no Wigwam; without the Wigwam we should have had no Abraham Lincoln; without a Lincoln we might have to day had no Government."

On the evening of November 13, 1869, at around nine o'clock, the great wooden building, even more of a tinderbox than it had been nine years earlier, caught fire. The blaze quickly swelled into a raging inferno, visible for miles around like a shining cloud in the night sky. Chicagoans poured from the theaters, the opera, and the lager beer saloons as soon as they learned that "the Wigwam was burning; that one of the very few historic landmarks which Chicago boasted was being swiftly and surely destroyed; that our Faneuil Hall, not in which Liberty was rocked, but in which she was clad with a giant's strength, would soon be no more. The effect was electric," the *Chicago Tribune* reported. One sentence in the news story had the ring of an epitaph: "Within its walls freedom was born, and it gave to America the most illustrious character in her history."

Many of the figures behind the Lincoln miracle at the Wigwam went on to play prominent roles in the 1860s.

Francis Blair, the seasoned political pro who had fought for Edward Bates, became a close advisor to Lincoln. Like presidents before him, Lincoln valued Blair's wisdom and experience. He sent Blair to offer the command of the Union armies to Robert E. Lee, before the Virginian chose to side with his state instead. He also enlisted Blair to send out peace feelers in 1865. Blair, occupying the house that still bears his name across Pennsylvania Avenue from the White House, could easily pop in to confer with the president.

Thurlow Weed, though farther away in New York, also advised Lincoln throughout his presidency on crucial matters of politics and patronage. He finally did go to Europe, explaining the Union cause to its governments, helping to stave off recognition of the Confederacy. A letter of praise he wrote to Lincoln in March 1865 spurred the president to reflect on his profound and moving second inaugural, in which Lincoln urged Americans to strive on "with malice toward none, with charity for all" as the savage war drew toward its end. Lincoln wrote Weed that he expected the address "to wear as well as—perhaps better than—anything I have produced; but I believe it is not immediately popular."

Shortly after Lincoln's second inauguration, Kansas editor John Alexander Martin and congressman Abel Carter Wilder, both of whom had been at the Chicago convention, paid Lincoln a visit at the White House. Leaving the meeting "vividly impressed . . . with the simple majesty of his presence, with his unaffected manner, his greatness, [and] his loving kindness," Martin recalled the "indignation with which the Kansas delegation received his nomination; and I said to Mr. Wilder, what I have always since felt, that probably the most fortunate thing that ever happened for the Nation was the chance which, at Chicago in 1860, committed its destiny to his strong, prudent, and loyal hands."

Stephen Douglas, Lincoln's fierce political enemy for decades, emerged from the 1860 election as a staunch defender of the Union. When Lincoln informed him that he would call for seventy-five thousand volunteers, Douglas suggested two hundred thousand, and he embarked on a Midwestern speaking tour on behalf of a bipartisan war effort. While many wondered whether Lincoln was up to the job, Douglas told a friend, "I've known Mr. Lincoln a longer time than you have, or than the country has. He'll come out all right, and we will all stand by him." But Douglas did not stand for long. His health undermined by years of smoking, hard drinking, and intense pressure, he contracted typhoid fever and died on June 3, 1861.

Norman B. Judd, who brought the convention to Chicago and created a seating chart designed to aid Lincoln, desperately hoped for a cabinet seat, and Illinois senator Lyman Trumbull pushed hard for him. But in the end, forces backing Simon Cameron and Caleb Smith worked against Judd, and Lincoln believed Illinois could not fairly claim both the presidency and a cabinet seat. Judd bitterly reflected to Trumbull that Lincoln "never had a truer friend than myself" but that the president-elect had opted for political "trimming and wants to get rid of me." He complained that even "female influence" had been active against him—code for Mary Lincoln, who never forgave him for his role in helping Trumbull win the Senate over her husband in 1855. Lincoln did award Judd a consolation prize, making him ambassador to Prussia—disappointing another friend, Gustave Koerner, the German

American who had fought hard in Chicago for Lincoln's nomination, and who believed he merited the post. Unfortunately, Lincoln had only so many jobs to give away. "He always had more horses than oats," as Leonard Swett put it.

Trumbull, who had contended that the frail, sickly Supreme Court justice John McLean would make a fine president—as it turned out, McLean died only one month into Lincoln's presidency—thought little of Lincoln as president. He called Lincoln "a follower and not a leader," noting his tendency to calibrate his actions to public opinion. While Lincoln would ultimately win the war and end slavery, Trumbull griped that "a man of more positive character, prompt and systematic action, might have accomplished the same result in half the time, and with half the loss of blood and treasure."

Henry S. Lane, who had jumped on a table and fanatically swung his cane to celebrate Lincoln in Chicago, served for all of two days as governor of Indiana before being elected a U.S. senator by the new Republican-dominated legislature. Though he did not achieve much distinction in his one term in the Senate, Lane zealously sustained Lincoln and the Union cause during the war, voting faithfully to back the war effort.

Andrew G. Curtin, who also warned the delegates in Chicago that he could not win with Seward heading the ticket, was elected governor of Pennsylvania. A strong and energetic war governor, he advanced the career of Union general George G. Meade, who beat back Robert E. Lee's invasion of his state at Gettysburg, perhaps the turning point of the war. Alexander K. McClure, who worked with Curtin to derail Seward in Chicago, later became a confidant of President Lincoln. In May 1864, when McClure assured Lincoln that he would be renominated by his party, the president reminded him of what had happened four years earlier: "Well, McClure, what you say seems to be unanswerable, but I don't quite forget that I was nominated for President in a convention that was two-thirds for the other fellow."

David K. Cartter of Ohio, who announced the votes putting Lincoln over the top at Chicago, won Lincoln's appointment as the minister to Bolivia. Later, Lincoln named him chief justice of the District of Columbia Supreme Court, overlooking complaints that Cartter was nothing but a blustering, ill-bred hack politician.

Elmer Ephraim Ellsworth, commander of the crack U.S. Zouave Cadets, who thrilled the Wigwam crowd with their maneuvers on Wednesday night of convention week, was the first noted casualty of the Civil War. The fiercely patriotic twenty-four-year-old was gunned down on May 24, 1861, while removing a Confederate flag from the roof of the Marshall House, in Alexandria, Virginia. Northerners revered Ellsworth as a martyr to the Union cause, and his body lay in state in the East Room of the White House.

Mary A. Livermore, the former Easterner who was appalled by Chicago's filth and who served as the sole woman reporter at the convention, fought tirelessly for better medical care for men wounded in the war. In November 1862, when the war was going badly, she and a friend met with the haggard president in Washington. "I shall never forget the shock which his presence gave us," Livermore recalled. "His introverted look and his half-staggering gait were like those of a man walking in his sleep. He seemed literally bending under the weight of his burdens." Lincoln brightened, though, when Livermore told him where she lived. "So you are from Chicago!" he exclaimed. "You are not scared by Washington mud, then, for you can beat us to pieces in that." In 1863, she organized the Northwestern Sanitary Fair in Chicago, which raised $86,000 for the cause of care for wounded soldiers. Lincoln donated his own manuscript copy of the Emancipation Proclamation, which sold for $3,000. Livermore's hard work as a nurse led some to call her "the American Florence Nightingale." She went on to fight for women's rights, including suffrage, and alcohol prohibition.

Carl Schurz, who rallied large numbers of German immigrants to support Lincoln, sought an appointment as an ambassador in Europe. Seward initially opposed it, fearing Schurz's revolutionary background would offend the courts, but Lincoln thought America should not "discriminate against men for having made efforts in behalf of liberty elsewhere." When two men lobbying on Schurz's behalf warned Seward that many people would be disappointed if the German American was denied a post, Seward exploded, "Disappointment! You speak to me of disappointment! To me, who was justly entitled to the Republican nomination for the presidency, and who had to stand aside and see it given to a little Illinois lawyer!" Schurz did obtain a fine position as ambassador to Spain, then returned to America to serve with distinction as a Union general, fighting at the Second Battle of Bull Run and at the Battles of Chancellorsville, Gettysburg, and Chattanooga, and on until the end of the war.

Jesse K. Dubois, who had fought hard for Lincoln's nomination in Chicago, was hurt and angered to find that his friend and former neighbor offered nothing for him or his son-in-law. "Uncle Jesse," Lincoln tried to explain, "there is no reason why I don't want to appoint you, but there is one why I can't,—you are from the town I live in myself." Dubois did not accept the explanation. He was "*mortified*," he wrote Lincoln, "more from the fact that I placed a too high estimate on my *relations* with you, and did not know my *position*. . . . I did suppose I had a right to a small share of the spoils, but let it pass." But Dubois did not let it pass. Four years later, he was still complaining. "Lincoln is a singular man and I must Confess I never Knew him: he has for 30 years past just used me as a plaything to accomplish his ends: but the moment he was elevated to his proud position he seemed all at once to have entirely changed his whole nature and become altogether a new being—Knows no one and the road to favor is always open to his Enemies whilst the door is hymetically [*sic*] sealed to his old friends."

Leonard Swett, another key player in Chicago, did not seek any office for himself, but he lobbied hard for David Davis, the manager of Lincoln's surprise victory. When a seat on the U.S. Supreme Court opened in 1862, there was fierce competition for the post. Lincoln was wary of awarding too many prized appointments to his Illinois allies, but Davis's friends went to work on the president. Iowa supporter Hawkins Taylor, who had attended the convention, reminded Lincoln that "but for the extraordinary effort of Judge Davis, you would not have received the nomination at the Chicago Convention. . . . I feel that it is due to yourself as well as to Judge Davis that you should tender him the appointment of Supreme Judge." Swett confronted Lincoln at the White House at seven o'clock one morning, before the president could turn to other business. "If Judge Davis, with his tact and force, had not lived, and all other things had been as they were, I believe you would not now be sitting where you are," Swett bluntly told him. "Yes, that is so," Lincoln replied gravely. In the end, he nominated the obscure circuit court judge for the lifetime position, and the Senate confirmed him. Davis proved an excellent justice. Ironically, he ruled against Lincoln in his best-known decision, *Ex Parte Milligan*, finding shortly after the president's death that, under the Constitution, civilians could not be tried in military courts—as many had been during the war—while civilian courts were in operation, unless Congress otherwise stipulated.

Illinois lawyer Orville H. Browning, initially a Bates supporter, visited Bates in St. Louis after the convention to ask that he support Lincoln. Bates coldly refused to take to the hustings, agreeing only to write a letter backing the nominee. After the death of Stephen Douglas, the Republican-led Illinois legislature elected Browning to fill his seat in the U.S. Senate. In Washington, he became close to the Lincolns socially. But Browning desperately wanted the Supreme Court job that went to Davis, and he could never quite rise above his initial instinct that Lincoln was not cut out for the presidency. He wrote to a friend in 1864: "You know, strange as it may seem to you, that I am personally attached to the President, and have faithfully tried to uphold him, and make him respectable; tho' I have never been able to persuade myself that he was big enough for his position. Still, I thought he might get through, as many a boy through college, without disgrace, and without knowledge; and I fear he is a failure."

Salmon P. Chase, who yearned to be president and believed Lincoln was not up to the task of saving the Union, mounted a sub-rosa campaign for the 1864 nomination while still serving as treasury secretary. Lincoln shrugged off reports of Chase's maneuvers. "I have determined to shut my eyes, as far as possible, to everything of the sort," he said. "Mr. Chase makes a good Secretary and I shall keep him where he is. If he becomes President, all right, I hope we never have a worse man." David Davis, on the other hand, was disgusted, comparing Chase's conduct to "eating a man's bread and stabbing him at the same time." In early 1864, Chase's efforts foundered, and Lincoln accepted his resignation. But, once again refusing to hold a grudge, Lincoln selected Chase to be chief justice of the Supreme Court after the death of Chief Justice Roger Taney in October 1864. Even on the bench, Chase never relinquished his dreams of being nominated and winning the White House, until he died of a stroke, at sixty-five, on May 7, 1873.

Edward Bates served as attorney general for much of the war, regarded as a moderate force in the cabinet. When Taney died, the Missourian begged Lincoln to name him to the post. "I desire it chiefly—almost wholly as the crowning retiring honor of my life," he wrote to the president. When Bates heard nothing on the appointment, he resigned his cabinet post in November 1864, a month before Lincoln named the more radical Chase. Bates died five years later, at seventy-five.

Ensconced in the office of vice president, Hannibal Hamlin complained that Lincoln, while treating him personally with "kindness and consideration," virtually ignored him. "Of course I am not consulted at all, nor do I think there is much disposition in any quarter to regard any counsel I may give much if at all," Hamlin grumbled in 1862. In 1864, the Republican Party, hoping to attract Democratic voters, changed its name to the National Union Party and dumped Hamlin at its 1864 national convention in favor of Democrat Andrew Johnson, the military governor of Tennessee. Johnson turned up at the inauguration on March 4, 1865, embarrassingly drunk. Six weeks later he was president.

On April 5, 1865, while Lincoln toured the captured Confederate capital of Richmond, Virginia, Seward was planning to take a carriage ride through the streets of Washington with his son and daughter. When the driver closed the door, the startled horses bolted. Seward tried to escape from the runaway carriage, only to be flung like a rag doll, breaking his arm and badly shattering his jaw. Four nights later, Lincoln returned to Washington and went to his weak and suffering friend, who was immobile in his bed at home. Lincoln stretched out next to Seward on the bed with his head in his hand. "I think we are near the end, at last," Lincoln told him. That day, Lee surrendered his Army of Northern Virginia, all but ending the war.

On April 14, Seward was still helpless in bed when a big man, claiming to have medicine for the patient, forced his way upstairs and stabbed Seward repeatedly. Though the assailant sliced open Seward's cheek and neck, the metal wires holding his jaw may have deflected the knife away from his jugular vein. After Seward's sons Frederick and Augustus fought with him, the man escaped into the night. The horribly injured secretary of state survived. It turned out the attack was coordinated. Around the same time, the leader of the conspiracy, famous and handsome actor John Wilkes Booth, entered the presidential box at Ford's Theatre and shot Lincoln in the back of his head, plunging him into darkness until his death the next morning. Andrew Johnson became president, Booth was hunted down and killed, and the oft-disparaged Lincoln became a martyr to the war, revered from that time on.

On the day that Lincoln died, his son Robert wired David Davis: "Please come at once to Washington to take care of my father's affairs." Robert later described Davis "as a second father, and this he was to me until his death." Administering the estate proved to be a thankless task in many ways. Dealing with a mountain of unpaid bills for extravagant clothes and furniture, and realizing Mary Lincoln had returned to Illinois with boxes of goods pilfered from the White House, Davis concluded that the former first lady was "a natural born thief."

During her marriage, Mary had had to deal with the darker side of her husband's nature—his bouts of depression, his gloomy sense that pain and failure were endemic to human life, his notion born of his Baptist upbringing that people could only do so much, and that the rest was in the hands of a just but inscrutable God. Perhaps Lincoln was able to withstand the disaster of bloodshed and defeats in the war because his own life had been haunted by sadness and loss after loss, including the difficulties in his married life. In the eyes of Illinois lawyer

Henry Clay Whitney, Mary Lincoln's "domestic discipline" trained her husband to endure difficult and unreasonable people, many of whom he needed in the war effort. "The nation is largely indebted to Mary Todd Lincoln for its autonomy," Whitney contended.

For his part, Lincoln believed his ability to handle clashing personalities was one of his greatest strengths. "I may not have made as great a President as some other men, but I believe I have kept these discordant elements together as well as anyone could," Lincoln told Swett one night in the middle of the war. He had a rare gift for overlooking even the contempt and betrayal of political associates, believing that ignoring slights and seeking to save relationships paid off in the end. "Do good to those who hate you and turn their ill will to friendship," he advised Mary. That approach helped Lincoln hold the Republican Party together in Washington and draw in Democrats to support the war.

With all her quirks, Mary Lincoln suffered unfathomably. Not only had she seen her husband assassinated at her side, but she and Abraham had lost their three-year-old son Edward to illness back in Springfield in 1850, and their beloved eleven-year-old Willie to typhoid fever in Washington in 1862. Tad, the boy who, with Willie, had greeted the Republican delegation at the gate of their home in Springfield, died in 1871 at eighteen. Mary's sole surviving son Robert—anguished by her dangerous paranoia and her recklessness with money—felt compelled to commit her for a time to a mental institution. On July 15, 1882, eleven years to the day after Tad's passing, Mary Todd Lincoln suffered a stroke at her sister's home and died the next day at sixty-three.

Robert Lincoln, who moved on from Phillips Exeter Academy to graduate from Harvard College, became a lawyer, Republican activist, U.S. secretary of war, ambassador to Britain, and president of the Pullman Palace Car Company. Sometime during the Civil War, he slipped on a railroad platform in Washington and was saved from injury or death when he was rescued by a well-known actor—Edwin Booth, brother of his father's later assassin. Robert lived long enough to attend the 1922 dedication of the Lincoln Memorial in Washington and see his all-too-human father turned into a marble god. He died at his Vermont home, Hildene, on July 26, 1926, a week before his eighty-third birthday.

In 1867, Thurlow Weed retired from politics. During his subsequent brief service as editor of the *New York Commercial Advertiser*, he incurred Mary Lincoln's wrath by exposing some of the ways she had cheated the taxpayers as first lady. With searing sarcasm, Weed thanked Mrs. Lincoln for her vitriol. "It is pleasant to remember that we were always out of favor in that quarter," he wrote. "It is equally pleasant to remember that we possessed the friendship and confidence of Mr. Lincoln to the last hour of his life, without paying court, as others did, to Mrs. Lincoln, and in spite of her constant effort to disturb our relations."

Weed's deteriorating health and failing eyesight finally drove him out of journalism, and he spent the last years of his life working on his memoirs and entertaining visitors at his apartment on Fifth Avenue in New York. "No stranger who called upon him could help but be impressed by the old gentleman's kindly and considerate manner," the *New York Times* reported. Hundreds of people came by. He liked to have young people around him, "and was always a sympathetic listener and advisor concerning their plans and desires." He recounted the stirring events of his lifetime, sharing "entertaining reminiscences of the noted men he had known so intimately," often inviting his visitors to "stay and have some little refreshment; take a dish of ice-cream with me." Weed retained his Christian faith to the end. "I cannot believe, and cannot be brought to believe that the purpose of our creation is fulfilled in our short existence here. To me the existence of another world is a necessary supplement of this, to adjust its inequalities and imbue it with moral significance." He died on November 22, 1882, at eighty-five. The daughter who accompanied him to Chicago, Harriet, never married. The *Buffalo Evening News* noted on her death in 1893 that "Miss Weed devoted the 75 years of her life entirely to the care of her father and his public work."

With Weed's support and advice, Seward served President Johnson through his tempestuous administration. Perhaps most famously, Seward initiated the farsighted purchase of the Russian territory of

Alaska for $7.2 million. Many at the time considered it a financial sinkhole, and the purchase later came to be called "Seward's Folly." But Alaska proved to be of immense value, not only for its natural resources but for its massive geopolitical importance, protecting the United States during the Cold War in the next century. Seward finally retired from politics at the end of Johnson's term, on March 4, 1869. On October 10, 1872, he worked as usual in the morning at his writing desk in Auburn, despite a cough, but grew weaker and more feverish as the day went on. Loved ones gathered around his bed, realizing the seventy-one-year-old was on the door of death. His daughter-in-law Jenny asked whether he had anything to tell them. "Nothing," Seward said, "only love one another."

The ever-ambitious Horace Greeley, who had helped ruin Seward's chances to be president at the Wigwam, ran for that office in 1872 as the nominee of the Liberal Republican Party, an amalgamation of Democrats and reformers opposed to the reelection of Republican president Ulysses S. Grant. His last desperate bid for political glory ended in disaster. In October, Greeley broke off campaigning to be with his desperately sick wife, Mary, who died a week before the election. Greeley not only lost in a landslide but faced the certain prospect that his beloved *New-York Tribune* would fall into other hands. He died on November 29, at sixty-one, six weeks after the passing of his old friend and adversary Seward.

That same year, the Labor Reform Party nominated David Davis for president. Davis sought the nomination of the Liberal Republican Party as well, only to lose to Greeley. In 1877, the Illinois legislature elected Davis to the position his old friend Abraham Lincoln had desperately coveted, U.S. senator. Davis left the Supreme Court to take the post. After serving one term, the senator retired to his home in Bloomington, where he died on June 26, 1886, at seventy-one. "David Davis did a great thing for this country when he went to the National Convention in 1860 to direct the campaign in the interest of his old friend Lincoln. When Lincoln was nominated, David Davis went to bed for the first time in six days," read his obituary in the *New York Sun*.

* * *

To this day, historians debate whether Davis and his cohorts made deals to secure the nomination. Less than a week after the convention, the Washington correspondent of the *New-York Tribune* recorded that Lincoln had explicitly barred his supporters from doing so: "It is known here, that on the night preceding the nomination, a letter was received from him at Chicago, expressly forbidding any combinations looking to his selection, and declaring in the strongest terms, that he would not consent to be the candidate, except as the free choice of a majority of the Convention." Certainly, Lincoln wrote as if he felt unencumbered by promises. Many who see Lincoln as a cut above grubby politicians still have difficulty regarding him as the beneficiary of shenanigans in Chicago and political trading in smoke-filled rooms, even though he was involved in logrolling from the early days of his political career in the Illinois legislature.

Arguing against that view is the testimony of allies of Edward Bates and Simon Cameron, the strong memories of Joseph Medill and Henry Clay Whitney, and the letters that Lincoln operatives wrote to the candidate from Chicago arguing patronage pacts would be required. Matilda Gresham, wife of a later secretary of state, insisted that Davis had promised a cabinet seat to Indiana's Caleb B. Smith. "That the pledge was made I have heard from Judge Davis's own lips. That it was kept, everybody knows, for Caleb B. Smith became the first Secretary of the Interior in Mr. Lincoln's Cabinet." Certainly, deals for patronage and position were at the very heart of president-making in the nineteenth century, if not to this day. And even if Lincoln objected, the pragmatic and problem-solving Davis was on the ground deciding what needed to be done to win his friend's nomination. In early 1861, Montgomery Blair complained that Lincoln, in forming his cabinet, had "suffered himself to be seduced by a grateful & unsuspicious heart into early commitments which he has had too much pride upon the point of honor involved in promises—although made by others—to revoke." Surely, he was referring, at the very least, to Cameron. While

Leonard Swett initially wrote to a friend, "No pledges have been made, no mortgages executed," Swett later spoke to a fellow lawyer "of his labors with Cameron; of the promises he made Pennsylvania on behalf of Mr. Lincoln, and of the subsequent difficulty he encountered in persuading Mr. Lincoln to carry out the contracts, or 'bargains,' as Mr. Lincoln called them."

James Parton, in an essay published two years after Lincoln's assassination (and almost instant deification), argued that the trading in Chicago was extensive. "There is a general impression that Abraham Lincoln was a kind of innocent lamb, who was elected and reelected without any agency of his own," Parton observed. The reality was very different. "Abraham Lincoln was not only a politician but a keen, able, and closely calculating politician. Were not the leading members of his cabinet—Seward, Chase, Cameron, Bates, (and Mr. Dayton, his Minister to France,) the chief competitors in the convention of 1860? And was it not the timely withdrawal of some of them, and the partial withdrawal of others, which secured his nomination? Does the reader suppose that there was no connection between these appointments and the change of votes in the convention? If the reader does suppose this, it is himself who is the innocent lamb."

In desperately offering public positions with time running out in May 1860, Davis and Swett might well have pledged more than they could deliver. Years later, at a dinner party at the summer lakeside home of Chicago soap mogul N. K. Fairbank, Davis frankly told Chicago lawyer Wirt Dexter that Lincoln's men had secured the support of delegates by "making promises to bring them into line. Sometimes the promises overlapped a little." Dexter gently suggested, "You must have prevaricated somewhat?"

"PREVARICATED?" Davis replied. "Prevaricated, Brother Dexter? We lied, lied like hell."

Though the Union had been victorious, Lincoln left behind a country facing terrible challenges. The South's economy was in ruins. Some four million African American slaves had to be employed, educated, and integrated into a free society if they were to become full citizens. With white Southerners fearing violence, destitution, and the loss of their remaining political power, this proved an ugly and agonizing process. They employed brutality and abused the voting rights of black men to retain their control. Though America adopted constitutional amendments to strike down slavery and secure constitutional rights for former slaves, the battle for equal justice continued well into the twentieth century. In many ways, the struggle continues. Yet African Americans did lift themselves up, defying prejudice, shouldering the responsibilities of citizenship, rising to leadership roles in every realm, and immeasurably enriching their nation.

Some observers, looking back, thought what happened at the Wigwam in Chicago in May 1860 was something of a miracle. While the delegates there understood some of Lincoln's strengths, journalist Isaac H. Bromley argued, they could not possibly have conceived how incredibly well suited this complex man was for the hard struggle ahead. The men at the Wigwam were "unconscious instruments of a Higher Power," Bromley believed. "They had nominated the plain, every-day, story-telling, mirth-provoking Lincoln of the hustings; the husk only of the Lincoln of history. It took four fearful years to give the event its true relations and right proportions, and it was not until the veil was drawn by an assassin's hand that the real Lincoln was revealed."

Acknowledgments

It has been one of the greatest privileges of my life to immerse myself in the world of Abraham Lincoln, whose humanity, integrity, and courage shine forth no matter how earnestly one searches for his flaws. I am grateful to people who made this possible.

My first debt of gratitude must be to my father, Robert Achorn, who gave me the greatest gift I think I ever received as a boy: Bruce Catton's three-volume *Centennial History of the Civil War*. Catton's beautiful prose, his mastery of storytelling, and his eye for compelling detail moved me greatly. His accounts of the 1860 Democratic and Republican national conventions especially have stayed with me for decades, certainly informing this work.

I am forever grateful to Gordon S. Wood for his friendship and conversation, and especially for his brilliant insights into the young country that shaped Lincoln.

Frank J. Williams, former chief justice of the Rhode Island Supreme Court and founder of the Lincoln Forum, encouraged me to make this attempt, then read the manuscript and made many suggestions for improvement.

Michael Burlingame, president of the Abraham Lincoln Association, and author or editor of many books I found essential—including his massive, unexpurgated Lincoln biography, available through the

Knox College website—generously read the entire manuscript, prevented some missteps, and improved it in myriad ways.

Jeffrey Ludwig, education director of the must-see Seward House Museum in Auburn, New York, scanned the manuscript under a very tight schedule and made much-appreciated suggestions for improvement.

Any errors that stubbornly survived are, of course, mine.

I found Walter Stahr's magnificent *Seward: Lincoln's Indispensable Man* immensely helpful, in both pointing to original sources in his voluminous research and shaping my understanding of the stature and greatness of the man. Stephen Boothroyd, an expert on nineteenth-century train travel, helped me better understand the "race" to the Chicago convention, including the switching of locomotives without stopping the train. Susan M. Haake, curator of the Lincoln Home National Historic Site, in Springfield, Illinois, shared her insights about the way the house looked in 1860. Sylvia Hasenkopf, president of the Cairo (New York) Historical Society, guided me to Thurlow Weed's birthplace and the haunts of his boyhood, with the assistance of Cairo town historican Robert Uzzilia. I am grateful for help from experts, past and present, at the Abraham Lincoln Presidential Library, in Springfield, and the David Davis Mansion and the McLean County Museum of History, in Bloomington, Illinois. The Library of Congress's digitized Abraham Lincoln Papers collection was, of course, invaluable. Those of us looking back at the political conventions of 1860 will always owe a particular debt to Murat Halstead of the *Cincinnati Commercial*, who covered them with unflagging energy, intelligence, and panache.

Karen Potter, who boldly earned her master's degree in history at seventy, tracked down leads for me until illness led to her untimely death during this project. I miss her keenly and could never thank her sufficiently for her kindness, friendship, humor, and support.

J. William Middendorf II, former secretary of the navy and U.S. ambassador to the European Union, helped inform my judgments about the cabinet-level politics that went into Lincoln's nomination. Llewellyn King, the executive producer and host of PBS's *White House Chronicle*, was greatly encouraging. I am also grateful for the opportunities I had to glean insights about practical politics from former Rhode Island House Speaker Nicholas Mattiello and attorney Mark Ryan, a former colleague and executive at the *Providence Journal*.

I have had the great fortune now to work twice with a wonderful editor at Grove Atlantic, George Gibson, whose wisdom and artistry made the book much stronger. Thanks also to Assistant Editor Emily Burns. Alicia Burns's close copy editing saved me from many an embarrassment.

I am grateful too for the help of my agents Lisa Adams and David Miller at the Garamond Agency, who have now steered four of my books to successful publication. Author Ken Dooley was always supportive. John Arnold helped me with myriad questions about IT, interspersed with essential discussions about the Beatles. Several other friends kept me sane during crazy times over the last few years, most notably Helen and Jim Glover, Todd Johnson, and my sister Susan Achorn.

In writing this book, I thought often about the country we are leaving behind for the young, including our grandchildren Jacee and Ramona. Exploring the events of one week in May 1860 renewed my sense of how fate, or Providence, has stepped in at critical times to rescue the United States and its ideals from destruction. I send this volume out with deep love for the nation that the Founders created, and that Abraham Lincoln was able to sustain, through a new birth of freedom.

Special thanks to my wife, Valerie. She graciously accompanied me on my travels, including to Chicago, Central Illinois, St. Louis, Auburn, Niagara Falls, and the birthplaces of Horace Greeley and Thurlow Weed, as I mulled this book. I read every chapter aloud to her, which helped immeasurably in improving the clarity, sound, and pacing of the writing. When she couldn't wait to hear what happened next, I concluded I was on the right track. I could not have written this without her love, faith, and support. To her *The Lincoln Miracle* is dedicated.

Illustration Credits

Image credits for the insert section are as follows:

Image 1.1: National Portrait Gallery, Smithsonian Institution; gift of Marvin Sadik.

Image 2.1: Brady-Handy photograph collection, Library of Congress, Prints and Photographs Division, LC-BH82-5006 A [P&P].

Image 2.2: Library of Congress, Prints and Photographs Division, LC-BH82-5251 A [P&P].

Image 2.3: Abraham Lincoln Presidential Library and Museum.

Image 3.1: Library of Congress, Prints and Photographs Division, LC-BH83-45 [P&P].

Image 3.2: *Transactions of the Illinois State Historical Society for the Year 1928.*

Image 3.3: Chicago History Museum, ICHi-064454; Charles R. Clark, photographer.

Image 4.1: Chicago History Museum, ICHi-002001.

Image 4.2: Library of Congress, Prints and Photographs Division, Illus. in AP2.H32 1860 (Case Y) [P&P].

Image 5.1: Library of Congress, Prints and Photographs Division, LOT 14043-2, no. 991 [P&P].

Image 5.2: Brady-Handy photograph collection, Library of Congress, Prints and Photographs Division, LC-BH82-4505 A [P&P].

Image 6.1: Library of Congress, Prints and Photographs Division, LC-B813-1599 B [P&P].

Image 6.2: Library of Congress, Prints and Photographs Division, LC-B813-1747 B [P&P].

Image 6.3: Library of Congress, Prints and Photographs Division, LC-B813-1741 A [P&P].

Image 6.4: Library of Congress, Prints and Photographs Division, LC-BH82-5052 B [P&P].

Image 7.1: Library of Congress, Prints and Photographs Division, LOT 13301, no. 232 [P&P].

Image 7.2: *Woman's Work in the Civil War: A Record of Heroism, Patriotism and Patience*, by L.P. Brockett and Mary C. Vaughn (Philadelphia: Zeigler, McCurdy & Co., 1867).

Image 7.3: U.S. National Archives, #527435.

Image 8.1: Library of Congress, Geography and Map Division, G4104.C6A3 1857.P3.

Image 8.2: Library of Congress, Prints and Photographs Division, Illus. in AP2.L52 1856 (Case Y) [P&P].

Image 8.3: Amon Carter Museum of American Art, Fort Worth, Texas (1970.189).

Image 9.1: University of Iowa Libraries, Special Collections Department.

Image 10.1: Boston Public Library, #13_05_000727.

Image 10.2: American Antiquarian Society.

Image 10.3: Smithsonian American Art Museum. The Ray Austrian Collection, gift of Beatrice L. Austrian, Caryl A. Austrian, and James A. Austrian

Image 11.1: Library of Congress, Prints and Photographs Division, PGA - Currier & Ives—Impending crisis (A size) [P&P].

Image 12.1: Library of Congress, Prints and Photographs Division, PRES FILE - Lincoln, Abraham—Portraits—Meserve no. 22 [item] [P&P].

Image 13.1: National Park Service.

Image 13.2: Library of Congress, Prints and Photographs Division, Unprocessed in PR 13 CN 1972:018 [item] [P&P].

Image 13.3: National Park Service.

Image 14.1: Library of Congress, Prints and Photographs Division, PH - Whipple (J.), no. 1 (A size) [P&P].

Image 15.1: Library of Congress, Prints and Photographs Division, PGA - Currier & Ives—National game . . . (B size) [P&P].

Image 16.1: Library of Congress, Prints and Photographs Division, PGA - Rease—Union must . . . (B size) [P&P].

Bibliography

Collections

Abraham Lincoln Papers, Library of Congress, Manuscript Division

Blair Family Papers, Library of Congress

David & Sarah Davis Family Correspondence, Illinois Wesleyan University

E. B. Washburne Papers, Library of Congress

The Ida M. Tarbell Collection, Allegheny College Pelletier Library

John Mather Austin Journals 1832–1877, Andover-Harvard Theological Library, Harvard Divinity School, Cambridge, MA

Salmon P. Chase Papers, Library of Congress

Seward Family Archives, University of Rochester

Newspapers and Periodicals

Adams Sentinel (Gettysburg, PA)

Alexandria (VA) *Gazette*

Alleghenian (Ebensburg, PA)

Alton (IL) *Weekly Telegraph*

Anti-Slavery Bugle (Lisbon, OH)

Atchison (KS) *Daily Champion*

Boston Evening Transcript

Brandon (VT) *Gazette*

Brooklyn Daily Eagle

Buffalo Daily Courier

Buffalo Evening News

Buffalo Morning Express

Buffalo Weekly Express
Burlington (IA) *Weekly Hawk-Eye*
Burlington (VT) *Daily Times*
Cadiz (OH) *Sentinel*
Charleston (SC) *Mercury*
Chicago Democrat
Chicago Journal
Chicago Press and Tribune
Chicago Sunday Times-Herald
Chicago Tribune
Cincinnati Commercial
Cincinnati Daily Gazette
Cincinnati Daily Press
Cincinnati Enquirer
Cleveland Daily Leader
Congressional Globe
Daily American Organ (Washington, DC)
Daily Democrat and News (Davenport, IA)
Daily Evening Express (Lancaster, PA)
Daily Exchange (Baltimore)
Daily Milwaukee News
Daily Missouri Republican (St. Louis, MO)
Daily Nashville (TN) *Patriot*
Daily Pantagraph (Bloomington, IL)
Davenport (IA) *Daily Gazette*
Detroit Free Press
Douglass Monthly
Elyria (OH) *Independent Democrat*
Erie (PA) *Observer*
Evening Star (Washington, DC)
Fayetteville (NC) *Observer*
Franklin Repository and Transcript (Chambersburg, PA)
Fremont (OH) *Weekly Journal*
Grand Haven (MI) *News*
Harper's Weekly
Hartford (CT) *Daily Courant*
Holmes County Farmer (Millersburg, OH)
Illinois Citizen (Danville, IL)

Illinois State Journal (Springfield, IL)
Indianapolis Daily Journal
Janesville (WI) *Daily Gazette*
La Grange (MS) *Weekly National American*
Lancaster (PA) *Examiner*
Lewistown (PA) *Gazette*
Liberator (Boston)
Lima (OH) *Weekly Gazette*
Los Angeles Times
Louisville Daily Courier
Missouri Democrat (St. Louis, MO)
Montgomery (AL) *Weekly Advertiser*
Nebraska State Journal (Lincoln, NE)
New Bern (NC) *Daily Progress*
New Orleans Bee
New York Daily Herald
New York Log Cabin
New York Sun
New York Times
New-York Tribune
North Iowa Times (McGregor, IA)
North Star (Danville, VT)
Oregon Argus (Oregon City, OR)
Our Constitution (Urbana, IL)
Peoria (IL) *Transcript*
Philadelphia Inquirer
Philadelphia Press
Pittsburgh Daily Post
Plymouth (IN) *Democrat*
Portland (ME) *Evening Express*
Poughkeepsie (NY) *Journal*
Racine (WI) *Advocate*
Racine (WI) *Daily Journal*
Racine (WI) *Democrat*
Raleigh (NC) *Register*
The Republic: A Monthly Magazine of American Literature, Politics & Art
Richmond (VA) *Dispatch*
Rock Island (IL) *Argus*

St. Joseph (MO) *Weekly Free Democrat*

St. Louis Daily Globe-Democrat

San Francisco Call

Saturday Evening Express (Lancaster, PA)

Spirit of Democracy (Woodsfield, OH)

Syracuse (NY) *Daily Courier and Union*

Urbana (IL) *Union*

Wabash Express (Terre Haute, IN)

Weekly Atchison (KS) *Champion*

Weekly Mississippian (Jackson, MS)

Weekly Ottumwa (IA) *Courier*

Weekly Pioneer and Democrat (St. Paul, MN)

Western Railroad Gazette (Chicago)

Wheeling (VA) *Daily Intelligencer*

White Cloud Kansas Chief (Abilene, KS)

Wisconsin State Journal (Madison, WI)

Yonkers (NY) *Examiner*

Magazine Articles

Basler, Roy P. "James Quay Howard's Notes on Lincoln." *Abraham Lincoln Quarterly*, December 1947.

Bromley, Isaac H. "Historic Moments: The Nomination of Lincoln." *Scribner's Magazine*, November 1893.

Casdorph, Paul Douglas. "The Bogus Texas Delegation to the 1860 Republican National Convention." *Southwestern Historical Quarterly* 65, no. 4 (April 1962): 480–86.

Clark, Mary King. "Lincoln's Nomination as Seen by a Young Girl from New York." *Putnam's Magazine*, February 1909.

Clason, A. W. "The Split at Charleston in 1860." *Magazine of American History*, November 1886.

Currey, J. Seymour. "Mr. Lincoln's Visit to Waukegan in 1860." *Journal of the Illinois State Historical Society*, April 1911–January 1912.

Davis, Reuben. "Speech of Hon. Reuben Davis, of Mississippi, in the House of Representatives, December 8, 1859." *Congressional Globe*.

Davis, Stephen M. "'Of the Class Denominated Princely': The Tremont House Hotel." *Chicago History*, Spring 1982.

Douglas, Stephen A. "The Dividing Line Between Federal and Local Authority. Popular Sovereignty in the Territories." *Harper's Magazine*, September 1859.

Dudley, Thomas H. "The Inside Facts of Lincoln's Nomination." *Century Magazine* 40 (1890).

Elliff, John T. "Views of the Wigwam Convention: Letters from the Son of Lincoln's 1856 Candidate." *Journal of the Abraham Lincoln Association* 31, no. 2 (Summer 2010): 1–11.

Herriott, F. I. "The Conference in the Deutsches Haus, Chicago, May 14–15, 1860." *Transactions of the Illinois State Historical Society for the Year 1928* (Springfield, IL: Phillips Bros., 1928).

———. "Memories of the Chicago Convention of 1860." *Annals of Iowa*, October 1920.

"Horace White," *Journal of the Illinois State Historical Society*, October 1916.

Illinois Scrapbook. "The 'Ups and Downs' of the Windy City." *Journal of the Illinois State Historical Society*, March 1948.

Keith, Elbridge G. "A Paper on the National Republican Convention of 1860." *University of Illinois Bulletin*, May 15, 1904.

Lamb, Martha J. "Thurlow Weed's Home in New York City." *Magazine of American History*, January 1888.

Luthin, Reinhard H. "Indiana and Lincoln's Rise to the Presidency." *Indiana Magazine of History* 38, no. 4 (December 1942): 385–405.

———. "Pennsylvania and Lincoln's Rise to the Presidency." *Pennsylvania Magazine of History and Biography* 67, no. 1 (January 1943).

Mires, Austin. "Jesse Applegate, of Umpqua Valley, Oregon, and the Part He Played in the First Nomination of Abraham Lincoln—a Bit of Unwritten History." *Congressional Record: Proceedings and Debates of the Second Session of the Seventieth Congress of the United States of America*, February 26–March 4, 1929.

Olden, Peter H. "Anton C. Hesing: The Rise of a Chicago Boss." *Journal of the Illinois State Historical Society* 35, no. 3 (1942): 260–87.

Parton, James. "Chicago." *Atlantic Monthly*, March 1867.

———. "Past Presidential Nominations, Part IV." *Northern Monthly*, October 1867.

Robeson, George F. "John Johns of Webster County." *The Palimpsest*, November 1924.

Schwartz, Thomas F., and Kim M. Bauer. "Unpublished Mary Todd Lincoln." *Journal of the Abraham Lincoln Association* 17, no. 2 (Summer 1996).

Scott, Leslie M. "Oregon's Nomination of Lincoln." *Quarterly of the Oregon Historical Society*, September 1916.

Staudenraus, P. J. "'The Empire City of the West'—A View of Chicago in 1864." *Journal of the Illinois State Historical Society* 56, no. 2 (Summer 1963): 340–49.

Stevens, Lucia A. "Growth of Public Opinion in the East in Regard to Lincoln Prior to November, 1860." In *Transactions of the Illinois State Historical Society for the Year 1906* (Springfield, Illinois: Illinois State Journal).

Swett, Leonard Herbert. "Leonard Swett." In *Transactions of the McLean County Historical Society* 2 (Bloomington, Illinois: McLean County Historical Society, 1903).

Van Deusen, Glyndon G. "Thurlow Weed's Analysis of William H. Seward's Defeat in the Republican Convention of 1860." *Mississippi Valley Historical Review* 34, no. 1 (June 1947): 101–04.

Books

Adams, Charles Francis. *An Autobiography* (Boston: Houghton Mifflin, 1916).

Adams, Henry. *The Education of Henry Adams* (Washington, DC, self-published, 1907).

Arnold, Isaac N. *The Life of Abraham Lincoln* (Chicago: Jansen, McClurg, 1885).

Baringer, William. *Lincoln's Rise to Power* (Boston: Little, Brown, 1937).

Bates, Edward. *The Diary of Edward Bates, 1859–1866*. Edited by Howard K. Beale (Washington, DC: United States Government Printing Office, 1933).

Baxter, Maurice G. *Orville H. Browning: Lincoln's Friend and Critic* (Bloomington: Indiana University Press, 1957).

Beecher, Henry Ward. *Eyes and Ears* (Boston: Ticknor and Fields, 1862).

Blaine, James G. *Twenty Years of Congress: From Lincoln to Garfield*. 2 vols. (Norwich, CT: Henry Bill, 1884).

Brooks, Noah. *Abraham Lincoln and the Downfall of American Slavery* (New York: G. P. Putnam's Sons, 1895).

Brooks, Noah. *Washington in Lincoln's Time* (New York: Century, 1895).

Bross, William. "Extracted from 'What I Remember of Early Chicago.'" In *Reminiscences of Chicago During the Forties and Fifties* (Chicago: Lakeside Press, 1913).

Brown, John. *The Life and Letters of John Brown: Liberator of Kansas, and Martyr of Virginia*. Edited by F. B. Sanborn (Boston: Roberts Brothers, 1891).

Browning, Orville H. *The Diary of Orville Hickman Browning*. Edited by Theodore Calvin Please and James G. Randall. 2 vols. (Springfield: Illinois State Historical Library, 1927).

Brownlow, William Gannaway. *Sketch of Parson Brownlow, and His Speeches at the Academy of Music and Cooper Institute, New York, May, 1862* (New York: E. D. Barker, 1862).

Burlingame, Michael. *Abraham Lincoln: A Life*. Vol. 1 (Baltimore: Johns Hopkins University Press, 2008).

Burlingame, Michael, ed. *Abraham Lincoln: The Observations of John G. Nicolay and John Hay* (Carbondale: Southern Illinois University Press, 2021).

Burlingame, Michael. *An American Marriage: The Untold Story of Abraham Lincoln and Mary Todd* (New York: Pegasus, 2021).

Burlingame, Michael, ed. *At Lincoln's Side: John Hay's Civil War Correspondence and Selected Writings* (Carbondale: Southern Illinois University Press, 2000).

Burlingame, Michael. *The Inner World of Abraham Lincoln* (Urbana: University of Illinois Press, 1997).

Cain, Marvin R. *Lincoln's Attorney General Edward Bates of Missouri* (Columbia: University of Missouri Press, 1965).

Carlyle, Thomas, and Ralph Waldo Emerson. *The Correspondence of Thomas Carlyle and Ralph Waldo Emerson, 1834–1872*. 2 vols. (London: Chatto & Windus, 1883).

Carpenter, Francis Bicknell. *Six Months at the White House with Abraham Lincoln* (New York: Hurd and Houghton, 1866).

Carr, Clark E. *The Illini: A Story of the Prairies* (Chicago: A. C. McClurg, 1908).

Carwardine, Richard. *Lincoln's Sense of Humor* (Carbondale: Southern Illinois University Press, 2017).

Catton, Bruce. *The Centennial History of the Civil War*. Vol. 1, *The Coming Fury* (Garden City, NY: Doubleday, 1961).

Catton, Bruce. *This Hallowed Ground: A History of the Civil War* (Garden City, NY: Doubleday, 1956).

Clay, Cassius M. *The Life of Cassius Marcellus Clay: Memoirs, Writings, and Speeches*. 2 vols. (Cincinnati: J. Fletcher Brennan, 1886).

Cook, Frederick Francis. *Bygone Days in Chicago: Recollections of the 'Garden City' of the Sixties* (Chicago: A. C. McClurg, 1910).

Cook, Robert. *Civil War America: Making a Nation, 1848–1877* (London: Routledge, 2003).

Croffut, William A. *An American Procession, 1855–1914: A Personal Chronicle of Famous Men* (Boston: Little, Brown, 1931).

Davis, J. McCan. *How Abraham Lincoln Became President* (Springfield, IL: The Illinois Company, 1909).

Derby, J. C. *Fifty Years Among Authors, Books and Publishers* (New York: G. W. Carleton, 1884).

Doster, William E. *Lincoln and Episodes of the Civil War* (New York: G. P. Putnam's Sons, 1915).

Douglas, Stephen A. *Remarks of the Hon. Stephen A. Douglas, on Kansas, Utah, and the Dred Scott Decision* (Chicago: Daily Times, 1857).

Douglass, Frederick. *The Frederick Douglass Papers, Series One: Speeches, Debates, and Interviews*. Vol. 2, *1847–54*. Edited by John Blassingame (New Haven: Yale University Press, 1982).

Duis, E. *The Good Old Times in McLean County, Illinois* (Bloomington, IL: Leader Publishing, 1874).

Ecelbarger, Gary. *The Great Comeback* (New York: St. Martin's Press, 2008).

Eckley, Robert S. *Lincoln's Forgotten Friend Leonard Swett* (Carbondale: Southern Illinois University Press, 2012).

Flint, Henry M. *Life of Stephen A. Douglas, United States Senator from Illinois. With His Most Important Speeches and Reports* (New York: Derby & Jackson, 1860).

Foster, Lillian. *Way-Side Glimpses, North and South* (New York: Rudd & Carlton, 1860).

Freeman, Joanne B. *The Field of Blood: Violence in Congress and the Road to Civil War* (New York: Farrar, Straus & Giroux, 2018).

Fuess, Claude M. *Carl Schurz: Reformer* (New York: Dodd, Mead, 1932).

Gale, Edwin O. *Reminiscences of Early Chicago and Vicinity* (Chicago: Fleming H. Revell, 1902).

Gienapp, William E. *The Origins of the Republican Party, 1852–1856* (New York: Oxford University Press, 1987).

Good, Timothy S. *Lincoln for President: An Underdog's Path to the 1860 Republican Nomination* (Jefferson, NC: McFarland, 2009).

Greeley, Horace: *Horace Greeley's Jokes* (New York: Journeymen Printers' Co-operative, 1872).

Greeley, Horace. *Recollections of a Busy Life* (New York: J. B. Ford, 1869).

Gresham, Matilda. *Life of Walter Quintin Gresham, 1832–1895*. 2 vols. (Chicago: Rand, McNally, 1919).

Hale, William Harlan. *Horace Greeley: Voice of the People* (New York: Harper & Brothers, 1950).

Halstead, Murat. *Three Against Lincoln: Murat Halstead Reports the Caucuses of 1860*. Edited by William B. Hesseltine (Baton Rouge: Louisiana State University Press, 1960).

Hamlin, Charles Eugene. *The Life and Times of Hannibal Hamlin* (Cambridge, MA: Riverside Press, 1899).

Harper, Robert S. *Lincoln and the Press* (New York: McGraw-Hill, 1951).

Hay, John. *Inside Lincoln's White House: The Complete Civil War Diary of John Hay*. Edited by Michael Burlingame and John R. T. Ettlinger (Carbondale: Southern Illinois University Press, 1999).

Hayes, Melvin L. *Mr. Lincoln Runs for President* (New York: Citadel, 1960).

Hayes, Rutherford Birchard. *Diary and Letters of Rutherford Birchard Hayes: Nineteenth President of the United States* (Columbus: Ohio State Archeological and Historical Society, 1922).

Herndon, William H., and Jesse William Weik. *Herndon's Lincoln: The True Story of a Great Life*. 3 vols. (Chicago: Belford-Clarke, 1889).

Hesseltine, William B., and Rex G. Fisher, eds. *Trimmers, Trucklers & Temporizers: Notes of Murat Halstead from the Political Conventions of 1856* (Madison: State Historical Society of Wisconsin, 1961).

Hill, Alice Polk. *Tales of the Colorado Pioneers* (Denver, CO: Pierson & Gardner, 1884).

Hollister, O. J. *Life of Schuyler Colfax* (New York: Funk & Wagnalls, 1886).

Holzer, Harold. *Father Abraham: Lincoln and His Sons* (Honesdale, PA: Calkins Creek, 2011).

Hone, Philip. *The Diary of Philip Hone*. Edited by Bayard Tuckerman. 2 vols. (New York: Dodd, Mead, 1889).

Humphrey, Zephaniah Moore. *Memorial Sketch. Zephaniah Moore Humphrey and Five Selected Sermons* (Philadelphia: J. B. Lippincott, 1883).

Hunt, Harry Draper. *Hannibal Hamlin of Maine, Lincoln's First Vice-President* (Syracuse, NY: Syracuse University Press, 1969).

Jenkins, John S. *The Life of John Caldwell Calhoun* (Auburn, NY: John E. Beardsley, 1850).

Johannsen, Robert W. *Stephen A. Douglas* (Urbana: University of Illinois Press, 1997).

Johnston, Richard Malcolm, and William Hand Browne. *Life of Alexander H. Stephens* (Philadelphia: J. B. Lippincott, 1884).

Karamanski, Theodore J. *Rally 'Round the Flag: Chicago and the Civil War* (Chicago: Nelson-Hall, 1993).

King, Willard L. *Lincoln's Manager: David Davis* (Cambridge, MA: Harvard University Press, 1960).

Koerner, Gustave. *Memoirs of Gustave Koerner, 1809–1896*. Edited by Thomas J. McCormack. 2 vols. (Cedar Rapids, IA: Torch Press, 1909).

Krisher, Trudy. *Fanny Seward: A Life* (Syracuse, NY: Syracuse University Press, 2015).

Lamon, Ward H. *The Life of Abraham Lincoln; from His Birth to his Inauguration as President* (Boston: James R. Osgood, 1872).

Lincoln, Abraham. *The Collected Works of Abraham Lincoln*. Edited by Roy P. Basler. 8 vols. (New Brunswick, NJ: Rutgers University Press, 1953–55).

Lincoln, Abraham, and Stephen Douglas. *Political Debates between Hon. Abraham Lincoln and Hon. Stephen A. Douglas in the Celebrated Campaign of 1858, in Illinois* (Columbus, OH: Follett, Foster, 1860).

Linder, Usher F. *Reminiscences of the Early Bench and Bar of Illinois* (Chicago: Chicago Legal News Co., 1879).

Linn, William Alexander. *Horace Greeley: Founder and Editor of the New York Tribune* (New York: D. Appleton, 1903).

Livermore, Mary A. *My Story of the War: A Woman's Narrative* (Hartford, CT: A. D. Worthington, 1889).

Livermore, Mary A. *The Story of My Life* (Hartford, CT: A. D. Worthington, 1897).

Logan, Mrs. John A. *Reminiscences of a Soldier's Wife: An Autobiography* (New York: Scribners, 1926).

Luebke, Frederick C., ed. *Ethnic Voters and the Election of Lincoln* (Lincoln: University of Nebraska Press, 1971).

Luthin, Reinhard H. *The First Lincoln Campaign* (Gloucester, MA: Peter Smith, 1944).

McCall, Samuel W. *Thaddeus Stevens* (Boston: Houghton Mifflin, 1909).

McClure, Alexander K. *"Abe" Lincoln's Yarns and Stories* (Henry Neil, 1904).

McClure, Alexander K. *Abraham Lincoln & Men of War-Times*, 4th ed. (Philadelphia: Times Publishing, 1892).

Merriam, George S. *The Life and Times of Samuel Bowles*. 2 vols. (New York: Century, 1885).

Miller, Donald L. *City of the Century: The Epic of Chicago and the Making of America* (New York: Simon & Schuster, 1996).

Monaghan, Jay. *The Man Who Elected Lincoln* (Indianapolis: Bobbs-Merill, 1956).

National Democratic Executive Committee. *Proceedings of the Conventions at Charleston and Baltimore* (Washington, DC, 1860).

Neely, Mark E. *The Last Best Hope of Earth: Abraham Lincoln and the Promise of America* (Cambridge, MA: Harvard University Press, 1993).

Nichols, T. L. *Forty Years of American Life*. 2 vols. (London: John Maxwell, 1864).

Nicolay, John G. *An Oral History of Abraham Lincoln: John G. Nicolay's Interviews and Essays*. Edited by Michael Burlingame (Carbondale: Southern Illinois University Press, 2006).

Nicolay, John G. *With Lincoln in the White House: Letters, Memoranda, and Other Writings of John G. Nicolay, 1860–1865*. Edited by Michael Burlingame (Carbondale: Southern Illinois University Press, 2000).

Nicolay, John G., and John Hay. *Abraham Lincoln: A History*. 10 vols. (New York: Century, 1890).

Oldroyd, Osborn H., ed. *The Lincoln Memorial: Album Immortelles* (New York: G. W. Carlton, 1882).

Page, Edwin L. *Abraham Lincoln in New Hampshire* (Boston: Houghton Mifflin, 1929).

Parton, James. *The Life of Horace Greeley: Editor of the New York Tribune* (Boston: Fields, Osgood, 1869).

Pike, James S. *First Blows of the Civil War* (New York: American News Company, 1879).

Pratt, Harry E. "David Davis, 1815–1886," PhD diss. (University of Illinois, 1930).

Pratt, Harry E. *The Personal Finances of Abraham Lincoln* (Chicago: Lakeside Press, 1943).

Procter, Addison G. *Lincoln and the Convention of 1860: An Address Before the Chicago Historical Society, April 4, 1918* (Chicago: Chicago Historical Society, 1918).

Ray, P. Orman. *The Convention That Nominated Lincoln* (Chicago: University of Chicago Press, 1916).

Republican National Convention. *Proceedings of the Republican National Convention Held at Chicago, May 16, 17 and 18, 1860* (Albany, NY: Weed, Parsons, 1860).

Rhode Island Historical Society. *Slavery in Rhode Island*. Publications of the Rhode Island Historical Society. New Series. Vol. 2 (Providence, RI, 1894).

Rice, Allen Thorndike, ed. *Reminiscences of Abraham Lincoln by Distinguished Men of His Time* (New York: Harper & Brothers, 1909).

Sandburg, Carl. *Abraham Lincoln: The Prairie Years* (New York: Blue Ribbon Books, 1926).

Schurz, Carl. *The Reminiscences of Carl Schurz*. 3 vols. (New York: McClure, 1907).

Schurz, Carl. *Speeches, Correspondence and Political Papers of Carl Schurz*. Edited by Frederic Bancroft. 6 vols. (New York: G. P. Putnam's Sons, 1913).

Schwartz, Bernard. *A History of the Supreme Court* (New York: Oxford University Press, 1993).

Seward, Frederick W. *Seward at Washington as Senator and Secretary of State*, 2 vols. (New York: Derby and Miller, 1891).

Seward, William H. *Early Days and College Life of the Late William H. Seward*. Collections of the Cayuga County Historical Society (Auburn, New York: Knapp, Peck & Thomson, 1889).

Seward, William H. *The Works of William H. Seward*. Edited by George E. Baker. 5 vols. (Boston: Houghton, Mifflin, 1887).

Seward, William H., and Frederick W. Seward. *Autobiography of William H. Seward, 1801–1834* (New York: D. Appleton, 1877).

Sheahan, James W., and George P. Upton. *The Great Conflagration. Chicago: Its Past, Present and Future* (Philadelphia: Union Publishing, 1871).

Smiley, David L. *Lion of White Hall: The Life of Cassius M. Clay* (Madison: University of Wisconsin Press, 1962).

Smith, William Ernest. *The Francis Preston Blair Family in Politics*. 2 vols. (New York: McMillan, 1933).

Stahr, Walter. *Seward: Lincoln's Indispensable Man* (New York: Simon & Schuster, 2012).

Stampp, Kenneth M. *The Causes of the Civil War* (New York: Touchstone, 1986).

Stanton, Henry B. *Random Recollections* (New York: Harper & Brothers, 1887).

Stillman, William James. *The Autobiography of a Journalist*. 2 vols. (Boston: Houghton, Mifflin, 1901).

Stirling, James. *Letters from the Slave States* (London: John W. Barker & Son, 1857).

Stoddard, Henry Luther. *Horace Greeley: Printer, Editor, Crusader* (New York: G. P. Putnam's Sons, 1946).

Stovall, Pleasant A. *Robert Toombs: Statesman, Speaker, Soldier, Sage* (New York: Cassell, 1892).

Strong, George Templeton. *The Diary of George Templeton Strong*. Edited by Allan Nevins and Milton Halsey Thomas. 4 vols. (New York: Macmillan, 1952).

Sumner, Charles. *Speech of Hon. Charles Sumner in the Senate of the United States, 19th and 20th May, 1856* (Boston: John P. Jewett, 1856).

Swett, Leonard. "Memorial Address: The Life and Services of David Davis." In *Proceedings of the Illinois State Bar Association, at its Tenth Annual Meeting, Held at the City of Springfield, January 11 and 12, 1887, with the Constitution, Officers, Standing Committees and Roll of Members for the Year 1887* (Springfield, IL: H. W. Rokker, 1887).

Taylor, John M. *William Henry Seward: Lincoln's Right Hand* (Washington: Brassly's, 1991).

Thoreau, Henry D. *Walden; or, Life in the Woods* (Boston: Ticknor and Fields, 1854).

Turner, Justin G., and Linda Leavitt Turner. *Mary Todd Lincoln: Her Life and Letters* (New York: Alfred A. Knopf, 1972).

Twain, Mark. *Roughing It* (Hartford, CT: American Publishing Company, 1872).

Van Deusen, Glyndon G. *Horace Greeley: Nineteenth-Century Crusader* (New York: Hill and Wang, 1953).

Van Deusen, Glyndon G. *Thurlow Weed: Wizard of the Lobby* (Boston: Little, Brown, 1947).

Van Evrie, John H. Introduction to *The Negro's Place in Nature: A Paper Read Before the London Anthropological Society*, by James Hunt (New York: Van Evrie, Horton, 1864).

Villard, Henry. *Memoirs of Henry Villard, Journalist and Financier, 1835–1900*. 2 vols. (Boston: Houghton, Mifflin, 1904).

Wakefield, Sherman Day. *How Lincoln Became President* (New York: Wilson-Erickson, 1916).

Wallace, Irving. *The Fabulous Showman: The Life and Times of P. T. Barnum* (New York: Knopf, 1959).

Wallace, Joseph. *Sketch of the Life and Public Services of Edward D. Baker* (Springfield, Illinois: Journal Company, 1870).

Weed, Thurlow. *Autobiography of Thurlow Weed*. Edited by Harriet A. Weed and Thurlow Weed Barnes. 2 vols. (Boston: Houghton, Mifflin, 1884).

Weik, Jesse W. *The Real Lincoln: A Portrait* (Boston: Houghton Mifflin, 1922).

Welles, Gideon. *Lincoln and Seward* (New York: Sheldon, 1874).

Wentworth, John. *Early Chicago, Fort Dearborn, An Address* (Chicago: Fergus, 1881).

White, Horace. *The Life of Lyman Trumbull* (Boston: Houghton Mifflin, 1913).

Whitney, Henry Clay. *Life on the Circuit with Lincoln: with Sketches of Generals Grant, Sherman and McClellan, Judge Davis, Leonard Swett, and Other Contemporaries* (Boston: Estes and Lauriat, 1892).

Whitney, Henry Clay. *Lincoln the Citizen (February 12, 1809 to March 4, 1861)* (New York: Current Literature, 1907).

Whitney, Thomas R. *A Defence of the American Policy* (New York: De Witt & Davenport, 1856).

Williams, Robert C. *Horace Greeley: Champion of American Freedom* (New York: New York University Press, 2006).

Wilson, Douglas L., and Rodney O. Davis, eds., *Herndon on Lincoln: Letters* (Urbana: University of Illinois Press, 2016).

Wilson, Douglas L., and Rodney O. Davis, eds. *Herndon's Informants: Letters, Interviews, and Statements about Abraham Lincoln* (Urbana: University of Illinois Press, 1997).

Wilson, Rufus Rockwell. *Intimate Memories of Lincoln: A Companion Volume to Lincoln Among His Friends* (Elmira, NY: Primavera Press, 1945).

Wilson, Rufus Rockwell. *Lincoln Among His Friends: A Sheaf of Intimate Memories* (Caldwell, ID: Caxton Printers, 1942).

Wood, James Playsted. *One Hundred Years Ago: American Writing of 1848* (New York: Funk & Wagnalls, 1948).

Woollen, William Wesley. *Biographical and Historical Sketches of Early Indiana* (Indianapolis: Hammond & Co., 1883).

Online Sources

Burlingame, Michael. *Abraham Lincoln: A Life*. Unedited Manuscript. Accessed January 31, 2022. https://www.knox.edu/about-knox/lincoln-studies-center/burlingame-abraham-lincoln-a-life.

United States Congress. *The Congressional Globe: Containing the Debates and Proceedings of the First Session of the Thirty-Sixth Congress: Also of the Special Session of the Senate*, book, 1860; Washington, D.C. Accessed April 15, 2022. https://digital.library.unt.edu/ark:/67531/metadc30806/.

Notes

ABBREVIATIONS USED IN THE NOTES

ALP: Abraham Lincoln Papers, Library of Congress, Manuscript Division

CW: Lincoln, Abraham. *The Collected Works of Abraham Lincoln.* Edited by Roy P. Basler. 8 vols. (New Brunswick, NJ: Rutgers University Press, 1953–55)

DFC: David & Sarah Davis Family Correspondence, Illinois Wesleyan University

The man that thinks: William H. Herndon and Jesse William Weik, *Herndon's Lincoln: The True Story of a Great Life*, 3 vols. (Chicago: Belford-Clarke, 1889), 2:375.

It is my belief: Leonard Swett, "Memorial Address: The Life and Services of David Davis," in *Proceedings of the Illinois State Bar Association, at its Tenth Annual Meeting, Held at the City of Springfield, January 11 and 12, 1887, with the Constitution, Officers, Standing Committees and Roll of Members for the Year 1887* (Springfield, IL: H. W. Rokker, 1887), 79.

Without Chicago we: *Chicago Tribune*, March 25, 1867.

Had Abraham Lincoln died: Mark E. Neely, *The Last Best Hope of Earth: Abraham Lincoln and the Promise of America* (Cambridge, MA: Harvard University Press, 1993), vii.

PROLOGUE: Such a Sucker as Me

1 *The young reporter stood*: Vignette drawn from Henry Villard, *Memoirs of Henry Villard, Journalist and Financier, 1835–1900*, 2 vols. (Boston: Houghton, Mifflin, 1904), 1:96–97.

2 *"Lincoln has made"*: David Davis to Julius Rockwell, Danville, IL, October 26, 1858, DFC.

2 *"If the* Irish*"*: David Davis to William Perrin Walker, Bloomington, IL, November 16, 1840, DFC.

3 *"I must say frankly"*: Villard, *Memoirs*, 1:93.

4 *"lay floating"*: Herndon and Weik, *Herndon's Lincoln*, 3:587.

CHAPTER 1: Unconscious Strength

9 *"sluggish river . . . winds"*: *Atchison* (KS) *Daily Champion*, May 24, 1868.

9 *"greasy to the touch"*: James W. Sheahan and George P. Upton, *The Great Conflagration. Chicago: Its Past, Present and Future* (Philadelphia: Union Publishing, 1871), 46.

9 *"in color and consistency"*: James Parton, "Chicago," *Atlantic Monthly*, March 1867, 336.

11 *"too much of a candidate"*: Leonard Swett to Josiah Drummond, May 27, 1860, *Portland* (Maine) *Evening Express*, July 22, 1891.

11 *"the humblest of all"*: CW, 4:53.

11 *That morning's edition*: *Harper's Weekly*, May 12, 1860.

11 *"Our delegates have left"*: Rutherford B. Hayes to S. Birchard, May 11, 1860, Rutherford Birchard Hayes, *Diary and Letters of Rutherford Birchard Hayes: Nineteenth President of the United States* (Columbus: Ohio State Archeological and Historical Society, 1922), 555.

11 *bustling Tremont House*: Stephen M. Davis, "'Of the Class Denominated Princely': The Tremont House Hotel," *Chicago History*, Spring 1982, 26–36.

12 *"calling out"*: Lillian Foster, *Way-Side Glimpses, North and South* (New York: Rudd & Carlton, 1860), 123.

12 *"the most ultra"*: *New York Daily Herald*, May 5, 1860.

13 *"Such a motley"*: Foster, *Way-Side Glimpses*, 123.

13 *"This town is a"*: Harold Holzer, *Father Abraham: Lincoln and His Sons* (Honesdale, PA: Calkins Creek, 2011), 63.

13 *preconvention guide*: *New York Daily Herald*, May 5, 1860.

13 *After Davis reached*: Swett, "Memorial Address," 79.

14 *"If I were asked"*: Swett, "Memorial Address," 80.

14 *had "that way"*: Henry Clay Whitney, *Life on the Circuit with Lincoln: with Sketches of Generals Grant, Sherman and McClellan, Judge Davis, Leonard Swett, and Other Contemporaries* (Boston: Estes and Lauriat, 1892), 734.

15 *"He had a big head"*: Mrs. John A. Logan, *Reminiscences of a Soldier's Wife: An Autobiography* (New York: Scribners, 1926), 377.

15 *"He is the only"*: Swett, "Memorial Address," 81.

15 *"two Negro Boys"*: Willard L. King, *Lincoln's Manager: David Davis* (Cambridge, MA: Harvard University Press, 1960), 4.

15 *"honest in their motives"*: Ibid., 51.

16 *"to support a wife"*: David Davis to William Perrin Walker, Lenox, MA, May 1, 1835, DFC.

17 *"Lincoln is the best"*: David Davis to William Perrin Walker, Decatur, IL, May 4, 1844, DFC.

17 *"Mrs. Lincoln is not"*: David Davis to Sarah W. Davis, Springfield, IL, August 2, 1846, DFC.

17 *"wishes to loom"*: David Davis to Sarah W. Davis, Springfield, IL, August 8, 1847, DFC.

17 *"The Salary"*: David Davis to William Perrin Walker, Paris, IL, May 16, 1848, DFC.

17 *"Arriving at the county"*: Swett, "Memorial Address," 76.

18 *"He had not great"*: Whitney, *Life on the Circuit*, 55.

18 *"shunned and abhorred all"*: Ibid., 58.

18 *"knew just enough law"*: Swett, "Memorial Address," 76.

18 *"Before this court"*: Ibid., 78.

18 *"This court is loaded"*: Harry E. Pratt, "David Davis, 1815–1886," PhD diss. (University of Illinois, 1930), 58.

18 *"If any of the lawyers"*: Ibid., 76.

18 *"Judge Davis was"*: *Urbana* (Illinois) *Union*, April 15, 1858.

18 *"be confined in"*: Swett, "Memorial Address," 77.

19 *"the quail whistled"*: Leonard Herbert Swett, "Leonard Swett," in *Transactions of the McLean County Historical Society* 2 (Bloomington, IL: McLean County Historical Society, 1903), 339.

19 *"This thing of travelling"*: David Davis to Sarah W. Davis, Bloomington, IL, July 16, 1848, DFC.

19 *"perhaps the hardest"*: David Davis to Sarah W. Davis, Clinton, IL, April 24, 1851, DFC.

19 *"old pioneer" told*: E. Duis, *The Good Old Times in McLean County, Illinois* (Bloomington, IL: Leader Publishing, 1874), 287–88.

20 *"In my opinion"*: Douglas L. Wilson and Rodney O. Davis, eds., *Herndon's Informants: Letters, Interviews, and Statements about Abraham Lincoln* (Champaign: University of Illinois Press, 1997), 349.

20 *"and would read and study"*: Herndon and Weik, *Herndon's Lincoln*, 2:308–09.

21 *"a bobtail sack coat"*: King, *Lincoln's Manager*, 74.

21 *"I dread your going"*: Sarah W. Davis to David Davis, Lenox, MA, May 19, 1848, DFC.

21 *"But instead of"*: David Davis to Julius Rockwell, Bloomington, IL, February 10, 1841, DFC.

21 *"I am going to be"*: Michael Burlingame, *An American Marriage: The Untold Story of Abraham Lincoln and Mary Todd* (New York: Pegasus, 2021), 82.

21 *"I mean to make"*: Ibid.

21 *"the most ambitious"*: Ibid.

21 *"had the fire"*: Ibid.

21 *"the most reticent"*: Wilson and Davis, *Herndon's Informants*, 348.

21 *"done to whistle off sadness"*: Ibid., 350.

22 *"Lincoln had no spontaneity"*: Ibid., 348.

22 *"Lincoln hadn't the manhood"*: Ibid., 349.

22 *"Rough, uncouth and unattractive"*: *Illinois Citizen* (Danville, IL), May 29, 1850.

23 *"There is not much"*: CW, 3:511.

23 *"not in battle"*: Autobiographical account, Ibid, 3:511–12.

25 *"The panther's scream"*: CW, 1:386.

25 *"I used to be"*: *Chicago Sunday Times-Herald*, August 25, 1895.

25 *"Say to him that"*: CW, 2:97.

25 *"I am now the most"*: CW, 1:229.

25 *"His melancholy dripped"*: Herndon and Weik, *Herndon's Lincoln*, 3:588.

26 *"She insisted"*: Henry Clay Whitney, *Lincoln the Citizen (February 12, 1809 to March 4, 1861)* (New York: Current Literature, 1907), 150.

26 *"the saddest man"*: Wilson and Davis, *Herndon's Informants*, 266.

26 *"I never saw"*: Michael Burlingame, *The Inner World of Abraham Lincoln* (Urbana: University of Illinois Press, 1997), 244.

27 *"Dickey," Lincoln said*: Alexander K. McClure, *"Abe" Lincoln's Yarns and Stories* (Henry Neil, 1904), 73–74.

27 *"Lincoln is undoubtedly"*: *Our Constitution* (Urbana, IL), July 4, 1857.

27 *"Twenty-two years ago"*: CW, 2:382–83.

28 *"A house divided"*: Ibid., 461.

29 *"It gave me"*: CW, 3:339.

29 *"The path had been"*: John Hay, *Inside Lincoln's White House: The Complete Civil War Diary of John Hay*, ed. Michael Burlingame and John R. T. Ettlinger (Carbondale: Southern Illinois University Press, 1999), 244.

29 *"Lincoln has only"*: *Daily Missouri Republican* (St. Louis, MO), May 15, 1860.

29 *"You damned fools"*: Jay Monaghan, *The Man Who Elected Lincoln* (Indianapolis, IN: Bobbs-Merill, 1956), 36.

30 *bedecked its building:* William Baringer, *Lincoln's Rise to Power* (Boston: Little, Brown, 1937), 213.

CHAPTER 2: The Irrepressible Conflict

32 *"The beauty and importance"*: *Chicago Press and Tribune*, May 29, 1860.

32 *"Join the Wide Awakes!"*: *Yonkers* (NY) *Examiner*, November 15, 1860.

32 *"all of the rowdies"*: *Fayetteville* (NC) *Observer*, October 25, 1860.

32 *"that he will refrain"*: *Chicago Press and Tribune*, May 29, 1860.

33 *"I have yet to"*: *Louisville Daily Courier*, November 26, 1856.

34 *"where caucuses were held"*: Martha J. Lamb, "Thurlow Weed's Home in New York City," *Magazine of American History*, January 1888, 3.

34 *"exceedingly busy"*: *New York Daily Herald*, May 5, 1860.

34 *"clamorous as crows"*: Montgomery Blair to his wife, Chicago, May 11, 1860, Blair Family Papers, Library of Congress.

35 *"heard that a neighbor"*: Thurlow Weed, *Autobiography of Thurlow Weed*, 2 vols., ed. Harriet A. Weed and Thurlow Weed Barnes (Boston: Houghton, Mifflin, 1884), 1:12–13.

35 *"That was night"*: Ibid., 1:20.

36 *"We communed together"*: Ibid., 1:74.

36 *"During the winter"*: Ibid., 97.

36 *that he had "commenced life"*: *Alleghenian* (Ebensburg, PA), May 31, 1860.

36 *"I saw in him"*: Ibid., 423.

37 *"Weed is very much"*: William H. Seward and Frederick W. Seward, *Autobiography of William H. Seward, 1801–1834* (New York: D. Appleton, 1877), 166.

37 *"never uttered an expression"*: Ibid., 28.

38 *"William, unlike most"*: William H. Seward, "Early Days and College Life of the Late William H. Seward," *Collections of the Cayuga County Historical Society* (Auburn, New York: Knapp, Peck & Thomson, 1889), 26.

38 *"so vast, so splendid"*: Seward, *Autobiography*, 29.

38 *"again embarked on"*: Seward, *Autobiography*, 374.

38 *"God bless Thurlow"*: J. C. Derby, *Fifty Years Among Authors, Books and Publishers* (New York: G. W. Carleton, 1884), 58.

39 *"that our race"*: Seward, *Autobiography*, 386–87.

39 *Seward on one trip*: Ibid., 395.

40 *"This right hand drops"*: William H. Seward, *The Works of William H. Seward*, ed. George E. Baker, 5 vols. (Boston: Houghton, Mifflin, 1887), 3:388.

40 *including $11,000*: John M. Taylor, *William Henry Seward: Lincoln's Right Hand* (Washington: Brassly's, 1991), 55.

40 *"Without your aid"*: Seward, *Autobiography*, 642.

40 *"late Dictator"*: Ibid., 648.

40 *"my first last"*: Walter Stahr, *Seward: Lincoln's Indispensable Man* (New York: Simon & Schuster, 2012), 105.

40 *"abandon the"*: Ibid., 102.

41 *"a lone voice was"*: John Mather Austin, July 4, 1846, Journals 1832–1877, Andover-Harvard Theological Library, Harvard Divinity School, Cambridge, MA.

41 *"exhausted in mind"*: Stahr, *Seward*, 105.

41 *On his way home*: Weed, *Autobiography*, 1:602–603.

41 *"as a fanatic"*: *Weekly Mississippian* (Jackson, MS), March 2, 1849.

42 *"excepting the people"*: Stahr, *Seward*, 119.

42 *By the 1850s*: Robert Cook, *Civil War America: Making a Nation, 1848–1877* (London: Routledge, 2003), 15.

43 *"We cannot, in our"*: Seward, *Works*, 1:67.

44 *"given me much pain"*: Stahr, *Seward*, 127.

44 *"Yes, in spite of you"*: Ibid., 131.

44 *"blighted the hopes"*: George Templeton Strong, *The Diary of George Templeton Strong*, ed. Allan Nevins and Milton Halsey Thomas, 4 vols. (New York: Macmillan, 1952), 2:19.

44 *"Standing upon the rock"*: *New York Times*, April 1, 1853.

44 *"good volumes to"*: Stahr, *Seward*, 141.

45 *"thinks your speech"*: Ibid., 143.

45 *"whipped or coaxed"*: Ibid., 151.

45 *"to express not so"*: Weed, *Autobiography*, 2:231.

46 *"We do not want"*: William E. Gienapp, *The Origins of the Republican Party, 1852–1856* (New York: Oxford University Press, 1987), 311.

46 *"did not think anybody"*: Stahr, *Seward*, 163.

46 *"unfaithful to a purpose"*: Ibid., 170.

46 *"It is an irrepressible"*: Seward, *Works*, 4:56.

47 *"guns firing, bells ringing"*: Frederick William Seward to Francis Miller, May 8, 1859, Seward Family Archives, University of Rochester.

47 *"higher advancement"*: Frederick W. Seward, *Seward at Washington as Senator and Secretary of State*, 2 vols. (New York: Derby and Miller, 1891), 1:405.

47 *violent westerly gales, snowstorms*: *New-York Tribune*, December 29, 1859.

48 *"Be much happier"*: Quoted in the *Burlington* (VT) *Daily Times*, January 2, 1860.

48 *"God bless you all"*: Stahr, *Seward*, 181.

49 *"sectional candidate" elected*: *The Congressional Globe: Containing the Debates and Proceedings of the First Session of the Thirty-Sixth Congress: Also of the Special Session of the Senate* (Washington, D.C., 1860), Appendix, 36.

49 *"lady correspondent"*: Quoted in *Cadiz* (OH) *Sentinel*, May 16, 1860.

49 *"threw off restraint"*: Henry Adams, *The Education of Henry Adams* (Washington, self-published, 1907), 88–89.

50 *"If I succeed in"*: *Congressional Globe*, op. cit., 69.

50 *"until I read in Europe"*: *New York Times*, August 18, 1860.

50 *"remove all the obstacles"*: Henry B. Stanton, *Random Recollections* (New York: Harper & Brothers, 1887), 212.

50 *"not unlike a straw"*: Murat Halstead, *Three Against Lincoln: Murat Halstead Reports the Caucuses of 1860*, ed. William B. Hesseltine (Baton Rouge: Louisiana State University Press, 1960), 119.

51 *"a small, nervous mouth"*: *New York Times*, February 10, 1860.

51 *"frequently fumbled with"*: Noah Brooks, *Washington in Lincoln's Time* (New York: Century, 1895), 28.

51 *"Nothing can be sweeter"*: *New York Times*, February 10, 1860.

51 *"as an act of sedition"*: *New York Daily Herald*, March 1, 1860.

51 *"So calm in temper"*: *New-York Tribune*, March 1, 1860.

51 *"ashamed that I am"*: Michael Burlingame, *Abraham Lincoln: A Life*, vol. 1 (Baltimore: Johns Hopkins University Press, 2008), 604.

52 *"As he handed me"*: Stanton, *Random Recollections*, 213.

52 *"grand wire-puller"*: *Brandon* (VT) *Gazette*, May 31, 1860.

52 *"He is a great man"*: George S. Merriam, *The Life and Times of Samuel Bowles*, 2 vols. (New York: Century, 1885), 1:302.

52 *March 5 letter*: Weed, *Autobiography*, 2:260–61.

52 *"Not a single move"*: *New Bern* (NC) *Daily Progress*, April 30, 1860.

53 *"Seward is Weed"*: Gideon Welles, *Lincoln and Seward* (New York: Sheldon, 1874), 23.

53 *"Weed seems to be"*: *New York Daily Herald*, May 16, 1860.

53 *"hopelessly split"*: *Cincinnati Daily Gazette*, May 14, 1860.

53 *"the crowning opportunity"*: Weed, 2:260.

CHAPTER 3: Temple of Liberty

54 The Hidden Hand: *Chicago Press and Tribune*, May 12, 1860.

54 *"a decided sensation"*: *Chicago Press and Tribune*, January 6, 1860.

54 *"And still they came"*: *Chicago Press and Tribune*, May 14, 1860.

55 *"fixed by good judges"*: Ibid.

55 *"ample enough to"*: Ibid.

56 *"a large, cheap"*: Ibid.

56 *"with boyish enthusiasm"*: Elbridge G. Keith, "A Paper on the National Republican Convention of 1860," *University of Illinois Bulletin*, May 15, 1904, 3.

57 *"against it forever, and"*: *Chicago Press and Tribune*, May 19, 1860.

57 *In 1831, when Chicago*: Donald L. Miller, *City of the Century: The Epic of Chicago and the Making of America* (New York: Simon & Schuster, 1996), 56–58.

57 *named after big men*: John Wentworth, *Early Chicago, Fort Dearborn, An Address* (Chicago: Fergus, 1881), 68.

57 *"their eyes wild"*: Miller, *City of the Century*, 63–64.

58 *William W. Boyington, whose majestic*: *Chicago Press and Tribune*, May 14, 1860.

58 *"rough and unplaned"*: Ibid., 1860.

58 *"any others who"*: *Chicago Press and Tribune*, May 9, 1860.

58 *"A bevy of ladies"*: Quoted in *Janesville* (WI) *Daily Gazette*, May 11, 1860.

59 *"miserable abortion"*: *Daily Milwaukee News*, May 19, 1860.

59 *"when for the first"*: *Chicago Press and Tribune*, May 14, 1860.

59 *"The sight was a"*: *Chicago Journal*, May 14, 1860.

59 *"must have been one"*: Bruce Catton, *The Centennial History of the Civil War*, vol. 1, *The Coming Fury* (Garden City, NY: Doubleday, 1961), 49.

59 *"worthy object of pride"*: *Chicago Press and Tribune*, May 14, 1860.

60 *"tax private liberality"*: *Chicago Press and Tribune*, May 12, 1860.

60 *"Come up and put"*: *Chicago Journal*, May 12, 1860.

60 *Robert Wilson Patterson*: *Chicago Tribune*, March 1, 1894.

61 *general assembly in 1857*: *Chicago Tribune*, June 9, 1857.

61 *"Oh God, we pray"*: *Chicago Press and Tribune*, May 14, 1860.

61 *"a happy tribute"*: Ibid.

61 *famous for a horror*: Bruce Catton, *This Hallowed Ground: A History of the Civil War* (Garden City, NY: Doubleday, 1956), 6.

62 *"a mistress . . . who"*: Charles Sumner, *Speech of Hon. Charles Sumner in the Senate of the United States, 19th and 20th May, 1856* (Boston: John P. Jewett, 1856), 9.

62 *"I rejoice in the"*: *Chicago Press and Tribune*, May 14, 1860.

62 *Republican "treasure"*: *Cleveland Daily Leader*, June 15, 1860.

63 *message of William Lloyd Garrison*: David L. Smiley, *Lion of White Hall: The Life of Cassius M. Clay* (Madison: University of Wisconsin Press, 1962), 21.

63 *"the convention of gallant"*: *Chicago Press and Tribune*, May 14, 1860.

63 *"the ladies for their"*: Ibid.

64 *"It is now twenty-five"*: Ibid.

65 *"Its bustle and life"*: *Louisville Daily Courier*, November 26, 1856.

66 *purchase seventy-five acres*: Robert W. Johannsen, *Stephen A. Douglas* (Urbana: University of Illinois Press, 1997), 335–36.

66 *"As I was sitting still"*: Carl Schurz, *The Reminiscences of Carl Schurz*, 3 vols. (New York: McClure, 1907), 2:43–44.

67 *"The river is choked"*: Henry Ward Beecher, *Eyes and Ears* (Boston: Ticknor and Fields, 1862), 100.

67 *"no sooner discharge"*: P. J. Staudenraus, "'The Empire City of the West'—A View of Chicago in 1864," *Journal of the Illinois State Historical Society* 56, no. 2 (Summer 1963): 344.

67 *"green and black slime"*: Mary A. Livermore, *The Story of My Life* (Hartford, CT: A. D. Worthington, 1897), 457–58.

68 *"aggregation of vileness"*: Frederick Francis Cook, *Bygone Days in Chicago: Recollections of the 'Garden City' of the Sixties* (Chicago: A. C. McClurg, 1910), 158–59.

68 *terrifying visitation of cholera*: Miller, *City of the Century*, 122–23.

69 *"When you walk"*: James Stirling, *Letters from the Slave States* (London: John W. Barker & Son, 1857), 2–3.

69 *"sidewalk oglers"*: "The 'Ups and Downs' of the Windy City," *Journal of the Illinois State Historical Society*, March 1948, 82–83.

70 *"It was no uncommon"*: William Bross, "Extracted from 'What I Remember of Early Chicago,'" in *Reminiscences of Chicago During the Forties and Fifties* (Chicago: Lakeside Press, 1913), 18–19.

70 *Norman B. Judd*: *Chicago Tribune*, November 12, 1878; *Wisconsin State Journal* (Madison, WI), November 12, 1878.

70 *"a contemptible fellow"*: King, *Lincoln's Manager*, 108.

71 *"I am astonished"*: *Nebraska State Journal* (Lincoln, NE), April 15, 1881.

71 *"It seems to me"*: Ibid.

71 *"Any effort to put"*: CW, 3:355.

71 *"I find some of"*: Ibid., 3:509.

72 *show of "bravado"*: *New-York Tribune*, December 22, 1859.

72 *"selection of Chicago"*: *Spirit of Democracy* (Woodsfield, OH), December 28, 1859.

72 *hoarse from "hallooing"*: *Chicago Press and Tribune*, May 14, 1860.

73 *"He wore a 'knitted"*: George F. Robeson, "John Johns of Webster County," *Palimpsest*, November 1924, 425–27.

73 *"He is a live"*: *Burlington* (IA) *Weekly Hawk-Eye*, May 19, 1860. Ingersoll wrote under the nom de plume of Linkensale.

73 *"brief remarks that were"*: *Chicago Press and Tribune*, May 14, 1860.

74 *"poorly veiled under"*: Joseph Wallace, *Sketch of the Life and Public Services of Edward D. Baker* (Springfield, IL: Journal Company, 1870), 57.

74 *"the* honor *to his* memory": *Chicago Press and Tribune*, May 16, 1860.

74 *"a thin, angular man"*: *New York Daily Herald*, May 16, 1860.

74 *"ugliest man in Indiana"*: *Burlington* (IA) *Weekly Hawk-Eye*, May 26, 1860.

74 *"having traveled two hundred"*: *Chicago Press and Tribune*, May 14, 1860.

75 *"You embarrass me"*: Ibid.

CHAPTER 4: Star after Star

79 *"to open their hands"*: *Chicago Press and Tribune*, May 10, 1860.

80 *"The news to-night"*: *Chicago Press and Tribune*, May 9, 1860.

80 *"never omitted an opportunity"*: *Weekly Pioneer and Democrat* (Saint Paul, MN), January 3, 1860.

81 *"We do not wish"*: Johannsen, *Stephen A. Douglas*, 296.

81 *"sad and melancholy results"*: *Remarks of the Hon. Stephen A. Douglas, on Kansas, Utah, and the Dred Scott Decision* (Chicago: Daily Times, 1857), 11.

83 *"This is* fact, *unchanging"*: John H. Van Evrie, introduction to *The Negro's Place in Nature: A Paper Read Before the London Anthropological Society*, by James Hunt (New York: Van Evrie, Horton, 1864), 4.

84 *"cannot be destroyed"*: John S. Jenkins, *The Life of John Caldwell Calhoun* (Auburn, NY: John E. Beardsley, 1850), 423.

84 *"highly respected elder"*: Rhode Island Historical Society, *Slavery in Rhode Island*, Publications of the Rhode Island Historical Society, New Series, vol. 2 (Providence, RI, 1894), 143.

85 *"I will never surrender"*: Pleasant A. Stovall, *Robert Toombs: Statesman, Speaker, Soldier, Sage* (New York: Cassell, 1892), 78.

85 *"had for more than"*: Bernard Schwartz, *A History of the Supreme Court* (New York: Oxford University Press, 1993), 119.

86 *"noisy, brawling, roistering"*: Kenneth M. Stampp, *The Causes of the Civil War* (New York: Touchstone, 1986), 106.

86 *"The intolerance of"*: Ibid., 203–04.

86 *"an exhausted soil"*: Seward, *Autobiography*, 268.

87 *"the very worst enemies"*: Quoted in *Alabama Beacon* (Greensboro, AL), May 25, 1860.

87 *"shall fall into black"*: *Detroit Free Press*, April 8, 1860.

87 *"I am opposed to"*: *Political Debates between Hon. Abraham Lincoln and Hon. Stephen A. Douglas in the Celebrated Campaign of 1858, in Illinois* (Columbus, OH: Follett, Foster, 1860), 30.

87 *"I am not, nor"*: CW, 3:145–46.

88 *"beyond all doubt the"*: *New Orleans Bee*, May 21, 1860.

88 *"A reaction has begun"*: *New York Daily Herald*, April 10, 1860.

89 *The son of an Ohio*: *New York Times*, July 3, 1908.

89 *bottle of "private whiskey"*: Halstead, *Three Against Lincoln*, 4.

90 *"and talked of stormy"*: Ibid., 5.

90 *"There must be no"*: Ibid., 6.

91 *"She has now no"*: *Charleston Mercury*, April 16, 1860.

91 *"He is a compact"*: Halstead, *Three Against Lincoln*, 8.

91 *"with white spreads and"*: Ibid., 7–8.

91 *"They were full of"*: Ibid., 9.

92 *"on the platform that"*: Henry M. Flint, *Life of Stephen A. Douglas, United States Senator from Illinois. With His Most Important Speeches and Reports* (New York: Derby & Jackson, 1860), 216.

92 *"nor any power to"*: A. W. Clason, "The Split at Charleston in 1860," *Magazine of American History*, November 1886, 459.

93 *"the speech of the Convention"*: Halstead, *Three Against Lincoln*, 54.

93 *"Mr. Yancey is a"*: Ibid., 52.

93 *"Ours is the property"*: National Democratic Executive Committee, *Proceedings of the Conventions at Charleston and Baltimore* (Washington, 1860), 69.

93 *"put their hands on"*: Halstead, *Three Against Lincoln*, 54–56.

94 *SLAVES FOR SALE*: Ibid., 67.

94 *"with a curious mingling"*: Ibid., 68.

95 *"the Cincinnati swindle"*: Ibid., 72.

95 *"There was a shudder"*: Ibid., 83–84.

95 *"to join in fraternal"*: Ibid., 76.

95 *After adjournment that day:* Ibid., 86–87.

96 *When the convention reconvened*: Ibid., 88–89.

97 *Douglas received only 145 ½*: National Democratic Executive Committee, *Proceedings*, 141.

97 *Many delegates were coming around*: Halstead, *Three Against Lincoln*, 100–01.

98 *"that men will be"*: Richard Malcolm Johnston and William Hand Browne, *Life of Alexander H. Stephens* (Philadelphia: J. B. Lippincott, 1884), 355–56.

98 *"the Chicago Convention has"*: Halstead, *Three Against Lincoln*, 101.

98 *a crowd gathered*: *Chicago Press and Tribune*, May 15, 1860.

98 *"I neither feel mortified"*: John Brown, *The Life and Letters of John Brown: Liberator of Kansas, and Martyr of Virginia*, ed. F. B. Sanborn (Boston: Roberts Brothers, 1891), 594.

99 *"Something of the sturdy"*: Zephaniah Moore Humphrey, *Memorial Sketch. Zephaniah Moore Humphrey and Five Selected Sermons* (Philadelphia: J. B. Lippincott, 1883), 4.

99 *"the necessity of a"*: *Chicago Press and Tribune*, May 15, 1860.

CHAPTER 5: The Man in the White Coat

100 *"redolent with antediluvian": Brandon* (VT) *Gazette*, May 31, 1860.

100 *"His dilapidated hat"*: *Brooklyn Daily Eagle*, May 28, 1860.

101 *"a gangling, wispy-haired"*: Irving Wallace, *The Fabulous Showman: The Life and Times of P. T. Barnum* (New York: Knopf, 1959), 65.

101 *"is personally as placid"*: *Richmond* (VA) *Dispatch*, May 24, 1860.

101 *"I can write better"*: William Harlan Hale, *Horace Greeley: Voice of the People* (New York: Harper & Brothers, 1950), 85.

101 *"virtuous and refined"*: Announcement in *Log Cabin* (New York, NY), April 3, 1841.

101 *"public teacher"*: William Alexander Linn, *Horace Greeley: Founder and Editor of The New York Tribune* (New York: D. Appleton, 1903), 76.

102 *"Mr. Greeley, I like"*: Robert C. Williams, *Horace Greeley: Champion of American Freedom* (New York: New York University Press, 2006), 80.

102 *"Had God granted him"*: Strong, *Diary of George Templeton Strong*, 4:459.

102 *well over 200,000*: Linn, *Horace Greeley*, 70.

102 *"the right spiritual father"*: Thomas Carlyle and Ralph Waldo Emerson, *The Correspondence of Thomas Carlyle and Ralph Waldo Emerson, 1834–1872*, 2 vols. (London: Chatto & Windus, 1883), 2:234.

102 *"I undertook the task"*: James Parton, *The Life of Horace Greeley: Editor of the New York Tribune* (Boston: Fields, Osgood, 1869), v.

103 *"good load of delegates"*: *Cleveland Daily Leader*, May 14, 1860.

103 *"lugging a huge leather satchel"*: Whitney, *Lincoln the Citizen*, 288.

103 *twenty-three-year-old Frank Johnson*: *Chicago Tribune*, May 18, 1907; Leslie M. Scott, "Oregon's Nomination of Lincoln," *Quarterly of the Oregon Historical Society*, September 1916, 201–14.

104 *"he has empowered"*: *Oregon Argus* (Oregon City, OR), March 31, 1860.

104 *"I did not feel"*: Scott, "Oregon's Nomination," 205.

104 *Jesse Applegate*: Austin Mires, "Jesse Applegate, of Umpqua Valley, Oregon, and the Part He Played in the First Nomination of Abraham Lincoln—a Bit of Unwritten History," *Congressional Record: Proceedings and Debates of the Second Session of the Seventieth Congress of the United States of America*, February 26–March 4, 1929, 4810–11.

104 *"She worked," one resident recalled*: Parton, *The Life of Horace Greeley*, 37.

105 *"a natural fool"*: Ibid., 64.

105 *"The parting was a"*: Williams, *Horace Greeley*, 14–15.

106 *"I doubt if, in the"*: Parton, *The Life of Horace Greeley*, 90.

106 *"He came, at length"*: Ibid., 95.

107 *"because her fire"*: Williams, *Horace Greeley*, 47.

107 *"often said she wished"*: Hale, *Greeley: Voice of the People*, 119.

107 *"When beaten, as he"*: Henry Luther Stoddard, *Horace Greeley: Printer, Editor, Crusader* (New York: G. P. Putnam's Sons, 1946), 116.

108 *"with light hair and"*: Weed, *Autobiography*, 1:466.

108 *"the finest fellow"*: Williams, *Horace Greeley*, 45.

108 *"filth, squalor, rags, dissipation"*: Horace Greeley, *Recollections of a Busy Life* (New York: J. B. Ford, 1869), 145.

108 *"I am ever ready"*: Weed, *Autobiography*, 2:97.

109 *"The laws of Heaven"*: *New-York Tribune*, May 13, 1846.

109 *"The nation cannot afford"*: Marvin R. Cain, *Lincoln's Attorney General Edward Bates of Missouri* (Columbia: University of Missouri Press, 1965), 64.

109 *"Every word that [Greeley]"*: Weed, *Autobiography*, 2:148.

110 *"The usually travelled route"*: Robert S. Harper, *Lincoln and the Press* (New York: McGraw-Hill, 1951), 10–11.

110 *"the most thoroughly"*: James Playsted Wood, *One Hundred Years Ago: American Writing of 1848* (New York: Funk & Wagnalls, 1948), xxiii.

110 *"He won't let them"*: Frederick W. Seward, *Seward at Washington*, 1:92.

111 *"the* Times *is your special"*: Hale, *Greeley: Voice of the People*, 151.

111 *"the time and circumstances"*: Weed, *Autobiography*, 2:225.

111 *"It seems to me"*: Ibid., 2:277–81.

112 *"The Republican standard"*: Herndon and Weil, *Herndon's Lincoln*, 2:64.

113 *"What does* The*"*: CW, 2:430.

113 *"Who would know by"*: Williams, *Horace Greeley*, 200.

113 *"Greeley is not doing"*: Herndon and Weil, *Herndon's Lincoln*, 2:60.

113 *"Our business is war"*: John Wentworth to Abraham Lincoln, April 19, 1858, ALP.

113 *"Chocolate and morning journals"*: Greeley, *Recollections*, 372.

114 *"Friends, I have been"*: Villard, *Memoirs*, 1:124.

114 *"salting" a mine*: Alice Polk Hill, *Tales of the Colorado Pioneers* (Denver: Pierson & Gardner, 1884), 29–32.

114 *"Horace Greeley went over"*: Mark Twain, *Roughing It* (Hartford, CT: American Publishing Company, 1872), 153.

115 *"If some of you"*: Justin G. Turner and Linda Leavitt Turner, *Mary Todd Lincoln: Her Life and Letters* (New York: Alfred A. Knopf, 1972), 46.

116 *"Madame Bates"*: Quoted in *Detroit Free Press*, May 12, 1860.

116 *he was "old-fogish"*: Hale, *Greeley: Voice of the People*, 216.

116 *"fossil of the Silurian"*: Glyndon G. Van Deusen, *Horace Greeley: Nineteenth-Century Crusader* (New York: Hill and Wang, 1953), 242.

116 "a little old gentleman": William B. Hesseltine and Rex G. Fisher, eds., *Trimmers, Trucklers & Temporizers: Notes of Murat Halstead from the Political Conventions of 1856* (Madison: The State Historical Society of Wisconsin, 1961), 92.

116 *"The old fellow's big"*: Ibid., 103.

116 *"the ugliest man in"*: *Cincinnati Enquirer*, May 13, 1860.

117 *"the ultra Republicans"*: William Ernest Smith, *The Francis Preston Blair Family in Politics*, 2 vols. (New York: McMillan, 1933), 1:465.

117 *"the same clique"*: Herriott, F. I. "The Conference in the Deutsches Haus, Chicago, May 14–15, 1860," *Transactions of the Illinois State Historical Society for the Year 1928*, 115.

117 *"Who can believe that"*: *New York Daily Herald*, March 5, 1860.

118 *"hisses . . . as prominent"*: Ibid., March 9, 1860.

118 *"Devotion to the success"*: *New York Times*, April 21, 1860.

118 *"And that, considering"*: Edward Bates, *The Diary of Edward Bates, 1859–1866*, ed. Howard K. Beale (Washington, DC: United States Government Printing Office, 1933), 107.

119 *"There were crowds of"*: Halstead, *Three Against Lincoln*, 121.

119 *"'ye Old Fogie' Convention"*: *Oregon Argus* (Oregon City, OR), July 14, 1860.

119 *"kangaroo ticket, with all"*: William Gannaway Brownlow, *Sketch of Parson Brownlow, and His Speeches at the Academy of Music and Cooper Institute, New York, May, 1862* (New York: E. D. Barker, 1862), 23.

119 *"the Constitution as it is"*: *Baltimore Daily Exchange*, May 10, 1860.

119 *"With what face could"*: Halstead, *Three Against Lincoln*, 136.

120 *"harmonious" Democrats*: Ibid., 124.

120 *"are not demagogues"*: Quoted in *Louisville Daily Courier*, May 25, 1860.

120 *"This whole movement"*: Quoted in *Burlington* (IA) *Weekly Hawk-Eye*, May 19, 1860.

121 *"I could not be a"*: *Liberator* (Boston), May 18, 1860.

121 *"Every one knows"*: *Anti-Slavery Bugle* (Lisbon, OH), May 26, 1860.

121 *"We love liberty, equality"*: *Liberator* (Boston), May 18, 1860.

122 *"I tell you we shall"*: Smith, *Blair Family in Politics*, 1:468.

122 *"this was a church service"*: Horace Greeley, *Horace Greeley's Jokes* (New York: Journeymen Printers' Co-operative, 1872), 24–25.

123 *"shan't nominate Seward"*: Weed, *Autobiography*, 2:268–69.

123 *"when State after State"*: Quoted in James S. Pike, *First Blows of the Civil War* (New York: American News Company, 1879), 519.

123 *"Horace Greeley is a human"*: James Parton, "Past Presidential Nominations, Part IV," *Northern Monthly*, October 1867, 451.

124 *his "sharp voice"*: *New York Daily Herald*, May 16, 1860.

124 *"It would seem that"*: Quoted in *Rock Island* (IL) *Argus*, May 30, 1860.

124 *"Much as success is"*: Quoted in *New York Daily Herald*, May 16, 1860.

124 *"remarked . . . with evident"*: *Missouri Democrat* (St. Louis, MO), May 15, 1860.

125 *"orders to his faithful"*: *New York Daily Herald*, May 16, 1860.

CHAPTER 6: The Taste *Is* in My Mouth

127 *blue-eyed, auburn-haired*: Usher F. Linder, *Reminiscences of the Early Bench and Bar of Illinois* (Chicago: Chicago Legal News, 1879), 68.

127 *"But in reality we"*: John G. Nicolay, *An Oral History of Abraham Lincoln: John G. Nicolay's Interviews and Essays*, ed. Michael Burlingame (Carbondale: Southern Illinois University Press, 2006), 30.

127 *"by the arm with"*: Whitney, *Life on the Circuit*, 77–78.

128 *"Lincoln, what are you"*: Wilson and Davis, *Herndon's Informants*, 441–42.

128 *"your wife, whom I"*: Thomas F. Schwartz and Kim M. Bauer, "Unpublished Mary Todd Lincoln," *Journal of the Abraham Lincoln Association* 17, no. 2 (Summer 1996), 15.

128 *"Mrs. Lincoln was a"*: Rufus Rockwell Wilson, *Lincoln Among His Friends: A Sheaf of Intimate Memories* (Caldwell, ID: Caxton Printers, 1942), 96–99.

129 *some "aristocratic company"*: Wilson and Davis, *Herndon's Informants*, 692.

129 *"rough and cold" month*: Ibid., 718–19.

130 *Shortly after Lincoln delivered*: Whitney, *Life on the Circuit*, 78–80.

131 *"I have a decided"*: Osborn H. Oldroyd, ed., *The Lincoln Memorial: Album Immortelles* (New York: G. W. Carlton, 1882), 473–76.

132 *"putting Lincoln up for"*: Whitney, *Life on the Circuit*, 83.

132 *"that he felt like"*: *Cincinnati Commercial*, January 12, 1859.

132 *"His ambition was a"*: Herndon and Weik, *Herndon's Lincoln*, 2:375.

132 *"He had his burning"*: Douglas L. Wilson and Rodney O. Davis, eds., *Herndon on Lincoln: Letters* (Urbana: University of Illinois Press, 2016), 130.

133 *"I must, in candor"*: CW, 3:377.

133 *"I must say I do not"*: Ibid., 3:395.

133 *"consider whether it would"*: Ibid., 3:366.

133 *"I hate to see"*: Ibid., 2:320.

134 *"already damaging"*: Ibid., 3:384.

134 *"hedge against divisions"*: Ibid., 3:390–91.

135 *densely argued 18,000-word*: Stephen A. Douglas, "The Dividing Line Between Federal and Local Authority. Popular Sovereignty in the Territories," *Harper's Magazine*, September 1859, 519–37.

135 *"without a salutation"*: Michael Burlingame, ed., *At Lincoln's Side: John Hay's Civil War Correspondence and Selected Writings* (Carbondale: Southern Illinois University Press, 2000), 115–16.

135 *"a policy restricting the"*: CW, 3:407.

135 *"they must go back"*: Ibid., 3:424.

135 *"He is so put up by"*: Ibid., 3:410.

136 *"Send Abram Lincoln to"*: Thurlow Weed to Norman B. Judd, October 20, 1859, ALP.

136 *"What it means I don't"*: Norman B. Judd to Abraham Lincoln, October 21, 1859, ALP.

136 *"As to the ticket you"*: CW, 3:491.

137 *Lincoln got welcome news*: Ibid., 3:510.

137 *"It contains, perhaps"*: *Chicago Press and Tribune*, February 25, 1860.

137 *"No former effort in"*: Herndon and Weik, *Herndon's Lincoln*, 3:455.

138 *"They can't drive me"*: Smiley, *Lion of White Hall*, 164.

138 *"Lincoln's face brightened"*: Michael Burlingame, *Abraham Lincoln: A Life*, unedited manuscript (https://www.knox.edu/about-knox/lincoln-studies-center/burlingame-abraham-lincoln-a-life), 1592–93.

139 *"I was greatly disappointed"*: Noah Brooks, *Abraham Lincoln and the Downfall of American Slavery* (New York: G. P. Putnam's Sons, 1895), 186–87.

139 *"Go back to that old"*: CW, 3:522–50.

141 *"idea that slavery is right"*: Ibid., 4:17.

141 *"Seward was the great"*: Herndon and Weik, *Herndon's Lincoln*, 3:456.

141 *"You must get yourself"*: Horace White to Abraham Lincoln, February 10, 1860, ALP.

141 *"There was more difference"*: "Horace White," *Journal of the Illinois State Historical Society*, October 1916, 388–98.

142 *"'blew me up' tremendously"*: Lucia A. Stevens, "Growth of Public Opinion in the East in Regard to Lincoln Prior to November, 1860," in *Transactions of the Illinois State Historical Society for the Year 1906* (Springfield, IL: Illinois State Journal), 296–97.

142 *"a most corrupt liar"*: Quoted in *Rock Island* (IL) *Argus*, April 7, 1859.

143 *"whoring after Strange"*: Norman B. Judd to Abraham Lincoln, May 13, 1859, ALP.

143 *"Do like Seward does"*: Whitney, *Life on the Circuit*, 146.

143 *"you could not have"*: David Davis to Abraham Lincoln, April 23, 1860, ALP.

143 *"I am not in a position"*: CW, 3:517.

144 *"You saw what the"*: Norman B. Judd to Abraham Lincoln, February 21, 1860, ALP.

144 "*Look out for* prominence": John Wentworth to Abraham Lincoln, February 7, 1860.

144 "*He thinks I may*": Orville H. Browning, *The Diary of Orville Hickman Browning*, ed. Theodore Calvin Please and James G. Randall, 2 vols. (Springfield: Illinois State Historical Library, 1927), 1:395.

144 "*If he were ten years*": CW, 4:40.

144 "*It seems to me*": David Davis to Henry E. Dummer, February 20, 1860, Chicago Historical Society.

145 "*Lincoln himself entertained*": Whitney, *Life on the Circuit*, 72.

145 "*Well, gentlemen, let us*": J. Seymour Currey, "Mr. Lincoln's Visit to Waukegan in 1860," *Journal of the Illinois State Historical Society*, April 1911–January 1912, 182.

145 "*Lincoln was perfectly 'taken'*": Whitney, *Life on the Circuit*, 86–88.

146 "*Everyone who has seen*": *Chicago Press and Tribune*, May 5, 1860.

146 "*no greater exemption*": CW, 4:43.

146 "*Cannot a quiet combination*": Reinhard H. Luthin, "Pennsylvania and Lincoln's Rise to the Presidency," *Pennsylvania Magazine of History and Biography* 67, no. 2 (January 1943), 67.

146 "*the only person who*": Baringer, *Lincoln's Rise*, 207.

146 "*When urging your claims*": Lyman Trumbull to Abraham Lincoln, April 24, 1860, ALP.

147 "*The taste* is *in my mouth*": CW, 4:45–46.

148 "*My name is new*": Ibid., 4:34.

148 "*present Mr. Lincoln as*": James G. Blaine, *Twenty Years of Congress: From Lincoln to Garfield*, 2 vols. (Norwich, CT: Henry Bill, 1884), 1:168.

148 "*one or both*": CW, 4:46–47.

148 "*men who ought to*": Ibid., 4:47–48.

150 *lifted the gangly lawyer*: Wilson and Davis, *Herndon's Informants*, 462–63.

150 "*an old Democrat of*": *Illinois State Journal* (Springfield, IL), May 11, 1860.

150 "*How are you, Abe?*": J. McCan Davis, *How Abraham Lincoln Became President* (Springfield, IL: Illinois Company, 1909), 69.

151 "*We are here in*": Jesse K. Dubois to Abraham Lincoln, May 13, 1860, ALP.

151 "*can not enter the ring*": CW, 4:32.

152 "*keep cool under all*": Ibid., 4:49.

152 "*Don't stir them up*": Ibid., 4:44.

152 "*telling a Crowd now*": Mark W. Delahay to Abraham Lincoln, May 13, 1860, ALP.

152 "*we want all our deligates*": William Butler to Abraham Lincoln, May 14, 1860, ALP.

153 "*The pressure against him*": Herriott, "Deutsches Haus," 127–28.

153 "*we will do our best*": Jesse K. Dubois to Abraham Lincoln, May 13, 1860, ALP.

CHAPTER 7: River of Iron

157 *"Long John made his"*: Edward Hempstead to Elihu B. Washburne, May 14, 1860, E. B. Washburne Papers, Library of Congress.

157 *"the new and costly"*: *Chicago Times* quoted in *Rock Island* (IL) *Argus*, May 18, 1860.

157 *national news in 1857*: *Alexandria* (VA) *Gazette*, June 15, 1857.

158 *"our Brobdingnagian Mayor"*: *Western Railroad Gazette* (Chicago), May 19, 1860.

158 *two "monster trains"*: *Chicago Press and Tribune*, May 14, 1860.

159 *"of the richest silk"*: *Buffalo Weekly Express*, May 15, 1860.

159 *"that such bodies were"*: *Poughkeepsie* (NY) *Journal*, May 26, 1860.

160 *"By what mysterious power"*: CW, 2:10.

161 *"tall, dark, superbly built"*: Mary King Clark, "Lincoln's Nomination As Seen By a Young Girl from New York," *Putnam's Magazine*, February 1909, 536–38.

161 *"on a scale to match"*: T. L. Nichols, *Forty Years of American Life*, 2 vols. (London: John Maxwell, 1864), 1:400.

162 *"Niagara scenery possessed"*: *Chicago Press and Tribune*, May 15, 1860.

162 *"A hurried breakfast"*: *Poughkeepsie* (NY) *Journal*, May 26, 1860.

162 *"trial of speed"*: *Buffalo Daily Courier*, May 15, 1860.

162 *"It will be run through"*: *Chicago Press and Tribune*, May 14, 1860.

163 *"presented a beautiful"*: *Cleveland Daily Leader*, May 15, 1860.

163 *"The gaily decorated"*: *Chicago Press and Tribune*, May 16, 1860.

163 *"there were gathered the"*: *Wheeling* (VA) *Daily Intelligencer*, May 18, 1860.

163 *"gazed with amazement"*: *Chicago Press and Tribune*, May 16, 1860.

163 *"went merry as a"*: Ibid.

163 *"The whistle nearly blew"*: *New York Times*, May 18, 1860.

164 *"But man proposes and"*: *Chicago Press and Tribune*, May 16, 1860.

164 *"If I had not broken"*: *Buffalo Daily Courier*, May 15, 1860.

165 *"all heavily loaded"*: Ibid.

165 *"wonder of the world"*: *Poughkeepsie* (NY) *Journal*, May 26, 1860.

165 *"decorated everyone who"*: *New York Daily Herald*, May 19, 1860.

166 *"to see what a Massachusetts"*: *Detroit Free Press*, May 15, 1860.

167 *"The Michigan Central"*: *Cleveland Daily Leader*, May 21, 1860.

167 *"long lines of furrows"*: *Buffalo Daily Courier*, May 18, 1860.

167 *"They come, they come"*: *Buffalo Weekly Express*, May 15, 1860.

168 *"So harness the steam"*: *Chicago Press and Tribune*, May 15, 1860.

169 *"The eyes of the nation"*: *Franklin Repository and Transcript* (Chambersburg, PA), May 16, 1860.

169 *"along the whole line"*: *Chicago Press and Tribune*, May 30, 1860.

169 *"met always by crowds"*: Clark, "Lincoln's Nomination," 536.

169 *"and from farm houses"*: *Chicago Press and Tribune*, May 15, 1860.

170 *"Our train was obliged"*: *Buffalo Daily Courier*, May 18, 1860.

170 *"it was necessary to"*: *Cincinnati Daily Press*, May 29, 1860.

170 *On board, the passengers*: *Chicago Press and Tribune*, May 15, 1860.

170 *"less of that annoying"*: *Weekly Atchison* (KS) *Champion*, May 19, 1860.

171 *"If you will put yourself"*: *Chicago Tribune*, July 14, 1878.

172 *"saw a tall, gaunt"*: Swett, "Leonard Swett," 337.

172 *"In response to my"*: Wilson and Davis, *Herndon's Informants*, 731–32.

173 *"the great triumvirate"*: Whitney, *Life on the Circuit*, 67.

173 *"I know him as intimately"*: Leonard Swett to Josiah Drummond, May 27, 1860, *Portland* (ME) *Evening Express*, July 22, 1891.

173 *"very anxious to take"*: CW, 3:508.

174 *"tireless, sleepless, unwavering"*: Swett to Drummond.

174 *"committees of visitation"*: Swett, "Memorial Address," 79.

175 *"there were eight who"*: Swett to Drummond.

175 *"would split rails by"*: I.e., *Lancaster* (PA) *Examiner*, February 22, 1860; *Weekly Ottumwa* (IA) *Courier*, February 2, 1860; and *Lima* (OH) *Weekly Gazette*, February 10, 1860.

175 *"Constables are worth more"*: *Chicago Press and Tribune*, May 14, 1860.

176 *"Nearly the entire delegation"*: Whitney, *Lincoln the Citizen*, 288.

176 *"a set of Pollitical"*: Glyndon G. Van Deusen, *Thurlow Weed: Wizard of the Lobby* (Boston: Little, Brown, 1947), 211.

176 *"He took me to his"*: Weed, *Autobiography*, 2:256.

177 *"You know why we"*: Glyndon G. Van Deusen, "Thurlow Weed's Analysis of William H. Seward's Defeat in the Republican Convention of 1860," *Mississippi Valley Historical Review* 34, no. 1 (June 1947), 103.

177 *"Everybody who knows"*: *Chicago Tribune*, July 14, 1878.

177 *"Things are working"*: Nathan M. Knapp to Abraham Lincoln, May 14, 1860, ALP.

178 *"at work for you"*: Charles H. Ray to Abraham Lincoln, May 14, 1860, ALP.

178 *"Sir I wrote you"*: William Butler to Abraham Lincoln, May 14, 1860, ALP.

178 *"He was as ruff a"*: Roy P. Basler, "James Quay Howard's Notes on Lincoln," *Abraham Lincoln Quarterly*, December 1947, 396.

178 *"You know he was"*: Nicolay, *An Oral History*, 23.

179 *"He came to me with"*: Balser, "James Quay Howard's Notes," 396–97.

179 *"The Stock is gradually"*: Mark W. Delahay to Abraham Lincoln, May 14, 1860, ALP.

180 *"To A Lincoln"*: Jesse K. Dubois and David Davis telegram to Abraham Lincoln, May 14, 1860, ALP.

180 *"Strangers are respectfully"*: *Chicago Press and Tribune*, May 14, 1860.

180 *"expecting that his nomination"*: Stahr, *Seward*, 188.

180 *"In all probability"*: *New York Daily Herald*, May 19, 1860.

180 *"a thousand times declared"*: *New-York Tribune*, May 22, 1860.

180 *"His popularity is universal"*: *New York Daily Herald*, August 27, 1860.

181 *"He appears entirely cool"*: Austin, Journals, May 14, 1860.

181 *"emerged on to the shore"*: *Buffalo Daily Courier*, May 18, 1860.

181 *"and a most magically"*: *Chicago Press and Tribune*, May 15, 1860.

182 *"fairly shook the earth"*: *Poughkeepsie* (NY) *Journal*, May 26, 1860.

182 *"The cannons began to"*: *New York Daily Herald*, May 19, 1860.

182 *"Terrified, I stared at"*: Clark, "Lincoln's Nomination," 536–37.

183 *"Long John Wentworth is"*: *Burlington* (VT) *Times*, May 23, 1860.

183 *"the bulk of the party"*: *Janesville* (WI) *Daily Gazette*, May 15, 1860.

183 *"The advent of the"*: Addison G. Procter, *Lincoln and the Convention of 1860: An Address Before the Chicago Historical Society, April 4, 1918* (Chicago: Chicago Historical Society, 1918), 5.

183 *"went to Chicago with"*: *New York Daily Herald*, May 22, 1860.

183 *"The New York delegation"*: Isaac H. Bromley, "Historic Moments: The Nomination of Lincoln," *Scribner's Magazine*, November 1893: 649.

184 *"I too rely on the"*: Van Deusen, "Weed's Analysis," 102.

CHAPTER 8: Deutsches Haus

185 *"Allow me to introduce"*: CW, 4:50.

186 *"I look upon this"*: *Burlington* (IA) *Weekly Hawk-Eye*, May 26, 1860.

187 *"addressed him in a"*: Schurz, *Reminiscences*, 2:89–91.

187 *"She was then about"*: Ibid., 2:169–72.

188 *"From him we received"*: Ibid., 2:173–74.

188 *"take the boldest course"*: Ibid., 2:175.

189 *issued a circular*: *Louisville Daily Courier*, May 15, 1860.

190 "strange, discordant, *and even"*: CW, 2:468.

191 *"Our own children are"*: Frederick C. Luebke, ed., *Ethnic Voters and the Election of Lincoln* (Lincoln: University of Nebraska Press, 1971), 80.

191 *strong arm descending*: See *Republic Monthly Magazine of American Literature, Politics & Art*, January 1852, 50.

192 *"It was enough to"*: Strong, *Diary*, 1:94.

192 *"These Irishmen, strangers"*: Philip Hone, *The Diary of Philip Hone*, ed. Bayard Tuckerman, 2 vols. (New York: Dodd, Mead, 1889), 1:184.

192 *"Mr. Seward had been"*: Blaine, *Twenty Years of Congress*, 1:165.

193 *"I am not a Know-Nothing"*: CW, 2:323.

193 *"were not fortunate enough"*: *Los Angeles Times*, June 20, 1894.

193 *"still being told, and"*: CW, 3:333.

194 *"Germans were persecuted"*: Peter H. Olden, "Anton C. Hesing: The Rise of a Chicago Boss," *Journal of the Illinois State Historical Society* 35, no. 3 (1942), 267.

194 *"Ten years ago it"*: *New York Daily Herald*, June 10, 1859.

195 *"malcontents of the"*: Thomas R. Whitney, *A Defence of American Policy* (New York: De Witt & Davenport, 1856), 171.

195 *"busy-bodies, and"*: Quoted in *Davenport* (IA) *Daily Gazette*, August 6, 1859.

195 *"almost every grog"*: Quoted in *Lancaster* (PA) *Saturday Evening Express*, September 23, 1854.

196 *"The Germans turned out"*: Gustave Koerner, *Memoirs of Gustave Koerner, 1809–1896*, ed. Thomas J. McCormack, 2 vols. (Cedar Rapids, IA: Torch Press, 1909), 1:623.

196 "ein verdammter Republikaner": Olden, "Anton C. Hesing," 264.

197 *"imported barbarians"*: Quoted in *Chicago Press and Tribune*, March 9, 1860.

197 *"peculiarly flattered"*: *Montgomery* (AL) *Weekly Advertiser*, August 6, 1856.

197 *In 1856, Lincoln worked*: Burlingame, *Abraham Lincoln* Unedited, 1170.

198 *"I have started a"*: CW, 2:376.

198 *"Massachusetts is a sovereign"*: Ibid., 3:380.

198 *"Herndon, I gave"*: Carl Sandburg, *Abraham Lincoln: The Prairie Years* (New York: Blue Ribbon Books, 1926), 330.

199 *"instructing the delegates"*: *Indianapolis Daily Journal*, February 21, 1860.

199 *"the finest models of"*: Herriott, "Deutsches Haus," 135.

199 *"Americans must rule"*: *Daily American Organ* (Washington, DC), August 8, 1856.

199 *"truly, faithfully and vigorously"*: Herriott, "Deutsches Haus," 140–41.

200 *"If Bates, Banks, or any"*: *Cleveland Daily Leader*, March 23, 1860.

200 *"no man who has not"*: *Richmond* (VA) *Dispatch*, February 29, 1860.

200 *"We have dallied and"*: *Peoria* (IL) *Transcript*, March 5, 1860.

200 *"For God's sake let us"*: Pike, *First Blows*, 484.

201 *"the Republic of equal rights"*: Carl Schurz, *Speeches, Correspondence and Political Papers of Carl Schurz*, ed. Frederic Bancroft, 6 vols. (New York: G. P. Putnam's Sons, 1913), 1:57.

201 *"generally recognized by"*: Herriott, "Deutsches Haus," 148.

202 *"If it is taken from"*: *Detroit Free Press*, April 17, 1860.

202 *"greatest affair of the"*: *Chicago Press and Tribune*, February 17, 1860.

202 *a "Seward move"*: Quoted in *Burlington* (VT) *Free Press*, May 18, 1860.

202 *"The German convention is"*: *New-York Tribune*, May 14, 1860.

203 *"The German convention today"*: *New-York Tribune*, May 15, 1860.

203 *"There was no convention"*: *Detroit Free Press*, May 15, 1860.

203 *"recognizing perfect equality"*: *New-York Tribune*, May 15, 1860.

203 *"Greeley is hard at"*: *Daily Democrat and News* (Davenport, IA), May 18, 1860.

204 *"the sentiment of the"*: Herriott, "Deutsches Haus," 189.

204 *"The feeling for Seward"*: Koerner, *Memoirs*, 2:85.

204 *"tried to defend their"*: *Detroit Free Press*, May 17, 1860.

CHAPTER 9: Moving Heaven and Earth

210 *"While one train was"*: *Daily Evening Express* (Lancaster, PA), May 14, 1860.

210 *"No one, who has"*: *Franklin Repository and Transcript* (Chambersburg, PA), May 30, 1860.

210 *"boast of their morality"*: *Holmes County Farmer* (Millersburg, OH), May 17, 1860.

210 *equipped with "private bottles"*: Halstead, *Three Against Lincoln*, 141–42.

211 *"After arriving at the"*: *Daily Evening Express* (Lancaster, PA), May 15, 1860.

212 *"a splendid man, when"*: *Burlington* (IA) *Weekly Hawk-Eye*, May 26, 1860.

212 *"smooth-shaven, classical"*: Bromley, "Historic Moments," 650.

212 *"Even those who most"*: Blaine, *Twenty Years of Congress*, 1:166.

212 *"No one who then"*: Clark E. Carr, *The Illini: A Story of the Prairies* (Chicago: A. C. McClurg, 1908), 271.

213 *"The city swarms like"*: *Chicago Press and Tribune*, May 16, 1860.

213 *"The weather is warm"*: *New York Daily Herald*, May 16, 1860.

213 *"He would kindle as much"*: *New York Daily Herald*, May 10, 1860.

214 *"It strikes me that"*: Quoted in *Cadiz* (OH) *Sentinel*, May 9, 1860.

214 *"a brother lawyer's office"*: John T. Elliff, "Views of the Wigwam Convention: Letters from the Son of Lincoln's 1856 Candidate," *Journal of the Abraham Lincoln Association* 31, no. 2 (Summer 2010), 5–6.

215 *"Babel was never so"*: *Erie* (PA) *Observer*, May 19, 1860.

215 *"claims of Senator Seward"*: *Poughkeepsie* (NY) *Journal*, May 26, 1860.

216 *"some of whom did"*: Schurz, *Reminiscences*, 2:176–79.

216 *"assume an air of"*: Burlingame, *Abraham Lincoln* Unedited, 1657.

216 *"a whole squad of"*: *Detroit Free Press*, May 16, 1860.

217 *"Mr. Weed, though unable"*: Blaine, *Twenty Years of Congress*, 1:166.

217 *"motions are as rapid"*: Burlingame, *Abraham Lincoln* Unedited, 1647.

218 *"corruption and bribery"*: *Detroit Free Press*, May 6, 1860.

218 *"money or stocks"*: Quoted in *Daily Evening Express* (Lancaster, PA), May 2, 1860.

218 *"He won't steal, himself"*: William James Stillman, *The Autobiography of a Journalist*, 2 vols. (Boston: Houghton, Mifflin, 1901), 1:374.

219 *"surrounded by a corrupt"*: Burlingame, *Abraham Lincoln* Unedited, 1655.

219 *"The convention would"*: *New York Daily Herald*, May 10, 1860.

219 *Weed with Mephistopheles*: Schurz, *Reminiscences*, 2:178.

219 *"He was so robust"*: Van Deusen, *Weed: Wizard*, 185.

220 *dying slowly with excruciating*: Ibid., 233.

220 *author was Charles Dickens*: Weed, *Autobiography*, 2:570.

220 *"of intemperate habits"*: Ibid., 1:563–67.

222 *"We had a touch"*: Procter, *Lincoln and the Convention*, 6.

223 *"dressed in his light"*: Ibid., 7–9.

224 *Montgomery Blair recalled*: Burlingame, *Abraham Lincoln* Unedited, 1713.

224 *"and pleaded with him to"*: Alexander K. McClure, *Abraham Lincoln & Men of War-Times*, 4th ed. (Philadelphia: Times Publishing, 1892), 31.

225 *"Elections in the city"*: *Wabash Express* (Terre Haute, IN), May 16, 1860.

225 *"few pens could do"*: *Poughkeepsie* (NY) *Journal*, May 26, 1860.

225 *"They did, however, assure"*: Van Deusen, "Weed's Analysis," 103.

226 *"cold ingratitude"*: *Philadelphia Press*, May 21, 1860.

226 *"All honor to glorious"*: *Rock Island* (Illinois) *Argus*, April 9, 1860.

226 *"It was most emphatically"*: Quoted in *Danville* (VT) *North Star*, April 14, 1860.

226 *"To me, Governor Seward"*: F. I. Herriott, "Memories of the Chicago Convention of 1860," *Annals of Iowa*, October 1920, 455.

227 *"You delegates all say"*: Thomas H. Dudley, "The Inside Facts of Lincoln's Nomination," *Century Magazine* 40 (1890), 478.

227 *"The Seward men are"*: *New York Daily Herald*, May 16, 1860.

227 THE WINNING MAN: *Chicago Press and Tribune*, May 15, 1860.

228 *"The New York men were"*: Carr, *Illini*, 271.

229 *"no material change in"*: William Butler to Abraham Lincoln, May 14, 1860, ALP.

229 *vast sum in 1860*: $100,000 would be worth more than $3 million today, an enormous amount of campaign money in an age before broadcast or digital media buys.

230 *"Wentworth has come out"*: Herman Kreismann to Elihu B. Washburne, May 15, 1860, Washburne Papers.

230 *"I for one think"*: Mark W. Delahay to Abraham Lincoln, May 13, 1860, ALP.

230 *"around the hotels talking"*: "Senator Palmer on the Chicago Convention of 1860," The Ida M. Tarbell Collection, Allegheny College Pelletier Library.

231 *"strengthen our organization"*: Browning, *Diary*, 1:407.

232 *him and Tom Marshall*: Ibid., 1:469.

232 *"more friends than all"*: *Wheeling* (VA) *Daily Intelligencer*, May 19, 1860.

232 *"Prospects very good"*: Jesse K. Dubois telegram to Abraham Lincoln, May 15, 1860, ALP.

233 *"moving heaven & Earth"*: Jesse K. Dubois and David Davis telegram to Abraham Lincoln, May 15, 1860, ALP.

233 *"curiosity of the town"*: Halstead, *Three Against Lincoln*, 142.

233 *firebrand's hair come off*: Joanne B. Freeman, *The Field of Blood: Violence in Congress and the Road to Civil War* (New York: Farrar, Straus & Giroux, 2018), 240.

233 *"vulgar, barbarous, and inhuman"*: *Baltimore Daily Exchange*, April 17, 1860.

234 *"A very pretty compliment"*: *Buffalo Daily Courier*, May 18, 1860.

234 *"It is a rather significant"*: *Janesville* (WI) *Daily Gazette*, May 16, 1860.

234 *"irrepressible badge"*: *Wheeling* (VA) *Daily Intelligencer*, May 18, 1860.

234 *But "the truth is"*: *Cincinnati Enquirer*, May 13, 1860.

235 *"liked wines and Kentucky"*: Herriott, "Memories," 462.

235 *"magnificent rally"*: *Chicago Press and Tribune*, May 16, 1860.

236 *"The chances appear to"*: *Detroit Free Press*, May 16, 1860.

236 *"sake of spoils"*: *New York Times*, May 16, 1860.

236 *"decidedly in the foreground"*: *Cincinnati Enquirer*, May 13, 1860.

237 *"The last thing I"*: Elliff, "Views of the Wigwam," 6.

237 *"were in magnificent condition"*: Halstead, *Three Against Lincoln*, 144.

CHAPTER 10: Things Is Working

241 *people "stowed away"*: Halstead, *Three Against Lincoln*, 143.

241 *"Our street cars run"*: *Western Railroad Gazette* (Chicago), May 19, 1860.

241 *"thousands and tens of"*: *Wheeling* (VA) *Daily Intelligencer*, May 19, 1860.

241 *cashier at one saloon*: *North Iowa Times* (McGregor, IA), May 23, 1860.

242 *"It seems almost fabulous"*: *Wabash Express* (Terre Haute, IN), May 16, 1860.

242 *"The surprise of strangers"*: *Cleveland Daily Leader*, May 21, 1860.

242 *"not half finished, and"*: *Boston Evening Transcript*, May 21, 1860.

242 *"scores of palatial dwellings"*: *Franklin Repository and Transcript* (Chambersburg, PA), May 30, 1860.

242 *"has had its ups and"*: *New York Daily Herald*, May 19, 1860.

243 *"perhaps as fine a"*: *Chicago Times*, May 18, 1860.

244 *"as if the fate of"*: Halstead, *Three Against Lincoln*, 143–44.

244 *"This is the city where"*: *Cincinnati Enquirer*, May 13, 1860.

244 *a "telling effect"*: James Elliott to Salmon P. Chase, May 21, 1860, Salmon P. Chase Papers, Library of Congress.

245 *"trickster . . . who envied"*: Cassius M. Clay, *The Life of Cassius Marcellus Clay: Memoirs, Writings, and Speeches*, 2 vols. (Cincinnati, OH: J. Fletcher Brennan, 1886), 1:248.

245 *"position was humiliating"*: F. M. Wright to Salmon P. Chase, May 21, 1860, Salmon P. Chase Papers, Library of Congress.

245 *"hatched wooden eggs"*: Roger Hosea to Salmon P. Chase, May 16, 1860, Salmon P. Chase Papers, Library of Congress.

245 *"Mr. Lincoln was either"*: *Chicago Democrat*, May 16, 1860.

245 *"The friend of some"*: *Cincinnati Daily Press*, May 17, 1860.

246 *"if I had neither"*: *Chicago Press and Tribune*, May 17, 1860.

246 *"The change of time"*: *Racine* (WI) *Democrat*, March 21, 1860.

247 *"Since the [Democratic] Convention"*: *White Cloud Kansas Chief* (Abilene, KS), May 10, 1860.

247 *anniversary of Napoleon's debacle*: I.e., *Lewistown* (PA) *Gazette*, May 10, 1860.

247 *"a competent corps"*: *Chicago Press and Tribune*, May 16, 1860.

247 *"being squeezed almost"*: *North Iowa Times* (McGregor, IA), May 23, 1860.

247 *"Irrepressible Conflicters"*: *Racine* (WI) *Daily Journal*, May 17, 1860.

248 *"The door keepers were"*: *Chicago Press and Tribune*, May 17, 1860.

248 *all wearing white hats*: According to Joseph Medill, *Chicago Tribune*, February 7, 1909.

248 *"making a very impressive"*: *Pittsburgh Daily Post*, May 17, 1860.

248 *"the delegates could be"*: Bromley, "Historic Moments," 647.

248 *"father returned home late"*: Rufus Rockwell Wilson, *Intimate Memories of Lincoln: A Companion Volume to Lincoln Among His Friends* (Elmira, NY: Primavera Press, 1945), 4.

249 *"It was the meanest"*: *San Francisco Call*, April 21, 1895.

249 *"The scene is such"*: P. Orman Ray, *The Convention That Nominated Lincoln* (Chicago: University of Chicago Press, 1916), 18.

249 *"has fallen the duty of"*: *Buffalo Morning Express*, May 16, 1860.

250 *"a grand and inspiring"*: Schurz, *Reminiscences*, 2:179–80.

250 *"10,000 people were gathered to-day"*: *New-York Tribune*, May 17, 1860.

250 *a "barn-like structure"*: Bromley, "Historic Moments," 647.

251 *"It stuck like wax"*: CW, 2:252.

251 *"He is a dull, chuckel headed"*: Browning, *Diary*, 1:407.

252 *"His appearance does not"*: *Brandon* (VT) *Gazette*, May 31, 1860.

252 *"It is our purpose"*: National Republican Convention, *Proceedings of the Republican National Convention Held at Chicago, May 16, 17 and 18, 1860* (Albany, NY: Weed, Parsons, 1860), 5–6.

253 *"to amend the proposition"*: Ibid., 12.

253 *"Horace Greeley was the"*: Bromley, "Historic Moments," 649.

254 *"Our object here is"*: National Republican Convention, *Proceedings*, 22.

254 *"Today all is confusion"*: Elliff, "Views of the Wigwam," 6–8.

255 *"Other girls, those of"*: Halstead, *Three Against Lincoln*, 147–48.

256 *"They say that if we"*: National Republican Convention, *Proceedings*, 27–28.

256 *"gentle, manly, affable"*: *Brandon* (VT) *Gazette*, May 31, 1860.

256 *"the one short and"*: Halstead, *Three Against Lincoln*, 145.

256 *"The suggestion of Don Quixote"*: Schurz, *Reminiscences*, 2:180.

257 *"could only have been"*: National Republican Convention, *Proceedings*, 30–31.

257 *"He certainly could not"*: Halstead, *Three Against Lincoln*, 145–46.

257 *"should be a motto"*: National Republican Convention, *Proceedings*, 35.

258 *"Make it ten!"*: Ibid., 39.

258 *"a long and pleasant"*: Austin, Journals, May 16, 1860.

259 *"no cause for doubting"*: Stahr, *Seward*, 188.

259 *"very much discouraged"*: Procter, *Lincoln and the Convention*, 9–10.

259 *GOV. SEWARD'S NOMINATION*: *New-York Tribune*, May 17, 1860.

259 *"The Republicans have all"*: Halstead, *Three Against Lincoln*, 148.

260 *"The greatest excitement prevails"*: *Racine* (WI) *Daily* Journal, May 21, 1860.

260 *"strength was augmenting"*: Leonard Swett to Abraham Lincoln, May 25, 1860, ALP.

261 *"dead cock in the pit"*: *Erie* (PA) *Observer*, May 19, 1860.

262 *"This change from Cameron"*: *Daily Evening Express* (Lancaster, PA), May 19, 1860.

262 *"Unless Seward has strength"*: Mark W. Delahay to Abraham Lincoln, May 16, 1860, ALP.

262 *"wrighting in the Room"*: William Butler to Abraham Lincoln, May 16, 1860, ALP.

263 *"the West should be"*: Isaac N. Arnold, *The Life of Abraham Lincoln* (Chicago: Jansen, McClurg, 1885), 166–67.

263 *"looking after the wants"*: *St. Louis Daily Globe-Democrat*, January 31, 1909.

264 *George Blakey, handling*: Baringer, *Lincoln's Rise*, 252.

264 *"spoke up in a hard"*: Wilson, *Intimate Memories*, 11.

264 *"They literally overwhelmed us"*: "Senator Palmer on the Chicago Convention of 1860," The Ida M. Tarbell Collection, Allegheny College Pelletier Library.

265 *"Prospects fair friends at"*: Jesse K. Dubois telegram to Abraham Lincoln, May 16, 1860, ALP.

265 *"Dont be frightend"*: Norman B. Judd telegram to Abraham Lincoln, May 16, 1860, ALP.

265 *"prominent citizens from"*: *Chicago Press and Tribune*, May 17, 1860.

266 *"with any degree of"*: Koerner, *Memoirs*, 2:86.

266 *"seize all the chances"*: *Western Railroad Gazette* (Chicago), May 19, 1860.

267 *"They fall prostrate in"*: *Cleveland Daily Leader*, May 22, 1860.

267 *"Every one of their"*: *Poughkeepsie* (NY) *Journal*, May 26, 1860.

267 *"braves" and "squaws"*: *Democrat and News* (Davenport, IA), May 18, 1860.

268 *"At two o'clock this"*: Halstead, *Three Against Lincoln*, 149.

268 *"from the fatigues of"*: *Chicago Press and Tribune*, May 17, 1860.

268 *"the only really quiet"*: Elliff, "Views of the Wigwam," 8.

CHAPTER 11: For Want of Tally Sheets

271 *"expecting the nomination"*: Halstead, *Three Against Lincoln*, 148–49.

271 *"transcendent interest"*: *Wisconsin State Journal* (Madison, WI), May 19, 1860.

271 *some local attractions*: *Chicago Press and Tribune*, May 17, 1860.

273 *"upon a door-step"*: Halstead, *Three Against Lincoln*, 149.

273 *"immediately ruined"*: Ibid., 149–50.

274 *"have no doubt of"*: Elliff, "Views of the Wigwam," 9.

275 *"The moment I named"*: Koerner, *Memoirs*, 2:87–89.

276 *"Both sides are trying"*: *New York Daily Herald*, May 18, 1860.

276 *"Sir—Can you not arrange"*: National Republican Convention, *Proceedings*, 42.

276 *Shortly after ten o'clock*: Ibid., 42–49.

277 "Where is the old Virginia": Quoted in the *St. Joseph* (MO) *Weekly Free Democrat*, May 19, 1860.

277 *"Roughs" and "hard boys"*: *New York Times*, April 28, 1860.

278 *"I faced the mob"*: National Republican Convention, *Proceedings*, 49–50.

278 *"I have seldom heard"*: Halstead, *Three Against Lincoln*, 150.

279 *"The Newyork men will"*: William Butler to Abraham Lincoln, May 17, 1860, ALP.

279 *"I agree with Seward"*: CW, 4:50.

280 *"are desperate gamblers"*: Mark W. Delahay to Abraham Lincoln, May 17, 1860, ALP.

281 *"Much discussion was going"*: Dudley, "Inside Facts," 478.

281 *"twice as many honest"*: National Republican Convention, *Proceedings*, 68–70.

282 *a horrifying report by: New-York Tribune*, May 14, 1860.

283 *"No man could have"*: Paul Douglas Casdorph, "The Bogus Texas Delegation to the 1860 Republican National Convention," *Southwestern Historical Quarterly* 65, no. 4 (April 1962), 480.

284 *"I now think the Tariff"*: CW, 4:49.

284 *"We did not consider"*: Koerner, *Memoirs*, 2:87.

285 *"Teutonic naturalization"*: *New York Daily Herald*, May 18, 1860.

285 *"rising tide of conservative"*: *New York Daily Herald*, May 19, 1860.

285 *"Its sentiments are plain"*: *Daily Pantagraph* (Bloomington, IL), May 19, 1860.

285 *"Pennsylvania went into"*: Halstead, *Three Against Lincoln*, 152.

285 *"I'll shoot him!"*: *New-York Tribune*, February 22, 1859.

286 *"convention was not willing"*: Arnold, *Life of Abraham Lincoln*, 165–66.

286 *"That we solemnly re-assert"*: National Republican Convention, *Proceedings*, 86–87.

287 *"The signers of the"*: Frederick Douglass, *The Frederick Douglass Papers, Series One: Speeches, Debates, and Interviews*, vol. 2, 1847–54, ed. John Blassingame (New Haven: Yale University Press, 1982), 359–87.

287 *"I hate it because of"*: CW, 2:255.

288 *"Now, I say to you"*: Ibid., 3:113.

288 *"If you have been inclined to"*: Ibid., 2:547.

288 *"into a merely revolutionary"*: Ibid., 3:376.

289 *"his negro-equality doctrines"*: Ibid., 3:262–63.

289 *"I offer this because"*: National Republican Convention, *Proceedings*, 87.

289 *"Everybody knew him"*: Schurz, *Reminiscences*, 2:181–83.

289 *"It is not the business"*: National Republican Convention, *Proceedings*, 88–89.

289 *"But he considered everything"*: Halstead, *Three Against Lincoln*, 154.

290 *Wilmot objected to the*: National Republican Convention, *Proceedings*, 89–92.

290 *"The German Republicans of"*: Ibid., 92–95.

290 *"slimly built, with a bright"*: *Daily Evening Express* (Lancaster, PA), May 21, 1860.

291 *"That will never do!"*: Koerner, *Memoirs*, 2:90.

292 *"No man was ever"*: Henry D. Thoreau, *Walden; or, Life in the Woods* (Boston: Ticknor and Fields, 1854), 49.

292 *He proposed an amendment*: National Republican Convention, *Proceedings*, 95–98.

292 *"a sturdy sandy-haired man"*: *Harper's Weekly*, August 7, 1875, 634–35.

293 *"This was a strong appeal"*: Halstead, *Three Against Lincoln*, 155–56.

293 *"from one of the negro-hating"*: *Atchison* (KS) *Daily Champion*, May 24, 1868.

293 *"There was such earnestness"*: Bromley, "Historic Moments," 653.

294 *"lugs in the lofty"*: Bates, *Diary*, 129.

294 *"a negro is as good"*: *Cincinnati Enquirer*, May 18, 1860.

294 *"All the thousands of"*: Halstead, *Three Against Lincoln*, 158–59.

294 *"sprang to their feet"*: *Chicago Journal*, May 18, 1860.

294 *Aaron Goodrich stood up*: National Republican Convention, *Proceedings*, 98–99.

295 *"Seward would have been"*: Wilson, *Lincoln Among*, 196.

296 *"you have to lift"*: Wilson and Davis, *Herndon's Informants*, 452–53.

296 *"It was a very strenuous"*: Wilson, *Lincoln Among*, 97.

297 *"His legs seemed to"*: William E. Doster, *Lincoln and Episodes of the Civil War* (New York: G. P. Putnam's Sons, 1915), 15.

297 *"His agility was surprising"*: Wilson, *Lincoln Among*, 89.

297 *"loved this game"*: Wilson and Davis, *Herndon's Informants*, 492.

297 *"This intimacy with Gov. Seward"*: Austin, Journals, May 17, 1860.

297 *"Your friends are firm"*: Elbridge Spaulding telegram to William H. Seward, Chicago, May 17, 1860, Seward Papers, University of Rochester.

297 *"We have no doubt"*: Edward D. Morgan telegram to William H. Seward, Chicago, May 17, 1860, Seward Papers, University of Rochester.

298 *"Am very hopeful dont"*: David Davis telegram to Abraham Lincoln, May 17, 1860, ALP.

CHAPTER 12: Lincoln Ain't Here

301 *"seemed to electrify"*: Halstead, *Three Against Lincoln*, 158–60.

301 *"We became friends then"*: Schurz, *Reminiscences*, 2:183.

302 *"known ability, of great"*: Procter, *Lincoln and the Convention*, 14.

302 *At 10:30 p.m., Weed*: Van Deusen, "Weed's Analysis," 103.

303 *"The Seward men are"*: *Elyria* (OH) *Independent Democrat*, May 23, 1860.

304 *"stentorian voices"*: Arnold, *Life of Abraham Lincoln*, 167.

304 *"we were aided"*: Leonard Swett to Josiah Drummond, May 27, 1860.

304 *"Everybody was mad"*: Whitney, *Lincoln the Citizen*, 289.

305 *"was pledging everything"*: Matilda Gresham, *Life of Walter Quintin Gresham, 1832–1895*, 2 vols. (Chicago: Rand McNally, 1919), 1:110–11.

305 *"go through a dark alley"*: *New York Times*, May 22, 1882.

306 *"I don't think he would"*: Samuel W. McCall, *Thaddeus Stevens* (Boston: Houghton Mifflin, 1909), 311–12.

306 *"very name stinks in"*: Nicolay, *An Oral History*, 41.

306 *"a mere sham"*: Ward H. Lamon, *The Life of Abraham Lincoln; from His Birth to his Inauguration as President* (Boston: James R. Osgood, 1872), 449.

306 *"had been fed upon"*: Halstead, *Three Against Lincoln*, 162.

307 *"were not free from"*: Bromley, "Historic Moments," 647.

308 *GOV. SEWARD WILL BE*: *New-York Tribune*, May 18, 1860.

308 *"The opposition to Seward"*: *New York Daily Herald*, May 18, 1860.

308 *"every one of the"*: Halstead, *Three Against Lincoln*, 161.

308 *"It is impossible to"*: *New York Times*, May 18, 1860.

308 *"the skillful and practical"*: *Illinois State Journal* (Springfield, IL), May 18, 1860.

309 *"The committee from Pennsylvania"*: Dudley, "Inside Facts," 478.

310 *"There were hundreds of"*: Halstead, *Three Against Lincoln*, 161–62.

310 *"a grand opening"*: *Wisconsin State Journal* (Madison, WI), May 19, 1860.

311 *"They are both glorious"*: *Elyria* (OH) *Independent Democrat*, May 23, 1860.

312 *"Damned if we haven't"*: *Chicago Tribune*, February 7, 1909.

312 *"bought all my men"*: Nicolay, *An Oral History*, 43.

312 *"after everything was arranged"*: Burlingame, *Abraham Lincoln* Unedited, 1686.

312 *"commerce between"*: Bromley, "Historic Moments," 653.

313 *"Judge Davis, Lamon, and Swett"*: Burlingame, *Abraham Lincoln* Unedited, 1667–68.

313 *"But Cameron was in"*: Lamon, *Life of Abraham Lincoln*, 449.

313 *"All Hail Pennsylvanians!"*: *Chicago Press and Tribune*, May 18, 1860.

313 *"I feel more confident"*: *Wisconsin State Journal* (Madison, WI), May 19, 1860.

314 *"Hangman's Day"*: Quoted in *Rock Island* (IL) *Argus*, May 21, 1860.

314 *"To-day I presume Seward"*: Charles Eugene Hamlin, *The Life and Times of Hannibal Hamlin* (Cambridge, MA: Riverside Press, 1899), 345.

314 *A LAST ENTREATY*: *Chicago Press and Tribune*, May 18, 1860.

314 *"It was evidently written"*: Halstead, *Three Against Lincoln*, 163.

316 *"A cannon was taken"*: Quoted in *Buffalo Daily Courier*, May 31, 1860.

316 *"poured itself into Auburn"*: Stanton, *Random Recollections*, 215.

316 *the* Journal, *local businesses*: *Illinois State Journal* (Springfield, IL), May 18, 1860.

317 *"Excellent & neat Beer Saloon"*: Wilson and Davis, *Herndon's Informants*, 435.

317 *"was very nervous"*: Ibid., 437–38.

318 *"The bargain was fulfilled"*: Lamon, *Life of Abraham Lincoln*, 449.

318 *"Badger Boys"*: *Racine* (WI) *Advocate*, May 23, 1860.

318 *"abounded in confidence"*: Halstead, *Three Against Lincoln*, 163–64.

319 *"a political 'turn of"*: Whitney, *Lincoln the Citizen*, 290.

319 *"I got our hooters in"*: *St. Louis Daily Globe-Democrat*, January 31, 1909.

320 *"which, all through the"*: Wilson, *Intimate Memories*, 5.

320 *"curbstone enthusiasm"*: Lamon, *Life of Abraham Lincoln*, 448.

320 *"It was plain to see"*: *Poughkeepsie* (NY) *Journal*, May 26, 1860.

320 *"Stores were closed"*: Leonard Swett to Josiah Drummond, May 27, 1860.

320 *"Gaily attired ladies"*: *Daily Evening Express* (Lancaster, PA), May 21, 1860.

320 *"When the door was"*: *Elyria* (OH) *Independent Democrat*, May 23, 1860.

321 *"In stentorian tones that"*: Mary A. Livermore, *My Story of the War: A Woman's Narrative* (Hartford, CT: A. D. Worthington, 1889), 550–51.

321 *"Looked at from the stage"*: Bromley, "Historic Moments," 654.

322 *"the battle of the ballot"*: Procter, *Lincoln and the Convention*, 14.

322 *"Their countenances were beaming"*: *Brandon* (VT) *Gazette*, May 31, 1860.

322 *"I could not see how"*: *New-York Tribune*, May 22, 1860.

322 *"Lincoln will be nominated"*: John Farnsworth telegram to E. B. Washburne, May 18, 1860, E. B. Washburne Papers.

322 *"the Republican side of"*: Schuyler Colfax to Abraham Lincoln, May 18, 1860, ALP.

323 *"Mr. Weed's hand directed"*: Weed, *Autobiography*, 2:262.

323 *"All right. Everything indicates"*: Stahr, *Seward*, 188.

CHAPTER 13: Yonder Goes Lincoln

327 *"O, we entreat Thee"*: National Republican Convention, *Proceedings*, 99–100.

328 *five additional delegates*: Ibid., 102–06.

328 *"I rise—"*: Ibid., 107–08.

329 *"I took my seat among"*: *Philadelphia Inquirer*, April 21, 1895.

329 *"In the order of"*: National Republican Convention, *Proceedings*, Nominations and voting, 108–26.

329 *"with a deafening shout"*: Leonard Swett to Josiah Drummond, May 27, 1860.

330 *"The response was prodigious"*: Halstead, *Three Against Lincoln*, 164–71.

330 *"one might have supposed"*: Bromley, "Historic Moments," 654–56.

332 *"and were carried from"*: *Chicago Press and Tribune*, May 19, 1860.

334 *"Our programme was to"*: Leonard Swett to Josiah Drummond, May 27, 1860.

334 *"He was sanguine"*: Austin, Journals, May 18, 1860.

335 *"Loud shouts rent the"*: Quoted in *Buffalo Daily Courier*, May 31, 1860.

335 *"somewhat dilapidated, consisting"*: Jesse W. Weik, *The Real Lincoln: A Portrait* (Boston: Houghton Mifflin, 1922), 106–07.

335 *dust in a corner grew*: *Brooklyn Daily Eagle*, October 16, 1887.

335 *"Well boys, what do"*: Wilson and Davis, *Herndon's Informants*, 490–91.

338 *"neither honest brave or"*: O. S. Comestock to Abraham Lincoln, January 29, 1861, ALP.

339 *"have anything he wants"*: *Philadelphia Inquirer*, April 21, 1895.

339 *"the first to catch"*: *New York Times*, May 24, 1860.

339 *"It did not look to me"*: *Poughkeepsie* (NY) *Journal*, May 26, 1860.

339 *"by the artful contrivance"*: *New York Daily Herald*, May 23, 1860.

341 *"Nearly every member of"*: *New York Daily Herald*, May 19, 1860.

341 *"Standing next to the"*: *Burlington Weekly Hawk-Eye*, May 26, 1860.

341 *"a peal of human voices"*: *Chicago Press and Tribune*, May 30, 1860.

342 *"In that direction shouts"*: Edwin O. Gale, *Reminiscences of Early Chicago and Vicinity* (Chicago: Fleming H. Revell, 1902), 401–02.

342 *"men yelled like incarnate"*: *Franklin Repository and Transcript* (Chambersburg, PA), May 30, 1860.

342 *"The billows of this"*: Livermore, *My Story*, 552.

342 *"demanded by gestures"*: Halstead, *Three Against Lincoln*, 171.

342 *"a hundred thousand"*: Arnold, *Life of Abraham Lincoln*, 169.

342 *"Babel of joy and"*: *Chicago Press and Tribune*, May 19, 1860.

343 *"The whole house was"*: Quoted in *Western Reserve Chronicle* (Warren, OH), May 30, 1860.

343 *"before the surging and"*: Halstead, *Three Against Lincoln*, 172.

343 *"The New Yorkers sat"*: *New York Daily Herald*, May 19, 1860.

343 *"like Rachel, weeping"*: *New York Daily Herald*, May 22, 1860.

343 *"It seemed to me"*: Livermore, *My Story*, 552.

343 *"threw his great arms"*: Swett, "Memorial Address," 80.

344 *"his fingers* hard *upon"*: Allen Thorndike Rice, ed., *Reminiscences of Abraham Lincoln by Distinguished Men of His Time* (New York: Harper & Brothers, 1909), 170.

344 *"Well, Curtis, we have"*: Keith, "Paper on the National Republican Convention," 14.

344 *"who, I imagined, sat"*: Schurz, *Reminiscences*, 2:186–87.

344 *"Western fellows" were different*: *Buffalo Daily Courier*, May 21, 1860.

345 *"Physically," observed*: *Burlington* (IA) *Weekly Hawk-Eye*, May 26, 1860.

345 *"so profound that you"*: *Brandon* (VT) *Gazette*, May 31, 1860.

345 *"Mounting a table"*: *New York Times*, May 21, 1860.

345 *"brief and beautiful eulogy"*: *North Iowa Times* (McGregor, IA), May 23, 1860.

346 *"All this time, there sat"*: *Burlington* (IA) *Weekly Hawk-Eye*, May 26, 1860.

346 *"the speech of the hour"*: Halstead, *Three Against Lincoln*, 173.

347 *"almost disabled" by emotion*: *Chicago Press and Tribune*, May 19, 1860.

347 *"No human body could"*: *New York Times*, May 21, 1860.

348 *"crinoline which entered in"*: *Brandon* (VT) *Gazette*, May 31, 1860.

348 *"There were bands of"*: Halstead, *Three Against Lincoln*, 173–74.

348 *"The anxiety was by"*: *Cleveland Morning Leader*, May 19, 1860.

349 *"As he drew near"*: Austin, Journals, May 18, 1860.

349 *"so pale, trembling and"*: Quoted in *Buffalo Daily Courier*, May 31, 1860.

350 *"The flags were furled"*: Stanton, *Random Recollections*, 216.

350 *"We have no time"*: Quoted in *Buffalo Daily Courier*, May 31, 1860.

350 *"told Mother and I"*: Trudy Krisher, *Fanny Seward: A Life* (Syracuse, NY: Syracuse University Press, 2015), 50.

351 *"This I thought from"*: Wilson and Davis, *Herndon's Informants*, 491.

351 *handed it to a messenger*: *Journal* quoted in the *Burlington* (IA) *Weekly Hawk-Eye*, May 26, 1860.

351 *"YOU ARE NOMINATED"*: J. J. A. Wilson telegram to Abraham Lincoln, May 18, 1860, ALP.

351 *"Abe Lincoln: We did it"*: Nathan M. Knapp telegram to Abraham Lincoln, May 18, 1860, ALP.

351 *"Abraham Lincoln: You're"*: J. J. Richards telegram to Abraham Lincoln, May 18, 1860, ALP.

352 *"Hon. A. Lincoln: You"*: Ibid.

352 *"Hon. A. Lincoln: Vote"*: J. J. A. Wilson telegram to Abraham Lincoln, May 18, 1860, ALP.

352 *"you had better come"*: Wilson and Davis, *Herndon's Informants*, 492.

352 *"agitated—turned pale"*: Ibid., 453.

CHAPTER 14: The Dirty-Shirt Ticket

354 *"much to the amusement"*: *Chicago Press and Tribune*, May 19, 1860.

354 *"The steamtugs are whistling"*: *New York Daily Herald*, May 19, 1860.

354 *"Talk of your money"*: Halstead, *Three Against Lincoln*, 174.

355 *"City wild with Excitement"*: Jesse W. Fell telegram to Abraham Lincoln, May 18, 1860, ALP.

355 *"God bless you we"*: Ward Hill Lamon and William W. Orme telegram to Abraham Lincoln, May 18, 1860, ALP.

355 *"My humble congratulations"*: William M. Dickson telegram to Abraham Lincoln, May 18, 1860, ALP.

355 *"we have announced your"*: Follet, Foster & Company telegram to Abraham Lincoln, May 18, 1860, ALP.

355 *"I shall probably be"*: Horace White telegram to Abraham Lincoln, May 18, 1860, ALP.

355 *"Engaged to Edit a"*: D. B. Cooke and Company telegram to Abraham Lincoln, May 18, 1860, ALP.

356 *"There is great of"*: J. J. A. Wilson to Abraham Lincoln, May 18, 1860, ALP.

356 *"The Republicans of"*: J. J. Richards telegram to Abraham Lincoln, May 18, 1860, ALP.

356 *"I congratulate you. Shall"*: Charles H. Ray telegram to Abraham Lincoln, May 18, 1860, ALP.

356 *"A special train has"*: Quoted in *Chicago Press and Tribune*, May 19, 1860.

356 *"Dont come here for"*: David Davis telegram to Abraham Lincoln, May 18, 1860, ALP.

356 *"Dont let any one"*: Leonard Swett telegram to Abraham Lincoln, May 18, 1860, ALP.

356 *Similar telegrams*: Norman B. Judd telegram to Abraham Lincoln; Jesse Dubois and William Butler telegram to Abraham Lincoln; Solomon Sturgis telegram to Abraham Lincoln; Gustave Koerner telegram to Abraham Lincoln; Charles H. Ray, John Locke Scripps, and Joseph Medill telegram to Abraham Lincoln, all May 18, 1860, ALP.

356 *"Write no letters &"*: David Davis telegram to Abraham Lincoln, May 18, 1860, ALP.

357 *"The nomination of Abram"*: *Philadelphia Press*, May 21, 1860.

357 *"The rooms of the"*: *New York Times*, May 21, 1860.

357 *"I am excited &"*: Mark W. Delahay to Abraham Lincoln, May 18, 1860, ALP.

358 *"such another sorry set"*: *Buffalo Daily Courier*, May 21, 1860.

358 *"brought about by the"*: *Poughkeepsie* (NY) *Journal*, May 26, 1860.

359 *"by apprehensions created"*: Quoted in *Brooklyn Daily Times*, May 26, 1860.

359 *"a scene of madness"*: *North Iowa Times* (McGregor, IA), May 23, 1860.

359 *"This illustrious personage"*: *Richmond* (VA) *Dispatch*, May 24, 1860.

360 *"in that endeavor, Mr. Greeley"*: *New York Times*, May 24, 1860.

361 *"Greeley slaughtered Seward"*: O. J. Hollister, *Life of Schuyler Colfax* (New York: Funk & Wagnalls, 1886), 148.

361 *"I was never insensible"*: *New-York Tribune*, June 14, 1860.

361 *"considering where I live"*: Hollister, *Schuyler Colfax*, 148.

362 *"Governor Morgan not only"*: McClure, *Abraham Lincoln*, 40.

362 *"was to declare that"*: *New York Times*, May 24, 1860.

362 *"a pleasant, good looking"*: *New York Daily Herald*, May 22, 1860.

363 *"standing as a parliamentarian"*: Hamlin, *Hannibal Hamlin*, 344.

363 *"the Illinois delegation was"*: Arnold, *Life of Abraham Lincoln*, 168.

364 *"several forged ones"*: Schuyler Colfax to Abraham Lincoln, May 18, 1860.

364 *"By most people it"*: *New York Daily Herald*, May 22, 1860.

365 *"seemed delighted"*: Lyman Trumbull to Abraham Lincoln, May 18, 1860.

365 *"stentorian voice"*: *Daily Evening Express* (Lancaster, PA), May 21, 1860.

366 *"At the head was a"*: *North Iowa Times* (McGregor, IA), May 23, 1860.

366 *PENNSYLVANIA GOOD FOR*: *Elyria* (OH) *Independent Democrat*, May 23, 1860.

366 *nomination of a vice president*: National Republican Convention, *Proceedings*, 127–34.

367 *"If the multitude could"*: Halstead, *Three Against Lincoln*, 174.

367 *"The faithful yelled themselves"*: *New York Daily Herald*, May 19, 1860.

367 *"Senator Hamlin is Vice"*: John Wentworth telegram to Abraham Lincoln, May 18, 1860, ALP.

367 *"nobody ever seriously thought"*: *Plymouth* (IN) *Democrat*, June 7, 1860.

367 *"a shrill, musical and clear"*: *Burlington* (IA) *Weekly Hawk-Eye*, May 26, 1860.

368 *"was a matter of surprise"*: *Daily Evening Express* (Lancaster, PA), May 21, 1860.

368 *Howard lost a bet*: *New York Times*, May 21, 1860.

368 *Tying up loose ends*: National Republican Convention, *Proceedings*, 134–44.

369 *"When he becomes fully"*: *Burlington* (IA) *Weekly Hawk-Eye*, May 26, 1860.

370 *"Applause and hisses"*: *New York Daily Herald*, May 19, 1860.

371 *"Torrents of liquor"*: Halstead, *Three Against Lincoln*, 177.

371 *"Everybody seems to"*: *Illinois State Journal* (Springfield, IL), May 19, 1860.

371 *"their echoes caught up"*: P. Orman Ray, *The Convention That Nominated Lincoln*, 36.

371 *"From turret to foundation"*: *Chicago Press and Tribune*, May 19, 1860.

372 *"for* the whole fence*"*: *Chicago Press and Tribune*, May 21, 1860.

372 *"Misrepresentation has achieved"*: Quoted in *New York Daily Herald*, May 23, 1860.

372 *"The New Yorkers are"*: Quoted in *Rock Island* (IL) *Argus*, May 23, 1860.

373 *"I found them generally"*: Koerner, *Memoirs*, 2:92.

373 *"a large procession"*: *Buffalo Morning Express*, May 19, 1860.

373 *"to forget their disappointments"*: Procter, *Lincoln and the Convention*, 15.

373 *"generally remarked that Lincoln"*: *North Iowa Times* (McGregor, IA), May 23, 1860.

374 *"He treated me civilly"*: McClure, *Abraham Lincoln*, 41.

374 *"spread like wildfire"*: *Philadelphia Press*, May 21, 1860.

374 *Weed was "feeling badly"*: *Chicago Tribune*, July 14, 1878.

375 *"I informed them very"*: Weed, *Autobiography*, 1:602.

375 *the ratification rally*: *Chicago Press and Tribune*, May 19, 1860.

376 *"Seward had shaken the"*: *New York Daily Herald*, May 19, 1860.

376 *"as though they have"*: Quoted in *Syracuse* (NY) *Daily Courier and Union*, May 23, 1860.

376 *"Chicago is in a blaze"*: *New-York Tribune*, May 19, 1860.

377 *"'the dirty-shirt ticket'"*: *New York Daily Herald*, May 22, 1860.

377 *"pleasant and genial in"*: *Chicago Press and Tribune*, May 24, 1860.

377 *Hamlin was in his rooms*: Hamlin, *Hannibal Hamlin*, 346.

377 *"Well, dear," Hamlin wrote*: Ibid., 347.

378 *"I could not believe it"*: Ibid., 351.

378 *"We at Washington had"*: Ibid., 347.

378 *"You have assembled to"*: *New York Times*, May 21, 1860.

379 *"For nearly five minutes"*: *Chicago Press and Tribune*, May 24, 1860.

379 *"to stand firm and"*: *Wisconsin State Journal* (Madison, WI), May 23, 1860.

379 *"The outrage has caused"*: *Chicago Press and Tribune*, May 24, 1860.

380 *"in a blaze of excitement"*: *Illinois State Journal* (Springfield, IL), May 19, 1860.

380 *"I will write home"*: Edwin L. Page, *Abraham Lincoln in New Hampshire* (Boston: Houghton Mifflin, 1929), 134.

381 *"We place the names"*: Quoted in *Wisconsin State Journal* (Madison, WI), May 28, 1860.

382 *"My dear Weed"*: Weed, *Autobiography*, 2:270.

382 *"I never before saw"*: Halstead, *Three Against Lincoln*, 177.

CHAPTER 15: Six Feet Four

387 *"This morning, we of"*: *Yonkers* (NY) *Examiner*, May 24, 1860.

387 "bow to the decision": Quoted in *New York Times*, May 21, 1860.

388 *"We have summered and"*: Quoted in *Wheeling* (VA) *Daily Intelligencer*, May 24, 1860.

388 *"transplant Thurlow Weed"*: Quoted in *New York Times*, May 21, 1860.

388 *"The People want one"*: *Hartford* (CT) *Daily Courant*, May 19, 1860.

388 *"Lincoln is a traitor"*: *Daily Democrat and News* (Davenport, IA), May 19, 1860.

389 *"does not look right"*: Quoted in *La Grange* (MS) *Weekly National American*, May 26, 1860.

389 *"Lincoln—ignorant of"*: *Daily Democrat and News* (Davenport, IA), May 19, 1860.

389 *"The latter has talents"*: *Richmond* (VA) *Examiner*, May 22, 1860.

389 *"rough-hewn village politician"*: *Lancaster* (PA) *Intelligencer*, May 29, 1860.

390 *"When your mother wants"*: *Western Railroad Gazette* (Chicago), May 26, 1860.

390 *"the institution of slavery"*: *New Orleans Daily Crescent*, May 21, 1860.

390 *"men of marked ability"*: *Adams Sentinel* (Gettysburg, PA), May 21, 1860.

390 *"air was fairly blue"*: Weed, *Autobiography*, 2:273.

391 *"buy Greeley a new suit"*: *New York Daily Herald*, May 23, 1860.

391 *"upon two grounds"*: Joshua Reed Giddings to Abraham Lincoln, May 19, 1860, ALP.

391 *"without conditions"*: CW, 4:52–53.

391 *shouts of "Old Abers"*: *New York Times*, May 25, 1860.

391 *"As seems to be the custom"*: Ibid.

393 *reported on the booming*: *Daily Democrat and News* (Davenport, IA), May 21, 1860.

393 *"There was a fair"*: *Rock Island* (IL) *Argus*, May 21, 1860.

393 *"the nomination was coldly"*: Van Deusen, "Weed's Analysis," 104.

394 *"meet the train with"*: Procter, *Lincoln and the Convention*, 15–16.

395 *"abundantly provided against"*: *Daily Evening Express* (Lancaster, PA), May 24, 1860.

395 *"At every railroad station"*: Schurz, *Reminiscences*, 2:187–88.

395 *crowd "was irrepressible"*: *Chicago Press and Tribune*, May 22, 1860.

396 *"on which stood many"*: Koerner, *Memoirs*, 2:93–94.

396 *"almost the whole population"*: *Chicago Press and Tribune*, May 22, 1860.

397 *"three cheers and a tiger"*: *Chicago Press and Tribune*, May 21, 1860.

397 *"Rails formed a prominent"*: *Daily Evening Express* (Lancaster, PA), May 24, 1860.

397 *"the presence of Mrs. Lincoln"*: Weik, *The Real Lincoln*, 272–73.

398 *"Good morning, gentlemen"*: Report by *Chicago Journal* quoted in *Janesville* (WI) *Daily Gazette*, May 23, 1860.

400 *"The lines upon his face"*: Rice, *Reminiscences of Abraham Lincoln*, 173–74.

400 *"His rough and ready"*: *Daily Evening Express* (Lancaster, PA), May 24, 1860.

401 *"My eyes were never feasted"*: *Chicago Press and Tribune*, May 30, 1860.

403 *"electrified his audience"*: *Illinois State Journal* (Springfield, IL), May 21, 1860.

CHAPTER 16: The People Decide

407 *"I have slight inclination"*: Van Deusen, "Weed's Analysis," 103.

408 *"The disappointment, therefore"*: *New York Times*, May 25, 1860.

408 *"The rail candidate forsooth!"*: Stahr, *Seward*, 194.

408 *"When I got the news"*: Frederick W. Seward, *Seward at Washington*, 1:453.

408 *"When I went out"*: Ibid., 453–54.

409 *"It jars harshly"*: Quoted in *Buffalo Morning Express*, June 18, 1860.

409 *"The past is dead"*: *New-York Tribune*, May 23, 1860.

409 *"smeared with the"*: *Daily Milwaukee News*, May 30, 1860.

409 *"Both men were remarkable"*: *Chicago Tribune*, July 14, 1878.

410 *"I found Mr. Lincoln"*: Weed, *Autobiography*, 2:603.

410 *"saw me; but he showed"*: CW, 4:71.

410 "fairness, *and fairness only*": Ibid., 4:57.

410 *"kind and generous"*: Weed, *Autobiography*, 2:270.

411 *"Weed was subdued, gentle"*: Frederick W. Seward, *Seward at Washington*, 1:454–56.

412 *"Your services are more"*: Stahr, *Seward*, 195.

412 *"A horrid looking wretch"*: *Charleston* (SC) *Mercury*, June 7, 1860.

412 *"Who is this huckster"*: *Liberator* (Boston), June 8, 1860.

412 *Alas for the Democrats*: Halstead, *Three Against Lincoln*, 185–278.

413 *a section of the floor*: Ibid, 211.

413 *"If my enemies are"*: Ibid, 231.

414 *"In the name of"*: Ibid, 237.

414 *"If . . . Douglas would now"*: Catton, *Coming Fury*, 68.

414 *"No one, this side"*: CW, 4:118.

415 *"Well, wife, there is"*: Francis Bicknell Carpenter, *Six Months at the White House with Abraham Lincoln* (New York: Hurd and Houghton, 1866), 113.

415 *"where there was more"*: John G. Nicolay, *With Lincoln in the White House: Letters, Memoranda, and Other Writings of John G. Nicolay, 1860–1865*, ed. Michael Burlingame (Carbondale: Southern Illinois University Press, 2000), 7.

415 *"procession moved along"*: Strong, *Diary*, 3:41.

415 *"That's all right"*: *Holmes County Farmer* (Millersburg, OH), June 21, 1860.

416 *"a genial, pleasant, and kind"*: David Davis to Abraham Lincoln, August 5, 1860, ALP.

416 *"He was well pleased"*: Thurlow Weed to Abraham Lincoln, August 13, 1860, ALP.

416 *William B. Astor*: I.e., *Daily Nashville* (TN) *Patriot*, October 31, 1860.

416 *"in great danger"*: Reinhard H. Luthin, "Indiana and Lincoln's Rise to the Presidency," *Indiana Magazine of History* 38, no. 4 (December 1942), 398.

417 *"some part, perhaps a"*: Stahr, *Seward*, 197.

417 *"I never could understand"*: Charles Francis Adams, *An Autobiography* (Boston: Houghton Mifflin, 1916), 62.

417 *"You are doing more"*: *New York Times*, September 29, 1860.

417 *"The truth is, we"*: James E. Harvey to Abraham Lincoln, July 27, 1860, ALP.

417 *"had very little to say"*: *New York Daily Herald*, August 27, 1860.

417 *"I shall be personally"*: CW, 4:86–87.

418 *"elbowed his way up"*: *New York Daily Herald*, October 20, 1860.

418 *"'old Abe' was a revelation"*: Charles Francis Adams, *An Autobiography*, 64–65.

418 *Seward-mania erupted*: *Chicago Press and Tribune*, October 3, 1860.

419 *"Oh, how lonesome"*: David Davis to Sarah W. Davis, Bloomington, IL, September 30, 1860, DFC.

419 *"it is right hard to"*: David Davis to Sarah W. Davis, Clinton, IL, October 10, 1860, DFC.

419 *"Mr. Lincoln is the next"*: Johannsen, *Stephen A. Douglas*, 797–98.

420 *"the Union maintained and"*: *Richmond* (VA) *Dispatch*, August 29, 1860.

420 *"Yes, my friends, I would"*: *Raleigh* (NC) *Register*, September 2, 1860.

420 *"His wife is very"*: David Davis to Sarah W. Davis, Clinton, IL, October 12, 1860, DFC.

420 *"What delightful rambles"*: David Davis to Sarah W. Davis, Urbana, IL, October 22, 1860, DFC.

420 *"Mr. Lincoln looked as"*: David Davis to Sarah W. Davis, Urbana, IL, October 15, 1860, DFC.

420 *"A fearful responsibility"*: David Davis to Sarah W. Davis, Danville, IL, November 4, 1860, DFC.

421 *"Have you any little"*: CW, 4:129–30.

421 *"direct and haughty attempt"*: *New York Times*, November 2, 1860.

421 *"So be it, good friends"*: *Charleston* (SC) *Mercury*, November 6, 1860.

421 *that "elections were like"*: Michael Burlingame, ed., *Abraham Lincoln: The Observations of John G. Nicolay and John Hay* (Carbondale: Southern Illinois University Press, 2021), 19.

421 *"accepted everything with"*: *New-York Tribune*, November 12, 1860.

422 *"was satisfactory so far"*: Wilson, *Intimate Memories*, 327–28.

422 *"I feel a great responsibility"*: *Observations of John G. Nicolay and John Hay*, 23.

423 *"cursed—swore and held"*: Ibid.

423 *"All through the campaign"*: Nicolay, *An Oral History*, 41.

423 *"From the things that"*: Robert S. Eckley, *Lincoln's Forgotten Friend Leonard Swett* (Carbondale: Southern Illinois University Press), 79.

423 *"Yet on the whole"*: Ibid.

424 *"every thought that we"*: William H. Seward to Abraham Lincoln, January 27, 1861, ALP.

424 *"hold firm, as with"*: CW, 4:151.

425 *"regards himself as the"*: *New-York Tribune*, February 27, 1861.

425 *"I can't afford to"*: John G. Nicolay and John Hay, *Abraham Lincoln: A History*, 10 vols. (New York: Century, 1890), 3:371.

425 *"so many battle fields"*: Two documents from February 1861, ALP.

425 *"I am loath to close"*: CW, 4:271.

425 *"Some thoughts for the"*: Ibid, 4:317–18.

426 *Lincoln wrote out a reply*: Ibid., 4:316–17.

426 *WANTED—A POLICY*: *New York Times*, April 3, 1861.

426 *"Executive skill and vigor"*: Frederick W. Seward, *Seward at Washington*, 590.

426 *"combinations too powerful"*: CW, 4:332.

426 *"If anyone had said"*: Bromley, "Historic Moments," 647–48.

EPILOGUE: Unconscious Instruments

428 *"Pale as ashes"*: Stanton, *Random Recollections*, 218.

429 *"paid the* first *installment"*: Van Deusen, *Greeley*, 257.

429 *"What in the world"*: William A. Croffut, *An American Procession, 1855–1914: A Personal Chronicle of Famous Men* (Boston: Little, Brown, 1931), 123.

429 *"every drop of blood henceforth"*: Horace Greeley to Abraham Lincoln, July 29, 1861, ALP.

429 *"The Prayer of 20 Millions"*: *New-York Tribune*, August 20, 1862.

429 *"As to the policy"*: CW, 5:388–89.

430 *"There is no time for delay"*: *Douglass Monthly*, March 1863.

430 *"took him everywhere"*: *New York Times*, September 25, 1860.

430 *"Without Chicago"*: *Chicago Tribune*, March 25, 1867.

431 *"the Wigwam was burning"*: *Chicago Tribune*, November 14, 1869.

431 *"to wear as well as"*: CW, 8:356.

431 *"vividly impressed . . . with"*: *Atchison* (KS) *Daily Champion*, May 24, 1868.

432 *"I've known Mr. Lincoln"*: Johannsen, *Stephen A. Douglas*, 860.

432 *"never had a truer"*: Norman B. Judd to Lyman Trumbull, January 3, 1861, Trumbull Papers, Library of Congress.

432 *"He always had more"*: *Herndon's Lincoln*, 3:534.

433 *"a follower and not"*: Horace White, *The Life of Lyman Trumbull* (Boston: Houghton Mifflin, 1913), 428.

433 *achieve much distinction*: William Wesley Woollen, *Biographical and Historical Sketches of Early Indiana* (Indianapolis, Hammond & Co., 1883), 124.

433 *"Well, McClure, what you"*: McClure, *Abraham Lincoln*, 137.

434 *"I shall never forget"*: Livermore, *My Story*, 555.

434 *which sold for $3,000*: Ibid., 430.

434 *"the American Florence Nightingale"*: *Evening Star* (Washington, DC), January 24, 1915.

434 *"discriminate against men"*: Schurz, *Reminiscences*, 2:221.

434 *"Disappointment! You speak"*: Ibid., 2:221–22.

435 *"there is no reason"*: *New-York Tribune*, May 4, 1865.

435 *He was* "mortified": Jesse K. Dubois to Abraham Lincoln, April 6, 1861, ALP.

435 *"Lincoln is a singular man"*: Jesse K. Dubois to Henry Clay Whitney, April 6, 1865, Albert J. Beveridge Papers, Library of Congress.

435 *"but for the extraordinary"*: Pratt, "David Davis, 1815–1886," 82.

436 *"If Judge Davis, with"*: Herndon and Weik, *Herndon's Lincoln*, 3:503.

436 *"You know, strange as"*: Maurice G. Baxter, *Orville H. Browning: Lincoln's Friend and Critic* (Bloomington: Indiana University Press, 1957), 158.

436 *"I have determined to"*: Nicolay and Hay, *Abraham Lincoln*, 8:316.

436 *"eating a man's bread"*: David Davis to Julius Rockwell, Washington, DC, January 24, 1864, DFC.

437 *"I desire it chiefly"*: Edward Bates to Abraham Lincoln, October 13, 1864, ALP.

437 *"kindness and consideration"*: Nicolay, *An Oral History*, 68.

437 *"Of course I am not consulted"*: Harry Draper Hunt, *Hannibal Hamlin of Maine, Lincoln's First Vice-President* (Syracuse, NY: Syracuse University Press, 1969), 155.

438 *"I think we are near"*: Frederick W. Seward, *Seward at Washington*, 2:271.

438 *"Please come at once"*: Harry E. Pratt, *The Personal Finances of Abraham Lincoln* (Chicago: Lakeside Press, 1943), 131.

438 *"as a second father"*: Ibid., 141.

438 *"a natural born thief"*: Michael Burlingame, *At Lincoln's Side*, 187.

438 *"domestic discipline"*: Whitney, *Life on the Circuit*, 99.

439 *"I may not have"*: Wilson and Davis, *Herndon's Informants*, 165.

439 *"Do good to those"*: Ibid., 358.

440 *"It is pleasant to remember"*: Quoted in *Chicago Press and Tribune*, October 8, 1867.

440 *"No stranger who called"*: *New York Times*, November 23, 1882.

440 *"Miss Weed devoted the"*: *Buffalo Evening News*, November 4, 1893.

441 *"only love one another"*: Stahr, *Seward*, 543.

441 *"David Davis did a great"*: *New York Sun*, June 27, 1886.

442 *"It is known here"*: *New-York Tribune*, May 24, 1860.

442 *"That the pledge was"*: Gresham, *Life of Walter Quintin Gresham*, 1:110–11.

442 *"suffered himself to be"*: Burlingame, *Abraham Lincoln* Unedited, 1670.

442 *"No pledges have been"*: Leonard Swett to Josiah Drummond, May 27, 1860.

442 *"of his labors with Cameron"*: *Chicago Times*, June 9, 1889.

443 *"There is a general impression"*: Parton, "Past Presidential Nominations," 542.

443 *"making promises to bring"*: Burlingame, *Abraham Lincoln* Unedited, 1668.

444 *"unconscious instruments of"*: Bromley, "Historic Moments," 656.

Index